# The Kifuliiru Language: Volume 2

# A Descriptive Grammar

SIL International®
Publications in Linguistics

Publication 147

Publications in Linguistics are published by SIL International®. The series is a venue for works covering a broad range of topics in linguistics, especially the analytical treatment of minority languages from all parts of the world. While most volumes are authored by members of SIL, suitable works by others will also form part of the series.

**Series Editor**
Mike Cahill

**Volume Editors**
Rhonda Hartell Jones
Mary Huttar

**Production Staff**
Bonnie Brown, Managing Editor
Lois Gourley, Compositor
Barbara Alber, Cover design

**Cover Photograph**
Roger Van Otterloo

# The Kifuliiru Language: Volume 2

# A Descriptive Grammar

Roger Van Otterloo

SIL International®
Dallas, Texas

© 2011 by SIL International®
Library of Congress Catalog No: 2011929643
ISBN: 978-1-55671-270-8 (volume 2)
ISBN: 978-1-55671-279-1 (two-volume set)
ISSN: 1040-0850

Printed in the United States of America

All rights reserved

No part of this publication may be reproduced, stored in a retrieval system, or transmitted in any form or by any means—electronic, mechanical, photocopy, recording, or otherwise—without the express permission of SIL International®. However, short passages, generally understood to be within the limits of fair use, may be quoted without written permission.

Copies of this and other publications of SIL International® may be obtained from:

SIL International Publications
7500 W. Camp Wisdom Road
Dallas, TX 75236-5629

Voice: 972-708-7404
Fax: 972-708-7363
publications_intl@sil.org
www.ethnologue.com/bookstore.asp

# Dedication

This book is dedicated to Robert E. Longacre and Stephen H. Levinsohn, trailblazers in discourse linguistics.

# Contents

Dedication . . . . . . . . . . . . . . . . . . . . . . . . . . . . . . . . . . . . . . . . . . . . . . v
List of Tables . . . . . . . . . . . . . . . . . . . . . . . . . . . . . . . . . . . . . . . . . . . xv
Preface . . . . . . . . . . . . . . . . . . . . . . . . . . . . . . . . . . . . . . . . . . . . . . . . xvii
Acknowledgments . . . . . . . . . . . . . . . . . . . . . . . . . . . . . . . . . . . . . xix
Bafuliiru Foreword . . . . . . . . . . . . . . . . . . . . . . . . . . . . . . . . . . . . . xxi
A Brief Background to Writing Grammars in Africa
    by Derek Nurse . . . . . . . . . . . . . . . . . . . . . . . . . . . . . . . . . . xxiii
Contributing to Language Revitalization and Maintenance
    by John Watters . . . . . . . . . . . . . . . . . . . . . . . . . . . . . . . . . xxix
Abbreviations . . . . . . . . . . . . . . . . . . . . . . . . . . . . . . . . . . . . . . xxxiii
Maps . . . . . . . . . . . . . . . . . . . . . . . . . . . . . . . . . . . . . . . . . . . . . xxxvii
1 Introduction . . . . . . . . . . . . . . . . . . . . . . . . . . . . . . . . . . . . . . . . . 1
    1.1 Language name and classification . . . . . . . . . . . . . . . . . . . . . . . . 1
    1.2 Dialects . . . . . . . . . . . . . . . . . . . . . . . . . . . . . . . . . . . . . . . . . . . . 2
    1.3 Previous language work; contributors to the present work . . . . . . . . . 2
    1.4 Inventory of parts of speech . . . . . . . . . . . . . . . . . . . . . . . . . . . . . 3
    1.5 Conventions . . . . . . . . . . . . . . . . . . . . . . . . . . . . . . . . . . . . . . . . 5
        1.5.1 Texts and their numbering . . . . . . . . . . . . . . . . . . . . . . . . . 5
        1.5.2 Transcription conventions . . . . . . . . . . . . . . . . . . . . . . . . . 6
    1.6 Possible mismatches between Kifuliiru and other languages . . . . . . . 10
        1.6.1 Reduplication . . . . . . . . . . . . . . . . . . . . . . . . . . . . . . . . . 10
        1.6.2 Pronouns . . . . . . . . . . . . . . . . . . . . . . . . . . . . . . . . . . . . 11
        1.6.3 "Expressive" nouns communicating adjectival concepts . . . . . . 11
        1.6.4 Locative phrases with cl. 16 **ha** . . . . . . . . . . . . . . . . . . . . 11
        1.6.5 Ideophones and interjections . . . . . . . . . . . . . . . . . . . . . . 12
        1.6.6 Verbs . . . . . . . . . . . . . . . . . . . . . . . . . . . . . . . . . . . . . . . 12
        1.6.7 Clauses . . . . . . . . . . . . . . . . . . . . . . . . . . . . . . . . . . . . . 14

    1.6.8 Interclausal relations .................................... 15
    1.6.9 Textlinguistics ........................................... 15
    1.6.10 Proverbs .............................................. 17
**2 Nouns** ................................................................. **19**
  2.1 Constituent structure of the noun............................. 19
    2.1.1 Singular-plural correspondences ......................... 21
    2.1.2 Examples of count nouns by gender....................... 22
    2.1.3 Non-count nouns........................................ 23
  2.2 Class agreement triggered by noun gender-number .............. 24
    2.2.1 Gender-number prefixes by grammatical grouping .......... 24
    2.2.2 Agreement for conjoined NPs with different GNPs: cl. 8 (**bi**-) .... 28
    2.2.3 Two different GNPs referring to same real-world referent ...... 28
    2.2.4 Mismatches between noun classes ........................ 29
    2.2.5 Lexicalized noun prefixes................................ 30
    2.2.6 Personification of noun by addition of **wa** clitic............... 30
  2.3 Semantic categories typically found in various Kifuliiru
       noun classes............................................... 31
**3 Pronouns and Demonstratives** ..................................... **37**
  3.1 Previous reference: the morpheme **e** / **o** ........................ 37
  3.2 Verb prefix pronouns and enclitic pronouns.................... 38
    3.2.1 Bound subject pronominal prefixes ........................ 39
    3.2.2 Bound object pronominal prefixes ........................ 39
    3.2.3 Object enclitics.......................................... 41
  3.3 Personal pronouns ........................................... 42
    3.3.1 Structure of personal pronouns .......................... 42
    3.3.2 Functions of personal pronouns ......................... 45
  3.4 Interrogative pronouns....................................... 51
    3.4.1 Structure of interrogative pronouns ...................... 51
    3.4.2 Functions of interrogative pronouns ...................... 53
  3.5 Demonstratives............................................... 56
    3.5.1 Structure of demonstratives ............................. 56
    3.5.2 Function of demonstratives............................... 64
    3.5.3 Set demonstrative function .............................. 75
    3.5.4 Locative demonstrative pronouns formed with -**mûndà** ....... 78
**4 Adjectives, Numbers, and Quantifiers** ............................. **81**
  4.1 Adjectives................................................... 81
    4.1.1 Lexical adjectives....................................... 81
    4.1.2 Stative verbal adjectives................................. 85
    4.1.3 Special adjective –**zira** 'without'........................... 88
    4.1.4 Comparison strategies .................................. 89
  4.2 Quantifiers.................................................. 91

  4.2.1 Quantifier -óshì 'all' ........................................ 92
  4.2.2 Quantifier -ómbì 'both' ....................................... 93
 4.3 Cardinal numbers ................................................. 93
  4.3.1 Numbers 1–7 .................................................. 93
  4.3.2 Numbers 8–10 ................................................. 95
  4.3.3 Numbers 11–99 ................................................ 96
  4.3.4 Numbers 100–999 .............................................. 96
  4.3.5 Numbers 1,000–1,000,000 ...................................... 97
 4.4 Ordinal numbers .................................................. 97

# 5 Adverbs .............................................................. 99
 5.1 Temporal adverbs ................................................. 99
 5.2 Positional adverbs .............................................. 102
 5.3 Manner adverbs .................................................. 102
 5.4 Intensifier and limiter adverbs ................................. 104
 5.5 Confirmatory adverbs ............................................ 105
 5.6 Additive adverbs ................................................ 105

# 6 Ideophones, Interjections, and Greetings ............................ 107
 6.1 Ideophones ...................................................... 108
  6.1.1 General characteristics of ideophones ...................... 109
  6.1.2 Ideophones: a sample of meanings by domain ................. 112
  6.1.3 Ideophone examples in context .............................. 116
 6.2 Interjections ................................................... 124
  6.2.1 General characteristics of interjections ................... 124
  6.2.2 Interjections: a sample of meanings by domain .............. 125
 6.3 Greetings ....................................................... 134
  6.3.1 Greetings at encounter ..................................... 134
  6.3.2 Leave-taking ............................................... 135
  6.3.3 Forms of address ........................................... 135

# 7 Noun Phrases ........................................................ 137
 7.1 Noun phrase structure ........................................... 137
  7.1.1 Constituent structure of noun phrases ...................... 137
  7.1.2 Marked order of the NP ..................................... 139
  7.1.3 Noun phrase constituents used substantively ................ 140
  7.1.4 Infinitives in noun phrases ................................ 143
 7.2 Augments ........................................................ 143
  7.2.1 Augment structure .......................................... 143
  7.2.2 Augment function ........................................... 145
 7.3 Associative phrases ............................................. 150
  7.3.1 Associative phrase structures .............................. 150
  7.3.2 Associative phrase functions ............................... 151
  7.3.3 Frozen associative structure with special focus ............ 154

7.4 Associative pronouns . . . . . . . . . . . . . . . . . . . . . . . . . . . . . . . . . . . . . . . . 157
7.5 Conjunctives used with noun phrases. . . . . . . . . . . . . . . . . . . . . . . . 158
   7.5.1 Conjunctive **na** . . . . . . . . . . . . . . . . . . . . . . . . . . . . . . . . . . . . . . . . . 158
   7.5.2 Conjunctive **kandi iri** 'or' . . . . . . . . . . . . . . . . . . . . . . . . . . . . . . 162
   7.5.3 Conjunctive **nga** 'like, as' . . . . . . . . . . . . . . . . . . . . . . . . . . . . . . 163
7.6 Noun phrases involving **mwene** 'ownership'. . . . . . . . . . . . . . . . . . 164
   7.6.1 Ownership or authority . . . . . . . . . . . . . . . . . . . . . . . . . . . . . . 164
   7.6.2 Family members. . . . . . . . . . . . . . . . . . . . . . . . . . . . . . . . . . . . . 165
   7.6.3 Comparative 'like X' . . . . . . . . . . . . . . . . . . . . . . . . . . . . . . . . . 166
7.7 Noun phrases with following nouns of apposition . . . . . . . . . . . . . 166
7.8 Multiple noun phrase embedding . . . . . . . . . . . . . . . . . . . . . . . . . . . 167

**8 Locative Phrases** . . . . . . . . . . . . . . . . . . . . . . . . . . . . . . . . . . . . . . . . . . . . .**169**
8.1 Locative markers . . . . . . . . . . . . . . . . . . . . . . . . . . . . . . . . . . . . . . . . . 169
   8.1.1 Locative marker structure . . . . . . . . . . . . . . . . . . . . . . . . . . . . 169
   8.1.2 Locative marker function. . . . . . . . . . . . . . . . . . . . . . . . . . . . . 176
   8.1.3 Idioms involving frozen locative markers. . . . . . . . . . . . . . . 192
8.2 Position nouns. . . . . . . . . . . . . . . . . . . . . . . . . . . . . . . . . . . . . . . . . . . . 195
   8.2.1 Position noun structure . . . . . . . . . . . . . . . . . . . . . . . . . . . . . . 195
   8.2.2 Position noun functions . . . . . . . . . . . . . . . . . . . . . . . . . . . . . . 199
   8.2.3 Forms resembling position nouns. . . . . . . . . . . . . . . . . . . . . . 201

**9 Verb Words and Phrases**. . . . . . . . . . . . . . . . . . . . . . . . . . . . . . . . . . . . .**203**
9.1 Overview of verb form types. . . . . . . . . . . . . . . . . . . . . . . . . . . . . . . . 204
   9.1.1 Basic affixation for verb words . . . . . . . . . . . . . . . . . . . . . . . . 204
   9.1.2 Single-word verbs . . . . . . . . . . . . . . . . . . . . . . . . . . . . . . . . . . . 208
   9.1.3 Grammaticization of auxiliaries . . . . . . . . . . . . . . . . . . . . . . . 213
   9.1.4 Multiword verbs in which only one word is inflected . . . . . . . . . 215
   9.1.5 Multiword verbs which include two inflected forms. . . . . . . . . . 217
   9.1.6 Adverbial auxiliaries which precede an uninflected
        verb stem. . . . . . . . . . . . . . . . . . . . . . . . . . . . . . . . . . . . . . . . . . 221
   9.1.7 Negation . . . . . . . . . . . . . . . . . . . . . . . . . . . . . . . . . . . . . . . . . . . 225
9.2 Detailed inventory of TAM form/meanings. . . . . . . . . . . . . . . . . . . . 227
   9.2.1 Tense . . . . . . . . . . . . . . . . . . . . . . . . . . . . . . . . . . . . . . . . . . . . . . 228
   9.2.2 Aspect . . . . . . . . . . . . . . . . . . . . . . . . . . . . . . . . . . . . . . . . . . . . . 237
   9.2.3 Mood . . . . . . . . . . . . . . . . . . . . . . . . . . . . . . . . . . . . . . . . . . . . . . 248
   9.2.4 TAM in auxiliaries . . . . . . . . . . . . . . . . . . . . . . . . . . . . . . . . . . . 264
   9.2.5 TAM with -**ba**- auxiliary in compound verb phrases . . . . . . . . . . 292
   9.2.6 Focus . . . . . . . . . . . . . . . . . . . . . . . . . . . . . . . . . . . . . . . . . . . . . . 298

**10 Clauses and Information Structure** . . . . . . . . . . . . . . . . . . . . . . . . . .**301**
10.1 Syntactic structure of independent clauses. . . . . . . . . . . . . . . . . . . 301
   10.1.1 Non-verbal clauses . . . . . . . . . . . . . . . . . . . . . . . . . . . . . . . . . 301
   10.1.2 Verbal clause nucleus . . . . . . . . . . . . . . . . . . . . . . . . . . . . . . . 305

Contents     xi

    10.1.3 Obliques. . . . . . . . . . . . . . . . . . . . . . . . . . . . . . . . . . . . . . . . . . . . . . . . . 317
    10.1.4 Polar questions. . . . . . . . . . . . . . . . . . . . . . . . . . . . . . . . . . . . . . . . . . 323
  10.2 Information structure . . . . . . . . . . . . . . . . . . . . . . . . . . . . . . . . . . . . . . 324
    10.2.1 Summary of information structure terminology . . . . . . . . . . . 324
    10.2.2 Pauses . . . . . . . . . . . . . . . . . . . . . . . . . . . . . . . . . . . . . . . . . . . . . . . . . . 329
    10.2.3 Topic-comment articulation . . . . . . . . . . . . . . . . . . . . . . . . . . . . . 335
    10.2.4 Point of departure. . . . . . . . . . . . . . . . . . . . . . . . . . . . . . . . . . . . . . 338
    10.2.5 Presentational articulation . . . . . . . . . . . . . . . . . . . . . . . . . . . . . 343
    10.2.6 Identificational articulation. . . . . . . . . . . . . . . . . . . . . . . . . . . . . 344
  10.3 Alternations of basic constituent order . . . . . . . . . . . . . . . . . . . . . . 348
    10.3.1 Preposing a clause constituent . . . . . . . . . . . . . . . . . . . . . . . . . . 348
    10.3.2 Postposing a clause constituent . . . . . . . . . . . . . . . . . . . . . . . . . 357
    10.3.3 Promoting to clause object. . . . . . . . . . . . . . . . . . . . . . . . . . . . . . 359
    10.3.4 Marked placement of pronominal elements . . . . . . . . . . . . . . . 361

**11 Dependent Clauses and Interclausal Relations** . . . . . . . . . . . . . . . . .**365**
  11.1 Dependent adverbial clauses . . . . . . . . . . . . . . . . . . . . . . . . . . . . . . . 365
    11.1.1 Conditional clauses . . . . . . . . . . . . . . . . . . . . . . . . . . . . . . . . . . . . 367
    11.1.2 Contrary-to-fact conditional/result clauses . . . . . . . . . . . . . . . 368
    11.1.3 Temporal clauses . . . . . . . . . . . . . . . . . . . . . . . . . . . . . . . . . . . . . . 371
    11.1.4 Concessive clauses. . . . . . . . . . . . . . . . . . . . . . . . . . . . . . . . . . . . . 383
    11.1.5 Logical clauses . . . . . . . . . . . . . . . . . . . . . . . . . . . . . . . . . . . . . . . . 384
    11.1.6 Purpose/result clauses . . . . . . . . . . . . . . . . . . . . . . . . . . . . . . . . . 385
    11.1.7 Focus clauses . . . . . . . . . . . . . . . . . . . . . . . . . . . . . . . . . . . . . . . . . 387
    11.1.8 Purpose/result clauses, together with focus. . . . . . . . . . . . . . . 390
    11.1.9 Manner clauses . . . . . . . . . . . . . . . . . . . . . . . . . . . . . . . . . . . . . . . 393
    11.1.10 Reason clauses . . . . . . . . . . . . . . . . . . . . . . . . . . . . . . . . . . . . . . . 394
  11.2 Analytic causatives. . . . . . . . . . . . . . . . . . . . . . . . . . . . . . . . . . . . . . . . 397
  11.3 Reduced clauses indicating concomitant "state" . . . . . . . . . . . . . . . 398
  11.4 Complement clauses. . . . . . . . . . . . . . . . . . . . . . . . . . . . . . . . . . . . . . 399
    11.4.1 Classes of complement clauses . . . . . . . . . . . . . . . . . . . . . . . . . 400
    11.4.2 Idiom of attempt . . . . . . . . . . . . . . . . . . . . . . . . . . . . . . . . . . . . . . 405
    11.4.3 Idiom of number . . . . . . . . . . . . . . . . . . . . . . . . . . . . . . . . . . . . . . 405
    11.4.4 Idiom of comparison with **kè=tàlì yò=háàhè**
            'isn't it all the more'. . . . . . . . . . . . . . . . . . . . . . . . . . . . . . . . . 406
  11.5 Relative clauses. . . . . . . . . . . . . . . . . . . . . . . . . . . . . . . . . . . . . . . . . . . 407
    11.5.1 Subject relative clauses. . . . . . . . . . . . . . . . . . . . . . . . . . . . . . . . . 408
    11.5.2 Object or complement relative clauses . . . . . . . . . . . . . . . . . . 410
    11.5.3 Null relativizers . . . . . . . . . . . . . . . . . . . . . . . . . . . . . . . . . . . . . . . 413
    11.5.4 Headless relative clauses . . . . . . . . . . . . . . . . . . . . . . . . . . . . . . . 416
    11.5.5 **kútì** 'how' grammaticized in a relative construction . . . . . . . . 416
    11.5.6 Relative clause function: denoting thematic salience. . . . . . . . . . . . . . 417

11.6 Relations between independent clauses . . . . . . . . . . . . . . . . . . . . . . . 419
   11.6.1 Coordination between clauses . . . . . . . . . . . . . . . . . . . . . . . . . . . 419
   11.6.2 Contrast between clauses . . . . . . . . . . . . . . . . . . . . . . . . . . . . . . . . 421
   11.6.3 Clause level alternatives: **ìrí...kàndí írí** 'if...or' . . . . . . . . . . . . . . . 422
11.7 Pauses at the sentence level . . . . . . . . . . . . . . . . . . . . . . . . . . . . . . . . . . 423

# 12 Narrative Forms . . . . . . . . . . . . . . . . . . . . . . . . . . . . . . . . . . . . . . . . . . . . . 429
12.1 Speech register summary . . . . . . . . . . . . . . . . . . . . . . . . . . . . . . . . . . . . 429
12.2 Narrative text units . . . . . . . . . . . . . . . . . . . . . . . . . . . . . . . . . . . . . . . . . 431
   12.2.1 Story introduction . . . . . . . . . . . . . . . . . . . . . . . . . . . . . . . . . . . . . . 431
   12.2.2 Story body . . . . . . . . . . . . . . . . . . . . . . . . . . . . . . . . . . . . . . . . . . . . 434
   12.2.3 Peak . . . . . . . . . . . . . . . . . . . . . . . . . . . . . . . . . . . . . . . . . . . . . . . . . 445
   12.2.4 Story conclusion . . . . . . . . . . . . . . . . . . . . . . . . . . . . . . . . . . . . . . . 445
12.3 Highlighting . . . . . . . . . . . . . . . . . . . . . . . . . . . . . . . . . . . . . . . . . . . . . . . 447
   12.3.1 Demonstratives as thematic salience markers . . . . . . . . . . . . . . 447
   12.3.2 Thematic salience expressed by the cl. 16 locative marker
      **ha** 'place' . . . . . . . . . . . . . . . . . . . . . . . . . . . . . . . . . . . . . . . . . . . . 467
   12.3.3 Emphatic prominence (-**ag**) . . . . . . . . . . . . . . . . . . . . . . . . . . . . . . 468
   12.3.4 Slowing-down devices . . . . . . . . . . . . . . . . . . . . . . . . . . . . . . . . . . 472
   12.3.5 Songs which provide key information . . . . . . . . . . . . . . . . . . . . . 475
12.4 Reporting of conversation . . . . . . . . . . . . . . . . . . . . . . . . . . . . . . . . . . . 480
   12.4.1 Reported speech in quite formal written register . . . . . . . . . . . 480
   12.4.2 Direct versus indirect speech . . . . . . . . . . . . . . . . . . . . . . . . . . . 482
   12.4.3 Reported speech in informal registers . . . . . . . . . . . . . . . . . . . . 483
12.5 Participant reference . . . . . . . . . . . . . . . . . . . . . . . . . . . . . . . . . . . . . . . 491
   12.5.1 Introduction of participants . . . . . . . . . . . . . . . . . . . . . . . . . . . . 491
   12.5.2 Tracking of major participants . . . . . . . . . . . . . . . . . . . . . . . . . . 495

# 13 Proverbs and Riddles . . . . . . . . . . . . . . . . . . . . . . . . . . . . . . . . . . . . . . . . 497
13.1 Proverbs . . . . . . . . . . . . . . . . . . . . . . . . . . . . . . . . . . . . . . . . . . . . . . . . . . 497
   13.1.1 Proverb formal considerations . . . . . . . . . . . . . . . . . . . . . . . . . . 497
   13.1.2 Proverb meaning considerations . . . . . . . . . . . . . . . . . . . . . . . . 502
13.2 Riddles . . . . . . . . . . . . . . . . . . . . . . . . . . . . . . . . . . . . . . . . . . . . . . . . . . . 504
   13.2.1 Riddle formal considerations . . . . . . . . . . . . . . . . . . . . . . . . . . . 505
   13.2.2 Riddle meaning considerations . . . . . . . . . . . . . . . . . . . . . . . . . 508

# 14 Reduplication . . . . . . . . . . . . . . . . . . . . . . . . . . . . . . . . . . . . . . . . . . . . . . 509
14.1. Reduplication structural considerations . . . . . . . . . . . . . . . . . . . . . . 510
   14.1.1 Parts of speech where reduplication occurs . . . . . . . . . . . . . . . 510
   14.1.2 Two phonological constraints affecting reduplication . . . . . . . 512
   14.1.3 Reduplicating only part of the stem . . . . . . . . . . . . . . . . . . . . . . 513
14.2. Functions of reduplication . . . . . . . . . . . . . . . . . . . . . . . . . . . . . . . . . . 513
   14.2.1 Repetition . . . . . . . . . . . . . . . . . . . . . . . . . . . . . . . . . . . . . . . . . . . 513
   14.2.2 Extensiveness (or the lack of it) . . . . . . . . . . . . . . . . . . . . . . . . . 518

    14.2.3 Reduplication expressing emphasis . . . . . . . . . . . . . . . . . . . . . . . 523
    14.2.4 Reduplication (usually) expressing pejorative . . . . . . . . . . . . . . 525
**Appendix: Texts** . . . . . . . . . . . . . . . . . . . . . . . . . . . . . . . . . . . . . . . . . . . . . 529
**References** . . . . . . . . . . . . . . . . . . . . . . . . . . . . . . . . . . . . . . . . . . . . . . . . . 551
**Person index** . . . . . . . . . . . . . . . . . . . . . . . . . . . . . . . . . . . . . . . . . . . . . . . 555
**Language index** . . . . . . . . . . . . . . . . . . . . . . . . . . . . . . . . . . . . . . . . . . . . 559
**Overall index** . . . . . . . . . . . . . . . . . . . . . . . . . . . . . . . . . . . . . . . . . . . . . . 561

# List of Tables

Table 1.1. Kifuliiru consonant symbols...............................6
Table 1.2. Kifuliiru vowels............................................7
Table 2.1. Kifuliiru noun classes....................................20
Table 2.2. Mapping of singular/plural noun class pairings..............22
Table 2.3. Gender-number prefixes by grammatical grouping...........24
Table 3.1. Personal pronoun examples for all noun classes .............44
Table 3.2. Functions of personal pronouns .........................45
Table 3.3. Default and emphatic demonstratives for all classes..........61
Table 3.4. Summary of demonstrative pronoun meaning components....65
Table 4.1. Lexical adjectives .......................................82
Table 7.1. Constituents of the noun phrase ..........................138
Table 7.2. Augment form relative to noun class ......................144
Table 8.1. Co-occurrence restrictions for LMs and NP complements .....175
Table 8.2 Summary of LM semantics..............................176
Table 8.3. Inventory of position nouns..............................197
Table 8.4. Co-occurrences of various locative markers
    with position nouns..................................198
Table 8.5. Position noun functions .................................200
Table 9.1. Basic affixation for verb words ...........................205
Table 9.2. Adverbial auxiliaries which require inflection on main verb ..220
Table 9.3. Adverbial auxiliaries which precede an uninflected verb stem 222
Table 9.4. Verbs that occur before infinitives ........................265
Table 9.5. Auxiliaries dealing with relative time......................268
Table 9.6. Auxiliaries dealing with relative location .................277
Table 9.7. Auxiliaries dealing with relative time plus location..........287
Table 9.8. Auxiliaries dealing with mood ..........................289
Table 9.9. TAM of auxiliary.......................................293

Table 9.10. Stative verb frames that may follow the auxiliary -**ba**- ...... 297
Table 11.1. Conjunctions which may introduce dependent
adverbial clauses ................................... 366
Table 11.2. Dependent adverbial clauses which do not
involve conjunctions............................... 367
Table 12.1. Speech register summary ............................... 431
Table 14.1. Parts of speech exhibiting reduplication ................... 510

# Preface

This volume describes the grammar of Kifuliiru, a Bantu language of zone J. Included are linguistic levels from words, phrases, clauses, through to narrative text linguistics. A companion volume describes Kifuliiru phonology, tone, and derivation. The goal of these two volumes is not only to depict the linguistic richness of this language, but to further research in related Bantu languages as well. Of course all languages, even closely related ones, have their own distinctives. Nevertheless, there is a huge set of features that Bantu languages share, and it is hoped that these two volumes will assist researchers in unlocking the secrets of those languages, or at least suggest potential areas of linguistic investigation.

In this volume, well-known Bantu distinctives, such as the noun class system, are extensively documented. There are many less-investigated areas of research, where Bantu forms and meanings differ significantly from Indo-European ones. Of particular note is the systemic study of pronouns, demonstratives, locatives, and the highly complex verbal system. Clause structure is also researched, including information structure within the clause, and alternations of basic constituent word order, based on discourse parameters. Conjunctions and inter-clausal connections are thoroughly presented, as well as many discourse considerations within narrative texts. Finally, there is an overview of ideophones and interjections and proverbs and riddles, which are all significant within the African communication style. These distinctions are all summarized in 6.1 and 13, respectively.

Just one case in point involves the correct use of Kifuliiru information structure (see 10.2). For example, in Kifuliiru, the topic (established information) is typically presented at the beginning of the sentence. This topic is isolated by a following pause, and the new information is presented at the end of the clause in focus position. There are many strategies for maneuvering the constituents of the default SVO order, to ensure that the new information is presented at the end, where it belongs based on discourse considerations. Included are various types of preposing, postposing, promoting to object, and marked placement of pronouns and quantifiers. The study of topic-comment is just one of the many linguistic areas where investigation bore rich, and often unexpected, fruit!

The present time reflects a key turning point for the language. With most of the children now attending elementary school, and with fourteen secondary schools in the area, the original richness of the language is being increasingly compromised by an overlay of the national language, French, which is from a totally different linguistic family. Much of the Kifuliiru grammar and vocabulary is in real danger of vanishing. This present grammatical description, at the request of the Bafuliiru people, reflects the classic language spoken by the recent generation which did not mix the language with French or a trade language.

Insofar as possible, the examples provided are taken from spoken folktales or other natural texts. This is to ensure that the language described is authentic and genuine. By contrast, we did not come at the language from a "Can you say this?" or "How do you say that?" viewpoint. Paradigms were elicited only to fill in comparable forms not found in the texts.

To maximize its viability over time, this description reflects a theory-neutral perspective wherever possible. We have attempted to avoid technical jargon or obtuse diagrams intelligible only to the linguistic elite. At the same time, established nomenclature has been followed where appropriate. In addition, wherever we thought it helpful, we have separated form from function, describing each in turn. It is our sincere hope that this grammar will benefit the intended audiences, and serve as a springboard for further research.

Roger Van Otterloo
June 2008

# Acknowledgments

It was a privilege to live and work among the Bafuliiru people. We thank them for their warm welcome and many kindnesses over the sixteen years we resided among them (1980–1996), and for their patience in teaching us their language. We are honored that all our sons had the privilege of speaking Kifuliiru as one of their two "first" languages. Special thanks goes to the family of the late Kashindi Ye'Mwana Adrien, on whose compound we lived. Their children were some of the many playmates for our five boys growing up there.

The Bafuliiru have a proverb: "No one shaves the back of his own neck". Everyone needs help at some point. That proverb can be applied to this volume, since so many people have made a significant contribution. Deep appreciation goes to SIL International Linguistics Coordinator Mike Cahill, who supervised this work and provided much wisdom, encouragement, and logistical help. In addition we are grateful to our Eastern Congo Group, and especially our former group directors, Jon Hampshire, and Ed Lauber, for setting aside time for us to write. Without that, this book would never have seen the light of day.

This work is the second of two volumes. The writing of these two volumes was a joint effort. I wrote the present volume, covering nouns, pronouns, adjectives and numerals, adverbs, ideophones and interjections, noun phrases, locative phrases, verb words and phrases, clauses, interclausal relations, narrative texts, proverbs and riddles, and reduplication. My wife, Karen, wrote the volume on phonology, tone, and derivational processes. We each read and made comments on the other's work. However, there are many ways to cut (and serve) the "linguistic pie", and each of us remains responsible for the content of our respective volumes.

We are grateful to the many Bafuliiru who provided the texts we used for this work. Our original texts and other data were collected before the days of computers and were all lost in the looting which took place at the beginning of the war in 1996. Thus we are grateful to Kibambazi Zihindula for the collection of many new stories to analyze. Thanks goes to Juma Kinyamagoha for transcribing the texts, and to Sengoronge Katyera for dictating all the recordings used to mark tones in this volume. During the process of recording, Kamaro Busongoye assisted, and made many corrections and clarifications regarding the examples.

Although this book is on the whole as theory-neutral as possible, there are two chapters where it seemed necessary to approach the material from a more defined theoretical perspective. The chapter on clauses is based on information theory, which, among other things, sorts out the proper placement of old and new information. The chapter on narrative texts owes much to the work of Robert Longacre, Stephen Levinsohn and other discourse scholars.

This work has received extensive input. We are grateful to Derek Fivaz, who visited us more than once during our early period of Kifuliiru analysis, and introduced us to Bantu linguistics. Our heartfelt thanks also goes to all those who carefully read early drafts of all or parts of this volume, providing much invaluable feedback. These include Maryanne Augustin, Cheri Black, Sebastian Floor, Carl Follingstad, Leoma Gilley, Loren Koehler, Lana Martens, Derek Nurse, Kent Rasmussen, Oliver Stegen, and Rhonda Thwing. A special word of thanks goes to Stephen Levinsohn, and Doris Payne, who suggested major revisions. Our heartfelt thanks also goes to Mary Ruth Wise, George Huttar, Bonnie Brown, Rhonda Hartell Jones, Margaret González, Lois Gourley, and the rest of the staff at the editing and publishing department at Dallas SIL for their labor in bringing this work to publication. All of the above people not only corrected many earlier errors, but also provided additional information and insights, and we are deeply grateful for the expertise they shared. In the end we take full responsibility for the choices made and any shortcomings.

Our ultimate thanks goes to God, our creator and sustainer, who not only led us to Africa in the first place, but also protected and provided for us all along the way, and by whose enabling we have been able to document what is in this work. To him be all the glory!

# Bafuliiru Foreword

Kifuliiru is a Bantu language spoken by more than 400,000 people, in the Uvira Territory of the Democratic Republic of Congo. In the beginning, Kifuliiru did not have the good fortune to be written. Nor was it taught in the schools. In fact when children spoke Kifuliiru on the school ground, they sometimes had a dead rat tied around their neck as punishment. There were many other types of punishment as well, such as writing lines over and over, saying "I will not speak Kifuliiru". As a result of such cultural arrogance on the part of teachers, some Bafuliiru no longer appreciate their mother-tongue. Many make mistakes when speaking it, mixing it indiscriminately with other languages.

Since Kifuliiru was not written down, people got used to speaking the trade language, Kiswahili. Kiswahili became the language of the primary school, and even the language for teaching God's Word in church. Everyone who could not speak Kiswahili well was viewed as an ignorant, backward person. Students were also taught in French, which further compromised the mother-tongue. Many children now speak Kifuliiru with French word order and mix words haphazardly from other languages. It's a very sad situation to find oneself in, losing one's language and cultural heritage!

All the same, most Bafuliiru living in their homes have continued to guard their language. And they now have the good fortune to have it written down, thanks to the work of SIL International. Many have begun to wake from sleep, and want to see their language given its proper place. In addition, many Bafuliiru are now happy to speak Kifuliiru even in church services. Kifuliiru has also begun to be resurrected in the area primary schools. The goal is that the children, from an early age, will be fluent in reading and writing their mother-tongue, as well as Kiswahili and French. This bodes well for generations to come.

In addition the Kifuliiru cultural association (Case Culturelle Fuliiru, or CACF) has published a variety of books to resurrect the language, including traditional stories, proverbs, and riddles, as well as books about traditional culture. The thirst to guard the language is now great!

This linguistic book is a like big sickle, to help the Bafuliiru harvest the riches of their language. Between its covers the essence of Kifuliiru is described at all levels, with all the original nuances. This will help all those writing the language to write with a pleasing style. Our desire is to adapt parts of this book into a form from which all the Bafuliiru people can benefit. This includes writing books for teaching the Kifuliiru language and culture in the primary schools. A Writer's Manual has also been produced, based on this grammar, for all who are interested in producing authentic literature that is sweet and clear.

The Bafuliiru, when they see this book, will laugh and dance, rejoicing in all the work that Roger and Karen Van Otterloo have done. Our language has been taken out of obscurity, and out of a slow death, and has been given a place among the languages of Africa. May God bless this work!

Elie Mushonio Banyimwire Rusati, President of Kifuliiru Cultural Association (CACF)
Phanuël Kibambazi Zihindula, Kifuliiru project director
December 2006, City of Uvira, Democratic Republic of Congo

# A Brief Background to Writing Grammars in Africa

by Derek Nurse

When asked by the authors to contribute a short preface to this grammar, I thought it appropriate to set it in a historical context and sketch the evolution of the writing of grammars of sub-Saharan African languages, and of East African and Bantu languages in particular.

African languages and western writing systems came together in the mid nineteenth century, and over the following century they fused in several forms.

Churches were among the first developers of written material in the Roman script. They recognized the need to put the Scriptures, hymns, and later, other material into writing. Scriptures, containing as they do the same text across many languages, are not only a fine repository of classical language but also an invaluable source of comparative material, currently underused, for linguists. Equally important, and relevant here, churches saw that their representatives sent from Europe were eventually replaced by others, and that these successors needed instruction in the language, rather than reinventing the wheel every few years. So teaching materials, at first quite short and elementary, were developed, and some eventually developed into fuller grammars. These were often written by missionaries who had spent a long time in Africa and felt it would be a shame for their knowledge of the language to go to waste. From short teaching materials to a more complete grammar is a large step. Fine examples of more complete material by church representatives are the works of Barlow (1914, Great Britain), Hulstaert (1938, 1965, Belgium), Sacleux (1909, 1939, France) and Raum (1909, Germany). Raum's work on the Moshi dialect of Chaga resulted from many years' living on Kilimanjaro. Marred only by its lack of a list of contents, it is a real treasure trove, both of linguistic material and of stories. In the 1970s Gérard Philippson and I translated one of these stories for a student in Dar es Salaam, who was the grandson of the Chaga who had recorded them originally with Raum. The tradition of storytelling had meanwhile died out, and the grandson told us it was a fine story, that he had never heard, and that it even contained one or two names he recognized, and he asked where had it come from?!

Schools were initially run by the churches, later by the government. Schools had to have reading and instructional materials, which posed technical questions of how to reduce to writing languages which involved new difficulties not faced by those writing Western European languages. It also raised the issue of which variety or dialect to use, and what was to be the standard.

Professional administrators, established a little later, needed to communicate. With other senior administrators they used the colonial language but with junior, local employees they used a local language. Colonial administrators had limited tours of duty, and their replacements had to acquire that language. Both in Africa and Europe, pedagogical grammars were written and used, at first for major languages, later for the languages of some smaller communities.

The need on the part of the churches and of colonial governments for people who could speak African languages and thence for descriptive and instructional materials led gradually to the involvement of European universities. They sometimes absorbed clergy (Guthrie, for example) and administrators who had spent time in Africa, and they eventually set up institutes and departments of African languages, to produce pedagogical material, to write grammars, to broaden the general knowledge base. Invariably, most of the descriptions and grammars relied on the linguistic heritage and insights of the authors, most of whom had grown up in the Latin and Greek grammatical tradition and had only come to African languages later in life. Not surprisingly, many of these grammars use Latin models and theoretical terminology. Although some of their insights had to do with what we would now call linguistic universals, others look dated. It is appropriate here to mention the central role of the linguists at Tervuren and Brussels, under whose supervision a torrent of descriptions and theses on Bantu languages poured out in the second half of the twentieth century.

These strands continued and evolved until the dust of World War II settled and revealed a new world, where new factors came into play. The most obvious ones were the independence of African nations, coupled with the loss of a sense of colonial mission among western nations and a loss of Christian faith in Western Europe. These led to several immediate results: a drying up of the supply of the kinds of Western European individuals willing and able to write grammars, the establishment of African language departments in Africa, the emergence of African scholars, and the increased role of Americans in matters of faith and scholarship in Africa. A less salient factor was the emergence of linguistics, especially theoretical linguistics, as a discipline. Theoretical linguistics is primarily concerned with advancing the theoretical enterprise, and tends to produce short pieces—chapters, articles, squibs. It does not have the writing of grammars as a priority, and few of the theoretical grammars of African languages written during the heyday of transformational theory during the 1960s and 1970s have stood the test of time.

Have the changes just outlined led to an upsurge in the production of grammars? Put another way, are there enough grammars of sub-Saharan African, especially Bantu, languages? The answer is no. In preparing a forthcoming book, I wanted to do a survey of verbal phenomena in the languages of Guthrie's 85 Bantu groups, covering the whole Bantu area. Since no one can know so many languages, I had to rely on grammars and descriptions written by others. I made a list of all work I could find dealing with verbs in Bantu languages—books (especially), chapters in books, articles, theses, short discussions, unpublished work by others, my own work, and minor sources. Three rough general descriptive categories emerged: those groups of languages well described, those poorly described, and those in between, 'average'. These categories are relative. 'Well described' means that the verb system of at least one language in the group is reasonably described and that there exist descriptions for most of the other members of the group (some 20%); 'poorly described' means there is no good analysis of the verb system for any of the languages in the group and the whole group is poorly described (some 25%): 'average' is the remainder, the largest set of groups and languages (the rest, some 55%). Even the "well described' languages often suffer from a lack of examples, by which to test the descriptive or theoretical claims. I assume that what is true of the description or analysis of verb systems would in general be true of the rest of the grammatical system. So only 20% of the groups surveyed were reasonably described, and many languages were entirely undescribed or analysed. There is reason to think that non-Bantu languages or languages in other areas of Africa score even less well, using similar criteria. A few years ago Larry Hyman gave the keynote address at the Annual Conference for African Linguistics, and those who knew him expected a theoretical content. They were surprised to hear a speech strongly advocating the need for descriptive grammars (Hyman 2004).

If we compare who has written these grammars in the last fifty years, who are the authors? I examined a fairly comprehensive bibliography of Bantu languages for grammars of Bantu languages. With 'grammars' it is hard to know where exactly to draw the line. I included only published works which aimed at presenting all or most of the grammar, and excluded those which presented only partial analyses—sketches, descriptions or analyses of parts of the grammar, theoretical tracts, and most university theses. Most theses are excluded because writing grammars takes years, far longer than the time allowed for most theses, which concentrate on some aspect of the target language. The largest single producer of grammars over the last half century is still Europe, followed at some distance by Africa (especially South Africa) and then North America. The overwhelming impression is that of the small number of real grammars, and the number is not increasing. It is apparently so hard to write a grammar because certain conditions have to be met. The author needs to know the target language well, which means Africans, or non-Africans who have spent long years in Africa. The author needs courage, to venture into a language for which there is no grammatical tradition and little or no existing literature. Since writing a grammar takes years, the author needs a stable and adequate income over a long period. For many Africans and some non-Africans, that cannot be guaranteed, which is why most theses go no further. It also requires incentive, and neither African nor non-African universities encourage or reward the spending of long years on a grammar. Above all, it takes a certain kind of individual, an individual who is inspired, who loves language in general, the target language in particular, and is trained and happy to spend time doing this work. Small wonder that few grammars get written. No one forced the few authors, whether in the nineteenth or the twenty-first century, to do this work—they just want to do it.

And so it is with the two volumes of this grammar, too. The Van Otterloos spent thirteen years living with the Fuliiru, interspersed with three one-year periods of leave, plus several following years in Nairobi, a total of some twenty years each, forty in total, testimony to their amazing dedication, determination, and hard work, resulting in two extensive volumes, and 1,300 examples. This monumental reference work represents one of the most comprehensive grammars of any East African Bantu language. It combines masses of data and examples with linguistic argumentation and statements about all the basic topics to be expected in this kind of grammar: phonology, various word classes (noun, verb, pronoun/demonstrative, adjective, adverbials, and locatives), and sentence structure. It contains sections on topics not always adequately covered in conventional grammars: tone (a very long chapter), reduplication, ideophones, information theory (chapter 10), text analysis (chapter 12). To keep happy those who would say that grammars often make claims but do not show data to justify or falsify the claims, it provides many pages of examples and texts. It also deals with minor topics that do not often appear elsewhere: many 'adverbial auxiliaries' (fully grammaticalised auxiliaries expressing mainly aspect and mood), two verb forms expressing 'frustrated results', and the reduplication of nouns (the reduplication of 'mango' expresses multiple mangoes given out, one at a time, one to each worker, and successively acted on in the same way).

This grammar has been more than an academic exercise. Much of this material has already been adapted into a set of presentations in Swahili and French, for the benefit of the Bafuliiru themselves, as well as speakers of dozens of other Bantu languages East Africa. The idea is to stimulate local language awareness for mother-tongue speakers through a set of appropriately-graded seminars, so that this linguistic knowledge be brought back to the language communities themselves.

These two volumes would be a valuable addition to any Africanist's or linguist's bookshelf, appealing to several audiences. The general reader will find it very useful for reference and general interest. Theoretical linguists will find material and discussion for many current topics. Comparativists will find it a useful source for information on many topics.

**References**

Barlow, A. R. 1914 (reprinted 1951, 1960). *Studies in Kikuyu grammar and idiom.* Edinburgh: Blackwood.

Hulstaert, G. 1938. *Praktische grammatika van het Lonkundo (Lomongo).* Antwerp: De Sikkel.

Hulstaert, G. 1965. *Grammaire du Lomongo, 2eme partie, morphologie.* Tervuren: MRAC.

Hyman, L. H. 2005. Why describe African languages? In A. Akinlabi and O. Adesola (eds), *Proceedings of the 4th World Congress of African Linguistics.* New Brunswick 2003, 21–42. Cologne: Ruediger Köppe Verlag.

Raum, J. 1909. *Versuch einer Grammatik der Dschaggasprache (Moschi-Dialekt).* Berlin: G. Reimer. 1964 reprint. Farnborough: Gregg Press reprint.

Sacleux, C. 1909. *Grammaire des dialectes Swahilis.* Paris: Procure des R. P. du Saint Esprit.

Sacleux, C. 1939. *Dictionnaire Kiswahili-Francais.* Paris: Institut d'Ethnologie.

# Contributing to Language Revitalization and Maintenance

by John Watters
Past President, SIL International®

Over the past two decades the general public has become increasingly aware that numerous languages currently spoken are said to be in danger of disappearing. Some linguists suggest that as many as 90% of the languages currently spoken in the world will no longer be spoken by the year 2100. For example, Krauss (1992, *Language* 68(1):4-10) suggests that 50% of the languages currently spoken are "moribund". That is, they are not being learned by the children of the language community. Another 40% of all languages are "endangered". That is, conditions are such that children in some generation in the next 100 years will stop learning their parents' language. That leaves 10% that might be considered "safe". In comparison, others have suggested languages with fewer than 100,000 speakers are in danger of disappearing, or about 80% of languages currently spoken. Others suggest a more conservative number of 50%. Whatever the number, the clear concern is that current conditions pose a significant danger to the linguistic diversity in the world.

In today's world, the process of globalization generally favors the languages of wider communication in place of the lesser known or minoritized languages. Economics, national politics, formal education, and media reinforce the value of languages of wider communication. As these languages expand their domain of use, an increasing reduction in the linguistic diversity around the world is likely to occur. In addition, national language policies for various reasons generally favor the languages of the majority or the greater plurality. Even those nations that have policies that recognize the value of the lesser known languages within their boundaries and seek to treat them as part of their national heritage often find it difficult in practice to provide the resources needed to strengthen their role in the local community and nation. They can often adopt procedures and practices that in fact undermine their continued existence.

There is no easy or failsafe pathway that can guarantee the renewal or indefinite use of a given language. However, it is safe to say that to ignore the smaller languages and their current endangerment is not the pathway. Policy and decision makers in government institutions are generally able to make a significant difference by securing domains within the society for the use of the given language. One example would be the consistent professional support of these languages in their educational systems, as in multi-lingual educational systems. In addition, linguistic research and the development of linguistically based products in the language can strengthen their potential to survive. These products may serve educational purposes, reference and research purposes, socio-economic and political purposes, religious purposes, and so on.

The preservation of languages is not easily accomplished. Like anything of value it takes hard work. For the many unwritten languages it requires developing a linguistically and sociolinguistically based writing system if they are to be used in education, for example. The development of dictionaries and grammars as well as the preparation of collections of local proverbs, cultural stories and village histories take significant time and persistent effort. These serve as records of the linguistic and cultural knowledge of the speakers of these languages. The grammar of Kifuliiru found in this volume is just such a product. It represents the work of speakers of the Kifuliiru language and SIL International field linguists, Roger and Karen Van Otterloo. The Preface written by the Bafuliiru speaks to the importance of this grammar for the language community itself.

This grammar is presented in such a way as to benefit the Bafuliiru people. Its presence in the community will serve the current and future generations in providing them a better understanding of their language and appreciating it for the treasure it is. In particular it can serve as a basis for the development of a pedagogical grammar and literacy materials that would help Bafuliiru speakers, especially school children, to distinguish their language from French and Swahili. Such contrasts benefit the use of all three languages, minimizing confusion and allowing each language to serve its role relative to the community. The hope is that this grammar would benefit not only this generation but the coming generations of Bafuliiru.

Given the endangered nature of many languages spoken in the world today, the sooner we are able to assist language communities using their languages in written form and in various domains the better. In SIL International we are concerned to see as much done as possible in the first quarter of the 21st century so that the current and future generations of children do not start down the path of losing their language.

As with this Kifuliiru grammar, SIL is assisting with research in various Bantu languages in conjunction with scholars and others who speak these languages. As much as possible, these efforts are being done via clusters of related languages. This provides the greatest possibility of sharing what is learned in one language of the cluster with other language communities in the same cluster and so increases the efficiency of the related efforts. In this way educational and other materials might be produced more quickly for speakers of these languages.

The Kifuliiru grammar is particularly helpful in this regard within the Bantu zone. Instead of concentrating on just the morpheme and word level, it includes a detailed description of the variant sentence structures and word orders as well as discourse features. The Kifuliiru grammar should serve as a reference point in the study of closely related Bantu languages and hopefully beyond. This is a potentially significant contribution to the possibilities of seeing many Bantu languages survive the 21st century.

In conclusion, SIL International would like to see such a product serve the speakers of the Bafuliiru community in profound ways as well as serve neighboring languages through comparative research and the stimulation of similar language programs. I congratulate the Bafuliiru community and the Van Otterloos on their significant work.

# Abbreviations

| | |
|---|---|
| 1PL / 1.PL | first-person plural |
| 1SG / 1.SG | first-person singular |
| 2PL / 2.PL | second-person plural |
| 2SG / 2.SG | second-person singular |
| A.M | associative marker |
| ADD.P | additive pronoun |
| ADD.V | additive verb |
| Adv | adverb |
| ALT.P | alternative pronoun |
| APL | applicative |
| AU | augment |
| AUX | auxiliary |
| C | consonant / predicate complement |
| C.F | contrary-to-fact |
| C.V | copy vowel |
| (cl.) 1, (cl.) 2, etc. | noun class 1, class 2, etc. |
| CMP | complementizer |
| CND | conditional |
| CND.C.F | conditional, contrary-to-fact, (pres.) |
| CND.C.F.PST | conditional, contrary-to-fact, past |
| CNJ | conjunctive |
| COM | comitative |
| CON | continuative |

| | |
|---|---|
| COP | copula |
| CS | causative |
| CTR.P | contrastive pronoun |
| D | distal / direct speech |
| DFE | dominant focal element |
| DIF.SET | different-set pronoun |
| DM | development marker |
| EMP / E | emphatic |
| F1 | future, imminent |
| F2 | future, default |
| F3 | future, remote |
| Fa | final vowel -**a** |
| Fe | final vowel -**e** |
| Fi | final vowel -**i** |
| FOC | focus |
| FRUS | frustrated |
| FV | final vowel |
| GNP | gender-number prefix |
| H | high tone |
| HL | falling contour on a single syllable |
| I | indirect speech |
| IMMED | immediately |
| IMP.P | imperative plural |
| IMP.S | imperative singular |
| INTL | intentional |
| INTS | intensive |
| INTV | intervening time |
| L | low tone |
| LH | underlying L and H tone on a single syll. |
| LM | locative marker |
| MUT | mutual |
| N | nearby / nasal |
| NEG | negative |
| NEG.FOC | negative focus |
| NEU | neuter |

## Abbreviations

| | |
|---|---|
| O1, O2, etc. | object marker cl. 1, cl. 2, etc. |
| O.P | object prefix |
| O.R | object relative marker |
| Obj. | object |
| Obj.1 | first object |
| Obj.2 | second object |
| OBV | obvious |
| P | proximal |
| P.C | proximal contrast |
| P.R | previous reference |
| P1 | past, recent |
| P2 | past, unmarked |
| P3 | past state |
| PERS | persistively |
| PoD | point of departure |
| POS | positional |
| POT | potential |
| PREV | previously |
| PRO | pronoun |
| PROG | progressive |
| PS | passive |
| Q | question marker |
| R | remote |
| RCP | reciprocal |
| RDP | reduplication |
| REP | repeatedly |
| RFX | reflexive |
| RS | resultative |
| RV.I | reversive intransitive |
| RV.T | reversive transitive |
| S.P | subject prefix |
| S.R | subject relative marker |
| SAME.SET | same-set pronoun |
| SBSQ | subsequent |
| SBV | subjunctive |

| | |
|---|---|
| SF | surface form |
| SQ | sequential |
| Sw. | Kiswahili |
| TAM | tense/aspect/mood |
| TL | timeless |
| TRANS | transitive |
| TSM | thematic salience marker |
| UF | underlying form |
| V | vowel |
| VIP | very important person |
| YET | (not) yet |
| ~ | alternate pronunciation/form |
| \| | short pause |
| \|\| | long pause |

# Maps

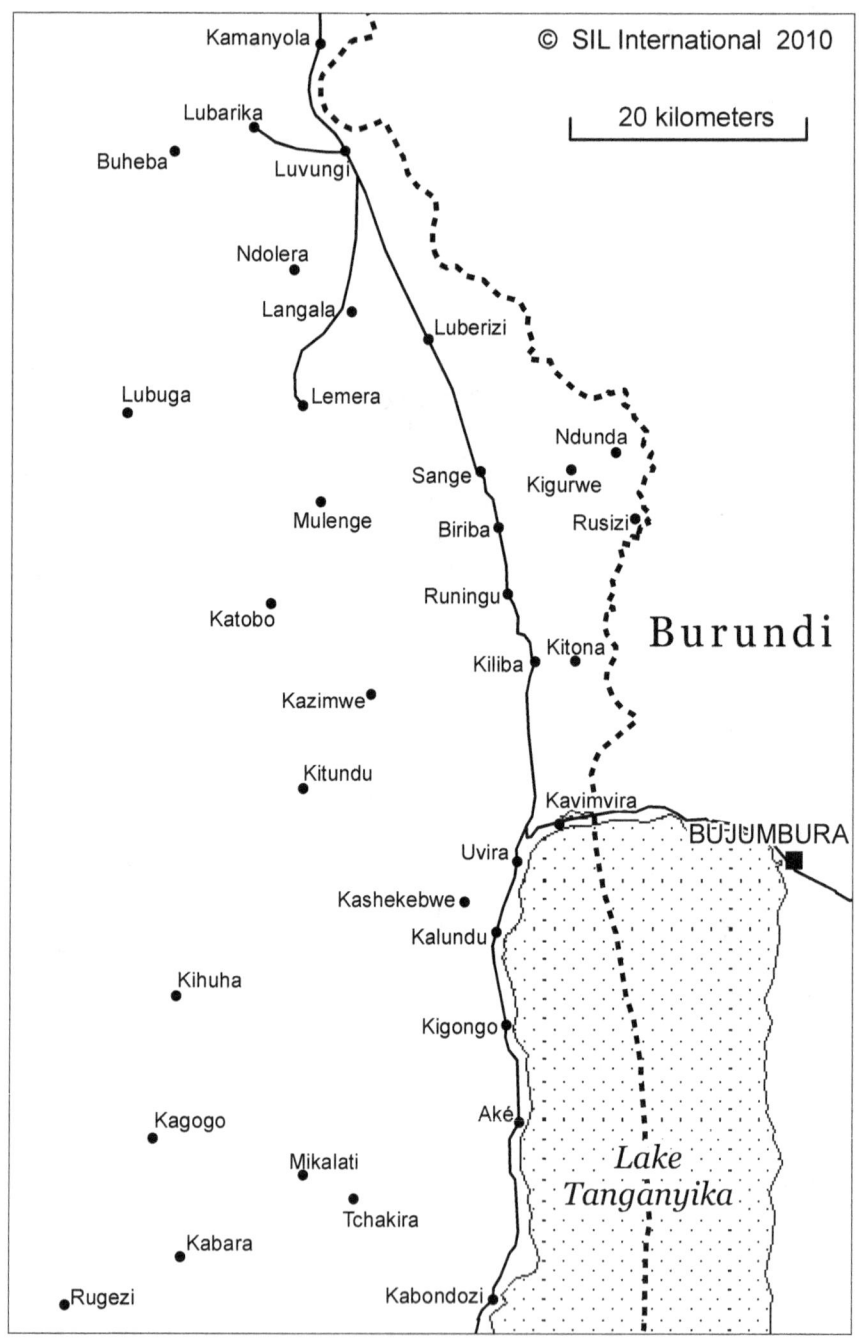

# 1

# Introduction

## 1.1 Language name and classification

**Kífùlìirû** (complete with the cl. 7 prefix **kí-**) is the name the Bafuliiru people always use for their language. For reasons of convenience, linguists often reduce the name to **Fuliiru**. Non-speakers often pronounce the name with a short penultimate vowel, and often substitute **e** for **i** in that position, producing the variants of **Kifuliru, Fuliru, Kifulero,** or **Fulero**. The code letters in the *Ethnologue* are FLR (Gordon 2005).

Guthrie (1971) classified Kifuliiru in zone D as D.63 in the Ha group, which also includes Kinyarwanda, D.61 and Kirundi, D.62 among others.

Later this group was reorganized by Meeussen and is now commonly known as Zone J, also called "Great Lakes," or "Lacustrine." In the current classification, Kifuliiru is labeled as one of the J(D)50 languages (Bastin 2003) along with Kivira, Kinyindu, Mashi, Havu, Chitembo, and Kihunde, all situated along the eastern border of the Democratic Republic of Congo (DRC). Included in the larger J group, further north within the eastern DRC border, are Kinande, Talinga, and Hema. Other languages within the larger J group include Kirundi and Kinyarwanda, as well as all the languages of southern Uganda, the Luhya and Gusii groups of Kenya, and a number of languages in northern Tanzania. Geographically these languages are all in the area of the Great Lakes: Lake Albert, Lake Edward, Lake Kivu, Lake Tanganyika, and Lake Victoria.

Kifuliiru is most closely related to Kinyindu (80–90% cognate),[1] followed by the Mashi-Havu cluster.

---

[1] This is based on personal research.

## 1.2 Dialects

Kifuliiru enjoys a high degree of cohesiveness. Although the Bafuliiru people to the south are marginally influenced by Kivira, to the west by Kinyarwanda, and to the north by Mashi, still as a whole they are quite homogeneous; the language is easily understood across the area, with only minor phonological and vocabulary differences.

In this regard, there are a few words that vary relative to sounds which are otherwise contrastive in the language: **s/sh**, e.g. **múshósì** 'man' and **músósi**, **shéshēēzì** 'morning' and **sésēēzì**. The sound **n** alternates in a few words with **ny**, such as **nyínà** 'his/her mother' and **nínà**, or **nyândì** 'who' versus **nândì**. Most say **bángérè** 'shepherds', but a few say **béngérè**. The word meaning 'a younger same-sex sibling' is pronounced either as **múlùmùnà** or **múlùmùlà**. Speakers from most areas delete a nasal before a fricative in verb forms such as **àgéézìrì** 'he has gone', from **-génd-** 'go', while a few do not delete it, e.g. **àgéénzìrì**. People influenced by Kivira use the **-ngwà** exclusive pronoun set, e.g. the cl. 2 **bóòngwâ** 'themselves' as well as the **-nyènè** set with the same meaning, e.g. **bóónyènè** 'themselves'. Such differences affect a few specific lexical items, or the presence/absence of a specific phonological rule, but there are no major differences that affect intelligibility.

## 1.3 Previous language work; contributors to the present work

The only scholarly publication focused on Kifuliiru is the French volume called *Phonologie du kifuliru: langue bantoue du groupe J* by Francis Jouannet. This volume primarily consists of a listing of the phonemes of Kifuliiru with examples demonstrating the phonemic contrasts. Some of the vocabulary and tone listed in this book seems to reflect Mashi influence. One unpublished work on Kifuliiru grammar also exists. In 2004, as a part of his master's degree program at the Nairobi Evangelical Graduate School of Theology, Kamaro Busongoye produced a thesis entitled "Complement Clauses in Kifuliiru".

Kifuliiru speakers whose input has contributed directly to this study of their language, listed alphabetically by second name, include Rev. Mushonio Banyimwire wa'Rusati, Pastor Kamaro Busongoye, Birunga Kaneneka, Asile Kashindi, Sengoronge Katyera, Pastor Juma Kinyamagoha, Kifuvyo Kwangiba, the late Pastor Kazera Kyula, the late Rev. Bahabwa Musobwa, Pastor Bugulube Mwemera, the late Pastor Nakalali Bukuru, Rev. Mulubi Ngalonga, Rev. Mulogoto Yunga, and Pastor Kibambazi Zihindula. Many others have contributed indirectly.

## 1.4 Inventory of parts of speech

The following parts of speech[2] are presented here for Kifuliiru:

ADJECTIVES are a closed set of approximately thirty-nine items. They differ from nouns in that they may be used attributively, juxtaposed to a noun and agreeing in gender and number with the noun they modify. The meanings of the adjectives are all quite general in nature, as exemplified by the stems -**bi** 'bad', -**ija** 'good', -**hamu** 'large', -**niini** 'small'.

More specific adjectival meanings are expressed by stative verbal adjectives, which are productively derived from verbs. These derived forms use the adjective prefixes and agree with some nominal referent in gender and number, but are generally used as predicate adjectives rather than in attributive position with nouns, e.g. **bì-yándìké** (8-written) (from -**yándik**- 'write') in the relative clause **byóshí íbìrì bìyándìké** 'everything which is written'. The actual occurrences of stative verbal adjectives in Kifuliiru literature are relatively infrequent.

ADVERBS include about twenty common terms describing time, manner, etc., as well as many others that occur less frequently.

ASSOCIATIVE MARKERS mark the initial element of the associative phrase which connects (or associates) one noun with another. Structurally they are clitics, formed by the gender-number prefix (GNP) + -**a**. Thus in **bíhé byá=kàbìgìngwê** 'the time of afternoon', the cl. 8 noun **bíhê** 'time' is associated with the cl. 12 noun **kàbìgìngwê** 'afternoon' by means of the associative marker **bya**, which is composed of the cl. 8 associative prefix **bi-** (agreeing with the cl. 8 **bíhê**) and the following -**a**.

ASSOCIATIVE PRONOUNS are formed from an associative marker and a pronominal suffix. They are the form used wherever a pronoun follows an associative marker. For example **há=bútámbí lyé=nyûmbà** 'beside (of) the house' is pronominalized as **há=bútámbí lyáyò** 'beside (of) it', where **lyáyò** represents the associative pronoun.

AUGMENTS are structurally clitics, occurring as the initial element of most noun phrases. Thus the initial **a** in **á=bándù** 'the people' is an augment, as is the initial **a** in **á=bàndì bándù** 'the other people'.

AUXILIARIES include verbal forms derived from the copula verb -**ba** 'be/become', which are used to set the tense/aspect/mood of stative verb phrases. They also include the adverbial auxiliaries. In addition, there are the progressive auxiliaries **mú**, **bú**, and -**gweti**.

COMPLEMENTIZERS introduce complement clauses (e.g. "that" in the clause "that he had arrived" as used in the sentence "I was not aware that he had

---

[2] Listed under parts of speech are word-level units which function as syntactic classes. Most sub-lexical word-building units, such as "prefixes" or "clitics" are not included.

arrived"), and include only three forms: **kwo, mbu,** and **ngu,** all with the English translation 'that'.

CONJUNCTIONS can be divided into those that join phrases, and those that express relationships between clauses and sentences.

DEMONSTRATIVES are deictic[3] (pointing) words such as 'this' and 'that'. Kifuliiru has five different demonstratives, in addition to two set selectors. Demonstratives may be used pronominally, or as modifiers of a following noun.

IDEOPHONES are usually found outside the clause nucleus (mostly on the right side) and involve quite a large set of words, most of which "sound like" what they are describing. Many are reduplicated forms, and they are often introduced by a quote marker.

INTERJECTIONS are also usually found outside the clause nucleus (usually on the left side, and without an introductory quote marker) and express surprise, derision, pain, surprise, etc.

LOCATIVE MARKERS are a closed set of seven different items that are used at the beginning of a locative phrase. (They contrast with the true noun class prefixes, which are prefixed to noun roots.) Only one of the locative classes (cl. 16) actually includes a noun, **hándù** 'place'. The four markers are 16 **há**, 17 **kú**, 18 **mú**, and 23 **í**. The three additional locative forms are frozen compound forms of which the initial element is the cl. 23 **í**.

NOUNS belong to one of seventeen noun classes[4] (1–16, 19), and trigger noun class agreement on the various components of the noun phrase, as well as on the verb. Each class tends to cover a certain semantic category, such as people (cl. 1–2), masses (cl. 6), abstracts (cl. 14), diminutive (cl. 19), etc. A great number of nouns are derived from verbs, other nouns, formatives, and even phrases.

NUMBERS are found in both cardinal and ordinal forms, and include structurally diverse forms: some are technically adjectives, while others are numerals or nouns. **Múgùmà** 'one' is an adjective, **bàbìrì** 'two', **bàshàtù** 'three' (both numerals) are cardinal numbers. The ordinal numbers such as **ú=(múndú) wà mbérè** 'the first (person) (lit., the one of front/ahead)', **ú=wá kàbìrì** 'second' and **ú=wá kàshàtù** 'third', are formed by the use of associative constructions in which the number is the nominal element of the associative phrase.

POSITION NOUNS are a closed class of about fifteen nouns which function almost exclusively in locative phrases. These words have characteristics of both nouns and prepositions, and so are given a name that reflects them both.

---

[3] In narrative texts, the Nearby and Remote demonstratives mark thematic salience.

[4] Cl. 1a is a special form of cl. 1, and includes some proper names, kinship terms, etc. For cl. 1a, the normal cl. 1 singular prefix **mu-** is absent, e.g. **nyina** 'mother', although the plural **ba-** prefix is present, e.g. **banyina** 'mothers'.

PRONOUNS are of many types, including verbal subject and object prefixes, verbal object suffixes, five kinds of personal pronouns, and eight kinds of interrogative words.

QUANTIFIERS include **bóóshì** 'all', **bómbì** 'both', and **ngiisi** 'each', and occur after the noun in the noun phrase.

The QUESTION WORD **ka** is a clitic located at the beginning of the clause and turns the whole clause into a question. E.g. **Ká=nààwè úgáàlyà kú=bítólè** 'And you, will you eat (some of) the bitter eggplant?'

QUOTE MARKERS **ti** ‹quote›, **mbu** ‹quote›, **ngu** ‹quote› and **kwókùnô** ‹quote. MARKED› are used to introduce quotes.

VERBS include single-word forms, such as **bà-tá-gá-ná-kì-mú-shúlìk-àg-à** (2-NEG-F2-ADD.V-PERS-O1-hit-EMP-Fa) 'and they will not still hit him EMP' and multiword forms. The latter, involving auxiliaries, are also very common, e.g. **á-báà-lí kìzì génd-á bá-gá-hììv-à** (S.R-2-P3 REP GOING-Fa 2-INTL-hunt-Fa) 'they who were in the state of repeatedly going to hunt'. The basic structure of a verb includes a root, which can be modified by various extensions to form a base. The base plus the final vowel forms the stem. The stem plus the object prefixes forms the macrostem. That unit in turn is inflected by a wide variety of prefixes which serve as subject marker, negative marker, additive, tense/aspect/mood markers, etc.

## 1.5 Conventions

### 1.5.1 Texts and their numbering

One hundred and fifty-three texts were employed for this study, all narrative. The sources of these texts are shown in the chart below. The majority of the texts were spoken by a 55-year-old man named Sengoronge Katyera, a master of classic Kifuliiru discourse. It is because he has provided so many of the texts that he is listed separately from the rest of the men aged 50–70.

| Source | Age | People | Texts | Text numbers |
|---|---|---|---|---|
| Women | 20–45 | 4 | 13 | 101-113 |
| Women | 50–70 | 4 | 10 | 201-210 |
| Men | 20–45 | 5 | 27 | 301-303, 501-524 |
| Men | 50–70 | 6 | 12 | 401-412 |
| Sengoronge | 55 | 1 | 91 | 01-56, 601-635 |
| Total | | 20 | 153 | |

In the relatively few cases where language data to exemplify a certain Kifuliiru grammatical construction could not be found in those texts, examples were taken from the Kifuliiru New Testament. It is our opinion that such material, translated meaning-for-meaning, is much more valid than data elicited word-for-word, where one asks, "Can you say ....(a certain form)?" or "Can you make that verb phrase into a passive?" These latter methods of data gathering seem to be much more open to the label of "translationese" than the use of material which was translated broadly, meaning-for-meaning and not form-for-form. For the chapter on interjections and ideophones, most examples were not found in the texts, so we asked Kifuliiru speakers to give various examples in a natural context.

The text references are listed as (01 033), where 01 stands for the story number, and 033 stands for the line number in the story. Biblical references are listed as Gen 1:3 (Genesis chapter 1, verse 3) where the book abbreviation comes first, followed by the chapter, and then the verse number.

### 1.5.2 Transcription conventions

The consonant symbols used in this book are here related to the places and manners of articulation in table 1.1.

Table 1.1. Kifuliiru consonant symbols

|  | Labial | Labio-dental | Alveolar | Pre-palatal | Velar | Laryn-geal |
|---|---|---|---|---|---|---|
| Plosives, voiceless | p |  | t |  | k |  |
| Plosives, voiced |  |  | d |  | g |  |
| Fricatives, voiceless |  | f | s | sh |  | h |
| Fricatives, voiced |  | v | z | j |  |  |
| Plosives, pre-nasalized | mb |  | nd |  | ng |  |
| Nasals | m |  | n | ny |  |  |
| Liquids |  |  | l/r |  |  |  |
| Approximants | b |  |  |  |  |  |
| Glides | w[a] |  | y |  |  |  |

[a] The sound w, although present in Kifuliiru, is very rare, occurring as w only in pronominal/prefixal forms. When it occurs without a preceding consonant, it is always synchronically traceable to a high back vowel, u, which has undergone glide formation. Thus w is included in the phoneme inventory only in a marginal way.

The phoneme l alternates non-contrastively with r between front vowels. The phoneme l also contrasts with r in other environments. This situation is the result of borrowings, especially from Kinyarwanda.

## 1.5 Conventions

The vowels (short and long) are as in table 1.2:

Table 1.2. Kifuliiru vowels

|     | Front | Central | Back  |
|-----|-------|---------|-------|
| Hi  | i ii  |         | u uu  |
| Mid | e ee  |         | o oo  |
| Low |       | a aa    |       |

VOWEL COALESCENCE is represented in the data only where it is mandatory in the pronunciation of the language. This means that it is indicated up to the level of the phonological word, which includes the cliticization of monosyllabic forms. In the following example, ba+i (associative marker **ba**+ cl. 23 clitic **i**) surfaces as **be**, and coalescence is mandatory: **á=bándú bé̱=kāāyà** 'people of the compound'. Coalescence is not written at the level of the phrase, however, so that **ànágêndà í=kāāyà** 'he went home' is not written as usually pronounced at normal speed (i.e. **ànágêndé=kāāyà**), since it can also be pronounced in deliberate speech as two words without coalescence.

SURFACE TONE is marked in all data, as follows. The acute accent (**é**) is used to indicate high tone, e.g. **ú=múké̱ngè** 'hollow grass used as straw'. The grave accent (**è**) indicates low tone, e.g. **ú=múkè̱ngè** 'monitor lizard'. The circumflex (**ê**) is used to indicate a phonetic falling contour on a phonologically conditioned long vowel (which is not written as a double vowel), e.g. **ú=múkê̱ngè** 'wooden trough for making banana beer'. On a long vowel written as VV, a falling contour is marked with an acute accent on the first vowel and a grave accent on the second (**áà**). Such a contour reflects a lexical HL sequence, e.g. **túgágáàjà** 'we will count'. Mid tone (the phonetic realization of an underlying low-high sequence, **ǐ**) is indicated by a macron (**ī**),[5] whether on a single vowel, e.g. **ú=múvī̱ndì** 'grasshopper dropping', or on a double vowel **á=mī̱ījì** 'water'. In Kifuliiru there are no rising tones in the surface pronunciations.

A non-conjugated VERB BASE has tone indicated only on the first syllable (e.g. **-fùkam-** 'kneel') because this is where the underlying tone of a verb always surfaces. The tone of the following syllables within the verb stem will vary according to the tense/aspect/mood of a specific conjugated form. A verb base on which there is no tone indicated is underlyingly toneless, e.g. **-laalik-** 'invite', since its tone depends completely on its TAM environment. Other toneless morphemes include certain prefixes, certain suffixes (including most verbal suffixes) and many single-syllable words.

---

[5] Kifuliiru has no phonemic rising contours. Rather any underlying LH is pronounced on the surface as a level mid tone.

DIRECT QUOTES are introduced by a colon ( : ) then set off by double chevrons: ( « ) for opening the quote, and ( » ) for closing it, e.g. **Ànádètà: « Yîjâ! »** 'And he said: « Come! »' This follows one of the French standards. The introductory quote markers **ti, mbu, ngu** are glossed with the word "quote", surrounded by single chevrons like this: ‹quote›.

IDEOPHONES AND INTERJECTIONS are also marked in examples by double chevrons, e.g. **Lèèzà náyè ngwà=vwómè, « shóóbè »**. 'Leeza, and she also, when she tried to get water, « frustration »'.

HYPHENS ( - ) are used to separate affixes from each other and from roots, when morphemes are separated for glossing purposes, e.g. **mú-kèngè** (3-monitor.lizard). They are also used to separate the parts of reduplicated items, e.g. **ká-síngé-síngè** (12-speedily-RDP), as well as to indicate morphemes or groups of morphemes which do not comprise whole words, e.g. the verb root -**génd**- 'go'.[6] Prefixes are followed by a hyphen, and suffixes are preceded by one. Verb bases are both preceded and followed by one.

EQUAL SIGNS ( = ) are used to join clitics to the word on which they depend, thus clearly distinguishing affixes and clitics. Clitics include separate words like **na** 'and' and **nga** 'like'. The initial augment **á** in **á=bándù** 'people' is also a clitic. In Kifuliiru, uninflected monosyllabic verb stems which follow an auxiliary are all clitics, and are also set off by an equal sign, e.g. the monosyllabic verb -**ly**- 'eat' in the phrase **ànákìzíí=ryà** 'he repeatedly ate'.

Regarding the parsing of words into morphemes for glossing purposes, it should be noted that there are some forms where there is a PORTMANTEAU[7] effect, often as a result of vowel coalescence, where the meaning of a whole form cannot be reduced to a sum of the individual parts. This happens for example, with the proximal and nearby demonstratives, as well as with the object relative. In such forms, the surface forms cannot always be parsed into "morpheme" sections which have a one-to-one correspondence with the underlying meanings. In such cases we have tried to make an approximation which reflects the basic underlying meanings but does not necessarily reflect underlying forms of the actual morphemes. In cases where what appears to be one morpheme in the parsing represents more than one underlying morpheme, the gloss includes a plus sign: e.g. **Yìbyó** (those.N+8).

---

[6] Verb roots and bases generally end in a consonant, e.g. the root -**gend**- 'go'. There are, however, a limited number of CV roots. Most of these end in a vowel which is changed by phonological rule to a glide preceding the obligatory FV, e.g. -**mo**- > -**mw**- 'shave'. Unless the underlying vowel is in focus in the discussion, we normally indicate these by a -**Cw**- or -**Cy**-. Two verbs with CV roots, the copula -**ba**- 'be, become' and the verb -**ha**- 'give', end in /a/, which does not undergo glide formation. Since long vowels are not used word finally, the addition of a FV to these does not result in a surface long vowel.

[7] Portmanteau (Crystal 2003:360) is "a term used in morphological analysis...where a single morph can be analyzed into more than one MORPHEME..."

## 1.5 Conventions

The FINAL VOWEL of verbs is parsed as a separate morpheme for purposes of morpheme-by-morpheme glossing. However in the case of adverbial auxiliaries ending in final vowel -**i**, e.g. **gendi** 'GOING', and the copula -**li**, the final vowel is not separated. This is merely a convention, for the sake of brevity, since each of these auxiliary forms is considered a unit, and cannot be interrupted by derivational extensions[8] or other suffixes, as non-auxiliary verbs can.

However, the final vowel is separated off in auxiliaries ending in -**a**, e.g. -**genda** 'going', as that form can alternatively surface with a final -**e**, e.g. in the subjunctive auxiliary -**gende** in (1.1).

(1.1) **Yìbyó**       **by-óshì** ||   **ù-Ø-génd-è**          **w-à-bì-hàmb-à** |   **mú**=
      those.N+8      8-all          2SG-SBV-GOING-Fe        2SG-P1-O8-put.in-Fa   18=

**kí-tútúlúgù**.
7-big.container

'All those (cl. 8 things) || you go and put them | in a big container.'
(208 056)

The term RESULTATIVE[9] (RS) is used to refer to Kifuliiru verb forms with the final -**ir-i**, which is the Kifuliiru reflex of the Proto-Bantu *- **i̧d-e** (or *- **i̧de**). In using the term resultative (related to, but not equal with "anterior") we follow Bybee, who uses this term for a verb where "an action in the past produces a state that persists into the present" (Bybee, Perkins, and Pagliuca 1994:318); for example the resultative **àtèzírì** 'he has set the trap, and the resulting state still obtains, the trap remains set'. Thus **à-tèz-ír-ì** is glossed morpheme-by-morpheme as (1-trap-RS-Fi).

The **e/o** morpheme of PREVIOUS REFERENCE (P.R) is a word-building component that is found in several kinds of words in Kifuliiru, including many pronouns and qualifiers, as well as the focus copulas. In the morpheme glosses, these P.R morphemes are usually not specified, as the previous reference is already

---

[8] Except for the emphatic suffix.

[9] The term "perfective", rather than resultative is often used in Bantu literature to refer to the final -**ir-i** suffix. It is also commonly used in reference to forms of the verb which include this morpheme. However, grammarians are quick to point out that this suffix is usually not associated with perfect aspect, as the name might imply, which "presents an event as an undifferentiated and time-bounded whole" (Nurse 2003:96) but rather with anterior, which "refers to an earlier action which produced a state which either lives on or whose consequences or relevance live on" (ibid.). Thus both in reference to tense/aspect forms created by the use of this suffix, and in reference to the suffix itself, we have used the term "resultative" (which is a subset of anterior) when referring to any inflected verb form which includes the use of this suffix. We also use RS as the gloss for this suffix in morpheme-by-morpheme glosses.

clear, and to add an additional P.R tends to clutter the gloss, making it more difficult to follow.

The glosses of most free (whole word) personal pronouns are written in caps, e.g. "THEY", to demonstrate the emphatic nature of the pronoun.

The third singular is glossed as cl. 1 (not 3SG), and the third plural is glossed as cl. 2 (not 3PL). Note that third-person singular pronouns are free-glossed 'he', 'she', or 'it', depending on the context from which the example is taken.

(Sw.) following a word indicates a direct borrowing from Kiswahili.

PAUSES in Kifuliiru are important in isolating various components of information structure at the clause and sentence level. Thus all clause and sentence examples in this book have been carefully marked for pause. Long pauses of one-half second or longer are marked with two vertical lines ( ‖ ). Pauses shorter than one-half second are marked with one vertical line ( | ).

SQUARE BRACKETS ( [ ] ), besides indicating phonetic transcription, are also used to separate morphemes within word formulas. In formulas, every prefix is marked only by a left bracket ( [ ) and every suffix is marked only by a right bracket ( ] ). The root has a bracket both preceding and following ( [ ] ). The parentheses in formulas represent optional morphemes. Thus the formula for the direct imperative singular is: [verb base] -**a**]. The formula for the simple subjunctive is: [S.P [ (NEG) [ Ø [ (O.P) [ (RFX) [base] -**e**], which means obligatory subject prefix, optional negative prefix, null TAM prefix, optional object prefix, optional reflexive prefix (or 1SG object), base, and -**e** final vowel.

## 1.6 Possible mismatches between Kifuliiru and other languages

When writing in Kifuliiru, or when translating something into Kifuliiru, the writer must be constantly aware when the linguistic systems of Kifuliiru diverge from those of other languages, including French (the national language of the Democratic Republic of Congo), English, biblical Greek, biblical Hebrew, etc. If the grammar of the source language is merely translated word for word, much of the Bantu essence is stripped away in the resultant Kifuliiru translation, leaving a bland resemblance that often miscommunicates. Some of the main Kifuliiru distinctives are summarized in this section, and dealt with in greater detail throughout the book.

### 1.6.1 Reduplication

Reduplication is a rich and pervasive feature of Kifuliiru, and is found in nouns, verbs, adverbs, adjectives, locative phrases, numbers, associative pronouns, different-set pronouns, and demonstrative pronouns. Reduplication is part of the language's tendency to grammaticize real-world phenomena that reflect repetition, extensiveness, emphasis, etc. Reduplication should

## 1.6 Possible mismatches between Kifuliiru and other languages

be incorporated into Kifuliiru texts wherever the natural context implies it, whether or not it is found in French or other source languages.

### 1.6.2 Pronouns

Pronouns in some languages function largely to keep track of referents. However in Kifuliiru, free (whole word) pronouns never serve just to keep references clear; rather they are highly marked. Thus, whether in composition or in translation, pronouns should be used only in places where they would naturally occur, and must be chosen carefully from among the various possibilities. As is typical in Bantu, each person and each noun class has its own pronoun set. The basic personal pronoun in Kifuliiru is contrastive, and here represented by the cl. 2 **bóòhê** 'THEY', in capital letters to mark contrast. This pronoun always marks a clear contrast between the referent and other similar items or groups. The ALTERNATIVE PRONOUN **bóókì** 'THEY' (again in capital letters) marks a contrast to some other set which would otherwise mistakenly be assumed. The ADDITIVE PRONOUN **nábò** is in addition to a similar item which has already been mentioned. The SAME SET PRONOUN **ábààbò** refers to members of the same set, or similar items of the same kind. Each of these pronouns, as well as many others not mentioned here, has a strong rhetorical function, and should be used only when, and always when, that rhetorical context is triggered.

### 1.6.3 "Expressive" nouns communicating adjectival concepts

In Kifuliiru, the closed set of thirty-nine adjectives is typically quite generic, e.g. 'good', 'bad', 'long', 'short', etc. To communicate a specialized or emphatic adjectival meaning, "expressive" nouns are often used with following associative phrases. They are called "expressive" because they all have quite colorful adjectival meanings. For example **nángùngùbàngà wé**=**nyûmbà** refers to 'a huge thing of a house'. In this case the first noun **nángùngùbàngà** 'the huge thing', although technically a noun, has a descriptive or attributive function. It expresses an attribute of the noun which is found in the following associative phrase. Such attributive nouns are quite common in Kifuliiru, and provide for a lively discourse. Since in other languages such "expressive" nouns may not be used as often, the use of this device should be kept in mind.

### 1.6.4 Locative phrases with cl. 16 *ha*

In Kifuliiru there is more than one locative marker meaning 'place', including cl. 16 **há** and cl. 23 **í**, e.g. **há**=**lwījì** 'at the river' versus **í**=**rwījì** 'at the river'. Of these two, the cl. 16 **há** marks a location in the story where a new development of the story theme is *about to* take place. By marking such a location with the locative marker **há**, the speaker is in effect shining a spotlight on that place in the story, encouraging the hearer to pay special attention to what will follow. The cl. 23 **í** (although it has the identical meaning 'place') lacks the component of "new thematic development."

### 1.6.5 Ideophones and interjections

Most ideophones are intended to mimic the sounds of what they describe, e.g. **boom!** in English. In typical Bantu fashion, Kifuliiru boasts an extensive list of ideophones, which are used to describe various phenomena including animal sounds, being bitten, eating, escaping, falling, grabbing, many kinds of movement, doing something quickly, being sick, striking, tripping, water sounds, doing things without care, etc.

Interjections are also very common in Kifuliiru, and include many words expressing implication, surprise, derision, pain, etc. Both ideophones and interjections can do much to bring life to the text.

### 1.6.6 Verbs

#### *1.6.6.1 Tense/aspect/mood*

In Kifuliiru, the TAM slot includes many categories not found in other languages, especially non-African languages. These include various types of mixed imperatives, where two imperatives are joined together for various effects. There are also several kinds of contrary-to-fact conditionals. Besides the unmarked future, there are also several kinds of immediate futures, as well as the new future, and the remote future. For the past tense, there are multiple recent pasts, including a frustrated past, and the unmarked past. The resultative (past action with present implications) is also of special note, as well as the various progressives, including the progressive intentional. Continuative marks predictable items. There are also several kinds of copulas. This list is just a sample of the many kinds of specialized verb forms. If the language is to be used effectively, these forms must each be employed in the proper communicative context.

#### *1.6.6.2 Auxiliary* **ba**

Stative phrases have their TAM set by the auxiliary verb **-ba-** 'become', with the lexical stative verb following, e.g. **ìrí ákábá àkòlà mú=bìtááhánà** 'when he was now going home with them (cl. 8 things)', where **ákábà** 'he was' sets the past tense, while **àkòlà mú=bìtááhánà** is the main stative (lexical) verb meaning 'he is now (but not before) returning home with them'. Whenever a stative lexical verb is found, this auxiliary must be used, if the time includes any of the ten triggering TAM possibilities.

### 1.6.6.3 Adverbial auxiliaries

The Kifuliiru verb phrase also includes a set of sixteen adverbial auxiliaries, most of which end in -**a**, which can be followed by a conjugated verb. These are: -**kìri** 'persistive', -**kòla** 'newly (now, not before)', -**shùba** 'previously (before, not now)', -**gáluka** 'returning', -**génda** 'going', -**lènga** 'passing', -**shiiba** 'all day', -**sìgala** 'remaining', -**taaha** 'going home', -**tuula** 'habitual', -**yàma** 'immediately', -**yàma/yàmiri** 'always', -**yíja** 'coming', -**gwanwa** 'encountered', -**kèngeera** 'unintended', and -**laala** 'one day ago'.

There are also twenty-five adverbial auxiliaries ending in -**i**: -**géndi** 'going', -**híkiri** 'arriving', -**lèngi** 'passing', -**sìgali** 'remaining', -**yíji** 'coming', -**búli** 'subsequently', -**kì** 'persistive', -**kìzi** 'repeated/habitual', -**kòli** 'newly (now, not before)' -**máli** 'already', -**shúbi** 'previously (before, not now)', -**shúbi** 'again', -**támi** 'finally', -**tàngí** 'first', -**té** 'prior', -**yàmi** 'immediately', -**zíndi** 'lastly', -**zíndukiri** 'early in morning', -**hámbiri** 'almost trouble', -**líndi** 'after duress', -**lóózi** 'as if wanted', -**lúnguli** 'prematurely', -**ményi/-yíji** 'knowing', -**zì/-záàzi** 'not yet', -**zìndi** 'ever'. The above auxiliaries can be sorted according to relative time, relative location, relative time/location, and mood. All of them have been highly grammaticized.

Of interest are -**géndì** 'going' and -**yíjì** 'coming', often used "redundantly" (relative to other languages) before an independent verb with the very same meaning. This is seen in (1.2) where the adverbial auxiliary -**yíjì** 'coming' is followed by the main lexical verb **yíjà** 'come'.

(1.2)  **Hà-ná-yîjì**    **yíj-à**   ‖  **mú-tàbánà   mú-gùmà**.
      16-SQ-COMING   come-Fa   1-young.man  1-one

'And there coming came ‖ one young man.' (101 009)

In addition, the choice of -**géndì** 'going' versus -**yíjì** 'coming' is triggered by whether the action is seen as moving toward, or away from, the deictic center. There is likely to be a mismatch here with many non-Bantu languages. All of these auxiliaries are an integral part of Kifuliiru, and "conventionalize implicatures," i.e. they grammaticize forms that other languages do not overtly state. Effective Kifuliiru will employ all these forms in a meaningful and natural way.

In addition to the above, Kifuliiru also includes roughly fifty verbs which can be followed by an infinitive clause. These include verbs of relative time, such as 'begin' and 'finish'. The rest all deal with commonly accepted modal categories such as 'be able', 'behoove', 'want', 'add to', 'refuse/accept', 'leave', 'allow', 'know/forget', 'be afraid', 'change/stay the same', 'be born/die', and 'lack'.

#### 1.6.6.4 Concomitant phrases

Two verb phrases can be joined by the conjunction **ìrí** 'while' to show that the actions of those clauses are occurring at the same time. In addition, **mú** plus the infinitive can be used either preceding or following the verb, to indicate the *state* in which the main verb of the clause occurs. All of these forms need to be employed naturally, and where appropriate to the context.

### 1.6.7 Clauses

#### 1.6.7.1 Topic-comment articulation

In topic-comment articulation the topic (understood information) comes at the beginning of the clause, isolated by a following pause, while the comment (new information) follows, with the dominant focal element (DFE) coming at the very end of the clause. There are many ways to alter the clause order, so that the topic is positioned at the beginning of the clause, and comment at the end, including various types of preposing, postposing, promoting to object, and marked placement of pronouns and quantifiers. Topic-comment articulation affects the large majority of clauses, and must be employed correctly if Kifuliiru is to be clear and natural. When translating phrase by phrase from a non-Bantu language, a relatively minor point in the clause is often placed in the comment position at the end, where it is completely out of place. This is a very common translation mistake, and makes the material in the receptor language much more difficult to understand.

Pauses are typically employed to separate topic from comment, in ways that are very unnatural in many Indo-European languages. The implications of pause relative to Kifuliiru orthography need to be taken into account.

#### 1.6.7.2 Identificational articulation

Identificational articulation involves a presupposed proposition. The focus, then, is on "the element that was lacking in the presupposed proposition" Levinsohn (2006:5). In the sentence "Sengoronge is the one who was throwing up", the reader/addressee is already aware that someone was throwing up, and "Sengoronge" identifies who it was. Using identificational articulation for the presentation of material is a very common device in Kifuliiru, but is not necessarily common in unrelated languages.

*1.6 Possible mismatches between Kifuliiru and other languages*

*1.6.7.3 Locative inversion*

Locative inversion frequently signals the introduction of a major participant. In locative inversion, a locative phrase is found in the position of surface subject. The verb is followed by the "real" (or underlying) subject of the sentence, which is in focus at the end of the clause, in the position of dominant focal element. Whether by means of locative inversion, or another strategy, the main participant needs to be introduced at the end of the clause, in focal position, if the reader is to process the participant as being "major" in the story.

### 1.6.8 Interclausal relations

Dependent clauses include ten types of adverbial clauses, including several with compound conjunctions to communicate two ideas at once. There are also analytic causatives. Among the dependent clauses are at least eight different kinds of temporal clauses, each one used in its own context. The conjunctions (and types of clauses) must be chosen carefully if the concepts being expressed are to come across naturally.

Clauses employing negative verbs with the additive morpheme can be used concessively, and they can also be used to communicate contrast.

Relative clauses are basically restrictive in Kifuliiru. In addition, Kifuliiru relative clauses are typically used to mark items or events of thematic salience, i.e. they highlight material that is central to the theme of the story. This often occurs in the introductory sentence of the story.

### 1.6.9 Textlinguistics

*1.6.9.1 Speech registers*

Though the terms admittedly refer to phenomena on a continuum, for our discussion, Kifuliiru narrative texts can be classified into three different speech registers: quite formal, somewhat informal, and quite informal. These different registers are distinguished by the ways they use thematic salience markers, speech verbs, emphatic prominence, and the continuative aspect.

*1.6.9.2 Paragraphs*

One of the main ways to mark a discontinuity in narrative flow, and therefore a new paragraph, is by the use of the conjunction **ìrí** 'when' followed by a verb in the 'unmarked past tense (P2)', indicated in the verb by the TAM prefix **ka-**. In many cases such a clause does not present new information, but merely repeats old information. For example in (1.3) the clause **ànáyàmì géndá ágálóòzá Wàngáàvù** 'and he immediately went looking for Cow' is followed by the seemingly redundant statement **Ìrí ákáhíká mú=njírà** 'When he arrived in the road'. This phrase marks a temporal discontinuity, introducing a new episode. In typical narratives, well over half of the new episodes are marked in this way. In translating material into Kifuliiru from other language families which do not include such a device for introducing episodes, there will likely be a mismatch, resulting in unnatural Kifuliiru text, unless a conscious effort is made to include the natural Kifuliiru discourse features.

(1.3) À-ná-yàmì   **génd-á**   á-gá-lóòz-á |   W-à-n-gáàvù. ||   **Ìrí**
      1-SQ-IMMED  going-Fa   1-INTL-seek-Fa  1-A.M-9-cow          when

**á-ká-hík-á**   mú=   n-jírà ||   à-ná-hùlúk-ír-à |   k-û=   lyá
1-P2-arrive-Fa  18-path= 9-path   1-SQ-appear-APL-Fa   17-1=   that.R

mú-sháàjà.
1-old.man

'He immediately went looking | for Cow. || When he arrived in the path || he appeared | to that old man.' (105 025-26)

### 1.6.9.3 Use of continuative in informal register

The continuative verb form marks predictable sequences in informal text and can be used very effectively in Kifuliiru.

### 1.6.9.4 Thematic salience markers

Two of the demonstrative pronouns, when used in narrative discourse, function to mark the thematic salience of characters and events in the story. The nearby demonstrative (e.g. cl. 2 **yàbô**) marks DEFAULT thematic salience, while the remote demonstrative (e.g. cl. 2 **bàlyâ**) marks MAJOR thematic salience. This use of demonstrative pronouns is quite different from that in some other languages and can present a major mismatch.

### 1.6.9.5 Use of the emphatic extension

The derivational emphatic extension **-ag** is used in informal narratives to mark emphatic prominence, meaning 'pay attention to what is coming'. This device can be used very effectively in the right context.

### 1.6.9.6 Songs which provide key information

In Kifuliiru folk tales, one common highlighting strategy is to introduce a song, consisting of a few clauses, often with a few Kiswahili loan words, and usually repeated more than once in the story. These short songs function to give an insider's view of the story, usually hinting at the problem in the story, so the addressee can be of help. In oral texts, these songs are always sung by the storyteller, while the rest of the story is spoken.

### 1.6.9.7 *Reported speech*

Different speech registers use different styles for expressing reported speech. In the formal written register almost every quote is introduced by a speech verb such as 'said, told, asked', etc. Direct quotes are used for more thematic events, while indirect quotes are used more for background information. In the informal registers on the other hand, speech verbs are used only at the beginning of a tight-knit conversation, with the remaining speeches in that conversation introduced by a variety of reduced forms, but with no speech verb.

### 1.6.9.8 *Participants*

Major participants are typically introduced at the end of a clause, in focal position. In addition, participants are often repeated in a noun phrase when they begin a new conversation, or at the beginning of a new episode. It should also be noted that participants are usually tracked using a consistent term. The major participant "cow" will be called "that cow", or just "cow" many times in the story, but will not typically be referred to as the "lazy bovine", or "the calf's mother", etc.

### 1.6.10 Proverbs

Typical for Africa, there are thousands of proverbs in Kifuliiru, and they are used often in texts. To use them naturally is a very effective rhetorical device.

# 2

# Nouns

In typical Bantu fashion, Kifuliiru has an extensive set of seventeen noun classes. The noun classes trigger agreement with augments, adjectives, demonstratives, pronouns, possessives, subject and object verb prefix pronouns, etc.

There is a tendency to put elements of the same type together in one noun class, e.g. humans (cl. 1/2), liquids (cl. 6), plants (cl. 7/8), abstractions (cl. 14), diminutives (cl. 19/13), etc. Although the system has broken down somewhat, there are still significant tendencies toward grouping like items together in the same noun class.

## 2.1 Constituent structure of the noun

The structure of the Kifuliiru noun word[1] is: [noun class prefix[2] [noun stem]. The class prefix can also be termed a gender number prefix (GNP),[3] which is a type of portmanteau morpheme. That is to say it indicates not only the grammatical gender of the word, but also indicates whether the noun is singular or plural.[4]

---

[1] Isolated nouns are often preceded by an augment. However, this augment is not a prefix, but a clitic. While phonologically part of the noun word, syntactically the augment is a component of the noun phrase, and is thus discussed in chapter 7.

[2] Nouns belonging to cl. 1a, and some nouns in cl. 9/10 have no class prefix.

[3] The term "gender-number prefix" was first introduced to us by Derek Fivaz.

[4] The exceptions to this include the mass nouns, mostly found only in cl. 6, cf. **á=mìíjì** 'water'. The other exception is cl. 9/10, where the nominal prefixes are identical (e.g. **nyûmbà** 'house/houses'), so that the number of the noun is not discernable without observing the agreements triggered elsewhere in the phrase or sentence.

At least twenty-three noun classes can be reconstructed for Proto-Bantu[5] (Welmers 1973:165). In a tradition starting with Bleek, expanded by Meinhof (1899, 1932), and modified slightly by others, each class is assigned a number. Of these, Kifuliiru has all but cls. 20-22. Of the twenty classes occurring in Kifuliiru, seventeen can be accurately categorized as noun classes,[6] and are illustrated in table 2.1. Notice that for singular of cl. 1a[7] nouns, e.g. **dáàtà** 'my father', the GNP is a zero morpheme.

Table 2.1. Kifuliiru noun classes

| Cl. | GNP | Noun stem | Noun word | Gloss |
|---|---|---|---|---|
| 1 | mú- | -ndù | múndù | 'person' |
| 1a | --- | dáàtà | dáàtà | 'father' |
| 2 | bá- | -ndù | bándù | 'people' |
| 3 | mú- | -kóndè | múkóndè | 'banana' |
| 4 | mí- | -kóndè | míkóndè | 'bananas' |
| 5 | í-[a] | -búyè | ííbúyè | 'stone' |
| 6 | má- | -búyè | mábúyè | 'stones' |
| 7 | kí- | -hándò | kíhándò | 'sore' |
| 8 | bí- | -hándò | bíhándò | 'sores' |
| 9 | N-[b] | -gòkò | ngòkò | 'chicken' |
| 10 | N- | -gòkò | ngòkò | 'chickens' |
| 11 | lú- | -lìmì | lúlìmì | 'tongue' |
| 12 | ká- | -fùlò | káfùlò | 'turtle' |
| 13 | tú- | -fùlò | túfùlò | 'turtles' |
| 14 | bú- | -lâ | búlâ | 'intestine' |
| 15 | kú- | -twīrì | kútwīrì | 'ear' |
| 16 | há- | -ndù | hándù | 'place' |
| 19 | hí- | nyûmbà | hínyûmbà | 'small house' |

[a]In one observed case in Kifuliiru, the cl. 5 GNP is **li-**, i.e. **lí-íno** (5-tooth).
[b]Cl. 9 and cl. 10 are the same for both singular and plural forms. As seen in the following example the cl. 9/10 concord prefix N-, which is an

---

[5]Though Ziervogel (1971) posits two more locative classes: cl. 24 ***ka-** and cl. 25 ***n(I)**.

[6]The cl. 17 **ku**, cl. 18 **mu**, and cl. 23 **i** are never used as noun prefixes. When they are attached to nouns, it is always as a clitic at the phrase level. Thus they are discussed at more length in chapter 8. Like the other classes, however, these locative classes do function as agreement prefixes in other word classes, e.g. as demonstrative prefixes, e.g. cl. 17 **kúnò** 'this.P.C (place)', cl. 18 **múnò** 'this.P.C (place)', cl. 23 **îinò** 'this.P.C (place)', etc., and trigger agreement in verbs, pronouns, etc.

[7]Nouns in cl. 1a are typically kinship terms, personifications, and proper names (Welmers 1973:166).

unspecified nasal consonant, assimilates to the place of articulation of a consonant which directly follows it. Since the augment is generally a copy of the vowel of the noun prefix, the use of the augment **í** with these classes indicates that historically the noun prefix may have been **N(i)-**.

| Cl. | GNP | Stem | Gloss | Word | Gloss |
|---|---|---|---|---|---|
| 9/10 | N- | **hìngírò** | 'farm' | **mbìngírò** | 'field' |
| 9/10 | N- | **láhírò** | 'deny' | **ndáhírò** | 'oath' |
| 9/10 | N- | **gòkò** | 'chicken' | **ngókò** | 'chicken' |

The meaning of the noun is inextricably linked to the GNP associated with a given stem. In (2.1) are presented pairs of noun roots that are identical in every way (including vowel length and tone) except for the GNP that they are linked to.

(2.1) **mú-<u>bìbì</u>**   **bú-<u>gángà</u>**   **bú-<u>húnì</u>**
1-seed.scatterer   14-malaria   14-rebellion

**lú-<u>bìbì</u>**   **má-<u>gángà</u>**   **mú-<u>húnì</u>**
11-boundary   6-cow.urine   3-sadness

There are also homophonous noun stems which have a common semantic element. In Kifuliiru -**ndu** is the most widely used homophonous noun stem. Using this stem we find six separate meanings with a total of nine different possible class prefixes (counting singulars and plurals). All these words share a meaning something like "the generic, lowest-common-denominator item".

| (2.2) | Cl. | Noun | Gloss | Cl. | Noun | Gloss |
|---|---|---|---|---|---|---|
| | 1 | **mú-<u>ndù</u>** | 'person' | 2 | **bá-<u>ndù</u>** | 'people' |
| | 7 | **kí-<u>ndù</u>** | 'thing' | 8 | **bí-<u>ndù</u>** | 'things' |
| | 14 | **bú-<u>ndù</u>** | 'ugali' | 6 | **má-<u>ndù</u>** | 'old ugali' |
| | 15 | **kú-<u>ndù</u>** | 'essence' | | | |
| | 16 | **há-<u>ndù</u>** | 'place' | | | |
| | 19 | **hí-<u>ndù</u>** | 'small thing' | | | |

### 2.1.1 Singular-plural correspondences

Different Bantu languages match singular and plural concord classes in various ways. In the standard Bantu system of numbering noun classes, as a general rule singular classes have odd numbers, and plural classes have even numbers. In Kifuliiru each singular class is intrinsically linked to one, and only one, plural class.[8] Thus all nouns associated with a cl. 1 singular prefix **mú-** have cl. 2 plural prefix **bá-** and no other. Likewise all nouns with a cl. 5 singular prefix **í-** have a cl. 6 plural prefix **má-**, etc.

On the other hand, many prefixes having a plural meaning are linked to more than one singular prefix. As can be seen in table 2.2, the cl. 2 prefix **bá-** is the plural form for the cl. 1 singular (prefix **mú-**), or the cl. 1a singular (null prefix). In the same way the cl. 6 prefix **má-** is the plural for the singular classes 5 **(l)í-**, 14 **bú-**, and 15 **kú-**. The cl. 10 N- plural is shared by the singular cl. 9 N- and cl. 11 **lú-**. Finally, the cl. 13 **tú-** plural is shared by the singular cl. 12 **ká-** and cl. 19 **hí-**. The cl. 16 prefix **há-** is used for either singular or plural.

Table 2.2. Mapping of singular/plural noun class pairings

| SG cl. | GNP | Noun | Gloss | PL cl. | GNP | Noun | Gloss |
|---|---|---|---|---|---|---|---|
| 1 | mú- | mú-ndù | 'person' | 2 | bá- | bá-ndù | 'people' |
| 1a | --- | dáàtà | 'father' | | | bá-dáàtà | 'fathers' |
| 3 | mú- | mú-kóndè | 'banana' | 4 | mí- | mí-kóndè | 'bananas' |
| 5 | (l)í- | í-búyè | 'rock' | 6 | má- | má-búyè | 'rocks' |
| 14 | bú- | bú-lâ | 'intestine' | | | má-lâ | 'intestines' |
| 15 | kú- | kú-twīrì | 'ear' | | | má-twīrì | 'ears' |
| 7 | kí- | kí-hándò | 'sore' | 8 | bí- | bí-hándò | 'sores' |
| 9 | N- | ny-ûmbà | 'house' | 10 | N- | ny-ûmbà | 'houses' |
| 11 | lú- | lú-lìmì | 'tongue' | | | n-dímì | 'tongues' |
| 12 | ká- | ká-bwâ | 'dog' | 13 | tú- | tú-bwâ | 'dogs' |
| 19 | hí- | hí-nyûmbà | 'sm. house' | | | tú-nyûmbà | 'sm. houses' |
| 16 | há- | hándù | 'place' | 16 | há- | há-ndù | 'places' |

### 2.1.2 Examples of count nouns by gender

Count nouns have a both a singular and a plural form, as can be seen in (2.3).

| (2.3) | Cl. | Singular | Plural | Gloss |
|---|---|---|---|---|
| | 1/2 | mú-shààjà | bá-shààjà | 'old person(s)' |
| | | mú-zìmbà | bá-zìmbà | 'thief(s)' |
| | 1a/2 | dáàtà | bá-dáàtà | 'father(s)' |
| | | máàwê | bá-máàwê | 'mother(s)' |
| | 3/4 | mú-mbátì | mí-mbátì | 'cassava(s)' |

---

[8]The partial exception to this is the cl. 19 diminutive, which generally takes its plural in cl. 13 (**tú-**), but sometimes (especially when the original class of the diminutive noun is cl. 12) has its plural in cl. 14 (**bú-**).

## 2.1 Constituent structure of the noun

| Cl. | Singular | Plural | Gloss |
|---|---|---|---|
|  | **mú-lóngè** | **mí-róngè** | 'bamboo(s)' |
| 5/6 | **í-kéétà** | **má-kéétà** | 'knife(s)' |
|  | **í-síìbù** | **má-síìbù** | 'wasp(s)' |
| 7/8 | **kí-bùzì** | **bí-bùzì** | 'goat(s)' |
|  | **kí-shìmbò** | **bí-shìmbò** | 'bean(s)' |
| 9/10 | **n-gòkò** | **n-gòkò** | 'chicken(s)' |
|  | **n-gwârè** | **n-gwârè** | 'quail(s)' |
| 11/10 | **lú-hàzì** | **m-bázì** | 'rooster(s)' |
|  | **lw-âlà** | **ny-áàla** | 'rock(s)' |
| 12/13 | **ká-bwâ** | **tú-bwâ** | 'dog(s)' |
|  | **ká-fwérò** | **tú-fwérò** | 'calf of leg(s)' |
| 14/6 | **bú-dìkù** | **má-dìkù** | 'liver(s)' |
|  | **bú-lwàzì** | **má-lwàzì** | 'sickness(s)' |
| 15/6 | **kú-twīrì** | **má-twīrì** | 'ear(s)' |
|  | **kú-gúlù** | **má-gúlù** | 'leg(s)' |
| 19/13 | **hí-nyûmbà** | **tú-nyûmbà** | 'small house(s)' |
|  | **hí-ngóró-ngórò** | **tú-ngóró-ngórò** | 'small coin(s)' |

### 2.1.3 Non-count nouns

Non-count nouns have only one form, i.e. they do not have both a singular and plural form. This includes mass nouns, liquids, abstracts, etc. These forms are concentrated in cl. 6 and cl. 14, but can occur in other classes as well. Examples of non-count nouns are given in (2.4).

| (2.4) | Cl. | Noun | Gloss |
|---|---|---|---|
|  | 3 | **mú-únyù** | 'salt' |
|  | 4 | **mí-sî** | 'strength' |
|  | 6 | **mì-gírízô** | 'teaching' |
|  | 6 | **mí-íjì** | 'water' |
|  | 6 | **má-vùtà** | 'oil' |
|  | 6 | **má-shê** | 'manure' |
|  | 7 | **Kí-fùlììrû** | 'Kifuliiru language' |
|  | 7 | **Kí-bèmbê** | 'Kibembe language' |
|  | 9/10 | **shéshēēzì** | 'morning' |
|  | 14 | **bú-ményì** | 'knowledge' |
|  | 14 | **bú-lìgò** | 'evil' |

## 2.2 Class agreement triggered by noun gender-number

### 2.2.1 Gender-number prefixes by grammatical grouping

The gender and number associated with each noun triggers concord agreement over a wide range of constructions, including adjectives, demonstratives, numerals, associative pronouns, focus pronouns, associative noun phrases, copulas of all types, clitics at the end of verbs, subject and object markers on verbs, subject and object relative constructions, etc.

Table 2.3 lists the various concord prefixes. This table provides a separate column wherever a difference occurs in any class among the concord forms. The column on the right summarizes the total number of different forms for each class, not counting the augment, which is basically a copy of the vowel of the noun prefix. For many of the classes all the prefixes have the same form, e.g. for cl. 7 there is only one underlying form, **ki-**. For cl. 1, by contrast, there are six different forms, so "6" is the total given in the right-hand column. Besides the numbered noun classes, table 2.3 also includes the "personal classes", i.e. first- and second-persons singular and plural.

Table 2.3. Gender-number prefixes by grammatical grouping

| Cl. | A | B | C | D | E | F | G | H | I | # |
|---|---|---|---|---|---|---|---|---|---|---|
| 1SG | --- | --- | --- | --- | ni- | n- | -ní | n- | --- | 2 |
| 2SG | --- | --- | --- | --- | u- | u- | -ú | kú- |  | 2 |
| 1 | ú | mú- | mú- | ú | i- | a- | -g | mú- | gú- | 6 |
| 1a | --- | Ø | mú- | ú- | i- | a- | -g | mú- | gú- | 7 |
| 1PL | --- | --- | --- | --- | tu- | tu- | -itu | tù- | --- | 1 |
| 2PL | --- | --- | --- | --- | mu- | mu- | -inyu | mù- | --- | 2 |
| 2 | á | bá- | bá- | ba- | ba- | ba- | -ba | bà- | bà- | 1 |
| 3 | ú | mú- | mú- | gu | gu- | gu- | -gu | gù- | gù- | 2 |
| 4 | í | mí- | mí- | í | i- | i- | -í | gì- | gí- | 3 |
| 5 | í | (l)í- | lí- | li | li- | li- | -li | lì- | lì- | 1 |
| 6 | á | má- | má- | ga | ga- | ga- | -ga | gà- | gà- | 2 |
| 7 | í | kí- | kí- | ki- | ki- | ki- | -ki | kì- | kì- | 1 |
| 8 | í | bí- | bí- | bi- | bi- | bi- | -bi | bì- | bì- | 1 |
| 9 | í | N- | N- | í- | i- | i- | -í | gì- | gí- | 3 |
| 10 | í | N- | N- | zi- | zi- | zi | -zi | zì- | zì- | 2 |
| 11 | ú | lú- | lú- | lu- | lu- | lu- | -lu | lù- | lù- | 1 |
| 12 | á | ká- | ká- | ka- | ka- | ka- | -ka | kà- | kà- | 1 |

## 2.2 Class agreement triggered by noun gender-number

| Cl. | A | B | C | D | E | F | G | H | I | # |
|-----|---|---|---|---|---|---|---|---|---|---|
| 13 | ú | tú- | tú- | tu- | tu- | tu- | -tu | tù- | tù- | 1 |
| 14 | ú | bú- | bú- | bu- | bu- | bu- | -bu | bù- | bù- | 1 |
| 15 | ú | kú- | kú- | ku- | ku- | ku- | -ku | kù- | kù- | 1 |
| 16 | á | há- | há- | ha- | ha- | ha- | -ha | hà- | hà- | 1 |
| 17 | --- | --- | --- | ku- | ku- | ku- | --- | kù- | --- | 1 |
| 18 | --- | --- | --- | mu- | mu- | mu- | --- | mù- | --- | 1 |
| 19 | í | hí- | hí- | hi- | hi- | hi- | -hi | hì- | hì- | 1 |
| 23 | --- | --- | --- | i- | i- | i- | --- | ì- | --- | 1 |

Note: A-augment, subject relative; B-noun; C-adjective, etc.; D-demonstratives, A.M; E-pronouns, etc.; F-subject prefix of verb; G-associative pronoun; H-object prefix of verb; I-different-set pronoun; #-number of different underlying forms.

### 2.2.1.1 Representative constructions where different GNPs occur

One example from each of the columns above is presented in (2.5). Examples are taken from cl. 2, 4, and 1, listed in that order to reflect the increasing number of distinct prefixes. In cl. 2 the concordial prefixes for all constructions take the same shape (**ba**-). The prefixes for cl. 4 have three distinct forms (**i**-, **mi**-, and **gi**-). The prefixes for cl. 1 are maximally differentiated with six different forms (**u**-, **mu**-, **i**-, **a**-, **-g**, and **gu**-).

The following layout is not exhaustive. For example, it includes only one of five possible demonstratives, the proximal contrastive -**nò**, (see 2.5D), and only one of four personal pronouns, the contrastive -**hê**, (see 2.5E). However, each of the forms included in (2.5) does exemplify the forms that are not included.

(2.5) Cl. 2, 4, and 1 examples for each column of Table 2.3

| Col | Exemplified | Cl. 2 | Cl. 4 | Cl. 1 |
|-----|-------------|-------|-------|-------|
| A | Augment | **á**=**bá-ndù**<br>AU=2-person<br>'the people' | **í**=**mí-tègò**<br>AU=4-trap<br>'the traps' | **ú**=**mú-ndù**<br>AU=1-person<br>'the person' |
| B | Noun | **bá-ndù**<br>2-person<br>'people' | **mí-tègò**<br>4-trap<br>'traps' | **mú-ndù**<br>1-person<br>'person' |

| Col | Exemplified | Cl. 2 | Cl. 4 | Cl. 1 |
|---|---|---|---|---|
| C | Adjective | bá-ndú bá-là<br>2-person 2-tall<br>'tall people' | mí-tègò mí-là<br>4-trap 4-long<br>'long traps' | mú-ndú mú-là<br>1-person 1-tall<br>'tall person' |
| D | Demonstrative | bà-nó bá-ndù<br>2-these.P.C<br>2-person<br>'these people' | ì-nó mí-tègò<br>4-these.P.C. 4-trap<br>'these traps' | ù-nó mú-ndù<br>1-this.P.C<br>1-person<br>'this person' |
| E | Pronoun | bó-òhê<br>(UF: bá-ó-hé)<br>2-CTR.P<br>'THEY (contrast to others)' | y-ôhê<br>4-CTR.P<br>'THEY (contrast to others)' | y-êhê<br>1-CTR.P<br>'HE (contrast to others)' |
| F | Subject of verb | á=bá-ndú bá-ká-fw-à<br>AU=2-person 2-P2-die-Fa<br>'the people died' | í=mí-tègó í-ká-fw-à<br>AU=4-trap 4-P2-die-Fa<br>'the traps died' | ú=mú-ndú á-ká-fw-à<br>AU=1-person 1-P2-die-Fa<br>'the person died' |
| G | Associative pronoun | í=bí-ndú by-à-bò<br>AU=8-thing 8-A.M-2<br>'the things of them' | í=bí-ndú by-á-yò<br>AU=8-thing 8-A.M-4<br>'the things of them' | í=bí-ndù by-à-gè<br>AU=8-thing 8-A.M-1<br>'the things of him' |
| H | Object of verb | bá-ká-bà-yít-à<br>2-P2-O2-kill-Fa<br>'they killed them' | bá-ká-gì-yít-à<br>2-P2-O4-kill-Fa<br>'they killed them' | bá-ká-mú-yít-à<br>2-P2-O1-kill-Fa<br>'they killed him' |
| I | Different set | á=bà-ndì bá-ndù<br>AU=2-other 2-person<br>'other people' | í=gî-ndì mí-tègò<br>AU=4-other 4-trap<br>'other traps' | ú=gû-ndì mú-ndù<br>AU=1-other 1-person<br>'another person' |

## 2.2 Class agreement triggered by noun gender-number

From table 2.3 we see that in the majority of the classes (14 of the total 20) the GNP has the same underlying form wherever it occurs. This is true of cl. 2 **ba-**, 5 **i-**, 7 **ki-**, 8 **bi-**, 11 **lu-**, 12 **ka-**, 13 **tu-**, 14 **bu-**, 15 **ku-**, 16 **ha-**, 17 **ku-**, 18 **mu-**, 19 **hi-**, 23 **i-**.

In (2.6) for example, only the cl. 7 prefix **kí-** is used for each word in the sentence. This includes the noun **kítì** 'tree', the demonstrative **kínò** 'this.C.P', the demonstrative **kìndì** 'other', the associative pronoun **kyákyò** 'of it' (**í-** changes to the glide **y-** before vowel-initial stems), the adjective **kíhámù** 'large', the contrastive pronoun **kyôhê** 'IT', and the subject agreement on the verb **ky-à-ná-ból-à** 'and it rotted'.

(2.6) **Kí-nó     kî-ndì     kí-tí     ky-á-kyò | kí-hámù ‖ ky-ôhê**
     7-this.P.C  7-other   7-tree   7-A.M-7      7-large        7-CTR.P

**ky-àná-ból-à.**
7-SQ-rot-Fa

'This other tree of it | large ‖ IT rotted. (This other large tree of it rotted.)'

For three of the classes (3 **mú-**, 6 **má-**, and 10 **N-**) there are two segmentally different underlying forms of the GNP, i.e. for cl. 3 they are **mu-** and **gu-**, for cl. 6 they are **ma-** and **ga-**, and for cl. 10 they are **N-** and **zi-**.

For two of the classes (4 **mi-** and 9 **N(i)**) there are three underlying shapes of the GNP. This is exemplified in (2.7) where **mí-** is prefixed to the noun root **-ímbù** 'harvest', and to the adjective **-nììnî** 'small'. When the cl. 4 and cl. 9 are associated with **-ndì** 'other', they take the form **gí-**. Finally, they take the form **i-** when it is prefixed to the demonstrative **-ryá** 'that.R', the associative pronoun **yàyò** 'of them' (again, palatalized to **y-** preceding vowels), the contrastive pronoun **yôhê** 'THEY', or used as the subject prefix on the verb **yànáfwà** 'and they died'.

(2.7) **Ì-ryá     gî-ndì     mí-ìmbù   y-à-yó | mí-nììnî ‖ y-ôhé | y-àná-fw-à.**
     4-that.R  4-other    4-harvest  4-A.M-4    4-small       4-CTR.P  4-SQ-die-Fa

'Those other harvests of them | small ‖ THEY | died. (Their other small harvests died.)'

Focusing on the prefixes associated with the animate singular classes, we notice greater diversity, in that there are six segmentally different forms in cl. 1, and seven different forms in cl. 1a (counting the null marker).

As seen in (2.8), for cl. 1 the GNP assumes the form of **ù-** in **ùlyâ** 'this', **gú-** in **gûndì** 'other', **-g** in **wàgè** 'of his', **mú-** on **múkáyù** 'fierce', **i-** (palatalized before the vowel) in **yêhê** 'he.CTR.P', and **a-** as subject prefix for **ànágêndà** 'and he went'.

(2.8) Ù-lyá    gû-ndì    mú-ndú    w-à-gé |    mú-káyù ||    y-ê-hé |    à-ná-gênd-à.
1-that.R  1-other   1-person  1-A.M-1     1-fierce       1-CTR.P     1-SQ-go-Fa

'That other person of his | fierce || HE | went. (That other fierce person of his went.)'

### 2.2.2 Agreement for conjoined NPs with different GNPs: cl. 8 (*bi-*)

Each Bantu language with a developed concord system needs a strategy for choosing a subject concord when conjoined subject nouns belong to different classes. The class chosen is said to be highest in the class hierarchy for that language. In Kifuliiru, the concord chosen for conjoined nouns of differing classes is cl. 8. In (2.9) the cl. 10 **njóvù** 'elephants' is of a different class from the cl. 4 **míjōkà** 'snakes'. The subject concord on the verb is neither cl. 10 nor cl. 4, but rather the cl. 8 bi-.

(2.9) **N**-jóvú    n-é=    **mí**-jōkà |    **bí**-ká-yìt-w-á    mú=    kí-shùkà.
10-elephant  CNJ-AU=  4-snake         8-P2-kill-PS-Fa       18=    7-bush

'Elephants and snakes | were killed in the bush.'

In (2.10) the conjoined nouns, cl. 4 **míkéékê** 'fish' and cl. 14 **búndù** 'ugali (stiff porridge)' are again represented by the cl. 8 subject prefix **bi-** on the verb. The same cl. 8 prefix is also employed with the predicate adjective **bínúnù** 'delicious'.

(2.10) **Mí**-kééké    n-ó=    **bú**-ndù ||    **bì**-rí    **bí**-núnù.
4-fish            CNJ-AU=  14-fufu          8-be      8-delicious

'Fish and stiff porridge || are delicious.'

### 2.2.3 Two different GNPs referring to same real-world referent

The subject prefix of a verb agrees in gender and number with the noun which is the subject of that verb, whether expressed or understood. For example in (2.11) the cl. 1 subject prefix **a-** on the copula **àlì** 'is' agrees with the cl. 1 antecedent **múhyà** 'new wife'.

(2.11) À-ná-búùz-à: || «**Mú**-hyà    **à**-lì    háyì?»
1-SQ-ask-Fa           1-new.wife  1-is   where

'And he asked: || «Where is the new wife?»' (624 030)

With a copula, however, the subject prefix "looks forward" and agrees with its complement. In (2.12) the mother is talking about her son named **Bíkòbà**

## 2.2 Class agreement triggered by noun gender-number

(a cl. 1a noun) who is referred to by the cl. 1a object **mú-** 'him' in the verb form -**múhánúúlà** 'advise him'. However, in the next clause the subject prefix changes to the cl. 7 **ki-**, which agrees with the following noun in the complement, **kízéèzè** 'simpleton'.

(2.12) **Nyínà**     | **à-ná-dèt-à** ‖ **kw-â**= **tà-gá-kì-shùbì**
 1a+his.mother   1-SQ-speak-Fa   CMP-1=   NEG-F2-PERS-AGAIN

**mú-hánúúl-á** ‖ **mú=kúbá   kì-rì   kí-zéèzè**.
O1-advise-Fa    because   7-is    7-simpleton

'The mother | said ‖ that she would no longer again advise him ‖ because he is a simpleton.' (07 036)

In (2.13) the subject is a cl. 14 noun **ú=búgùmâ** 'unity', but the cl. 4 focus copula **yó** agrees with the following cl. 4 complement **mísî** 'strength'.

(2.13) **Ú=bú-gùma     y-ó=     mí-sî.**
 AU=14-oneness   4-FOC=   4-strength

'Unity is the one that is strength.' (02 026)

Example (2.14) demonstrates the same phenomenon with the copula -**kòla** (is.NEWLY). Both elements of the noun phrase **í=byámbàlwà byàgè** 'his clothing' are marked by the cl. 8 GNP **bi-**. In the next clause, that clothing is now predicated, via the aspectual copula -**kòla** (is.NEWLY), to be rags. Once again, the cl. 14 subject pronoun **bu-** 'it' agrees with the following noun **bú-sángánírà** 'ragged clothing', and not with the previous cl. 8 antecedent **bi-**.

(2.14) **À-ná-lól-èèkèz-á     í=by-ámbàlwà  by-à-gè** ‖ **à-ná-bòn-à   kwó=**
 1-SQ-look.at-INTS-Fa   AU=8-clothing   8-A.M-1     1-SQ-see-Fa   CMP=

**bù-kòlá** |       **bú-sángánírà.**
14-is.NEWLY    14-ragged.clothing

'And he looked carefully at his clothing ‖ and he saw that it is now | tattered rags.' (33 022)

### 2.2.4 Mismatches between noun classes

In traditional narratives, a non-cl. 1 animal character sometimes triggers the cl. 1 verbal subject agreement. Thus in (2.15) the cl. 11 **lúkwàvù** 'rabbit' does not take the cl. 11 **lu-** agreement on the verb. Instead the cl. 1 subject prefix **a-** is found on the verb **ànáyîjà** 'and he came'. This can be seen as a relaxing of the agreement rules in some contexts, in taking a noun which is a still a synchronically valid member of another noun class, and using it as if it were a proper name, which then falls in cl. 1a.

(2.15) Há-àhô   lú-kwàvù |   à-ná-yîj-à.
        E-then.N   11-rabbit      1-SQ-come-Fa

'Right then the rabbit | came.' (627 015)

### 2.2.5 Lexicalized noun prefixes

With many cl. 1a nouns, there might appear to be skewing in GNP agreement. This is because though cl. 1a nouns have no segmental prefix, they often begin with what appears to be the prefix of another class, which has been lexicalized as a part of the name or title. All agreements with cl. 1a nouns are of cl. 1 (e.g. verbal subject and object prefixes, demonstratives, associative, etc.) For example though **bùlàmbê** might appear to begin with a cl. 14 prefix **bu-**, it is still a cl. 1a noun (note the plural **bábùlàmbê**), and never cl. 14. This is observed in a phrase like **ùyó bùlàmbé wó=múkàzì** 'that.N depraved one of a woman', where the cl. 1a **bùlàmbê** 'depraved one' does not trigger the cl. 14 **bu-** agreements; rather the agreements for this word are those of cl. 1a. The same situation is found for most personal proper names, all of which are of cl. 1a. For instance, the name **Kályôshò**, starts with **ká-**, but does not take cl. 12 agreements, as seen by the verbal subject agreement in (2.16).

(2.16) Kályôshò |   à-ná-bwîr-à   náákùlù:        || «É=   mú-gààkà ||
        Kalyosho    1-SQ-tell-Fa   1a+his.grandmother   O=   1-old.lady

   má-kì gá-nò?»
   6-what 6-here.P.C

'Kalyosho | told his grandmother: || «O grandma || what's going on here?»' (619 060)

### 2.2.6 Personification of noun by addition of *wa* clitic

In some narratives, animal names, and even nouns which denote people but which are not personal names, can have the cl. 1 associative marker **w-a** added as a clitic[9] before the regular GNP, which then triggers agreement with the cl. 1 verbal subject prefix **a-**. The addition of the **w-a** marker causes the noun to be treated as a proper name, signifying a particular referent. For example

---

[9]These seem to be clitics (i.e. not prefixes) just as the more typically-used associative markers are. Tonally they act just like the associative markers, having H tone before a word with initial L tone, and L tone before a word with an initial H tone.

## 2.3 Semantic categories typically found in various Kifuliiru noun classes

the cl. 11 **lúkwàvù** 'rabbit' becomes the cl. 1 **W-à=lúkwàvù**,[10] as in (2.17), and agrees with the cl. 1 **a-** subject prefix found on the verbs **ákáyúsâ** 'he finished' and **ànádètà** 'and he said'.

(2.17) W-à=lú-kwàvú | ìrí à-ká-yùs-á ú=kú-ly-â ‖ à-ná-dèt-à:...
 1-A.M=11-rabbit when 1-P2-finish-Fa AU=15-eat-Fa 1-SQ-speak-Fa

'Rabbit | when he finished eating ‖ he said:..' (627 036)

In some cases even a noun which is already cl. 1, like **múndù** 'person', is given the **w-a** clitic, and thus acts as a "proper name", cf. **wà=múndù** 'person' in (2.18).

(2.18) É= W-à=mú-ndù ‖ ù-yú mw-àná w-é= n-gáàvù | ú-lí
 O= 1-A.M=1-person this.P-1 1-child 1-A.M+AU= 9-cow S.R+1-is

 yà-hà ‖ à-lí w-à-nî.
 here.P-16 1-is 1-A.M-1SG

'Mr. person ‖ this cow's child | which is here ‖ belongs to me.' (631 010)

## 2.3 Semantic categories typically found in various Kifuliiru noun classes

As is typical of Bantu languages, Kifuliiru groups words of the same semantic type into the same noun class. For example, nouns denoting humans belong for the most part to cl. 1. Kinship terms, proper names (including those of the various types of cassava) and many of the large birds belong to cl. 1a. Small birds, parts of the body belong to cl. 12, etc. A summary of these distinctions, with representative examples, is presented here in (2.19).

(2.19) Semantic categories typically found in various Kifuliiru noun classes

| Cl. | Category | Examples |
|---|---|---|
| 1/2 | Humanness | **múngérè** 'shepherd', **múkōzì** 'servant', **múhwîjà** 'foolish one', **múbìbì** 'sower', **múfùmù** 'doctor', **mwìgéndérézì** 'patient person', **múgùndà** 'commoner', **múná-bwêngè** 'intelligent person', **múná-mwétè** 'energetic person', **múzìmbà** 'thief', **músháàjà** 'old person', **mwāmì** 'king', **múnyérè** 'girl', **mútàbánà** 'boy', **mwānà** 'child', **múgândà** 'royal messenger', **múgéézì** 'traveler' |

---

[10] **Wà=lúkwàvù** could be glossed as 'Mr. Rabbit', although in most stories we gloss it simply as 'Rabbit'.

| Cl. | Category | Examples |
|---|---|---|
| 1a/2 | Names | nágáhébà 'self-sacrificing person', Nákálémékà 'God' |
| | Kinship terms | náhánò 'lord', náákùlù 'their grandmother', návyàlà 'their mother-in-law', dáàtà 'our father' |
| | Large birds | nákásàrè 'hawk', nálúhàzê 'hawk', námúlòbâ-fwì 'fish hawk', námújòngò 'crow', náfúúfúlù 'owl' |
| | Characters | nákáhùkù 'destitute one', nákáhâmbà 'criminal', nákándákálà 'lazy person', nákímíníkà 'mass murderer', námāānà 'obstinate person', námúfwìrì 'widow', nángòrá-mábì 'wicked person', nápéèyâ 'ill-mannered woman' |
| 3/4 | Plants | múmbátì 'cassava plant', múbérè 'papyrus', múdyô-tyô 'banana', múhándá-njóvù 'thorn bush', múkóbè 'a kind of tree', mútíìnì 'fig tree' |
| | Round items | mwézì 'moon', múshàhò 'pot', múgóbà 'udder', mubágò 'lid' |
| | Long items | mùgózì 'rope', múgúfúlì 'chain', mújòkà 'snake', múnwê 'finger', múnyáàfù 'flexible stick or whip', músî 'blood vessel', mútàlímbwà 'road', múzììzì 'line', mwâgì 'maize stalk', mútéérà-tèèrà 'flute', múshùùgì 'long thorn', múshánízô 'rope for carrying basket', múshábíírò 'long shield', múhétò 'bow', múgwánò 'eel', múfúlégè 'long narrow village' |
| | Liquid masses | músáàmà 'pure banana juice', mútóbò 'fruit juice', mwítà 'soup', múgêngè 'tear' |
| | Non-liquid masses | múshèènyù 'sand', múshyánò 'flour', mútókīīkò 'ashes', mútēēkò 'bunch', múgómbà 'banana beer', múgètè 'cake of dry blood' |
| 5 | Body parts | íìsû 'eye', ízūūlù 'nose', íbēērè 'breast', íbíngà 'gall bladder', íbûndà 'abdomen', ííffkò 'kidney', íìdwî 'knee', íígósì 'neck', íkôndò 'navel', íìtàmà 'cheek' |
| 6 | Liquid masses | mííjì 'water', mávùtà 'oil', mátê 'saliva', mágángà 'urine of cow', mágòlóóvì 'water', mánjòká-njòkà 'venom', máshwî 'urine', mátà 'milk', máávù 'beer', mázòngòròkò 'chicken feces' |

## 2.3 Semantic categories typically found in various Kifuliiru noun classes

| Cl. | Category | Examples |
|---|---|---|
| 7/8 | Body parts | **kíbùnò** 'waist', **kífúnè** 'fist', **kígèré-gérè** 'wrist or ankle', **kíkòrò-kòrò** 'throat', **kímbìrí-mbīrì** 'headless body', **kínwànwâ** 'animal mouth', **kínògòshò** 'hoof', **kípùùpù** 'headless thing', **kírúmbù** 'body part', **kírūndà** 'corpse', **kíságè** 'long hair', **kítùgò** 'shoulder', **kítúmbà** 'animal corpse', **kívíngá-vîngà** 'large intestines', **kízéétè** 'cattle rump', **kíbérò** 'thigh' |
| | Trees | **kítì** 'tree', **kíròndò-lòndò** 'cloth tree', **kígázì** 'palm tree', **kígûndù** 'banana plant', **kíshàngé-shāngè** 'tree species', **kíbómbó-shólyô** 'tree with sap for glue' |
| | Long items | **kíbâmbà** 'banana rope', **kíjángálà** 'banana leaf' |
| 9/10 | Man-made items | **ndágírírò** 'grazing area', **ndándà** 'journey food', **ndáárò** 'extra house', **nzógérà** 'dog bell', **nyûmbà** 'house', **ngéngérè** 'bell', **ngíngò** 'bed', **ngóférà** 'hat', **ngóókô** 'ugali bowl', **ngómà** 'drum', **ngòòtì** 'long knife', **ngóvì** 'baby sling', **ngwétò** 'shoe', **síríbò** 'shield', **sháhò** 'bag' |
| | Larger animals | **mbálágà** 'large fish (sp.)', **mbénè** 'goat', **mbóngò** 'antelope', **mbwá-kázì** 'female dog', **mbwá-rúmè** 'male dog', **ndàrè** 'lion', **níngù** 'large fish', **njómbò** 'large fish (sp.)', **njóvù** 'elephant', **nóózì** 'large fish (sp.)', **fíízì** 'big bull', **nyáàbù** 'cat', **nyánà** 'calf', **ngáàvù** 'cattle', **ngóónà** 'crocodile', **ngúhê** 'large fish' (sp.), **ngúngù** 'hornless cow', **ngwî** 'leopard', **nyûndà** 'eagle', **ngúlúbè** 'pig' |
| | Sensation | **ndúúbánò** 'sweat', **ndéngéérwà** 'empathy', **ngéránià** 'worry', **nzígò** 'vindictiveness', **nzíkírà** 'hatred' |
| 11/10 | Long items | **lúgéézì** 'journey', **lúbáhwâ** 'board', **lúsîngà** 'long string from palm leaf', **lúshààlì** 'firewood', **lúzìzì** 'long thin sticks', **lwíjì** 'river', **lútálíro** 'foundation', **lúsésémà** 'robe', **lúsáàtì** 'walking stick with spear tip', **lúngù** 'squash vine', **lúkòbà** 'rope', **lúhíkù** 'string from plant', **lúbìbì** 'boundary' |

| Cl. | Category | Examples |
|---|---|---|
| | Personal names (cl. 1a but **Ru-** pfx) | **Rúgóndéshà, Rúshálìkà, Rúhíndííshà, Rúrèshà, Rúsárázâ, Rúshúkírà, Rúnyérérà, Rúréézâ, Rútúkù, Rútúúbániâ, Rúbúngêngà, Rúmwémúzâ** |
| | Place names | **í=Lúvùngì** Luvungi, **í=Lúbárίkà** Lubarika, **í=Lúbèríízì** Luberizi, **í=Rúbángà** Rubanga, **í=Rúbùgà** Rubuga, **í=Rùníngù** Runingu, **í=Rwénéénà** Rweneena, **í=Rwéngérò** Rwengero, **lúbàkò** 'forest' |
| 12/13 | Small animals | **kábwâ** 'dog', **kánjèrèrè** 'cockroach', **kárámátà** 'small crocodile', **kásàmúnìgà** 'mongoose', **kávùtáàlè** 'chameleon' |
| | Birds | **kányúnì** 'bird', **kálèmbé-rêmbè** 'sparrow', **káshííshî** 'pied wagtail', **kashuuta** 'bird that takes chickens', **kahezi** 'small bird that runs on ground' |
| | Lesser body parts | **káfwôgê** 'gizzard', **kágúmà** 'animal heart', **káhângà** 'skull', **káhólé-hóòlê** 'soft spot in child's skull', **kámírá-búndù** 'esophagus', **kánwâ** 'mouth', **kálédù** 'chin', **káfwérò** 'calf of leg' |
| | Personal names (all cl. 1a, but have **ka-** pfx) | **Kazeera, Kanwesa, Kashombani, Kamaro, Kahaalwe, Kashindi, Kalyosho, Kanyola, Kananiro, Kahindiisa** |
| | Place names† | **kádótà** 'small spring', **kágóngò** 'corner of house', **kágúlìrò** 'market place', **kāāyà** 'compound, village, town'; as well as village names: **í=Kábóndóózì, í=Kálùndù, í=Kábùngùlù, í=Kávínvírà** (all with obligatory cl. 23 clitic) |
| 14 | Abstracts | **búsōrè** 'youth', **búhììvì** 'hunting', **búkēnì** 'poverty', **búkìzè** 'salvation', **búlámú** 'life', **búlìgò** 'evil', **búlwāzì** 'sickness', **búngérè** 'watching animals', **búshóbózì** 'ability', **bútábáázì** 'help', **búzìmbà** 'thievery', **búhwìjà** 'ignorance', **búményì** 'knowledge', **búngùkè** 'profit', **búráákárì** 'wrath', **búsàmbánì** 'adultery', **búsììmè** 'liking', **búnyérè** 'girlhood', **búshàmbààlè** 'rejoicing', **búshòmbánì** 'hatred', **bútùùdù** 'humility' |

## 2.3 Semantic categories typically found in various Kifuliiru noun classes

| Cl. | Category | Examples |
|---|---|---|
|  | Place names | **bútàmbì** 'edge', **bútéréèrè** 'uninhabited wilderness', **í=Búvīīrà, í=Búrùndì, í=Búkàfù, í=Búhéébà, í=Bújúmbúrà, í=Búhēnà, í=Búlááyà** (all with cl. 23 locative clitic) |
| 15 | Verbal infinitive | **kúgéndà** 'to go', **kúgálúkà** 'to come back' |
| 19 | Diminutive | **híbwâ** 'small dog', **híngóró-ngórò** 'coin', **hífúmbà** 'small bundle', **híhândè** 'small bit', **híhwá-hwâ** 'thin person', **híjéré-jérè** 'small specks', **híkérè** 'small leaf', **híkòòjòkà** 'small broken off piece', **hílàbìkê** 'small mark', **hínónógórò** 'small bird claw', **hítúùkù** 'fruitfly larva' |

† Some or all of these could be considered reflexes of the cl. 24 *ka- locative class which Ziervogel (1971) posits for Proto-Bantu.

# 3

# Pronouns and Demonstratives

Kifuliiru is rich in pronouns and demonstratives. There are five free (self-standing) pronouns. Their function is not primarily to keep track of referents; rather, all are highly marked, each with a special function in the broader text. In addition, there are two kinds of set pronouns and many interrogative pronouns. There are also five kinds of demonstratives, each of which can be emphasized and then reduplicated. It should be noted that when used in texts, demonstratives can indicate different degrees of thematic salience.

## 3.1 Previous reference: the morpheme *e* / *o*

Before describing the pronouns and demonstratives, we will first look at the morpheme **e** / **o** 'previous reference' (P.R). This is a formative (word-building component) that is found in several kinds of words in Kifuliiru, including many pronouns and quantifiers, as well as the focus copulas. This form is referred to by Ashton (1959:19) as the "**o** of reference," and always points to a referent which is already mentioned in the previous context, or assumed to be known. In Kifuliiru, the "**o** of reference" takes the form **e** in the personal classes (first-person singular through second-person plural), and is realized as **o** for third-person plural (cl. 2) and all the non-personal classes. In the morpheme glosses, these P.R morphemes are usually not specified, because the previous reference is already clear, and to add an additional "P.R" tends to clutter the gloss, making it hard to follow.

 Twelve distinct sets of reference words are formed using this morpheme. They include the demonstratives (shown here in cl. 2 form): **yàbô** 'nearby', **báàbô** 'nearby reduplicated'; the personal pronouns: **bóòhê** 'contrastive', bóókì 'alternative', bóónyènè 'exclusive', bóngwà 'exclusive', and nábo̱ 'additive'; the set pronouns: ábààbo̱ 'same set'; the quantifiers: bó̱mbì 'both', bóóshì 'all'; the copulas: bô̱ 'focus' (also functioning as an object relative pronoun) and ndáábo̱ 'negative focus'. In (3.1) the underlying and surface forms are shown for cl. 8, and for the personal cl. 1PL.

(3.1) Previous reference morpheme in different parts of speech

|     | UF Cl. 8 | SF Cl. 8 | Gloss |
|-----|----------|----------|-------|
| a.  | y-i-bi-o̱<br>EP-C.V-8-P.R | yìbyô̱ | dem.: nearby |
| b.  | bi-o̱-(y)i-bi-o̱<br>8-P.R-EP-C.V-8-P.R | byêbyô̱ | dem.: nearby reduplicated |
| c.  | bi-o̱-he<br>8-P.R-CTR.P | byô̱hê | pronoun: contrastive |
| d.  | bi-o-ki<br>8-P.R-ALT.P | byó̱kì | pronoun: alternative |
| e.  | bi-o̱-nyene<br>8-P.R-self | byónyènè | pronoun: exclusive |
| f.  | bi-o-ngwa<br>8-P.R-self | byô̱ngwâ | pronoun: exclusive |
| g.  | na-bi-o̱<br>ADD.P-8-P.R | nábyò | pronoun: additive |
| h.  | i=bi-a-ba-o̱<br>AU=8-A.M-2-P.R | í=byàbo̱ | pronoun: same set |
| i.  | bi-o̱-mbi<br>8-P.R-both | byó̱mbì | quantifier: both |
| j.  | bi-o̱-shi<br>8-all | byó̱shì | quantifier: all |
| k.  | bi-o̱<br>8-P.R | byô̱ | copula: focus |
| l.  | ndaa-bi-o̱<br>NEG.FOC-8-P.R | ndáábyò | copula: neg. focus |

## 3.2 Verb prefix pronouns and enclitic pronouns

As is typical of Bantu languages, the noun phrase naming the subject or object can be dropped, leaving only the subject or object prefix on the verb, or an enclitic at the end of the verb, to refer to the argument in question. These pronominal prefixes and encliters are described in section 3.2.1–3.2.3.

## 3.2.1 Bound subject pronominal prefixes

Every verb phrase, with the exception of the direct imperative, involves at least one bound pronoun in the form of a subject prefix which agrees in noun class with the expressed or understood subject. The subject NP itself may be omitted if discourse considerations allow, leaving only the subject prefix on the verb to represent it. The bound verbal subject pronouns are as follows: 1SG **n-**, 2SG **u-**, cl. 1 **a-**, 1PL **tu-**, 2PL **mu-**, cl. 2 **ba-**, cl. 3 **gu-**, cl. 4 **i-**, 5 **li-**, cl. 6 **ga-**, cl. 7 **ki-**, cl. 8 **bi-**, cl. 9 **i-**, cl. 10 **zi-**, cl. 11 **lu-**, cl. 12 **ka-**, cl. 13 **tu-**, cl. 14 **bu-**, cl. 15 **ku-**, cl. 16 **ha-**, cl. 17 **ku-**, cl. 18 **mu-**, cl. 19 **hi-**, cl. 23 **i-**. All are analyzed as underlyingly toneless, but may bear either H or L tone depending on the form of the verb.

In (3.2) the noun phrase **ùyó múkàzì** 'that.N woman' is the free (self-standing) NP subject of the first clause, and is cross-referenced in the same clause via the cl. 1 subject prefix pronoun **a-** at the beginning of the verb **ànátàngírà ú=kújúgúmà** 'and (she) began to shake'. Since that same referent is understood to be the subject of the following clause, the noun phrase itself is not repeated. Only the subject prefix pronoun **a-** is seen on the verb **ànáyìbúúzà** 'and she asked herself'. Thus subjects in Kifuliiru must always be marked by a pronominal prefix on the verb, whether or not a free NP subject also occurs.

(3.2) Ùyó  mú-kàzì ‖ à-ná-tàngír-à  ú=kú-júgúm-à ‖
 that.N+1 1-woman 1-SQ-began-Fa AU=15-shake-Fa

 à-ná-yì-búúz-à:...
 1-SQ-RFX-ask-Fa

'That woman ‖ began to shake ‖ and she asked herself:...' (04 18-19)

## 3.2.2 Bound object pronominal prefixes

An object noun phrase can also be represented by an object prefix incorporated into the verb. This incorporated prefix is used only when the noun phrase serving as the object is omitted or when it is presented as a preposed topic. The bound object pronouns are as follows: cl. 1SG **ń-**, cl. 2SG **kú-**, cl. 1 **mú-**, cl. 1PL **tù-**, cl. 2PL **mù-**, cl. 2 **bà-**, cl. 3 **gù-**, cl. 4 **gì-**, cl. 5 **lì-**, cl. 6 **gà-**, cl. 7 **kì-**, cl. 8 **bì-**, cl. 9 **gì-**, cl. 10 **zì-**, cl. 11 **lù-**, cl. 12 **kà-**, cl. 13 **tù-**, cl. 14 **bù-**, cl. 15 **kù-**, cl. 16 **hà-**, cl. 19 **hì-**, cl. 23 **gì-**. Note that the cl. 1 singular prefixes **ń-**,[1] **kú-**, and **mú-** have high tones, while the rest of the object prefixes have low tones.

In (3.3) the first clause contains the full direct object NP **mwámì** 'king', while the second clause contains only the object prefix **mú-** 'him', standing for the same referent. In Kifuliiru, when the full object referent is expressed

---
[1] The tone of the 1SG **ń-** prefix is realized on an adjacent syllable, usually to the left.

in a clause, the object pronoun is not used in the verb. Thus the free object NP/pronoun or the object pronoun prefix, but not both, can occur in the same clause. Thus we find **bànábwîrà mwámì** 'they told (the) king', but not ***bànámúbwîrà mwámì**, where **mú** is the cl. 1 object prefix.[2]

(3.3) Yàbó      bà-àná |   bà-ná-bwîr-à   mw-ámì ||   kwó=   bá-ká-kòl-á |
      those.N+2  2-children 2-SQ-tell-Fa   1-king       CMP=   2-P2-work-Fa

   kw-á=    ká-bà-bwír-à. ||   Nè=    rí   â-ngà-lóóz-à ||
   CMP-1=   P2-O2-tell-Fa      CNJ=   if   1-CND-want-Fa

   bá-gá-<u>mú</u>-lèèt-èr-á |   í=bí-rùndá |   gírà     à-Ø-bì-bòn-è.
   2-F2-O1-bring-APL-Fa       AU=8-corpse   so.that   1-SBV-O8-see-Fe

'Those children | told the king || that they (had) worked | as (a mutually known young man) told them. || And if he (king) wished || they would bring him | the corpses | so that he could see them.' (23 042)

In general, there is only one incorporated object pronoun per verb. Kifuliiru allows two incorporated object pronouns in a single verb only if one of the two is either first-person singular **n-** or the reflexive **yi-**. When there are two incorporated objects, the first-person or reflexive object is always the one which is placed closest to the verb stem, while the other occurs to its left. This can be observed in (3.4), in the verb **yé=wàbìmbééréz**â 'he's the one who gave them (cl. 8) to me'. Here both the cl. 8 **bì-** 'them' and cl. 1 **m-** 'me'[3] are incorporated as object prefixes. The leftmost object is the cl. 8 **bì-** 'them (things)', and the one closest to the verb stem is the first-person singular **m-**.

(3.4) N-à-gwán-án-à            ná=    mw-ìrá    w-à-nì ||   y-é=
      1SG-P1-encounter-RCP-Fa  CNJ=   1-friend  1-A.M-1SG   1-FOC=

   w-à-<u>bì</u>-<u>m</u>-bééréz-â.
   1-P1-O8-O1.SG-give-Fa

'I encountered my friend || he's the one who gave me them.' (12 011)

In (3.5) both cl. 11 **lù-**, referring to **lwíjì** 'river' and the reflexive **yì-** are incorporated into the verb, in the object position.

---

[2] This is in contrast to Kiswahili, where both the object noun and the object prefix are often included in the same clause, e.g. **wa-ka-<u>mw</u>-ambi-a m-falme** (2-SQ-O.1-tell-Fa 1-king) 'they told (him) the king', where the cl. 1 verbal object prefix **mw-** appears in addition to the object itself, **mfalme** 'king'.

[3] Here the 1SG object appears as **m-** because **n-** assimilates to the place of articulation of the following consonant.

(3.5) **Ú-w-áàlí kìzí lù-yì-làsh-á       =mwò ‖ lù-ná-yàm-é |**
S.R-1-P3   REP   O11-RFX-throw-Fa   =18   11-CON-IMMED-Fe

**lw-à-mú-twâl-à.**
11-P1-O1-carry-Fa

'The one who threw himself in it ‖ it immediately | carried him away.'
(603 063)

### 3.2.3 Object enclitics

If there are two pronominal objects, neither of which is first-person singular or reflexive, and both are required by discourse constraints to be pronominalized and incorporated, then one object is marked by a pronominal prefix within the verb, and the second object is marked at the end of the verb as an enclitic. The structure of the object enclitic is not the same as that of the object prefix marked within the verb. Rather it is a fuller pronominal form, consisting of the GNP plus the previous reference marker -**o** / -**e**. These forms are identical in shape to the object relative markers: cl. 1 **ye**, cl. 2 **bo**, cl. 3 **gwo**, cl. 4 **yo**, cl. 5 **lyo**, cl. 6 **go**, cl. 7 **kyo**, cl. 8 **byo**, cl. 9 **yo**, cl. 10 **zo**, cl. 11 **lwo**, cl. 12 **ko**, cl. 13 **two**, cl. 14 **bwo**, cl. 15 **kwo**, cl. 16 **ho**, cl. 17 **kwo**, cl. 18 **mwo**, cl. 19 **hyo**, cl. 23 **yo**. Their tone seems to be polar: H when following a L tone, or L when following a H tone.

Hierarchy determines the decision regarding which of the two pronouns is to be incorporated as an object prefix within the verb and which is to be encliticized. The higher ranking one is incorporated as a prefix, while the lower ranking one becomes an enclitic. This hierarchy for incorporation into the verb is second person › third person (cl. 1/2) › other classes. If both referents are from non-personal classes, an animate referent preempts a non-animate referent. In (3.6) the verb **ngéndì kúshàhúlírá=yè** '(that) I go put him in his place for you' demonstrates that the second-person singular object **kú-** 'you', outranks the third-person singular object **yè** 'him' which is cliticized at the end of the verb.

(3.6) **Ø-M-bóh-èr-á |           mú=   yìbyó     bí-jángálà ‖     gírà**
IMP.S-O1.SG-wrap-APL-Fa    18=   that.N+8   8-banana.leaves   so.that

**n-Ø-géndí           kú-shàhúl-ír-á         =yè.**
1SG-SBV-GOING       O2.SG-belittle-APL-Fa   =O1

'Wrap me up | in those banana leaves ‖ so that I (may) go and put him in his place for you.' (14 029)

It is also common for a locative object to be expressed as an enclitic, even when there is no incorporated object in the verb. (Locative objects may sometimes be incorporated into the verb as well, but it is much more common to encliticize them.) In (3.7) the cl. 23 locative object **yo** is encliticized.

(3.7) **Í=mûndà    n-gwétì     n-gá-hìng-ìr-à ||    n-gá-kìzí**
      23=place    1SG-PROG    1SG-INTL-farm-APL-Fa    1SG-F2-REP

**dùg-ír-á           =yò ||    nì-Ø-yím-é**
make.porridge-APL-Fa    =23      1SG-SBV-refuse.to.give-Fe

**mù-ká-à-niè.**
1-wife-A.M-1SG

'At the place where I farm || I will always make stiff porridge there || (so) I may refuse to give (it to) my wife.' (14 029)

## 3.3 Personal pronouns

Free (self-standing) personal pronouns are always highly marked, both in regard to their location in the clause and to their meaning. (This is distinct from pronouns in many other languages.)

There are several types of personal pronouns. CONTRASTIVE pronouns focus on the referent as opposed to other possibilities. ALTERNATIVE pronouns indicate that the referent is in contrast to what is wrongly assumed. EXCLUSIVE pronouns indicate the referent himself. ADDITIVE pronouns show that the referent is in addition to another of the same kind already described. All members of this set of four personal pronouns contain the previous reference morpheme **e-** / **o-**.

### 3.3.1 Structure of personal pronouns

The structure of the various free pronouns is presented in (3.8)–(3.12), and representative samples are provided from cl. 1, 4, 7, 12. All of these pronouns include the pronominal GNP, as well as the **e-** / **o-** previous reference morpheme.

Bracketing is done as follows: a form with only a left bracket represents a prefix, a form with only a right bracket represents a suffix, a stem has both a left and right bracket. The initial and final brackets are the boundaries of the entire word. Note that in each case the GNP and previous reference morpheme are treated as prefixes or suffixes, while the unique element which sets the word apart from the others is treated as the stem.

## 3.3 Personal pronouns

The contrastive pronouns are formed by the pronoun GNP, followed by the previous reference morpheme **e-** / **o-**, and then the morpheme **-he**, according to the following formula:

[pronoun GNP [P.R [**he**]

| (3.8) | | Cl. 1 | Cl. 4 | Cl. 7 | Cl. 12 |
|---|---|---|---|---|---|
| | UF | [i [e [he] | [i [o [he] | [ki [o [he] | [ka [o [he] |
| | SF | **yêhê** | **yôhê** | **kyôhê** | **kóòhê** |

Similarly, the alternative pronouns begin with the GNP, followed by the previous reference morpheme **e-** / **o-**, and finally the morpheme **-ki**, according to the following formula:

[pronoun GNP [P.R [**ki**]

| (3.9) | | Cl. 1 | Cl. 4 | Cl. 7 | Cl. 12 |
|---|---|---|---|---|---|
| | UF | [i [e [ki] | [i [o [ki] | [ki [o [ki] | [ka [o [ki] |
| | SF | **yékì** | **yókì** | **kyókì** | **kóókì** |

Likewise, the exclusive pronouns begin with the GNP, followed by the previous reference morpheme **e-** / **o-**, and finally the morpheme **-nyènè**, according to the following formula:

[pronoun GNP [P.R [**nyènè**]

| (3.10) | | Cl. 1 | Cl. 4 | Cl. 7 | Cl. 12 |
|---|---|---|---|---|---|
| | UF | [i [e [nyènè] | [i [o [nyènè] | [ki [o [nyènè] | [ka [o [nyènè] |
| | SF | **yényènè** | **yónyènè** | **kyónyènè** | **kóónyènè** |

There is another set of exclusive pronouns, which was borrowed from Kiviira, and which is now also used in Kifuliiru. They are formed with the morpheme **-ngwâ** in place of **-nyénè**, according to the following formula:

[pronoun GNP [P.R [**ngwâ**]

| (3.11) | | Cl. 1 | Cl. 4 | Cl. 7 | Cl. 12 |
|---|---|---|---|---|---|
| | UF | [i [e [ngwâ] | [i [o [ngwâ] | [ki [o [ngwâ] | [ka [o [ngwâ] |
| | SF | **yêngwâ** | **yôngwâ** | **kyôngwâ** | **kóòngwâ** |

The additive pronouns begin with the conjunctive **na** 'CNJ', followed by the GNP, and finally the previous reference morpheme **e-** / **o-**,[4] according to the following formula:

---

[4]The first-person singular additive pronoun **nààní** 'and I' is the exception to this. It lacks the

[**na**] pronoun GNP P.R]

(3.12)  | Cl. 1 | Cl. 4 | Cl. 7 | Cl. 12
UF | [na] i] e] | [na] i] o] | [na] ki] o] | [na] ka] o]
SF | **náyè** | **náyò** | **nákyò** | **nákò**

Table 3.1 includes a list of all of the personal pronouns in all classes, referred to in this section.

Table 3.1. Personal pronoun examples for all noun classes

| GNP | Contrastive | Alternative | Exclusive | Exclusive (from Kiviira) | Additive |
|---|---|---|---|---|---|
| 1SG | niêhê | niékì | niényènè | niêngwâ | nàànî |
| 2SG | wêhê | wékì | wényènè | wêngwâ | nààwê |
| 1 | yêhê | yékì | yényènè | yêngwâ | náyè |
| 1PL | twêhê | twékì | twényènè | twêngwâ | nyììtú |
| 2PL | mwêhê | mwékì | mwényènè | mwêngwâ | nììnyú |
| 2 | bóòhê | bóókì | bóónyènè | bôngwâ | nábò |
| 3 | gwôhê | gwókì | gwónyènè | gwôngwâ | nágwò |
| 4 | yôhê | yókì | yónyènè | yôngwâ | náyò |
| 5 | lyôhê | lyókì | lyónyènè | lyôngwâ | nályò |
| 6 | góòhê | góókì | góónyènè | gôngwâ | nágò |
| 7 | kyôhê | kyókì | kyónyènè | kyôngwâ | nákyò |
| 8 | byôhê | byókì | byónyènè | byôngwâ | nábyò |
| 9 | yôhê | yókì | yónyènè | yôngwâ | náyò |
| 10 | zóòhê | zóókì | zóónyènè | zôngwâ | názò |
| 11 | lwôhê | lwókì | lwónyènè | lwôngwâ | nálwò |
| 12 | kóòhê | kóókì | kóónyènè | kôngwâ | nákò |
| 13 | twôhê | twókì | twónyènè | twôngwâ | nátwò |
| 14 | bwôhê | bwókì | bwónyènè | bwôngwâ | nábwò |
| 15 | kwôhê | kwókì | kwónyènè | kwôngwâ | nákwò |
| 16 | hóòhê | hóókì | hóónyènè | hôngwâ | náhò |
| 18 | mwôhê | mwókì | mwónyènè | mwôngwâ | námwò |
| 19 | hyôhê | hyókì | hyónyènè | hyôngwâ | náhyò |
| 23 | yôhê | yókì | yónyènè | yôngwâ | náyò |

previous reference morpheme, at least in its surface form.

### 3.3.2 Functions of personal pronouns

In Kifuliiru all free personal pronouns have a marked meaning, which are presented in table 3.2. Each of these pronouns provide more than just reference; they add some other meaning, focusing on how a referent is "special."

Table 3.2. Functions of personal pronouns

| Cl. 2 form | Definition |
| --- | --- |
| bóòhê | CONTRASTIVE referent, relative to others |
| bóòkì | ALTERNATIVE referent, in contrast to what is assumed |
| bóónyènè/bôngwâ | EXCLUSIVE referent "itself" (**bôngwâ** from Kiviira) |
| nábò | ADDITIVE referent, in addition to others |

#### 3.3.2.1 Contrastive pronouns

Contrastive pronouns are not normally used unless there is contrastive focus involved. In (3.13) the daughter of a certain king was available for marriage, and several young men were chasing her. As they did, she would throw money over her back, and when they would stop to pick it up she would escape. One young man, *he* (by contrast) did not pay attention to the money, but continued chasing the princess until he caught up with her. Then she was given to him as his bride. The use of the pronoun **yêhê** (HE.CTR.P)[5] (reflecting the young man who was undistracted) is being *contrasted* with the others, who were distracted.

The sentence examples in (3.13)–(3.15) would be perfectly grammatical without the inclusion of the contrastive pronoun since the anaphoric subject pronoun prefix on the verb already clearly points to the referent. The addition of the pronoun serves to contrast the subject of this verb with another referent.

(3.13) Ùyó    mú-nyérè ‖ à-ná-shùbì  mwágúl-á    í=fwáràngà ‖
      that.N+1  1-girl      1-SQ-AGAIN  throw.down-Fa  AU=10+money

      hálìkó  ùyó    mú-tàbánà |  y-ê-hé  à-tà-ná-zì-twáz-à.
      but    that.N+1  1-young.man  1-CTR.P  1-NEG-SQ-O10-care-Fa

'And that girl ‖ again threw down the money ‖ but that young man | HE did not pay attention to it.' (06 022)

In (3.14) the pronoun **yêhê** 'SHE (in contrast to others)' refers to the twelfth wife of a certain king in a story. The other wives had all given birth to girls,

---

[5] For contrastive, alternative, and additive pronouns, the focus is communicated by the use of capitalization in the free gloss line, e.g. "HE".

but the twelfth wife **yêhê** (SHE.CTR.P) gave birth to a boy, throwing the other wives into fits of jealousy.

(3.14) Yàbó      bá-kà-à-gè      bòò-shì ‖   bá-ká-bùt-á          bà-ánà
      N+2       2-wife-A.M-1    2-all       2-P2-give.birth-Fa   2-child

      bá-nyérè ‖   sì=   w-í=       kùmì   ná=   bà-bìrì ‖   y-êhè ‖
      2-girl       But   1-A.M+AU   ten    CNJ=  2-two       1-CTR.P

      á-ká-bùt-à           ú=mw-ānà     mú-tàbánà.
      1-P2-give.birth-Fa   AU=1-child   1-boy

'All those wives ‖ they gave birth to girl children ‖ but the twelfth | SHE | gave birth to a boy child.' (107 004)

In (3.15) a woman had protected a leopard from hunters by hiding it in her house. By describing the leopard with the contrastive pronoun **yôhê** 'IT (in contrast to others)' the speaker is focusing on the fact that the leopard, by contrast, would not later protect the woman.

(3.15) Yéwè     mú-kàzì! ‖   W-à-bìsh-à         iyó         =n-gwî. ‖     Hálìkò
      Oh.my    1-woman      2SG-P1-hide-Fa     that.N+9    =9-leopard    but

      ú-gáá-bòn-à |   y-ôhê |    ì-tá-gá-kú-bìsh-à |          kírí    ú=lú-sìkù
      2SG-F2-see-Fa   9-CTR.P    9-NEG-F2-O2.SG-hide-Fa       even    AU=11-day

      lú-gùmà.
      11-one

'Oh my, woman! ‖ You hid (i.e. protected) that leopard. ‖ But you will see | IT | will not hide you | (not) even one day!' (04 010)

### 3.3.2.1.1 No contrast when preceded by **kuguma na** 'together with' and **nga** 'like'

When the contrastive pronoun denotes accompaniment and is preceded by **na** 'with' or states a comparison and is preceded by **nga** 'like', it no longer communicates the notion of contrast. In this case, the pronoun is not glossed as contrastive (CTR) but merely as a pronoun (PRO).

In (3.16) **bóòhê** 'them' is the complement of **na** 'with' in the accompaniment phrase **nà=bóòhê** 'with them'. In this construction there is no implication that **bóòhê** 'they' is being contrasted with any other referent.

## 3.3 Personal pronouns

(3.16) **Ná-yè** | **à-ná-bwátál-á**    **gírà**    **à-Ø-shòl-è** ||    **à-ná-tàngír-à**
ADD.P-1    1-SQ-sit.down-Fa    so.that    1-SBV-play-Fe    1-SQ-began-Fa

**ú=kú-vùn-á** |    **kúgúmá**    **nà=**    **bó-òhê**.
AU=15-play.game-Fa    together    CNJ=    2-PRO

'And HE | as well sat down in order to play mankala || and he began to start the game | together with them.' (30 004-005)

### 3.3.2.2 Alternative pronouns

The alternative pronouns have a very distinct meaning: they point to the fact that the referent is not the one who is mistakenly assumed, but another. Alternative pronouns are often used at crucial turning points in the plot of a story.

In (3.17) the first character boastfully employs the contrastive pronoun **yêhê** (HE.CTR.P), saying that it was impossible for anyone to trick *him* (implying that *others* could be tricked.) The second person reciprocates with a boast of his own, signified by the additive **náyè** 'and he also'. Then by employing the alternative pronoun **yékì** (HE.ALT.P) (in contrast to what was mistakenly expected) he communicates that he will trick the first person, in contrast to the mistaken assumption that no one would be able to do so. Note that each of these pronouns could be removed and it would still be clear who the referents were.

(3.17) **Mú-gùmà**    **à-ná-bwîr-à**    **ú=w-àbò** |    **kwó=**    **y-ê-hé**    **ndáá-yé**
1-one    1-SQ-tell-Fa    AU=1-SAME.SET    CMP=    1-CTR.P    NEG.FOC-1

**ú=w-àbò**    **mú-ndú**    **ú-w-àngà-mú-téb-à.** ||    **Ná-yé**
AU=1-SAME.SET    1-person    S.R-1-POS-O1-trick-Fa    ADD.P-1

**ú=w-àbò** |    **à-ná-mú-bwîr-à** |    **kwó=**    **y-ékì** |    **à-ngà-mú-téb-à**.
AU=1-SAME.SET    1-SQ-O1-tell-Fa    CMP=    1-ALT.P    1-POT-O1-trick-Fa

'A certain person told his fellow | that HE, there's no other person who would be able to trick him. || And HE that fellow | told him | that HE (unexpected alternative) | would be the one who would trick him.'

This same morpheme **-ki** 'alternative' is commonly associated with the cl. 5 contrastive copula **lyô** 'that's when', forming the related contrastive copula **lyókì** 'that's when (in contrast to what has been mistakenly assumed)'. In (3.18) a common assumption is stated, i.e. that it's impossible to take by force what's in the house of a mighty man. However, the contrastive copula **lyókì** 'that's when (in contrast to what was mistakenly assumed)' puts special focus on the fact that the things of a mighty man, contrary to normal expectation, can be plundered.

(3.18) **Ndáá-yé** | ú-w-àngà-nyág-á | í-bì-rì mú= ny-ûmbà y-é=
NEG.FOC-1   S.R-1-POS-steal-Fa   S.R-8-be   18=   9-house   9-A.M+AU=

kí-hàgàngè. ‖ Hálìkò | á-málí | kì-kón-à | <u>ly-ókí</u> |
7-mighty.man   but   1-ALREADY   O7-tie.up-Fa   5-ALT.C

à-ngà-kì-sháhùl-á | í-bì-rì =mwó.
1-POS-O7-plunder-Fa   S.R-8-be   =18

'There's no one | who can take by force | the (things) that are in the house of a mighty man. But | when one has already tied him up | THAT'S WHEN | he could plunder him | what's inside.' (Mat 12:29)

### 3.3.2.3 Exclusive pronouns

The exclusive pronouns **nyene** and **ngwa** denote 'self/selves (to the exclusion of others)'. They emphasize either (a) that the referent (or group of referents) is unaccompanied, i.e. 'by himself', or (b) that the referent 'himself as opposed to any other', is being referred to.[6]

In (3.19) a lion has promised a certain cow that he will not eat it. The lion's friends, an eagle and a leopard, are trying to figure out how they might get the lion to kill the cow anyway (as they would get to share in the meal!) The scheming eagle asks if the lion wouldn't agree to eat the cow if the cow *itself* were to ask him to eat it. Eagle thus refers to the cow with the exclusive pronoun **yónyènè** 'it itself'.

(3.19) Ì-yí n-gáàvù | ìrí y-àngà-dèt-à | y-ónyènè | kw-ó=
this.P-9   9-cow   if   9-CND-say-Fa   9-self   CMP-2SG=

Ø-gì-ly-è ‖ h-ó= w-àngà-fw-à | ná= yù-gú mw-énà ‖
SBV-O9-eat-Fe   16-O.R=   2SG-POS-die-Fa   CNJ=   this.P-3   3-hunger

k-ó= tà-ngà-gì-ly-à?
Q-2SG=   NEG-POS-O9-eat-Fa

'This cow | if it would say | itself | that you (should) eat it ‖ rather than dying | from this hunger ‖ wouldn't you eat it?' (11 026)

---

[6]These pronouns are not used to indicate that an action is reflexive. Reflexivity is expressed only by the use of the reflexive object **yì-** directly preceding the verb stem.

## 3.3 Personal pronouns

In (3.20) the second-person singular exclusive pronoun **wényènè** 'yourself' is used, in the context that someone has judged *himself*.

(3.20) **Kéérà**       w-à-yì-twír-à         ú=lú-bààjá |   w-ényènè ||   kw-ó=
       ALREADY        2SG-P1-RFX-cut-Fa     AU=11-law      2SG-self       CMP-AU=

   **mú-shósí** | à-tà-Ø-kìzí       bùt-à.
   1-man          1-NEG-TL-REP      give.birth-Fa

'Already you yourself have judged | for yourself || that a man | does not habitually give birth.' (631 023)

In (3.21) the first-person singular pronoun **niényènè** 'myself' focuses attention on the fact that the lion is living *all by itself*, unaccompanied.

(3.21) **Ù-Ø-lék-é**        tù-Ø-túúl-ánw-è ||      mú=kúbá      nàà-ní ||
       2SG-SBV-allow-Fe    1PL-SBV-live-MUT-Fe    because       ADD.P-1

   **n-dúúz-ír-í**     **ni-ényènè**.
   1SG-live-RS-Fi      1SG-self

'Allow that we live together || because and ME || I am living all by myself.' (11 013)

The alternate form of the exclusive pronoun, originally borrowed from Kiviira, is exemplified in (3.22). The alternate form occurs very infrequently in the corpus of our texts, but it is commonly used in Kifuliiru conversation. In this example the king is upset that the people he has sent to kill a certain person have not done so. He then asserts, by the use of the exclusive pronoun, that he *himself* will do the job.

(3.22) **Mwámì** || tì=       **Ni-êhê** |   n-gá-mú-yì-yìt-ìr-à   |   **ni-êngwâ**.
       1-king        ‹quote›  1SG-CTR.P     1SG-F2-O1-RFX-kill-APL-Fa    1SG-self

'The king || said ME | I will just kill him for myself | I myself.' (210 108)

In (3.23) a fox came and chased away all the wedding guests from their dancing, leaving behind only the bride by *herself* in the shelter they had built for the occasion.

(3.23) **Sì**=    **ú=mú-hyà** ||    à-ná-sìgàl-è        hí=    bándá       **y-êngwâ**.
       but       AU=1-bride         1-CON-remain-Fe    16+5   shelter     1-self

'But that bride || remained behind in the shelter by herself.' (102 008)

### 3.3.2.4 Additive pronouns

The additive pronoun, e.g. **nábo** 'they also' states that the referent(s) is involved in the very same situation/action as a previous, just mentioned referent.

In (3.24) a king offered his sad daughter in marriage to anyone who could make her laugh. When finally a young man was able to make the daughter laugh, the king laughed as well. The pronoun **náyè** 'he also' draws special focus to the fact that the king *also* laughed, just like his daughter had just done.

(3.24) Mw-ámì | à-ná-yîj-à ‖ à-ná-gwân-à ùyó mú-lùzìnyérè
1-king 1-SQ-come-Fa 1-SQ-encounter-Fa that.N+1 1-king's.daughter

à-kì-gwétí á-gáá-shék-à ‖ <u>ná-yè</u> à-ná-shék-à.
1-PERS-PROG 1-INTL-laugh-Fa ADD.P-1 1-SQ-laugh-Fa

'The king | arrived ‖ and found that princess still laughing ‖ and HE ALSO he laughed.' (07 051)

In (3.25) we return to the story of the lion, leopard, eagle, and cow. In order to trick the cow into being eaten, both the eagle and the leopard have offered themselves to the poor starving lion, so that he could eat them. When the cow saw that the lion had refused to eat his friends even though they offered themselves, it lost its fear and it too offered itself as a meal for the starving lion. The pronoun **náyò** 'and it also' draws special focus to the fact that the cow is now doing the very same thing that the eagle and leopard have just done.

(3.25) Ìyó n-gáàvú | ìrí í-ká-yùvw-á kw-á= bà-àbò
that.N+9 9-cow when 9-P2-hear-Fa CMP-AU= 2-SAME.SET

bà-dèt-á | kw-é= bà-Ø-ly-è | í-tà-ná-bà-ly-à ‖ <u>ná-yó</u> |
2+P1-say-Fa CMP-9= O2-SBV-eat-Fe 9-NEG-SQ-O.2-eat-Fa ADD.P-9

y-àná-dèt-à: ‖ «Ím-Ø-b-é ni-ó= gáà-ly-à.»
9-SQ-say-Fa 1-SBV-become-Fe 1-O.R+FOC+2SG= F2-eat-Fa

'That cow | when it heard its fellows say | that it (the lion) eat them | and it did not eat them ‖ and IT ALSO (Cow) said: ‖ «Let me be the one whom you will eat.»' (11 037)

In (3.26) the wedding host tells the common people who are assisting him to do just as he does when attending to the wedding guests. The additive pronoun

## 3.4 Interrogative pronouns

**nábò** 'and they' draws attention to the fact that the peasants followed on in doing just what the wedding host had already done.

(3.26)  À-ná-lámùs-à    yàbó           bá-génì |   ìrí        à-ná-hún-ìz-à      î-twè. ‖
       1-SQ-greet-Fa   THOSE.N+2    2-guests    while    1-SQ-bow-CS-Fa    5-head

       Yàbó         bá-gùndà ‖    í=ky-ânyà        bá-ká-bà-lámús-â ‖   ná-b-ó
       THOSE.N+2    2-peasants    AU=7-time        2-P2-O2-greet-Fa          ADD.P-2

       bà-nà-gír-á |   kwô-kw-ò.
       2-SQ-do-Fa       E-15-thus

'And he (wedding host) greeted those guests | while bowing his head. ‖ Those common folk ‖ when they greeted them (the guests) ‖ and THEY ALSO did | the same thing.' (34 009-010)

## 3.4 Interrogative pronouns

Kifuliiru has interrogative pronouns which agree in noun class with the antecedent and which mean 'Which kind?', 'Which one?', and 'How many?' There are also non-agreeing interrogatives which ask: 'When?', 'Why?', 'Who?', 'Where?', and 'How?'.

### 3.4.1 Structure of interrogative pronouns

#### 3.4.1.1 Agreeing forms

The variable (agreeing) interrogative pronouns are all of the form GNP plus stem. They are: -**ki** 'which type', -**hi** 'which one', -**nga** 'how many'.

The pronoun meaning 'which type?' is formed with the nominal/adjectival GNP prefix followed by -**ki**, according to the following formula:

    [GNP [**ki**]

(3.27) | | Cl. 1 | Cl. 4 | Cl. 7 | Cl. 9 | Cl. 11 |
|---|---|---|---|---|---|
| UF | [mú [ki] | [mí [ki] | [kí [ki] | [nyí [ki] | [lú [ki] |
| SF | múkì | míkì | kíkì | nyíkì | lúkì |

The pronoun meaning 'which one' is formed with the nominal/adjectival GNP prefix plus -**hi**, according to the following formula:

    [GNP [**hi**]

(3.28)

|     | Cl. 1 | Cl. 4 | Cl. 7 | Cl. 11 | Cl. 12 |
|-----|-------|-------|-------|--------|--------|
| UF  | [mú [hi] | [mí [hi] | [kí [hi] | [lú [hi] | [ká [hi] |
| SF  | múhì  | míhì  | kíhì  | lúhì   | káhì   |

The pronoun meaning 'how many?' is formed with the numeral GNP prefix, which has L tone, followed by -**nga**, according to the following formula:

[GNP [**nga**]]

These forms, which use the demonstrative prefixes, occur only with the plural classes. That these do not use the adjectival prefixes can be seen from the cl. 10 prefix, which is **zi**- with demonstratives but **nyi**- with the adjectival pronouns.

(3.29)

|     | Cl. 2 | Cl. 4 | Cl. 8 | Cl. 10 | Cl. 13 |
|-----|-------|-------|-------|--------|--------|
| UF  | bà [ngá] | [í [ngá] | [bì [ngá] | [zì [ngá] | [tù [ngá] |
| SF  | bàngâ | îngâ  | bìngâ | zìngâ  | tùngâ  |

(3.30) Interrogative pronouns for all classes

| GNP | Which type? | Which one? | How many? |
|-----|-------------|------------|-----------|
| 1SG |             |            |           |
| 2SG |             |            |           |
| 1   | múkì        | múhì       |           |
| 1PL |             |            |           |
| 2PL |             |            |           |
| 2   | bákì        | báhì       | bàngâ     |
| 3   | gúkì        | gúhì       |           |
| 4   | míkì        | míhì       | îngâ      |
| 5   | líkì        | líhì       |           |
| 6   | mákì        | máhì       | gàngâ     |
| 7   | kíkì        | kíhì       |           |
| 8   | bíkì        | bíhì       | bìngâ     |
| 9   | nyíkì       | nyíhì      |           |
| 10  | nyíkì       | nyíhì      | zìngâ     |
| 11  | lúkì        | lúhì       |           |
| 12  | kákì        | káhì       | kàngâ     |
| 13  | túkì        | túhì       | tùngâ     |
| 14  | búkì        | búhì       | bùngâ     |
| 15  | kúkì        | kúhì       |           |

*3.4 Interrogative pronouns* 53

| GNP | Which type? | Which one? | How many? |
|---|---|---|---|
| 16 | **hákì** | **háhì** | **hàngâ** |
| 17 | --- | --- | --- |
| 18 | --- | --- | |
| 19 | **híkì** | **híhì** | |
| 23 | --- | --- | |

### 3.4.1.2 Non-agreeing interrogative forms

In addition to the above variable forms that can be associated with many different classes, there are several forms that are invariable, or that have only singular/plural forms: **kítùmà kíkì** 'why?', **háyì**[7] 'where?', **mángókì** 'when?', **kútì** 'how?', **nyândì / bányândì** 'who? (SG/PL)'.

The interrogative **mángókì** 'when?' is a combination of the temporal complementizer **mángò** '(at the time) when' and interrogative suffix -**ki**. The -**ki** suffix is used only in this temporal interrogative and in the interrogative pronoun set asking 'what kind?'. The personal interrogative, **nyândì** 'who?' serves as a cl. 1a pronoun which has its plural in cl. 2 **bányândì**.

### 3.4.2 Functions of interrogative pronouns

#### 3.4.2.1 Agreeing forms

The interrogative set of which the cl. 8 form **bíkì** 'what (things)?' is a member asks 'which kind?' or 'which type?'. These forms are often used in a verbless clause. In (3.31) the interrogative **bíkì** 'what (kind of thing)' refers to what has made him skinny.

(3.31) **Bì-kí**   í-by-à-kú-jáàv-y-â   kwókùnô?
       8-what    S.R-8-P1-O2.SG-get.skinny-CS-Fa   like.this.P.C

'What has caused you to be skinny like this?' (11 018)

The interrogative pronoun may also be used following a verb, serving as its object. In (3.32) the interrogative pronoun means: "*What* will I hide for you?".

---

[7]The interrogative **háyì** 'where?' is also sometimes pronounced as **háhì**, which is probably the original form of this cl. 16 locative interrogative. The second **h** has merely undergone softening and voicing between the vowels, resulting in **háyì**, and the **y** is sometimes softened even to the extent that it is reduced to zero in quick speech: **háì**.

(3.32) Ùyó      mú-sháàjá    à-ná-gì-búúz-à: ‖ «N-gá-kú-bìsh-ìr-à
      that.N+1  1-old.man    1-SQ-O9-ask-Fa   1SG-F2-O2.SG-hide-APL-Fa

   bí-kì?»
   8-what

'And that old man asked it (Cow): ‖ «What (things) will I hide for you?»'
(105 017)

In (3.33) the commonly heard phrase **mákì gánò?** 'what's going on here? (lit., what are these matters?)' is used. This cl. 6 construction is somewhat idiomatic, and shows that the speaker does not expect the situation or approve of it and is asking for an explanation.

(3.33) **Kályôshò** | à-ná-bwîr-à  nááкùlù:      ‖ «É=  mú-gààkà ‖
       Kalyosho    1-SQ-tell-Fa   1a+his.grandmother   O=  1-old.lady

   **má-kì**  gá-nò?»
   6-what    6-here.P.C

'Kalyosho | told grandmother: ‖ «O grandma ‖ what's going on here?»'
(619 060)

When the referent of the interrogative is expressed as a noun, then the interrogative follows it, as in (3.34).

(3.34) É=   mw-âná  w-à-nì  ‖ bú-twâlì     **bú-kì**    bw-ó=
       O=   1-child  1-A.M-1SG  14-rulership  14-which   14-O.R=

   n-gá-kú-hèèrèz-â?
   1SG-F2-O2.SG-give-Fa

'O my child ‖ what kind of authority (is it) which I will give to you?'
(607 023)

The interrogative pronoun set of which **kíhì** is a member asks 'which one'? In (3.35) the speaker asks 'Which one will I choose?'. This pronoun is used relatively rarely.

(3.35) Ààhó! ‖ **Lì-hí**  ly-ó=   n-àngà-tóól-à? ‖ N-dá-yì-j-ì.
       OK.then  5-which   5-O.R=  1SG-POT-choose-Fa  1SG-NEG-know-RS-Fi

'Okay then! ‖ Which one would I choose? ‖ I don't know.' (Php 1:22)

The interrogative pronoun set of which **bàngâ** is a member asks the question 'how many?'. In (3.36) the question is 'How many children are these?'.

(3.36) **Yà-bá   bà-ánà   ‖   bà-lì   bà-ngâ?**
       these-2  2-children   2-are   2-how.many

   'These children ‖ are how many?' (46 009)

### 3.4.2.2 Non-agreeing forms

The interrogative pronoun **kítùmà kíkì** 'why? (lit., reason which kind?)' is a "frozen" case of the 'which type?' pronoun above, which questions the purpose of an event, asking 'why'. In (3.37) the question is asked why the father cut the vine.

(3.37) **É=   dáàtà   ‖   kí-tùmà   kí-kì       w-à-tèm-á   |   yùgwó**
       O=   1a+father    7-reason   7-what    2SG-P1-cut-Fa    that.N+3

   **mú-lándírà?**
   3-vine

   'O father ‖ why (lit., (for) what kind of reason) have you cut | that vine?' (32 026)

The interrogative pronoun **háyì** asks the question 'where?'. In (3.38) Kalyosho is asked: "Where are you running to?".

(3.38) **É=   Kályôshò ‖ háyí      h-ô=           lì    mú=    tíbít-ír-à?**
       O=   Kalyosho   where   16-O.R+2SG=   are   PROG=  run-APL-Fa

   'O Kalyosho ‖ where is it you are running to?' (17 010)

In (3.39) the question **háyì** 'where' is found at the end of the clause.

(3.39) **É=   mú-nyérè ‖   ú=mú-kùlù       ‖   w-à-mú-sìg-à        háyì?**
       O=   1-girl       AU=1-great.one       2SG-P1-O1-leave-Fa   where

   'O girl ‖ the older brother ‖ where did you leave him?' (303 030)

The interrogative pronoun **mángókì** asks the question 'when?'. In (3.40) the speaker asks how long he will need to be patient.

(3.40) **N-gá-yàm-à       |    n-gwétì       n-gá-mù-gòòyèr-á   |   hàlíndé**
       1SG-F2-ALWAYS-Fa      1SG-PROG      1SG-INTL-O1-endure-Fe    until

   **màngókì?**
   when

   'I will always be | enduring you | until when?' (Luk 9:41)

The interrogative pronoun **nyândì** (SG) or **bányândì** (PL) asks 'who?'. In (3.41) the speaker asks "'who reached into my pot?'".

(3.41) É bà-ánà ‖ nyândì ú-w-à-húm-á | mú= yà-ká ká-bìndì
O 2-children who S.R-1-P1-touch-Fa 18= this.P-12 12-pot

kà-à-nî?
12-A.M-1SG

'O children ‖ who touched | in this pot of mine?' (33 010)

The interrogative pronoun **kútì** asks 'how?'. In (3.42) the speaker asks "how could my husband have changed into a pig?".

(3.42) Yóò! ‖ Kútì kù-nó yíbà-niè à-híndùk-à
Oh.me how 15-this.P.C husband-1SG 1+P1-turn.into-Fa

n-gúlúbè?
9-pig

'Oh me! ‖ How is this my husband has turned into a pig?' (01 027)

The pronoun **kútì** can also be translated 'what?' when used to ask about an action. In (3.43) the rabbit is asked what should be done to his friend hedgehog, who was caught stealing.

(3.43) Éwè ‖ ù-yú mw-ìrá w-à-wè ‖ tù-Ø-mú-gír-àg-è kútì?
hey.you this.P-1 1-friend 1-A.M-2SG 1PL-SBV-O1-do-EMP-Fe how

'Hey you ‖ this friend of yours ‖ what (how) shall we do to him?' (09 020)

The form **kútì** can also be used as an informal greeting: **Kútì?** 'How (is it)?' to which the reply is either (**Nângà**), **kwókùnô** '(No), just like this' or **Ndáákwò** 'There's nothing'.

### 3.5 Demonstratives

### 3.5.1 Structure of demonstratives

Kifuliiru is rich in demonstratives, having five basic sets, and four degrees of distance. Structurally, two of these sets (here shown with cl. 2 prefixes), **yábà** (these.PROXIMAL+2), **yàbô** (those.NEARBY+2) do not have a stem as such. Their base form is a prefix, and they can be considered composite forms rather than as being analyzable into more than one meaningful morpheme. The three other demonstratives, **bá-nò** (2-these.PROXIMAL.CONTRASTIVE), **bà-lyâ**

## 3.5 Demonstratives

(2-these.REMOTE), **bà-líírà** (2-those.DISTAL) do have a stem. The structures of all five sets are discussed below.

Each of these five sets can be used to derive an emphatic form which indicates focus. For example, the cl. 2 **yàbô** 'those.NEARBY', when emphasized becomes **báàbò** 'those.NEARBY very ones (focal)'. The focus form can then be reduplicated, to produce a reduplicated focal form **báàbò-báàbò** 'those very ones (emphasized focal)'.

The basic demonstrative forms often precede a noun, e.g. **yàbó bándù** 'those.NEARBY people'. However, they can be used substantively, especially preceding a copula. In (3.44) **yàbá** 'these.PROXIMAL' is used substantively. The emphatic demonstratives are most often used substantively.

(3.44)  <u>Yà-bá</u>      bà-lí     bà-ánà       bà-à-nî.
   these.P-2   2-are   2-children   2-A.M-1SG

'These are my children.'

### 3.5.1.1 Forms with no stem

The nearby and proximal demonstratives are composed of two syllables. Depending on the noun class of the referent, the second syllable of the demonstrative always corresponds phonologically to the form of a corresponding GNP. For example **ùyú** is the proximal demonstrative for cl. 1 (**u-** is the GNP prefix for cl. 1 nouns); **yábà** is the proximal demonstrative for cl. 2 (**ba-** is the GNP prefix for cl. 2 nouns). Since these two forms have no stem, the language employs copy vowels[8] and an epethentic **y-** to fulfill syllable structure constraints. This produces composite forms, i.e. forms which cannot be analyzed as a series of distinct morphemes but rather as portmanteau forms.

The PROXIMAL DEMONSTRATIVES for classes 1, 4, 9, and 23 are formed according to the following formula:

  [copy vowel [epenthetic **y**[9] [demonstrative GNP]

The proximal demonstratives for the remaining classes, all of which have CV- prefixes, follow the formula:

  [epenthetic-**y** [copy vowel [demonstrative GNP]

In each case, the gender and number of the referent is conveyed by the GNP on the right, while the notions of "proximity" are conveyed by the combination of the GNP with the units on the left. In the parsing of these forms, e.g. **y-á-bà** (2.this.P), the first two hyphens do not really refer to morpheme breaks,

---

[8] Alternatively, the copy vowel could be analyzed as an augment.
[9] This could also be considered an epenthetic **i** which is changed to **y** by the rule of glide formation when it precedes another vowel.

but only to a segmentation of the structure. The forms and GNP numbers for which this second formula is used are: -**bà** (2), -**gà** (6), -**kà** (12), -**hà** (16), -**lì** (5), -**kì** (7), -**bì** (8), -**zì** (10), -**hì** (19), -**gù** (3), -**lù** (11), -**tù** (13), -**bù** (14), -**kù** (15), -**mù** (3,18).

Forms for representative classes of proximal demonstratives with V-only and CV prefixes are shown in (3.45).

(3.45)

|  | Cl. 1 | Cl. 4 | Cl. 7 | Cl. 12 |
|---|---|---|---|---|
| UF | u-y-u | i-y-i | y-i-ki | y-a-ka |
| SF | úyù | íyì | yíkì | yákà |

The NEARBY DEMONSTRATIVE is identical to the proximal demonstrative described above, but with the addition in final position of the previous reference (P.R) morpheme -**o**.[10]

Because its base is the same as the proximal demonstrative, the formula for the nearby form of cl. 1, 4, 9, and 23 differs from that of the other classes in exactly the same way that the formulas for the proximal demonstratives differed. The formula for nearby demonstratives of cl. 1, 4, 9, and 23 is:

[copy vowel [epenthetic **y** [demonstrative GNP] P.R]

The formula for the nearby demonstrative of the other classes is:

[epenthetic **y** [ copy vowel [demonstrative GNP] P.R]

Note that when the proximal forms end in a consonant plus high vowel **i** or **u**, the rule of glide formation causes the nearby forms to end with -**yo** or -**wo**: e.g. cl. 7 **yìkyô** and cl. 11 **yùlwô**. In nearby forms for which the proximal forms end with **a**, vowel coalescence takes place: e.g. the cl. 12 **ya-ka-o** becomes **yà-kô** because of the rule of "lexical unlike vowel assimilation," which states: A non-high, non-back vowel (**e** or **a**) assimilates totally to a following vowel at morpheme boundaries within the word. In the case of **uyu-o** > **úyù**, there is a process of absorption by which **uyu-o** > **uywo** > **ùyô**. Forms for representative classes of nearby demonstratives are shown in (3.46).

(3.46)

|  | Cl. 1 | Cl. 4 | Cl. 7 | Cl. 12 |
|---|---|---|---|---|
| UF | u-y-u-ó | i-y-i-ó | y-i-ki-ó | y-a-ka-ó |
| SF | ùyô | ìyô | yìkyô | yàkô |

In nearby demonstrative forms, the noun class is conveyed in the UF by the penultimate morpheme, while the notion of "nearby" is conveyed by the

---

[10] The previous reference morpheme normally takes two forms, -**e** and -**o**. The -**e** is used only with first- and second-person forms and third-person singular (cl. 1). However, the nearby demonstrative does not have a first- or second-person form, and thus the -**e** form of the previous reference marker is not used. The cl. 1 form, the only one in which -**e** would be the expected form, takes -**o** instead, probably by analogy.

## 3.5 Demonstratives

combination of the two segments on the far left and the previous reference morpheme on the far right.

### 3.5.1.2 Forms based on demonstrative stems

The remaining three demonstratives all have a stem: **-no** for proximal contrastive forms, **-lyá** for remote forms, and **-lììrà** for distal forms. The formula for all forms is:

[demonstrative GNP [demonstrative stem]

Example forms in are given with the cl. 2 prefix **ba-**. The free glosses of the first two are 'those', and the last, 'these'.

(3.47)

| | Distal | Remote | Proximal contrastive |
|---|---|---|---|
| UF | **ba-liira** | **ba-lya** | **ba-no** |
| SF | **bàlíírà** | **bàlyâ** | **bánò** |

### 3.5.1.3 Emphatic forms of the demonstrative

The five demonstrative pronouns described above all have derived emphatic forms. There is a single formula for deriving the emphatic form of any of the five demonstratives. The underlying morphology involves the combination of a focus copula (which itself is formed from a pronoun prefix plus the previous reference morpheme) followed by a relativizer (which could also be considered the augment for that class, or simply a copy vowel),[11] and then by the unmarked form of the demonstrative pronoun in question, but minus any initial **y**. This can be formalized as follows:

[pronoun prefix [-**e** / -**o**] [relativizer [unmarked demonstrative (minus any initial epenthetic **y**)]

That the emphatic demonstrative, which consists of a focus copula plus vocalic prefix plus the unmarked demonstrative, is synchronically lexicalized as a single word is shown by the fact that it can itself be preceded by the focus copula/object relative. In (3.48) the emphatic demonstrative **yôyù** 'this VERY one' is placed between the object relative/focus copula and the verb.

---

[11] It is necessary to assume this extra vowel because of the coalescence found in the forms which have a stem with a CV prefix, e.g. cl. 7 **kínò**, **kìryá**, **kìríírà**, etc. In these cases, when the focus pronoun is added, there is coalescence between the focus copula and the added vowel. This can be seen in the cl. 7 emphatic forms: **kyékìnó**, **kyékìryá**, **kyékìríìrâ**, where the coalescence between the **o** of the focus copula (**kyó**) and the added **i**, yields **e** (underlined in the forms just listed). If there were no added **i**, the result would instead be *kyokino, *kyokirya, etc. In the forms without stems, the resulting vowel would be the same whether one assumes an extra vowel or not, so for consistency in the derivation, we assume it in all the forms.

(3.48) Yé=   y-ô-yú | tw-à-hééréz-á | í-tùmù.
       1-FOC  E-this.P-1  1PL-P1-give-Fa  5-spear

'He is this very one | to whom we gave | the spear.' (06 013)

There is considerable vowel coalescence involved in these intensified forms, as shown in the examples below. This vowel coalescence follows the rule of "postlexical unlike vowel coalescence," since each form involves more than one lexical unit, i.e. the focus copula and the demonstrative form with its added vocalic prefix. This post-lexical coalescence can be described as follows: when two unlike vowels coalesce, the resultant vowel exhibits the height of the first vowel, and the frontness/backness of the second vowel. Thus: e + u→o, a + o→o, o + a→a, o + i→e. High vowels (**i** and **u**) become **y** and **w**, respectively, when they precede an unlike vowel.

The underlying morphology of various emphatic demonstratives, together with the phonological derivations necessary to arrive at the surface form, is presented in (3.49)–(3.53). Examples from five different noun classes are presented. Forms of all other classes can be extrapolated from these. The basic formulas above each set of examples are presented using the cl. 1 example of each form.

The emphatic form of the PROXIMAL demonstrative 'this one' is:

[pronoun prefix [previous reference] [relativizer [**úyù**]

(3.49)    Cl. 1              Cl. 4              Cl. 7               Cl. 12
          [í [e] [ú [úyù]    [í [o] [í [íyì]    [kí [o] [í [íkì]    [ká [o] [á [ákà]
          [yé] [úùyù]        [yó] [îìyì]        [kyó] [îìkì]        [kó] [áàkà]
          **yôyù**           **yêyì**           **kyêkì**           **káàkà**

The emphatic form of the NEARBY demonstrative 'that.N very one' is:

[pronoun prefix [previous reference] [relativizer [**ùyó**]

(3.50)         Cl. 1              Cl. 4              Cl. 7                Cl. 12
       UF      [í [e] [ú [ùyó]    [í [o] [í [ìyó]    [kí [o] [í [ìkyó]    [ká [o] [á [àkó]
       Step 1  [yé] [úùyó]        [yó] [îìyó]        [kyó] [îìkyó]        [kó] [áàkó]
       SF[12]  **yôyó**           **yêyó**           **kyêkyó**           **káàkó**

---

[12] Vowels are compensatorily lengthened following a glide (**w** or **y**) as well as preceding a NC (e.g. **mb, nd, ng**). Any long vowel is shortened, however, when followed by three or more morae within the word. Such lengthening will be assumed in surface forms, and double vowels will only be used to indicate length which is not conditioned.

## 3.5 Demonstratives

The emphatic form of the PROXIMAL CONTRASTIVE demonstrative **uno** 'this one (compared with others)' is:
[pronoun prefix [previous reference] [relativizer [ùnó]]

| (3.51) | Cl. 1 | Cl. 4 | Cl. 7 | Cl. 12 |
|---|---|---|---|---|
| UF | [í [e] [ú [ùnó] | [í [o] [í [ìnó] | [kí [o] [í [kìnó] | [ká [o] [á [kànó] |
| Step 1 | [yé] [úùnó] | [yó] [îìnó] | [kyó] [íkìnó] | [kó] [ákànó] |
| SF | yônó | yênó | kyêkìnó | káákànó |

The emphatic form of the REMOTE demonstrative **ùlyá** 'that.R one' is:
[pronoun prefix [previous reference] [relativizer [ùlyá] N14

| (3.52) | Cl. 1 | Cl. 4 | Cl. 7 | Cl. 12 |
|---|---|---|---|---|
| UF | [í [e] [ú [ùlyá] | [í [e] [í [ìryá] | [kí [o] [í [kìryá] | [ká [o] [á [kàlyá] |
| Step 1 | [yé] [úùlyá] | [yé] [îìryá] | [kyó] [íkìryá] | [kó] [ákàlyá] |
| SF | yôlyá | yêryá | kyékìryá | káákàlyá |

The emphatic form of the DISTAL demonstrative **ùlííra** 'that.D one (away from speaker and hearer)' is:
[pronoun prefix [previous reference] [relativizer [úlīírá]]

| (3.53) | Cl. 1 | Cl. 4 | Cl. 7 | Cl. 12 |
|---|---|---|---|---|
| UF | [í [e] [ú [úlìírá] | [í [o] [í [írìírá] | [kí [o] [í [kìlìírá] | [ká [o] [á [kàlìírá] |
| Step 1 | [yé] [úlìírá] | [yó] [írìírá] | [kyó] [íkìlìírá] | [kó] [ákàlìírá] |
| SF | yólîìrá | yérîìrá | kyékìlîìrá | kákàlîìrá |

Table 3.3 lists the surface forms for all five types of default and emphatic demonstratives for all noun classes.

Table 3.3. Default and emphatic demonstratives for all classes

| Noun Cl. | Dem. Affix | Proximal | Nearby | Proximal contrastive | Remote | Distal |
|---|---|---|---|---|---|---|
| 1 Default[a] | ú | úyù | ùyô | únò | ùlyâ | úlīìrà |
| 1 Emph. | | yôyù | yôyô | yônô | yôlyâ | yólīìrà |
| 2 Default | bà | yábà | yàbô | bánò | bàlyâ | bàlíírà |
| 2 Emph. | | báàbà | báàbô | báábànò | báábàlyâ | bábàlíírà |
| 3 Default | gù | yúgù | yùgwô | gúnò | gùlyâ | gùlíírà |
| 3 Emph. | | gwôgù | gwôgwô | gwógùnô | gwógùlyâ | gwógùlíírà |

| Noun Cl. | Dem. Affix | Proximal | Nearby | Proximal contrastive | Remote | Distal |
|---|---|---|---|---|---|---|
| 4 Default | í | íyì | ìyô | ínò | ìryâ | íriirà |
| 4 Emph. | | yêyì | yêyô | yênô | yêryâ | yériirà |
| 5 Default | lì | yírì | yìryô | línò | lìryâ | lìríírà |
| 5 Emph. | | yérì | lyêryô | lyélìnô | lyélìryâ | lyélìríírà |
| 6 Default | gà | yágà | yàgô | gánò | gàlyâ | gàlíírà |
| 6 Emph. | | gáàgà | gáàgô | gáágànô | gáágàlyâ | gágàlíírà |
| 7 Default | kì | yíkì | yìkyô | kínò | kìryâ | kìríírà |
| 7 Emph. | | kyêkì | kyêkyô | kyékìnô | kyékìryâ | kyékìríírà |
| 8 Default | bì | yíbì | yìbyô | bínò | bìryâ | bìríírà |
| 8 Emph. | | byêbì | byêbyô | byébìnô | byébìryâ | byébìríírà |
| 9 Default | í | íyì | ìyô | ínò | ìryá | íriirà |
| 9 Emph. | | yêyì | yêyô | yênô | yêryâ | yériirà |
| 10 Default | zì | yízì | yìzô | zínò | zìryâ | zìríírà |
| 10 Emph. | | zéèzì | zéèzô | zéézìnô | zéézìryâ | zézìríírà |
| 11 Default | lù | yúlù | yùlwô | lúnò | lùlyâ | lùlíírà |
| 11 Emph. | | lwôlù | lwôlwô | lwólùnô | lwólùlyâ | lwólùlíírà |
| 12 Default | kà | yákà | yàkô | kánò | kàlyâ | kàlíírà |
| 12 Emph. | | káàkà | káàkô | káákànô | káákàlyâ | kákàlíírà |
| 13 Default | tù | yútù | yùtwô | túnò | tùlyâ | tùlíírà |
| 13 Emph. | | twôtù | twôtwô | twótùnô | twótùlyâ | twótùlíírà |
| 14 Normal | bù | yúbù | yùbwô | búnò | bùlyâ | bùlíírà |
| 14 Emph. | | bwôbù | bwôbwô | bwóbùnô | bwóbùlyâ | bwóbùlíírà |
| 15 Default | kù | yúkù | yùkwô | kúnò | kùlyâ | kùlíírà |
| 15 Emph. | | kwôkù | kwôkwô | kwókùnô | kwókùlyâ | kwókùlíírà |
| 16 Default | hà | yáhà | yàhô | hánò | hàlyâ | hàlíírà |
| 16 Emph. | | háàhà | háàhô | hááhànô | hááhàlyâ | háhàlíírà |

## 3.5 Demonstratives

| Noun Cl. | Dem. Affix | Proximal | Nearby | Proximal contrastive | Remote | Distal |
|---|---|---|---|---|---|---|
| 18 Default | kù | yúmù | yùmwô | múnò | mùlyâ | mùlíírà |
| 18 Emph. | mù | mwômù | mwômwô | mwómùnô | mwómùlyâ | mwómùlíírà |
| 19 Default | hì | yíhì | yìhyô | hínò | hìryâ | hìríírà |
| 19 Emph. |  | hyêhì | hyêhyô | hyéhìnô | hyéhìryâ | hyéhìríírà |
| 23 Default[b] | í | --- | ìyô | ínò | ìryâ | íríīrà |
| 23 Emph. |  | --- | yêyô | yênô | yêryâ | yéríīrà |

[a]This includes 1a forms.

[b]These cl. 23 forms are used only with -**mûndà** 'place'; see 3.5.4 for locative demonstratives with -**mûndà**.

### 3.5.1.4 Set demonstratives

The forms meaning 'same-set' and 'different-set' are classified as demonstratives, since they employ the demonstrative GNPs. The same-set demonstratives are formed according to the following formula. Examples are shown in (3.54).

[AUG [GNP [ A.M [**ba**] P.R]

The cl. 2 [**ba**] GNP in the formula can also be replaced by the 1PL -**tu** e.g. á=**bììtù** 'our fellow' or the 2PL -**nyu**, e.g. á=**bììnyù** 'your (PL) fellow'. When one of these two is used, the final previous reference marker -**o** is either underlyingly absent or absorbed by the back round vowel of the -**tu** or -**nyu**.

(3.54)    Cl. 1      Cl. 4      Cl. 7      Cl. 12
     UF   [u [u [a [ba] o]   i [i [a [ba] o]   [i [ki [a [ba] o]   [a [ka [a [ba] o]
     SF   ú=wàbò      í=yàbò      í=kyàbò      á=kààbò

The different-set demonstratives are formed according to the following formula:

[AUG [GNP [**ndi**]

Note that the augment can be attached to this demonstrative, to form, for example, the cl. 1 **úgûndì** 'other'.

(3.55)    Cl. 1      Cl. 4      Cl. 7      Cl. 12
     UF   [u [gu [ndi]   [i [gi [ndi]   [i [ki [ndi]   [a [ka [ndi
     SF   ú=gûndì      í=gîndì      í=kìndì      á=kàndì

(3.56) Same-set and different-set demonstrative forms

| GNP | Same-set | Different-set |
|---|---|---|
| 1 (of 1PL) | ú=wìtù | |
| 1 (of 2PL) | ú=wìnyù | |
| 1 | ú=wàbò | ú=gûndì |
| 2 (of 1PL) | á=bììtù | |
| 2 (of 2PL) | á=bììnyù | |
| 2 | á=bààbò | á=bàndì |
| 3 | ú=gwàbò | ú=gùndì |
| 4 | í=yàbò | í=gîndì |
| 5 | í=ryàbò | í=rìndì |
| 6 | á=gààbò | á=gàndì |
| 7 | í=kyàbò | í=kìndì |
| 8 | í=byàbò | í=bìndì |
| 9 | í=yàbò | ú=gîndì |
| 10 | í=zààbò | í=zìndì |
| 11 | ú=lwàbò | ú=lùndì |
| 12 | á=kààbò | á=kàndì |
| 13 | ú=twàbò | ú=tùndì |
| 14 | ú=bwàbò | ú=bùndì |
| 15 | ú=kwàbò | ú=kùndì |
| 16 | á=hààbò | á=hàndì |
| 19 | í=hyàbò | í=hìndì |

### 3.5.2 Function of demonstratives

The classic definition of demonstratives is that they "point" to the objects they refer to, pointing out objects that are near, far away, etc. This is one of their basic functions in Kifuliiru. In the process of pointing, the various factors that come into play are: orientation of speaker relative to hearer, discourse remoteness, and contrast with alternatives.

In addition, in narrative discourse contexts, some demonstratives function as thematic salience markers (TSM) (12.3.1). A summary of the various components of meaning for Kifuliiru demonstratives is presented in table 3.4.

## 3.5 Demonstratives

Table 3.4. Summary of demonstrative pronoun meaning components

|  | Demonstrative | Cl. 2 examples | Speaker/hearer orientation | Contrast | Theme marking (narrative) |
|---|---|---|---|---|---|
| a. | Proximal contrastive | bánò | at speaker location | contrast, alternative | |
| b. | Proximal | yábà | at speaker location | | |
| c. | Nearby | yàbô | at hearer location | | |
| c¹. | Nearby, TSM | yàbô | near in story | | default thematic salience |
| d. | Distal | bàlíírà | away from speaker and hearer | | |
| e. | Remote | bàlyâ | temporally remote | | |
| e¹. | Remote, TSM | bàlyâ | near in story | | major thematic salience |

Two of the demonstratives point to a referent at the same location as the speaker (table 3.4a, b). The distinction between these two is not a matter of degrees of distance from the speaker; the distance is exactly the same. Rather, the proximal demonstrative focuses attention on the referent as being 'here' where the speaker is. The proximal contrastive demonstrative, while also pointing to a referent which is at the location of the speaker, focuses on 'this particular referent, usually in contrast to possible alternatives'. That contrast can be quite marked at times, though in other cases it is subtle.

The nearby demonstrative refers to something at the location of the hearer (but not of the speaker).

The distal demonstrative (table 3.4d) refers to a referent that is positionally distant from both speaker and hearer. The remote demonstrative (table 3.4e) points to a referent which is temporally distant, i.e. prior to the present discourse, but which is shared in the common experience of both the speaker and hearer. It refers to "that thing that we both know about, and have already dealt with together".

Finally, both the nearby and remote demonstrative (table 3.4c¹, e¹) can also be thematic salience markers (TSM). The nearby demonstrative marks thematic salience in a default way, while the remote marks it in a major way (12.3.1).

### 3.5.2.1 Proximal demonstrative function

The proximal demonstrative focuses attention on the fact that the referent is in the same location as the speaker. This involves more than just identifying a participant as 'the one here'; it draws considerable attention to the fact, and is commonly used for rhetorical effect.

In (3.57) the king states that he will not demand a dowry for his daughter. He then uses the proximal demonstrative **úyù** 'this.P', making it clear that he's not just talking theoretically, but specifically of *this* daughter of his who is right there with him.

(3.57) **Mw-àmí**　　à-ná-dèt-à: ||　　«Ngíìsì　　ú-gá-yâng-à　　<u>ù-yú</u>
　　　　1-king　　　　1-SQ-say-Fa　　　each　　　S.R+1-F2-marry-Fa　this.P-1

　　　　**mú-lùzìnyérè** |　n-dá-gá-mú-hùùn-à　　í-bí-ndù.»
　　　　1-king's.daughter　1-NEG-F2-O1-request-Fa　AU=8-thing

'And the king said: || «Whoever will marry this princess | I won't ask him for things (bride price).»' (25 006)

In (3.58) the leopard and eagle want to help the lion eat the cow. Thus they come whispering to the lion: "Would you not eat this cow?" By using the proximal form **íyì** 'this.P' they are in effect saying "this one right under our noses".

(3.58) **Ìyó**　　　n-gwí |　　n-ó=　yò　　　nyûndà ||　bà-ná-hwéhwétéz-á |
　　　　that.N+9　9-leopard　CNJ=　that.N+9　eagle　　　2-SQ-whispered.to-Fa

　　　　**ìyó**　　　n-dàrè ||　bà-ná-gì-bwír-à: ||　«K-ó=　　tà-ngà-ly-à　|
　　　　that.N+9　9-lion　　　2-SQ-O9-tell-Fa　　　Q-2SG=　NEG-POT-eat-Fa

　　　　<u>ì-yí</u>　　　n-gáàvù?»
　　　　this.P-9　9-cow

'That leopard | and that eagle || whispered | to that lion || and they told it: || «Would you not eat | this cow?»' (11 021)

In (3.59) the king is again faced with potential suitors wanting to marry his beautiful daughter. This time he gives them a seemingly impossible task of trapping **ìyí mbúúsì** 'this.P wind' that felled **yìbí bígûndù** 'these.P banana trees'. By using the proximal demonstrative, the king makes the whole scene tangible and the challenge more actual.

## 3.5 Demonstratives

(3.59) **Mw-àmì** | **à-ná-shúbì**  **bà-bwír-à:** || «**Mù-Ø-tég-è**   **ì-yí**
1-king   1-SQ-AGAIN   O2-tell-Fa   2PL-SBV-trap-Fe   this.P-9

**m-búsi** | **í-y-á-n-gw-ìk-ìz-á**   |   **y-ì-bí**   **bí-gûndù**
9-wind   S.R-9-P1-O1.SG-fall-APL-CS-Fa   these.P.8   8-banana.tree

**by-à-nì.**»
8-A.M-1SG

'The king | told them again: || «Trap this wind | which has caused to fall (for me) | these banana trees of mine.»' (25 013)

In (3.60) the proximal demonstrative is used for rhetorical effect with the cl. 15 infinitive. The dog and the bull are living together in the same place, and dog starts barking. By the use of **yúkù** 'this' in the phrase **yùkú kúmóká kwàwè** 'this barking of yours', the bull draws attention to the dog's barking which is going on right there where they are, and thus bringing them in danger of an attack from the lion.

(3.60) **ìyó**   **shúúlí**   **y-àná-dèt-à:** || «**É=**   **mááshì**   **yâgà!** ||
that.N+9   bull   9-SQ-speak-Fa   O=   for.goodness.sake!   comrade

**Yù-kú**   **kú-mók-á**   **kw-à-wè** |   **kú-gáá-tùm-à**   **í=n-dàrè** |
this.P-15   15-bark-Fa   15-A.M-2SG   15-F2-cause-Fa   AU=9-lion

**ì-gá-yîjí**   **tù-téér-á**   **há-nò.**»
9-F2-COMING   O1.PL-attack-Fa   16-here.P.C

'That bull said: || «Oh for goodness sake my companion! || This barking of yours | will cause the lion | to come and attack us here.»' (45 006)

In (3.61) the leopard, which usually bullies the other animals, is now caught in a trap, thanks to the cleverness of the rat. The rat then says to the trapper: "Quick! Kill this leopard!" By using the proximal demonstrative **íyì** 'this', the rat is emphasizing that the leopard is right there where they are and within their power.

(3.61) **Í=m-bébá**   **y-àná-bwîr-à**   **ùyó**   **mú-tèzì:** ||   «**Ø-yàm-á**
AU=9-rat   9-SQ-tell-Fa   that.N+1   1-trapper   IMP.S-IMMED-Fa

**w-à-yìt-á** |   **ì-yí**   **n-gwî!**»
2SG-P1-kill-Fa   this.P-9   9-leopard

'The rat told that trapper: || «Quickly kill | this leopard!»' (35 031)

### 3.5.2.2 Proximal contrastive demonstrative function

The proximal contrastive demonstratives point to something "here", in usually *implicit* (i.e. not strong) contrast with possible alternatives.

In (3.62) the crocodile, after eating some fruit, takes the rest home to his children. When the children taste it, they exclaim: "O comrade! This food which you've brought us, this time it's really tasty!" The proximal contrastive demonstrative **bínò** 'this.P.C' refers to **byókúlyâ** 'food'. The emphasis is not so much on *this food right here*. Rather **bínò** 'this.P.C' focuses on this food in contrast to other food, as a way of exclaiming how tasty the food is. The contrast is further reinforced by the use of the adverb **lééèrò** 'this time (in contrast to other times)'.

(3.62) **Bà-ná-dèt-à:** ‖ «**É yâgà** ‖ **bì-nó by-ókúlyá** | **by-ó=**
2-SQ-speak-Fa   O  comrade  8-this.P.C  8-food   8-O.R=

**w-à-tù-lééét-ér-à** ‖ **lééèrò** | **by-à-mét-èèrèr-á bwènèènè!**»
1-P1-O1.PL-bring-APL-Fa   this.time   8-P1-be.tasty-INTS-Fa  very.much

'And they said: ‖ «O comrade ‖ this food | which you've brought us ‖ this time around | it's really tasty!»' (12 010)

In (3.63) the rat is shocked to see how skinny the frog has become. So he asks the frog: "O frog, what's *this*, which has caused you to get skinny like this?" The use of the proximal contrastive demonstrative **bínò** 'this.P.C' expresses disapproval, implying there are alternatives to what is found here.

(3.63) **Éé= kèrê** ‖ **bí-kí bì-nó** | **í-by-à-túm-à**
O=   frog    8-what  8-this.P.C   S.R-8-P1-cause-Fa

**w-à-jàmb-à kwókùnò?**
2SG-P1-get.skinny-Fa   like.this.P.C

'O frog ‖ what's this | which has caused you to get so skinny like this?' (20 006)

In (3.64) the frog answers: "This hunger is what has caused me to get skinny." The use of the proximal contrastive demonstrative **gúnò** 'this.P.C' following **mwénà** 'hunger' has the effect of saying 'hunger this (is)'. That is to say, it's not the alternative of sickness, or anything else, but it's *this* hunger here.

## 3.5 Demonstratives

(3.64)  **Kèré   à-ná-shùvy-à:** ‖ «**Mw-éná   gù-nô** ‖ **ú-gw-à-túm-á**
frog     1-SQ-answer-Fa         3-hunger   3-this.P.C   S.R-3-P.1-cause-Fa

**n-à-jàmb-à.**»
1SG-P1-get.skinny-Fa

'Frog answered: ‖ «It's this hunger ‖ which caused me to get skinny.»'
(20 007)

In (3.65) a dog has gone to live with a lion. But when the dog began to bark at night, the lion becomes afraid and tells the dog: "O comrade, you're really barking! The man will come and spear us here." In using the proximal contrastive demonstrative **hánò** 'here.P.C', the lion is saying that this is the particular place where the man will spear us, here (where we would be safe if you were quiet).

(3.65)  **É=   yâgà**  ‖ **ù-gwétí    ú-gáá-mók-à.** ‖ **Ú=mú-ndú** |
O=    comrade   2SG-PROG   2SG-INTL-bark-Fa    AU=1-person

**á-gá-yíjí      tù-tùmít-ír-á      há-nò.**
1-F2-COMING  1PL-spear-APL-Fa  16-here.P.C

'O comrade ‖ you are barking. ‖ A person | will come and spear us here!'
(45 016)

### 3.5.2.3 Nearby demonstrative function

One of the two functions[13] of the nearby demonstrative is to point to a referent which is perceived as being away from the speaker, and at the location of the hearer. Normally this involves a situation where the speaker and hearer are between approximately one and twenty meters apart from each other. A typical example, shown in (3.66), would be where a person is walking along the road and passes a village compound five to twenty meters away. As the speaker passes, he says **músìngó yàhô** 'greetings over there (where you are, but I'm not)'.

(3.66)  **Mú-sìngó   yà-hô!**
3-greeting   there.N-16

'Greeting (to) over there!'

In (3.67) a speaker, addressing a hearer across the room, says **Ùté mbèèrèzá yìkyó kítáábò** "First give me that.N book". The nearby demonstrative **yìkyô**

---

[13]The nearby demonstrative is also a thematic salience marker (TSM) in the discourse context.

'that.N (there where you are)' is employed, as the book is perceived as being away from the speaker, and at the location of the hearer.

(3.67) Ù-Ø-té       m-bèèrèz-á      yìkyó       kí-táábò.
      2SG-SBV-PRIOR  O1.SG-give-Fa   that.N+7    7-book

'(You) first give me that book.'

The greeting shown in (3.66) can also be used by a speaker on one mountain ridge who yells across to his friend on another mountain ridge one hundred meters away. What governs the use of this form is not the degree of physical distance between the speaker and the hearer, but rather whether the speaker is perceived as being in a different location from the hearer.

### 3.5.2.4 *Distal demonstrative function*

The distal demonstrative points to a referent that is perceived as being away from both speaker and hearer. The extent of distance does not matter; the referent may be a few meters from both, or far off in the distance.

In (3.68) a man is telling his wife to go to the foot of a mountain, in order to retrieve his stick of bamboo. As the mountain is far away from where both of them are located, the distal demonstrative is used to describe it.

(3.68) À-ná-híkìrì      bwír-á    nákìrìrí        w-à-gè: ‖ «Ù-Ø-génd-é
       1-SQ-ARRIVING    tell-Fa   favorite.wife   1-A.M-1    2SG-SBV-go-Fe

   mw-í=   dàkò    ly-á=    gù-lììrá    mú-gàzì ‖
   18-5=   under   5-A.M=   3-that.D    3-mountain

   ú-Ø-n-dèèt-èr-è              ú=mú-lóngé |      gw-ó=    n-à-sìg-à
   2SG-SBV-O1.SG-bring-APL-Fe   AU=3-bamboo       3-O.R=   1SG-P1-leave-Fa

   =hô.
   =16

'And arriving he told his favorite wife: ‖ «Go to the foot of that mountain ‖ bring me the bamboo | that I left there.»' (27 007)

In (3.69) a poor widow summons her son,[14] saying: "Go to that village of rich people and try to get some work, so we can buy some food." The use of the distal demonstrative **kàlíírà** 'that.D (there away from both of us)' signifies that neither of the ones involved in the conversation is at the place of the rich village.

---

[14] The mother addresses her son here as "father", as is common in the Kifuliiru culture.

## 3.5 Demonstratives

(3.69) **Lú-sìkù     lú-gùmà |   nyínà           |  à-ná-mú-bwîr-à: ||   «É=**
      11-day     11-one         1a+his.mother      1-SQ-O1-tell-Fa         O=

      **dáàtà          || ù-Ø-génd-é        mú=   kà-lììrá      kà-àyá |**
      1a+my.father       2SG-SBV-go-Fe    18=   12-that.D    12-village

      **k-à=         bá-gàlè || ù-Ø-húún-é               mw-ó=   mú-kòlwà.**
      12-A.M+AU=   2-rich.one  2SG-SBV-request-Fe   18-AU=  3-work

'One day | his mother | said to him: || «O my father || go into that village | of rich people || ask for work there.»' (07 007)

### 3.5.2.5 Remote demonstrative function

One of the two functions of the remote demonstrative is to refer to the common experience of both the speaker and hearer, at a time prior to the present discourse. It refers to "that referent which we have both dealt with together at another time, and which we still remember."

For example, if someone comes to your door and employs the remote demonstrative **bìryâ** 'those.R' referring to **bíndù** 'things' you had better do some fast thinking, because by use of the pronoun **bìryâ** he is signaling things which have previously been discussed between the two of you and (it can be assumed) which you both are still aware of, e.g. you may have promised him some money, or a favor!

Example (3.70) is taken from a story of two characters named Beard and Heart. One day Beard said: "Hey my friend, let's begin to farm and plant some maize." When Heart refused, saying that he didn't have the strength to dig up the soil, Beard went by himself, loosened up the soil and planted the maize.

In the next sentence, Beard tells Heart: "Go with me and help me pull the weeds out of *that* field of maize". In referring to the **ndálò** 'field', Beard uses the remote demonstrative **ìryâ** 'that.R'. What triggers the use of the remote demonstrative here is that a period of time has elapsed since they last had talked together about the field (as long as it takes for weeds to grow up). But they both still remember the maize field very well, as well as the experience they shared in regard to that field.

(3.70) Í=ky-ânyà   ky-ó=       kú-yúfír-à |  lw-ânwà   à-ná-bwîr-à
       AU=7-time    7-A.M+AU=   15-weed-Fa    12-beard  1-SQ-tell-Fa

      mú-tìmà: ||  «Ù-Ø-gêndì        n-dàbáál-ág-à |  ú=kú-yúfír-à |
      3-heart       2SG-SBV-GOING    O1-help-EMP-Fa   AU=15-weed-Fe

      ì-ryá       n-dáló    y-é=      bí-góòjè.»
      9-that.R    9-field   9-A.M+AU= 8-maize

'At the time of weeding | Beard told Heart : || «You go and help me | weed | that field of maize.»' (50 006)

Example (3.71) is taken from the story of "The Cow That Didn't Fear the Lion". The middle of the story finds the cow weak from hunger during a famine, and the lion's friends make the suggestion to the lion that it satisfy its gnawing hunger by eating the cow. But the lion refuses to do so, as it has already promised the cow that the two of them will live together as neighbors.

The leopard and eagle go home. In a few days they return. In this new discourse setting the leopard asks the lion: "Hey you, why didn't you do *that* which we told you?" In this sentence, the leopard uses the cl. 15 remote demonstrative **kùlyâ** 'that.R'. The demonstrative is pointing back to a referent that originally occurred totally outside the context of their present discourse, but which was in the shared experience of the speaker and hearer, and still remembered well by both.

(3.71) Í=n-gwí          y-àná-búùz-à   í=n-dàrè: || «Éwè |     kí-tùmà    kí-kí |
       AU=9-leopard     9-SQ-ask-Fa    AU=9-lion    hey.you    7-reason   7-what

       ù-tá-ká-gír-à |        kù-lyá       tú-ká-kú-bwír-à?»
       2SG-NEG-P2-do-Fa       15-that.R    1PL-P2-O2.SG-tell-Fa

'Leopard asked the lion: || «Hey you | for what reason | did you not do | that (which) we told you?»' (11 032)

### 3.5.2.6 *Emphatic demonstrative function*

Each of the five demonstrative pronoun forms can be used as the base for deriving an emphatic demonstrative pronoun. For example, **bánò** 'these.P.C (in contrast to others)' when emphasized becomes **báábànô** 'these very same (emphatic focus)', while **bàlíírà** 'those ones, away from speaker and hearer' becomes **bábàlíírà** 'those very same ones, away from speaker and hearer', etc. As can be seen, the meaning of every emphatic focal demonstrative is exactly the same as the meaning of the default form, with the additional

## 3.5 Demonstratives

component of meaning 'these/those very same ones, with implicit contrast to any other possibility'.

The sentence in (3.72) is taken from the story of the king's daughter who was being sought by many young men who wanted to marry her. After much arguing, the king finally said: "Whoever runs after her and catches her, *that is the one who will be her husband*." In using the cl. 1 **yôyô** 'that.N very same one', the king is emphasizing the fact that it's the young man who catches his daughter who will become her husband; no other alternative will be considered.

(3.72) **Ngíìsì** | **ú-gá-mú-tíbìt-à** =kwô || **à-ná-mú-gwàt-è** || **y-ôyó** |
each S.R-F2-O1-run-Fa =17 1-CON-O1-grab-Fe E-that.N+1

**y-é=** **gáà-b-à** **yîbà**.
1-FOC= F2-become-Fa her.husband

'Whoever | will run after her || and catch her || that very same one | is the one who will be her husband.' (06 013)

In (3.73) the wife of the crocodile got sick and went to a **múlágúzì** 'fortune-teller' for help. The **múlágúzì** told her to bring him the heart of a **híkólò** 'monkey', so her husband went and got a monkey, and brought it to him, still alive. The crocodile then tells the fortune-teller: "The things you sent me for, they are these very things I have brought". By using **byébìnò**, the cl. 8 emphatic version of the proximal contrastive demonstrative, the crocodile is saying 'these very same things'.

(3.73) **Ì=by-ó=** **w-á-n-dùm-à** || **by-é-bìnó**
AU=8-O.R= 2SG-P1-O1.SG-send-Fa E-8-these.P.C

**n-à-léét-ág-à**.
1SG-P1-bring-EMP-Fa

'Those (things) which you sent me for || they are these very same things I've brought.' (12 023)

Example (3.74) follows right on from the previous one. The monkey, realizing that they're about to cut his heart out, does some fast thinking and says to the crocodile: "You're acting just like a child. If you had told me right there at that very place, I would not have left it (my heart) at that tree. Let's go back there and bring it." By using **hááhàlyâ** 'right there at that very same place' (the cl. 16 emphatic version of the remote demonstrative) the monkey is in effect saying: "We were *right there* where my heart was. (So why didn't you ask me for it then and there, so we wouldn't have to go to all this trouble?)".

(3.74) **Ù-kí-m-bwìr-ìr-è**　　**háá-hà-lyá** ‖　**ngà**=
2SG-C.F-O1.SG-tell-APL-Fe　E-16-there.R　then=

**n-dà-gù-sìg-à** │ **kú**= **kì-ryá kí-tì.**
1SG-NEG-O3-leave-Fa　17=　7-that.R　7-tree

'If you had told me at that very same place ‖ I would not have left it (heart) │ at that tree.' (12 026)

### 3.5.2.7 Reduplicated emphatic demonstrative function

The emphatic demonstratives can in turn be reduplicated, so that **báábànò** becomes **báábànò-báábànò**, etc. The meaning of the emphatic demonstratives, when reduplicated, focuses even more heavily than the non-reduplicated emphatic on the notion of "sameness", stressing that the referent being discussed is the 'very, very' same one as was mentioned before.

In (3.75) a man is sitting at home when a messenger comes from the king, telling him to go to the king's compound early the next morning to do some work. Right then (at the very same time) another messenger comes from his in-laws, telling him to report for work at his father-in-law's early the next morning. This presents a real dilemma, as in Kifuliiru culture both the father-in-law and the king must be highly respected.

By employing **háàhò-háàhò** 'at that.N very same time', which is the reduplicated version of the emphatic nearby demonstrative **háàhò**, the speaker is placing special emphasis on the fact that the two messages came at the very same time (and are therefore in competition with each other). This is central to the theme of the story, which is: "Who is more important, the king or father-in-law?".

*3.5 Demonstratives*

(3.75) **Ìrí    á-ká-b-á         à-bwàt-íír-ì  há=  mw-à-gè ‖  í=n-dùmwá**
       when  1-P2-become-Fa  1-sit-RS-Fi   16=  place-A.M-1  AU=9-messenger

   **y-é=   bw-àmí |        y-àná-yîj-à |     kw-â=**
   9-A.M+23=  14-king's.place  9-SQ-come-Fa      CMP-1=

   **Ø-zíndúkírí           gêndì   kòl-á |      í=bw-āmì. ‖**
   SBV-EARLY.MORNING   GOING    work-Fa    23=14-king's.place

   <u>**Háà-hò-háàhò**</u> ‖   **í=gî-ndí       n-dùmwà      y-àná-lyôk-à**
   E-16.there.N-RDP     AU=9-other    9-messenger    9-SQ-come.from-Fa

   **í-mw-à-bò-vyàlà |     kw-â=    Ø-zíndúkírí           géndì**
   23-home-A.M-2-in.law   CMP-1=   SBV-EARLY.MORNING   GOING

   **kòl-ér-á |       shé-vyàlà.**
   work-APL-Fa    1a+father-in.law

'When he was sitting at home ‖ a messenger from the king | came | (saying) that he should go early the next morning and work for | the king. Right then and there ‖ another messenger came from the home of his in-laws | (saying) that he should go early the next morning and work for | his father-in-law.' (44 005-006)

### 3.5.3 Set demonstrative function

The "same-set" and "different-set" demonstratives are polar opposites: the same-set demonstratives refer to another member of the same set (not another). The different-set demonstratives refer to a member of another set (not this same one). Either of these may be used as a modifier, preceding a noun, and occur in the second position in the noun phrase, just after any demonstrative and before the noun. They can also be used substantively with no following noun, either with or without a preceding demonstrative.

#### 3.5.3.1 Same-set demonstrative function

Same-set demonstratives refer to member(s) of the same set. The nearest English equivalent might be 'fellow', where what is marked is a member of the same set or grouping. The term does not imply any close camaraderie or personal relationship, only membership in the same set of things.

In (3.76) there are two billy goats who have encountered each other on a felled tree which is used as a bridge to cross a river. These goats are not friends, but only belong to the same set, 'billy goat' (**kí-hèbè**). The fact that they are not friends is seen by the ensuing argument over who should back up so that the other can cross the bridge first.

(3.76) Í=ky-áàlí    fììs-ír-ì ‖    ky-àná-bwîr-à    í=ky-àbò |
     AU=7-P3    be.muscular-RS-Fi    7-SQ-tell-Fa    AU=7-SAME.SET

     ky-ó=    lú-jógótì ‖    kwó=    kí-Ø-kì-hìndù-s-é |
     7-A.M+AU=    11-thinness    CMP=    7-SBV-O7-turn.around-CS-Fe

     kì-téé    Ø-yì-lèng-ér-à.
     7-PRIOR    SBV-RFX-pass-APL-Fa

'The one which was muscular ‖ told his fellow (billy goat) | the thin one ‖ to turn itself around | so he (the muscular goat) could first just pass over.' (08 006)

Though the English term *fellow* implies humanness or at least animacy, this is not true of the same-set demonstratives in Kifuliiru. Inanimate referents of the same type are also referred to by these same-set demonstratives. Thus in (3.77) laws are said to have 'fellow laws', implying that there are others just like them.

(3.77) É=    Mw-ígìrìzà ‖    mú=    màajà    zó-óshì ‖    lú-hí    |
     O=    1-teacher    18=    10+laws    10-all    11-which

     ú-lù-kùl-íír-í    í=z-āābò?
     S.R-11-surpass-RS-Fi    AU=10-SAME.SET

'O teacher ‖ in all the laws ‖ which one | is the one that surpasses its fellows?' (Mat 22:36)

In (3.78) the frog gathers all his "fellows" of the set of frogs.

(3.78) Kèré    ná-yè ‖    à-ná-kùùmán-i-á    á=bà-ábò    bá-kèrè
     1a+frog    ADD.P-1    1-SQ-gather-CS-Fa    AU=2-SAME.SET    2-frog

     bó-óshì.
     2-all

'The frog ‖ and HE ALSO gathered all his fellow frogs.' (21 012)

In (3.79) the **káshiishi** 'pied wagtail bird' speaks to all of his 'fellow' birds.

## 3.5 Demonstratives

(3.79) **W-á-ká-shììshì**    ná-yè |    à-ná-yíìj-à ||    à-ná-bwíìr-à
1-A.M-12-pied.wagtail    ADD.P-1    1-SQ-come-Fa    1-SQ-tell-Fa

**ú=tw-àbò**    tú-nyúnì ||  kwó=  tù-Ø-lék-é    ná-yè |
AU=12-SAME.SET    12-birds    CMP=  12-SBV-allow-Fe    ADD.P-1

à-Ø-yímb-è.
1-SBV-sing-Fe

'The pied wagtail bird and HE ALSO | came || and he told his fellow birds || that they allow that he ALSO | sing.' (614 039)

Though the -**abo** portion of this form does not change to agree with a referent in any noun class, there are forms which are used for the personal classes (plural only).[15] As seen in (3.80), the same set demonstratives which agree with first-person plural and second-person plural are -**iitu** 'our fellow...' and -**iinyu** 'your (PL) fellow...'. These, like -**abo** 'their fellow', are formed using the associative marker, -**a**, but due to the rule of lexical level vowel coalescence, the associative -**a** assimilates completely to the following vowel in the suffix -**itu**, or -**inyu**, e.g. -**a-itu** > **iitu**. In (3.80) we see the example **ú=wìtù** 'our fellow'. The initial GNP in the term "fellow" agrees with cl. 1, i.e. the augment **u** and prefix **u** > **w** on **ú=w-ìtù** 'fellow'. It is by the ending, -**itu** that the fellow is marked as being 'one of our set'.

(3.80) **Ú=kú-yíjì**    hík-ír-à    há= kā-āyà ||  à-ná-búúz-àgy-é
AU=15-COMING    arrive-APL-Fa    16= 12-village    1-CON-ask-EMP-Fe

nyínà:     || «Hàyí  **ú=w-ì-tù**    à-lól-à?»
1a+his.mother  where  AU=1-SAME.SET-1PL  1+P1-head.to-Fa

'Upon coming to arrive at the village || he asked the mother emphatically: || «Where did our fellow go?»' (205 028)

### 3.5.3.2 Different-set demonstrative function

In a word, the different-set demonstratives mean 'other(s)'. It refers to another item of the same type as was just referred to, but which is distinct. In (3.81) we see the different-set demonstrative **bándì** 'others' used with a preceding demonstrative and a following noun. Here it refers to "other hunters".

---

[15] These forms which express mutual relationship have no singular possessive forms. There is no form in this set to express 'my fellow', but only 'our fellow, your (PL) fellow, their fellow'.

(3.81) **Ná=**   yàbó         **bá-ndí**      bá-hììvì ‖ mú-gùmà   á-àlí
       CNJ=     those.N+2    2-other         2-hunters   1-one    1-P3

   yì-yík-ììr-í                    |   ú=mù-mbátì.
   RFX-have.travel.food-APL+RS-Fi      AU=3-cassava

'And those other hunters ‖ one (of them) carried for himself | cassava.' (03 004)

In (3.82) **ú=gûndì** 'another' is the first element in its noun phrase, and thus bears the augment.

(3.82) **Ú=gû-ndì**   mú-tàbánà |  à-ná-yì-làsh-à    |  mú=   kí-shùkà.
       AU=1-other    1-boy       1-SQ-RFX-throw-Fa     18=   7-bush

'Another young man | threw himself | into the bush.' (01 028)

The different set demonstratives can also be used without a following noun, when the referent is clear, as in (3.83).

(3.83) **Ù-lyá**    mú-tàbánà ‖ à-ná-yábììr-é    **í=hí-nyúní** | à-ná-hèèrèz-é
       1-that.R    1-boy       1-CON-take-Fe    AU=19-bird     1-CON-give-Fe

   mú-gùmà ‖ à-ná-yábììr-é    **í=hì-ndì**   ‖ à-ná-hèèrèz-é | ú=gû-ndì
   1-one      1-CON-take-Fe   AU=19-other      1-CON-give-Fe   AU=1-other

'And that boy ‖ took a little bird | and gave it to one (person) ‖ *and* he took another (bird) ‖ and gave it to | another (person).' (210 062)

### 3.5.4 Locative demonstrative pronouns formed with *-mûndà*

#### 3.5.4.1 *Structure of locative demonstrative pronouns*

The locative phrase head **í=mûndà** (23=place), when preceded by a cl. 23 demonstrative pronoun, serves as a locative demonstrative pronoun. The cl. 23 forms are **iyí mûndà** 'this.proximal place (P)', **inó mûndà** 'this.proximal.contrastive place (P.C)', **iyó mûndà** 'that.nearby place (N)', **iryá mûndà** 'that.remote place (R)', and **iriirá mûndà** 'that.distal place (D)'.

The resulting emphatic forms are: **yêyì mûndà** 'this.EMPHATIC.PROXIMAL place', **yênò mûndà** 'this.EMPHATIC PROXIMAL.CONTRASTIVE place', **yêyò mûndà** 'that.EMPHATIC.NEARBY place', **yêryà mûndà** 'that.EMPHATIC.REMOTE place', **yérììrá mûndà** 'that.EMPHATIC.DISTAL place'. The proximal contrastive form **ínò**, e.g. **yîjá ínò** 'come over here' (phonetically [**yîjéènò**]), and the emphatic nearby form **yêyò** (see (3.88)) have been observed without the accompanying **mûndà**, but the other forms of the cl. 23 demonstrative are always found with the following **mûndà**. Unlike other emphatic demonstratives, the emphatic locative demonstratives formed with **mûndà** cannot be reduplicated.

### 3.5.4.2 Function of locative demonstrative pronouns

In (3.84) **ìnó mûndà** 'this contrastive place' functions as a locative demonstrative pronoun. The man asked what caused them to arrive at *this place*.

(3.84) **Mú-ndú  mú-gùmà  tî=     ‖ «Bí-kí    í-by-à-mù-hí-s-á**
       1-person  1-one    ‹quote›   8-what   S.R-8-P1-O2.PL-arrive-CS-Fa

   **ì-nó         mûndà?»**
   23-this.P.C   place

'One person said: ‖ «What has caused you (PL) to arrive here?»' (103 040)

In (3.85) the emphatic form of the proximal contrastive is used when the speaker says 'Let's remain at this very place'.

(3.85) **Tù-Ø-yì-bèèr-èr-è              y-ê-nò         mûndà ‖  tù-Ø-kízí**
       1PL-SBV-RFX-remain-APL-Fe      E-23-this.P.C  place     1PL-SBV-REP

   **yì-sháát-ír-à        mú=   lù-nò         lw-íjì.**
   RFX-play-APL-Fa      18=   11-this.P.C   11-river

'Let's just remain right here ‖ continuously just playing in this river.' (16 015)

In (3.86) the locative demonstrative pronoun **ìyó mûndà** 'that.N place' functions as the relativizer for the phrase **ìyó mûndà yìbyó byūlà byàláshwà**, 'where the peelings were thrown'.

(3.86) **Yàkó       ká-bwà ‖  kà-ná-tíbìt-ìr-à |    ìyó        mûndà |  yìbyó**
       that.N+12  12-dog    12-SQ-ran-APL-Fa     that.N+23  place     that.N+8

   **by-ùlá       by-à-lásh-w-à.**
   8-peelings   8-P1-throw-PS-Fa

'That dog ‖ ran over there | to the place where | those peelings were thrown.' (03 014)

In (3.87) the man made stiff porridge right there (in the cave.)

(3.87) À-ná-kìzí dùg-ír-à | y-êyò mûndà.
 1-SQ-REP make.porridge-APL-Fa E-that.N+23 place

'And he repeatedly made stiff porridge | right there.' (111 014)

In (3.88), which describes the same situation as the preceding example, we see the cl. 23 emphatic demonstrative **yêyò** 'right there' used without the following **mûndà**.

(3.88) À-ná-kìzí déék-ér-à y-êyò || nó=
 1-SQ-REP cook-APL-Fa E-that.N+23 CNJ+AU

 kú-dùg-ìr-à y-êyò.
 15-make.porridge-APL-Fa E-that.N+23

'And he kept cooking right there || and making stiff porridge right there.' (611 016)

In (3.89) we see a use of the distal form of the cl. 23 locative, as the people are told to go 'over there' in the Negev.

(3.89) Mù-Ø-génd-é | í-rì-ìrá mûndà | í= Négèbù.
 2PL-SBV-go-Fe 23-E-that.D place 23= Negev

'Go | over to there | to the Negev.' (Jhn 3:26)

# 4
# Adjectives, Numbers, and Quantifiers

There is a closed set of approximately thirty-nine lexical adjectives in Kifuliiru, all of which communicate general concepts such as -**îjâ** 'good', -**bì** 'bad', etc.

There are also stative verbal adjectives, which are productive, but rarely employed. Examples include cl. 9 **njwèkê** 'tied up' from **kúshwékà** 'to tie', and cl. 8 **bíyándìkê** 'written things' from **kúyándíkà** 'to write', etc.

The numbers are structurally a diverse group, taken from various grammatical categories. However, all the numbers, whether structurally nouns (like **múnààná** 'eight' and **ígáná** 'hundred' ) adjectives (like -**gùmà** 'one') or numerals (like -**bìrì** 'two') as well as the structurally pronominal quantifiers (-**óshì** 'all' and -**ómbì** 'both') have a common syntactic bond with adjectives: they can all modify nouns, and they occur immediately following the noun in the noun phrase (7.1.1).

## 4.1 Adjectives

### 4.1.1 Lexical adjectives

In typical Bantu fashion, there is a closed set of adjective stems found in the lexicon. So far only thirty-nine have been encountered in the data, all of which are listed in table 4.1. Most of these forms are related to a verb, but subsequently lexicalized. In some cases the adjective is the source from which the verb is derived (cf. column 3). Such derivation from adjectives to verbs is done via the inchoative -**h** extension (corresponding to the Proto-Bantu *-**p**-) which is added to the adjectival stems to derive verbs denoting the process of assuming some quality (Schadeberg 2003:84). Conversely, other adjectives are derived from verbs (cf. column 4). In the case of **nóvù** 'soft', *both* a derived verb and an apparent source verb exist.

Adjectives are of the structure: [Adjective GNP[1] [stem]. The class prefix of the adjective is identical to the nominal prefix[2], and agrees with the class of the noun which the adjective qualifies. For example, with a cl. 1 noun, such as **múndù** 'person', the adjective -**bí** 'bad' has a cl. 1 prefix: **múndú múbì** 'a bad person', while with the cl. 2 noun, **bándù** 'people', the adjective prefix has cl. 2 agreement: **bándú bábì** 'bad people'. The adjectives in table 4.1 express many *general* (not specific) adjectival qualities, e.g. light and heavy, good and bad, tall and short, etc.

Table 4.1. Lexical adjectives

|  | Adjective stem | Gloss | Verbs derived from adjectives | Verbs from which adjectives derived | Gloss |
|---|---|---|---|---|---|
|  | 1 | 2 | 3 | 4 | 5 |
| a. | -ángù | 'light' | -yánguh- |  | 'become light' |
| b. | -zítò | 'heavy' | -zídoh- |  | 'become heavy' |
| c. | -bì | 'bad' | -biih- |  | 'become bad' |
| d. | -îja | 'good' |  |  |  |
| e. | -òfì | 'short' | -yòfih- |  | 'become short' |
| f. | -là | 'long, tall' | -laah- |  | 'get long' |
| g. | -nììnî | 'small' | -niih- |  | 'be scarce' |
| h. | -kùlù | 'great' |  | -kùl- | 'grow big' |
| i. | -hámù | 'large' |  | -hám- | 'get big' |
| j. | -èrù | 'white, pure' |  | -yèr- | 'get white, pure' |
| k. | -ìrù | 'black' |  | -yìr- | 'get dark' |
| l. | -dúkùlà | 'red' |  | -dúkul- | 'be red' |
| m. | -gùmà | 'one, some' |  |  |  |
| n. | -lébè | 'a certain' |  |  |  |
| o. | -gérwà | 'a few' |  | -gér- | 'measure' |

---

[1] It should be noted that while a noun of cl. 1a has no segmental noun prefix, an adjective agreeing with a cl. 1a noun does have a segmental prefix, **mú**-, which is identical to that for agreement with nouns belonging to cl. 1.

[2] This true for all classes except cl. 1a.

## 4.1 Adjectives

|   | Adjective stem | Gloss | Verbs derived from adjectives | Verbs from which adjectives derived | Gloss |
|---|---|---|---|---|---|
|   | 1 | 2 | 3 | 4 | 5 |
| p. | -ìngì | 'many' | | | |
| q. | -hyàhyâ | 'new' | | -hy- | 'get ripe' |
| r. | -shààjà | 'old' | | -shaaj- | 'get old' |
| s. | -tíbíìrâ | 'dull' | | -tíb- | 'be lacking' |
| t. | -ùgì | 'sharp' | -yùgih- | | 'become sharp' |
| u. | -lúlù | 'bitter' | | -lúl- | 'be bitter' |
| v. | -núnù | 'sweet' | | -nún- | 'be sweet' |
| w. | -làngì | 'fierce' | | -làngam- | 'be fierce' |
| x. | -káyù | 'fierce' | | -káy- | 'be angry' |
| y. | -nóvù | 'soft' | -nóvúh- | -nóg- | 'become soft' |
| z. | -lêmbù | 'soft,' | | -lémb- | 'make limp' |
| aa. | -gùmààna̋ | 'alive, well' | | | |
| bb. | -lwāzì | 'sick' | | -lwal- | |
| cc. | -bìshì | 'unripe, wet' | | | |
| dd. | -ùmù | 'dry' | | -yùm- | 'dry out' |
| ee. | -gágù | 'spoiled' | | -gág- | 'spoil (food)' |
| ff. | -jààvù | 'not tasty' | -jààvuh- | | 'lack flavor' |
| gg. | -māātà | 'empty' | | -maat- | 'eat relish only' |
| hh. | -lyâlyà | 'deceptive' | | -lyalyani- | 'deceive' |
| ii. | -lèmà | 'crippled' | -lèmah- | | 'be crippled' |
| jj. | -òbà | 'fearful' | -yòboh- | | 'be afraid' |
| kk. | -òlò | 'lazy' | -yòloh- | | 'be lazy' |
| ll. | -sírè | 'possessed' | -síreh- | | 'be possessed' |
| mm. | -èngè | 'clever' | -yèngeh- | | 'be clever' |

A representative sample of the adjective prefixes, before both consonant and vowel adjective stems, is provided in (4.1).

(4.1) Adjective concord samples

| Cl. | -bì 'bad' | -káyù 'fierce' | -îjá 'good' | -òfi [3] 'short' |
|---|---|---|---|---|
| 1 | múbì | múkáyù | mwîjâ | mwófi |
| 2 | bábì | bákáyù | bíìjâ | bóófi |
| 3 | múbì | múkáyù | mwîjâ | mwófi |
| 4 | míbì | míkáyù | míìjâ | myófi |
| 5 | líbì | líkáyù | líìjâ | lyófi |
| 6 | mábì | mákáyù | míìjâ | móófi |
| 7 | kíbì | kíkáyù | kíìjâ | kyófi |
| 8 | bíbì | bíkáyù | bíìjâ | byófi |
| 9 | nyíbì | ngáyù | nyîjâ | nyófi |
| 10 | nyíbì | ngáyù | nyîjâ | nyófi |
| 11 | lúbì | lúkáyù | lwîjâ | lwófi |
| 12 | kábì | kákáyù | kíìjâ | kóófi |
| 13 | túbì | túkáyù | twîjâ | twófi |
| 14 | búbì | búkáyù | bwîjâ | bwófi |
| 15 | kúbì | kúkáyù | kwîjâ | kwófi |
| 16 | hábì | hákáyù | híìjâ | hóófi |
| 19 | híbì | híkáyù | híìjâ | hyófi |

The adjective follows the noun which it qualifies. In (4.2) the adjective **líbì** 'bad' follows the noun **ííhánò** 'advice'. For more information about the relative order of adjectives and other qualificatives, see (7.1.1).

(4.2) **Í-í-hánó**   **lí-bí** |   lì-kìzí   yìt-íís-áni-â.
AU=5-advice   5-bad   5-REP   kill-CS-RCP-Fa

'Bad advice | habitually causes (people) to kill each other.' (31 022)

In (4.3) the adjective **míkáyù** 'fierce' functions by itself as the entire NP, being the complement of the verb **yànáàlí rīīrì** 'and they were'. Its cl. 4 GNP agrees with its antecedent in the previous clause, **í=mívùnò** 'game strategy'.

---

[3] The tone markings in this column reflect the isolation form of the adjective. In context, these forms all have LL tone, e.g. **mwòfi**, etc., and the preceding noun will exhibit the left-shifted H tone of the adjective prefix, e.g. **úmúkàzì** 'woman' versus **úmúkàzí mwòfi** 'short woman'.

(4.3) Mú=kúbá á-àlí hì-ìt-í í=**mí**-vùnó **mì**-ngì ‖ **y**-àn-áàlí
because 1-P3 has-RS-Fi AU=4-game.strategy 4-many 4-ADD.V-P3

rì-ìr-í **mí**-káyù.
be-RS-Fi 4-fierce

'Because he had many game strategies ‖ and they were fierce.' (30 007)

Simple adjectives are sometimes found in reduplicated form. Some examples found in our texts are: **bòòló-bōōlò** 'weak, weak', **màkáyù-màkàyû** 'difficult, difficult', **mànúnù-mànùnú** 'sweet, sweet', **mbámù-mbàmú** 'large, large', **míkùlù-kúlù** 'great, great', **nyírà-nyìrá** 'long, long', etc.

**4.1.2 Stative verbal adjectives**

Besides the lexical adjectives listed above, there is also a set of derived stative verbal adjectives. These are formed in much the same way as a lexical adjective: The adjective prefix is followed by the verb base (radical plus extensions), with a high toned final suffix -**e** (8.1.2). The first syllable of the radical bears the lexical tone of the verb (if there is one) while any further non-final syllables have L tone. The structure is summarized by the formula:

[Adj. GNP [verb base] -**e**].

Though these forms retain a limited number of verbal characteristics,[4] the use of the adjective prefix rather than a verbal subject prefix shows that they are being treated as adjectives and not primarily as verbs.[5] For example, in cl. 10 we find the N- prefix (**m**- before following **b**), just like in nouns and adjectives, on the stative verbal adjective **m**-bàmìk-è (9-closed-e) 'closed in' í=**ny**-ííví z-áàlì **m**-bàmìk-è (AU=10-doors 10-P3 10-closed-e) 'the doors were closed'.

The stative verbal adjective can theoretically be derived from almost any verb, and thus would seemingly have the potential to be very common. In actual fact, however, it is fairly infrequently used, found only a dozen or so times in fifty-six folk tales. In over six hundred pages of Biblical text there are probably less than twenty different forms. The following are some of the stative verbal adjectives found in our data.

---

[4]They include any extensions found in the verb stem, and exhibit a verbal-type tone pattern, which includes the underlying tone of the verb radical, followed by a L tone which spreads rightward, and a H-tone suffix.

[5]For example, in a verb, the cl. 10 subject prefix would be **zi**- as in í=**ny**-ííví **zi**-ká-hàmík-w-â 'the doors (10) were closed (passive)'.

(4.4) Stative verbal adjectives examples

| Cl. | Verbal adjective | Gloss | Source verb | Gloss |
|---|---|---|---|---|
| 1 | ú=mú-shwèk-ê | AU=1-captive-e | kú-shwék-à | 15-tie-Fa |
| 2 | á=bá-làalìk-ê | AU=2-invitees-e | kú-láálík-à | 15-invite-Fa |
| 4 | mí-lámbìk-ê | 4-laid.down-e | kú-lámbík-à | 15-lay.down-Fa |
| 5 | lí-fùùnìk-ê | 5-covered-e | kú-fúúník-à | 15-cover-Fa |
| 6 | má-bààj-ê | 6-carved-e | kú-bāāj-à | 15-carve.wood-Fa |
| 6 | má-shùk-ê | 6-cleaned-e | kú-shùk-à | 15-clean-Fa |
| 6 | má-tèrèk-ê | 6-set.aside-e | kú-tèrék-à | 15-set.aside-Fa |
| 6 | má-yándìk-ê | 6-written.matters-e | kú-yándík-à | 15-write-Fa |
| 8 | bí-rûng-ê | 8-seasoned-e | kú-lúng-à | 15- season-Fa |
| 9 | m-bàngìk-ê | 9/10-firmly.placed-e | kú-bàngík-à | 15-place.firmly-Fa |
| 9 | m-bàmìk-ê | 9/10-closed-e | kú-hàmík-à | 15-close.tightly-Fa |
| 9 | n-jwèk-èr-ê | 9/10-tied.up.at-e | kú-shwék-ér-à | 15-tie.up-APL-Fa |
| 9 | n-zìngùùl-ê | 9/10-unwrapped-e | kú-zìng-úúl-à | 15-unwrap-RV-Fa |

In (4.5) the form **njwèkèrê** 'tied' is composed of the cl. 10 adjective prefix **n-**, the verb root **-shwek-**, the applicative extension **-er**, and the final **-é**. In (4.5) the stative verbal adjective **njwèkèrê** 'tied' is used as a substantive, serving as the complement of the copula **zìshùbà** 'they were'.

(4.5) Mù-tà-shóbòl-à     ú=kú-vùn-á     yì-zí     n-góní |
2PL-NEG+P1-be.able-Fa   AU=15-break-Fa   these.P-10   10-stick

í=ky-ànyà zì-shùbá     n-jwèk-èr-è     kúgùmà.
AU=7-time 10-PREV     10-tie-APL-e     together

'You were not able to break these sticks | when they were tied together.'
(02 018)

That these are not just random lexicalized forms, nor lexical nouns, is shown by the fact that the same verbal adjective stem can be used with different class agreements, e.g. cl. 6 **máyándìkê** or cl. 8 **bíyándikê** 'written', cl. 6 **mábààjê** or cl. 18 **múbààjê** 'carved', cl. 9 **mbàngìkê** or cl. 18 **múbàngìkê** 'firmly placed', cl. 4 **mílámbìkê** or cl. 7 **kílámbìkê** 'laid down', cl. 6 **mátèrèkê** or cl. 10 **ndèrèkê** 'set aside, stored', cl. 11 **lúhàmìkê** or cl. 10 **mbàmìkê** 'locked', depending on the noun or phrase that it modifies.

## 4.1 Adjectives

The following pair of examples illustrates two forms of the adjective derived from the verb -**hàmik**- 'lock'. In (4.6) the adjective takes the cl. 11 form **lúhàmìkê**, since it agrees with the cl. 11 **lwívì** 'door'.

(4.6) Írí        bá-ká-hík-á       há=mw-á=        Mú-gàngà ‖ bà-húmààn-á |
      when     2-P2-arrive-Fa   16-place-A.M=   1-doctor        2+P1-meet-Fa

    ú=lw-íví |     lù-lì    lú-hàmìk-ê.
    AU=11-door    11-is     11-locked-e

'When they arrived at doctor's place ‖ they found | the door | (it is) locked.' (103 087)

In (4.7) the cl. 10 form **mbàmìkê** is found, modifying the plural cl. 10 **í=nyíívì** 'doors'.

(4.7) Írí         bá-ká-hík-à ‖    bà-gwán-án-á |       í=ny-ííví         zé=
      when      2-P2-arrive-Fa    2+P1-meet-RCP-Fa    AU=11-door       10-A.M

    bí-síìkà ‖        zì-rí    m-bàmìk-ê.
    8-inner.room    10-is    10-locked-e

'When they arrived ‖ they found | the doors of the inner rooms ‖ (they are) locked.' (Jdg 3:24)

In (4.8) the verbal adjective describes a locative phrase and takes the cl. 18 locative agreement (**mu**-): **Mwí=yò ndálò mwâlì múbààjé í=shíndá mbyàhyâ** 'and in that.N garden there was *carved out* a new tomb'.

(4.8) **Mw-í**=      yò    n-dálò |    **mw**-áàlì    **mú-bààj-é**    í=shíndá    m-byàhyâ.
      18-there.N    9     9-field    18-P3           18-carve-e       AU=9+grave  9-new

'In that garden | there was carved out a new tomb.' (Jhn 19:41)

The stative verbal adjectives may also be used following a noun. In (4.9) the cl. 5 **lífùùnìkê** 'covered' is the final element in the phrase beginning with the cl. 5 **íréngò** 'bottle'.

(4.9) À-ná-lyôs-á        í-gérá       lyá=    kà-shàtù ‖   ly-àná-léèt-á
      1-SQ-go.out+CS-Fa  5-fish.hook  5-A.M=  12-three     5-SQ-bring-Fa

   í-réngó lí-ìjá    bwènèèné | ly-èrú   ly-ó=     lú-bùlà |
   5-bottle 5-good   very.much  5-white  5-A.M+AU= 11-pearl

   <u>lí-fùùnìk-é</u>   bwîjâ.
   5-covered-e    well

'And he took out the third fish hook ‖ and it brought a very nice bottle |
pearl white | well capped.' (56 008)

As is true of any adjectives, stative verbal adjectives can also be used substantively, filling nominal positions in the syntax. In (4.10) the cl. 2 **á=bálààlìkê** 'the invited ones' (derived from the toneless verb **kúláálíkà** 'to invite') is employed as the object of a verb.

(4.10) Ká=  w-àngà-shál-ìs-â         <u>á=bá-lààlìk-é</u> ‖   kú=   ky-ânyà
       Q=   2SG-POT-be.hungry-CS-Fa  AU=2-invited.ones-e  17=   7-time

   bà-kìrì  kúgùmá | ná=   nàhánó  w-ó=       bú-hyà?
   2-PERS   together  CNJ=  lord    1-A.M+AU=  14-wedding

'Would you make the invited ones fast ‖ at the time they are still together with | the lord of the wedding?' (Luk 5:34)

### 4.1.3 Special adjective –*zíra* 'without'

The root -**zírà** 'without' functions as an adjective, taking the obligatory adjective/nominal GNP which agrees with the noun being modified. However, -**zírà** is different from other adjectives in that it takes an obligatory NP complement.[6] This can be seen in (4.11) where the cl. 5 noun **îtwê** 'head' is modified by **lízírá kímbìrí-mbìrì** 'without a body'.

(4.11) À-ná-húmààn-àn-à |   í-ì-twé |   <u>lí-zírá</u> |  kí-mbìrí-mbìrì.
       1-SQ-encounter-RCP-Fa  AU=5-head  5-without    7-body-RDP

'And he encountered | a head | without | a body.' (503 010)

As is true of any adjective, -**zíra** may be used substantively, functioning, with its complement, as the nominal element of a noun phrase. In (4.12) -**zíra** takes the cl. 8 prefix **bi-** and bears the augment, to become **í=bízírà**. Its complement here is **kámárò** 'value'. The meaning is '(things) without value'.

---

[6] Its ability to take a complement is partly due to its derivation from a verbal construction using the verb -**zír-** 'refuse something (as taboo)'. It is related to the cl. 3 noun **múzírò** 'taboo'.

## 4.1 Adjectives

(4.12)  **Ìrí**  **w-àngà-b-à**          **ù-lóz-ììz-í**        **ú=kú-lóng-á**     **í=kí-ndú**
      if   2SG-CND-become-Fa     2SG-want-RS-Fi        AU=15-get-Fa         AU=7-thing

      **í-kì-rì**   **nà=**   **ká-márò |**   **ù-tá-Ø-téb-èèrèz-ìbw-é |**       **n-é=**
      S.R-7-is     CNJ=      12-value         2-NEG-SBV-trick-INTS-PS-Fe         CNJ-AU=

      **bí-zírá**   **ká-márò.**
      7-without    12-value

'If you would want to get a thing which has value | don't be deceived | by what is without value.' (06 027)

There is also a non-agreeing form of this word which is used as the head of an adverbial construction. With this non-agreeing adverbial form, the complement may be a simple NP, but it more often takes the form of a reduced clause of which the subject is an infinitive. In (4.13) the form **búzírà** 'without' is followed by the verb phrase **kúlàsá ú=túbwâ** 'causing the dogs to make noise'.

(4.13)  **Lyêryó |**   **bà-ná-gênd-à**   **bw-îjà-bwîjâ ||**   **bú-zírá**
      right.then    2-SQ-go-Fa         14-good-RDP           14-without

      **kú-làs-á |**           **ú=tú-bwâ.**
      15-to.make.noise+CS-Fa   AU=13-dogs

'Right then | they went slowly slowly || without causing to make noise | the dogs.' (206 096)

### 4.1.4 Comparison strategies

Here we present two ways to compare[7] one item with another.

  a) The locative head **ku** 'in connection' can be used to introduce a standard of comparison. In (4.14) it is stated that **shè=vyàlà** 'father-in-law' is the one who is greater than the king. The focus copula **ye** 'he's the one' works together with the cl. 17 **kú** 'in connection' in the phrase **yé=múkùlù kú=mwàmì** 'he's the one who is great relative to the king (i.e. he's greater than the king)'.

---

[7] The addition of a following adverb such as **bwénèènè** 'very much' or **hínììnî** 'a little' can also be used to qualify the degree of quality, e.g. **bínúnú bwénèènè** 'very sweet (lit., sweet very much)' but not generally to compare one item or group with another.

(4.14) **Shè-vyàlà**　　　w-ó=　　　**mú-ndù** ‖ y-é=　　**mú-kùlù**　kú=
　　　 1a+father-in.law　1-A.M+AU=　1-person　1-FOC=　1-great　　17=

**mw-àmì**.
1-king

'A person's father-in-law ‖ he's the one who's greater than the king.'
(44 012)

In (4.15) it is stated that the **ú=mwìgéndérézì** 'the patient one' is the one who is big relative to the fighter.

(4.15) **Ú=mw-ìgéndérézì** ‖　y-é=　　**mú-kùlù**　**kú=**　　**n-dwánì**.
　　　 AU=1-patient.one　　1-FOC=　1-great　17=　　9-fighter

'The patient one ‖ is the one who's greater than (great relative to) the fighter.' (Pro 16:32)

b) Another common way to express comparison is by means of the verb **-hím-** 'to surpass'. In (4.16) the leopard is said to have **mísî** 'strength' **ú=kúhímà ìyó shúúlì** 'surpassing that.N bull'.

(4.16) **Í=kí=shókómà** ‖　ky-ó=　　kì-rì　　né=　　　mí-sí ‖
　　　 AU=7-leopard　　7-FOC=　7-have　CNJ+AU　4-strength

**ú=kú-hím-à**　　　ìyó　　　shúúlì.
AU=15-surpass-Fa　that.N+9　9+bull

'The leopard ‖ is the one which has strength ‖ more than that bull.'
(45 007)

The verb **-hím-** 'surpass' is often expressed in the resultative (RS) form. Example (4.17) uses the RS of **-hím-** to express the superlative, **ìhímìrí í=zìndì zóóshì** 'surpassing all others'.

(4.17) **Ì-yí**　　yó=　　　ny-ámá |　ny-íìjá |　**ì-hím-ìr-í**　　|　í=zìndì
　　　 9-this.P　9-FOC=　9-meat　　9-good　　9-surpass-RS-Fi　AU=10-other

zó-óshì ‖　ì-ná-lí　　|　yô=　　m-bí |　kú-zì-hím-á　　　|　zó-óshì.
10-all　　9-ADD.V-is　9-FOC=　9-bad　15-O10-surpass-Fa　10-all

'This is the meat | good | surpassing all others ‖ and it is | bad | surpassing | all others.' (24 022)

## 4.2 Quantifiers

The quantifiers form a closed class of two different forms, both of which occur in the final position 6 of the noun phrase (7.1.1).[8] The quantifiers are given here in the cl. 2 form: **bóóshì** 'all' and **bómbì** 'both'. These forms take the demonstrative prefix.

The formula for -**shi** 'all' and -**mbi** 'both' is the demonstrative prefix, followed by the previous reference morpheme, and then the root, as follows:

[Demonstrative GNP [P.R[9] [Root]

(4.18)
| Cl. | 'all' | 'both' |
|---|---|---|
| 1PL | twéshì | twémbì |
| 2PL | mwéshì | mwémbì |
| 1 | yéshì | |
| 2 | bóóshì | bómbì |
| 3 | gwóshì | |
| 4 | yóshì | yómbì |
| 5 | lyóshì | |
| 6 | góóshì | gómbì |
| 7 | kyóshì | |
| 8 | byóshì | byómbì |
| 9 | yóshì | |
| 10 | zóóshì | zómbì |
| 11 | lwóshì[10] | |
| 12 | kóóshì | |
| 13 | twóshì | twómbì |
| 14 | bwóshì | |
| 15 | kwóshì | |
| 16 | hóóshì | hómbì |
| 19 | hyóshì | |

---

[8]These are a type of pronominal form (shown by the use of the pronominal prefixes (e.g. **y-(e)**- for cl. 1, rather than **mu**-, and by the presence of the **-e/-o** of reference). They can either modify a noun, e.g. **íbíndú byóshì** 'all things', or be used substantively as a pronoun, e.g. **bóóshì bàgéndà** 'all of them went'.

[9]The previous reference morpheme consists of **e** in 1PL, 2PL, and 1 (third-person singular), and **o** everywhere else. Interestingly, this same dichotomy in form is found in Basaá (A43) (Hyman 2003d:269).

[10]The cl. 11 form, **lwóshì** can be used to modify a cl. 11 noun, or can be used as an adverb, following a verb, and meaning 'completely'.

## 4.2.1 Quantifier -óshì 'all'

The quantifier **-óshì/-éshì** 'all' can be used with either singular or plural class agreement. When used with singular classes it is often best translated 'whole', while with plural classes, it is best expressed as 'all'. In either case the basic meaning is 'all', denoting total inclusion of the item or set of items referred to. In (4.19) the quantifier **bóóshì** 'all' modifies **yàbó báhyàkàzì** 'those.N new brides'.

(4.19) Yàbó         bá-hyàkàzì    bó-óshì ||   bà-ná-tàlík-à    á=má-bòkò    kú=
       those.N+2    2-new.wives   2-all        2-SQ-put.up-Fa   AU=6-hands   17=

       má-twè ||    írí      bà-nà-lír-à.
       6-head       while    2-ADD.V-cry-Fa

'Those new brides all of them || put their hands up on (their) heads || while crying.' (01 036)

In (4.20) the cl. 5 singular **lyóshì** 'all' refers to all of the **ííbúyè** 'rock'.

(4.20) Y-àná-tyábíríz-à ||   y-àná-làláng-á            |   yìryó       íí-búyé
       9-SQ-thunder-Fa       9-SQ-break.by.striking-Fa     that.N+5    5-rock

       ly-óshì.
       5-all

'And it thundered || and it struck and broke | that rock all of it.' (36 040)

Following a negative copula, **-óshì/-éshì** means 'at all'. In (4.21) it follows the negative copula **ndááyè** 'there is no one'.

(4.21) Ndáá-yè      y-éshì ||   ú-w-à-gí-m-bwéhúúk-à.
       NEG.FOC-1    1-all       1.S.R-P1-O9-O1.SG-whisper-Fa

'There was no one at all || who whispered it to me.' (1Sa 22:8)

The quantifier **-óshì/-éshì** 'all', when preceded by the invariable demonstrative **ngíìsì**[11] 'each' and followed by a relativized verb, means 'whoever/whichever', or 'any (x)'. This meaning of **-óshì/-éshì** 'whichever' is found with both singular and plural classes.

In (4.22) **ngíìsì yéshí úgámùtèèrà** means 'whoever will attack you (PL)' or 'anyone who will attack you'.

---

[11] **ngíìsì** is pronounced **kízì** by some people, exactly like the verbal aspect marker **kízì** which means 'repeatedly', etc.

## 4.3 Cardinal numbers

(4.22) **Ngíìsì y-éshí**    **ú-gá-mù-tèèr-à** |    **á-gá-mù-hím-à.**
     each    1-whoever    S.R+1-F2-O2.PL-attack-Fa    1-F2-O2.PL-defeat-Fa

'No matter who it is who will attack you | he will overcome you.' (02 019)

### 4.2.2 Quantifier -*ómbì* 'both'

The pronominal quantifier **-ómbì/-émbì** 'both' is formed from the previous reference marker plus the root **-mbì**. It, like the numerals, is used only with plural classes.

In (4.23) the cl. 10 quantifier **zómbì** 'both' modifies the NP **yìzó nyámíìshwà** 'those wild animals'.

(4.23) **Yìzó**    **ny-ámíìshwà**    **z-ómbì** ||    **z-àná-púmúk-ír-à**
     those.N+10    10-wild.animals    10-both    10-SQ-dashed.off-APL-Fa

    **mú=**    **kí-shúkà**.
    18=    7-bush

'Those wild animals both of them || dashed off into the bush.' (16 022)

## 4.3 Cardinal numbers

### 4.3.1 Numbers 1–7

The number **-gùmà** 'one' is an adjective (it takes adjective concord prefixes). It is also used in the plural classes, with the meaning 'some'. The numbers **-biri** 'two', **-shatu** 'three', **-ná** 'four', **-tāānu** 'five', **-(lí)ndàtù** 'six', and **-línda** 'seven' take the numeral class prefixes and are used only with the plural classes.[12] The numbers from one to seven are presented in (4.24).

---

[12] Cl. 16 is a locative class referring to 'specific location at a place' and may be used either as a singular or plural class: **ha-ndu** (16-place). Thus the numerals may be used with this class though it is not exclusively a plural class.

(4.24) Kifuliiru numbers 1–7

| Cl. | One[†] | Two | Three | Four | Five | Six | Seven |
|---|---|---|---|---|---|---|---|
|  | -gùmà | -biri | -shatu | -ná | -tāānu | -ndàtu | -lí=nda |
| 1 | múgùmà |  |  |  |  |  |  |
| 2 |  | bàbìrì | bàshàtù | bánà | bàtáánù | bàlí ndàtù | bàlí=ndà |
| 3 | múgùmà |  |  |  |  |  |  |
| 4 |  | íbírí | íshátù | ínà | ítāānù | (ìrí ndàtù) ndátù | írí=ndà |
| 5 | lígùmà |  |  |  |  |  |  |
|  | -gùmà | -biri | -shatu | -ná | -tāānu | -ndàtu | -lí=nda |
| 6 |  | gàbìrì | gàshàtù | gánà | gàtáánù | gàlí ndàtù | gàlí=ndà |
| 7 | kígùmà |  |  |  |  |  |  |
| 8 |  | bìbìrì | bìshàtù | bínà | bìtáánù | bìrí ndàtù | bìrí=ndà |
| 9 | ngúmà |  |  |  |  |  |  |
| 10 |  | zìbìrì | zìshàtù | zínà | zìtáánù | (zìrí ndàtù) ndátù | zìrí=ndà |
| 11 | lúgùmà |  |  |  |  |  |  |
| 12 | kágùmà |  |  |  |  |  |  |
| 13 |  | tùbìrì | tùshàtù | túnà | tùtáánù | tùlí ndàtù | tùlí=ndà |
| 14 | búgùmà |  |  |  |  |  |  |
| 15 | kúgùmà |  |  |  |  |  |  |
| 16 | hágùmà | hàbìrì | hàshàtù | hánà | hàtáánù | hàlí ndàtù | hàlí=ndà |
| 19 | hígùmà |  |  |  |  |  |  |

[†]There are also plural forms of this number, but when used in the plural it means 'some' or 'certain' rather than being a quantifier.

Note that the form of **ndàtù** 'six' is similar to the form of the number -**shatu** 'three'. -**ndàtù** 'six' is probably originally from a cl. 10 plural of -**shatu** meaning 'threes'.

Before **ndàtù** 'six', we often find an optional form: the usual numeral prefixes followed by the copula -**li**. (The number **zìríndà** (**zìrí=ndà**) 'seven' is formed in the same way.) This is because the number system is historically based on five, and only two through five are historically numerals. Thus we find forms like the following: cl. 2 **á=bàànà bàlí ndàtù** 'six children', cl. 4 **né=myèzì ìrí ndàtù** 'six months', cl. 6 **ná=mátàvì gàlí ndàtù** 'six branches', cl. 8 **bíhé bìrí ndàtù** 'the sixth hour', cl. 10 **bwé=gárámá zìrí ndàtù** 'of six grams', and cl. 13 **ú=túbìndì tùlí ndàtù** 'six pots'.

However, there are many times with the number six (but not with the monosyllabic -**nda** 'seven') where the whole prefix is dropped, especially in forms where the concord is in cl. 4, producing such forms as **í**=**myàká ndàtù** 'six years', **í**=**myèzí ndàtù** 'six months', **né**=**mìròndó ndàtù** 'six items of clothing'. The alternate forms, with the copula, e.g. **í**=**myèzí írí ndàtù** 'six months', are also attested, but less frequently. The copula is also often dropped for cl. 10 **sìkú ndàtù** 'six days', and in the number 'twenty six' **mákùmì gàlí ndàtù ná**=**ndàtù** rather than *****mákùmì gàlí ndàtù ná**=**gàlí ndàtù**. It is also possible to drop the copula in the case of the ordinal numeral; both **wá**=**kàlí ndàtú** 'sixth (person)' and **wé**=**ndàtù** 'sixth' are attested. See below for more ordinal numerals.

Reduplication of numbers is used in the case of *identical groups* of a certain number, or in pricing items *at so much each*. For example, there can be groups of five people each: **bàtáánú**-**bàtáánù** 'five people each', or piles of food priced at **mákùmì gàtáánú**-**gàtáánù** 'fifty each'.

The Kifuliiru numbers are expressed on the hands as follows:

(4.25) One    The index finger pointing up, with all the others closed in a fist.
Two    Index finger and one next to it pointing up, all the others closed.
Three    Three end fingers pointing up, thumb pulling index finger down.
Four    The index finger and the second finger crossed together.
Five    All fingers brought together in a fist, with thumb tucked inside.
Six    Three on each hand.
Seven    Three on one hand and four on the other.
Eight    Four on each hand.
Nine    Four on one hand and a five on the other.
Ten    Two fives (fists) tapped together (as many as there are tens).

## 4.3.2 Numbers 8–10

The numbers eight to ten are nouns and do not take numeral concord markers. They do not agree in any way with the nouns they modify. They are **múnààna** 'eight', **mwêndà** 'nine', and **í**=**íkùmì** 'ten', with its plural **mákùmì** 'tens'. We saw that with six and seven, the copula is usually used: **gàlí ndátù** 'six', **gàlí**=**ndà** 'seven', etc. With eight, nine, and ten, the copula is not used, e.g. **á**=**bándú múnààna** 'eight people'. The exception to this is with the numbers which are multiples of ten or of a hundred. In these cases the copula is used with **múnààná** 'eight' and **mwêndà** 'nine', e.g. **màkùmì gàlí múnààná** 'eight tens (80)', **mágáná gàlí mwêndà** 'nine hundreds (900)'.

### 4.3.3 Numbers 11–99

The numbers 11–19 make use of the cl. 5 noun **í=íkùmì** 'ten', followed by the additional number, e.g. 'ten and one', 'ten and two', etc. Though ten itself is non-agreeing, the additional number which follows the ten always agrees with the antecedent for any number between 1 and 7. Thus the number 'two' -**biri** in 'twelve (lit., ten and two)', when modifying the cl. 4 **í=myákà** 'years' is **ííkùmí ní=bírì** 'twelve *years*'. Likewise, it has the cl. 10 prefix **zì-** when modifying a cl. 10 noun, as in **í=ngúlíró íkùmì ná=zìbìrì** 'twelve *posts*', and the cl. 2 prefix **ba-** with the cl. 2 **á=bààná íkùmì ná bàbìrì** 'twelve *children*', etc.

The numbers 20–99 use the cl. 6 **màkùmì** 'tens', followed by the additional number, again agreeing with the antecedent where applicable. Thus we observe **máyíngà màkùmì gàlí ndàtù ná=gàbìrì** 'sixty-two weeks', in which **gabiri** takes the cl. 6 **ga-** prefix, agreeing with the cl. 6 **máyíngà** 'weeks'. Likewise, in **í=myáká màkùmì gàlí ndàtù ní=bírì**, meaning 'sixty-two years', it takes the cl. 4 prefix **í-**, agreeing with the cl. 4 **í=myákà** 'years'.

(4.26) | | | |
---|---|---|---
**màkùmì gàbìrì** | 'twenty' | **màkùmì gàlí ndàtù** | 'sixty'
**màkùmì gàshàtù** | 'thirty' | **màkùmì gàlí=ndà** | 'seventy'
**màkùmì gáná** | 'forty' | **màkùmì gàlì múnààná** | 'eighty'
**màkùmì gàtáánù** | 'fifty' | **màkùmì gàlì mwêndà** | 'ninety'

### 4.3.4 Numbers 100–999

The cl. 5/6 noun **íígánà/mágánà** 'hundred/hundreds', is used in the same way as **màkùmì** is used for 'tens'. Forms are given in (4.27):

(4.27) | | | |
---|---|---|---
**íígánà** | '100' | **mágáná gàlí ndàtù** | '600'
**mágáná gàbìrì** | '200' | **mágáná gàlí=ndà** | '700'
**mágáná gáshàtù** | '300' | **mágáná gàlì múnààná** | '800'
**mágáná gáná** | '400' | **mágáná gàlì mwêndà** | '900'
**mágáná gàtáánù** | '500' | | |

Once again, for numbers expressing the single digits, such as the five in three hundred thirty-five, the number between one and seven agrees with the antecedent. Here **zìtáánù** 'five' agrees with cl.10 **sìkú**.

(4.28)  sìkú mágáná gáshàtú nà=(mákùmì) gáshàtú ná=<u>zì</u>tāānù   '335 days'

### 4.3.5 Numbers 1,000–1,000,000

The number one thousand is the cl. 7 **kí-húmbì** with its plural, cl. 8 **bí-húmbì**. Thus we find **bíngóró-ngóró byàwè kíhúmbí nì=gánà** 'your 1,100 coins'. Other examples are seen in (4.29).

(4.29) ábándú bíhúmbí bìshàtù             '3,000 people'
        bíhúmbí íkúmí nà=bínà               '14,000'
        bíhúmbí mákùmì gàshàtù              '30,000'
        bíhúmbí ígáná ná=gàbìrì              '120,000'
        bíhúmbí igáná nà=mákùmì gáná nà=bínà   '144,000'

The cl. 3/4 noun **múlyònì/míryònì** 'million' is borrowed from French. It can be used to express numbers such as **míryònì mágáná gàbìrì** '200,000,000'.

## 4.4 Ordinal numbers

The ordinal numbers are formed by following the relevant noun with agreeing associative marker, which in 'second' through 'seventh' is followed by the number with the cl. 12 prefix **ka-**, as seen in (4.30). The number **ndátù** 'six' is sometimes an exception to the use of the **ka-** prefix. In (4.30) are examples agreeing with the cl. 11 noun **lúsìkù** 'day', and therefore involving the corresponding cl. 11 associative marker <u>lwa</u>/<u>lwo</u>/<u>lwi</u>. Note that in the case of first, the term **mbérè** 'front', is used (instead of any form of -**gùmà** 'one').

(4.30) ú=lúsìkù lwà=mbérè  '1st day'
ú=lúsìkù lwá=ká̱bìrì  '2nd day'
ú=lúsìkù lwá=ká̱shàtù  '3rd day'
ú=lúsìkù lwá=ká̱nà  '4th day'
ú=lúsìkù lwá=ká̱tāānù  '5th day'
ú=lúsìkù lwá=kà̱lí=ndàtù ~ ú=lúsìkù lwé=ndàtù  '6th day'
ú=lúsìkù lwá=kà̱lí=ndà  '7th day'
ú=lúsìkù lwó=múnààna  '8th day'
ú=lúsìkù lwó=mwêndà  '9th day'
ú=lúsìkù lwí=kùmì  '10th day'
ú=lúsìkù lwí=kùmì nà=lúgùmà  '11th day'
ú=lúsìkù lwí=kùmì ná=zìbìrì  '12th day'
ú=lúsìkù lwí=kùmì ná=zìshàtù  '13th day'
ú=lúsìkù lwí=kùmì nà=zínà, etc.  '14th day'

There is a cl. 14 noun **ú=búgírà** 'times' (which probably derives from the abstract cl. 14 relative of the verb **-gír-** 'do/make'). This is used with a numeral having cl. 12 agreement (or with a non-agreeing nominal number, such as **ííkùmì** 'ten') to tell how many times something has taken place. In expressing the term 'first time', **ú=bwà=mbérè**, the noun **ú=búgírà** itself is not generally used, but only referred to by the substantive use of the associative marker which agrees with it; nor does this construction use the cl. 12 prefix **ka-** nor the adjective **-gùmà** 'one'.

The terms for 'two times', 'three times', etc., all follow the pattern: **ú=búgírá kàbìrì** 'two times', **ú=búgírá kàshàtù** 'three times', **ú=búgírá kánà** 'four times', **ú=búgírá kàtáánù** 'five times', **ú=búgírá kàlíndàtù** 'six times', **ú=búgírá kàlíndà** 'seven times'. The higher numbers do not take the cl. 12 agreement: **ú=búgírá múnààna** 'eight times', **ú=búgírá mwêndà** 'nine times', etc.

The same cl. 12 agreement is found with the numeral question word **-ngâ** 'how many?', which takes numeral prefixes, and the adjectival quantifier **-ìngì** 'many': **ú=búgírá kàngâ?** 'how many times?' **ú=búgírá kìngì** 'many times'.

# 5

# Adverbs

Kifuliiru has a number of adverbs, which express time, position, and manner, etc. Many are very common, while others are quite rare. In the left hand column of the various lists below is the number of times each adverb occurs in the data (about 30,000 clauses) for a relative comparison of frequency.

Adverbs are invariable forms. They neither agree with any other element of the clause, nor do they trigger any agreement. Each adverb has its own unique class prefix, lexicalized as a part of the word. Included are prefixes from cl. 3, 5, 6, 7, 8, 9/10, 11, 12, 14, and 15. Thus the lexicalized prefixes found in adverbs include all of the classes except for the cl. 1/2 human, cl. 4 and 13, the cl. 19 diminutive, and the cl. 17, 18, and 23 locatives.

Kifuliiru adverbs normally occur either directly before or directly after the clause nucleus of S V O, but a few can occur within it, as will be seen below. Here follows a representative, but not exhaustive, list of Kifuliiru adverbs, sorted by various categories.[1]

## 5.1 Temporal adverbs

The temporal adverbs deal with time orientation. Quite a few of these are used as points of departure (10.2.4) at the beginning of the sentence, and so establish a starting point for the communication, relative to something already in the context.

---

[1] I am grateful to Stephen Levinsohn for his input in help with sorting out the various adverb categories.

(5.1) | No. | Adverb | Gloss |
|---|---|---|
| 1,720[2] | kéèrà | 'already, long ago' |
| 846 | lyêryô | 'right then' |
| 643 | há=nyúmà | 'afterwards' |
| 492 | háàhò | 'at that.N very time' |
| 270 | búnò | 'now' |
| 178 | lúsìkù lúgùmà, etc. | 'one day, etc.' |
| 171 | zèènê | 'today' |
| 111 | léèrò | 'this time' |
| 102 | shéshēēzì | 'morning' |
| 76 | lígùmà | 'once' |
| 47 | kúshéézì | 'tomorrow' |
| 31 | káré-kárê | 'early in morning' |
| 28 | háàhò-háàhò | 'right at that.N very same time' |
| 12 | bwóbùnô | 'right now' |
| 10 | ú=bwàkyá-ú=bwàyírà | 'day and night' |
| 3 | kínyà-lígùmà | 'at the same time' |
| 3 | lígúmà nà=lígúmà | 'right away' |

The adverb **kéèrà** 'ALREADY' indicates COMPLETIVE aspect. The meaning is to do something thoroughly and to completion (Bybee, Perkins, and Pagliuca 1994:318). **Kéèrà** usually occurs immediately before the verb, but in some cases it is preposed to the position preceding the subject noun.

The completed recent past consists of **kéèrà** 'ALREADY' followed by a conjugated verb in the recent past (P1) tense. Since the time frame of the recent past may include an action which occurred only seconds before, the addition of **kéèrà** is used to emphasize that something has *already* happened. In (5.2) the completed recent past form is **kéèrà nàkúláhìrìrà** 'I have already refused (to) you'.

---

[2]This combines the few times the adverbial **kéèrà** means 'long ago', as well as the much more common use meaning 'already'.

## 5.1 Temporal adverbs

(5.2) **Kéèrà**      n-à-kú-láhìr-ìr-à        ||        kwó=
      ALREADY    1SG-P1-O2.SG-refuse-APL-Fa         CMP=

   **n-dá-gáá-kú-ly-â**    |    w-é=    mw-ìrá  w-à-nì.
   1SG-NEG-F2-O2.SG-eat-Fa    2SG-FOC=    1-friend  1-A.M-1SG

'I have refused (for) you || that I will not eat you | you (who are) my friend.' (11 014)

In (5.3) we see an example where **kéèrà** precedes the nominal subject of the verb. Here **kéèrà** is preposed before **íngwî** 'leopard'. The effect is to give greater emphasis to **kéèrà** than it would have if it were placed immediately to the left of the verb.

(5.3) **Ù-kwìr-íír-ì**    **ù-Ø-lyók-è**    yà-hó    ||  mú=kúbá |  **kéèrà**
      2SG-must-RS-Fi    2SG-SBV-leave-Fe    there.N-16   because       ALREADY

   **í=n-gwí**    |    y-à-hà-híg-ìr-à.
   AU=9-leopard    9-P1-O16-purpose-APL-Fa

'You need to leave there || because | already the leopard | has made plans for that place.' (10 009)

The adverb **kéèrà** can also be used in conjunction with the unmarked past (P2) tense, which is marked by the verb prefix **ká**-. In (5.4) **kéèrà íkáhòngókà** means that the house 'had already fallen down (before yesterday)'.

(5.4) **Ìyó**       ny-ûmbà  ||  **kéèrà**  |    í-ká-hòngók-à.
      that.N+9    9-house       ALREADY       9-P2-fall.down-Fa

'That house || already | fell down (some time ago.)' (23 017)

In (5.5) the adverb **lyêryô** 'right then' indicates that there is no delay between what just happened and what is subsequently happening, thus functioning as a point of departure.

(5.5) **Lyêryó**    |    ìyó       m-bóngó  ná-yò  |  y-àná-náák-á:...
      right.then        that.N+9   9-gazelle  ADD.P-9    9-SQ-say.rudely-Fa

'Right then | that gazelle as well | also rudely stated:...' (21 004)

In (5.6) the adverb **há=nyúmà** 'afterwards' relates the statement to what happened before, thus again functioning as a point of departure.

(5.6) **Há=nyúmá** | yàbó      bá-túúlání   bà-à-gè |   bà-ná-kìzì
      Afterwards   those.N+2   2-neighbors  2-A.M-1    2-SQ-REP

   mú-yìm-a      í=by-ókúlyà |   í-shálì |   ly-àná-mú-yìt-à.
   O1-deny-Fa    AU=8-food      5-hunger    5-SQ-O1-kill-Fa

'Afterwards | those neighbors of his | continuously denied him food | and hunger | killed him.' (40 024)

## 5.2 Positional adverbs

Positional adverbs express the relative position of the action.

(5.7) | No. | Adverb | Gloss |
|---|---|---|
| 192 | **hááshì** | 'on ground or floor' |
| 20 | **bùùbì** | 'lying face down' |
| 11 | **kífúdéètê** | '(going) backwards' |
| 0 | **búgálàmà** | 'lying on back' |
| 0 | **kángálí-ngálì** | 'lying on back' |
| 0 | **lúgálì** | 'lying on back' |
| 0 | **bútùlì** | '(progressing) downwards' |

In (5.8) the man crashes down, and the word **hááshì** 'to the ground' describes *where* he landed.

(5.8) À-ná-yìbùmbúlík-á        **hááshì**   ||   í=by-ókúlyá   í=by-áà=    lì
      1-SQ-crash.down-Fa       on.ground        AU=8-food     S.R-8-O.R+1= P3

   hí-ít-ì   ||   by-àná-yòn-ék-à.
   has-RS-Fi    8-SQ-pour.out-NEU-Fa

'And he crashed down || and the food which he had || poured out.' (34 015)

## 5.3 Manner adverbs

There are many adverbs of manner, but most of them are rarely or never found in our texts.

## 5.3 Manner adverbs

(5.9)

| No. | Adverb | Gloss |
|---|---|---|
| 475 | **bwîjâ** | 'well' |
| 76 | **lwóshì** | 'completely' |
| 63 | **dúbà** | 'quickly' |
| 44 | **búshâ** | 'worthless' |
| 16 | **búkóndwè** | 'naked' |
| 14 | **bwíjà-bwîjâ** | 'slowly' |
| 6 | **lútó-lútô** | 'furtively' |
| 3 | **kínà-lígùmà** | 'all at one time' |
| 3 | **mákéngwà** | 'warily' |
| 2 | **múlîndì** | 'quickly' |
| 1 | **bígùgù-bígùgù** | 'in crowds' |
| 1 | **búlêmbè-rémbè** | 'full to brim' |
| 1 | **ínóòkà** | 'precisely' |
| 1 | **kásíngé-síngè** | 'very fast' |
| 1 | **tíítà** | 'plenty' |
| 0 | **kíjùgà** | 'almost full' |
| 0 | **kángúbí-ngúbì** | 'in a hurry' |
| 0 | **káshúùshì** | 'quickly, vigorously' |
| 0 | **kásúúlúlù** | 'very fast' |
| 0 | **kíbándè-bándè** | 'without waiting' |
| 0 | **kírámúkò** | 'periodic' |
| 0 | **lújóbé-jóbè** | 'in shame' |
| 0 | **nábágángà** | 'resolutely' |
| 0 | **ngórókà** | 'in one fell swoop' |
| 0 | **nvúùlì** | 'quickly' |
| 0 | **rúnùùkà** | '(deny) totally' |
| 0 | **ú=mújéèjè** | 'gently, just a little' |

As seen from the numbers above, the most frequently found adverb of manner is **bwîjâ** 'well'. In (5.10) this adverb modifies the passive verb -**yákiir-w**- 'received'.

(5.10) **Bà-ná-yákīīr-w-à    bwîjâ ||    bà-ná-háàb-w-à    í=kí-gòlò.**
2-SQ-receive-PS-Fa    well    2-SQ-give-PS-Fa    AU=7-guest.room

'They were received well || and they were given a guest room.' (36 017)

## 5.4 Intensifier and limiter adverbs

In this category, there are two forms which are quite common: **bwénēēnè** 'very much' and **nààhô** 'only'. The rest are specialized forms not exemplified in our texts, but recorded in the dictionary.

(5.11) | No. | Adverb | Gloss |
|---|---|---|
| 908 | **bwénēēnè** | 'very much' |
| 585 | **nààhô** | 'just, only' |
| 0 | **dwàvwé-dwàvwê** | 'very many' |
| 0 | **kásèmà** | 'great many' |
| 0 | **ngùmbí-ngùmbì** | 'with nothing at all' |
| 0 | **yòndó-yòndò** | 'great many' |

In (5.12) the commonly used adverb **bwénēēnè** 'very much' modifies -**bònà búlìgò** 'be annoyed, upset'.

(5.12) **Yîbà    || à-ná-bòn-à    bú-lìgò    bwénēēnè.**
her.husband    1-SQ-felt-Fa    14-annoyance    very.much

'Her husband || was very annoyed.' (27 021)

In (5.13) the adverb **nààhô** 'just, only' modifies a clause consisting of only the verb **ngámúyìtà** 'I will kill her'. The meaning is that there is no question about whether I will kill her, I will just do it.

(5.13) **N-gá-mú-yìt-à    nààhô.**
1SG-F2-O1-kill-Fa    just

'I'm just going to kill her.' (201 072)

In (5.14) **nààhô** 'only' indicates that it was only the old men who knew the marks.

(5.14) À-ná-yì-búúz-à | kútì bà-mény-á ú=tú-lángíkízô |
1-SQ-RFX-ask-Fa how 2+P1-know-Fa AU=13-mark

ú=tù-yìj-íbw-í | ná= bá-shààjà nààhô.
S.R-13-know+RS-PS-Fi CNJ 2-old only

'And he asked himself | how they knew the marks | that were known | by the old men only.' (23 040)

## 5.5 Confirmatory adverbs

There are two confirmatory adverbs. Among these, **kírî** 'even' is very common, but the other is relatively rare.

(5.15) No.   Adverb        Gloss
 887   **kírî**         'even'
   0   **méné-ménè**   'really, truly'

The adverb **kírí** 'even' expresses confirmation by adding the least likely possibility. In (5.16) the form **kírí ná nyììtù** means 'even us (contrary to expectation)'.

(5.16) <u>Kírí</u> ná= nyìì-tù ‖ í=mí-kòlwà | ì-rì mú= kízì =b-á
Even CNJ= ADD.P-1PL AU=4-work 4-is PROG= REP =be-Fa

mì-ngí bwénēēnè.
4-many very.much

'Even (for) us also ‖ the work | is habitually much very.' (113 014)

In (5.17) **kírí** 'even' indicates the lack of success the hunters had; that they did not scare up 'even one wild animal' (although it is expected that they would have).

(5.17) Bà-tà-ná-vyûl-à | <u>kírí</u> n-é= n-yámíìshwá n-gùmà.
2-NEG-SQ-get.up-Fa even CNJ-AU= 9-wild.animal 9-one

'They did not scare up | even one wild animal.' (03 006)

## 5.6 Additive adverbs

The common additive adverbs include **kwà=kúndì** 'also' and **kàndî** 'again'. These adverbs are unique, in that they all (as well as **ngànà** 'really') can occur between the subject and the verb.

(5.18) | No. | Adverb | Gloss
--- | --- | --- | ---
| 200 | **kwà=kúndì** | 'also'
| 148 | **kàndî** | 'again'
| 1 | **nyènê** | 'as well'

The additive form **kwà=kúndì** means 'also' in reference to an event. In (5.19) the adverb **kwà=kúndì** 'also' indicates that the third one, just like the other ones before, *also* did not spring loose (from trap).

(5.19) À-ná-hík-á      kú=   gw-á=   kà-shàtù ‖ nà-gwó   kwà=kúndì |
       1-SQ-arrive-Fa  17=   3-A.M=  12-third   ADD.P-3  also

   gù-tá-ká-hūk-à.
   3-NEG-P2-spring.loose-Fa

'He arrived to the third one (trap) ‖ and it (also) | did not spring loose.'
(632 036)

The adverb **kàndî** 'again' indicates the repetition of an event. This is exemplified in (5.20).

(5.20) Ù=bú-shígí   kàndì    bw-àná-yìr-a    ‖  kwó-kùlyà-kwókùlyà.
       AU=14-night  again    14-SQ-be.dark-Fa   E-thus.R-RDP

'Night again became dark ‖ in the very same way as before.' (632 036)

# 6
# Ideophones, Interjections, and Greetings

Ideophones, interjections, expressive nouns, and respect-sensitive greetings are all quite common in Bantu languages. The classic distinctive of ideophones is that they often mimic the sound of what they are describing. Interjections, on the other hand, express an interaction, usually emotive, with some situation. Expressive nouns tend to present extreme ideas. Greetings, including forms of address, are also discussed in this chapter.

In this chapter, the glosses of ideophones and interjections are always marked between double chevrons: « ». Both ideophones and interjections tend to occur outside of the clause nucleus, which is S V O. Ideophones tend to occur on the right side of the clause nucleus and are often introduced by a quote marker. Interjections tend to occur on the left side of the clause nucleus and are rarely associated with a quote marker. A high percentage of ideophones (but not interjections) have a corresponding verb.

In (6.1) the ideophone **jíì**[1] 'motor noise' occurs at the end of the sentence, on the right of the clause nucleus. Note that it is introduced by the quote marker **mbu**.

(6.1) N-àná-yùvw-á | ú=mú-dùgà gú-gá-yîj-à | mbú= «Jíì.»
   1SG-SQ-hear-Fa   AU=3-car   3-F2-come-Fa   ‹quote›= motor.noise

   'I heard | a car coming | ‹quote› «Vroom».'

---

[1] Though many of these forms are transcribed with only two vowels, the final vowel is often markedly extended and much longer than a standard phonemic long vowel.

In (6.2) we observe **àdètà kwâ=tàmúyìtà** 'he said that he did not kill him'. The interjection **mbàmbwê** 'not really!' begins the next sentence, on the left side of the clause nucleus. What follows is **Yé=wàmúyita!** 'He's the one who DID kill him!'

(6.2) À-dèt-à    kw-â=    tà-mú-yìt-à.    ‖    «Mbàmbwê!»  ‖  Y-é=
      1+P1-say-Fa  CMP-1=  NEG+P1-O1-kill-Fa    Not really!      1-FOC=

     w-à-mú-yìt-à!
     1-P1-O1-kill-Fa

'He said that he did not kill him. ‖ «Not really!» ‖ He's the one who killed him.'

There are cases, albeit much more rare, where ideophones can be used in place of nouns. Thus the form **búú** 'moo' can represent the sound of the cow, or by extension, the cow itself. In (6.3) **búú** occurs within the clause nucleus, in the object slot and before the oblique **há=mwàgè** 'at his home'.

(6.3) Bà-báág-à    «búú» |    há=    mw-à-gè.
      2+P1-slaughter-Fa  cow      16=    home-A.M-1

'They slaughtered a cow | at his home.'

## 6.1 Ideophones

Ideophones are "any vivid (**ideophonic**) representation of an idea in sound, such as occurs through onomatopoeia" (Crystal 2003:225). In other words, ideophones normally mimic the sound of what they are describing. They are commonly used to describe the sounds of animals, or the sounds of being bitten, breaking, eating, falling, fire, grabbing, moving, quickness, sickness, striking, stubbornness, suspicious noises, trips, water sounds, acting without care, etc.

Examples in English would be **boom**! or **bam**! In Kifuliiru **dítì!** stands for the sound of a thing that was in the air and has now dropped down to the ground. **Jíì** represents the noise of a motor. **Kàpààpwê** is used when a thing is snatched from another, etc. Sometimes, however, the ideophone does *not* represent a sound, as in **pépéépé** 'very dazzling white'. Ideophones are quite often reduplicated, and they are often related to an equivalent verbal form.

## 6.1 Ideophones

### 6.1.1 General characteristics of ideophones

#### 6.1.1.1 Ideophones often introduced by quote markers

Ideophones often represent the sound of something (as if it were talking) and are thus often introduced by a direct speech quote marker, e.g. **ti**, **mbu**, and **ngu** (17.4).

In (6.4) the quote marker **ti** introduces **gátá gátá** 'the sound of many things coming at once'.

(6.4) Há-ká-yíj-á    ú=tú-nyúní  tw-ìngì ‖ tw-àná-tw-à    hááshì    ‖
16-P2-come-Fa  AU=13-birds  13-many  13-SQ-land-Fa  down.on.ground

<u>tí</u>=    | «<u>Gátà</u>    | gátà».
‹quote›=  many.coming  many.coming

'There came many birds ‖ and they landed down on the ground ‖ ‹quote› | «Many | many».'

In (6.5) the quote marker **mbu** introduces **dútù** 'the sound of breaking'.

(6.5) Ú=mù-gózí  gw-àná-dúúdúk-à ‖ mbù=    «<u>Dútù</u>».
AU=3-rope  3-SQ-break-Fa    ‹quote›=  snap.

'The rope broke ‖ ‹quote› «snap».'

In (6.6) the quote marker **ngu** introduces **dítì** 'the sound of something hitting the ground'.

(6.6) Ú=mw-émbé |  gw-àná-yì-dìtúl-à    hááshì    ‖ <u>ngù</u>= |
AU=3-mango  3-SQ-RFX-plummet-Fa  down.on.ground  ‹quote›

«<u>Dítì</u>».
thud

'The mango | plummeted down to the ground ‖ ‹quote› | «thud».'

The quote formula can also be represented by the use of a "speech" verb, e.g. 'bark, make noise, yell'. In (6.7) the verb -**mók**- 'bark' introduces the ideophone **bwá, bwá** 'the sound of barking'.

(6.7) Á=ká-bwá |  kà-lì  mú=    <u>mók-á</u>: ‖  «<u>Bwá</u> |  <u>bwá</u>».
AU=12-dog  12-is  PROG=  bark-Fa    woof    woof

'The dog | is barking: ‖ «Woof | woof.»'

In (6.8) the verb -**yán**- 'bleat, low' introduces the ideophone **bàà**, which is the sound that a sheep makes.

(6.8) **Ká**= mù-yùvw-ít-ì ‖ kì-nó  kí-bùzí | kì-rì  mú=  yán-à |
Q=  2PL-hear-RS-Fi  7-this.P.C  7-sheep  7-is  PROG=  bleating-Fa

«**Bààà**»?
baa

'Do you hear | this sheep | bleating | «baaa»?'

In (6.9) the verb -**làk**- 'make sound' introduces the ideophone **jùlùlú jùlùlù** 'the sound of milk hitting the jug'.

(6.9) **À-ná-kàm-à  í=n-gáàvù** ‖ **á=má-tá** | **gà-ná-kìzí  làk-à**
1-SQ-milk-Fa  AU=9-cow  AU=6-milk  6-SQ-REP  make.noise-Fa

**mú**=  n-góngóóró: ‖ «**Júlúlúlû** | **júlúlúlúlû**».
18=  9-milk.container  squirt  squirt

'He milked the cow ‖ the milk | and it continuously made noise in the milk jug: ‖ «squirt | squirt».'

In (6.10) the verb -**gír**- 'do, make' introduces **fòròròrò** 'the sound of snoring'.

(6.10) **Ìrí  á-ká-b-à  à-gwèj-íír-ì** ‖ **tw-àná-yùvw-à  kw-â**=
When  1-P2-be-Fa  1-lay.down-RS-Fi  1PL-SQ-hear-Fa  CMP-1=

**kòlà  mú**=  **gír-á** | «**Fòròròrò** | **fòròròrò**».
be.NEWLY  PROG=  do-Fa  snore  snore

'When he was lying down ‖ we heard that he is doing | «snore | snore».'

In (6.11) the reduplicated ideophone **kágàtà-kágàtà** expresses the sound of someone swishing through water, while **vwò vwò vwò** expresses the sound of the river itself. In this example, there is no speech verb and no quote marker to introduce the ideophone. **Kágàtà-kágàtà** 'the swishing sound of going through' is introduced only by the locative phrase **mú=lwīj̀ì** 'in the river', while **vwò vwò vwò** 'sound of river' is introduced only by the noun **ú=lwīj̀ì** 'river'. Each of these ideophones occurs at the end of a verbless clause.

## 6.1 Ideophones

(6.11)  Ù-**lyá**   **mú-tàbánà** |   **à-ná-mú-bììk-é**   í=   **mú-góngò**. ‖ Mú=
        1-that.R   1-young.man    1-CON-O1-place-Fe    23=  3-back           18=

   **lw-ìjí** |  «**Kágàtà** | **kágàtà**»   ‖   ú=**lw-ìjí**   |
   11-river   swishing.sound.of.passing-RDP    AU=11-river

   «**vwò** | **vwò** | **vwò**»  ‖  bà-ná-**jábùk**-à |  ú=**lw-ījì**.
   sound.of.river-RDP-RDP         2-SQ-cross-Fa       AU=11-river

'And that young man | placed her on (his) back. ‖ In the river | «passing through swish | swish» ‖ the river | «gurgle | gurgle | gurgle» ‖ and they crossed | the river.' (112 015)

### 6.1.1.2 Forms not representing a sound

There are other cases, relatively less frequent, where an ideophone does not represent an actual sound. For example, in (6.12) **jábàtì** represents a dejected person, who is going home depressed. Although this does not represent the sound of something, it is still introduced by the quote marker **ti**.

(6.12)  N-à-**mú-bòn-à**      mú=   n-**jírà** ‖ à-lì **tí**=:  | «**Jábàtì** |  **jábàtì**».
        1SG-P1-O1-see-Fa      18=   9-path    1-is ‹quote›=    dejected    dejected

'I saw him in the path ‖ he is ‹quote›: |«dejected | dejected».'

In (6.13) **pépéépê** 'dazzling white' is introduced by the verb -**bònek**- 'be seen, appear' (which is *not* a verb dealing with sound).

(6.13)  Ú=**mú-shósì** |  à-ná-**yámbàl**-à  ‖  à-ná-**bòn-ék**-à |   «**Pépéépê**».
        AU=1-man         1-SQ-wear-Fa          1-SQ-see-NEU-Fa    dazzling white

'The man | got dressed ‖ and appeared | «dazzling white».'

### 6.1.1.3 Ideophones used nominally

As noted in the introduction of this chapter, besides occurring in the outer periphery at the end of the sentence, ideophones can occasionally be used nominally, or as a modifier following a copula. Thus besides being found in the periphery, they may also be found as a point of departure, or as a part of the clause nucleus, for example as a clause object, complement of an associative marker, etc.

In (6.14) the ideophone **gógí-gógì** 'crowding, crowding' occurs as a point of departure (10.2.4). **Ùyú gógì-gògí wìnyù** 'this crowding, crowding of yours'. It is interesting that the ideophone takes cl. 1a agreements, since this is a class which usually denotes animates and proper names.

(6.14) Ù-yú    «gógì    gògí»    w-ì-nyù ‖    háyì    mù-gá-kwìr-w-à?
this.P-1    crowding    crowding    1-A.M-2SG    where    2PL-F2-fit-PS-Fa

'This «crowding crowding» of yours ‖ where will you fit?'

In (6.15) the ideophone **gírí gìrì** 'hastily, hastily' occurs as a complement of the verb, just after **mùlì** 'you (PL) are'.

(6.15)  Mw-à-yíj-á    mù-lì    «gírí    gírí» ‖    mù-yíjî    =lyà
2PL-P1-come-Fa    2PL-are    hastily    hastily    2PL-COMING    =eat

í=by-ó=    búshâ    ‖    mù-Ø-génd-é    ìyó    mûndà!
AU=8-A.M+AU=    purposelessness    2PL-SBV-go-Fe    there.N    place

'You have come you are «hastily hastily» ‖ you have come to eat the things of worthlessness ‖ go over there!'

In (6.16) the ideophone **vúùjù, vúùjù** 'careless, careless' occurs as the object of the cl. 3 associative marker **gwa**, which refers to **múgánúúlò** 'conversation'.

(6.16) Ú=mú-gánúúló    gw-à-gè ‖    gù-shùbà    gw-à=    «vúùjù    vúùjù».
AU=1-speaking    3-A.M-1    3-was.PREV    3-A.M=    careless    careless

'His conversation ‖ was «careless careless».'

## 6.1.2 Ideophones: a sample of meanings by domain

Some common ideophones are listed in (6.17), sorted according to semantic domain. While the categories are somewhat arbitrary (e.g. **vwî** 'pass quickly in the air' could be included under "movement" or under "quickly") they do reflect an attempt to group the ideophones in like categories. Included is the related verb, if there is one.

(6.17)  Ideophones: a sample of meanings by domain

| Form | Related verb | Meaning |
|---|---|---|
| Animal sounds | | |
| bàà | | 'sound of a sheep' |
| méé | | 'sound of a goat' |
| búú | | 'sound of a cow, or "cow" itself' |
| bwá | | 'sound of a dog' |
| bwé | | 'sound of a fox, leopard' |
| híhíì-híì | | 'sound of an owl' |

## 6.1 Ideophones

| Form | Related verb | Meaning |
|---|---|---|
| **kòkyó-kòkyó** | | 'sound of a chicken clucking' |
| **nyááù** | | 'sound of a cat' |
| Sting | | |
| **zíbù** | -zìbul- | 'stung by a bee or bitten by a snake' |
| **zítù** | -zìtul- | 'stung by a small insect' |
| Break | | |
| **dútù** | -duuduk- | 'breaking of a rope, die suddenly' |
| **gútù** | -gùtul- | 'break a tree, or weak person' |
| **kótò** | -kòtok- | 'a tree breaking, when it is dry' |
| **pwá ~ pwí** | -pwamuuk- | 'breaking of egg, fruit, jug of water' |
| Colors | | |
| **pépéépê** | | 'very white' |
| Food/eating | | |
| **júlúlú-júlùlù** | -júlulund- | 'milk coming from a cow' |
| **kyó-kyó** | | 'noise of thick porridge in the throat' |
| **mátù-mátù** | -mátul- | 'noise by mouth in eating' |
| **mírù** | -mírangus- | 'to swallow quickly' |
| **shápù-shápù** | | 'a dog drinking' |
| Falling | | |
| **dítì** | -yìdìtul- | 'something high that has fallen down' |
| **kókò-kókò** | | 'a big thing falling down' |
| **kúù-kúù** | | 'a tree falling down' |
| **póó ~ púú** | | 'chopping a hard tree chop chop' |
| **pútì-pútì** | -tìbuk- | 'relatively small thing falling down' |
| Fire | | |
| **gúlù-gúlù** | -gúlumir- | 'roaring fire making noise' |
| **túlì-túlì** | -tùlik- | 'pop, as fire on wet firewood' |

| Form | Related verb | Meaning |
|---|---|---|
| Grab | | |
| kápáápwê | -paapul- | 'grab a thing from another by hitting it down' |
| pákù | -pákul- | 'grab a thing in the air' |
| shámwè | -shàmul- | 'snatch something from someone' |
| Movement | | |
| gátà-gátà | | 'many arriving in one place' |
| gógì-gógì | -yìgógombek- | 'going in of many people' |
| jíí | -jíjimb- | 'sound of a motor' |
| kágàtà-kágàtà | -kágaat- | 'swish (passing thru grass, or water)' |
| kólyò-kólyò | | 'many going into a place' |
| kótò-kótò | | 'heavy sound of goat or cow walking' |
| lálà-lálà | -lálaani- | 'going of a snake' |
| syé-syé | -syek-/-syekan- | 'rub two things together' |
| Quickly | | |
| gítì-gítì | | 'people in a hurry' |
| hwî | -hwikir- | 'to take something hurriedly' |
| pû | -puumuk- | 'running off in escape' |
| vwî | -yìvwim- | 'pass quickly in the air' |
| yùwí ~ zwî | -yìzwiririk- | 'small bird, or bullet going very fast' |
| zwírìrìrìrì | -zwiririk- | 'spurting out (e.g. blood)' |
| Sickness/struggle | | |
| ngágì-ngágì | -gàgik- | 'two people fighting' |
| pátì-pátì | -pàtika-patik- | 'difficult travel (in mud, blind person)' |
| párà-párà ~ púrù-púrù | -páraz- ~ -púruz- | 'sound of diarrhea' |
| húrù-húrù | -húruz- | 'sound of diarrhea' |
| shìshì-shìshì | -shuushirw- | 'shivering with a fever' |

## 6.1 Ideophones

| Form | Related verb | Meaning |
|---|---|---|
| **Snore** | | |
| fòròròròrò ~ fùrùrùrùrù | -fwij- | 'snore' |
| **Strike** | | |
| júgù-jùgù | -jùgumb- | 'noise of hitting or shaking something' |
| pútì ~ vútì | -vuudik- | 'strike without mercy' |
| shútù | -shuushul- | 'strike with a small, flexible stick' |
| vútù | -vùtul- | 'strike something harshly' |
| zíbù-zíbù | -zìbul- | 'strike with hand, or strike of an insect' |
| **Suspicious noise** | | |
| shólyò-shólyò | | 'thief, witch, etc. moving in dark' |
| tíì-tíì | | 'sound behind the house, etc.' |
| **Trip** | | |
| jábàtì-jábàtì | -jámbagir- | 'trip where lost something' |
| jébà-jébà | -jèba-jeb- | 'trip of s/o not strong, wandering' |
| nyáàfù-nyáàfù | -nyàvuuk- | 'trip of s/o strong, walks briskly' |
| shwé shwé | | 'trip where no strength' |
| tírì-tírì | -tiritimb- | 'trip of a well person' |
| **Water** | | |
| dàmbwî ~ dùmbwî | | 'kerplunk, fall in water' |
| gólò-gólò | -gòlomb- | 'flowing of water' |
| jágì-jágì ~ jógì-jógì | | 'the rain coming for a long time' |
| gólyò-gólyò | | 'water going in many channels' |
| shwá | | 'clothing with water in it, sloshing' |
| tóò-tóò | -tóny- | 'raining' |
| vwò vwò vwò | -vwogeer- | 'sound of going in river' |
| zóróróró | -zòrorond- | 'trickle of water about to be finished' |

| Form | Related verb | Meaning |
|---|---|---|
| Without carefulness | | |
| bàà-bàà ~ bwê bwê | | 'speaking without knowing what will say' |
| gúlìtì-gúlìtì | -gùlit- | 'go with a lot of noise' |
| hwî-hwî | -hwikir- | 'going without care, quickly' |
| hwîtì-hwîtì | -yìhwitik- | 'to go without care' |
| párà | -yìpálalik- | 'go from task to task without finishing' |
| shámwè-shámwè | -shàmul- | 'work or eat fast and sloppy' |
| vúùjù-vúùjù | -vùjuuk- | 'leave the path' |
| búhùshù-hùshù | -hùshuk- | 'go without stopping, pass on by' |

### 6.1.3 Ideophone examples in context

In this section are representative samples of ideophones in the context of sentences.

Many animal sounds are included among the ideophones. In (6.18) the ideophone **híhíì (híì), híhíì (híì)** represents the sound of an owl.

(6.18) **Náfúúfúlú    à-gwètì    á-gáá-làk-à:** ||    «**Híhíì** |    **híì** |    **híhíì** |
   1a+owl         1-PROG     1-INTL-make.noise-Fa    hiihii      hii       hiihii

**híì**».
hii

'The owl is making the noise: || «Hihii | hii | hihii | hii».'

In (6.19) the ideophone **nyáù nyáù** represents the sound of the cat and is introduced by the verb **-yamiz-** 'to cry loudly'.

(6.19) **Í=ny-áàbù    ì-gwètì    í-gá-yàmìz-â:**    || «**Nyáù** ||    **nyáù**».
   AU=9-cat       9-PROG     9-INTL-cry.loudly-Fa   meow        meow

'The cat is crying loudly: || «meow || meow».'

In (6.20) the ideophone **zíbù** 'zap' represents being bitten. Although the bite does not make a sound *per se*, the quote marker **mbu** is still used.

## 6.1 Ideophones

(6.20) Ú=lú-jùkí   lw-àná-n-zìbúl-à |   mbù=   «Zíbù ||   zíbù».
      AU=11-bee   11-SQ-O1.SG-bite-Fa   ‹quote›=   zap   zap.

'The bee stung me | ‹quote› «zap || zap».'

In (6.21) the ideophone **kótò** 'crack' represents the sound of a tree breaking, related to the verb **kúkòtókà** 'to break off'. In this example the quote marker is **ngù**.

(6.21) Í=kí-tí |   ky-àná-yàm-à   ky-à-kòtók-á || ngù=   «Kótò».
      AU=7-tree   7-SQ-IMMED-Fa   7-P1-broke-Fa   ‹quote›=   crack.

'The tree | immediately broke down || ‹quote› «Crack!»'

In (6.22) the ideophone **pwâ** 'burst' is also introduced by a quote marker, **ti**. **Pwâ** is related to **kúpwámúúká** 'to fall and burst'.

(6.22) Á=ká-bìndì ||   kà-ná-pwámúùk-á |   tì= |   «Pwá!»
      AU=12-jug   12-SQ-burst-Fa   ‹quote›=   burst!

'The jug || fell and burst | ‹quote› | «Burst!»'

Ideophones also includes the sounds of eating. In (6.23) the ideophone **mátù, mátù** 'smack, smack' represents the sound of someone eating stiff porridge.

(6.23) Ú=mú-shósì |   à-gwétí |   á-gá-mátùl-à   ú=bú-ndù |
      AU=1-man   1-PROG   1-INTL-eat.noisily-Fa   AU=14-stiff.porridge

    «Mátù |   mátù».
    smack   smack

'The man | is | noisily eating his stiff porridge | «Smack | smack».'

In (6.24) the ideophone **mírù, mírù** 'gulp, gulp' describes the sound of someone swallowing quickly.

(6.24) À-ná-míràngús-à   ||   «Mírù ||   mírù».
      1-SQ-quickly.swallowed-Fa   gulp   gulp

'He swallowed quickly: || «Gulp || gulp».'

In (6.25) the sound of a tree being cut down with an axe is represented by the ideophone **póó póó póó** 'hack, hack, hack'.

(6.25) À-ná-tòndéér-á   ú=kú-kùb-à         í=kí-tí=    n-é=      shèènyù: ‖
       1-SQ-begin-Fa    AU=15-cut.down-Fa   AU=7-tree   CNJ-AU=   9+axe

«Póó ‖   póó ‖   póó».
 Hack     hack    hack

'He began to cut down the tree with the axe: ‖ «Hack ‖ hack ‖ hack».'

In (6.26) the sound of blazing, roaring flames is represented by the ideophone **gúlù gúlù** 'blaze, blaze' and is introduced by the quote marker **ti**.

(6.26) Í=ny-ûmbà ‖   y-àná-yàm-á      y-à-híír-á        =tì:       ‖ «Gúlù
       AU=9-house    9-SQ-IMMED-Fa    9-P1-burn.up-Fa   ‹quote›=     blaze

gúlù    gúlù».
blaze   blaze

'The house ‖ immediately burned up ‹quote›: ‖ «Blaze blaze blaze».'

In (6.27) someone throws a dog a piece of stiff porridge, the act of the dog catching it in the air is represented by the ideophone **pákù** 'catch', (cf. -pàkul- 'catch in air') introduced by the quote marker **mbu**.

(6.27) N-à-kà-làsh-à       í=kí-tóló      ky-ó=       bú-ndù              ‖
       1SG-P1-O12-throw-Fa AU=7-piece     7-A.M+AU=   14-stiff.porridge

k-àná-yàm-à         kà-pàkúl-á          =mbù |       «Pákù».
12-SQ-IMMED-Fa      12-catch.in.air-Fa  ‹quote›=     catch

'I threw it (dog) a piece of stiff porridge ‖ and it immediately caught it in the air ‹quote› | «Catch».'

In (6.28) the ideophone **shámwè** 'snatch' is related to the verb **kúshàmúlà** 'to snatch' and is introduced by the quote marker **ti**.

(6.28) À-yì-léé-z-á          há=   bú-tàmbì    ly-à-gè ‖   à-ná-yàm-à
       1+P1-RFX-pass-CS-Fa   16=   14-beside   5-A.M-1     1-SQ-IMMED-Fa

à-shàmúl-á | ti=       | «Shámwè» ‖   à-ná-mú-twâl-à |
1-snatch-Fa  ‹quote›=    snatch        1-SQ-O1-carry-Fa

í=fwáráng à.
AU=10+monies

'He passed himself beside ‖ and he immediately snatched | ‹quote› | «Snatch» ‖ and he took his | money.'

## 6.1 Ideophones

In (6.29) the depressed feeling of having had something stolen is represented by the ideophone **pátì, pátì** 'loss, loss' introduced by the copula **-kòlà**.

(6.29) **Ú=mú-ndù** | **à-nyág-w-à** ‖ **á=má-gúlù mú= n-jírá** |
AU=1-person   1+P1-rob-PS-Fa   AU=6-feet  18=  9-path

**gá-tá-kòlá:** | «**Pátì pátì**».
6-FRUS.INTL-be.NEWLY   loss   loss

'A person | was robbed ‖ the feet in the street | were now: | «Loss loss».'

In (6.30) the ideophone **kótò, kótò** represents the heavy sound of animals going along, such as that of a cow, or a heavy goat. The quote marker **ngu** is used.

(6.30) **Í=n-gáàvù** ‖ **ì-rì mú= záát-á** ‖ **ngù=** «**Kótò** ‖ **kótò**».
AU=9-cow   9-is PROG= walk-Fa   ‹quote›= trample   trample

'The cow ‖ is walking ‖ ‹quote› «Trample ‖ trample».'

In (6.31) the ideophone **lálà, lálà** 'slithering along' represents the sound of a snake slithering. The quote marker **ti** is used.

(6.31) **Gù-shùbà mú= làlááni-â** | **tì=** «**Lá là là là là là là**».
3-was.PREV PROG= snake.along-Fa   ‹quote›= slither, slither

'It (snake) was snaking along | ‹quote› «Slither slither slither slither slither slither slither».'

When two things rub together, the ideophone **sye, sye** is used. This can include two pant legs, as well of branches of trees, etc. In (6.32) **syé, syé** 'rub, rub' is introduced by the quote marker **mbu**.

(6.32) **Yì-byó bí-tí= by-ómbì** ‖ **bì-kòlà** | **mbù=** «**Syê** | **syê**».
these.N-8  8-trees 8-both   8-be.NEWLY   ‹quote›= rub   rub

'These two trees ‖ are now | ‹quote› «Rub | rub».'

In (6.33) the ideophone **pú** 'zip' is used for the sound of zipping away, being related to the verb **kúpúúmúkà** 'dash off'.

(6.33) Ìrí     bá-ká-yíjí         m-bòn-à    ‖   bà-ná-yàm-à     bà-púúmúk-á
      when   2-P2-COMING        O1.SG-see-Fa    2-SQ-IMMED-Fa   2+P1-dash.off-Fa

   =tì:           «Pu».
   ‹quote›=       zip

'When they came to (the point where they could) see me ‖ they immediately dashed off ‹quote› «Zip».'

In (6.34) the sound of a fly buzzing past is represented by the ideophone **zwî** 'buzz'.

(6.34) Ú=rú-sáází   lw-á-n-dèng-à           =kwô |   n-àná-yîjì
      AU=11-fly    11-P1-O1.SG-pass-Fa     =17     1SG-SQ-COMING

   yùvw-â: ‖   «Zwî!»
   hear-Fa     buzz

'A fly passed by me | and I came to hear: ‖ «Buzz!»'

The Bafuliiru herdsmen used to drink the blood of their living cows by inserting a dart in the neck vein. In (6.35) the ideophone **zwírìrìrìrì** 'spurt' expresses the sound of the blood spurting out.

(6.35) Í=shúúlí    bà-gì-làsh-á        í-ráágò ‖   ú=mú-kó |   gw-àná-yîj-à: ‖
      AU=9+bull   2-O9-throw-Fa       5-dart      AU=3-blood  3-SQ-come-Fa

   «Zwírìrìrìrì».
   spurt, spurt

'The bull they threw a dart at it ‖ blood | came: ‖ «Spurt».'

In (6.36) the sounds of sickness, like the movement of diarrhea is represented by the ideophone **púrù, púrù** 'splatter, splatter' and is introduced by the quote marker **ngu**.

(6.36) N-à-láálà               n-gá-húrùz-á           bù-nó        bú-shìgì ‖
      1SG-P1-SPEND.NIGHT       1SG-INTL- diarrhea-Fa  14-this.P.C  14-night

   ngù=    «Púrùrù» |   ngù=     «púrùrù».
   ‹quote› splatter     saying   splatter

'I spent this night having diarrhea ‖ ‹quote› «Splatter» | ‹quote› «Splatter».'

## 6.1 Ideophones

In (6.37) the sounds of striking, like those of walking sticks being used as weapons in war is represented by the ideophone **pútì, pútì** and is introduced by the quote marker **ti**.

(6.37) Í=í-zíbó     ly-à-káy-à       ‖ í=n-góní       zì-kòlá         ny-ìngì |
      AU=5-war     5-P1-be.fierce-Fa   AU=10-sticks   10-be.NEWLY     10-many

   <u>tí</u>=    |    «<u>Pútì</u> |    <u>pútì</u>».
   ‹quote›=         whack          whack

'The war became fierce ‖ (walking) sticks were now many | ‹quote› | «Whack | whack».'

In (6.38) the ideophone **shútù, shútù** 'swish, swish' refers to running after a child with a small stick and hitting him repeatedly, just hard enough to scare him. The sound is introduced by the quote marker **ti**.

(6.38) **Tw-à-yúvw-á**   =<u>tì</u> |   «<u>Shútù</u> |   <u>shútù</u>» ‖   ú=mw-ānà ‖
      1PL-P1-hear-Fa    ‹quote›=    swish          swish         AU=1-child

   à-ná-tàngír-á   ú=kú-yàmíz-â.
   1-SQ-begin-Fa   AU=15-yell-Fa

'We heard ‹quote› | «Swish | swish» ‖ the child ‖ began to yell.'

In (6.39) the ideophone **vútù, vútù** 'whack, whack' refers to really hitting hard, to the point that the stick was broken.

(6.39) **Bà-gwétì**   **bá-gá-mú-vùtùl-à** ‖ «<u>Vútù</u> |   <u>vútù</u>» ‖   í=n-góní ‖
       2-PROG        2-INTL-O1-whack-Fa     whack          whack         AU=9-stick

   y-a-mú-mál-ìr-à            =kw-ò.
   9-P1-O1-finish.off-APL-Fa   =17

'They are whacking him: ‖ «Whack | whack» ‖ the stick ‖ is finished off on him.'

In (6.40) the ideophone **shólyò, shólyò** 'creep, creep' represents the suspicious noise heard behind the house.

(6.40) **Tw-àná-yùvw-à í= ny-úmá ly-é= ny-ûmbà:** ‖ «**Shólyò**
   1PL-SQ-hear-Fa  23=  9-behind  5-A.M+AU=  9-house  creep

**shólyò**».
creep

'We heard behind the house: ‖ «Creep creep».'

In (6.41) the ideophone **tíì**, meaning 'bang', is introduced by the quote marker **mbu**.

(6.41) **Bú-shìgì tw-àná-yùvw-â | mbù= | «Tíì!»**
   14-night  1PL-SQ-hear-Fa  ‹quote›=  bang

'In the night we heard | ‹quote› | «Bang».'

There are quite a few ideophones describing the state of a trip. In (6.42) the ideophone **jébà, jébà** 'feeble, feeble' refers to going along in a state of weakness.

(6.42) **À-lèng-à há-nó | à-lì «Jébà jébà»**.
   1+P1-pass-Fa  16-here.P.C  1-is  feeble  feeble

'He passed here | being «Feeble feeble».'

In (6.43) the ideophone **nyáàfù, nyáàfù** 'robust, robust' depicts a person who is strong and healthy.

(6.43) **À-kòlà «nyáàfù nyáàfù» mú= n-jírà.**
   1-be.NEWLY  robust  robust  18=  9-path

'He is now «robust robust» in the path.'

There are many ideophones for the sound of water. In (6.44) **dàmbwí** 'splash' describes the sound of one jumping into the water.

(6.44) **Mbw-à Ø-jábúk-é mú= lw-ījì** ‖ «**Dàmbwí**
   as.soon.as-1  SBV-cross.over-Fe  18=  11-river  splash

**dàmbwî**».
splash

'When he crossed over the river: ‖ «Splash splash».'

## 6.1 Ideophones

In (6.45) the ideophone **gólò, gólò** 'flow, flow' describes the flow of water, and is introduced by the quote marker **ti**.

(6.45) Gà-lyá   mì-ìjì    gó-óshì ‖ tì=        «Gólò    gólò    gólò».
       6-that.R 6-water  6-all     ‹quote›=   flow     flow    flow

  'That water all of it ‖ ‹quote› «Flow flow flow».'

In (6.46) the ideophone **jágì jágì** represents the sound of rain that has continued for a long time.

(6.46) Í=n-vùlà ‖ ì-géndèr-íír-í       ú=kú-ni-â |  «Jágì |   jágì».
       AU=9-rain  9-continue-RS-Fi   AU=15-rain-Fa  fall     fall

  'The rain ‖ continued to rain | «Fall | fall».'

In (6.47) the ideophone **pátì, pátì** represents the difficulty of sloshing through the mud.

(6.47) Y-ôyò     à-lì  mú=  bí-dákà: ‖  «Pátì |   pátì».
       E-that.N+1 1-is  18=  8-mud      slosh     slosh

  'That very one in the mud: ‖ «Slosh | slosh».'

In (6.48) the ideophone **zòròròrò** 'dripping sound at end of rain' is introduced by the quote marker **ti**.

(6.48) Ú=mú-làmbà ‖  gú-tá-kòlà              tî=         ‖ «Zòròròrò».
       AU=3-gutter    3-FRUS.INTL-be.NEWLY   ‹quote›=      drip, drip

  'The gutter ‖ was now ‹quote›: ‖ «Dripping».'

Kifuliiru has a wide range of verbs and ideophones dealing with something done carelessly. In (6.49) the ideophone **báà, báà** refers to 'blabbering speech' and is introduced by the quote marker **mbu**.

(6.49) À-lì  mbú=  ‖  «Báà |   báà». ‖  K-à=  dèt-à     bwîjâ?
       1-us  ‹quote›=   blabber  blabber    Q-1=  speak-Fa  well

  'He is saying: ‖ «Blabber | blabber». ‖ Is he speaking well?'

In (6.50) the ideophone **gúlìtì, gúlìtì** 'racket, racket' refers to a loud, boisterous movement.

(6.50) Kú-tì=    kù-nó    kw-ô=     lì     mú=     génd-á |   «Gúlìtì    gúlìtì».
      15-how    15-now   CMP-2SG=  are    PROG=   go-Fa       racket     racket

'How now that you are going | «Racket racket?»'

In (6.51) the verb **nàhùshúlà** 'I missed' is related to the ideophone **búhùshù, búhùshù** 'careless, careless'.

(6.51) N-à-kéngèèr-à              n-à-hùshúl-à ||    n-à-dèt-à: |    «Búhùshù
       1SG-P1-UNINTENDED-Fa       1SG-P1-miss-Fa      1-P1-say-Fa     careless

       búhùshù».
       careless

'I inadvertently miss || I said | «Careless careless».'

In (6.52) the ideophone **párà** reflects that much was done that is unfinished. The person referred to started many things that he couldn't finish.

(6.52) À-shùbá          =mbù |      «párà».
       1-was.PREV       ‹quote›=    unfinished

'He was previously ‹quote› | «Unfinished».'

## 6.2 Interjections

Interjections refer "to a CLASS OF WORDS which are UNPRODUCTIVE, do not enter into SYNTACTIC relationships with other classes, and whose FUNCTION is purely EMOTIVE" (Crystal 2003:239). Interjections typically occur in the clause periphery (outside of the S V O core). They differ from ideophones in that (a) they rarely involve the speech orienters **ti, mbu,** and **ngu,** and (b) they rarely are related to an equivalent verb form. By far most interjections are found *within* speech quotes. Included are words of comfort, delight, disgust, emotion, frustration, implication, provocation, scorning, surprise, and warning.

### 6.2.1 General characteristics of interjections

Interjections are found in the clause periphery, most commonly at the beginning of the clause. In (6.53) the interjection **éhéè!** 'oh my!' occurs at the beginning of the clause, before the clause core **twàsìgálà** 'we have remained'.

(6.53) «Éhéè!»     Tw-à-sìgál-à ||      kéèrà       á=bá-ndì       bà-génd-à.
       Oh.my!     1PL-P1-remain-Fa      ALREADY    AU=2-others    2+P1-go-Fa

'Oh my! || We have remained behind || the others have already gone.'

## 6.2 Interjections

In a few cases interjections also occur at the end of the clause, as in (6.54).

(6.54) N-gá-gír-à      m-bòh-é        ú=bú-lâ           | «Shóóbè!»
       1SG-P2-do-Fa    1SG-wrap-Fe    AU=14-intestines    unable

'I attempted to wrap the intestines | «Unable».'

### 6.2.2 Interjections: a sample of meanings by domain

Interjections normally have an emotive connotation and often involve interaction with something. A number of interjections are listed in (6.55) and in the following section some of them are exemplified.

(6.55) Interjections: a sample of meanings by domain

| Interjection | Related verb | Gloss |
|---|---|---|
| Comfort, empathy | | |
| **úúshì úshì** | | 'comfort a child, stop crying' |
| **yóò** | | 'empathy, shock' |
| Deny | | |
| **hòòbé-hòòbê** | | 'deny' |
| **kúùtù-kúùtù** | -yìkútumul- | 'deny with the armpit' |
| Delight | | |
| **àwíyíyíyí** | | 'ululation' |
| **àà** | | 'be pleased, agree' |
| **shòshó** | | 'now free of troubles, it is finished' |
| Disgust | | |
| **á** | | 'show disgust' |
| **hálìibwî** | | 'show surprise, point out weakness' |
| Emotion | | |
| **hee \| hehee \| yehee \| ehee** | | 'emotion' |
| Frustration | | |
| **áláàniê** | | '(Look at me!) anxiety of women' |
| **shóóbè** | | 'word to communicate inability' |
| **shòshó \| hongere** | | 'a frustrated person, like not giving birth' |

| Interjection | Related verb | Gloss |
|---|---|---|
| Implication | | |
| **ààhô** | | 'OK then' |
| **kízímà** | | 'so now (happy re. suffering of another)' |
| **máàshì** | | 'for goodness sake (shaming someone)' |
| **mbàmbwê** | | 'not really! (contradicting someone else)' |
| Provocation | | |
| **fyó-fyó** | | 'word of challenge' |
| **fyû ~ fyó** | | 'one says **fyu/fyo**, another **gaago**, fighting starts' |
| **móò** | -moomol- | 'laughing and the mouth wide open' |
| **júújì** | | 'jealousy because of what you are eating' |
| Scorn | | |
| **é=bòbô** | | 'a woman's small word of scorn' |
| **hóònyô** | -hónyolez- | 'poking fun, mocking of each other' |
| **hyéhyê** | | 'mocking laughter' |
| **níínò** | | 'derision (grab tooth as if tossing it out)' |
| **mhmm** | | 'others think he is unable to do sthg' |
| **yóhò ~ yúhù** | | 'shame a wrongdoer' |
| **yúbúbúbú ~ yúrúrúrú** | | 'scorn (hitting upper lip with fingers)' |
| Sickness, pain, anxiety | | |
| **áràràràrà** | | 'word showing great pain' |
| **lyâ-lyâ ~ kyâ-kyâ** | | 'noise after hearing bad news' |
| **mm hmm hmm** | | 'like when being stabbed' |
| **yáyébè ~ yáyéwè** | | 'shock and sadness' |
| **yóóò** | | 'the sound of a person in great pain' |
| **yóhòwê!** | | 'shock and sadness' |
| **yôwê** | | 'expression of pain, sadness' |

## 6.2 Interjections

| Interjection | Related verb | Gloss |
|---|---|---|
| Surprise | | |
| ééò | | 'is that right! (with surprise)' |
| kízígà | | 'surprise' |
| yéé | | 'expression of surprise and dismay' |
| Warning | | |
| e | | '(used following noun of direct address)' |
| ee! ngáhò! | | 'warn of danger; it's your business' |

In (6.56) the interjection **úshì** is used as a sound of comfort, to quiet a baby.

(6.56) «Úúshì | úshì» | ù-Ø-lék-é | ú=kú-lír-à || máàwè
      Calm.down  calm.down  2SG-SBV-stop-Fe  AU=15-cry-Fa  1a+our.mother

à-yíj-à.
1+P1-come-Fa

'«Calm down | calm down» | stop crying || our mother has come.'

The high-pitched interjection **àwíyíyí** 'sound of ululation' represents a high-pitched trill, usually performed by women at celebrations. Ululation is a typical Bantu expression of exuberant joy. The action itself is termed **kúbándá á=kábúúlì** 'to ululate'. (In Kiswahili the equivalent is **kupiga vigele-gele**). In (6.57) a child is born and thus the women break out in ululation.

(6.57) «Àwíyíyíyî» || Ù-Ø-lám-é | é= mw-àná w-à-nì.
      ululation      2SG-SBV-live.long-Fe  oh= 1-child  1-A.M-1SG

'«Ululation» || May you live long | oh my child!' (410 008-010)

In (6.58) the interjection **shòshó** is an expression of delight, that the case has been closed.

(6.58) Nângà || éé= «Shòshô»|| Ú=lú-bààjà lw-à-yít-w-à.
      No      O=  delight      AU=11-case  11-P1-kill-Ps-Fa

'No! || Oh «Delight». || The case is closed!'

In (6.59) the interjection **a** expresses disgust. It is pronounced with a sharp glottal stop at the end.

(6.59) «Á̱» ‖ Ø-n-jáág-ìr-à       yá-hà!
      Disgust  IMP.S-O1.SG-leave-APL-Fa  here-16

'«Oh!» ‖ Just go away from me here!'

The interjection **hálììbwî** 'how stupid!' literally means 'there is eaten'. It is used to expose the weak position of a person. In (6.60) it is said that the person has already judged himself, as he has spread news (that should have remained hidden.)

(6.60) «Hálììbwî» ‖  Sí=   kéèrà    w-à-yì-hán-à           w-ényènè |
       How.stupid    OBV=  ALREADY  2SG-P1-RFX-punish-Fa   2SG-self

       w-à-yì-bàl-à               ú=mw-âzì.
       2SG-P1-RFX-disclose-Fa     AU=3-news

'«How stupid!» ‖ It's obvious that already you have punished yourself | you have disclosed news.'

The interjection **yóò** 'oh no!'[2] is an expression of empathy and shock. In (6.61) it is used when the woman discovers that her husband has turned into a gazelle.

(6.61) Ùyó      mú-hyàkàzì ‖ à-ná-tòndééz-à  ú=kú-lír-á    kwókùnò: ‖
       that.N+1 1-new.wife   1-SQ-begin-Fa   AU=15-cry-Fa  like.this.P.C

       «Yóò! |  Bí-kí   í-by-á-n-déét-à           wéè?    Yíb-à-niê |
       Oh.my    8-what  S.R-8-P1-O1.SG-bring-Fa   oh.my   husband-1SG

       kéèrà    à-híndùk-à          m-bóngò!»
       ALREADY  1-turned.into-Fa    9-gazelle

'That young wife ‖ began to cry like this: ‖ «Oh my! ‖What has brought me? Oh my! ‖ My husband | has already turned into a gazelle!»' (01 031)

The interjections **héé, hèè, yee, éhéè, héhéè, and yéhè** are all used to express emotive reaction and can be used in several contexts, including surprise, encouragement, and warnings. In (6.62) **yéé** is used to show surprise, since a woman does not normally go into the forest where traps are laid.

---

[2] This is lower pitched and has a shorter vowel than the **yoo** of wailing.

## 6.2 Interjections

(6.62) W-á=n-dàrè tì= ‖ «<u>Yéé</u>!» ‖ Kó= mú-kàzì à-kìzí lēng-à mú=
  1-A.M=9-lion  ⟨quote⟩ Oh.my  Q=  1-woman  1-REP  pass-Fa  18=

  mí-tēgò?»
  4-traps

  'The lion ⟨quote: ‖ «Oh my! ‖ Does a woman habitually pass in traps?»'
  (401 032)

The interjection **shóóbè** always comes at the end of the clause (all seventeen times in the data) and indicates a frustration of what was intended. In (6.63) Leeza goes to get water, but the water spills, because her pot has holes in it. The interjection **shóóbè** 'frustrated, unable' indicates that she did not successfully get water.

(6.63) Léèzà  ná-yé  ngw-à=  Ø-vwóm-è  |  «shóóbè» ‖
  Leeza  ADD.P-1  as.soon.as-1=  SBV-get.water-Fe  unable

  Yàgó  mà-àjí |  gà-ná-kìzí  yòn-ék-à.
  that.N+6  6-water  6-SQ-REP  spill.on.ground-NEU-Fa

  'Leeza and SHE when she attempted to get water | «unable». ‖ That water | repeatedly spilled (on the ground).' (409 024-025)

The interjection **ààhô** 'OK then' is used to shame people into accepting a statement as true. It communicates that given the facts, the conclusion, or implication, is obvious. In (6.64) **ààhô** is used to allow the people to draw their own conclusion.

(6.64) «<u>Ààhô</u>» ‖  bwó=  mù-y-ìj-í  |  kwó=  mú-sósì |
  OK.then  since=  2PL-know-RS-Fi  CMP=  1-man

  à-tà-Ø-bùt-à ‖  bí-k-àgì  mw-à-kùmán-ír-à  yà-hò?
  1-NEG-TL-give.birth-Fa  8-what-EMP  2PL-P1-gather-APL-Fa  there.N-16

  '«OK then» ‖ Since you know | that a man | does not give birth ‖ for what are you gathering together there?' (17 014)

The interjection **kízímà** 'so now, therefore' means prerequisites have been met, so now what is due is being claimed. In (6.65) **kízímà** implies that the first man should be given the child, as the other has already been given half of the country.

(6.65) N-gáá-lék-à         n-gá-kú-hèèrèz-â |        kí-hùgò    lú-hândè ||
      1SG-F2-allow-Fa     1SG-F2-O2.SG-give-Fa      7-country  11-half

   «kìzímâ» |     ú-Ø-m-bèèrèz-é |       ù-yú        mw-ānà.
   so.now         2SG-SBV-O1-give-Fe     this.P-1    1-child

'I will allow to give you | half of the country: || «so now» | give me | this child.' (210 124)

The interjection **máàshì** 'for goodness sake, listen (with shaming)' is one of supplication, based on the hearer's conscience. It implies that something is obviously in order and the hearer should follow through. In (6.66) others have already tried and so the speaker says **máàshì** 'let me try too'.

(6.66) É=     bà-lyà           «máàshì»              || mù-Ø-lék-é            nàà-n-î ||
       O=     2-comrades       for.goodness.sake        2PL-SBV-allow-Fe     ADD.P-1SG

   n-Ø-déé              gèz-à           ú=kú-dèt-à.
   1SG-SBV-PRIOR       attempt-Fa      AU=15-say-Fa

'O comrades «for goodness sake» || allow ME ALSO || to first try to speak.' (204 040)

The interjection **mbàmbwê** 'not really!' expresses a contradiction of what has been said. In (6.67) the person says that he did not hit him. The form **mbàmbwê** 'not really!' implies a contradiction to this statement.

(6.67) À-dèt-à         kw-â=       tà-mú-shúlìk-à. ||    «Mbàmbwê» |
       1+P1-say-Fa    CMP-1=      NEG+P1-O1-hit-Fa        Not really!

   À-mú-shúlìk-á   =mà.
   1-O1-hit-Fa     =confirmation

'He said that he did not hit him. || «Not really» | he has hit him all right.'

In (6.68) the interjection **hóòbê** implies that an 'oath is taking place'.

(6.68) «Hòòbé     hòòbé» ||    N-dà-lí      nà=     mí-sí         y-à=     kú-lw-à.
       Swear      swear        1-NEG-am    CNJ=    4-strength    4-A.M=   15-fight-Fa

'«I swear I swear» || I have no strength to fight.'

In (6.69) the interjection **kúútù** signifies an 'oath (or swearing)', which is established by moving the elbow of the bent arm up and down.

## 6.2 Interjections

(6.69) É=    mw-ànà ‖ «kúùtù    kúùtù» ‖ n-à-láhìr-à    kú=
     O=   1-child        swear         swear         1SG-P1-refuse-Fa   17=

by-à-nî.
8-A.M-1SG

'O child: ‖ «I deny» (by waving armpit) ‖ I deny relative to my matters.'

In (6.70) the interjection **fyô, fyô** 'dare, dare' is one that dares another to make a belligerent move. If that person does, then a fight will ensue.

(6.70) Ù-Ø-shùbí    dēt-à |  «Fyô    fyô!»‖   Ù-Ø-bòn-é    kwó=
     2SG-SBV-AGAIN   say-Fa   dare    dare     2SG-SBV-see-Fe   CMP=

n-gá-kú-gír-à!
1SG-F2-O2.SG-do-Fa

'Just say again | «I dare you!» ‖ You will see what I will do to you!'

The interjection **hóònyò** is a term of derision, related to the verb **kúhónyólézà** 'to disparage, taunt'. In (6.71) it can be roughly translated 'Nya nya!'

(6.71) Ìrí    gú-ká-bòn-á |   kwó=   lì-tà-támí        yì-shàg-àn-i-â ‖
     When   3-P2-see-Fa    CMP=   5-NEG-DARING    RFX-shake-RCP-CS-Fa

gw-àná-lì-hónyòléz-à | gw-àná-dèt-à: ‖ «Hônyô!»
3-SQ-O5-disparage-Fa    3-SQ-say-Fa       nya-nya

'When it (cl. 3) saw | that it (cl. 5) would not dare to still shake itself ‖ it disparaged it | and it said: ‖ «Nya | nya!»' (523 006)

The interjection **níínò** is one of derision, where the speaker is poking fun at the hearer. When **níínò** is used the finger is placed on the upper two front teeth and flicked out, implying that I will not give you anything, even as small as a tooth.

(6.72) Hy-àná-kì-máámír-à         =kwò ‖ hy-àná-dèt-à: ‖ «Níínò! ‖
     19-SQ-O7-scamper.up-Fa      =17      19-SQ-say-Fa      too.bad

W-à-lùmúúk-à».
2SG-P1-get.no.gain-Fa

'It scampered up (the tree) ‖ and it said: ‖ «Too bad!» ‖ You've got no gain».' (12 029)

In (6.73) the person is saying that he will not give even something as small as a tooth.

(6.73) «Níínò!» ‖ N-dà-ngà-shúbí      kú-hééréz-â |  kìrí  hì-nò!
       Too bad!    1SG-NEG-POT-AGAIN  O2.SG-give-Fa even  19-this.P.C

'«Too bad!» ‖ I would not again give you | even this small thing!'

In (6.74) the high-pitched interjection **yóhò ~ yúhù** 'shame' is one of contempt, confirming that the addressee is being shamed.

(6.74) «Yóhò!» ‖  Í=shònì            zí-gá-kú-gwàt-à! ‖  Á=bá-ndú
       Shame!    AU=10+humiliation  10-F2-O2.SG-seize-Fa  AU=2-people

bá-gá-kú-shék-èr-à.
2-F2-O2.SG-laugh-APL-Fa

'«Shame!» ‖ Humiliation will seize you! ‖ People will laugh at you.'

In (6.75) the alternate pronunciation **yúhù** 'shame!' is used.

(6.75) «Yúhù!»‖  À-ni-á           mú=  n-jírà!
       Shame!   1+P1-defecate-Fa 18=  9-path

'«Shame!» ‖ She has defecated in the path!'

In (6.76) the interjection **yúbùbùbùbù ~ yúrùrùrùrù** involves poking fun. When either of these words are spoken, the speaker also taps the side of his own mouth repeatedly with his hand or wrist.

(6.76) «Yúbúbúbú!»‖  Ká=  mw-àngà-yúvw-à!
       Oh, brother!  Q=   2PL-POT-hear-Fa

'«Oh brother!» ‖ Would you listen to that?'

The interjection **áràràràrà** 'ai yai yai' is used when one is in deep pain, as in (6.77).

(6.77) «Áràràràrà!»‖  Kéèrà    n-à-yì-tèm-à! ‖      N-à-yì-kómérés-à!
       Ai yai yai    ALREADY  1SG-P1-RFX-cut-Fa    1SG-P1-RFX-injure-Fa

'«Ai yai yai!» ‖ I have already cut myself! ‖ I've injured myself!'

The interjection **àláànìè** is probably derived from the informal **àlá** 'look' and **nie** 'me', i.e. 'just look at me' and is usually used in a negative context,

## 6.2 Interjections

as an expression of dismay. In (6.78) the effect is to say 'Look! Hey! I am now in need!'

(6.78) «<u>Àláànìè</u>   wê!» ‖ N-à-góórw-à         kwókùnò!
       Look at me!  Hey!   1SG-P1-be.in.lack-Fa   like.this.P.C

'«Look at me hey!» ‖ I am in need now!'

In (6.79) the interjection **yáyébè** 'oh my' is used to express 'anxiety and despair'.

(6.79) «<u>Yáyébè</u>!» ‖ Bì-ryá     bí-ndù     by-à-hómb-à.
       Oh no           8-those.R  9-things   8-P1-suffer.loss-Fa

'«Oh no!» ‖ Those things have suffered loss.'

In (6.80) the interjection **yóhòwê** 'oh my!" expresses anxiety over the fact that the person got lost.

(6.80) «<u>Yóhòwê</u>!» ‖ W-éhé       w-à-tèrék-à.
       Oh my            2SG-CTR.P   2SG-P1-be.lost-Fa

'«Oh my!» ‖ YOU have gotten lost.'

The interjection **kízīgà** means 'surprise!' In (6.81) **kízīgà** is used to convey the surprise the person felt to find Beard hiding in the field.

(6.81) À-ná-yégèèr-à        mú=   kà-tì=      k-é=        n-dálò ‖
       1-SQ-come.near-Fa    18=   12-middle   12-A.M+AU   9-field

       «<u>Kízìgà</u>!»   Lw-ânwâ ǀ    à-bìsh-àm-ír-ì      =mwò.
       surprise         11-beard     1-hide-POS-RS-Fi    =18

'He neared the middle of the field. ‖ «Surprise» Beard ǀ was hiding in there.' (50 020)

The interjection **e** after a noun of direct address, means 'look out' or 'pay attention', e.g. **é=mwānà=è** 'O child, look out!' **é=múshósì=è** 'O man, look out!' **é=múkàzì=è** 'O woman, look out!', etc. In (6.82) the **è** after **mwánà** 'child' is a warning for the child to look out.

(6.82) É=   mw-ānà   «=<u>è</u>!»    ‖ Ø-Shààg-á       yà-hô!       ‖ Á-gá-kú-gwàt-à.
       O=   1-child   =look out!      IMP.S-leave-Fa   there.N-16     1-F2-O2SG-seize-Fa

'O child «look out»! ‖ Leave there! ‖ He is going to seize you.'

In (6.83) the **e** after **múkàzì** 'woman' is also a warning for the woman to be alert.

(6.83) É= mú-kàzì «=ê̱!» ‖ Yíbàlò à-yíj-à.
       O= 1-woman =look out your.husband 1+P1-come-Fa

'O woman «look out»! ‖ Your husband is coming.'

## 6.3 Greetings

Kifuliiru speakers are very sensitive as to whether the listener is above, below, or equal in social status to the speaker,[3] and they have different greeting forms for each case.

### 6.3.1 Greetings at encounter

When two people encounter each other, they normally greet each other first and then ask about the news. Asking about the news is usually perfunctory, unless something special has just happened.

There are different kinds of greetings, depending on the social status of the recipient. The highly formal greeting **Twàlám(ú)sà**,[4] literally, 'We greet you' (using the first-person plural even though spoken by one person), is used to greet people who are of higher social status, or those of equal status whom you wish to honor. **Nàlám(ú)sà** the same verb but with a singular subject, is still respectful, but not as formal as **Twàlámúsà**. The reply to either is often **Músīngò** 'greeting'. This is the neutral greeting and says nothing about social respect, either one way or another.

The form **Kútì/kútàgì** 'how (is it going)' is a term used by the younger generation. It is quite an informal greeting, and if used to greet people of higher social status, is considered disrespectful. The reply may be **Nângà, ndáákwò** 'no, there isn't any' or alternatively, **kwokuno** 'just like this'.

Following the initial greeting, one asks about news. When asking about the news, the neutral greeting is **Myázì míkì?** 'What kind of news?' The normal answer is **(Nângà,) míìjà** '(No,) good.' If the news is not actually very good, the reply is often **Míìja hínììnî** 'a little good', or even **Málwàzì nààhô** 'Only sickness' if that is the case. If there has been a real problem, that will be described following the standard answer, for example if someone at home has died, or has been in an accident, but that is relatively rare.

---

[3] This sensitivity to status is also reflected when washing hands before a meal. Among the Bafuliiru the people of highest status (which includes guests) must wash their hands first.

[4] Though there is technically a **u** in this verb, the normally optional rule of **u**-deletion following a nasal is applied to this greeting nearly without exception. This same rule of **u**-deletion generally applies also to **m(ú)síngò** 'greetings'.

There are several alternatives to using **Myázì míkì?** to elicit news. If two people meet in the morning, they will say **Kútì wàvyúkà?** 'How did you get up?' Again, the normal answer is **Nàvyúkà bwîjà** 'I got up well.'

Alternatively, at the end of the day one can ask **Kútì wàshííbà?** 'How did you spend the day?' And the normal answer is **Nàshííbà bwîjà** 'I spent it well.'

If two people meet only in passing, the usual question to the one passing by is **Háyì wàsháágà?** 'Where are you coming from?' or **Hayi wagenda?** 'Where are you going?' And the answer may be the name of a place, such as 'the school', 'the market', 'the clinic', 'the field', or a full clause such as 'I'm going to farm'. However, it is not considered impolite to answer in a non-committal way, such as 'down there', 'back there', 'up ahead', etc.

If one is talking to children, one often asks **Bíkí wàlyà?** 'What did you eat?' and the answer would be something like **í=bíshìmbò né=bíjûmbù** 'beans and (sweet) potatoes', etc.

### 6.3.2 Leave-taking

For leave-taking, there are a number options, and with no particular reference to status. **Báàbà** simply means 'goodbye'.

The form **Ùndámùkìzê** ___ means 'Greet ___ for me'. (The name of the person to be greeted is inserted in the blank.)

The person leaving says **Ùsígálágè, (nàgéndà)** 'You remain behind, (I am going)'. The person remaining behind then responds **Ùgéndágè bwîjà!** 'You go well.'

### 6.3.3 Forms of address

There are quite a few forms of address, which are closely linked to the relative status of the speaker and the addressee. Kifuliiru speakers are very conscious whether they are speaking up to someone, down to someone, or speaking to an equal.

All nouns of direct address are preceded by **é** 'O'. For example, **É=Séngòròngê** 'O Sengoronge' is the form used when addressing a person whose name is Sengoronge. Besides proper names, most kinship terms and titles (such as teacher, pastor, etc.) may be used as nouns of direct address.

It is impolite for someone of lesser status to use the proper name of a person of higher status, either in direct address or in reference to that person. The use of a kinship term or other form of address is generally preferable, even in addressing an equal. Alternatively, a parent is often addressed by reference to their child, e.g. **E=nyina wa=Jooni** 'O mother of John', saying the name of the mother's child, instead of the name of the mother herself. The forms of address are summarized in (6.84).

(6.84) Common forms of address
- Addressing all
  - **ê**      'O' (introducing noun of direct address)
- Addressing those of lower status
  - **yê**      'I hear you (of a man, to equal or lower status)'
  - **wé wè**      'I hear you ! (of woman, castigating)'
  - **éwè ~ yéwè**      'Hey you! (to get attention)'
  - **wé**      'to a person you are speaking down to'
  - **sháhù**      'to a low person, or to insult an equal'
- Addressing equals
  - **é=yâgà**      'O comrade (SG)'
  - **é=bàlyá**      'O comrades (PL)'
- Addressing those of higher status
  - **é=wálíhà**      'a term of respect for a man or woman'
  - **kàrámè**      'I hear you (said by a woman, respectfully)'
  - **yàgìrwâ**      'honored one'
  - **mútààmà**      'respected one'
  - **múhāānyì**      'one who gives'
  - **dáàtà**      'father'
  - **máàwè**      'mother'
  - **múgólì**      'a term of respect for addressing a woman'

# 7
# Noun Phrases

This chapter discusses noun phrases, describing their constituent order, as well as the possible substantive use of various NP constituents. This is followed by a discussion of the augment, which is structurally a phrase level clitic.

This chapter also includes phrases which embed NPs, including associative phrases. One special kind of associative phrase involves the "expressive nouns", which though structurally functioning as nouns, from an underlying point of view function as adjectives.

Other elements that embed noun phrases are **na** 'CNJ', **kandi iri** 'or', and **nga** 'like, as'. We also discuss a few idiomatic uses of NPs, as well as NPs involving **mwene** 'one having'. Finally we describe nouns of apposition and multiple embedding.

## 7.1 Noun phrase structure

### 7.1.1 Constituent structure of noun phrases

A noun phrase (NP) prototypically includes a noun as head, with other possible constituents occurring before and after it in a phrase, e.g. **yìbyó bítúmbwé bínúnù** 'those sweet fruits'. However the noun is very often "understood" (not explicitly stated) and then other elements of the phrase take over the head position of the phrase. In this case an augment is no longer attached to the noun (as the noun is not mentioned) but rather it is now positioned before a non-noun, e.g. **í̠=bínúnù** 'sweets' (augment underlined). Constituents of this type could be said to function "substantively" and occur very frequently in

Kifuliiru. Any NP constituent (except for the augment or **ngíìsì** 'each') may be used nominally and in this usage may constitute the "head" of the noun phrase (7.1.3).

Table 7.1 lays out the possible constituents of the noun phrase (NP) in their default order. (The examples in the table all have the **ba-** GNP from cl. 2.) With one exception (7.1.2 "Marked orders") the ordering of NP constituents is very strict. Thus if the NP includes a constituent from position 1, that constituent will precede whatever else occurs in the NP. Likewise, any constituent from position 2 will follow whatever may occur in position 1 and precede any of the elements listed in positions 3–8 and so forth for all the columns.

In addition, any given NP can include no more than one representative from any of the eight positions. Looking at position 1, for example, this means that if an NP includes an augment,[1] it cannot also have a demonstrative, or the determiner **ngíìsì** 'each'.

The NP as a unit can occur as the clause subject, or as one of the two possible objects. An NP can also occur as the complement of a locative phrase, the complement of an associative phrase, or the complement of a phrase headed by one of the conjunctives (**na**) (7.5.1), **kàndí ìrí** (7.5.2), **nga** (7.5.3), or **mwènê/bèènê** (7.6).

Table 7.1. Constituents of the noun phrase
(in default order of occurrence)

| Pos. 1 | Pos. 2 | Pos. 3 | Pos. 4 | Pos. 5 | Pos. 6 | Pos. 7 | Pos. 8 |
|---|---|---|---|---|---|---|---|
| Augment **á, í, ú** | Set selector **bààbò** 'fellows' **bàndì** 'other' | Noun **bándù** 'people', etc. | Assoc. pronoun **bààwè** 'yours' **bààgè** 'his'... | Adjective **bálà** 'tall', etc. | Quantifier **bómbì** 'both' **bìngì** 'many' **bóóshì** 'all' | Assoc. phrase **ba=hano** 'of here', etc. | Relative clause **ábàyíjà** 'who came', etc. |
| **ngíìsì** 'each' |  |  |  | Verbal adjectives **bátèèrèkê** 'lost ones', etc. | Numbers **bágùmà** 'some' **bàbìrì** 'two', etc. |  |  |

---

[1] The augment is a phrase level clitic which joins to whatever constituent follows it within the noun phrase.

## 7.1 Noun phrase structure

| Pos. 1 | Pos. 2 | Pos. 3 | Pos. 4 | Pos. 5 | Pos. 6 | Pos. 7 | Pos. 8 |
|---|---|---|---|---|---|---|---|
| Dem. **yábà** 'these.P' **bánò** 'these.P.C' **yàbó** 'those.N' **bàlyâ** 'those.R' **bàlíírà** 'those.D' | | | | | Question words **bàngâ** 'how many' **bákì** 'which kind' **báhì** 'which ones' | | |

### 7.1.2 Marked order of the NP

There is one exception to the strict word order of the NP (as presented in table 7.1) i.e. a reversal of the default order of elements in position 3 (noun) and position 4 (associative pronoun), so that the associative pronoun precedes the noun it modifies. This reordering communicates a type of contrastive focus on the associative pronoun. It defines the modified item as "one's *own* item" as opposed to any similar items owned by others.[2]

In (7.1) instead of the default order **ú=mwîmbù gwàgè** 'her harvest (lit., the harvest of her)', we see the marked order **ú=gwàgè mwîmbù**, lit., 'of her the harvest' but now with the meaning 'her own harvest (as opposed to the similar harvests of others)'. Because the associative pronoun in this case is now first in the NP, the augment attaches to it, whereas in the default order, it attached to the noun.

(7.1)   **Ngíísì mú-gùmà ‖ à-ná-gú-z-á   ú=gw-à-gè   mw-îmbù ‖**
          each   1-one     1-SQ-buy-CS-Fa   AU=3-A.M-1   1-harvest

   **à-ná-kìzí yàmì gúl-á ǀ mw-é=   shúùlì.**
   1-SQ-REP    IMMED buy-Fa 18-O.R+AU=  9+bull

'Each one ‖ sold her own share of the harvest ‖ and immediately bought from (the payment) ‖ a bull.' (522 020)

In (7.2) the associative pronoun **á=bààgè** 'his' is again in marked position, preceding instead of following the noun it modifies (**bándù** 'people'). In the

---

[2] It is interesting to note that when positioned between the augment and the noun, the associative pronoun is filling the position usually filled by the set selectors. In this position it also has the same function as the set selectors, i.e. it defines the following noun as belonging to a specific set, as opposed to other similar items.

same way, **í=byàgè** 'his' is in marked position, preceding **bínyámíìshwà** 'wild animals'. This marked order communicates that the people and wild animals were the man's own, thus not only communicating that they belonged to him, but setting them apart from what belonged to others.

(7.2) À-ná-b-á          n-á=       bà-à-gè     bá-ndù |    n-é=       by-à-gè
      1-SQ-become-Fa    CNJ-AU=    2-A.M-1     2-people    CNJ-AU=    8-A.M-1

  bí-nyámíìshwà.
  8-wild.animals

  'And he had his own share of people | and his own share of wild animals.'
  (110 033)

### 7.1.3 Noun phrase constituents used substantively

A constituent from almost any of the noun phrase positions can function as the head of the NP.[3] Although not structurally nouns, these elements are nevertheless functioning syntactically as the head of a NP. They are thus said to be used *substantively*.

Example (7.3) presents a "default" NP, where the head of the NP is structurally a noun **bándù** 'the people' (from position 3). It is marked by the augment **a=** to become **á=bándù**.

(7.3) Ìrí    á=bá-ndú        bá-ká-yúvw-á    ìyó        n-dúùlù ||
      when   AU=2-people     2-P2-hear-Fa    that.N+9   9-wail

  bà-ná-shólòlòk-èr-à        =hô.
  2-SQ-all.head-APL-Fa       =16

  'When people heard that wail || they all headed in that direction.' (54 013)

In (7.4), the head of the NP is the cl. 1 demonstrative **ùyô** 'that.N', referring to an implicit person who is not expressly stated. In this case the head of the NP is no longer structurally a noun. The NP consists of a demonstrative (from position 1), **ùyô** 'that.N one' and the relative clause (from position 8), **úshùbà nákìrìrì** 'who used to be the favorite wife'.

---

[3] Exceptions to this are the augment and **ngíìisì** 'each'.

## 7.1 Noun phrase structure

(7.4) **Ùyó**     **ú-shùbà**    **nákìrìrì** ||   **à-ná-b-à**           **y-é=**
that.N+1   S.R+1-PREV    favorite.wife    1-SQ-become-Fa    1-FOC=

**gá-kòròr-à.**
F2-be.less.favored-Fa

'That one who was the favorite wife || became the one who will be the less favorite.' (27 032)

In (7.5) **í=byàbò** 'their fellow' (from position 2) is the sole constituent of the NP. Notice that it is now marked by the augment.

(7.5) **Í=by-àbò**         **by-àná-gì-búúz-à:** ||  «**Ká-máró ká-kí** |
AU=8-SAME.SET    8-SQ-O9-ask-Fa          12-value   12-what

**k-ô=**          **hí-ít-í** |   **ú=kú-tù-hím-à?**»
12-O.R+2SG=   have-RS-Fi    AU=15-O1.PL-surpass-Fa

'The fellows asked him: || «What value | do you have | more than us?»' (37 005)

In (7.6) we focus attention on **wàgè** 'of his/hers', the final NP of the example. In this noun phrase, preceded by the conjunct **na** 'and/with', the associative pronoun **wàgè** 'of his/hers' (from position 4) functions as the sole element of the NP. Notice that it is now marked by the augment, which changes the conjunctive **na** to **no**.

(7.6) **Yàbó**       **bá-nyéré**   **ná=**   **yàbó**        **bá-tàbánà** ||   **bà-ná-síím-án-à** ||
THOSE.N+2   2-girls       CNJ=   THOSE.N+2    2-young.men      2-SQ-like-RCP-Fa

**ngíìsì mú-ndú** |   **n-ó=**    **w-à-gè**.
each    1-person       CNJ-AU=   1-A.M-1

'Those girls and those young men || liked each other || each person | with his/her fellow (girlfriend/boyfriend).' (01 006)

In (7.7) the adjective **múnììní** 'small' (from position 5) functions as the head of the NP. Once again, because there is no preceding element in the NP, the augment attaches to the adjective. Here there is also an associative phrase following, which modifies the head of the NP **ú=múnììni**.

(7.7) Ngíìsì      by-ó=   mù-tá-ká-gír-ír-á  |   ú=mú-nììnì      w-à=
      whatever   8-O.R=  2PL-NEG-P2-do-APL-Fa   AU=1-small.one  1-A.M=

   mú=  yà-bà...
   18=  these.P-2

'Whatever thing which you did not do | for the least important (person) from among these (people)...' (Mat 25:45)

Example (7.8) includes three noun phrases. The first, **úlì mú=yìlógézá íbìngì** 'the one who wants for himself much' consists only of a relative clause (from position 8). Each of the next two NPs consists solely or primarily of a quantifier (whose default position is position 6). The augment plus quantifier, **í=bìngì** 'many (things)' comprises the NP which serves as the object of the relative clause. The quantifier **byóshì** 'all (things)' (also belonging to position 6) is the sole element of its NP, which serves as object of the main clause.[4]

(7.8) <u>Ú-lì</u>     <u>mú=</u>    <u>yì-lóg-éz-á</u>      <u>í=bì-ngì</u>  ||  à-lí  mú=
      S.R+1-is  PROG=   RFX-want-APL-Fa   AU=8-much      1-is  PROG=

   bùl-à       by-óshì.
   lacking-Fa  8-all

'The one who wants for himself many (things) || is lacking everything.' (22 036)

In (7.9) the quantifying adjective **múgùmà** 'one' (from position 6) is the central element of the NP, modified by the associative phrase **wà=mú=yàbó bátàbànà** 'from among those young men'.[5]

(7.9) <u>Mú-gùmà</u>  w-à=    mú=   yàbó       bá-tàbánà  ||
      1-one       1-A.M=  18=   those.N+2  2-young.men

   à-ná-yì-tòn-éés-à      kwókùnò:...
   1-SQ-RFX-think-CS-Fa   like.this.P.C

'One of those young men || thought to himself like this:...' (06 021)

---

[4] The quantifiers such as **by-o-shi** (8-P.R-all), which include the pronominal previous reference (P.R) marker **o/e**, are never used with the augment.

[5] In this case the associative phrase includes a locative phrase, which in turn includes an embedded NP, **yàbó bátàbánà** 'those young men'.

## 7.1.4 Infinitives in noun phrases

The infinitive form commonly functions as a cl. 15 noun, with the typical **ku**-class concord. For this reason, the infinitive may fill position 3 of table 7.1, modified by preceding demonstrative(s) and following modifiers. If used as the subject NP, it triggers cl. 15 subject agreement in the following verb, as exemplified in (7.10).

(7.10)  Yù-**kú**      kú-mók-á      **kw**-à-wè  ||  **kú**-gáá-tùm-à |   í=kí-shókómà |
       this.P-15   15-bark-Fa   15-A.M-2SG     15-F2-cause-Fa   AU=7-cheetah

       kí-gá-yîjì       tù-téér-á        há-nò.
       7-F2-COMING    O1.PL-attack-Fa   16-here.P.C

'This barking of yours || is going to make | the cheetah | come and attack us here.' (45 006)

An entire clause may also be nominalized by the use of an infinitive verb. In such a case, the entire nominalized clause, including the complement, functions as the NP. An example is found in (7.11) the phrase **ú=kúkàndá á=mààvú gó=múgómbà** 'to make banana beer (lit., to press the beer of the banana)' is the subject of the sentence.[6] In this case **á=mààvú gó=múgómbà** 'beer of bananas' is the object of the verb of the nominalized clause.

(7.11)  **Ú=kú-kànd-á** |      **á=má-ávú**      g-ó=          mú-gómbà ||   gù-lì
       AU=15-press-Fa      AU=6-beer       6-A.M+AU=      3-banana        3-is

       mú-kòlwà |   ú-gù-lì   mú=    gír-w-á |   mú=    sìkù       zì-shàtù.
       3-work        S.R-3-is   PROG=   do-PS-Fa    18=    10+days    10-three

'To press | beer of bananas || is work | which is done | in three days.' (411 008)

## 7.2 Augments

Here we discuss first the structure of the augment (AU) and then its function.

### 7.2.1 Augment[7] structure

The augment in Kifuliiru consists of a single H-tone vowel which is a phonological copy of the GNP vowel of the noun with which it agrees. The augment

---

    [6]Here, because the subject agreement of a copula is triggered not by what precedes, but by the noun class of the complement, the verb does not agree with the infinitive in this particular case.

    [7]In the literature the augment is commonly referred to as the "pre-prefix". This name reflects one of its formal characteristics: it precedes the gender-number prefix of a noun. However,

thus takes one of three shapes: **ú**, **í**, or **á**. Looking at table 7.2, we see that for cl. 1 the augment **ú** is identical to the vowel of the GNP **mú-**, for cl. 2 the augment **á** is identical to the vowel of the GNP **bá-**, and for cl. 4 the augment **í** is identical to the vowel of the GNP **mí-**. Note that cl. 1a has no augment and that the augment for cl. 9/10, in which there is synchronically no vowel in the GNP, is **i**.

Table 7.2. Augment form relative to noun class

| Cl. | AU | GNP | Root | Surface | Gloss |
|---|---|---|---|---|---|
| 1 | ú= | mú- | -ndù | ú=múndù | 'person' |
| 1a | --- | --- | dáàtà | dáàtà | 'father' |
| 2 | á= | bá- | -ndù | á=bándù | 'people' |
| 3 | ú= | mú- | -kóndè | ú=múkóndè | 'banana' |
| 4 | í= | mí- | -kóndè | í=míkóndè | 'bananas' |
| 5 | í= | í- | -búyè | í=íbúyè | 'word' |
| 6 | á= | má- | -búyè | á=mábúyè | 'words' |
| 7 | í= | kí- | -hándò | í=kíhándò | 'sore' |
| 8 | í= | bí- | -hándò | í=bíhándò | 'sores' |
| 9 | í= | N- | -gòkò | i=ngòkò | 'chicken' |
| 10 | í= | N- | -gòkò | í=ngòkò | 'chickens' |
| 11 | ú= | lú- | -lìmì | ú=lúlīmì | 'tongue' |
| 12 | á= | ká- | -fùlò | á=káfūlò | 'turtle' |
| 13 | ú= | tú- | -fùlò | ú=túfūlò | 'turtles' |
| 14 | ú= | bú- | -lâ | ú=búlâ | 'intestine' |
| 15 | ú= | kú- | -twìrì | ú=kútwīrì | 'ear' |
| 16 | á= | há- | -ndù | á=hándù | 'place' |
| 19 | í= | hí- | nyûmbà | í=hínyûmbà | 'small house' |

Cl. 5 presents an interesting situation where the augment is identical in shape to the GNP,[8] and thus it becomes difficult to tell in isolation whether or not an augment is present. As can be seen in the form **í=í-gámbò** (AU=5-word) the cl. 5 augment **í** takes the identical shape as the cl. 5 GNP **í**.

Evidence that the GNP for the word **ígámbò** 'word' is **í** is presented in (7.12). Note that there is no augment on the cl. 2 noun **bákàzì** 'women' or the cl. 8 noun **bíhíndà** 'storehouses' when they follow the demonstrative. When **ígámbò** 'word' follows the demonstrative **yìryó** 'that.N' the GNP **í-** remains, although the augment **í** is no longer present.

---

"pre-prefix" is not an accurate name, at least not for Kifuliiru, as the augment is not a prefix, but rather a clitic functioning at the phrase level.

[8] With the exception of one word, **í=rìínò** 'tooth', where the cl. 5 prefix is **lí-** rather than **í-**.

## 7.2 Augments

(7.12) a. **yàbó**     **bá-kàzì**     'those women'
       those.N+2    2-woman

    b. **yìbyó**     **bí-híndà**     'those storehouses'
       that.N+8    8-storehouse

    c. **yìryó**     **í-gámbò**     'that word'
       that.n+5    5-word

Structurally speaking, the most significant fact about the augment in Kifuliiru is that it is not a prefix (or pre-prefix); rather it is a *clitic*. The augment, when it occurs, is always the initial element in an NP and is cliticized to the first word in the NP. This is seen in (7.13a) where the augment is attached to the left of **bìngì** 'many'. In (7.13b), **bìngì** no longer holds the first position in the NP and the augment **í** shifts to what is now the first word, **bíndù** 'things'. When the set selector **bìndì** 'other' is added to the front of the noun phrase (7.13c), the augment **í** is no longer attached to **bíndù** 'things', but shifts to what is now the first word of the phrase, the demonstrative **bìndì** 'other'.

(7.13) a.              **í̱=bì-ngì**            'many (things)'
                  AU=8-many

    b. **í̱=bí-ndú**     **bì-ngì**            'many things'
       AU=8-thing    8-many

    c. **í̱=bì-ndì**      **bí-ndú bì-ngì**    'many other things'
       AU=8-other     8-thing 8-many

### 7.2.2 Augment function

The augment in Kifuliiru denotes specific *referentiality*, marking a nominal lexical item as a "real world referent" in time and space, or at least in the mind of the speaker. A noun without an augment, on the other hand, refers either to an empty set of referents, or refers generally to "any and all" of the items found in that set.

Example (7.14) relates how a man married a second wife after accumulating much wealth. Since the noun phrase **í=bíndú bìngì** 'many things' refers to the definite, concrete wealth that the man possessed, the augment clitic **í** is positioned at the beginning of the phrase. In the same way the augment **ú** occurs as the at the front of the phrase **ú=múkàzì wá=kàbìrì** 'a second woman', since she is also a real referent in time and space. Both the wealth the man now owned, and the woman he married, are presented as "real" things.

(7.14) Ìrí      á-ká-b-à          à-kòlí         gw-èt-í        í̱=bí-ndú     bì-ngì |
      when    1-P2-become-Fa   1-is.NEWLY    have-RS-Fi     AU=8-thing   8-many

   à-ná-yâng-à       ú̱=mú-kàzì        w-á=       kàbìrì.
   1-SQ-marry-Fa    AU=1-woman      1-A.M=     second

'When he was now having much wealth | he married a second woman.'
(27 003)

The presence of the augment in these noun phrases is representative of the vast majority of noun phrases that occur throughout the language.

### 7.2.2.2.1 Contexts where the augment is found

#### 7.2.2.1.1 Augment marks NPs occurring as clause subject

For all statements (including even the vast majority of proverbs) the augment is found marking any subject noun occurring at the beginning of the clause. Example (7.15) is a Kifuliiru proverb, where a predication of a general nature is laid out. In this case, the clause subject **í̱=kírēmà** 'lame person' takes the augment, even though it does not refer to a particular real-world referent. Note that in this case, the object, **bwēngè** 'intellect' has no augment.

(7.15) I̱=kí-rēmà ‖        kì-tà-∅-búl-á          bw-ēngè.
      AU=7-lame.person    7-NEG-TL-lack-Fa      14-intellect

'A lame person ‖ does not lack intellect.'

The fact that the augment marks the sentence subject can be confirmed by a studying the corpus of over 1,000 Kifuliiru proverbs. Though these proverbs are by definition general in nature, the clause subject involves an augment or equivalent in the overwhelming majority of cases.

#### 7.2.2.1.2 Augment on infinitives

The augment nearly always occurs on the cl. 15 infinitive. Thus in (7.16) the infinitive **ú̱=kúyīmbà** 'to sing' is the complement in the verb phrase **kànátòndéézá ú̱=kúyīmbà** 'and it began to sing', and it takes the augment.

(7.16) Yàkó     ká-fùló |    kà-ná-tòndééz-á |    ú̱=kú-yìmb-à     kwókùnò:...
      that.N+12  12-turtle   12-SQ-begin-Fa      AU=15-sing-Fa    ‹quote.marked›

'That.N turtle | began | to sing in this way:....' (05 008)

### 7.2.2.2 Contexts where the augment is precluded

Since the augment communicates that the noun has a specific "real world referent", there are several forms where that "referentiality" is already implied. To mark the augment in those forms becomes redundant. Such cases are now presented below.

(1) The *five demonstrative sets*, exemplified by the cl. 2 representatives **bánò** 'this.P.C', **yábà** 'this.P', **yàbô** 'this.N', **bàlyâ** 'this.R', and **bàlíírà** 'this.D', together with the emphatic forms of each demonstrative, e.g. **báábànô, báàbà, báàbô, báábàlyâ**, and **báábàlìirà**, do not themselves take the augment.[9] In addition, they preclude the use of the augment on a following element of the noun phrase. This is seen in (7.17), where none of the words in the noun phrase beginning with the demonstrative **bánò** 'these.P.C' takes the augment. The "referentiality" in the real world is already implied by the demonstrative **bánò** 'these.P.C'.

(7.17) Ni-ê-he ‖   n-gá-sìg-à      n-à-bwír-á     bà-nó        bá-kàzì
      1SG-CTR.P   1-P2-LEAVE-Fa   1SG-P1-tell-Fa  2-these.P.C  2-women

  bà-à-nî |   kwó=   bà-Ø-kálâng-é |   á=má-bènyè.
  2-A.M-1SG   CMP=   2-SBV-fry-Fe      AU=6-donuts

  'ME ‖ I left word with these women of mine | that they fry | donuts.' (01 005)

(2) The *determiner* **ngíìsì** 'each/every' precludes the use of the augment, as is seen in (7.18), where in **ngíìsì múnyérè** 'every girl' **ngíìsì** does not take the augment, nor does the following noun, **múnyérè**. The "referentiality" is already implied by the determiner **ngíìsì** 'each/every'.

(7.18) Ùyó       mú-tàbánà ‖    à-ná-hééréz-à   ngíìsì   mù-nyéré |
      that.N+1   1-young.man    1-SQ-give-Fa    each     1-girl

  á=ká-nyúnì.
  AU=12-bird

  'That young man ‖ gave each girl | a bird.' (617 032)

(3) *Some quantifiers*, i.e. **bóóshì** 'all', **bómbì** 'both', and **bágùmà** 'some', also preclude the use of the augment, in that they are all inherently referential. This is exemplified in (7.19), where **bóóshì** 'all' lacks the augment.

---

[9] Some of these can be analyzed as including a lexicalized instance of the augment in their structure, but it is not synchronically interpreted as an augment. See the formulas for formation of the demonstratives in (8.1.6.1).

(7.19) ...mú=kúbá   bó-ó-shí ‖   bá-àlí kómbèr-íín-í  |   mú=
       because     2-all         2-P3   be.together-RS-Fi   IN.STATE=

kú-rágír-á | yìzó      n-gáàvù zà-à-bò.
15-graze-Fa  those.N+10  10-cows  10-A.M-2

'...because all of them ‖ were together | in grazing | those cows of theirs.'
(02 006)

(4) *Nouns which follow one of the locative markers* **há, kú, mú, í,** *and* **í=wa** *do not take the augment.* The locative marker already refers to something at a particular location, and thus to mark the noun by an augment becomes redundant. In (7.20) the locative phrase **há=lwījì** 'at the river' exemplifies this.

(7.20) Ìrí   bá-ká-hík-à   yà-hó       há=   lw-ījì ‖   bà-ná-shàmát-à
       When  2-P2-arrive-Fa there.N-16  16=   11-river   2-SQ-scoop.up-Fa

á=mī-ījì.
AU=6-water

'When they arrived there at the river ‖ they scooped up water.' (409 017)

It should be noted however, that nouns following **í=mwa** or **í=mûndà** 'place of' usually *do* occur with an augment, e.g. **í=mûndà ú=mwānà àgéndà** 'the place where the child went'. We would argue here that **í=mwa** or **í=mûndà** each underlyingly include a morpheme (in the case of **mu=nda**, two morphemes) which intervene between the locative marker and the following noun. Apparently **í=wa**, though it may have originally consisted of the cl. 23 locative followed by an associative marker, has been reinterpreted as a single locative morpheme, since the nouns which follow it do take the augment.

(5) *None of the Kifuliiru cl. 1a nouns can take an augment.* This is common in Bantu languages which use the augment and goes all the way back to Proto-Bantu, where a noun cl. 1a (with no augment) has been reconstructed. The lack of augment in cl. 1a nouns in Kifuliiru is exemplified in (7.21), where neither cl. 1a **máàwé** 'my mother' nor its cl. 2 plural form **bamáàwé** 'our mothers' can take an augment. By contrast, the augment can be used with cl. 1 nouns, as in **ú=múkòzì** 'servant' and its cl. 2 plural **á=bákòzì** 'servants'.

## 7.2 Augments

(7.21)  Cl.  |  | Cl. |
--- | --- | --- | ---
 | 1a | **máàwé** | 2 | **bá-máàwé**
 |  | 1a+my.mother |  | 2-our.mothers
cf. | 1 | **ú=mú-kòzì** | 2 | **á=bá-kòzì**
 |  | AU=1-servant |  | AU=2-servant

(6) In Kifuliiru there are *a few special vocabulary items* which can be said to have inherently specific reference and may be used almost as a proper name (cl. 1a noun). One is the cl. 1/2 noun **mwámì** 'king'. In the Kifuliiru culture, there is only one king (at any given time) and he is very well known by everyone. Although the Bafuliiru kings all had proper names, those names were not normally used when referring to the king, except when distinguishing one king from another. Thus in (7.22) we see the noun **mwámì** 'king', not **ú**=mwàmì.

(7.22) **Mw-àmí** | **à-ná-hàmágál-à á=bá-tûngwà** || **gírá**
1-king  1-SQ-call-Fa  AU=2-counselors  so.that

**bà-Ø-bà-hámbùùl-è.**
2-SBV-O2-settle.argument-Fe

'And king | called the counselors || so that they might settle their argument.' (17 008)

(7) *Nouns of direct address* do not take the augment, as can be seen in (7.23), where **é**=**múnyérè** 'O girl' does not include the augment.

(7.23) «**É**= **mú-nyérè** || **n-à-kú-síìm-à** || **n-àmú**= **kú-yáng-à**.»
O=  1-girl  1SG-P1-O2.SG-like-Fa  1SG-F1=  O2-marry-Fa

'O girl || I like you || I am about to marry you.' (112 010)

(8) When a noun is *modified by a quantifier*, it is possible to omit the augment. Thus example (7.24) shows the noun **bándù** 'people' without the augment, as the specificity of the referents is implied by the number. It is more common however, for a noun modified by a number to have the augment.

(7.24) **Mbú**= **bà-Ø-kébáánúk-è** **kwókùnò** || **bá-ndú**
As.soon.as=  2-SBV-turn.around-Fe  like.this.P.C  2-people

**má-kùmì** **gá-nà** | **bà-hík-à.**
6-tens  6-four  2+P1-arrive-Fa

'When they turned around like this || forty people | arrived.' (201 093)

(9) The augment does not appear on a predicational noun or substantive adjective which follows a copula. This is true whether the copula is positive, such as **àlí mútàbánà** 'he is a boy' and **àkòlà músósì** 'he is now a man' or negative, such as **ndááyè músósì** 'there is no man'. In a presentational context, where the copula has a locative subject, the augment is often (but not always) used on the noun: **há àlí rììrí ú̲=mútàbánà múgúmà** 'there was a certain boy'.

## 7.3 Associative phrases

Associative phrases, as seen in (7.25), are a possible constituent of noun phrases. The associative phrase functions as a modifier of the noun in the NP of which it is a part. An associative phrase may be used substantively as the head of a noun phrase.

### 7.3.1 Associative phrase structures

The associative phrase acts as a modifier of the preceding noun and consists of associative marker (A.M) + NP, or A.M + locative phrase. In each case the associative phrase is defined by, and begins with, an associative marker (A.M), which consists of an associative prefix[10] followed by -**a**. For example, for the cl. 1 A.M, this consists of the cl. 1 associative prefix **u**- followed by -**a**, forming the clitic **wa**. The A.M has polar tone, which is to say that it has H tone preceding a word which has initial L tone, or L tone preceding a word which has initial H tone.

(7.25) Typical associative phrase constructions

| | A.M followed by | Example | Gloss |
|---|---|---|---|
| a. | Noun phrase | yîshè w̲á=yùgwó mújókà | 'the father of that.N snake' |
| b. | Associative pronoun[†] | múgálá w̲àgè | 'his/her son' |
| c. | Ordinal number | ú=múkàzì w̲á=kàbìrì | 'the second wife' |
| d. | Locative demonstrative | ú=múkwì w̲á=hànò | 'the son-in-law of here' |
| e. | Locative phrase | ú=múnyéré w̲à=mú=kànó kāāyà | 'the girl of, this village' |

[†]In the case of an associative pronoun, the associative marker is joined to the following pronominal element to form a single word. This word has a different position in the NP (see table 7.1 in this chapter) than

---

[10]The GNP used with the A.M is the same as the one that is used for the demonstratives (7.1.3.1).

*7.3 Associative phrases*

the associative phrases which are still analytic and have not been combined into a single word.

### 7.3.2 Associative phrase functions

#### 7.3.2.1 *Associating two items together*

Associative phrases in Kifuliiru "associate" one noun (phrase) with another. The semantic categories expressed by this structure include quite a broad range of meanings, including possession, description, relation, location, provenance, etc.

In (7.26) the associative phrase **wé=bíndú byàgè** 'of the things of him', indicates the association of the supervisor with the things he supervises. The official is called the supervisor "of his things".

(7.26) Ù-lyá      mú-gìngì ‖ à-ná-hàmágál-à  ú=mw-ímángízí |  w-é=
       1-that.R   1-official   1-SQ-call-Fa    AU=1-supervisor  1-A.M=

   **bí-ndú     by-à-gè**.
   8-things    8-A.M-1

'That official ‖ called the supervisor | of his property (lit., the things of him).' (514 016 )

In (7.27) the A.M **ba** in the phrase **bà=mú=yàkó kāāyà** associates the noun **á=bándù** 'people' with a location, expressed by the locative phrase **mú yàkó kààyà** 'within the bounds of that.N village'.

(7.27) Á=bá-ndú       b-à=     mú=    yàkó     kā-āyà ‖  bà-ná-kìzí
       AU=2-people   2-A.M=   18=    that.N+12  12-village  2-SQ-REP

   **mú-sìmbáh-à**.
   O1-obey-Fa

'The people of that village ‖ continuously obeyed him.' (40 006)

By using an associative phrase, one can use a noun to describe another noun. In (7.28) the associative phrase **lwà=búlyâlyà** 'of deceit (deceitful)' describes the abstract noun **Ú=rúkùndò** 'love' as deceitful, by using an associative phrase with another abstract noun, "deceitfulness", as its complement.

(7.28) Ú=rú-kùndò    lw-à-gè    í=mw-à-nì |   lù-lì    lw-à=      bú-lyâlyà.
       AU=11-love    11-A.M-1   23=CON-A.M-1  11-is    11-A.M=    14-deceit

'His love for me | is deceitful.' (54 024)

In (7.29) the associative phrase **kyà=búshìgì** 'of night' modifies the noun **í=kyànyà** 'time'.

(7.29) <u>í=ky-ànyà</u>  <u>ky-à=</u>  <u>bú-shìgì</u> ||  ùyó  mú-ndù |  á-àlì  rì-ìr-ì
   AU=7-time  7-A.M=  14-night  that.N+1  1-person  1-P3  is-RS-Fi

  mú=  ny-ûmbà.
  18=  9-house

'At the time of night || that person | was in the house.' (45 020)

### 7.3.2.2 Expressive nouns

In Kifuliiru there is a large, unbounded set of "expressive"[11] nouns, which are followed by an associative phrase. In these cases the default ordering of the associative phrase is skewed, so that instead saying "the man of peace" where "of peace" is attributed to "man", this type of construction turns it around to say "the peaceable one of a man". By switching the normal order and positioning the descriptive word before (not after) the noun, special focus is placed on the "expressive" noun. For example, in the first row of (7.30), the word **kíhàgàngè** 'a large, strong one' is followed by the associative phrase **kyó=múshosi** 'of a man' and functions to describe a man who is very large and strong.

Although the function of these words resembles that of adjectives, there are three important differences:
- Adjectives are a closed set, limited to about thirty-eight items, while expressive nouns are an open-ended set.
- Adjectives have very generic meanings, like -**hámù** 'large', -**nììnî** 'small', -**núnù** 'sweet', -**lúlù** 'bitter', while most expressive nouns have extremely specific meanings.
- Adjectives follow the noun being described. These expressive nouns, by contrast, precede the noun being described.

These expressive nouns tend to present "extreme" ideas and involve two main categories.

1) One category includes large, strong, or numerous things, such as people with strong bodies, very rich people, large houses, large fields, large rivers and roads, huge numbers of things, etc.

2) The other main category includes pejorative items, such as paths that are not traveled, fierce people, stubborn people, bad people who strike fear in others, adulterers, abnormally fat people, clever deceivers, foolish children, unsettled people, lazy people, ones who pick fights, loose women, extremely

---

[11] Instead of "expressive", we could also use the words "vivid" or "extreme".

## 7.3 Associative phrases

thin people, people who talk too much, men who only pretend that they want to marry, women who finish things off, weak ones who are sick many days, etc.

In (7.30) we provide a small sample of the many forms of this type found in the language. As can be seen in the following list, the class of the first noun always triggers agreement on the associative marker. Thus in the first row of (7.30) we see that the cl. 7 **kí** prefix on **kíhàgàngè** matches the cl. 7 prefix **ki** (palatalized before the vowel) on the A.M **kyó**.

(7.30) Examples of expressive nouns defined by associative phrases

| | Cl. | Form | Gloss |
|---|---|---|---|
| | | Long or large | |
| a. | 7 | **kíhàgàngè kyó=múshosi**<br>large.strong.one A.M=man | 'a large, strong man' |
| b. | 12 | **kányábúngàkà ké=bíndù**<br>huge.number A.M=things | 'a huge number of things' |
| c. | 14 | **búrúrúmá bwà=ngáàvù**<br>very.large.thing A.M=cow | 'a very large, fat cow' |
| | | Fierce | |
| d. | 1a | **bítàzé wà=nyámíìshwà**<br>clever.wild.animal A.M=wild animal | 'a fierce animal avoiding hunters' |
| e. | 1a | **máháàmà wà=múshósì**<br>hyena A.M=man | 'a fierce man' |
| | | Clever | |
| f. | 7 | **kíbíndà kyà=múshosi**<br>coveter A.M=man | 'a clever, covetous man' |
| g. | 9 | **ngéngyá yà=múndù**<br>clever.one A.M=man | 'a clever one not easily tricked' |
| | | Weak | |
| h. | 1a | **ndágáhàlàalà wó=múshósì**<br>about.to.die A.M=person | 'a person near death' |
| i. | 3 | **múbú gwà=múshósì**<br>mosquito A.M=man | 'man who is skinny and weak' |

|     | Cl. | Form | Gloss |
|---|---|---|---|
| j. | 11 | **lúgàtà lwà=múndù**<br>sickness.that.stays A.M=person | 'person who is sick many days' |

Foolish

|     | Cl. | Form | Gloss |
|---|---|---|---|
| k. | 1a | **mwólérá wó=múkàzì**<br>speaking.much.and.lying A.M=woman | 'jabbering woman' |
| l. | 19 | **híyàngá-yàngá hyá=mwānà**<br>lazy/without.benefit A.M=child | 'a lazy, unsettled young person' |
| m. | 1a | **ngómbékwá wà=múkàzì**<br>lazy.one.who.doesn't.work A.M=woman | 'a lazy woman' |
| n. | 7 | **kìgámbání kyó=múkàzì**<br>backbiter A.M=woman | 'a woman who backbites others' |
| o. | 19 | **hírwírwí hyà=mútwâlì**<br>small.intellect A.M=ruler | 'a foolish ruler who doesn't know his job' |

Adultery

|     | Cl. | Form | Gloss |
|---|---|---|---|
| p. | 1a | **nápéèyà wà=múkàzì**<br>disobedient/shameless A.M=woman | 'a shameless woman' |
| q. | 11 | **lúpépyá lwà=múshósì**<br>indiscriminant.adulterer A.M=man | 'a man sleeping with any woman' |

Narrow

|     | Cl. | Form | Gloss |
|---|---|---|---|
| r. | 3 | **múshòdòkó gwà=njírà**<br>small.path.off.big.one A.M=path | 'a small isolated path' |
| s. | 3 | **músheshero gwà=njírà**<br>narrow.thing.that.squeezes A.M=path | 'a narrow path not known' |

## 7.3.3 Frozen associative structure with special focus

### 7.3.3.1 *Form*

There is an idiomatic construction consisting of a normal associative construction (GNP + **a**-) followed by **í=mwà** and then the associative complement. This special construction is exemplified by the phrase **ú=bwàtó bwé=mwá=Símòònì** 'the boat belonging (particularly) to Simon' and conveys special *focus*, i.e. the boat is associated with Simon (and not another).

*7.3 Associative phrases*

The structure begins with **bwa-**, agreeing with the antecedent **ú=bwàtó** 'boat' and then followed by the cl. 23 **í-**, the cl. 18 **mú**, and finally another associative marker **-a**. After vowel coalescence, the resulting surface form is seen in (7.31).

(7.31)

|  | Antecedent | Cl. mkr. | A.M | Cl. 23 | Cl. 18 | A.M | Complement |
|---|---|---|---|---|---|---|---|
| Underlying | **bú**-**àtó**<br>14-boat | **bu**<br>14 | **a**=<br>A.M= | **í**=<br>23= | **mú**=<br>18= | **a**<br>A.M | **Símòònì**<br>Simon |
| Labialization and V elision | **bw**-**àtó**<br>14-boat | **bw**<br>14 | **é**=<br>A.M+23= | | **mw-á**=<br>18+A.M= | | **Símòònì**<br>Simon |
| Free gloss | the boat belonging to Simon | | | | | | |

The complement in this special construction with the locative marker **í=mwá** (8.1.2.8) is always personal. The complement can take the form of a noun, such as the proper name **Yónà** 'Jonah', seen in (7.32a) or it may be a pronominal formative such as the first-person singular **-ní** 'I, me' in the form **bé=mwànî** '(cl. 2) of mine' seen in (7.32b). The complement can also be compound, including the formative **-vyàlà** 'in-laws', as in (7.32c) where the cl. 2 associative pronoun **-àbò** combines with **-vyàlà**.

(7.32)

| | Antecedent | Idiomatic form | | Gloss |
|---|---|---|---|---|
| a. | **kyé-kì-ryá**<br>E-7-that.R | **ky-é**=<br>7-A.M+23= | **mw-á=Yōnà**<br>18-A.M=Jonah | 'that.R very one (sign) belonging to Jonah' |
| b. | **á=bà-ànà**<br>AU=2-child | **b-é**=<br>2-A.M+23= | **mw-à-nî**<br>18-A.M-1SG | 'children belonging to me (not another)' |
| c. | **ú=mú-kòlwà**<br>AU=3-work | **gw-é**=<br>3-A.M+23= | **mw-à-bò-vyàlà**<br>18-A.M-2-in.law | 'work belonging to in-laws (not another)' |

*7.3.3.2 Function: Contrastive possession*

This construction means 'associated with the personal referent X (in focused contrast to others)'. It highlights the fact that there could be an alternative to the personal referent who is mentioned.

In (7.33) a rabbit is asked about the parentage of certain children. The rabbit's answer, employing the locative construction **í=mwa**, in the phrase **bé=mwànî** 'the ones of me (focus)', marks the fact that the children belong "to me" rather than to anyone else. The unmarked form, by contrast, would be **yàbá bàlí bààná bàànî** 'these are my children'.

(7.33) **Lw-àná-mú-shùvy-à:** ‖ «**Yà-bá bà-ánà** ‖ **bà-lì b-é=**
     11-SQ-O1-answer-Fa     these-2  2-children  2-are  2-A.M+23=

**mw-à-nî.»**
belonging-A.M-1SG

'And it answered him: ‖ «These children ‖ are mine (focus).»' (46 007-008)

In (7.34) **gùlyâ** 'that' is followed by the associative phrase **gwé=mwàgè** 'of his (in contrast to that of others)'. The inclusion of the locative marker **í=mwa** in this associative phrase clearly indicates that there is a focused contrast between these clothes and any clothes belonging to others.

(7.34) **Gù-lyá gw-é= mw-à-gè** ‖ **ná-yè** | **à-ná-gù-kàbúl-ír-à** |
     3-that.R  3-A.M+23=  belonging-A.M-1  ADD.P-1  1-SQ-O3-threw-APL-Fa

**yà-hó** | **í= rú-tàndà.**
there.N-16  23=  11-shelf.above.fire

'That (clothing) of his (focus) ‖ and he also | he threw it | there | at the drying place above the fire.' (302 056)

The use of **í=mwa** to mark the contrast to alternatives depends on the speech context. As a consequence, virtually the same associative phrase can occur in the same sentence, once with **í=mwa** and once without it, depending on whether the contrast with alternative referents is relevant.

Thus in (7.35) the first associative construction **bààgè** 'of him' occurs without the LM (locative marker) head **í=mwa**. The context involves the writer's claim that in the past his readers were not "people of him" (i.e. of God). In this case there is not a contrast with people of somebody else. However in the second associative construction **bé=mwàgè**, **í=mwa** is included, to mark the contrast between the state just mentioned (i.e. not being his people) and the present state (i.e. being his people).

(7.35) **Yà-hó kéèrà** ‖ **mù-tá-àli rì-ìr-ì bá-ndú bà-à-gè** ‖
     there.N-16  past  2PL-NEG-P3  is-RS-Fi  2-people  2-A.M-1

**hálìkò bú-nò** ‖ **mù-kòlà b-é= mw-à-gè.**
but  14-now.P.C  2PL-are.NEWLY  2-A.M+23=  belonging-A.M-1

'There in the past ‖ you were not his people ‖ but now ‖ you belong to him (focus).' (1Pe 2:10)

## 7.4 Associative pronouns

As seen in table 7.1, the associative pronoun fills position 4 in the default order of noun phrase constituents. The associative pronoun is formed from the GNP of the first referent, followed by the associative marker (A.M) -**a** and the GNP of the second referent, followed by the previous reference (P.R) morpheme **e** / **o**. This form does not really have a "root" per se; however to show how the pieces fit together, we have defined the A.M as the root, as that is what distinguishes the associative pronouns from other similar forms. The formula then would be as follows:

[GNP [A.M] GNP] P.R

| (7.36) | | Cl. 1 | Cl. 4 | Cl. 7 | Cl. 12 |
|---|---|---|---|---|---|
| | UF | [ú [a] bà] o] | [í [a] bà] o] | [ki [a] bà] o] | [ka [a] bà] o] |
| | SF | wàbò | yàbò | kyàbò | kààbò |
| | | 'their' | 'their' | 'their' | 'their' |

Because the GNP occurs twice in the formula, the possibilities fill a chart that is roughly 18 by 22. For brevity, we provide only representative samples in (7.37), in which the GNP in final position is from cl. 1, 4, 7, and 12.

The GNPs found both in initial and final position in the associative pronouns are generally of the standard pronominal form for their classes. There is an exception to this in the case of the final-position GNP used for the first- and second-person plural forms. Rather than the basic **tu** '1PL' and **mu** '2PL', the forms instead both have an initial **i**, i.e. -**ìtù** '1PL' and -**ìnyù** '2PL'. The initial **i** coalesces with the associative marker, yielding forms like the cl. 1 **wìtù** 'our' and the cl. 8 **bììnyù** 'your (PL)'.

(7.37) Associative pronouns for selected noun classes

| GNP | Cl. 1 | Cl. 4 | Cl. 7 | Cl. 12 |
|---|---|---|---|---|
| 1 | wàgè | wáyò | wákyò | wákò |
| 2 | bààgè | bááyò | báákyò | báákò |
| 3 | gwàgè | gwáyò | gwákyò | gwákò |
| 4 | yàgè | yáyò | yákyò | yákò |
| 5 | lyàgè | lyáyò | lyákyò | lyákò |
| 6 | gààgè | gááyò | gáákyò | gáákò |
| 7 | kyàgè | kyáyò | kyákyò | kyákò |
| 8 | byàgè | byáyò | byákyò | byákò |
| 9 | yàgè | yáyò | yákyò | yákò |

| GNP | Cl. 1 | Cl. 4 | Cl. 7 | Cl. 12 |
|---|---|---|---|---|
| 10 | zààgè | zááyò | záákyò | zaákò |
| 11 | lwàgè | lwáyò | lwákyò | lwákò |
| 12 | kaàgè | kááyò | káákyò | káákò |
| 13 | twàgè | twáyò | twákyò | twákò |
| 14 | bwàgè | bwáyò | bwákyò | bwákò |
| 15 | kwàgè | kwáyò | kwákyò | kwákò |
| 16 | hààgè | hā̄āyò | háákyò | háákò |
| 18 | mwàgè | mwáyò | mwákyò | mwákò |
| 19 | hyàgè | hyáyò | hyákyò | hyákò |

The associative pronouns essentially pronominalize an associative phrase. Instead of a full noun following the A.M, there is a pronominal element. However, these are lexicalized as single words, as shown in (7.36) and (7.37). As single-word lexical items, they no longer function in the noun phrase in the same position as the more complex associative phrase (position 7 in table 7.1) but instead are placed immediately following the noun, and preceding the adjective modifier, quantifier, etc. (position 4). For example, the numeral follows the associative pronoun in: **á=bákàzì bààgè bàshàtù** 'his three women'.

Thus the associative pronoun, though semantically equivalent to an associative phrase, is not syntactically equivalent to such a phrase. This is substantiated by the fact that a single NP may include both an associative pronoun and an associative phrase: **ámálíbú gààgè gà=ngíìsì mwákà** 'his troubles of every year'.

### 7.5 Conjunctives used with noun phrases

There is a very limited number of conjunctive elements which embed noun phrases. These elements are discussed here.

### 7.5.1 Conjunctive *na*

The conjunctive clitic **na** basically *conjoins* two items. However, this conjunctive carries a much broader range of meanings than the English conjunction "and". Below we reduce these to coordination, addition, reciprocity, the agent of a passive construction, instrumental, and accompaniment (of various types). What all of these meanings have in common is the element of conjunction. English translations include 'and', 'also', 'with', 'by', etc., depending on the context. Payne (1997:339) states that such sameness or similarity of morphological shape "among the instrumental, comitative, and coordinating operators is extremely common in the world's languages". In all of our

## 7.5 Conjunctives used with noun phrases

texts, coordinate NPs never involve embedding of associative phrases or relative clauses.

### 7.5.1.1 Coordinated noun phrases

Kifuliiru NPs can be coordinated with **na** 'CNJ'. In (7.38) there are four NPs, and **na** is used preceding each one of them (in contrast to English, where the first words would be separated by commas, with only the last word marked by 'and').

(7.38) À-ná-láálík-à | á=bá-túúlání kúgùmà <u>n-á</u>= bá-gìngì |
1-SQ-invite-Fa AU=2-neighbors together CNJ-AU= 2-attendants

<u>n-á</u>= bà-àmì | <u>n-á</u>= bá-gùndà í-kùmì.
CNJ-AU= 2-kings CNJ-AU= 2-common.people 5-ten

'And he invited | the neighbors together with courtiers | and kings | and 10 common people.' (34 003)

Again in (7.39) **na** 'CNJ' occurs preceding each additional noun.

(7.39) Mú-ndú mú-gùmà || á-àlì tùùz-ír-í í=n-gáávù || <u>n-á</u>=
1-person 1-one 1-P3 keep-RS-Fi AU=9-cow CNJ-AU=

ká-bwâ || <u>n-é</u>= m-bènè || <u>n-é</u>= n-yáàbù || <u>nà</u>=
12-dog CNJ-AU= 9-goat CNJ-AU= 9-cat CNJ=

nálúhàzè.
rooster

'One man || was keeping a cow || and a dog || and a goat || and a cat || and a rooster.' (37 002)

### 7.5.1.2 Additive noun phrases

The additive use of **na** implies that something is being added to what is already there. In (7.40) **na** adds **á=bàndì bóóshí á=bàbàkùlíírì** 'all others who surpass them in status' to others mentioned earlier that are also to be obeyed.

(7.40) Bà-Ø-kízí   sìmbáh-à ‖ ná=   bà-ndì    bó-ó-shí |
      2-SBV-REP   obey-Fa     CNJ+AU= 2-others  2-all

   á-bà-bà-kùl-íír-ì.
   S.R-2-O2-surpass-RS-Fi

   'That they continuously obey ‖ also all the others | who surpass them in status.' (38 016)

In (7.41) he had already arrived somewhere else and now arrives at the village, as well.

(7.41) À-ná-hík-à  ‖ nà=   há=  kā-āyà.
      1-SQ-arrive-Fa  CNJ=  16=  12-village

   'He arrived ‖ also (lit. and) at the village.' (111 028)

### 7.5.1.3 Reciprocal noun phrases

The form **na** at the head of a noun phrase can work in conjunction with the reciprocal extension -**an**. In (7.42) the reciprocal extension -**an** on the verb **yànákòméérànà** 'it was familiar' communicates a reciprocal give-and-take with the **bítùgwà** 'farm animals', which is itself introduced by **na**.

(7.42) Ìyó       m-bébà ‖ y-àná-kòméér-án-à | ná=    yìbyò
      that.N+9  9-rat    9-SQ-familiar-RCP-Fa  CNJ=  those.N+8

   bí-tùgwà.
   8-farm.animals

   'That rat ‖ became familiar with | those farm animals.' (48 004)

### 7.5.1.4 Agent of passive construction

The **na** can also introduce the agent of a passive construction. In (7.43) **na** introduces **ngòkò** 'chicken', which is the agent of the verb **nàháábwà** 'I was given'.

(7.43) W-á-m-bèr-ér-à              í=ì-gì     ly-à-ní ‖  ly-ó=
      2SG-P1-O1.SG-break-APL-Fa   AU=5-egg   5-A.M-1SG  5-O.R=

   n-à-háá-bw-á           ná=    n-gòkò.
   1SG-P1-give-PS-Fa     CNJ=   9-chicken

   'You broke my egg ‖ which I was given by chicken.' (204 013)

### 7.5.1.5 Instrument noun phrases

The **na** can also indicate an instrument. In (7.44) the person remembers that he cut himself with a type of curved-bladed farm knife.

(7.44) **Nàà-ní** ‖ **n-à-málí** kèngéér-à | kw-ó= lú-sìkù
ADD.P-1SG 1SG-P1-ALREADY remember-Fa CMP-AU= 11-day

**lú-gùmà** | **n-gá-yì-tòl-á** yù-gú mú-nwé | <u>n-ó</u>=
11-one 1SG-P2-RFX-cut.off-Fa this.P-3 3-finger CNJ-AU=

**mú-gùshù.**
3-cutter

'And me also ‖ I already remember | that one day | I cut off this finger of mine | with a cutter.' (38 008)

In (7.45) the harvesters are harvesting the rice with their hands.

(7.45) É= **bá-géshì** ‖ mw-é= mù-lì mú= gésh-á
O= 2-grain.harvesters 2PL-FOC= 2PL-are PROG= harvesting.grain-Fa

**ú=mú-pûngâ** ‖ <u>n-á</u>= má-bòkò...
AU=3-rice CNJ-AU= 6-hands

'O harvesters ‖ you who are in harvesting the rice ‖ by hand...' (204 016)

### 7.5.1.6 Accompaniment noun phrases

1) The form **na** can function to introduce accompaniment, connecting two referents that are together. In (7.46) **na** shows that the man is with his two wives.

(7.46) **Ùyó** mú-shósì ‖ ìrì á-ká-b-â | à-lí <u>ná</u>= yàbó
that.N+1 1-man when 1-P2-become-Fa 1-is CNJ= those.N+2

**bá-kà-à-gè** bà-bìrì...
2-wife-A.M-1 2-two

'That man ‖ when he was | with those two wives of his...' (409 003)

In this section we include a few other accompaniment forms as well. Although some of these are technically not phrases including **na**, they are grouped together here because they show alternative ways of expressing accompaniment, and this seems the best place to group them together.

2) Likewise, accompaniment can be expressed by the oblique phrase **kúgùmà ná** 'together with', plus a complement (the participants involved). This is seen in (7.47), with the phrase **kúgùmà nà=bóòhè** 'together with them'.

(7.47)

| s V | | Oblique | | |
|---|---|---|---|---|
| **À-ná-tàngír-á** | **ú=kú-vùn-à** | **kúgùmà** | **nà=** | **bó-òhè.** |
| 1-SQ-began-Fa | AU=15-play-Fa | together | CNJ= | 2-PRO |

'And he began to play (mankala) | together with them.' (30 005)

3) Accompaniment can also be expressed by the copula -**li** 'to be' with the mutual extension, which means 'the ones we are together with'. In (7.48) this is seen in the relative clause with the resultative form of the copula, **bó=tùlíínwì** 'with whom we are together'.

(7.48)

| S | | Relative | | |
|---|---|---|---|---|
| **Bà-nó** | **bá-ndú** | **b-ó** | **tù-lí-ínw-ì** | ... |
| 2-these.P.C | 2-people | 2-O.R | 1PL-are-RS+MUT-Fi | |

'These people | with whom we are together...'. (Jdg 8:5)

4) Finally accompaniment can be expressed by the object relative marker, plus the copula -**li**, plus **kúgùmà** 'together'. This is seen in (7.49), where the phrase **bó=tùlì kúgùmà** 'with whom we are together', modifies the subject **á=bándú bóóshì** 'all the people'.

(7.49)

| S | | Relative | | | s V |
|---|---|---|---|---|---|
| **Á=bá-ndú** | **bó-ó-shí** | **b-ó=** | **tù-lì** | **kúgùmà** | **bà-kú-lámùs-à.** |
| AU=2-people | 2-all | 2-O.R= | 1PL-are | together | 2-O2.SG-greet-Fa |

'All the people whom we are together with | greet you.' (Tit 3:15)

### 7.5.2 Conjunctive *kandi iri* 'or'

Kifuliiru NPs can also be coordinated together with **kàndì írí** 'or' (phonetically usually pronounced as a single word [**kàndìrí**].) In (7.50) the phrase **kàndì irí mwàná wàgè** 'or his child' is presented as an alternative to **wà=mbébà** 'the rat'.

(7.50) **Vyúk-à!** ‖ **w-à-gwá-s-á** | **w-à=m-bébá** ‖ **kàndì ìrí**
get.up-Fa 2SG-P1-capture-CS-Fa 1-A.M-9-rat or

**mw-àná w-à-gè.**
1-child 1-A.M-1

'Get up! ‖ You have captured | the rat ‖ or its child.' (632 082)

In (7.51) **kàndì ìrí** provides the alternatives **mwèné wìnyù** 'your brothers' and **mwìrá wàwè** 'your friend'.

(7.51) **U-tá-Ø-shòmb-àn-è** **ná=** **mw-èné** **w-ì-nyù** ‖ **kàndì ìrí**
2SG-NEG-SBV-hate-RCP-Fe CNJ= 1-relative 1-A.M-2PL or

**mw-ìrá w-à-wè.**
2-friend 1-A.M-2SG

'Don't hate your brothers ‖ or your friends.' (39 033)

### 7.5.3 Conjunctive *nga* 'like, as'

The conjunctive **nga** 'like, as' can be used to communicate comparison or approximation.

1) The conjunctive **nga** can be used with noun phrases, where it means 'like', and is attached as a proclitic preceding the initial element of a noun phrase. It conjoins by comparing the two noun phrases. In (7.52) **nga** 'like' precedes the NP **nyókò** 'your mother' and expresses the lament of a mistreated girl, that another wife of one's father is not like one's own mother.

(7.52) **Mù-k-á** **yîshò** ‖ **à-tá-lí** **ngá=** **nyókò** ‖ **é=**
1-wife-A.M 1a+your.father 1-NEG-is like= 1a+your.mother O=

**bâbà** (Sw.) **Kàshéndwà.**
father Kashendwa

'The wife of your father ‖ is not like your mother ‖ O father Kashendwa!' (43 031)

In (7.53) it is stated that "those ones are like his children", implying that they resemble his children, (and might actually be them).

(7.53) **Bà-lyâ** | **bà-lí ngá=** **bà-ànà** **bà-à-gè.**
2-those.R 2-are like= 2-children 2-A.M-1

'Those ones | are like his children.' (201 098)

2) The term **nga** 'like' can also be used without a comparative NP, to indicate approximation. In (7.54) the NP **sìkù zìngâ** 'how many days' is preceded by **nga** 'like' to show that the number of days is approximate.

(7.54) Írí  há-ká-mál-á  ngá=  sìkù  zì-ngâ  ‖  mú-kàzì
When  16-P2-finish-Fa  like=  10+days  10-how.many  1-woman

mú-gùmà |  á-àli  kìzí  génd-á |  á-gá-tòl-èèr-à |
1-one  1-P3  REP  GOING-Fa  1-INTL-pick.up-APL-Fa

ú=tú-shààlì |  há=  má-tóngò.
AU=13-firewood  16=  6-trash.heap

'When there had finished off (passed) about how many days ‖ one woman | repeatedly went | picking up | small firewood | at the trash heap.' (607 014)

## 7.6 Noun phrases involving *mwènê* 'ownership'

The noun **mwènê** (PL **bèènê**) unlike most nouns, can take a complement.[12] It is used in several idiomatic expressions. 1) When followed by a noun, it indicates 'ownership of' or 'authority over' the referent of that noun. 2) When followed by an associative pronoun, it is a term meaning a 'family member' or 'relative'. 3) When used to express likeness, **mwènê** is followed not by an associative pronoun but by a demonstrative complement.

### 7.6.1 Ownership or authority

The noun **mwènê/bèènê**, followed by a noun phrase, indicates 'ownership' or 'authority'. Example (7.55) shows that **mwènê** functions as a noun, in that it can be preceded by the demonstrative **ùyó** 'that.N', but unlike most nouns, **mwènê** takes a noun phrase complement, as well, in this case **yàkó kábwâ** 'that.N dog'.

(7.55) Ùyó  mw-èné  yàkó  ká-bwâ ‖  à-ná-dèt-à ‖  kwó=
that.N+1  1-one.having  that.N+12  12-dog  1-SQ-say-Fa  CMP=

y-é=  mw-ènè  =yó  m-bóngò.
1-FOC=  1-having  =that.N+9  9-gazelle

'That owner of that dog ‖ said ‖ that he's the owner of that gazelle.' (03 018)

---

[12]This is perhaps due to its possible evolution from a form of the expression "to have" or "be with" something.

## 7.6 Noun phrases involving mwènê 'ownership'

The plural form is **bèènê**. In (7.56) the people are said to be the owners of (having authority over) **á=kāāyà** 'the village'.

(7.56) Yàbó    bè-èné    á=kā-āyà  ||  bà-ná-búùz-à  yùlwó
those.N+2    2-owner    AU=12-village    2-SQ-ask-Fa    that.N+11

lú-kwàvù:...
11-rabbit

'Those owners of the village || asked that rabbit:...' (09 019)

When **bèènê** is the complement of an associative phrase, it still stands for the owner, but in a more general sense. In (7.57) **í=byá bèènê** 'things of someone' has the sense of things that belong to someone (else), without specifying who that someone is.

(7.57) Ù-Ø-hús-é    yùgwó    mú-tègò    w-ényènè  ||  w-é=    rì
2SG-SBV-open-Fe    that.N+3    3-trap    2SG-self    2SG-FOC=    is

mú=    génd-á    ú-gáà-ly-à    í=by-á=    bè-ènè!
PROG=    GOING-Fa    2SG-INTL-eat-Fa    AU=8-A.M=    2-owners

'Open that trap yourself || you are the one who is going eating the things of others!' (48 010)

In the proverb in (7.58), the phrase **yá=bèènê** 'of someone' refers in a general way to other people.

(7.58) Í=m-bùùlà    yá=    bè-ènè  ||  ì-tá-Ø-yìg-w-â.
AU=9-quirk    9-A.M=    2-owners    9-NEG-TL-learn-PS-Fa

'The quirk of others (lit., the ones having it) || is not (i.e. should not be) learned.' (32 042)

### 7.6.2 Family members

The word **bèènê**, followed by an associative pronoun, is also used for family members. In (7.59) **bèèné wàbò** means 'their relatives'. Other forms are **bèèné wìnyù** 'your relatives' and **bèèné wìtù** 'our relatives'. These are all frozen forms; the **wàbò/wìnyù/wìtù** is not a simple associative pronoun since what appears to be the cl. 1 **w-** at the beginning of them does not match the cl. 2 at the beginning of **bèènê**.

(7.59) í=ky-ànyá  bè-èné  w-à-bò |  bá-àli kìzí bòn-à ùyó
     AU=7-time  2-relative 1-A.M-2  2-P3  REP  see-Fa that.N+1

mú-nyérè ...
1-girl

'The time their brothers | were repeatedly seeing that girl...' (624 010)

In (7.60) **mwèné wìnyù** 'your relative' is a singular form.

(7.60) Y-ô-nó  ||  kéèrà  à-yìt-á  mw-èné  w-ì-nyù.
     EMP-1-this.P.C  ALREADY  1-kill-Fa  1-relative  1-A.M-2.PL

'This very one || has already killed your brother.' (632 075)

### 7.6.3 Comparative 'like X'

The noun **mwènê** (PL **bèènê**) followed by a demonstrative pronoun, expresses 'likeness' or 'comparability'. This is probably an extension of the semantic meaning of "relative" noted just above. The demonstrative agrees in noun class with the item with which the comparison is being made. For example the cl. 9/10 **í=ngúlúbé mwènè íyò**; 'a pig like that.N', as opposed to the cl. 1 **ú=múshósí mwènè úyò** 'a man like that.N', etc. To express likeness of manner, the cl. 15 agreement is used: **ábàli mú=gírà mwènè yúkwò** 'those who do like that.N'; **náyè ànáyígà ú=kúlàmúsániá mwènè kwókwò** 'and he also learned to greet like that.N'.

### 7.7 Noun phrases with following nouns of apposition

Kifuliiru syntax allows nouns of apposition,[13] i.e. one noun following another and referring to the same real-world referent. Nouns of apposition most often occur when the main character is first presented in a narrative, as a way of identifying the theme of the story. The pause found in the phrasing of the words, as well as the fact that the noun of apposition may follow the quantifier which is the final constituent of the simple noun phrase, makes it clear that these are not just being used as adjectives to modify the noun.

In (7.61) the NP **músósí múgùmà** 'one man' is in apposition to the noun **múkénì** 'poor person'.

---

[13] It is quite possible that these are filling the same grammatical "slot" as the relative clause, if present. The relative clause is also often used in the introduction of a main character in a narrative.

(7.61) **Há-àlì   rì-ìr-í    mú-sósí    mú-gùmà | mú-kénì.**
      16-P3    is-RS-Fi   1-man      1-one     1-poor.one

'There was one man | a poor person.' (23 002)

In (7.62) the statement is made that there was a **mwàmì** 'king', which is in apposition to the following noun **mwìtánì** 'murderer'.

(7.62) **Kéèrà ‖ há-àlí   rì-ìr-í    ú=mw-àmí |  mw-ìtánì.**
      long.ago 16-P3   is-RS-Fi   AU=1-king    1-murderer

'In the past ‖ there was a king | a murderer.' (23 002)

## 7.8 Multiple noun phrase embedding

Since a noun phrase may include an associative phrase and the complement of an AP is, in turn, a NP, there may be multiple embeddings. On rare occasions, the sole noun in such a multiple embedding may follow up to five clitics.

In (7.63) the noun phrase **ná=bà=mú=ké=Léméérà** includes five clitics: 1) the conjunctive **na**, 2) the cl. 2 associative marker **ba**, 3) the locative cl. 18 **mú**, 4) the cl. 12 associative **ka**, 5) the cl. 23 locative **i**=.(These last two are collapsed by phonological vowel coalescence.) The **ba** refers to an understood **bándù** 'people' and the **ké** refers to an understood **kááyà** 'village'. This is clear from the fact that the preceding phrase is **ngá=bándú bà=mú=kààyá ké=Sângè** 'as the people of in the village of Sange'.

(7.63) **Tù-shùbà    tú-gá-shálìk-à    ‖   ngá=   bá-ndù    b-à=      mú=**
       1PL-PREV    1PL-F2-be.hungry-Fa     as=    2-people  2-A.M=    18=

      **kà-àyá      k-é=         Sângé ‖  ná=    b-à=      mú=     k-é=**
      12-village  12-A.M+23=   Sange     CNJ=   2-A.M=    18=     12-A.M+23=

      **Léméérà.**
      Lemera

'We would have been hungry ‖ like the people belonging to the village of Sange ‖ and those belonging to Lemera.'

Each phrase is a constituent of a higher phrase. Without drawing a tree diagram, we can still show the relationships. In (7.64) each line shows the constituents of the phrase mentioned in the preceding line:

(7.64) **ná=bá=mú=ké=Léméérà**
Conjunction (**na**) + NP
NP → AU (**a=**) + associative phrase
Assoc. phrase → A.M (**ba=**) + locative phrase
Locative phrase → locative marker (**mú=**)+ NP
NP → associative phrase
Assoc phrase → A.M (**ka=**) + locative phrase
Locative phrase → locative marker (**í=**) +NP
Noun phrase → noun (**Léméérà**)

Thus at each level, the phrases involved include a phrase as a complement, so that there is multiple embedding. However, each phrase is only embedded one level deep. A similar example is found in (7.65) the phrase **ná=bà=mú=mbàgà yàwè** 'and those of within your family' includes the clitic **na** 'CNJ', the cl. 2 associative marker **ba** 'of' and the cl. 18 locative **mu** 'in'.

(7.65) **W-êhê** ‖ **ná=** **b-à=** **mú=** **m-bàgá** **y-à-wè** ‖
2SG-CTR.P  CNJ+AU=  2-A.M=  18=  9-family  9-A.M-2SG

**n-gá-mù-hèèrèz-â** |  **yì-bí**  **bí-hùgò.**
1SG-F2-O2.PL-give-Fa  these.P-8  8-countries

'YOU ‖ and the ones of in your family ‖ I will give you | these countries.' (Gen 26:3)

# 8

# Locative Phrases

All locative phrases (LPs) have two obligatory components. First is the locative marker (LM), consisting of one of the following: a cl. 16 **há**, cl. 17 **kú**, cl. 18 **mú**, cl. 23 **í**, or a complex LM (**í=wa, í=mûndà**, or **í=mwá**). The second LP constituent (following the LM) is either a noun phrase (NP), or position noun phrase.

There are considerable co-occurrence restrictions between the various LMs and different semantic types of LP complements: some LMs can co-occur only with inanimate LP complements, some co-occur only with animate ones, some co-occur only with nouns referring inherently to places and others co-occur mainly with abstract forms such as infinitives, etc.

Stacked locative class markers can also be employed in idiomatic ways that that no longer carry typical locative meanings.

## 8.1 Locative markers

### 8.1.1 Locative marker structure

#### 8.1.1.1 Locative agreement

The locative marker is the head of a locative phrase.[1] As such it triggers class agreement with other constituents in the locative phrase (LP), as well as with other elements in the clause.

In (8.1) the cl. 18 prefix **mu-** in the proximal contrastive demonstrative **múnò** 'in here' agrees with the cl. 18 locative clitic **mú**=in the phrase **mú=kāāyà** 'in

---

[1] The head of the phrase is the element which determines the syntactic function of the phrase (Payne 1997:31).

the village'. (Other similar phrases found in the corpus include **yùmwó mú**=**ndâ** 'in there in the stomach', **yùmwó mú**=**lwījì** 'in there in the river', **hànó há**=**mbùgà** 'here outside', **hànó há**=**kāāyà** 'here at the village', etc.)

(8.1) Y-é=     ká-mál-á         á=bá-ndú       bó-óshì  b-á=   mù-nó
      1-FOC    P2-finish.off-Fa AU=2-people    2-all    2-A.M  18-here.P.C

   mú= kā-āyà.
   18= 12-village

   'He's the one who finished off all the people of in here in the village.'
   (202 033)

The same kind of locative class agreement can occur between a locative phrase and a subsequent enclitic pronoun referring back to that locative phrase. In (8.2) the cl. 18 locative marker **mú** 'within' heads the locative phrase **mú**=**kíshūkà** 'within the bush'. That same cl. 18 marker **mú** (labialized before the vowel) is part of the enclitic pronoun=**mwó** 'within there (bush)' at the end of the sentence, which refers back to the full antecedent **mú**=**kíshūkà**.

(8.2) Mú-gùmá   w-à-bò |   à-ná-yì-làsh-à       mú=   kí-shūka. ||
      1-one    1-A.M-2    1-SQ-RFX-throw-Fa    18=   7-bush

   Ú=mú-hyàkàzí |   ú-w-áàlì   málì       mú-síím-à ||
   AU=1-new.wife    S.R-1-P3   ALREADY    O1-like-Fa

   à-ná-mú-kùlíkír-à      =mwò.
   1-SQ-O1-follow-Fa      =18

   'One of them (young men) | threw himself into the bush. || The newly married woman | who had already liked him || she followed him in there.'
   (01 023-024)

In (8.3) the cl. 17 locative marker **kú** 'contact' heads the locative phrase **kú**=**yìkyó kítì** 'in contact with that.N tree'. That same **kú** (labialized before a vowel) is repeated as the subject marker in the verb **kw**-**áàlí shònírì** '(on there) had climbed', maintaining the cl. 17 concord class agreement between the locative phrase functioning as clause subject and the subject marker on the verb. This structure, termed locative inversion, is further discussed in (12.5.1.1).

(8.3) Kú=   yìkyó      kí-tì ||   kw-áàlì    shòn-ír-ì    ú=mú-lándírà.
      17=   that.N+7   7-tree     17-P3      climb-RS-Fi  AU=3-vine

   'On that tree || had climbed a vine.' (32 007)

### 8.1.1.2 Internal constituent structure of locative markers

Four of the LMs consist of a single locative class marker (one of the twenty markers in the Kifuliru concord system). These include the cl. 16 **há** 'place of, thematic salience marker (TSM)', the cl. 17 **kú** 'in contact/connection with', the cl. 18 **mú** 'within', and the cl. 23 **í** 'place of'. These synchronically productive LMs occur only one per locative phrase; that is to say, they are never "stacked" one after the other.

In Kifuliiru there are also three LMs which are lexicalized multi-morphemic forms: **í=mwa** 'in contact/connection with', **í=mûndà** 'place of', and **i=wa** 'place of'. These three all trigger cl. 23 agreement.

The frozen LM **í=mwá** 'in contact/connection with' appears to be derived historically from a combination of the cl. 23 locative marker **í**, followed by the cl. 18 locative marker **mú** and finally the associative marker -**a**. The underlying form **í-mú-a** surfaces as **í=mwà**.

The frozen LM **í=mûndà** 'place of' is likely derived historically from a combination of the cl. 23 locative marker **í**, followed by the cl. 18 locative marker **mú** and then the noun **ndá** 'stomach, abdomen', a body-part commonly used as a locative term in African languages.

The frozen LM **í=wa** 'place of' is very likely derived historically from a combination of the cl. 23 locative marker **í**, followed by the cl. 14 marker **bú** and the associative marker **a**. The original underlying form **í=búa** would be labialized by a phonological rule to **í=bwá**. Since the intervocalic **b** is pronounced as a bilabial approximant in Kifuliiru, it would be very natural to soften the **b**, with the resulting form **í=wa**. In fact some Bafuliiru claim that the fuller form, **í=bwa**, is the "real word", although few actually pronounce it this way in normal speech.

### 8.1.1.3 Contextual structure of locative markers

When viewing LMs vis-à-vis their surrounding grammatical context, two important structural facts become evident: 1) All LMs (except **í=mûndà** 'place of') from a strictly structural point of view, are not prefixes on a noun; rather, they are proclitics.[2] They function at the phrase level, immediately preceding the LP complement, and are attached to the initial element of that complement. 2) The non-compound LMs, as well as **í=wa**, disallow the occurrence of an augment which would otherwise occur at the beginning of the following LP complement. These two points will now be elaborated in turn.

1) All locative markers (except **í=mûndà** 'place of') are here analyzed as PROCLITICS, attaching to the initial element of the NP at the phrase level.[3] In

---

[2] The one exception to this is the single, non-analytic locative noun **há-ndù** (16-place).

[3] However, the agreement markers which mark concord with the locative classes on non-nominal

(8.4a) it can be seen that the LM **há** 'at' directly precedes the noun **mútēgò** 'trap', to form the phrase **há=mútēgò** 'at the trap'. In (8.4b) the demonstrative pronoun **gùndì** 'other' is now noun phrase initial. Thus the locative proclitic **há** shifts to **gùndì**, forming the locative phrase **há=gùndì mútēgò** 'at the other trap'. In (8.4c) the demonstrative pronoun **yùgwô** is noun phrase initial and so the locative proclitic **há** now shifts to that. The point is that the LM attaches to whichever word is initial in the LP complement and is thus classified as a proclitic.

(8.4) a. <u>há</u>= mú-tēgò   'at the trap'
        16=  3-trap

   b. <u>há</u>= gùndì mú-tēgò   'at another trap'
        16=  3-other 3-trap

   c. <u>há</u>= yù-gw-ò gù-ndì mú-tēgò   'at that.N other trap'
        16=  that.N-3  3-other 3-trap

2) In the case of all the non-compound LMs, as well as **í=wa**, the LM precludes the use of the augment on the following LP complement. In (8.5a) the augment **ú=** is attached as a proclitic to the noun **mútēgò** 'trap' and in (8.5c) to the demonstrative pronoun **gùndì** 'other'. However, when the locative class marker **há** 'at' is present, as in (8.5b, d), the augment is no longer allowed to occur.

(8.5) a. <u>ú</u>=mú-tēgò   'the trap'
        AU=3-trap

   b. <u>há</u>=mú-tēgò   'at the trap'
        16=3-trap

   c. <u>ú</u>=gù-ndì  mú-tēgò   'another trap'
        AU=3-other  3-trap

   d. <u>há</u>=gù-ndì  mú-tēgò   'at another trap'
        16=3-other   3-trap

In addition to the cl. 16 LM **há** 'at' shown in (8.5), four other LMs preclude a following augment. They are: **kú** 'in contact/connection (impersonal)', **mú** 'within', **í=wa** 'place of', and **í** 'place of'. By contrast, the two compound LMs **í=mwá** 'in contact/connection (personal)' and **í=mûndà** 'at (the place of)' do optionally allow a following augment.

---

parts of speech (e.g. verbs, pronouns, demonstratives etc.) are analyzed as prefixes.

## 8.1.1.4 Co-occurrence restrictions for locative markers and NP complements

There are clear collocational restrictions regarding possible combinations of LMs and noun phrase complements. The co-occurrence restrictions are summarized in table 8.1.

1) The LM **mú** 'within' occurs very commonly, as its possible complements are taken from large, boundless classes (animate and inanimate nouns, and inherent place nouns). Examples with NPs in which the noun is animate include **mú**=**bákìnì** 'among dancers', **mú**=**báhyàkàzì** 'among new wives', **mú**=**bányérè** 'among girls'. Examples with inanimate NPs include **mú**=**kábìgìngwê** 'in the afternoon', **mú**=**káshékò** 'in laughing', **mú**=**múgóngò** 'on the back'. Examples with inherent place nouns include **mú**=**lwījì** 'in the river', **mú**=**lúbākò** 'in the forest', **mú**=**kāāyà** 'in the village', **mú**=**kíshūkà** 'in the bush'.

2) The LM **kú** 'contact/connection' is also quite common, as it can co-occur with the large class of inanimate referents such as **kú**=**lúsìkù lúkùlù** 'in connection with the important day', **kú**=**múkìrà** 'in contact with the tail', **kú**=**mbékà** 'in contact with the end', **kú**=**múhàndà** 'in contact with the toilet', **kú**=**lúlìmì** 'in connection with the tongue', **kú**=**búgénì** 'in connection with the feast', **kú**=**mátwīrì** 'in contact with the ears', **kú**=**kírūndà** 'in contact with the corpse'. It can also co-occur with place referents such as **kú**=**múgāzì** 'in contact with the mountain', **kú**=**lwījì** 'in contact with the river'. It can also occur with animate referents if the contact is considered impersonal (8.1.2.7.1).

3) The LM **í**=**mwá** 'in contact/connection with' is limited to occurrence with animate nouns, such **í**=**mwá**=**mwìrà** 'in connection with the friend', **í**=**mwá**=**mwīzò** 'in connection with maternal uncle', **í**=**mwá**=**bándù** 'in connection with the people', **í**=**mwá**=**bánàhámwìnyù** 'in connection with your lords', **í**=**mwá**=**ngámíyà** 'in connection with the camel', as well as inanimate nouns with attributed personality, such as **í**=**mwé**=**mígìsì** 'in connection with the idols'.

4) The LM **há** 'place of, with thematic salience' occurs before noun phrases with inanimate referents, such as **há**=**múlyángò** 'at the door', **há**=**lúdáhà** 'at the bag', **há**=**mútēgò** 'at the trap', **há**=**kítì** 'at the tree', **há**=**kátàndà** 'at the table'. It can also occur with inherently locational nouns such as **há**=**bwàmì** 'at the king's place' and **há**=**lwījì** 'at the river', **há**=**bwérúùlà** 'at the open place', **há**=**kāāya** 'at the village', **há**=**ndálò** 'at the field'.

5) The LM **í** 'place of' occurs exclusively with nouns that are inherently locational. They may refer to geographical settings such as **í**=**búlámbò** 'at the dry land', **í**=**búngérè** 'at the pasture', **í**=**búzíbà** 'at the deep water', **í**=**bwàmì** 'at the king's place', **í**=**kāāyà** 'at the village', **í**=**kúzìmù** 'at the underground place', **í**=**nákwêrè** 'at the place of torment', **í**=**rúbàkò** 'at the forest', **í**=**rúbéngà** 'at the gully', **í**=**rúgûndù** 'at the banana grove', **í**=**rwīji** 'at the river'. Also

included are all proper place names such as **í=Búfùlììrù** 'at the Fuliiru homeland', **í=Búrùndì** 'at Burundi', **í=Búvīīrà** 'at Uvira', **í=Kìlìbâ** 'at Kiliba'.

6) The LM **í=mûndà** 'place where (is)' when followed by a non-clause complement, occurs only with animate referents, such as **í=mûndà yîshè** 'at the place where his father (is)', **í=mûndà ùyó wàbò** 'at the place where his fellow', **í=mûndà á=bìgìrìzìbwà** 'at the place where the disciples', **í=mûndà gúvùrúnéèrì** 'at the place where the governor', **í=mûndà Rúrémà** 'at the place where God', **í=mûndà ìyó mbébà** 'at the place where that.N rat', and **í=mûndà í=ndārè** 'at the place where the lion'. It can also include a corpse (which had been animate and is still treated as such) as in **í=mûndà yìkyó kírùndà** 'at the place of that.N corpse'. It is also used in cases where the complement is a clause rather than a phrase.

7) The LM **í=wa** 'place where' occurs in only two contexts. The first context involves abstract constructions, such as infinitive phrases (with optional auxiliaries and objects) or abstract nouns, e.g. **í=wà=kúhīīvà** 'at the place of hunting (where takes place)', **í=wà=kúgéndî=lyà** 'at place of going to eat', **í=wà=kúgúlá í=bítòrò** 'at place of buying kerosene', **í=wà=kútwírwá ú=lúbààjà** 'at the place of being judged', **í=wà=kúràgírá í=bíbùzì** 'at the place of grazing sheep', **í=wà=kúyònáná ú=múkò** 'at the place of shedding blood'. This also includes abstract deverbal nouns, such as **í=wà=búlámù** 'place where life', **í=wà=búshèrèrè** 'at the place of destruction', **í=wà=lúfû** 'at place of death'.

The second context where **í=wa** is found involves nouns which are inherently locational, and which are in classes which have an augment of the form **i**. Thus the addition of **wa** serves to distinguish locative-í-plus-noun from augment-plus-noun, such as **í=wà=ndálò** 'at the field' (cf. **i=ndalo** 'the field'), or **í=wá=yìkyó kírígò** 'at that.N well', **í=wà=shíndà** 'at the grave', **í=wà=nyáàjà** 'at the lake'. The aforementioned co-occurrence restrictions are summarized in table 8.1.

## 8.1 Locative markers

Table 8.1. Co-occurrence restrictions for LMs and NP complements

| Locative marker | Inherent place | Impersonal NP[a] | Personal NP | Abstracted place |
|---|---|---|---|---|
| mú= | mú=lú-gûndù<br>18=11-banana.grove<br>'in banana grove' | mú=mú-tēgò<br>18=3-trap<br>'in trap' | mú=bá-kìnì<br>18=2-dancers<br>'among dancers' | |
| kú= | kú=lw-ījì<br>17=11-river<br>'contact with river' | kú=lú-sìkù lú-kùlù<br>17=11-day 11-great<br>'contact with great day' | | |
| í=mwa= | | | í=mwá=mw-ìrà<br>23=CON=friend<br>'contact with friend' | |
| há= | há=bw-àmì<br>16=14-king<br>'at king's place' | há=mu-tēgò<br>16=3-trap<br>'at trap' | | |
| í= | í=rú-bākò<br>23=11-forest<br>'at the forest' | | | |
| í=mûndà | | | í=mûndà í=m-bébà<br>23=place of 9-rat<br>'place of the rat' | |
| í=wa= | | | | í=w-à=kú-hīīv-à<br>23=place-A.M=15-hunt-Fa<br>'place of hunting' |
| | | | | í=w-à=bú-lámù<br>23=place.A.M=14-life<br>'place of life' |

[a] For a discussion of what is meant by "impersonal", and why we use this term here rather than "inanimate", see (8.1.2.7.1).

## 8.1.2 Locative marker function

### 8.1.2.1 Summary of locative marker semantics

Table 8.2 summarizes the semantic contexts obtaining with the seven LMs.

Table 8.2 Summary of LM semantics

| | A | | B | | | |
|---|---|---|---|---|---|---|
| | LM head | Meaning | Possible directional contexts | | | |
| | | | Pointing | None | Towards | From |
| 1. | í= | place where inherent location X | | x | x | x |
| 2. | í=mûndà | place where animate X | | | x | |
| 3. | í=wa= | place where abstract X | | | x | rare |
| 4. | há= | place where X (with thematic salience) | | x | x | x |
| 5. | mú= | place within X | | x | x | x |
| 6. | kú= | in contact/connection with impersonal X | a | x | x | x |
| 7. | í=mwa= | in contact/connection with personal X | a | x | x | x |

Note: An "a" in table 8.2 indicates that this directional meaning occurs only in abstract contexts.

Column A: Five of the LMs, i.e. **í, há, í=mûndà, í=wa**, and **mú** (rows 1-5) mark *place* (location), while **kú** and **í=mwá** mark *contact* or *connection* with a referent.

Column B: Regarding possible directional contexts for LP complements, it can readily be seen that the LMs **í=mûndà** and **í=wa** occur primarily in one directional context, i.e. *towards (goal)*. The LM **í=wa** can occur in the directional context *to* as well as *from*, although the latter is very rare. The other five (**í, há, kú, mú**, and **í=mwá**) can each occur in three directional contexts, i.e. *at, towards*, and *from*. Interestingly, the latter two directional contexts, i.e. 'towards' and 'from', are opposites! In addition, **kú and í=mwá** can occur in the directional context of *pointing*, although that occurs only in abstract contexts.

### 8.1.2.2 No inherent directional orientation

LMs do not generally bear a "directional" meaning. Rather they usually occur in a context where directional orientation is already clearly implied by the verb. Evidence for this assertion is provided in the following three examples, each involving the identical locative phrase **í=rwījì** 'location of the river'. In the three examples, the directional orientations are 'at the river', 'towards the river', and 'from the river'.

In (8.6) we observe the clause **yàtíndà í=rwīji** 'it (gazelle) delayed at the river'. The implicit understanding is that when the verb base -**tínd**- 'delay' is associated with a locative phrase such as **í=rwīji** 'river', that "delay" happens at the location of the LP complement, i.e. 'the river'. One does not delay toward a river, or delay from a river.

(8.6)   **Í=n-dàrè y-àná-bòn-á kw-é=   n-zòbè |   y-à-tínd-à     í=     rw-ījì.**
      AU=9-lion 9-SQ-see-Fa   CMP-AU=  9-gazelle  9-P1-late-Fa   23=    11-river

'The lion saw that the gazelle delayed |at the river.' (16 012)

In (8.7) we observe the clause **yànágêndà í=rwīji** 'and it went to the river'. Again, the implicit understanding is that when the verb base -**génd**- 'go' is associated with a locative phrase such as **í=rwīji** 'river', that the subject of the clause is going to the location of the LP complement, i.e. 'to the river'. One does not typically go at a river, or go from a river.

(8.7)   **Ìyó       n-zòbé ||  y-àná-bètúl-à          yàkó       ká-bìndì ||**
      that.N+9   9-gazelle   9-SQ-carry.on.back-Fa   that.N+12   12-jug

      **y-àná-gênd-à     í=     rw-ījì.**
      9-SQ-go-Fa       23=    11-river

'That gazelle || carried that water jug || and it went to the river.' (16 007)

Finally, in (8.8) we observe the clause **ànályôkà í=rwīji** 'she left from the river'. The implicit understanding is that when the verb base -**lyok**- 'leave' is associated with a locative phrase such as **í=rwīji** 'river', that the subject of the clause is leaving from the location of the LP complement, in this case, 'from the river'.

(8.8)   **Kàshéndwá    ná-yè ||   à-ná-lyôk-à          í=     rw-ījì.**
      Kashendwa     ADD.P-1   1-SQ-come.from-Fa    23=    11-river

'Kashendwa and she also || left the river.' (43 022)

Since the same LM **í** is used in each of the above examples, it seems fairly obvious that the directional orientation of the clause is bound up in the clause verb, and not in the LM itself. The prepositional glosses 'at', 'to', and 'from' are necessitated by the grammatical strictures of English, not Kifuliiru.

As with the LM **í**, the LMs **há**, **kú**, **í=mwa**, and **mú** can also occur in the context of the directional orientations *no movement*, *movement towards*, and *movement from*. In addition the LMs **kú** and **í=mwa** can occur in the context of *pointing*. Any attempt to describe the meanings of LMs vis-à-vis word-for-word English glosses is therefore problematic, for at least two reasons.

1) Any given LM, when occurring in different contexts, is glossed in quite different ways, even to the extent of seemingly "opposite" meanings. As already noted above, the LM **í** can be glossed by 'at', 'towards', 'from', the latter two having opposite directional meanings. It seems highly improbable that these contrasting meanings could all be "basic".

2) In addition, several of the LMs can be assigned the very same set of English glosses. For example, not only can the LM **í** be glossed as 'at', 'towards', 'from', but we have also demonstrated that those very same glosses can also be applied to the LMs **há**, **kú**, **í=mwà**, and **mú**. This fact undermines the value of such directional glosses in distinguishing the LMs from each other.

### 8.1.2.3 Location, inherent: í

The cl. 23 LM **í** marks inherent location of the following referent. Since this LM requires a complement that is inherently locative, it does not really add locative meaning, except to communicate 'place of'. Thus it simply confirms the referent as already being locative. In (8.9) the cl. 23 marker **í** heads the locative phrase **í=rúbākò** 'at the location of the virgin forest', identifying the cl. 11 noun **rúbākò** 'virgin forest' as intrinsically locative.

(8.9) Í=ky-ànyà ùyó     mú-sósì | á-àlì kìzì génd-á í=     rú-bàkò...
      AU=7-time that.N+1  1-man   1-P3  REP  go-Fa 23=   11-forest

'The time that man | was repeatedly going to the place of the forest...'
(54 003)

Besides **í=rúbākò** 'place of virgin forest', other inherently locative nouns include **í=rwījì** 'place of river', **í=búlámbò** 'place of dry land', **í=búzíbà** 'place of deep water', etc. In addition, all proper names of locations are mandatorily preceded by **í** including **í=Búkàfù** 'place of Bukavu', **í=Kìlìbâ** 'place of Kiliba', **í=Shângê** 'place of Sange', etc.

Position nouns, like **mbérè** 'ahead', are also treated as inherently locative, and the majority of unmarked cases (i.e. those not involving thematic salience) are preceded by the cl. 23 LM **í**. In (8.10) the cl. 23 marker **í** precedes

**mbérè** 'before' in the locative phrase **í=mbéré lyá=yùlwò lúkwàvù** '(location) ahead of that.N rabbit'.

(8.10) Yìkyó     kí-shégèshè ‖ ky-àná-kúúdúk-à ‖ ky-àná-gênd-à   í=
       that.N+7  7-porcupine   7-SQ-ran.fast-Fa   7-SQ-go-Fa      23=

       m-béré |  ly-á=   yùlwó      lú-kwàvù.
       9-before  5-A.M=  that.N+11  11-rabbit

'That porcupine ‖ ran fast ‖ and went ahead | of that rabbit.' (09 023)

### 8.1.2.4 Location, abstract: í=wa

The LM **í=wa** marks 'a location where abstract X'. In addition, the use of **í=wa** normally implies movement, or pointing, in the direction towards that location, although on rare occasions it can imply movement from a location as well. In (8.11) the LM **í=wa** marks the place where hunting takes place, signified by the infinitive **yùkwó kúhīīvà** 'that.N hunting'.

(8.11) Á=ká-fùlò ‖  kà-ná-zì-bwír-à       kwó=  ná-kò  |  ká-gá-zì-kùlíkír-à
       AU=12-turtle  12-SQ-O10-tell-Fa    CMP=  ADD.P-12  12-F2-O10-follow-Fa

       í=    w-á=        yùkwó       kú-híív-à.
       23=   place-A.M=  that.N+15   15-hunt-Fa

'The turtle ‖ told them that and it also | would follow them to the place of that hunting.' (05 003)

Movement verbs found occurring before **í=wa** in the data include: **-twal-** 'carry', **-génd-** 'go', **-yìgénder-** 'go away', **-fùluk-** 'return from work', **-kùlikir-** 'follow', and **-tíbitir-** 'run to'.

The collocations of **í=wa** can also include abstract nouns, such as those of cl. 14. In (8.12) **í=wa** heads the locative phrase **í=wà=búshèrèrè** 'towards the location where destruction', which is the complement of the verb **kúlólà** 'pointing (in the direction of)'.

(8.12) Ú=mú-lyángó   gw-ó=        kú-lól-á      í=    w-à=
       AU=3-door    3-A.M+AU=    15-look-Fa    23=   place.A.M=

       bú-shèrèèrè ‖     gù-yájàbùs-ír-ì.
       14-destruction    3-is.wide-RS-Fi

'The door of heading to the place of destruction ‖ is wide.' (Mat 7:13)

### 8.1.2.5 Location of animate referent: í=mûndà

The LM **í=mûndà** marks 'location where animate X'. In (8.13) the LM **í=mûndà** occurs in the context of the dog's movement towards the location of the lion.

(8.13) Á=ká-bwá   kà-ná-yùvw-á   kw-é=   n-dàrè  y-é=   rí  n-é=
       AU=12-dog   12-SQ-hear-Fa   CMP-AU=   9-lion  9-FOC=   is  CNJ-AU=

      mí-sì |   ú=kú-hím-á |   yìkyó   kí-shókómà ||
      4-strength   AU=15-surpassing-Fa   that.N+7   7-cheetah

      kà-ná-bùng-ír-á |   í=   mûndá   í=n-dārè.
      12-SQ-move-APL-Fa   23=   place   AU=9-lion

    'The dog heard that the lion is the one having strength | more than | that cheetah || and it moved residence | to the place of the lion.' (45 012)

In (8.14) someone is going towards the person called **Kíshìrìrì**.

(8.14) À-ná-gênd-à   í=   mûndà   Kíshìrìrì ||   à-ná-mú-líbùùk-ìr-à |
      1-SQ-go-Fa   23=   place   Kishiriri   1-SQ-O1-tell.trouble-APL-Fa

      yàgó   má-líbù.
      those.N+6   6-trouble

    'And he went to the place where Kishiriri (was) || and he told him about | those troubles.' (40 019)

Other movement verbs found occurring before **í=mûndà** in the data include: -**génd**- 'go', -**hík**- 'arrive', -**twal**- 'carry'. It is interesting to note the high occurrence of the applicative extension on verb forms preceding **í=mûndà**, including the following forms involving the applicative extension -**ir**: -**zàmuukir**- 'rise up to', -**bùngir**- 'relocate to', -**púmukir**- 'run away to', -**gálukir**- 'return to', -**gálulir**- 'cause to return to', -**gúmuukir**- 'rush (in a big group) to', and -**tíbitir**- 'run to'.

It is important to note that while **í=mûndà** occurs in the context of "movement towards" an animate referent, the condition of movement towards an animate referent in itself does necessarily trigger the use of **í=mûndà**. When this condition is combined with a *thematic development*, the relative form **á=hàlì** 'where there is' may be used instead of **í=mûndà**.

As mentioned above, the meanings of **í=mûndà** are not restricted to only "movement" towards a goal, but can also mark a referent that is merely being pointed at. In (8.15) **í=mûndà** heads the phrase **í=mûndà á=bìgìrìzìbwà bààgè** 'towards (the location where) his students', where the subject is pointing his

## 8.1 Locative markers

hand in the direction of where the students are (cf. the verb **ànáshôngà** 'and he pointed').

(8.15) **Há-à-h-ô** ‖ **à-ná-shong-à ú=kú-bòkò** | **í=** **mûndà**
E-there.N-16   1-SQ-point-Fa   AU=15-hand   23=   place

**á=bì-gìrìzìbwà   bà-à-gè**.
AU=2-students   2-A.M-1

'Right then ‖ he pointed his hand | to the place (where) his students (were).' (Mat 12:49)

### 8.1.2.6 Location plus thematic salience: há

The cl. 16 LM **há** has two simultaneous components of meaning.

1) The first component of meaning can be expressed abstractly as "at the location where X". This meaning is relatively straightforward, identifying a location by simply linking it to a referent occurring at that location. The referent can be a standard noun like **múlyángò** 'door', as in the locative phrase **há=múlyángò** 'at the place where the door is'. The referent can also be an inherently locative noun like **lwīj̄ı̀** 'river', as in the phrase **há=lwīj̄ı̀** 'at the location where the river is'. It can also be an isolated position noun like **mbérè** 'front', as in the phrase **há=mbérè** 'at the place ahead', or a position noun with a complement as in the phrase **há=bútàmbí lyó=mútúmbá gwà=nyínà** 'at the place beside the (animal) corpse of its mother'.

2) In addition, the LM **há** marks a location or setting in the narrative where a *significant new development* of the story theme is *about to* take place. This is described in the section on thematic salience in (12.3.2).

### 8.1.2.7 Impersonal connection/contact: ku

The cl. 17 concord marker **kú** signals an *impersonal contact/connection*[4] with the referent named in the complement. This abstract definition can cover different relationships, as can be seen from the very many English glosses that occur with **kú** throughout the data. Depending on the context, **kú** can be glossed as 'at, on, upon, to, towards, from, away from, up, down, concerning, in connection with, in the direction of, beginning at, ending at', etc.

#### 8.1.2.7.1 "Impersonal" notion

The term "impersonal" is used (rather than inanimate) because there are cases where animate referents are spoken of in an impersonal way. In (8.18) **kú**

---
[4]The term "contact" fits the more tangible cases where movement is involved, while the term "connection" is better suited to the cases that point in the direction of a certain referent.

signals contact between two referents, the boy and the river. However, the complement of **kú**, i.e. **lwījì** 'river', is not involved with the boy in a way that is personal.

(8.16) Ìrì  á-ká-hík-á     kú=   lw-ījì   ‖ à-ná-nyóótérw-à ‖ à-ná-gír-á
      when 1-P2-arrive-Fa  17=   11-river   1-SQ-be.thirsty-Fa   1-SQ-try-Fa

      mbw-à=         Ø-nyw-é        á=mī-ījì.
      FRUS.INTL-1=   SBV-drink-Fe   AU=6-water

'When he arrived at the river ‖ he was thirsty ‖ and he attempted to drink water.' (07 026)

While the impersonal contact is with an inanimate complement in the vast majority of cases (which would be expected in the case of an "impersonal" contact) in a few cases **kú** can also indicate contact with an animate complement, just so long as the contact is considered impersonal.

In (8.17) the complement of the LM **kú** is **rúmûngù** 'hyena', an animate animal. In this context, the man merely "encountered" the hyena by chance, without any personal interaction at that point.

(8.17) Mú-sósí mú-gùmà ‖ á-àlì kìzì génd-á      á-gá-tàndùùl-àn-à   ‖
       1-man   1-one     1-P3  REP  GOING-Fa   1-INTL-check.out-RCP-Fa

       à-ná-hùlúk-ír-à      kú=   rú-mûngù.
       1-SQ-appear-APL-Fa   17=   11-hyena

'One man ‖ was repeatedly going checking out (other people) ‖ and he encountered a hyena.' (14 002)

Example (8.18) represents another case, this one a bit trickier, where the complement of **kú** is not only animate, but might be seen as involving a very "personal" interaction, i.e. a man producing offspring via a certain woman. In the example, which is one small part of a long Biblical genealogy, the man named Salmon produces an offspring, Boaz, vis-à-vis his relation with the woman Rahab. The reason this seemingly "personal" connection is couched in impersonal terms **kú=Ráhààbù** 'in connection with Rahab', or more naturally put in English, 'by Rahab' relates to the purpose of the utterance, which is not focusing on their personal relationship, but rather on the impersonal link in the long genealogical record.

## 8.1 Locative markers

(8.18) **nà**=   **Sálùmòònì** ‖ **à**-**ná**-**bùt**-**à**   **Bóàzì** ‖ **kù**=   **Ráhààbù**.
   CNJ=   Salmon   1-SQ-give.birth-Fa   Boaz   17=   Rahab

'and Salmon ‖ gave birth to Boaz ‖ in connection with Rahab' (Mat 1:5)

### 8.1.2.7.2 Various contexts where **ku** signals contact/connection

The LM **kú** 'in contact, connection' occurs in a wide variety of contexts, including the marking of physical contact, membership in the same group, a relation with time, a relation with location, pointing to a referent, pointing to a previous contexts, means, manner, removing a part from the whole, and comparison.

a) In many cases, **kú** implies making or breaking physical contact between referents X and Y. Example (8.19) presents a case where **kú**, together with its complement **ùyó mwàmì** 'that.N king', marks the breaking of a contact. In the context, when the snake sees a bunch of rats running around, it unwraps itself from around the king, thus breaking the contact it had with the king.

(8.19) **Ìyó**   **shàtò** ‖ **ìrì**   **í**-**ká**-**bòn**-**á**   **kwó**=   **zì**-**kòlà**   **mú**=
   that.N+9   9+python   when   9-P2-see-Fa   CMP=   10-NEW   PROG=

**tíbít**-**á**-**tíbìtà** ‖ **y**-**àná**-**yì**-**zìng**-**óól**-**à**   **kù**=   **yó**   **mw**-**àmì** ‖
run-Fa-RDP   9-SQ-RFX-wind-RV-Fa   17=   that.N+1   1-king

**gírá**   **ì**-**Ø**-**gwát**-**é** |   **kú**=   **yìzò**   **m**-**bébà**.
so.that   9-SBV-grab-Fe   17=   those.N+10   10-rats

'That python ‖ when it saw that they (rats) are now running around ‖ it unwound itself away from that king ‖ in order to grab | some of those rats.' (51 026)

b) The LM **kú** also marks "connection" by virtue of the fact that two referents are in physical proximity with each other. In (8.20) **kú** marks a state of ongoing physical proximity with its complement **ngóókóló** 'shoreline'. In this case the sailors keep their ship close to the shoreline because of a severe storm. The reduplicated form of the locative phrase **kú**=**ngóókóló kú**=**ngóókóló** indicates the state of continuous, ongoing proximity with the shore, as they pass by it.

(8.20) **Tw-àná-gênd-à** | **tú-gá-lêng-à** | **kú**= **n-góókólò**
1PL-SQ-GOING-Fa   1PL-INTL-pass-Fa   17=   9-shore

**kú=ngóókólò** | **mú**= **ká-tí**= **k-á**= **má-líbù**.
RDP   18=   12-middle   12-A.M+AU=   6-distress

'And we went | and passed | continuously along the shore | in the state of difficulty.' (Act 27:7)

c) The LM **kú** also may mark the making or breaking of contact with a group. The contact with a group is either established or dissolved. In (8.21), **kú** marks an establishment of membership with **yàbó Báyáhúdì** 'those Jews'. Others, by contrast, establish membership with the group of **yìzó ndùmwà** 'those apostles'.

(8.21) **Bá-gùmà bà-à-bò** | **bà-ná-yì-bíík-à** **kú**= **yàbó**
2-some   2-A.M-2   2-SQ-RFX-place-Fa   17=   those.N+2

**Bá-yáhúdì** || **ná**= **bà-ndì** **bà-ná-yì-bíík-à** | **kú**= **yìzó**
2-Jews   CNJ=   2-others   2-SQ-RFX-place-Fa   17=   those.N+10

**n-dùmwà**.
10-apostles

'Some of them | joined themselves to those Jews || and others joined themselves | to those apostles.' (Act 14:4)

d) The LM **kú** commonly marks a relation with a time. Time is something that can be measured, including such things as times of the day, years of life, generations, etc. In (8.22) **kú** marks an ending of a time connection, defined by the complement **kyànyà Héróòdè ákáfwà** 'the time (when) Herod died'. In this case the period of Joseph's stay in Egypt is ended at the time Herod died.

(8.22) **À-ná-béèr-à** **y-ê-yó** **mûndà** || **hàlíndé ú=kú-hí-s-á**
1-SQ-remain-Fa   E-there.N-23   place   until   AU=15-arrive-CS-Fa

**kú**= **ky-ànyà** **Héróòdè** | **á-ká-fw-à**.
17=   7-time   Herod   1-P2-die-Fa

'And he remained at that very place || until the time that Herod |died.' (Mat 2:15)

e) The LM **kú** can mark a connection with a location. In (8.23) **kú** marks an ongoing locative contact with its two complements: **múgàzì múgùmà** 'one mountain', and **gùndì** 'other (mountain)'.

## 8.1 Locative markers

(8.23) **Í**=**n-dàrè**   **y-àná-béèr-à**   **kú**=   **mú-gàzì**   **mú-gùmà** ||   **n-ê**=
AU=9-lion   9-SQ-remain-Fa   17=   3-mountain   3-one   CNJ-AU=

**n-gwì**   **y-àná-béèr-à** |   **kú**=   **gù-ndì**.
9-leopard   9-SQ-remain-Fa   17=   3-other

'The lion remained on one mountain || and the leopard remained | on the other.'

f) The LM **kú** sometimes marks pointing to a certain referent. In example (8.24) the LM **kú** points (negatively) to the referent **fwáráŋgà** 'money'. The speaker is saying that he will not look to money, but he's intending instead to grab the king's daughter so he can take her home.

(8.24) **Ni-êhê** |   **n-dá-gáá-lól-à**   **kú**=   **fwáráŋgà** ||
1SG-CTR.P   1SG-NEG-F2-look-Fa   17=   10+money

**n-gá-mú-gwàt-à**   **nààhó** ||   **gírá**   **nì-Ø-mú-tààh-àn-è**.
1SG-F2-O1-seize-Fa   only   so.that   1SG-SBV-O1-go.home-COM-Fe

'ME | I will not look to money || I will just grab her || so that I go home with her.' (06 021)

g) Sometimes **kú** makes a connection to a previous situation in the text and is used as a "point of departure" (10.2.4). In (8.25) the cl. 15 marker **kú** on the phrase **kú=yùkwô** 'therefore' marks a connection with the verbal proposition occurring in the immediately preceding context. In this case **ku=yukwo** (lit., 'in connection with that.N', or simply 'therefore').

(8.25) **Kú=yù-kwô** ||   **mù-tá-Ø-kìzì**   **kì-géráni-â** |   **mbù**=
therefore   2PL-NEG-SBV-REP   PERS-worry-Fa   ‹quote›=

«**Bí-kì** |   **by-ó**=   **tú-gáá-ly-à?**»
8-what   8-O.R=   1PL-F2-eat-Fa

'Therefore || you should not still be worrying | ‹quote›: «What | will we eat?»' (Mat 6:31)

h) The LM **kú** is commonly employed to mark the means by which something happened. In (8.26) **kú njírá yá=yùgwó múlírò** 'by means of that.N fire' shows the means by which the little turtle got some big meat.

(8.26) **Kú=**    **n-jírá**   **y-á=**   **yùgwó**   **mú-lírò** ||   **yàkó**     **ká-fùlò** ||
       17=       9-path      9-A.M=    that.N+3    3-fire           that.N+12    12-turtle

   **ká-ká-lóng-á** |   **í=n-yámá** |   **m-bámù**.
   12-P2-receive-Fa    AU=9-meat       9-big

   'By means of that fire || that turtle || got | big | meat.' (05 009)

i) The LM **kú** is also commonly employed to mark a manner. In (8.27) **kú** together with its complement **bútògê** 'calmness' shows that the man returned home with his cows in a calm manner.

(8.27) **À-ná-tááh-án-à**       ||   **yìzó**       **n-gáàvù**   **zà-à-gè** ||   **kú=**
       1-SQ-go.home-COM-Fa          those.N+10    10-cows      10-A.M-1        17=

   **bú-tògê**.
   14-calm

   'And he went home || with those cows of his || in calm.' (17 019)

j) The complement of **kú** can represent the original whole, from which a part has been removed. Thus in (8.28) **yìbyó ùgwétí úgáàlyà** 'that.N which you are eating' marks the original whole, from which a part is to be taken. In this case the crocodile asks the little monkey to give him a part of (piece taken from) the food the monkey is eating.

(8.28) **É=**   **mw-ìrá**   **w-à-nì**   ||   **ú-Ø-m-bèèrèz-é**        **nàà-n-î** |   **kú=**
       O=     1-friend    1-A.M-1SG        2SG-SBV-O1.SG-give-Fe    ADD.P-1SG      17=

   **yìbyó**     **ù-gwétí**    **ú-gáà-ly-à**.
   that.N+8    2SG-PROG     2SG-INTL-eat-Fa

   'O my friend || give and me also |some of what you are eating.' (12 006)

k) Another use of **kú** is to indicate the referent to which something else is being compared, i.e. X is bigger (or smaller, or lighter, etc.) than Y.

In (8.29) **mwàmì** 'king' is the referent that **shévyàlà wó=múndù** 'a person's father-in-law' is being compared to. In other words, "the father-in-law is the big one relative to/in connection with the king". The meaning is that the father-in-law of a person is more important than the king.

*8.1 Locative markers* 187

(8.29) Shévyàlà   w-ó=   mú-ndù ‖ y-é=   mú-kùlù | kú=
1a+father.in.law  1-A.M+AU=  1-person  1-FOC=  1-great.one  17=

mw-àmì.
1-king

'The father-in-law of a person ‖ is the one who is important | relative to the king.' (44 012)

### 8.1.2.8 Contact/connection with X that is personal: í=mwá

The LM **í=mwa** marks a *personal contact or connection* with its complement X.

#### 8.1.2.8.1 Various contexts where **í=mwá** signals contact/connection

a) The trigger for the LM **í=mwa** 'in contact/connection' (CON) is the personal involvement of its complement. This is demonstrated in (8.30), where **í=mwa** indicates personal involvement with the complement **mwìrá wàgè** 'his friend'.

(8.30) À-yúvw-á |   í=   mwá=   mw-ìrá   w-à-gè.
1+P1-hear-Fa  23=  CON=  1-friend  1-A.M-1

'He heard | from his friend.' (Ka 04 12)

In (8.31) there is a connection between **ú=rúkùndò lwàgè** 'the love of him' and 'me', signaled by the personal pronoun suffix **ni**- at the end of **í=mwànî** 'in connection with me'.

(8.31) Ú=rú-kùndò  lw-à-gè  í=   mw-à-nî ‖ lù-lí  lw-à=  bú-lyâlyà.
AU=11-love  11-A.M-1  23=  CON-A.M-1SG  11-is  11-A.M=  14-deceit

'His love in connection with me ‖ is deceitful.' (54 024)

b) In some cases the complement of **í=mwà** constitutes the goal of a transfer. This sense is found with such verbs as -**tùm**- 'send', -**haan**- 'give', -**ményees**- 'cause to know', -**ràmbulir**- 'pay taxes to', -**gálulir**- 'return to'.

In (8.32) the complement of **í=mwá**, i.e. **á=bákáláálíkwâ** 'the ones who were invited', constitutes the goal to which the king sent the servants. The servants are sent to personally interact with the invitees, telling them to come to the wedding.

(8.32) Ùyó      mw-àmì ‖ à-ná-tùm-à      á=bá-kòzì        bà-à-gé | í=
     that.N+1  1-king   1-SQ-send-Fa     AU=2-servants    2-A.M-1   23=

     mwá=      bá-ká-láálík-w-â ‖    bà-Ø-géndí       bà-bwír-á ‖  kwó=
     CON=+S.R  2-P2-invite-PS-Fa     2-SBV-GOING      O2-tell-Fa   CMP=

     bà-Ø-yíj-è        kú=   bú-hyà.
     2-SBV-come-Fe     17=   14-wedding

'That king ‖ sent his servants | to the invited ones ‖ (so) they could go and tell them ‖ to come to the wedding.' (Mat 22:3)

c) In other cases the complement of **í=mwà** constitutes the source of a transfer, with verbs such as **-yùvw-** 'hear', **-lóng-** 'receive', **-huun-** 'request'. In (8.33) the complements of **í=mwà**, i.e. **yîshò úlì mwí=gúlù** 'your father in heaven', constitutes the source from which the reward might be received.

(8.33) Írí    mw-àngà-kízí    bì-gír-á     kú=   ky-ènènèkê ‖  ndàà=kì-yó
     if    2PL-CND-REP    O8-do-Fa     17=   7-openly      NEG.FOC=PERS-9

     m-bèmbó |   y-ó=    mú-gá-lông-à |    í=    mwá=    Yíshò |
     9-reward    9-O.R=  2PL-F2-receive-Fa  23=   CON=    1a+your.father

     ú-lì       mw-í=   gúlù.
     S.R+1-is   18-5=   above

'If you would repeatedly do it openly ‖ there's no longer any reward | which you will receive | from your father | who is in heaven.' (Mat 6:1)

### 8.1.2.9 'within': mu

The core meaning of the Bantu cl. 18 concord marker **mú** is 'place within'. The LM **mú** can also convey several non-locational meanings, involving abstract state, time, means, and the marking of set members.

#### 8.1.2.9.1 Various contexts where mu indicates location

a) Many *geographical areas* can occur as the complement of the LM **mú**, including such things as **kāāyà** 'village', **kíhùgò** 'country', **lúgûndù** 'banana grove', **lúbàkò** 'virgin forest', **íshámbà** 'desert', **bwàmì** 'the king's headquarters', **ndálò** 'field', **njírà** 'path',[5] **kyànyààNYà** 'sky', **lwījì** 'river', etc. Each of these

---

[5] The noun **njírà** 'path', although not an area extending in all directions like the other place nouns in this group, can nevertheless be viewed as a geographical area, as it has boundaries (even on the side) and it extends ahead and behind. Thus one can be in the path for an extended period of time.

geographical areas has boundaries of some sort, and when they occur as the complement of **mu**, the understanding is that the referent is located physically within those boundaries.

In (8.34) the LM **mú** marks the area within its complement, which is **njírà** 'path'.

(8.34) **Ìrí    bá-ká-b-à          bà-kòlà      mú=    n-jírà** ||  **yàbó**
       when  2-P2-become-Fa  2-are.NEW  18=    9-path      those.N+2

   **bá-tàbánà | bà-ná-shálìk-à.**
   2-young.men   2-SQ-be.hungry-Fa

   'When they were now in the road || those young men | became hungry.'
   (01 022)

b) The LM **mú** sometimes refers to the *area perceived as within the boundaries of an object X* (X not being inherently locational). The referential contexts include rather interesting cases, such as within the area of a part of the body, e.g. *within the area* of the neck, waist, back, or feet.

Thus in (8.35) the LM **mú** marks placement within the area of the LP complement **ígósì** 'neck'. In this case the snake says that it will wrap itself in the area of the neck, obviously not meaning physically inside the flesh of the neck.

(8.35) **Yùgwó    mú-jōkà** ||  **gw-àná-bwîr-à** |  **ìyó        n-gwârè:** ||
       that.N+3  3-snake       3-SQ-tell-Fa         that.N+9  9-quail

   «**N-gá-kú-yì-zìng-ír-à**                          **mw-í=    gósì** |
   1SG-F2-O2.SG-RFX-wrap.around-APL-Fa  18-5=    neck

   **ù-ná-m-bálàl-àn-è**           |  **hàlíndé í=   ká-jábó** | **k-ó=**
   2SG-CON-O1.SG-fly-COM-Fe    until       23=   12-across    12-A.M+AU=

   **lw-ījì.**
   11-river

   'That snake || told | that quail: || «I will wrap myself around your neck | and you will fly with me | until across | the river.»' (13 005)

c) The LM can also refer to an interior area, which is completely surrounded on all sides, top, and bottom. Some nouns which by default refer to an object with an inside area include **kíshímò** 'hole', **lwâlà** 'cave/rock', **lúdáhà** 'bag', **kábìndì** 'water pot', and **nyûmbà** 'house'. In (8.36) the LM **mú** marks placement within the interior of the LP complement **nyûmbà** 'house'.

(8.36) Ùyó       mú-tàbánà ‖ ìrí    á-ká-b-á          à-kòlí         gw-ét-í
      that.N+1   1-young.man   when   1-P2-become-Fa   1-is.NEWLY   have-RS-Fi

      ùyó        mú-hyàkàzì  mú=     ny-ûmbà ‖        à-Ø-búlí       ményá |
      that.N+1   1-new.wife  18=     9-house          1-SBV-SBSQ     know

      kwó=       yò          mú-hyàkàzì |   à-lí   mú-lwàzí |   w-ó=
      CMP=       that.N+1    1-new.wife     1-is   1-sick.one   1-A.M+AU=

      mú-bêmbè.
      3-leprosy

'That young man ‖ when he now had that new wife in the house ‖ he then knew | that that new wife | was sick | with leprosy.' (53 012)

### 8.1.2.9.2 Contexts where **mu** does not indicate location

Presented below are contexts involving the LM **mú**, where location is not in focus. In these cases **mú** can mark an item as occurring within an abstract state, as well as within a period of time. It can also mark means, delimit set membership, mark previous referents that are about to be reactivated in a significant new development of the story, and mark an item from which something is extracted.

a) The LM **mú** 'within' can take complements representing *abstract states*, defined as referents that are neither material, nor directly measurable, such as: **kíhúlù** 'darkness', **búkénì** 'poverty', **mákùbà** 'hardship', **káshékò** 'laughter', **mágézô** 'trials/temptation', **lúfû** 'death', etc.

In (8.37) the LM **mú** marks placement within the abstract state represented by the LP complement **kíhúlù** 'darkness'. Because the man was within the state of darkness, he could not see the snake.

(8.37) Ìrì      á-ká-gír-á   mbw-à=       Ø-yábíìr-è |    ú=lú-shààlì         mú=
       when     1-P2-try-Fa  FRUS.INTL-1=  SBV-take-Fe    AU=11-firewood      18=

       kí-húlù ‖    à-ná-gù-hùm-à        =kwô ‖   gw-àná-mú-kòméérés-à |   kú=
       7-dark       1-SQ-O3-touch-Fa     =17      3-SQ-O1-bit-Fa            17=

       mú-nwê.
       3-finger

'When he tried to take | the piece of firewood in the dark ‖ he touched it (snake) ‖ and it bit him | on the finger.' (48 013)

b) The LM **mú** sometimes marks the time period within which something occurs. In (8.38) the LM **mú** marks placement within the time period **kábìgìngwê**

## 8.1 Locative markers

'late afternoon', i.e. the food was brought within the time of **kábìgìngwê** 'late afternoon'.

(8.38) **Mú**=    **ká-bìgìngwê**    ‖    **bà-ná-bà-léét-ér-à**    **í**=**by-ókúlyâ**.
      18=    12-late.afternoon    2-SQ-O2-bring-APL-Fa    AU=8-food

'In the late afternoon ‖ they brought them food.' (09 007)

c) The cl. 18 LM **mú** is often used to indicate *means*. In (8.39) the complement of **mú**, i.e. **bírōōtò** 'dream' indicates the means by which Joseph was warned.

(8.39) **N-é**=    **ky-ànyà**    **á-ká-kéngúl-w-á**    **mú**=    **bí-rōōtò** ‖
      CNJ-AU=    7-time    1-P2-warn-PS-Fa    18=    8-dream

      **à-ná-sháàg-à**    **yà-hô**.
      1-SQ-leave-Fa    there.N-16

'And (at) the time he was warned in a dream ‖ he left there.' (Mat 2:22)

d) Sometimes the LM **mú** serves to *delimit set membership* within the boundaries of a location, always in conjunction with a preceding associative marker. Inherently locative nouns with defined geographical boundaries include **kíhūgò** 'country', **kāāyà** 'village', **múgāzì** 'mountain', **kíshūkà** 'bush', **ndálò** 'field', **kyànyààǹyà** 'sky', etc.

In (8.40) the combination of the cl. 2 associative marker **ba**, together with the LM **mú**, serves to delimit the referents **á**=**báshààjà bóóshì** 'all the elders' to those being within the complement, i.e. **yàkó kààyá kô**=**yó mwàmì** 'that.N village of that.N king'.

(8.40) **Á**=**bá-shààjà**    **bó-óshì** |    **b-à**=    **mú**=    **yàkó**    **kà-àyá**    **k-ô**=
      AU=2-old.men    2-all    2-A.M=    18=    that.N+12    12-village    12-A.M=

      **yó**    **mw-àmì** ‖    **bà-ná-yît-w-à**.
      that.N+1    1-king    2-SQ-kill-PS-Fa

'All the old men | from within that village of that king ‖ were killed.' (51 009)

e) In conjunction with a preceding associative marker, the LM **mú** can also restrict members being within set X *according to certain non-locational parameters*, i.e. the referent is defined as being among X, as opposed to other sets.

In (8.41) the cl. 11 associative marker **lwa**, together with the LM **mú**, serves to delimit the referent **ú**=**lwīmbò** 'song' to those songs within the complement of **mú**: here, **mú nyìmbó zà**=**Dáùdì** 'songs of David'. The song is from within the songs of David, as opposed to other songs.

(8.41) Ú=lw-ìmbó | lw-á= bà-lì mú= zàmúúk-ír-á í=
 AU=11-song 11-A.M+S.R= 2-is PROG= go.up-APL-Fa 23=

 Yèrùsàléèmù || lw-à= mú= ny-ìmbò z-à= Dáùdì.
 Jerusalem 11-A.M= 18= 10-songs 10-A.M= David

'The song | of the ones going up to Jerusalem || from among the songs of David.' (Psa 122:1)

f) In some cases the locative phrase headed by **mú** mentions previous referents, which serves as a platform from which a subset of those referents is reactivated, emerging into focus again. In (8.42) the complement of the LM **mú**, i.e. the previously mentioned **yàbó báhyàkàzì** 'those.N newly-wed women' serve as the platform from which the subset **múgùmà** 'one' emerges into focus.

(8.42) **Mú-gùmà** | **mú**= **yàbò** **bá-hyàkàzì** || à-ná-dèt-à:...
 1-one 18= those.N+2 2-new.wives 1-SQ-speak-Fa

'One | from among those new wives || said:...' (01 011)

g) In (8.43) the complement of **mú**, i.e. **àrìjâ** 'silver' is the source from which the **í=bíngóró-ngórò** 'coins' are extracted.

(8.43) **Kwôkwó** | bà-ná-yàm-à bá-gá-mú-hèèrèz-á || í=bí-ngóró-ngóró
 thus.N 2-SQ-IMMED-Fa 2-INTL-O1-give-Fa AU=8-coin-RDP

 má-kùmì gà-shàtù || í-bí-ká-tùl-w-á | **mú**= **àrìjâ**.
 6-tens 6-three S.R-8-P2-smelt-PS-Fa 18= silver

'Thus | they immediately gave him || thirty coins || which were smelted | from silver.' (Mat 26:15)

### 8.1.3 Idioms involving frozen locative markers

There are two idioms (where the whole is not predictable from the sum of the parts) involving frozen locative concord markers.

#### 8.1.3.1 'on one's side': Cl. 16 há=, plus cl. 11 lu-

The frozen adverbial idiom with the meaning 'on one's own accord (unilaterally)' begins with a frozen set of "stacked" concord class markers, i.e. the cl. 16 **há** and the cl. 11 **lu-**, in reference to **lú-hândè** (11-side), followed by the associative marker -**a**, and finally the associative pronoun. The first three elements never change, while the associative pronoun varies, depending on its

*8.1 Locative markers*

antecedent. The idiom often communicates a deliberate, unilateral position, without reference to others, and as such can be used in a derogatory sense.

In (8.44) the frozen prefixes **há=lwa-** are followed by the cl. 1 pronoun -**gè** to form **há=lwàgè** 'on his own accord'. In this case, the point is that **Káyáfà** did not speak on his own accord, independently of others. The implication, rather, is that someone else was behind what he was saying.

(8.44)   **Yìryó**    **í-gámbó** ‖ **ly-ó=**    **yò**    **Káyáfá**    **á-ká-dèt-à** ‖
      that.N+5    5-word      7-A.M+=   that.N+1   Caiaphas   1-P2-speak-Fa

      **à-tá-ká-lì-dét-à**      **há=**    **lw-à-gè**    **y-ényènè**.
      1-NEG-P2-O5-speak-Fa   16=      11-A.M-1    1-self

'That word ‖ which Caiaphas spoke ‖ he did not speak it on his own accord by himself.' (Jhn 11:51)

### 8.1.3.2 'at home of': í=mwa, mú=mwa, há=mwa

The idiom based on the frozen cl. 18 locative marker **mú**, followed by the associative marker **a-**, means 'at the home of'. Although the heart of the idiom (i.e. **mwa**) is frozen, the LM at the beginning is still employed to make productive distinctions. Thus when this idiom begins with the class locative marker **mú** it means 'in the home of'. When it begins with the cl. 23 **í**, it means 'at the location of the home'. When beginning with the cl. 16 **há** it means 'at the location of home, with significant development of the theme'.

In (8.45) the cl. 23 LM **í**, followed by the frozen idiomatic form **mwa** and the cl. 1 associative pronoun -**gè**, combines to form **í=mwàgè**, meaning 'at his home'.

(8.45)   **Ùyó**      **mú-ndù** ‖ **à-ná-tááh-án-à**      **yàkó**    **ká-bwá** | **í=**
      that.N+1   1-person    1-SQ-go.home-COM-Fa   that.N+12   12-dog    23=

      **mw-à-gè**.
      home-A.M-1

'That person ‖ returned home with that dog | to his home.' (14 033)

In (8.46) the cl. 16 LM **há**, followed by the frozen idiomatic form **mwa** and the cl. 1 associative pronoun -**gè**, combines to form **há=mwàgè**, meaning 'at his home', and also marks 'a significant development of the theme line', i.e. while the man was sitting at home, a messenger came from the king's headquarters.

(8.46) Ìrí       á-ká-b-á       à-bwàt-íír-ì   há=     mw-à-gè   ‖   í=n-dùmwà
      when      1-P2-be-Fa    1-sit-RS-Fi    16=     home-A.M-1    AU=9-message

      y-é=            bw-àmì        |  y-àná-yîj-á  |   kw-â=
      9-A.M+AU=       14-kings.place   9-SQ-come-Fa     CMP-1=

      Ø-zíndúkírí              géndí     kòl-á |    í=   bw-āmì.
      SBV-EARLY.MORNING        GOING     work-Fa    23=  14-king's.place

'When he was sitting at his home ‖ a messenger of the king | came (saying) ‖ that he should go early in the morning to work | at the king's place.' (44 005)

In (8.47) the cl. 18 LM **mú**, followed by the frozen idiomatic form **mwa** and the cl. 1 associative pronoun -**gè**, combines to form **mú=mwàgè**, meaning 'in his home'. In this case the first instance of the cl. 18 locative marker **mú=** is productive, while the second instance, where it is found in the heart of the idiom (**mwa**) is frozen.

(8.47) Mbw-à=         Ø-hí-s-é           kàndì   yìzó       n-yámà    mú=
       as.soon.as-1=  SBV-arrive-CS-Fe   again   those.N+10  1-meat   18=

       mw-à-gè    ‖  mú-ká-à-gè    à-ná-ráákár-à       bwénèènè.
       home-A.M-1    1-wife-A.M-1  1-SQ-be.angry-Fa    very.much

'As soon as he again brought that meat into his home ‖ his wife became furious.' (35 014)

Although 'home' most commonly means 'the compound', it can also mean 'one's home city', or even 'heaven'.

### 8.1.3.3 'instead of' á=hándú ha

The cl. 16 locative noun **á=hándù** can be used in an idiomatic way with a following associative phrase to mean 'in the place of' i.e. 'instead of'. In (8.48) the phrase **hà=yîshè Hèróòdè** means 'in the place of his father Herod'.

(8.48) **Hálìkò** | **írí**    **Yúsèfù** | **á-ká-yùvw-â** | **kwó=**   **Àrìkèláò** | **y-é=**
 but         when    Joseph   1-P2-heard-Fa   CMP=   Archelaus   1-FOC=

**w-à-yìm-á**          | **í=**   **Bù-yàhúdì** | **á=hà-ndú**   **hà=**   **yîshè**    |
1-P1-take.rule-Fa    23=    14-Judea    AU=16-place    16=    1a+his.father

**Hèróòdè...**
Herod

'But | when Joseph | heard | that Archelaus | is the one ruling | Judea | in the place of his father | Herod...' (Mat 2:22)

In (8.49) the cl. 16 focal copula **hó** (here **há** because of vowel coalescence) is used in the same way. It represents **á=hándú hó** 'instead of the place where', and introduces an entire embedded clause.

(8.49) **Bùlí**   **bw-îjâ** || **kí-gùmà**   **ky-à=**   **mú=**   **bí-rúmbú**   **by-à-wè** |
 14-is    14-well       7-one        7-A.M=    18=    8-organs        8-A.M-2SG

**kì-téérék-è** || **há=**            **má-gálá**   **gà-à-wè**   **gó-óshì** |
7-get.lost-Fe   16-FOC+AU=    6-body     6-A.M-2SG    6-all

**gà-ngà-lásh-w-á** |   **í=**   **nàkwêrè.**
6-POT-throw-PS-Fa      23=    hell

'It's good || one of your organs | gets lost || instead of your whole body | being thrown | into hell.' (Mat 5:29)

## 8.2 Position nouns

### 8.2.1 Position noun structure

#### 8.2.1.1 *Position nouns, vis-à-vis the notions of "noun" and "preposition"*

The "position noun" is a major distinctive of the Bantu language family. In Kifuliiru this class includes forms such as **mbérè** 'in front' and **bútàmbí (lyé=nyûmbà)** 'beside (the house)'. Although the first tendency might be to refer to such words as "prepositions", in terms of their semantic meaning, there has been significant objection raised in the Bantu literature to that term, e.g. Doke (1943:31) with many preferring to categorize these words as nouns. A careful analysis shows that these words share characteristics of both nouns and prepositions.

Position nouns resemble "normal" non-position nouns, in that:
- Both can comprise the sole element of the LP complement. The cl. 16 LM **há** can take the NP complement **múlyángò** in the phrase **há=múlyángò** 'at the door' or the position noun complement **mbérè** in the phrase **há=mbérè** 'at the place ahead'.
- Both can be modified by associative phrases. Cf. the "normal" noun with associative **á=káshòngyá kê=yó nyûmbà** 'the peak of that.N house' and the position noun, **ká-tì** in **mú=kátì kè=ndálò** 'in the middle of the field'.
- Just like "normal" nouns, each position noun belongs to a particular noun class and can be analyzed as consisting of a GNP plus a stem.

Position nouns resemble prepositions, in that:
- They constitute a closed class (of only fifteen members).
- They occur in a very restricted grammatical position, i.e. they must be directly preceded by one of the LMs **há**, **mú**, or **í**, and are optionally followed only by an associative phrase.
- They may not co-occur with other standard noun phrase constituents, such as adjectives, quantifiers, etc. For example, **í=kígûndù kígùmà** 'one/a certain banana plant' is allowed, while *****ínyúmá ngùmà** 'one/a certain behind' is not. Again, **bìryá bigûndù** 'those banana plants' is allowed, but *****yìryó ínyúmà** 'that.N behind' is not.
- Besides having the three structural criteria just mentioned, position nouns also resemble prepositions in that they all carry a meaning of "relative position".

Based on the above, we have opted to employ the term "position noun", which seems to reflect more adequately the characteristics of both nouns and prepositions.

### 8.2.1.2 *Position noun concord class agreement*

Position nouns, as defined here, are limited to forms which meet all three of the following criteria: 1) they denote meanings of relative position; 2) they are always preceded by a LM; 3) they can be followed by an associative phrase.

Thus far in the data, according to this definition, we have encountered a total of fifteen position nouns, listed in table 8.3.

## 8.2 Position nouns

Table 8.3. Inventory of position nouns

|     | Cl. of root | Position noun | Gloss | Cl. of A.M |
|-----|---|---|---|---|
| a.  | 5 | í-dàkò | 'under' | 5 |
| b.  | 5 | í-fwò | 'below' | 5 |
| c.  | 5 | í-gúlù | 'above' | 5 |
| d.  | 9/10 | m-bùgà[a] | 'outside' | 5 |
| e.  | 9/10 | ny-úmà | 'behind' | 5 |
| f.  | 9/10 | m-bàsháánà | 'border' | 5 |
| g.  | 9/10 | n-dà | 'inside' | 5 |
| h.  | 9/10 | m-bérè | 'before' | 5 |
| i.  | 14 | bú-tàmbì | 'beside' | 5 |
| j.  | 12 | ká-jábò | 'across' | 12 |
| k.  | 12 | ká-tì= | 'middle' | 12 |
| l.  | 11 | lú-hândè | 'side/direction' | 11 |
| m.  | 11 | lú-lyò | 'right.side' | 11 |
| n.  | 11 | lú-móshò | 'left.side' | 11 |
| o.  | 6 | má-lángà[b] | 'front' | 6 |

[a]The cl. 5 **ímbùgà** 'outside' is probably related to the cl. 11/10 **lúbùgà/ mbùgà** 'courtyard'.

[b]When used as a position noun, it is always preceded by a locative marker. This noun is also used as a normal cl. 6 noun meaning 'the face'. When used as a regular noun, it is not preceded by a locative marker.

From table 8.3 we see that the majority of the position nouns (rows a–i) trigger the cl. 5 concord marker **li-** on the associative marker.[6] This is seen in the locative phrase **há=bútàmbí lyó=mútúmbà** 'beside the corpse', where the (apparently) cl. 14 position noun **bútàmbì** 'beside' is followed by the cl. 5 associative marker (A.M) **lya**.

For three of these, the position noun itself is also cl. 5, as in the cases of **ídàkò** 'under', **ífwò** 'below', and **ígúlù** 'above' (table 8.3a–c).

---

[6]When the position noun **bútàmbì** is used as a general position noun, meaning 'beside', the following associative marker generally has cl. 5 agreements. But when **bútàmbì** is used to mean 'at/along the edge', i.e. at the literal physical edge of something, such as a road, it takes the cl. 14, agreement, as can be seen below, where the cl. 14 A.M **bwa** (seen as **bwo** here because of vowel coalescence with the initial vowel of the demonstrative) is employed instead of the usual cl. 5 **lya**.

Y-àná-yì-nénèk-à |　　há=　　bú-tâmbì　　bw-ô=　　y-ó　　mú-tèzì.
9-SQ-RFX-tip.toe-Fa　　16=　　14-beside　　14-A.M-that.N　　1-P.R　　1-trapper
'And it tiptoed | at the side of that (TSM) trapper.' 49 009

Position nouns which trigger the cl. 5 A.M, but do not themselves belong to cl. 5, include the cl. 9/10 position nouns **mbúgà** 'outside', **nyúmà** 'behind', **mbàshààná** 'border', **ndâ** 'inside', and **mbérè** 'in front', see table (8.3d-h) as well as the cl. 14 **bútàmbì** 'beside'.

The remaining six position nouns do not trigger the cl. 5 associative marker; rather in each case the prefix of the position noun agrees with the corresponding A.M. Thus the cl. 12 position nouns[7] **kájábò** 'across' and **kátì** 'middle' trigger the cl. 12 associative marker (A.M) **ka**, the cl. 11 position nouns **lúhândè** 'side', **lúlyò** 'right side', and **lúmóshò** 'left side' trigger the cl. 11 A.M **lwa**, and the cl. 6 position noun **málángà** 'in front' triggers the cl. 6 associative marker **ga**.

### 8.2.1.3 Collocational restrictions of position nouns with locative markers

There are definite restrictions regarding the possible combinations of LMs and position nouns. The overall patterns stand out clearly in table 8.4, providing representative samples from the data. In this table, the examples all include a following associative phrase complement, although most of these position nouns can also stand by themselves.

Table 8.4. Co-occurrences of various locative markers with position nouns

|   | With cl. 16 **há** (all TSM) | With cl. 18 **mu** | With cl 23 **i** |
|---|---|---|---|
| a. | h<u>á</u>=m-bérè ly-á-byò<br>16=9-before 5-A.M-8 | | í=m-bérè ly-ó=lú-fù<br>23=9-front 5-A.M+AU=11-death |
| b. | h<u>á</u>=nyúmá ly-é=n-yûmbà<br>16=behind 5-A.M+AU=9-house | | í=n-yúmá ly-á=kā-āyà<br>23=9-outside 5-A.M+AU=23-village |
| c. | h<u>á</u>=m-bùgà ly-ó=lú-gò<br>16=9-outside 5-A.M+AU 11-perimeter | | í=m-bùgà ly-á-kò<br>23=9-outside 5-A.M-12 |
| d. | h<u>á</u>=ká-jábò k-ó=lw-ījì<br>16=12-across 12-A.M+AU=11-river | | í=ká-jabó k-ó=lw- ījì<br>23=12-across 12-A.M+AU=11-river |
| e. | h-<u>í</u>=fwó ly-á=kā-āyà<br>16-AU=below 5-A.M+AU=12-village | | í=fwo ly-é=Bétèèrì<br>23=below 5-A.M+23=Bethel |

---

[7]Some Bantu scholars have linked the class 12 prefix **ká-** found on the position noun stems **-jábò** 'across' and **-ti** 'middle' (as well as that in words such as **kā-āyà** 'home', **ká-gúlìrò** 'market', etc.) to an ancient class 24 locative reflex **ka** (Gauton 1999 and Ziervogel 1959).

## 8.2 Position nouns

|    | With cl. 16 **há** (all TSM) | With cl. 18 **mu** | With cl 23 **i** |
|----|------------------------------|---------------------|-------------------|
| f. | <u>há</u>=bú-tàmbì ly-à-gè<br>16=14-beside 5-A.M-1 |                     | <u>í</u>=bú-tàmbì ly-é=n-jírà<br>23=14-beside 5-A.M+AU=9-path |
| g. |                              | <u>mú</u>=m-bàshàànà lyé=ndáló zì-ì-tù<br>18=9-middle 7-A.M+AU=9-field 10-A.M-1PL |                   |
| h. | <u>há</u>=kátì kà-à-bò<br>16=12-middle 12-A.M-2 | <u>mú</u>=ká-tì k-é=n-dálò<br>18-12-middle 12-A.M+AU=9-field |                   |
| i. | h-<u>í</u>=dākò ly-é=shyókò<br>16-5=under 5-A.M+AU=spring | <u>mw</u>-í=dākò ly-ó=mu-gazi<br>18-AU=bottom 5-A.M+AU=3-mountain |                   |
| j. | ---                          | <u>mú</u>=ndá ly-ó=rú-sóòzò<br>18=inside 7-A.M+AU=11-cup |                   |
| k. | h-<u>í</u>=gúlú ly-é=n-yáàjà<br>16-5=top 5-A.M+AU=9-lake | ---                 |                   |
| l. |                              | ---                 | <u>í</u>=má-lángà<br>23=6-front |
| m. | ---                          | ---                 | <u>í</u>=lú-hândè lw-é=lú-lyò<br>23=11-right 11-A.M+AU=11-side |
| n. |                              |                     | <u>í</u>=lú-lyó lw-á=mw-àmì<br>23=11-right 11-A.M=1-king |
| o. |                              |                     | <u>í</u>=lú-móshó lw-à=nyínà<br>23=11-left 11-A.M=mother |

Note: The following observations can be made:
1) The only LMs that can occur[8] before position nouns[9] are cl. 16 **há**, 18 **mú**, and 23 **í**.
2) The majority of position nouns[10] (nine altogether) can be preceded by the cl. 16 **há**, as well as by either the cl. 23 **í** (see rows a–f), or the cl. 18 **mú** (see rows g–j).

### 8.2.2 Position noun functions

All position nouns can indicate relative locative position, featuring such notions as 'ahead', 'behind', 'outside', 'outer surface', 'above', 'below', 'inside',

---

[8] In addition, the cl. 17 **kú** can co-occurring with the position noun **bútàmbì** 'beside', but only when **bútàmbì** is modified by an associative phrase with cl. 14 agreement rather than cl. 5, and an inherently locational complement, e.g. **kú=bútàmbì bwé=nyáàjà** 'at the edge of the lake'.

[9] That is to say, the "frozen" locative marker combinations **í'mûndà** 'at', **í=wà** 'at', and **í'mwà** 'in connection' never occur with position nouns.

[10] The anomalous case of **kwí=dàkò**, which occurred once in all the data, can be considered "sub-standard".

'middle', 'across', 'adjacent', and 'in relative direction of', etc. Since all position nouns can carry locative meanings, these meanings will be considered here as "primary". Some of those same position nouns can also indicate relative time, e.g. 'time before', 'time after', or a 'middle point in time'.

In addition, many position nouns may also have secondary meanings that are neither locative nor temporal, and the link between the primary and secondary meanings is sometimes not totally transparent. For example, it would be impossible to predict that the position noun **ígúlù**, with the primary locative meaning of 'above', would also carry the secondary meanings of 'purpose', 'result', or 'concerning'.

Table 8.5 presents a summary of the possible position noun meanings. Both the primary locative meanings, as well as the non-locative meanings are detailed.

Table 8.5. Position noun functions

| Position noun | Locative meaning | Other meanings |
|---|---|---|
| **í=mbérè** | 'in front of; ahead' | 'time before' |
| **há=mbérè** | 'location ahead of, TSM' | |
| **í=málángà** | 'in front of' | |
| **í=nyúmà** | 'behind' | 'outside; outside (surface)' |
| **há=nyúmà** | 'location behind, TSM' | 'time after; other than' |
| **í=mbùgà** | 'outside' | 'outsiders, illegitimate' |
| **há=mbùgà** | 'outside, TSM' | |
| **hí=gúlù** | 'up, TSM' | 'concerning, purpose, result' |
| **há=lúgúlú** | 'above' | |
| **mwí=dākò** | 'at base of' | 'under authority' |
| **hí=dākò** | 'area below, TSM' | |
| **í=fwò** | 'lower place' | |
| **mú=ndâ** | 'inside (of object)' | |

| Position noun | Locative meaning | Other meanings |
|---|---|---|
| **mú=kātì** | 'in the middle' | 'middle time' 'set from which subset taken' |
| **há=kātì** | 'place in middle, TSM' | 'essential co-relation with' |
| **mú=mbàshààna̋** | 'at edge between' | |
| **í=kájábo** | 'across (a distance)' | |
| **há=kájábò** | 'location across, TSM' | |
| **í=bútàmbì** | 'adjacent to, beside' | |
| **há=bútàmbì** | 'place adjacent to, TSM' | |
| **í=lúhândè** | 'side, direction' | |
| **í=lúlyò** | 'right hand side' | |
| **í=lúmóshò** | 'left hand side' | |

### 8.2.3 Forms resembling position nouns

While most locative phrases fit into the categories described above, there are a few that diverge from the definition of position nouns in that they can never be followed an associative phrase. Thus one cannot say **\*í=múgóngó lyé=nyûmbà**. Forms in this category include **í=múgóngò** 'back, or outside surface', **há=lúgúlù** 'place above', and **hááshì** 'down on the ground'.

# 9

# Verb Words and Phrases

In the first half of this chapter we present an exhaustive list of types of verbal forms.[1] This begins with single-word forms. We then describe multiword forms with only one subject prefix, as well as multiword forms with the identical subject prefix on two words. Then we present verb phrases[2] involving auxiliaries which precede infinitives. Finally we present different kinds of adverbial auxiliaries.

In the second half of the chapter we present an exhaustive catalogue of all form-meanings for verbs and verb phrases. These forms are sorted by tense, aspect and mood.[3] By "tense" we mean the basic time referenced by the utterance. Tense in Kifuliiru includes varieties of unmarked past, recent past, immediate future, unmarked future, and remote future.[4]

Combined with these tenses are the traditional categories of aspect, including the notions of habitual, persistive, progressive, resultative, sequential, predictable continuation, etc.

---

[1] These forms are differentiated from each other by combinations of the following six factors: (a) the tense/aspect/mood (TAM) marker in the fourth prefix position of the verb, (b) the choice of final vowel, (c) the stem-tone pattern, (d) the verb stem form (default versus resultative), (e) the additions of various auxiliaries, (f) additional semantic nuances (conditional, contrary-to-fact, etc.) can also be created by the use of certain conjunctions before the verb form.

[2] In this book "verb words" refers to single-word verb forms, while "verb phrases" refers to a verb word with associated auxiliaries. "Verb phrase" here is *not* used in the generative grammar sense of an entire predicate, i.e. the verb together with any non-verbal complement(s).

[3] I am indebted to Bybee et al (1994) for many of the meaning labels employed for verbs and verb phrases.

[4] Note that I do not include a present tense here, as all verb forms in the present tense have aspectual qualities, and thus are listed under "aspect".

Mood categories include the broad category of purpose and intention, which include subjunctive, imperative, unrealized expectation, progressive intentional, intentional previous state, frustrated intention. Mood also covers potential/conditional, including several contrary-to-fact varieties.

## 9.1 Overview of verb form types

This section presents a general summary of the basic types of verb forms.

### 9.1.1 Basic affixation for verb words

The single-word verb consists of ten possible positions (or slots), which are laid out in table 9.1. Some of these positions can be filled by one of many different semantic forms, e.g. the subject GNP slot, the tense/mood slot, the object GNP slot, and of course, the verb base slot. The subject relative has three possibilities, and the final vowel can be filled by one of four possibilities. Each of the remaining slots each has only one possible filler. The only mandatory positions are the verb base and the final vowel. In table 9.1 we mark the base, the stem, and the macrostem. In addition, in order to simplify formulaic descriptions, we have used the term "initial prefixes" to denote any prefixes found in the first six slots, since they often function together.

In cases of analytic verb forms (i.e. those consisting of more than one word) the six initial prefixes occur on the first word (the initial auxiliary), while the object and reflexive prefixes are attached to the final word of the form. For example, in **tù-tà-kì-rí mú=mú-shúlík-à** (1PL-NEG-PERS-is PROG=O1-hit-Fa) 'We are not still hitting him', the initial prefixes, from positions 1–6, are attached to the auxiliary, while the object prefix **mú-** 'him', from position 7, is attached to the main (lexical) verb at the end.

Immediately following table 9.1, we briefly comment on each of the positions, though many categories are discussed in more depth in subsequent sections. Note the phonological rules[5] affecting the indication of vowel length in various prefixes, such as -**gáá-** 'F2', -**à-** 'P1', -**ááyè** 'F3', -**àná-** 'SQ', -**àngà-** 'CND/POT', etc.

---

[5]The long vowel **aa** formed by the coalescence of any prefix ending in **a-** with an **a**-initial TAM marker (**à-** 'recent past (P1)', **àná-** 'sequential (SQ)', -**ááli** 'unmarked past (P3)', -**àngà** 'conditional' (CND), -**ángá** 'conditional, past', -**ááyè** 'remote future (F3)' is shortened by phonological rule whenever three or more morae follow: e.g. the cl. 2 subject prefix **ba-** plus the sequential tense **àná-** produce a long underlying vowel in **ba-àná-génd-a** (2-SQ-go-Fa) 'and they went'. However, this is realized as a short **a-**, as in **bànágêndà**. Following the practical orthography, we simplify this to a rule that any long vowel in verb prefixes which is due to morpheme concatenation is written as a single vowel.

9.1 Overview of verb form types

Table 9.1. Basic affixation for verb words

| Initial prefixes | | | | | | Macrostem | | | |
|---|---|---|---|---|---|---|---|---|---|
| | | | | | | | | Stem | |
| 1 | 2 | 3 | 4 | 5 | 6 | 7 | 8 | 9 | 10 |
| S.R | S | NEG | TAM | ADD.V | PERS | Obj.1 | Obj. 2 | Base[a] | FV |
| á | Subj. | ta- | à- | ná-[b] | kì- | Obj. | yì- | | -a |
| í | GNPs | | ká- | | | GNPs | n- | | -e |
| ú | | | gáá-[c] | | | | | | -ir-i[d] |
| | | | àná- | | | | | | |
| | | | na- | | | | | | |
| | | | ángá- | | | | | | -i |
| | | | àngà- | | | | | | |
| | | | tá- | | | | | | |
| | | | kì- | | | | | | |
| | | | Ø[e] | | | | | | |

[a]The verb "base" is comprised of the verb "root", including the extensions, and any other non-final suffixes.
[b]The **ná-** (ADD.V) can also occur in the macrostem, just before the object.
[c]The future/intentional **gáá-** is shortened when there are three or more morae following within the word.
[d]The entire resultative morpheme is considered a "final element" (see Volume 1). It can however, be interrupted by other morphemes, so in glossing, the two parts are glossed separately, as RS (resultative) and Fi (final -i). The final -i alone is also used as a FV in non-resultative auxiliary forms, where it is not usually glossed separately, but may be separated from the rest of the auxiliary by the addition of the emphatic extension, e.g. **ágáyíjì gìgwátà** 'he will come and seize it' versus **ágáyíj-àg-ì gìgwátà** 'he will come EMP and seize it'. However, the final -i of the auxiliary has its historical roots in the cl. 5 infinitive prefix.
[e]The null morpheme is used, for example, in the timeless tense.

Position 1: The SUBJECT RELATIVE MARKER, which is homophonous with the nominal augment, is the only morpheme which may occur to the left of the subject prefix.

Position 2: The SUBJECT PREFIX normally agrees in noun class with its antecedent. The subject prefix carries no inherent tone and is found in all finite forms except for the imperative. The actual forms for the subject prefix are: 1SG **n-**, 2SG **u-**, cl. 1 **a-**, 1PL **tu-**, 2PL **mu-**, cl. 2 **ba-**, cl. 3 **gu-**, cl. 4 **i-**, cl. 5 **li**-, cl. 6 **ga**-, cl. 7 **ki**-, cl. 8 **bi**-, cl. 9 **i**-, cl. 10 **zi**-, cl. 11 **lu**-, cl. 12 **ka**-, cl. 13 **tu**-, cl. 14 **bu**-, cl. 15 **ku**-, cl. 16 **ha**-, cl. 17 **ku**-, cl. 18 **mu**-, cl. 19 **hi**-, cl. 23 **i**-.

In (9.1) the cl. 1 subject **ùyó mwàmì** 'that.N king' requires the cl. 1 subject prefix **a**- at the beginning of the verb **àtànáshóbòlà** 'and he was not able'.

(9.1)   **Ùyó**     **mw-àmì** ‖ **à-tà-ná-shóbòl-à**     **ú=kú-tàl-á** | **yùgwó**
     that.N+1  1-king     1-NEG-SQ-be.able-Fa   AU=15-dry-Fa  that.N+3

     **mw-ítà**.
     3-soup

'That king ‖ was not able to dry | that soup.' (25 032)

Position 3: The NEGATIVE PREFIX is **ta**-, with no inherent tone. In **à-tà-ná-shóbol-à** (1-NEG-SQ-be.able-Fa) 'and he was not able', the negative prefix **ta**- is the second morpheme of the word.

Position 4: The TENSE/ASPECT/MOOD (TAM) PREFIX can be one of 10 different possibilities (including null), as listed in table 9.1. Some of these forms mark tense (e.g. unmarked past (P2), unmarked future (F2), and remote future (F3). Others mix in aspect/mood (e.g. the **tá**- 'frustrated past', the conditionals **ángá**- 'potential contrary-to-fact past' and **àngà**- 'potential/conditional', etc.). It should be noted that the segmental representation **twangageeziri** may have one of two tone patterns; one refers to 'present contrary-to-fact' and the other refers to 'past contrary-to-fact'. Both the tones realized on the prefix **anga**-, and the grammatical stem-tone pattern[6] on the verb stem are different in these two forms. The meaning of verb forms in which the TAM prefix is **ká**- or **àná**- differs depending on whether the final vowel is -e or -a.

Position 5: The ADDITIVE PREFIX **ná**- 'ADD.V' is related to the conjunction **na** 'CNJ' and basically states that the action of the verb is "in addition" to something else. When it is used, it most often occurs immediately after the TAM marker; for example in (9.2) it follows the future marker **gá**.

(9.2) **Nângà** | **n-dá-gá-ná-kì-shèèny-à.**
     no     1SG-NEG-F2-ADD.V-PERS-cut.firewood-Fa

'No | and I will no longer cut firewood.' (201 054)

In (9.3) the additive **ná**- follows the intervening time (INTV) marker **ká**- in the word **tùkánágálùkè** 'and we will return'.

---

[6]Tone patterns found on verb stems will be noted primarily by title.

(9.3) **Bì-rì kwôkwò** ‖ **ly-ô**= **bùt-à** **dúbà** ‖ **gírá**
8-is thus.N 5-FOC+2SG= give.birth-Fa quickly so.that

**tù-ká-ná-gálùk-è.**
1PL-INTV-ADD.V-return-Fe

'It's thus ‖ that's when you give birth quickly ‖ so that we can also return.' (01 028)

However in (9.4) we see the sequential **àná-** in the auxiliary **ànákìzí** 'and she repeatedly', while the additive **ná-** in **nádētà** 'and said' is attached to the main verb, which follows the auxiliary. The presence of both the sequential and the additive in the same construction demonstrates that the additive **ná-** is distinct from the sequential **àná-**.[7]

(9.4) **À-ná-kìzì ná-det-à** ‖ **kw-é**= **mw-à-bò** | **bà-tà-ly-à**
1-SQ-REP ADD.V-say-Fa CMP-23= home-A.M-2 2-NEG+P1-eat-Fa

**í-sùùsì.**
10-fly

'And she repeatedly also said ‖ that at their home | they do not eat flies.' (41 005)

Position 6: The PERSISTIVE PREFIX **kì-** means 'still', or with the negative, 'no longer'.[8] In (9.5) the **kì-** occurs just before the verb base -**mény-** 'know'.

(9.5) **Bà-tà-ná-kì-mény-à** ‖ **háyì** **h-ó**= **bà-lì mú**= **génd-à.**
2-NEG-ADD.V-PERS-know-Fa where 16-O.R= 2-is PROG= go-Fa

'And they no longer knew ‖ where they are going.' (01 038)

Position 7: The OBJECT PREFIX occurs at the beginning of the macrostem, just before the reflexive prefix or 1SG prefix,[9] and the lexical verb. The various forms of the object prefix have different inherent tones, as follows: 1SG **ń-**, 2SG **kú-**, 1 **mú-**, 1PL **tù-**, 2PL **mù-**, 2 **bà-**, 3 **gù-**, 4 **gì-**, 5 **lì-**, 6 **gà-**, 7 **kì-**, 8 **bì-**, 9 **gì-**,

---

[7] It seems that the final **a** both of the sequential **àná-** and of the additive **ná** is lengthened when followed by fewer than three morae within the word. This behavior is the same as that of clitics. The lengthening is not indicated in our transcription.

[8] Besides the possible meaning of 'no longer', the negative plus additive can also have concessive meaning, e.g. '(even so) he still did not...'

[9] The first-person singular object marker and the reflexive are the only ones which can co-occur with another object marker. This may reflect a hierarchy in which these two have the highest status. The 1SG and RFX never co-occur, so the maximum number of morphemes in the object slots is two. The first singular and reflexive always occur in the second object slot when they co-occur with another object marker.

10 **zì-**, 11 **lù-**, 12 **kà-**, 13 **tù-**, 14 **bù-**, 15 **kù-**, 16 **hà-**, 17 **kù-**, 18 **mù-**, 19 **hì-**, and 23 **gì-**.

Note that the cl. 1 **mú-** and the 2PL **mù-** are distinguished only by tone. In the speech of the younger generation, many are substituting the cl. 2 **bà-** for the 2PL **mù-**, following the usage in Kiswahili, which uses the cl. 2 marker **wa-** for both cl. 2 and 2PL objects.

Position 8: The REFLEXIVE PREFIX **yì-** 'RFX' occurs just before the verb stem.[10] This is seen in the following example, where the cl. 1 object prefix **mú-** precedes the reflexive prefix **yì-** and the verb stem -**lyos**-[11] 'cause to leave'.

(9.6)  À-tà-ná-kì-shóbòl-à ‖   ú=kú-mú-yì-lyó-s-á         =kwò.
       1-NEG-SQ-PERS-be.able-Fa   AU=15-O1-RFX-leave-CS-Fa   =17

'And he was no longer able ‖ to remove himself from on him (another person).' (53 013)

Position 9: The VERB BASE is made up of the verb root, plus a variable number of possible suffixes (including all extensions), but does not include the final vowel.

Position 10: The FINAL VOWEL may be -**a**, -**e**, **ir-i**, or -**i**, depending on the TAM involved.

### 9.1.2 Single-word verbs

In single-word verbs, the subject prefix, plus a variable number of other prefixes may be found on the verb.

#### 9.1.2.1 Infinitives

The infinitive is essentially a nominalized verb form. The verbal infinitives usually exhibit the augment **ú=** and obligatorily include the cl. 15 prefix **kú-**, followed by the macrostem with the final vowel -**a**. Infinitives may also optionally include the negative **ta-**, as well as an optional object prefix and the reflexive prefix. The grammatical tone pattern of the infinitive is the SIMPLE stem-tone pattern, primarily characterized by the lexical tone of the verb plus a following H tone. The chart in (9.7) includes three examples of infinitives:

---

[10] Though the reflexive prefix occurs in the same position as an object (and the same position as the second of two objects), its meaning does not always reflect the grammatical category of object, and sometimes does not even reflect the reflexive meaning. Thus we distinguish it from the other morphemes which occur in the object position.

[11] Note that any morpheme, whether affix or stem, which has no underlying tone will be left unmarked for tone unless found in a conjugated form or in context. Verb stems whose first (or rarely second) syllable has a double vowel, (e.g. -**taah**- 'go home'), a -CyV- (e.g. -**lyos**- 'remove') or -CwV- (e.g. **gwan**- 'encounter') are generally toneless. An unconjugated verb stem which is not toneless will be marked only with its underlying tone (found on the first syllable of the stem).

| (9.7) | 1 | 2 | 3 | 4 | 5 | 6 | 7 | |
|---|---|---|---|---|---|---|---|---|
| | | | Prefixes | | | Base | Suffixes | Gloss |
| | AU | Cl. 15 | (Neg) | (Object) | (RFX) | | FV | |
| | ú= | kú- | tà- | Obj. GNPs | yì- | | -à | |
| Examples | | | | | | | | |
| | ú= | kú- | | mú- | | -shékééréz- | -â | 'to mock him' |
| | ú= | kú- | tà- | | | -sìmbáh- | -à | 'to not obey' |
| | ú= | kú- | | mú- | yì- | -lyós- | -â | 'to remove oneself from him' |

### 9.1.2.2 Copulas

Kifuliiru has five different copulas, each with the basic meaning of either 'is' or 'be/become'. Four of them operate identically: the equational copula -**li**[12] 'is', -**kòla**[13] 'be.NEWLY (is now, but not before)', -**shùba** 'was.PREV (was, but is not now)', and -**kìri**[14] 'is.PERS (is still)'. Each member of this set of four forms shares the same unique characteristics, which is evidence for listing all of these forms as copulas.

- Each can stand by itself preceding a nominal complement, e.g. **àlì múlwāzì** 'he is (always) a sick person',[15] **àkòlà múlwāzì** 'he be.NEWLY (now, but not before) a sick person', **àshùbà múlwāzì** 'he was.PREVIOUSLY (before, but not now) a sick person', **àkìrì múlwāzì** 'he is.PERS (still) a sick person'. In these examples, -**li** refers to an unmarked, non-temporary state, while -**kòla**, -**shùba**, and -**kìri** refer to a state relative to some previous or present state.
- Each of these copulas (but no other verb) may occur before the progressive auxiliary **mú**. Thus we find **àlì mú=géndà** 'he is going', **àkòlà mú=géndà** 'he is now (but not before) going', **àshùbà**

---

[12] The copula -**li** (-**ri** following a high vowel) resembles the resultative ending -**ir-i**, which often bears a stative meaning.

[13] There is also an active verb -**kòl-** 'work'. This may be the source of this copula, but the copula has been lexicalized with a different meaning/function.

[14] The -**kiri** 'is still' is historically derived from the persistive prefix **ki-**, plus the -**li** copula. We consider the form -**kiri** to have been grammaticized.

[15] The use of this copula with the noun "sick person" implies that the sickness is a chronic condition, like diabetes, leprosy, etc. It is more typically used of a permanent characteristic such as **àlì múshósì** 'he is a man'.

**mú=géndà** 'he was (but is not now) going', and **àkìrì mú=géndà** 'he is still going'.

- All of these copulas are limited, in that they are intransitive and take no object.[16] Also, they cannot take extensions. In addition, they are not inflected for TAM. They only occur either unmarked for tense, or following the past P3 auxiliary **-áàli**. When used in any other temporal sense, the tense marking is placed on a preceding stative auxiliary copula **-ba-**.[17] In addition, with one exception, they are not found in the resultative form.[18] None of these forms (in contrast to all other verbs) has an infinitive form or can take the subjunctive **-e** final vowel.
- Each of these forms has a copular meaning, i.e. some form of 'to be'.

The fifth copula, **-ba-** 'be, become' (together with **-li** 'is') is well attested as a copula, having been reconstructed for Proto-Bantu. It stands in complementary distribution with **-li**. While **-li** is best translated 'is', **-ba-** can have the sense of 'be' or 'become'. It differs from the copulas described above in the following ways:

- It does not occur uninflected for TAM preceding a nominal complement. Rather, it only occurs before a nominal complement when it is in some form marked for tense or aspect, e.g. past tense, future tense, conditionality, etc., as shown in examples (9.8)–(9.11).

---

[16] However, the copulas, though intransitive, may have incorporated objects when used with a following locative phrase with cl. 18 **mú**, or when the locative is pronominalized as an encliticized object, e.g. the cl. 2 object **bà-** in **Samweli áàlì bàlììrì'mwó** 'Samuel was among them' or the cl. 1 **mú-** in **úwáàlì múlììrì mú=mwēndà** 'who was in debt to him'. It would seem that in these cases, perhaps there is also an assumed applicative extension (the morphology is ambiguous).

[17] Proto-Bantu reconstructions include only verb roots of -CV- or longer. The underlying root of this form is **-ba-**, as seen by the long vowel in the resultative form, **-biiri**, in which the **-a** of the root assimilates to the place of articulation of the vowel of the resultative **-iri** (**-ba-iri > biiri**). Long vowels are not permitted word-finally, however, so the addition of the final vowel never results in a long FV in the surface form, e.g. **ànábà** 'and he became', or the subjunctive form **ànábé** 'that he be(come)'.

[18] Again, the one exception is that **-li** can take the resultative ending (as can the copula **-ba-**, see preceding footnote). We find the **-iri** ending in the form **à-lí-ír-ì** 'she is RS'. (In the case shown in the example below, it could instead be interpreted as an applicative extension indicating location at a place. When used with P3 verb forms, this same form is clearly resultative. Morphologically the resultative form of this copula and the applicative form are identical.) The other three copulas are invariable.

| Háyì | nyínà | w-ò= | lyá | mú-nyérè | à-lí-ír-ì? |
|---|---|---|---|---|---|
| where | the.mother | 1-A.M+AU | that.R | 1-girl | 1-is-RS-Fi |

'Where is the mother of that girl?' (106 067)

## 9.1 Overview of verb form types

- It never occurs preceding the progressive auxiliary **mú**. It can, however, in contrast to the copulas above, follow the **mú** as the main lexical verb in a progressive form, e.g. **ìyó ndángó ìrì mú**=**bà ndérèkè** 'That.N jar is (in a state of being) ready'.
- It does have an infinitive form, and in its non-infinitive form it is always inflected for TAM. It may also take the subjunctive final vowel, -**e**.

In (9.8) the copula -**ba**- occurs with the P2 unmarked past **ìrí hákábà** 'when it was'. Together with **lúsìkù lúgùmà** 'one day', the meaning is 'when it was one day'.

(9.8) **Írí   há-ká-b-á     lú-sìkù   lú-gùmà...**
      when 16-P2-was-Fa 11-day    11-one

 'When it was (became) one day...' (628 007 )

In (9.9) the copula -**ba**- occurs with the potential form **àngà**- in the negative verb form **ndàngàbà** 'I would not be'.

(9.9) **À-ná-bà-shùvy-à: ‖ «N-dà-ngà-b-à        mú-ká    mú-gângà.»**
      1-SQ-O2-answer-Fa   1SG-NEG-POT-be-Fa  1-wife   1-witch.doctor

 'And she answered them: ‖ «I would not be (am not) the wife of a witch doctor.»' (603 047)

In (9.10) the copula -**ba**- is used with the sequential form in the verb **kànábà** 'and it became'.

(9.10) **Kà-lyá   ká-bwâ ‖ kà-ná-b-à       ng-á=   kà-yúvw-à.**
       12-that.R 12-dog   12-SQ-was-Fa  like-1= 12+P1-hear-Fa

 'That dog ‖ became as if it heard.' (106 155)

In (9.11) the copula -**ba**- occurs with the F2 future tense in the verb **ngáábà** 'I will be'.

(9.11) **Ú=lú-kwàvù   ná-lwò  ‖  lw-àná-dèt-à: ‖ «Ni-ê-hé**
       AU=11-rabbit  ADD.P-11  11-SQ-speak-Fa   1SG-CTR.P

 **n-gáá-b-à          mú-génì.»**
 1SG-F2-become-Fa  1-guest

 'The rabbit ‖ and HE ALSO said: ‖ «ME | I will be(come) the guest.»' (09 005)

### 9.1.2.3 Focus copulas: Positive and negative

In this section, we describe "focus copulas". They are, in fact, copular constructions in which some constituent is in positive or negative focus.

The POSITIVE FOCUS COPULAS are formed by the GNP, followed by the -e / -o previous reference marker. All have a high tone. The forms are: 1SG **nié**, 2SG **wé**, cl. 1 **yé**, 1PL **twé**, 2PL **mwé**, cl. 2 **bó**, cl. 3 **gwó**, cl. 4 **yó**, cl. 5 **lyó**, cl. 6 **gó**, cl. 7 **kyó**, cl. 8 **byó**, cl. 9 **yó**, cl. 10 **zó**, cl. 11 **lwó**, cl. 12 **kó**, cl. 13 **twó**, cl. 14 **bwó**, cl. 15 **kwó**, cl. 16 **hó**, cl. 17 **kwó**, cl. 18 **mwó**, cl. 19 **hyó**, and cl. 23 **yó**.

Focus copulas can occur alone before a NP, (as in 9.12) or they can be involved in cleft constructions before a verb. In (9.12) the cl. 1 **yé** occurs before the NP **Bíkòbà**, the name of a boy.

(9. 12) Há-àlí   rì-ìr-í    ú=mú-tàbánà      mú-gùmà |   í-zììnà   ly-à-gé |
       16-P3    is-RS-Fi   AU=1-young.man   1-one       5-name    5-A.M-1

y-é=    Bíkòbà.
1-FOC=  Bikoba

There was one young man | his name | (he) is Bikoba.' (07 002)

When used in cleft constructions,[19] they entail identificational articulation (see 10.2.6), where every element of the sentence, except for one, is assumed to be known. The focus, then, is on the missing element. In (9.13) the fact that someone told the speaker something is given information. The question is: 'who told him?' The answer is provided **yêhé yényènè** 'he himself'.

(9.13) Y-ê-hé      y-ényènè |   y-é=     w-á-m-bwír-à.
       1-CTR.P    1-self       1-FOC=   S.R+1-P1-O1.SG-tell-Fa

'HE himself | he's the one who told me.' (40 021)

When the focus copula is part of a verb phrase, the same concord prefix occurs on both the focus marker and the following verb.[20] This can be seen in (9.14), where the subject is cl. 11. Thus we find the cl. 11 focus copula **lwó** 'it's the one' and the cl. 11 subject marker **lu-** in the verb **lùlì mú=bàtééránià** 'is causing them to attack each other'.

---

[19] The definition of a cleft construction is "where a single CLAUSE has been divided into two separate sections, each with its own VERB, one of which appears in a dependent *wh*-clause" (Crystal 2003:75).

[20] Although as seen in (9.14), in the case of cl. 1 agreements, the subject agreement is **u-** (realized as **w-** preceding a vowel) as it is in relative verbs, rather than **a-**, the normal cl. 1 subject agreement.

## 9.1 Overview of verb form types

(9.14) **B-ómbì** ‖ **bà-ná-mény-á kw-ó=**    **lú-kwàvù** ‖ **lw-ó=**    **lù-lì**
  2-both    2-SQ-know-Fa   CMP-AU=   11-rabbit   11-FOC=   11-is

  **mú=**    **bà-téér-án-i-à.**
  PROG=    O2-attack-RCP-CS-Fa

'Both of them ‖ knew that the rabbit ‖ is the one who is causing them to attack each other.' (39 028)

The NEGATIVE FOCUS COPULAS consist of the formative **ndaa**[21] plus the focus marker, which is the GNP plus the **-e** / **-o** of previous reference. The resulting form is cl. 1 **ndááyè**, cl. 2 **ndáábò**, cl. 3 **ndáágwò**, cl. 4 **ndááyò**, cl. 5 **ndáályò**, cl. 6 **ndáágò**, cl. 7 **ndáákyò**, cl. 8 **ndáábyò**, cl. 9 **ndááyò**, cl. 10 **ndáázò**, cl. 11 **ndáálwò**, cl. 12 **ndáákò**, cl. 13 **ndáátwò**, cl. 14 **ndáábwò**, cl. 15 **ndáákwò**, cl. 16 **ndááhò**, cl. 17 **ndáákwò**, cl. 18 **ndáámwò**, cl. 19 **ndááhyò**, cl. 23 **ndááyò**.

The negative focus copulas often occur clause finally, as in (9.15), where **ndáábyò** 'there is none' occurs after **ibyokulya** 'food'.

(9.15) **Ì-nó**    **mûndà** | **nyì-ìtù**    **í=by-okúlyâ** | **ndáá-byò**.
  23-this.P.C   place   ADD.P-1PL   AU=8-food   NEG.FOC-8

'Here at this place | and US as well | there is no food.' (111 025)

They also can occur as the main verb,[22] as seen in (9.16). Here **ndáábyò** 'there is none' occurs before the NP **bíndú byó=gátùlèètèrà** 'things which you will bring us'.

(9.16) **Ndáá-byò**    **bí-ndú**   **by-ó=**    **gá-tù-lèèt-èr-à**    ‖   **há=**   **ny-úmà** |
  NEG.FOC-8   8-things   8-O.R+2s   F2-O1.PL-bring-APL-Fa   16   5-beside

  **ly-é=**    **n-gúlúbè.**
  5-A.M+AU   9-pig

'There's nothing which you will bring to us ‖ besides | a pig.' (501 014)

### 9.1.3 Grammaticization of auxiliaries

Before discussing the auxiliaries in the following sections, we would first note that all these auxiliaries are here considered to have been grammaticized as parts of various verb constructions. This applies to the progressive auxiliaries, the **-ba-** auxiliaries, all the adverbial auxiliaries, and the focus copula plus main verb.

---

[21] The **ndaa-** form is related to the negative prefix **ta-** in a regular verb.

[22] When followed by a relative clause of which the head (NP constituent which the relative clause modifies) is co-referential with the *object* of the verb of the relative clause.

To establish that a form is grammaticized (and thus is not lexical in nature) we need to evaluate each form according to commonly established criteria for grammaticization. The following four criteria for grammaticized forms are taken from Bybee, et al. (1994:38-39):

- "The gram[23] must belong to a closed class." The class of Kifuliiru adverbial auxiliaries, for example, includes 16 auxiliaries that precede an inflected verb and 26 adverbial auxiliaries that precede an uninflected stem, making 42 in all.[24] This is a closed set and is typical for a Bantu language.[25]
- "The gram must have fixed position in relation to the verb."
  (a) The Kifuliiru forms classed as auxiliaries occur in strict positions within the verb phrase. For example the adverbial auxiliaries occur after the initial prefixes in the verb word, i.e. after the subject, negative, tense/mood, and additive prefixes. In addition they always occur before the object prefix which is part of the macro-stem of the final, lexical verb in the phrase.
  (b) Nothing else can occur within the verb phrase except auxiliaries and the main verb, e.g. nouns, adjectives, etc. are not allowed to intervene.[26]
  (c) If an auxiliary entails a second subject prefix, that subject prefix must agree both in person and number with the original subject prefix of the initial word of the verb phrase.

---

[23] "Formally grammatical morphemes may be affixes, stem changes, reduplication, auxiliaries, particles, or complex constructions such as English 'be going to'. We refer to all of these types equally as grammatical morphemes and for convenience shorten this term to 'gram'" (Bybee et. al. 1994:2).

[24] In Bybee et. al. (1994:38) it is stated: "Occasionally...one encounters a closed class that is quite large. For instance, the category of 'modal verb' in Cambodian is described by Huffman in 1967 as a closed class, even though it contains some twenty-seven different verbs." Thus a number of 43 adverbial auxiliaries is apparently quite large relative to the world's language families. At the same time, it is still common to find such a large number of adverbial auxiliaries in Bantu languages.

[25] Examples of the extensive nature of Bantu adverbial auxiliaries (called by some "defective" verbs) can be found in Doke (1938), Meeussen (1959), Alexandre (1966), Dugast (1971), Carter (1973), to mention just a few.

[26] The only exceptions are a few adverbs, like **ngànà** 'really', **kàndî** 'again', which can occasionally occur between an auxiliary and the main verb, in cases where the main verb as well as the auxiliary is inflected for subject.

- "The gram must be lexically general." The Kifuliiru auxiliaries all have relatively broad semantic content. For example we find **-géndi** 'going', **-yíji** 'coming', **-lèngi** 'passing', but no auxiliary with a meaning such as 'trudging', or 'skipping', etc.
- "The gram must have a predictable meaning in most contexts…. excluding unproductive and idiosyncratic lexical derivations, as well as frozen phrases and idioms."[27] This is always true for the Kifuliiru auxiliaries.

### 9.1.4 Multiword verbs in which only one word is inflected

There are two types of multiword verbs in which inflection is found only on the initial word. These are discussed here.

#### 9.1.4.1 Progressive verbs

As already noted in 9.1.2.2, the unmarked progressive is an analytic form which employs one of four copulas: **-li** 'is', **-kòla** 'be.NEWLY (now, but not before)', **-shùba** 'was.PREVIOUSLY (before, but not now)', or **-kìri** 'is.PERS (still)'. The copula, inflected with initial prefixes which include a subject prefix and optionally an additive morpheme **ná-** comprises the first word of the verb phrase. It is then followed by the progressive marker **mú**,[28] which is cliticized to the macrostem.

In (9.17) the verb **úshùbà mú=múlyâ** 'who was (but is not now) eating him' includes the copula **úshùbà**, the progressive clitic **mú**, and the macrostem (which begins with the cl. 1 object prefix **mú-**).

(9.17) **Ìrí       á-ká-hík-á      =hò ‖   à-ná-gwán-án-à |   ù-lyá     nyûndà |**
       when     1-P2-arrive-Fa  =16      1-SQ-find-RCP-Fa   1-that.R   1a+eagle

   **ú-shùbà              mú=    mú-ly-á |   á=bā-ānà.**
   1+S.R-was.PREV        PROG   O1-eat-Fa   AU=2-children

'When he arrived there ‖ he found | that eagle | which had been eating | his children (lit., eating to him the children).' (610 023 )

---

[27] While the Kifuliiru adverbial auxiliaries might resemble serial verbs in some ways, there are also important differences: (1) The set of adverbial auxiliaries is a closed set (only 43) while serial verbs are typically a more open set. (2) Each of the adverbial auxiliaries in a verb phrase has a meaning that is independent of the co-occurring lexical verb. Serial verbs, on the other hand, often combine together to express one meaning, e.g. the two serial verbs "turning" and "going" might be juxtaposed to communicate the idea of "roll."

[28] **mú** is also the cl. 18 locative marker which means 'in' or 'within'. Such use of locative terms in progressive forms is extremely common in the world's languages and especially so in African languages (Bybee et al. 1994:129).

### 9.1.4.2 Semi-grammaticized auxiliaries followed by infinitives

Infinitives[29] can occur in a verb phrase, following a closed set of auxiliaries. In such constructions, the initial prefixes are found on the auxiliary. Following that is the infinitive, to which the incorporated object, if any, is prefixed, following the infinitive prefix and immediately preceding the verb stem.

In (9.18) the initial prefixes (cl. 2 subject prefix **ba-** and sequential prefix **àná-**) are found on the auxiliary **-tàngir-** 'begin', while the cl. 2 object prefix **bà-** appears on the infinitive of **-fùng-** 'stop someone from fighting'.

(9.18) Á=bá-fūūzì  ‖  bà-ná-tàngír-à  ú=kú-bà-fúng-à  |
  AU=2-ones.stopping.fighters  2-SQ-begin-Fa  AU=15-O2-stop.fighters-Fa

  tì=:  ‖  «Ø-Fùngwí  fùngwî.»
  ‹quote›  IMP.PL-don't.fight  RDP

'The ones stopping the fighter ‖ began to stop them | ‹quote›: ‖ «Stop fighting, stop fighting.»' (520 033)

In (9.19) the auxiliary verb **-hèzâ** 'finish (doing something)' is followed by the infinitive **ú=kúgùnywâ** 'to drink it' (which includes the cl. 3 object prefix **gù-**).

(9.19) Ìrí  á-ká-hèz-á  ú=kú-gù-nyw-â  |  mú=  ndá
  when  1-P2-finish-Fa  AU=15-O3-drink-Fa  18  stomach

  mw-àná-tòndéér-à  ú=kú-kér-à.
  18-SQ-begin-Fa  AU=15-cut-Fa

'When she finished drinking it | in her stomach it began to cut (cause sharp pains).' (628 045)

The verbs which introduce infinitives fulfill most (but not all) of the requirements of grammaticization and are thus called semi-grammaticized. They are grammaticized in that:
- The list of auxiliary forms is a closed class. In the data found in over 1,000 pages of text,[30] there are just under 50 different auxiliaries preceding infinitives, all presented in table 9.4.

---

[29] The verb constructions that today end in infinitives (beginning with **ú=kú-**) are probably on a grammaticization track similar to that followed by the adverbial auxiliaries ending in **-i**. The latter are followed by prefixless infinitives, which at an earlier stage, were infinitives beginning with **i-** (cl. 5, or perhaps cl. 23). That **i-** later shifted to the end of the previous auxiliary word.

[30] The text involves the entire New Testament and large parts of the Old Testament in Kifuliiru.

## 9.1 Overview of verb form types

- The gram has a fixed position in relation to the verb,[31] i.e. nothing can come between the auxiliary and the infinitive.[32] Also noteworthy is that object is attached to the following word in the phrase (the infinitive), as shown in (9.18) and (9.19).
- The auxiliaries which come before the infinitive have predictable meanings in all contexts.

The auxiliaries that introduce infinitives are not tightly grammaticized, in that:

- There are some auxiliaries which have quite specific meanings. The verbs -**twikir**- 'stop completely'; -**yìkaany**- 'cease (with startlement)' are rather particular.
- These auxiliaries, besides occurring before infinitives in verb phrases, can also occur by themselves as the main verb in a verb phrase, e.g. preceding a (non-infinitive) NP.[33]

### 9.1.5 Multiword verbs which include two inflected forms

There are four types of multiword constructions in which both the initial auxiliary and the main lexical verb are inflected. These are discussed in this section.

#### 9.1.5.1 -ba- 'to be' auxiliaries

The auxiliary verb -**ba**- 'be/become' can be used before stative[34] verb forms, to serve as a holder for the TAM inflection of the multiword verb phrase. Both

---

[31] Comment on "...in relation to the verb." Here the "verb", being an infinitive, also has nominal qualities. However, many verb forms (progressives, forms with adverbial auxiliaries, etc.) have a main lexical verb which is, for all practical purposes, an infinitive.

[32] The only exceptions are a few adverbs, like **ngana** 'really' and **kandi** 'again'.

[33] The -**ba**- 'be' copular auxiliary, as well as the adverbial auxiliaries which precede an inflected verb, can all be used as main verbs.

[34] "Stative" verbs describe an unchanging situation which will continue unless something happens to change it. "Dynamic" verbs, by contrast, depict one action as a unit, and typically describe a situation which involves some sort of change (Bybee et al. 1994:55). Dahl (1985:28) contrasts dynamic and stative verbs saying, "we distinguish those situation descriptions that involve change or movement from those that do not".

When a verb is dynamic, all the prefixes, including the object prefix, are prefixed directly onto the main verb. This is seen in the following example, where the action of the verb **twànáhìtááhánà** 'and we went home with it' is viewed as one unit. Note that the object prefix **hì**- is part of the main verb macrostem.

Tw-àná-tóòl-à    hí-nyínà,    tw-àná-hì-bòh-à,
1PL-SQ-pick.up-Fa 19-mother 1PL-SQ-O.19-wrap-Fa

tw-àná-hì-tááh-án-à.
1PL-SQ-O.19-go.home-COM-Fa

'We picked up the little mother, and we wrapped it up, and we went home with it.'
(635 009)

the -**ba**- auxiliary and the verb which follows must have the same subject prefix.

In (9.20) the time element is established by the auxiliary verb -**ba**- 'be/become' used in the P2 past form **ìrí ákábà** 'when he was'. The stative[35] verb follows: **àkòlà mú=kàtááhánà** 'he be.NEWLY (now, not before) in the state of going home with it (cl. 12)'. In this verb phrase the cl. 1 subject prefix **a**- is seen on the copular auxiliary **ákábà** 'he had become' as well as in the stative construction **àkòlà mú=kàtááhánà** 'he be.NEWLY going home with it'. Notice that the cl. 12 object **kà**-, referring to a certain animal, is prefixed to the main lexical verb.

(9.20) Ìrí  á-ká-b-á    à-kòlà    mú=    kà-tááh-án-à    ||
      when 1-P2-become-Fa 1-is.NEW PROG= O12-go.home-COM-Fa

   í=n-vúlá    ny-ìngì |   y-àná-yîj-à.
   AU=9-rain   9-much      9-SQ-come-Fa

'When he was now going home with it || much rain | came.' (49 004)

### 9.1.5.2 Progressive intentional verbs

The progressive intentional is formed by the auxiliary -**gwétì**[36] followed by a conjugated verb marked with the intentional **gáá**- TAM prefix. Both the auxiliary and the main verb must have the same subject prefix, and any object prefixes are attached to the lexical verb.

In (9.21) the verb phrase **ngwétì ngákúbùùzâ** means 'I am (intentionally) asking you'. (This meaning is different from that found in the other progressive form, **ndì=mú=kúbúúzâ** 'I am asking you', since the latter form has no overt intentional connotation.) Note that the cl. 1SG subject prefix **n**- occurs on both the auxiliary and the main verb. In addition, the 2SG object prefix **kú**- is prefixed to the second form, the lexical verb.

(9.21) K-ò=   tà-yúvw-à    kwó=   n-gwétì |   n-gá-kú-bùùz-â?
       Q-2SG  NEG-hear-Fa  CMP=   1SG-PROG    1SG-INTL-O2.SG-ask-Fa

'Don't you hear that I am (intentionally) | questioning you?' (627 017)

---

[35] Notice that the stem -**taah**- seen in this "stative" verb is the same stem which is used in the "dynamic" verb in **twànáhìtááhánà** 'and we went home with it' (see previous footnote). Thus we see that the labels "stative" and "dynamic" relate to the aspectual inflection of the verb and not to semantic content of the lexical verb itself.

[36] The auxiliary -**gweti** 'having' is the irregular resultative of the verb -**gwat**- 'grasp'. This helps to explain the grammaticized "intentional" meaning.

As seen in (9.22), the progressive intentional can also occur with the remote (P3) resultative form, as exemplified in the form **báàlì gwètì bágáhàmbànwâ** 'they were contending'.

(9.22) Yìkyó       ky-ànyà |   W-á-n-dàrè ||   bá-àli    gwètì
      that.N+7   7-time       1-A.M-9-lion      2-P3       PROG

      bá-gá-hàmbànw-â |    nô=    yó          mú-shósì...
      2-INTL-contend-Fa     CNJ=   that.N+1    1-man

'At that time | the lion || was (intentionally) contending | with that man...' (621 030)

#### 9.1.5.3 Adverbial auxiliaries which precede an inflected verb

In Kifuliiru there are 16 adverbial[37] auxiliaries which have the same subject markers as the following inflected verb form. All but one[38] of these auxiliaries ends with the invariable FV **-a**.[39] That all of these end with the FV **-a** would not be so significant, except that this distinguishes them structurally from the related adverbial auxiliaries which all end in **-i**, and which precede a *non-*inflected verb form.

The inflected verb forms which follow these auxiliaries are rather limited: verbs having the intentional **gáá-**, the progressive intentional (using **-gweti gáá-**), the resultative, the recent past (P1), or the progressive **mú**. Not every adverbial auxiliary can co-occur with each of these forms.

Among the **-a** final adverbial auxiliaries, there are two semantically "opposite" pairs, that is **-gwanwa** 'encounter/find' and **-sìga** 'leave behind'; as well as **-génda** 'going' and **-yíja** 'coming'.

For five of the **-a** final forms (**-génda**, **-lènga**, **-sìgala**, **-yàma**, and **-yíja**) there are equivalent adverbial auxiliaries which end in **-i**.

The **-a** final auxiliary **-yàma** has two very different meanings, depending on the type of verb which follows it.[40] When followed by a stative verb, it has the meaning of 'always', or 'enduring'. When followed by a dynamic verb form, the meaning is 'immediately'. Because there are two very different meanings, we list this auxiliary twice, even though the two are segmentally and tonally

---

[37] Both the **-a** final set and the **-i** final set are all called *adverbial* auxiliaries, since many of them have semantic content that is carried by adverbs in other languages, e.g. 'being somewhere all day', 'immediately'.

[38] The resultative form **-yàmiri** 'is always' ends with **-ir-i**.

[39] The source verb for any of these auxiliaries, when used with a non-auxiliary function, can of course have any of the final morphemes, **-a**, **-e**, or **-ir-i**.

[40] There is also one **-i** final adverbial auxiliary (**-shùbi**) which has two different meanings, dependent on the very same parameter.

identical. The resultative form, **yàmiri**, is always followed by a stative verb and always has the meaning 'always'.

The last four in table 9.2, i.e. **-gwanwa** 'encounter (state already begun)', **-kéngeera** 'unintended results', **-laala** 'state remains after one day ago', and **-sìga** 'leave (in a state)' are followed by main verbs that generally take the recent past (P1) tense form.

The forms in table 9.2 can be sorted relative to the possible forms of the following lexical verb. Forms (a–b) may be followed only by INTL, PROG; (c) PROG INTL, PROG; (d–g) INTL, PROG INTL, RS; (h) PROG, PROG INTL, RS, P1; (i, k) INTL, RS, P1; (j) INTL, PROG INTL, PROG, RS; (l) INTL, PROG INTL, RS, P1; (m) RS, P1; (n–p) only P1. The source verb is listed if there is a currently used verb which still has the same basic meaning. If there is a related -**i** final auxiliary, that is also listed.

Table 9.2. Adverbial auxiliaries which require inflection on main verb

|   | Auxiliary | Gloss | Source verb | Related **i**-final auxiliary |
|---|---|---|---|---|
| a. | -kòla | 'be.NEWLY' |  | -kòli |
| b. | -shùba | 'be.PREV' |  | -shúbi |
| c. | -gáluka | 'RETURNING' | -galuk- |  |
| d. | -génda | 'GOING' | -gend- | -géndi |
| e. | -lènga | 'PASSING' | -leng- | -lèngi |
| f. | -shiiba | 'ALL.DAY' | -shiib- |  |
| g. | -sìgala | 'REMAINING' | -sigal- | -sìgali |
| h. | -taaha | 'RETURN.HOME' | -taah- |  |
| i. | -tuula | 'HABITUAL' | -tuul- |  |
| j. | -yàma | 'IMMED' | -yàm-[a] | -yàmi |
| k. | -yàma/yàmiri | 'ALWAYS' | -yàm- |  |
| l. | -yíja | 'COMING' | -yij- | -yíji |
| m. | -gwanwa | 'ENCOUNTERED' | -gwanw- |  |
| n. | -kéngeera | 'UNINTENDED' | -kéngeer- |  |
| o. | -laala | 'ONE.DAY.AGO' | -laal-[b] |  |
| p. | -sìga | 'LEAVING' | -sìg- |  |

[a]The gloss for this verb is 'remain long-term, endure (in a state or place)'. This verb is intransitive.
[b]This verb means to 'stay overnight somewhere'.

### 9.1.5.4 Focus copula plus verb

The positive focus copula (9.2.6.1), when followed by a conjugated lexical verb, has the same subject prefix as that lexical verb. In (9.23) the cl. 7 prefix is found on the focus copula **kyó** 'it is', as well as on the main verb **kìtùmírì** 'that's the cause'.

(9.23) **Ky-ó**=   **kì-tùm-ír-ì** |   **á=ká-nwá**   **k-ó**=   **mú-ndù** |
      7-FOC   7-cause-RS-Fi   AU=12-mouth   12-A.M+AU   1-person

      **kà-zùngúlús-ír-w-ì** |   **n-ó**=   **lw-ânwâ.**
      12-circle-RS-PS-Fi   CNJ-AU=   11-beard

'That's the reason | that the mouth of a person | is surrounded | by a beard.' (50 026 )

### 9.1.6 Adverbial auxiliaries which precede an uninflected verb stem

Adverbial auxiliaries can precede an uninflected verb, which may be a copula, a main lexical verb, or even another auxiliary. Thus these auxiliaries can occur singly, or in a string of two or three. The first auxiliary always bears the initial prefixes, and is followed directly by *the uninflected macrostem* (which optionally includes object and reflexive prefixes) with final -**a**.[41] This macrostem displays the simple stem-tone pattern characteristic of the Kifuliiru infinitive. The group of 27 adverbial auxiliaries is listed in table 9.3. Note that they all have a final vowel -**i**.

When an adverbial auxiliary is present, the final verb in the construction not only lacks prefixes, but in a subjunctive form, which would normally have the final vowel -**e**, the final verb instead exhibits the final vowel -**a**. For example, the single-verb subjunctive form **ìmútìbùlìrè** '(may) it cause something to fall down to him', has the typical subjunctive final vowel -**e**, but when the addition of the adverbial auxiliary makes it a two-word form, the subjunctive final -**e** no longer appears anywhere in the form: **ìkízì mútìbúlírà** '(may) it continuously cause something to fall down to him'. This is because the auxiliary has an invariable ending, while the main verb which follows such an auxiliary is uninflectable: a prefixless infinitive. All prefixes, as well as the grammatical tonal pattern, fall on the auxiliary which precedes the main verb.

---

[41]This infinitive historically had an **i**- prefix, but over time, the **i**-initial infinitives fell out of use in the language, and the **i**- was reinterpreted as an ending on the preceding auxiliary. Because of this, all these forms (except for **tee** 'PRIOR', which has undergone more extensive modification) end with the vowel -**i**. Infinitives with a cl. 5 prefix consisting of **i**- are still in use in related Bantu J languages such as Kinande.

Table 9.3. Adverbial auxiliaries which precede an uninflected verb stem

| | Adverbial auxiliary | Gloss | Source verb | Gloss |
|---|---|---|---|---|
| Relative location | | | | |
| a. | géndi | 'GOING' | -génd- | 'go' |
| b. | híkiri | 'ARRIVING' | -hík- | 'arrive' |
| c. | lèngi | 'PASSING' | -lèng- | 'pass' |
| d. | sìgali | 'REMAINING' | -sìgal- | 'remain' |
| e. | yíji | 'COMING' | -yíj- | 'come' |
| Relative time | | | | |
| f. | búli | 'SUBQ (subsequently)' | -bùl- | 'lack' |
| g. | kì | 'PERS (persistently)' | | |
| h. | kìzi | 'REP (repeatedly)' | | |
| i. | kòli | 'NEWLY' | -kòl- | 'work' |
| j. | máli | 'ALREADY' | -mál- | 'be finished off' |
| k. | shúbì | 'PREV (PREVIOUSLY)' | | |
| l. | shúbì | 'AGAIN' | | |
| m. | tàngí | 'FIRSTLY' | -tàng- | 'be first' |
| n. | té(e) | 'PRIOR' | | |
| o. | yàmì | 'IMMED (IMMEDIATELY)' | | |
| p. | zíndi | 'LASTLY' | -zínd- | 'be last' |
| q. | zíndukiri | 'EARLY.IN.MORNING' | -zínduk- | 'be early in morning' |
| Mood | | | | |
| r. | hámbiri | 'ALMOST.TROUBLE' | | |
| s. | líndi | 'AFTER.EFFORT' | -línd- | 'wait' |
| t. | támi | 'AFTER.ALL.THAT' | -tám- | 'after all that' |
| u. | lóózi | 'AS.IF.WANTED.TO' | -lóóz- | 'want' |
| v. | lúnguli | 'PREMATURELY' | -lúngul- | 'move ahead' |
| w. | ményi/yìji | 'KNOWING' | -mény- / -yìj- | 'know' |
| Negative marker[a] | | | | |
| x. | zì/zâzì | 'NOT.YET (with NEG)' | | |
| y. | zìndi | 'NOT.EVER (with NEG)' | -zìnd- | |

[a] Two of the adverbial auxiliaries taking the final vowel **i** occur only in the context of the negative verbal prefix **ta-**. They are **-zíndi** 'ever' and **-zaazi / -zì** 'not yet' (**-zaazi** used with remote past, stative (P3), and **zi** used with P1 recent past tense).

*9.1 Overview of verb form types* 223

Examples of the use of these -**i**-final adverbial auxiliaries in various environments are given in (9.24)–(9.33). In (9.24) the auxiliary **kìzi** 'repeatedly', has been incorporated into the single-verb form **ìmútìbùlìrè** '(that) it cause something to fall down to him', to form the two-word verb **ìkízì mútìbúlírà** '(that) it repeatedly cause something to fall down to him'. Thus the subject prefix is now attached to the auxiliary, while the cl. 1 object prefix **mú**- 'him' is attached to the lexical verb at the right of the phrase.

(9.24) À-ná-bwîr-à    ìyó        m-bébà |   kw-ê=   Ø-shón-è   |   ì-Ø-<u>kízì</u>
      1-SQ-tell-Fa   that.N+1   9-rat        that-9    SBV-climb-Fe    9-SBV-REP

      mú-tìbúl-ír-à         |   í=bí-gázì.
      O1-knock.down-APL-Fa     AU=8-palm.fruits

      'He told that rat to climb | (so) it would repeatedly knock down for him | palm fruits.' (20 013 )

In (9.25) the form which without an auxiliary would appear as **ù-tá-ná-kì-bù-tàndùùl-è** (2SG-NEG-ADD.V-PERS-O14-check.out-Fe) 'don't still also check it out' appears as a multiword verb modified by two auxiliaries: **shúbi** 'again' and **géndi** 'going'. The prefixes **u** '2SG', **ta** 'NEG', **ná** 'ADD.V', and **kì** 'PERS' are all attached to the left-most auxiliary, while the macrostem **bù-tànduul-a** 'check it out' (including the cl. 14 object prefix **bù**-) is the right-most element in the phrase.

(9.25) Ìrí   w-àngà-kèngúl-w-à|     ù-ná-hùng-è          ú=bú-gómà ||
      if     2SG-CND-warn-PS-Fa       2SG-CON-avoid-Fe      AU=14-enmity

      ù-tá-ná-Ø-kì-<u>shúbì</u>              géndí   bù-tàndúúl-à.
      2SG-NEG-SBV-ADD.V-AGAIN        GOING   O14-check.out-Fa

      'If you are warned | and you avoid the enemy || don't you still again go and check it out.' (10 032 )

In (9.26) the PROGRESSIVE aspect verb **àlì mú=tēgà** 'he is trapping' has two adverbial auxiliaries inserted into it: **kìzi** 'repeatedly' and **yíji** 'coming'. They both occur after the progressive aspect marker **mú** 'PROG', and just before the macrostem **tèg-a** 'trap'.

(9.26) Mú-tàbáná    mú-gùmà ||    à-lì    mú=    <u>kìzì</u>    <u>yíjí</u>        tèg-à |
      1-young.man    1-one              1-is    PROG=    REP      COMING    trap-Fa

      ú=bú-nyúnì.
      AU=14-birds

      'One young man || is repeatedly coming trapping | little birds.' (210 075)

In (9.27) the FINITE VERB PLUS INFINITIVE **ànátòndéézá ú=kúgìláíírà** 'and he began to stay awake to guard it' has two adverbial auxiliaries **kìzi** 'repeatedly' and **géndi** 'going' inserted into it. They both come to the right of the **ú=kú**-infinitive marker, and to the left of the macrostem **gì-láliira** 'it-guard' (which includes the cl. 9 object prefix **gì-**).

(9.27) À-ná-tòndéézá | ú=kú-<u>kìzí</u>   géndí |   gì-lálíír-à.
       1-SQ-begin-Fa  AU=15-REP   GOING     O9-guard-Fa

'And he began | to repeatedly go | guard it.' (50 016)

In (9.28) the AUXILIARY **yàmi** 'immediately' occurs just before the stem **lék-a** 'give up' (which in turn acts an auxiliary preceding the infinitive **ú=kúshéényà** 'to cut firewood').

(9.28) Há-àhô || n-àná-<u>yàmì</u>   lék-à   | ú=kú-shéény-à.
       E-then.N  1-SQ-IMMED  give.up-Fa  AU=15-cut.firewood-Fa

'Right then || I immediately gave up | cutting firewood.' (201 107)

In (9.29) the PROGRESSIVE INTENTIONAL verb **bàgwétì bágágáyìrìzìbwâ** 'they are being despised' has the auxiliary **kizi** 'repeatedly' inserted in the middle, after the intentional marker **gáá-** and before the stem **-gáyirizibwa** 'despised'.

(9.29) Bà-gwétì |   bá-gáá-<u>kìzì</u>  gáyíríz-íbw-á || n-á=       bá-ndú |
       2-PROG       2-INTL-REP     despised-PS-Fa   CNJ-AU=  2-people

       b-á=        má-hângà            gó-óshì.
       2-A.M+AU=   6-foreign.nations   6-all

'There are | continuously being despised || by people | of all nations.' (Dan 9:16)

In (9.30) the VERB WITH -**ba**- AUXILIARY **múgáàbá mùgwèjíírì** 'you will be having lain down' has the adverbial auxiliary **kìzi** repeatedly inserted into it, just *before* the stem of the auxiliary -**ba**.

(9.30) Kú=   ky-ànyà  mú-gá-<u>kìzíì</u>  =bà |   mù-gwèj-íír-ì...
       17=   7-time   2PL-F2-REP       =be      2PL-lay.down-RS-Fi

'At the time you will be repeatedly | lying down...' (Psa 4:4)

In (9.31) the adverbial auxiliary **kòli** 'be.NEWLY' occurs within the lexical verb **àyázìrì** 'he is married' in the complex form **ìrí ákábá à(kòlì)yázìrì**. In

## 9.1 Overview of verb form types

this case, the adverbial auxiliary is inserted into the first word of the verb form which *follows* the -**ba**- auxiliary **ákábà** 'he was'.

(9.31) Ùyó    mw-ānà |   ìrí    á-ká-b-á           à-<u>kò</u>lì       yáz-ìr-ì...
       that.N+1  1-child  when  1-P2-become-Fa   1-be.NEWLY   marry-RS-Fi...

'That child | when he had now gotten married...' (52 003 )

In (9.32) the auxiliary **shúbi** 'again' occurs in the main verb of a PROGRESSIVE INTENTIONAL form, immediately following the intentional mood marker **gáá**- and preceding the prefixless form **yìmba** 'sing'.

(9.32) Bà-gwétì  | bà-gáá-<u>shù</u>bí  yīmb-à |  kwó-kù-nô:...
       2-PROG        2-INTL-AGAIN     sing-Fa     ‹quote.marked›

'They are intentionally | again singing | like this:...' (206 073 )

In (9.33) the auxiliary **shúbi** 'again' is found in the auxiliary form of **génda** 'going', following the subject prefix **mu**- and preceding the prefixless infinitive form **génda** 'going'. This whole polite imperative construction then serves as the auxiliary which precedes the intentional[42] **múgáhììvà** 'you (PL) intentionally hunt'.

(9.33) Mù-Ø-<u>shú</u>bì    génd-à |    mú-gá-hìiv-à.
       2PL-SBV-AGAIN    GOING-Fa    2PL-INTL-hunt-Fa

'Go again | and hunt.' (206 036 )

### 9.1.7 Negation

In Kifuliiru negation is expressed in two different ways:
One way to express negation is to include the NEGATIVE PREFIX **ta**- in the verb. In (9.34) the negative prefix **ta**- is seen in the verb **gàtàlííbwà** 'they are not eaten'.

(9.34) Á=má-fúmbà   gà-bìrì ||   gà-<u>tà</u>-lí-íbw-à.
       AU=6-bundle    6-two       6-NEG-eat-PS-Fa

'Two bundles || are not eaten.' (01 044)

It should be noted that the use of a speech verb with a negative connotation does not eliminate the need for basic negation in a following complement clause. Note in (9.35) that when the verb -**láhir**- 'deny, refuse' is used,

---

[42] The intentional **gáá**- only has intentional meaning (as opposed to the default F2 future meaning) when it follows an auxiliary.

the negative is still used in its complement clause. Here the lion denies (or refuses) that it will *not* eat the leopard, which is to say that he refuses to eat it. In this case the "double" negative does not produce a positive meaning, but remains negative.

(9.35) Í=n-dàrè ‖ y-àná-láhìr-à ‖ kw-é= tá-gáà-ly-à | ìyó
      AU=9-lion   9-SQ-refuse-Fa   CMP-9=  NEG-F2-eat-Fa  that.N+9

**n-gwî.**
9-leopard

'The lion ‖ refused ‖ that it will not eat | that leopard.' (11 035)

The other way to express negation is to use the NEGATIVE FOCUS COPULA **ndaa-** 'there is no'. In this case, the form **ndaa-** (which is a derivative of the negative marker **ta**)[43] is linked to the appropriate focus copula, to negate the existence of the referent(s) which the focus copula's prefix agrees with. Thus in (9.36) it is stated that there is no one: **ndáá-yè** 'there is no cl. 1', not even one of them, who got something.

(9.36) **Ndáá-yè** ‖ kìrì n-ó= mú-gùmá w-à-bò ‖ ú-ká-gì-gwát-à.
      NEG.FOC-1   even  and-AU=  1-one   1-A.M-2   S.R+1-P2-O9-grab-Fa

'There is not ‖ even one of them ‖ who grabbed it.' (25 019)

In informal register, the negative focus copula is sometimes shortened from **ndáá-kò, ndáá-yè**, etc. to just the **ndáá** formative followed by a noun. In (9.37) instead of **ndáá=kò kááyà** 'there is no village', we find the shortened form **ndá=kāāyà** 'there is no village'.[44]

(9.37) N-í= shùlè ly-é= lú-móshò ‖ **ndá**= kà-àyá
      CNJ-AU+5=  dreadlock  5-23=  11-left   NEG.FOC=  12-village

**á-kà-bùl-á | ú-yìmáng-îir-ì.**
S.R-12-lack-Fa   S.R+1-supervise-RS-Fi

'And the (meaning of) the dreadlock on the left ‖ there's no village which lacks | one who supervises it.' (506 035)

---

[43] The **a** of **ta-** is lengthened because this form, rather than being a prefix, is a single-syllable formative which is cliticized to the focus copula, another single-syllable formative. The final vowel of a word or formative preceding an enclitic is lengthened if fewer than three morae follow it.

[44] Note the difference in the length of the vowel in **nda/ndaa**. Clitics are lengthened when followed by fewer than three morae, but remain short if followed by three or more.

In (9.38) instead of **ndááː-kyò kígázì** 'there is no palm fruit', the writer shortens the form to **ndà=kígázì** 'there is no palm fruit'.

(9.38)  Ù-Ø-káni-é         ú=mú-tīmà ‖   ndà=       kí-gází
        2SG-SBV-grab-Fe    AU=3-heart    NEG.FOC=   7-palm.fruit

   n-gá-kú-hèèrèz-à.
   1SG-F2-O2.SG-give-Fa

'Steel yourself! ‖ There's no palm fruit (that) I will give you.' (629 014)

## 9.2 Detailed inventory of TAM form/meanings

This section details the meanings of Kifuliiru verb forms, separated here by the parameters of time, aspect, and mood (TAM), as well as focus. It should be noted that there are many portmanteau forms that simultaneously involve tense/aspect/mood categories so a total separation is not possible. [45]

The way tense, aspect, and mood occur on matrix verbs is structurally and functionally distinct from the way it occurs on auxiliaries. Thus the two will be treated separately here.

'Tense' deals with the temporal setting, that is, the time when an event or state occurs. Kifuliiru makes the distinction between immediate (in past and future), unmarked (in past and future), and remote (in past and future).

'Aspect' deals with the 'temporal contours', e.g. habitual, progressive, completive, resultative, narrative, predictable continuation, intervening time, etc. Each of these aspects can occur with a variety of tenses.

'Mood' deals with the categories of 'purpose and expectation', as well as 'conditional and potential'. Again, these moods can occur with a variety of tenses.

Finally, 'focus' in verbs deals with placing one item at the center of communicative interest, e.g. 'these very ones, as opposed to all others' or negatively stated 'there are none of these, as opposed to the possibility that some might exist'.

---

[45] For example, **tùshùbà túgágêndà** 'we (previously) would have gone (but did not)' includes the notion of recent past time, plus the notions of ongoing state, potentiality, intention, and often of contrary-to-fact. One cannot factor out various morphemes for each of these meanings. They are all communicated in the total sum of the verb phrase.

Likewise, in the portmanteau verb phrase **àgwétì ágáshèènyà** 'she is (intentionally) cutting firewood' the "present" time is combined with the "progressive" aspect, and the "intentional" mood. This is in contrast to the unmarked progressive **àlí mú shéényà** 'she is cutting firewood', where intentional does not come into play.

## 9.2.1 Tense

Tense, according to (Bybee et al. 1994:316) involves "those terms establishing the temporal setting of the situation with regard to the moment of speech".

For the purposes of this description of Kifuliiru, tense relates only to past and future types. All would-be present tenses are intertwined with notions of aspect, and thus are not listed in this section.

### 9.2.1.1 Past

The past tense forms in Kifuliiru include a recent past (P1) form. They also include an unmarked past (P2), which indicates a single action in the past. Finally, the P3 denotes the remote past, and is usually a state.

#### 9.2.1.1.1 Recent past

The default recent past (P1) is formed by the initial prefixes (including the TAM prefix **à-**) followed by the macrostem with final vowel **-a**, as indicated in the following formula:

[S.P [ (NEG) [**à**- [ (ADD.V) [ (PERS) [ (O.P) [ (RFX) [base] -**a**]

This verb form exhibits the Complex HL stem-tone pattern.

The recent past (P1) is a very common form which indicates that something has just happened[46] today, or yesterday. In (9.39) the verb **àhíndùkà** 'he turned into' is in the P1 tense, showing that the event happened today or yesterday.

(9.39) **Yóò!** || **Kútì ku-nó yíb-à-niè à-híndùk-à**
Oh.my how 15-this.P.C husband-A.M-1SG 1+P1-change-Fa

**n-gúlúbè!**
9-pig

'Oh my! || How (is) this (that) my husband has turned into a pig!' (01 027)

In (9.40) the recent past (P1) tense on **àlàkírà** 'he made noise' indicates that the gazelle, in the process of trying to win a race against the frog, heard the sound of the frog right then.

---

[46]Because the recent past (P1) can indicate actions which are just barely past, or even ones in process (but without noting any ongoing nature of the event), Kifuliiru speakers often perceive this form as present tense, bordering on unmarked for time.

## 9.2 Detailed inventory of TAM form/meanings

(9.40) Y-àná-yùvw-á kwó= kèré | à-làk-ír-à      í= m-bèrè
      9-SQ-hear-Fa   CMP=  1a+frog  1+P1-make.noise-APL-Fa  23=  9-before

ly-á-yò.
5-A.M-9

'And it heard that the frog | has just made a noise up ahead of it.' (21 022)

In (9.41) the recent past (P1) verb **àsúmīrwà** 'it was bought for her (lit., she was bought for)' shows that the meat had been bought for her recently.

(9.41) Ùyó     mú-ká-à-gè  ú=mú-kùlù |  ú-ká-b-á        nákòròrò ||
      that.N+1  1-wife-A.M-1  AU=1-great.one  S.R+1-P2-be-Fa  despised.wife

à-ná-bòn-à  kwó=  w-àbò     |  à-súm-ìr-w-á
1-SQ-see-Fa  CMP=  1-SAME.SET  1+P1-buy.food-APL-PS-Fa

í=n-yámà.
AU=9-meat

'That wife of his the older one | who became despised || she saw that her fellow (wife) | has had meat bought for her.' (26 004)

In (9.42) the verb **àdètà** 'he said' shows that the king had just spoken.

(9.42) Kályôshò || mbw-à=    Ø-yúvw-è    yùkwó     mw-āmì
      Kalyosho   as.soon.as-1=  SBV-hear-Fe  that.N+15  1-king

à-dèt-à      ||  à-ná-bà-bwír-à:...
1+P1-speak-Fa    1-SQ-O2-tell-Fa

'Kalyosho || when he heard that which the king said || he told them:...' (17 014)

### 9.2.1.1.2 Unmarked past (P2)

The default unmarked past form (P2) is comprised of the initial prefixes, including the temporal TAM prefix **ká-**, followed by the macrostem, with the final vowel -**a**, as indicated in the following formula:

[S.P [ (NEG) [ká- [ (ADD.V) [ (PERS) [ (O.P) [ (RFX) [base] -**a**]

This verb form exhibits the Simple stem-tone pattern. In addition, it should be noted that the H tone of the tense prefix **ká-** is realized not only on the tense prefix itself, but also on syllable that precedes it. In non-negative forms, this preceding syllable is the subject prefix, but in negative forms, it is the negative marker.

(a) This tense, without any other context, means 'unmarked past'. As such it can be used at the very beginning of stories, to set the stage. Thus in (9.43) the verb **ákáyábíírà** 'and he took (his dog)' is found in the first line of a narrative, letting the listener know that it took place "before yesterday".

(9.43) Lú-sìkù    lú-gùmà    Nàlwáhì |    á-ká-yàbíír-á      á=ká-bwá    kà-à-gè ||
       11-day    11-one      Nalwahi      1-P2-take-Fa       AU=12-dog   12-A.M-1

       à-ná-gênd-à    í=w-à=         kú-hīv-à.
       1-SQ-go-Fa    23=place-of=   15-hunt-Fa

'One day Nalwahi | took his dog || and he went to the place of hunting.' (29 002)

(b) Besides marking unmarked past, this tense is also used with tail-head sequences, a construction in which the 'tail' of one sentence is repeated at the head of the next one, often used to mark new paragraphs or episodes (Dooley and Levinsohn 2001:16). In such a case the time frame is not literally "before yesterday", but merely refers to the previous paragraph, as will be seen below.

In (9.44) there is an example of a tail-head sequence.[47] The tail, **ànáláhìrà** 'and she refused' comes at the tail (end) of the first clause. That same verb is repeated in the head (beginning) of the following sentence, in the dependent temporal clause **ìrí áká̱láhírà** 'when she had refused'. This marks a discontinuity in the narrative, marking a change in time/location, and thus the beginning of a new episode.

(9.44) Ùyó       mú-kí-ì-bà             à-ná-láhìr-à. ||   Ìrí      á-ká-láhír-à |
       that.N+1  1-wife-A.M-husband     1-SQ-refuse-Fa     when     1-P2-refuse-Fa

       ù-lyá      mú-kàzì    à-ná-gálùk-ìr-à |    í=mûndà     ù-lyá      mú-fùmú
       1-that.R   1-woman    1-SQ-return-APL-Fa   23=where    1-that.R   1-doctor

       w-à-gè.
       1-A.M-1

'That co-wife refused. || When she refused | that woman returned | to where that doctor of hers (was).' (107 037-038)

---

[47] Tail-head linkage involves "the repetition in a subordinate clause, at the beginning (the 'head') of a new sentence, of at least the main verb of the previous sentence (the 'tail')" Dooley and Levinsohn (2001:16).

### 9.2.1.1.3 Remote past

The remote past, state (P3) tense is used to express background information in discourse. The P3 is characterized by the use of the auxiliary -**áàlí** 'was',[48] which precedes a limited variety of forms.

The P3 -**áàli** auxiliary is most often followed by a verb in its resultative form. This resultative verb denotes the state produced by the action of the verb. The P3 construction is formed by the initial prefixes attached to the tense marker -**áàli**.[49] This is followed by a second verb word with the resultative base and final -**i**, as indicated in the following formula:

[S.P [ (NEG) [ (ADD.V) [-**áàlí**] [ (O.P) [ (RFX) [base] -**ir**-**i**]

The auxiliary -**áàlí** exhibits a HL tone contour on the **áà**, and a high tone on the second syllable. Though the P3 form in its basic form is a two-word construction with no subject prefix on the main verb, the main verb is not reduced to the form of a prefixless infinitive as it is in some forms. Instead, it is still inflected with the resultative ending, and exhibits not the stem-tone pattern of the infinitive, but the $V_2$ stem-tone pattern common to the irrealis forms.

Besides the usual construction with the main verb in the form of a resultative base, this time frame can also involve the adverbial auxiliary **kizi** followed by a default main verb in the form of a prefixless infinitive (not in the resultative) e.g. **áàlí kìzí sálírà** 'he repeatedly thought'.

In addition, this auxiliary can be followed either by one of two copulas (**kola** 'be.NEWLY' or **kiri** 'is.PERS') followed by a progressive form, e.g. **kyáàlí kòlá mú=híírà** 'it was newly burning', **áàlí kìrí mú=dētà** 'he was still speaking', or by the structurally resultative auxiliary **gweti** 'PROG', followed by a verb inflected for subject, and having the intentional **gáá-**, e.g. **áàlí gwètí ágáhìngà** 'she was (intentionally) farming'. These are exemplified below.

The P3 tense is used to present background information. This is exemplified in (9.45), where the P3 using the RS form of the copula -**li** 'is' introduces the main characters of a story.

(9.45) **Há-àlí**   **rì-ìr-í** |   **í=bí-hèbè**   **bì-bìrì.**
   16-P3      is-RS-Fi      AU=8-he.goats   8-two

'There were | two he-goats.' (08 002)

---

[48] This form, inflected with a subject prefix and optional negative, can be used on its own as a P3 copula, but in our texts is found very rarely with this usage; these rare occurrences are mostly in relative verb forms (e.g. **ábáàlí í=nyùmá lyàgè** 'the ones who were behind him').

[49] This is historically a form of the copula -**li**, but since it functions here as a single grammaticized auxiliary unit, we do not gloss the parts separately. Note that as seen in (9.45), the RS form of the copula -**li** is frequently used as the main verb which follows the auxiliary -**áàlí**.

In (9.46) we see the **-áàli** auxiliary used with the resultative form **tuuziri** 'he was keeping'.

(9.46) <u>À-ná-àlí</u>   <u>tùùz-ír-í</u>   |   í=n-gáàvù  y-à-gé   n-gùmà  nààhô.
1-ADD.V-P3   look.after-RS-Fi   AU=9-cow   9-A.M-1   9-one   only

'And he was keeping | his one cow only.' (42 004)

In (9.47) we see the use of the **-ààlí** auxiliary followed by the copula **kòla** 'be.NEWLY', in turn followed by its progressive form. As always, it signals background information, here in an explanatory clause.

(9.47) ...**mú=kúbá** |   í=kí-shùkà   gw-á=   à-lí   rì-ìr-í   =mwò   ||   <u>ky-áàlí</u>
because   AU=7-bush   3-O.R=   1-P3   is-RS-Fi   =18   7-P3

<u>kòlà</u>   <u>mú=</u>   <u>híír-à</u>.
be.NEWLY   PROG=   burn-Fa

'...because | the bush which it (snake) was in || was now burning up.' (13 002)

The example in (9.48) shows the P3 auxiliary followed by the progressive persistive. Here the P3 auxiliary **gàtáàlí** 'they were not' provides the temporal orientation for the progressive persistive **kìrì mú=bònà** 'still seeing'.

(9.48) N-á=   má-sú   gà-à-gè   ||   <u>gà-tá-àlí</u>   <u>kìrì</u>   <u>mú=</u>   <u>bòn-à</u>
CNJ-AU=   6-eyes   6-A.M-1   6-NEG-P3   be.PERS   PROG=   see-Fa

bw-îjâ.
14-good

'And his eyes || were no longer seeing well.' (Gen 27:1)

The P3 auxiliary can also be completed by the progressive intentional, as in (9.49), where the remote past **ààlí** forms the inflection for the phrase **gwètí ágáhìngà** 'she is farming'.

(9.49) **Lw-àná-bà-hí-s-à** |   h-ô=   yò   mú-kàzì   <u>á-àlí</u>   <u>gwètí</u>
11-SQ-O2-arrive-CS-Fa   16-O.R=   that.N+1   1-woman   1-P3   PROG

<u>á-gá-hìng-à</u>.
1-INTL-farm-Fa

'And it took them | to where that woman was (actively) farming.' (04 007)

### 9.2.1.2 Future

The future tenses include two immediate future (F1) forms: the simple immediate future and the immediate future, newly; two unmarked future forms: the unmarked future (F2) and the unmarked future, newly; and the remote future (F3).

#### 9.2.1.2.1 Immediate future

##### 9.2.1.2.1.1 Simple immediate future

The "immediate future" (F1) is comprised of the initial prefixes (including the P1 tense marker **à**-) followed by the clitic **mú** and then the macrostem, with the final vowel -**a**, as indicated in the following formula:

[S.P [à- [**mú**=[ (O.P) [ (RFX) [base] -**a**]

The subject prefix and tense marker **à**- have L tone, the **mú** has high tone, and the macrostem, acting as an infinitive form, exhibits the Simple stem-tone pattern.[50]

This is the one form where the status of **mú** is irregular, since there is no separate auxiliary (with following word break) preceding it, as is found in the progressive forms. Instead it is preceded simply by the subject and tense prefixes. Thus the prefixes are prefixed or cliticized directly to **mú**, which in turn is cliticized to the macrostem. Therefore the whole form before the macrostem could be called a clitic complex.

The "immediate future" refers to something about to happen imminently, but without marking it as being something new. In (9.50) the phrase **kútàgì kwó**=**nàmú**=**gírà?** 'what am I about to do?' refers to something just about to happen.

(9.50) À-ná-yì-búúz-à: || «Kút-àgì   kw-ó=   n-àmú=   gír-à?»
1-SQ-RFX-ask-Fa   what-EMP   15-O.R=   1SG-F1=   do-Fa

'And she asked herself: || «What will I now do?»' (04 019)

##### 9.2.1.2.1.2 Immediate future, newly

The "immediate future, newly" (F1 NEWLY) is a two-word phrase. The first word is comprised of the subject prefix, followed by the auxiliary copula -**kòla**. The

---

[50]The fact that the main verb stem takes the Simple stem-tone pattern, like the infinitive, rather than the Complex HL stem-tone pattern triggered by the -**à** tense marker indicates that there is an underlying word break between the prefixes and **mú**, and the verb stem. The **mú** is not a morphological part of the final word of the verb but rather, a proclitic.

second word begins with the clitic **bú=**, followed by the macrostem, with the final vowel **-a**, as indicated in the following formula:

[S.P [kòla] [bú=[ (O.P) [ (RFX) [base] -a]

The first word has all L tones, the **bú=** clitic has a H tone, and macrostem exhibits the Simple stem-tone pattern.

The 'immediate future, newly' refers to a *new* state that is about to begin *right now*. In (9.51) the phrase **ìkòlá bú=dèndúúkà** 'it is (newly) about to die' refers to a time that is imminent, and is contrasted with a former time.

(9.51) **Bà-ná-gwân-à**     **léèrò**   | **ìyó**     **n-dàrè** || **ì-kòlá**     **bú=**
2-SQ-encounter-Fa    this.time   that.N+9   9-lion     9-be.NEWLY   F1=

**dèndúúk-à**    | **ná=**    **yùgwó**    **mw-énà.**
be.finally.cut.off-Fa    CNJ=    that.N+3    3-hunger

'And they encountered this time | that lion || is newly about to finally die | from that hunger.' (11 030)

This imminent state can be denoted as having taken place in past time by adding the P3 auxiliary **-áàli**. This is seen in (9.52) in the phrase **ànáàlí kòlá bú=fwà** 'and he was (newly) about to die'.

(9.52) **Bì-rí**    **ú=kù-lì**    || **kw-á=**    **àlì**   **lémb-ìr-ì**     **bwénèènè** ||
8-is    AU=15-truth    CMP-1=    P3   be.very.sick-RS-Fi    very.much

**à-ná-àlí**    **kòlá**   | **bú=**    **fw-à.**
1-ADD.V-P3    be.NEWLY   F1=    die-Fa

'It's true || that he was very sick || and he was (newly) | about to die.' (Php 2:27)

*9.2.1.2.2 Unmarked future*

The 'unmarked future' (F2) is formed by the initial prefixes, including the future tense marker **gáá-**[51] followed by the macrostem, with the final vowel **-a**, as indicated in the following formula:

[S.P [ (NEG) [**gáá-** [ (ADD.V) [ (PER) [ (O.P) [ (RFX) [base] -a]

This verb form exhibits the $V_2$ stem-tone pattern.

---

[51] As noted above, the future/intentional **gáá-** is shortened when there are three or more morae following within the word.

### 9.2.1.2.2.1 Simple unmarked future

The unmarked future refers to an event that will happen, without any comment about whether it is immediate or remote. In (9.53) the unmarked future verb **ngákúhèèrèzâ** 'I will give you' refers to the future, with no other connotations involved.

(9.53) É= má-háàmà || ú-Ø-m-bèèrèz-é  íyò  m-bóngò ||
O=  6-bush.dog  2SG-SBV-O1.SG-give-Fe  that.N+9  9-gazelle

**n-gá-kú-hèèrèz-á**  í=n-dándà.
1SG-F2-O2.SG-give-Fa  AU=9-reward

'O bush dog || give me that gazelle || I will give you a reward.' (18 005)

In (9.54) the unmarked future auxiliary copula **ígáàbà** 'it will be' sets the time frame for the main verb **kéèrà yàtérà** 'it's already slackened'.

(9.54) N-é=  ky-ànyà  í=mí-sí  í-gáà-b-à  kéèrà
CNJ-AU=  7-time  AU=4-strength  4-F2-become-Fa  ALREADY

y-à-tér-à ||  ù-tá-Ø-n-yíbàgìr-è.
4-P1-be.lost-Fa  2SG-NEG-SBV-O1.SG-forget-Fe

'At the time (my) strength will already be slackened || don't forget me.'
(Psa 71:9)

### 9.2.1.2.2.2 Unmarked future, newly

The "future, newly" (F2 NEWLY) is a two-word form that begins with the subject prefix on the auxiliary copula -**kòlà**. The second word is an inflected form comprised of the same subject prefix, followed by the future **gáá-** prefix, followed by the macrostem, with the final vowel -**a**, as indicated in the following formula:

[S.P [**kòlà**] [S.P [**gáá-** [ (O.P) [ (RFX) [base] -**a**]

The first word has low tone, and the second word exhibits the V$_2$ stem-tone pattern.

The unmarked future, newly refers to a *new* state that has not occurred to that point, but which will occur. In (9.55) the phrase **kwâ=kòlà ágáákìzì géndá búkóndwè** 'that he will *newly* be going naked' refers to a new state which (though not occurring in the past) is about to take place.

(9.55) **mú=kúbá** | **á-ká-bōn-à** || **kw-â=** **kòlá** **á-gáá-kìzì** **génd-á** |
because 1-P2-see-Fa CMP-1= be.NEWLY 1-F2-REP go-Fa

**bú-kóndwè.**
14-naked

'because | he saw || that he will newly continuously go | naked.' (33 023)

In (9.56) **àkòlà ágáálúhà,** means 'is now (but not before) about to get tired'.

(9.56) **À-ná-bòn-à** | **ù-lyá** **mú-nyérè** | **à-kòlà** **á-gáá-lúh-à**.
1-SQ-see-Fa 1-that.R 1-girl 1-be.NEWLY 1-F2-get.tired-Fa

'He saw | that girl | is newly about to get tired.' (207 042)

### 9.2.1.2.3 Remote future

The "remote future" (F3) is a two-word form. The first word consists of the initial prefixes followed by the auxiliary form **-ááye**. The second word consists of the macrostem, with the final vowel **-e**, as indicated in the following formula:

[S.P [ (NEG) [**ááyè**] [ (O.P) [ (RFX) [base] **-e**]

The auxiliary has a H tone on its first syllable (the preceding prefix as well as the long **a** of **ááyè**) and a L tone on the second syllable. The second word of the two-word form, if unprefixed (i.e. no object markers) exhibits the Complex HH stem-tone pattern characteristic of minimally prefixed subjunctive forms. If there are any prefixes on the verb stem, the tone of the second word reverts to the $V_2$ stem-tone pattern, as happens in all subjunctive forms.

The remote future refers to an event that is far away in time. This event may occur at an imprecise, unpredictable time in the future. In the negative, this form by implication, means "never".

In (9.57) the father giving advice to his sons uses a relative clause in the remote future, **úwááyè bàtèèrè** 'who would (someday) attack them' to express a time in the remote, indeterminate future.

(9.57) ...**bà-ká-kìzí** **sìnd-á** **ú=mú-góm-á** | **ú-w-ááyè** **bà-tèèr-è**.
2-INTV-REP overcome-Fa AU=1-enemy S.R-1-F3 O2-attack-Fe

'...(that) they then repeatedly overcome the enemy | who would (someday) attack them.' (02 008)

In (9.58) the negative form of the remote future is used to imply that the young man will never again go to the place of the in-laws (not even in the remote future).

## 9.2 Detailed inventory of TAM form/meanings

(9.58) **Yùgwó mú-sòrè ‖ gw-àná-yàmì bíík-á í=n-dáhírò ‖ kwó=**
that.N+3   3-young-man   3-SQ-IMMED   place-Fa   AU=9-oath   CMP=

**gù-tá-áyè kì-génd-é | ì-yó mûndá | í-mw-à-bò-vyàlà.**
3-NEG-F3   PERS-go-Fe   there.N-23   place   23-place-A.M-2-in.law

'That young man ‖ immediately placed an oath ‖ that he will never any longer go | to that place | of the in-laws.' (36 061)

### 9.2.2 Aspect

Aspects function to "describe the temporal contours of a situation..." (Bybee 1994:317). Kifuliiru verbs exhibit eight different aspects, discussed in this section.

#### 9.2.2.1 Timeless / habitual

The timeless form (TL) is comprised of the initial prefixes, including a null morpheme in the TAM slot, which are attached to the macrostem, with the final vowel -**a**, as indicated in the following formula:

[S.P [ (NEG) Ø [ (ADD.V) [ (O.P) [ (RFX) [base] -**a**]

This verb form exhibits the Complex HL stem-tone pattern.

Thus the unmarked copula (COP) -**li** 'is' is not marked for past, present or future; it has no TAM marking. In (9.59) the unmarked -**li** form is equative and does not reference time at all.

(9.59) **Ú-nò à-tà-lì mú-ndù ‖ kì-rì kí-nyámíìshwà.**
1-this.P.C   1-NEG-is   1-person   7-is   7-wild.animal

'This one is not a person ‖ it's a wild animal.' (202 026)

The timeless form often marks habitual. In (9.60) **tùtúúlà nyûmbá ngùmà** means 'we live in one house' (without noting the time). The one speaking, and the person mentioned, habitually live in the same house.

(9.60) **Ú=mú-ndú tù-Ø-túúl-à ny-ûmbá n-gùmà.**
AU=1-person   1PL-TL-live-Fa   9-house   9-one

'The man we (with him) live (habitually) in one house.' (14 014)

Timeless forms are also found in many proverbs, as in (9.61), where **ìvùnà** 'it breaks' as well as the negative form **ìtàvùnà** 'it doesn't break' are both timeless.

(9.61) Í=n-gónì ‖ ì-Ø-vùn-à   í-vùhà ‖ sì=   ì-tà-Ø-vùn-à
AU=9-stick  9-TL-break-Fa  5-bone  OBV=  9-NEG-TL-break-Fa

n-géshò.
9-habit

'A stick ‖ breaks a bone ‖ but it doesn't break habits.'

### 9.2.2.2 State changes / continues

The copulas -kòla 'is (now not before)', -shùba 'was (before not now)' both denote state changes, and are polar opposites of each other. The auxiliary -kìri 'is (still)' denotes a lack of change. In (9.62) the copula ìkòla means 'it is (now, but not before)'. This indicates a *new state* which did not previously obtain.

(9.62) Nê=  yò     n-gwî |  i-kòlà        há=  bú-tàmbì  ly-à-gè.
and=  that.N+9  9-leopard  9-be.NEWLY  16=  14-beside  5-A.M-1

'And that leopard | is now beside him.' (35 020)

In (9.63) the copula gùshùbà means 'it was (before, but not now)'. This indicates a *previously occurring state* which no longer obtains.

(9.63) Ú=mú-gánúúló  gw-à-gè ‖ gù-shùbà   gw-à=  «vúùjù   vúùjù».
AU=1-speaking   3-A.M-1   3-was.PREV  3-A.M=  careless  careless

'His conversation ‖ was «careless careless».'

In (9.64) àkìrì means that 'he is (still)', indicating a *persisting state*.

(9.64) Ìyó      n-dàrè |  y-àná-mú-gwân-à |   à-kìrì     yà-hô.
that.N+9  9-lion   9-SQ-O1-encounter-Fa  1-is.PERS  there.N-16

'That lion | encountered him | he's still there.' (46 015)

### 9.2.2.3 Progressive

The "present progressive" (PROG) aspects are all multiword forms. The initial auxiliary is a copula (COP) (either -li 'is' or -kìri 'is (still)' or -kòla 'is (now, but not before)') which is inflected by the initial prefixes. Following is the auxiliary clitic mú 'PROG' (identical to the cl. 18 locative mú, but here grammaticized as a progressive marker). This clitic attaches to the following macrostem, with the final vowel -a, as indicated in the following formula:

[S.P [ (NEG) [COP] mú=[ (O.P) [ (RFX) [base] -a ]

## 9.2 Detailed inventory of TAM form/meanings

This first word exhibits all low tones (no identifiable stem-tone pattern).[52] The auxiliary PROG clitic **mú** has a high tone, and the second word exhibits the Simple stem-tone pattern.

### 9.2.2.3.1 Progressive, unmarked

The "progressive, unmarked" communicates an ongoing state *without* commenting on whether that state is new, persisting, intentional, etc. In (9.65) the unmarked progressive occurs twice using the copula -**li** 'is' in **bàlì mú=shéényà** 'they are cutting firewood' and **àlì mú=yītà** 'he is killing'.

(9.65) **Bà-lì**   **mú=**   **shéény-à** ‖ **ú-w-àbò**   **ná-yè** ‖ **à-lì**
      2-is    PROG   cut.firewood-Fa  AU=1-SAME.SET  ADD.P-1  1-is

      **mú=**   **yīt-à** |  **ú=bú-nyúnì.**
      PROG  kill-Fa  AU=14-birds

'They are cutting firewood ‖ their fellow and HE ‖ is killing | birds.' (210 059)

### 9.2.2.3.2 Progressive recent past

This verb form exhibits the Complex HL stem-tone pattern on the first word and the Simple stem-tone pattern on the second.[53]

The copula -**shùbà** refers to a recent state which 'previously obtained, but does not any more'. Thus in (9.66) the progressive phrase **tùshùbà mú=sháátà** 'we were playing' means that the speakers were in the process of playing recently, but are no longer doing so.

(9.66) **Í=ky-ànyà**  **tù-shùbà**  **mú=**  **sháát-à** ‖ **í=n-vùlà**  **y-àná-yàmí**
      AU=7-time   1PL-be.PREV  PROG=  play-Fa   AU=9-rain  9-SQ-IMMED

      **yíj-à.**
      come-Fa

'The time we were playing ‖ rain immediately came.' (113 008)

In (9.67) the husband has found his wife caught in a trap in the forest, where she should never have been. Here **ùshùbà mú=géndà** means 'you were (but are no longer) in state of going'.

---

[52] Because of the brevity of these forms, and their general lack of variability by the addition of optional morphemes etc., it is not possible to observe the tonal alternations which would serve to distinguish one pattern from another.

[53] The second word of such constructions takes the form of a prefixless infinitive, and thus exhibits the Simple stem-tone pattern which is characteristic of the infinitive.

(9.67) **Yîbà**    | à-ná-mú-bwîr-à: || «É= mú-kàzì || háyì h-ô=
her.husband   1-SQ-O1-tell-Fa    O=   1-woman    where  16-OR+2SG=

**shùbà**   **mú**=   **génd-à**?»
be.PREV    PROG=    go-Fa

'Her husband | told her: || «O woman || where was it you were
going?»' (632 040)

### 9.2.2.3.3 Progressive, persistive

The "progressive, persistive" refers to a state which is *still* happening. This implies that the state has been ongoing for some period of time previous to the statement. In (9.68) **bàkìrì mú=tùgírírà** 'they are still doing for us', the implication is the parents were doing something for us, and are still doing it.

(9.68) **Bí-kí    by-á=    bá-bùsì    bì-ì-tù |   bà-kìrì    mú**=
8-what   8-O.R+AU=   2-parents   2-A.M-1PL   2-be.PERS   PROG=

**tù-gír-ír-à**?
O1.PL-do-APL-Fa

'What are our parents | still doing for us?' (38 015)

### 9.2.2.3.4 Progressive, newly

The "progressive, newly" uses the copula **-kòla** to communicate that the state referred to is new, i.e. it did not obtain before, but does now. In (9.69) the use of **àkòlà** 'he is (now, not before)' in the form **àkòlà mú=dèta** 'he is newly speaking' communicates that the action is something new: Kishiriri was not speaking secrets before, but is now.

(9.69) **Bà-ná-mény-à   kwó=   Kíshìrìrì ||   à-kòla       mú=     dēt-à**
2-SQ-know-Fa   CMP=   Kishiriri    1-be.NEWLY   PROG=   speak-Fa

**ú=tú-mbíshwà**.
AU=13-secrets

'They knew that Kishiriri || is now speaking secrets.' (40 025)

In (9.70) **bàkòlà mú=sháátà** means that 'they are (now, not before) in the state of playing'.

9.2 Detailed inventory of TAM form/meanings   241

(9.70) **Ìrí    bá**-ká-b-á     **bà**-kòlà      **mú**=    **sháát**-à |    ìyó
       when    2-P2-become-Fa   2-be.NEWLY       PROG=      play-Fa       that.N+9

**ny**-ámîishwà |   **y**-àná-yîj-à.
9-wild.animal       9-SQ-come-Fa

'When they were now playing | that wild animal | came.' (619 037)

### 9.2.2.3.5 Progressive, intentional

The "progressive, intentional" is a two-word form. The first word is comprised of the initial prefixes followed by the progressive auxiliary **gweti**. The second word begins with the same subject prefix repeated, plus the intentional prefix **gáá**- and the macrostem with the final vowel -**a**, as indicated in the following formula:

[S.P [ (NEG) [ (ADD.V) [ (PERS) [**gwétì**] [S.P [**gáá**- [ (O.P) [ (RFX) [base] -**a**]

The first word exhibits the Complex HL tone pattern, and the second word exhibits the V$_2$ stem-tone pattern.

In (9.71) the verb **ábàgwétì bágáyìmbà** 'who are (intentionally) singing' shows that (a) something is in the state of happening now and (b) it is happening "intentionally" or "actively", i.e. the person is seen as singing with purpose and objective, and not just by happenstance. Usually this "intentional" meaning is not highly marked, but rather is somewhat subtle. (This is in contrast to the corresponding unmarked progressive form **ábàlì mú**=**yīmbà** 'who are singing', which is neutral, i.e. without indicating "intention".)

(9.71) **Há**-nò       **mú**=   **kì**-nó     **kí**-tì ||   **hà**-lì   **á**=bá-ndú |
       16-here.P.C    18=       7-this.P.C    7-tree         16-is       AU=2-people

**á**-bà-gwétì |      **bá**-gá-yìmb-à.
S.R-2-PROG           2-INTL-sing-Fa

'Here in this tree || are people | who are (intentionally) | singing.' (206 050)

In (9.72) the progressive intentional **àgwétì ágáshèènyà** 'she is (intentionally) gathering firewood' is used to communicate that something is in the process of happening now, and with intention. (This is in contrast to the corresponding unmarked progressive **àlì mú**-**shéényà** 'she is collecting firewood'.)

(9.72) **Bà-ná-mú-shùvy-à:** ‖ «**À-sìgál-à      à-gwétì**
      2-SQ-O1-answer-Fa        1+P1-remain-Fa     1-PROG

  **á-gá-shèèny-à.**»
  1-INTL-gather.firewood-Fa

  'And they answered him: ‖ «He remained collecting firewood.»' (25 010)

In (9.73) we see an alternative form of the progressive intentional form, in which the **gweti** auxiliary is not present: **ànákìzì géndá ágáyìfúndà** 'he was (intentionally) going forcing himself in.' Instead of **gweti**, the repetitive auxiliary **kizi** is followed by an auxiliary use of the verb 'to go.' This is inflected by the sequential prefix **àná-** at the beginning of the verb phrase.

(9.73) **À-ná-kìzì   génd-á | á-gá-yì-fúnd-à         mú=  n-yûmbà    zà-à-bò.**
      1-SQ-REP    go-Fa    1-INTL-RFX-force.in-Fa   18   10-houses  10-A.M-2

  'And he continuously went | forcing himself into their houses.' (Act 8:3)

### 9.2.2.4 Completive

The completive can occur with recent past (P1) or unmarked past (P2) forms. In (9.74) the completive auxiliary **kéèrà** 'already' emphasizes that the act of eating is already completed. The adverb **kéèrà** 'already' usually comes directly before the verb as seen in (74).

(9.74) **Yéhéè!** ‖ **Ì-ryá    n-gòkò    kéèrà      y-à-gì-ry-à.**
        oh.my!    9-that.R  9-chicken  ALREADY    9-P1-O9-eat-Fa

  'Oh my! ‖ That chicken has already eaten it (a certain piece of meat).' (204 008)

In (9.75) the auxiliary **kéèrà** 'already' emphasizes that the the old men were 'already' killed in past (P2) time.

(9.75) **Á=bá-shààjá   á-bá-àlì    gì-y-íj-ì     ‖ bà-tà-kírí         =hò ‖**
      AU=2-old.men   S.R-2-P3    O9-know-RS-Fi    2-NEG-is.PERS      =16

  **kéèrà  |  bá-ká-yìt-w-â.**
  ALREADY    2-P2-kill-PS-Fa

  'The old men who knew it ‖ no longer exist ‖ already | they were killed.' (23 025)

### 9.2.2.5 Resultative

The "resultative" (RS) is formed by the initial prefixes, followed by the resultative macrostem, as indicated in the following formula:

[S.P [ (NEG) [ (ADD.V) [ (PERS) [ (O.P) [ (RFX) [base] -**ir**-**i**]

This verb form exhibits the Complex HL stem-tone pattern in the simple one-word resultative form. When the resultative serves as the final word of a multiword form such as that in (9.114), it instead displays the Complex LH pattern. The verb base in these resultative forms typically undergoes a phonological modification, especially spirantization of the final consonant. These modifications are discussed at some length in Volume 1.

This form of the verb expresses what Bybee, et al. term "resultative". This means that it describes an action in the past which produces a state that persists into the present (Bybee, et al. 1994:318). The focus in this form is on the present state, rather than on the past action, and there is no indication as to when in the past the action might have taken place.

In (9.76) the resultative form **àbwátíìrì** 'she is sitting' (derived from -**bwátal**- 'sit') shows that the girl sat down in the past, and the results of that action are still present, i.e. she is sitting there.

(9.76)  À-húmààn-á |   ú=mú-nyérè ‖   à-bwát-íìr-ì   mw-í=   dàkò
        1-encounter-Fa  AU=1-girl       1-sit-RS-Fi    18-AU=  5+under

   ly-é=        kí-tì.
   5-A.M+AU=    7-tree

'He encountered | the girl ‖ is sitting under the tree.' (112 008)

The resultative -**bwìni** 'seeing' (derived from -**bòn**-) occurs twice in (9.77), in **mùbwíní** 'are you seeing' and **tùbàbwíní** 'we are seeing them'. The implication is that the persons being addressed had already caught sight of the children and can still see them.

(9.77)  «Ká=    mù-bw-ín-ì    yà-bá      bà-ánà?» ‖  Tì=
        Q=      2PL-see-RS-Fi these.P-2  2-children   ‹quote›

   «Tù-bà-bw-ín-ì.»
   1PL-O2-see-RS-Fi

'«Do you see these children?» ‖ ‹quote› «We see them.»' (522 043)

In (9.78) the resultative verb -**lwàzírì** 'is sick' indicates that the husband had got sick and was still in that condition.

(9.78) **Mú-ká-à-gê** ‖ **à-ná-mény-á** kwó= yîbà | **à-kòlí**
1-wife-A.M-1  1-SQ-know-Fa  CMP= her.husband 1-be.NEWLY

**lwàz-ír-ì**.
be.sick-RS-Fi

'His wife ‖ knows that her husband | is now sick.' (54 006)

### 9.2.2.6 *Sequential*

The sequential past (SQ) is comprised of initial prefixes, including the prefix **àná-**,[54] followed by the macrostem with final vowel **-a**, as indicated in the following formula:

[S.P [ (NEG) [**àná-** [ (PERS) [ (O.P) [ (RFX) [base] -**a**]

This verb form exhibits the Complex HL stem-tone pattern.

The sequential does not express specific time-orientation, but instead receives its time-orientation from a preceding verb.

In Kifuliiru narrative texts, the sequential form is the most common of the narrative tenses, marking the fact that one event is following another. In (9.79) the verbs **kyànámúkáyìrà** 'it was fierce to him' and **ànábùlà** 'and he lacked' are both sequential and serve to move the event line forward.

(9.79) Yìkyó    kí-tēērò ‖ **ky-àná-mù-káy-ìr-à**    bwénèènè |
that.N+7  7-attack    7-SQ-O1-be.fierce-APL-Fa  very.much

**à-ná-bùl-à**   kw-á=  gáá-gír-à.
1-SQ-lack-Fa  what-1= F2-do-Fa

'That attack ‖ was very fierce to him | and he had nothing he could do.' (19 003)

### 9.2.2.7 *Continuative*

The continuative (CON) is defined by Bybee, et al (1994:164) as meaning 'continue' or 'keep on doing'. The continuative is comprised of the initial prefixes, including the **ná-**, which is followed by the macrostem, with the final vowel -**e**, as indicated in the following formula:

[S.P [ (NEG) [ **ná-** [ (PERS) [ (O.P) [ (RFX) [base] -**e**]

---

[54] Alternatively, the **àná-** prefix could be considered as a composite of the P1 past (TAM prefix **à-**) with a following (contiguous) additive prefix **ná-**. These two would have been combined into a single form which has a sequential meaning. Because of the single meaning of these two morphemes when used in conjunction with each other, we gloss the recent past prefix and the additive prefix together as seqential (SQ).

## 9.2 Detailed inventory of TAM form/meanings

Like the other members of the subjunctive family having overt TAM marking plus the final -**e**, this verb form exhibits the V$_2$ stem-tone pattern.

The continuative has two uses, both of which include the notion of predictability:

(a) Especially in informal registers, it can occur on the event line of a narrative text, in places where the events are somehow "predictable". (b) It can also indicate an unrealized action that follows some subjunctive, conditional, future, or habitual verb. Again, the time or aspect can be predicted by that previous verb.

In (9.80) the continuative is used as a predictable continuation of a previous verb. In the first clause (SQ) the new wife sends the children to the river. The next clause (CON) begins **á=bààná bànágêndè** 'and the children went'. This is not really new information, but is already established in the hearer's mental representation, since it is an expected outcome of the previous statement. Thus the continuative form **bànágêndè** is used.

(9.80) ...(**mú**-**hyà**) | à-ná-kìzì tùm-à | bà-lyá   bà-ánà | í=   rw-ījì. ||
       (1-new.wife) 1-SQ-REP   send-Fa  2-those.R 2-children 23= 11-river

   **Á=bà-àná** || **bà-ná-gênd-è** b-ômbì | n-é=   n-dèhà  zì-bìrì.
   AU=2-children   2-CON-go-Fe    2-both   CNJ-AU= 10-gourds 10-two.

 '...(the new wife) | and she sent | those children | to the river. ||
   The children || went both (of them) | with two gourds.' (205 08-09)

The continuative can also be used as a continuation of the TAM of the previous verb, i.e. of the unmarked future (F2), the conditional (CND), etc. These are now exemplified below.

In (9.81) the verb of the initial relative clause **ngíìsì úgátàngì híká hànò** 'whoever will first arrive here' is in the future tense, and the second verb **ìnábè** 'and it be' is in the continuative: **í=ndèhá yàgè ìnábè ìyìjwírì** 'and her gourd is filled'. Thus the second clause is understood to be in the same future time frame, and a continuation of the condition begun by the relative clause. When the two parts of the condition are met, then the conclusion follows: **ngámútùmá í=mwá=mwìzó wàgè** 'I will send her to her maternal uncle'.

(9.81) **Ngíìsì ú-gá-tàngí**     **hík-á    há-nò**  ||  **í=n-dèhá    y-à-gè**
each    S.R+1-F2-FIRST    arrive-Fa  16-here.P.C    AU=9-gourd  9-A.M-1

<u>**ì-ná-b-è**</u>        **ì-yìjw-ír-ì**      **mw-á=    mī-ījì**   ||   **n-gá-mú-tùm-à** |
9-CON-become-Fe   9-fill-RS-Fi   18-AU=   6-water    1SG-F2-O1-send-Fa

**í=      mw-á=       mw-ìzó          w-à-gè.**
23=    place-A.M=  1-maternal.uncle   1-A.M-1

'Whoever will first arrive here || and her gourd is filled with water || I will send her | to her maternal uncle.' (43 017)

In (9.82) the verb in the first clause is the CONDITIONAL **ìrí bàngàlóngà í=kíndù** 'if they would get a thing'. The continuative **bàtànáyùvàànwê** 'and they don't get along' forms the second part of the conditional clause, and follows in the conditional mood of the first verb. When both of those of those conditions are met, then the conclusion, expressed by the timeless verb **bàkìzì nyágwá** 'they are repeatedly robbed of' follows.

(9.82) **Á=bá-ndù**  ||  **ìrí     bà-ngà-lóng-à       í=kí-ndù**  ||
AU=2-people   if    2-CND-receive-Fa    AU=7-thing

<u>**bà-tà-ná-yùvà-ànw-ê**</u>  ||   **bà-kìzì   nyág-w-á** |  **ì-by-ó=**
2-NEG-CON-hear-MUT-Fe        2-REP   grab-PS-Fa   AU=8-O.R=

**bà-ngà-lí-ír-ì.**
2-CND-eat-RS-Fi

'People || if they would get a thing || and they do not get along || they are habitually robbed | (of) the (things) they would have eaten.' (03 023)

In (9.83) the phrase **mángò wámbímà** 'if/when you defeat me' sets up a hypothetical CONDITIONAL state, and the following clause occurs in the continuative as an extension of that time frame.

(9.83) **Mángò   w-á-m-bím-à**          ||        <u>**ù-ná-b-è**</u>
when   2SG-P1-O1.SG-surpass-Fa        2SG-CON-become-Fe

**yíb-à-niè.**
husband-A.M-1SG

'If/when you defeat me || you will be my husband.' (30 009)

*9.2 Detailed inventory of TAM form/meanings* 247

In (9.84) there is a sequence of three commands. Here the first two are polite imperatives while the final one, **ùnámúbwìrè** 'and you tell him' is in the continuative .⁵⁵

(9.84)   U-Ø-bóh-è        í=ny-ámá     yó=         lú-lìmí ||
        2SG-SBV-wrap-Fe   AU=9-meat    9-A.M+AU=   11-tongue

        ù-Ø-gì-twàl-ìr-é           mw-àmí ||    ù-ná-mú-bwìr-è
        2SG-SBV-O9-carry-APL-Fe   1-king         2SG-CON-O1-tell-Fe

        kwókùnô:...
        ‹quote.MARKED›

'Wrap meat of the tongue || take it to the king || and tell him just like this:...' (24 022)

### 9.2.2.8 Intervening time

The aspect of intervening time (INTV) is comprised of the initial prefixes, including the distal **ká-** prefix, followed by the macrostem, including final vowel -e, as indicated in the following formula:

[S.P [**ká** [ (ADD.V) [ (O.P) [ (RFX) [base] -e]⁵⁶

As is typical of other subjunctive tenses, this verb form exhibits the V₂ stem-tone pattern. In contrast to the P2 tense, where the prefix preceding the P2 **ká-** exhibits a H tone, the H tone of the intervening time prefix **ká-** is *not* realized on the prefix which precedes.

The intervening time is always unrealized at the time of speaking and indicates a (subjunctive) time in the future which *follows an intervening time*. Thus in (9.85) one time period is represented by **ànábàtèndéérà kwó=bàté gēndà** 'and he begged them that they first go'. Here the verb **bàté gēndà** 'that they first go' is a simple subjunctive form.⁵⁷ The following verb is then expressed using the intervening time: **bàkáyîjè gûndì múlègè-règè** 'they will come another daytime'. The use of the intervening time indicates that there is a time period between the first action (their leaving) and their return on another day.

---

⁵⁵In other cases, the second command would be in the continuative, and the third in the intervening time. It is not clear why the first two here are both in the simple subjunctive.

⁵⁶There are no cases of negative forms of the intervening time in our texts, so we have not included the NEG marker as a possibility in the formula.

⁵⁷When an adverbial auxiliary intervenes between the prefixes and the main verb, the main verb is no longer inflected, and may not then exhibit the subjunctive final -e. Here the adverbial auxiliary is **búlí** 'SBSQ'.

(9.85) Ùyó    mw-àmì | à-ná-bà-tèndéér-à | kwó= bà-∅-té
     that.N+1  1-king    1-SQ-O2-beg-Fa    CMP=  2-SBV-PRIOR

     gēnd-à || **bà-ká-yîj-è** | gù-ndì mú-lègè-règè.
     go-Fa    2-INTV-come-Fe   3-other 3-day-RDP

'That king | begged them | that they first go || and then come back | another day.' (24 007)

In (9.86) the speaker says that she will first cook stiff porridge so she can eat, and after an intervening time has passed, she will then begin to cry. The **k** of the intervening time **ká-** in this example is voiced by phonological rule, becoming **g** when it directly follows the first-person singular subject marker **n-**. Furthermore, the final **-e** of the intervening time does not appear in this example, due to the intervening adverbial auxiliary which precludes the inflection of the main verb stem.

(9.86) N-àmú=  téé    dùg-á         n-∅-dy-è  ||
     1SG-F1=  PRIOR  cook.porridge-Fa  1SG-SBV-eat-Fe

     **n-gá-búlí**    tòndéér-á    ú=kú-lír-à.
     1SG-INTV-SBSQ  begin-Fa    AU=15-cry-Fa

'I will first cook porridge (in order that ) I eat || then I will begin to cry.' (54 009)

When there is to be an intervening time period between the execution of the two unrealized actions, the second verb is marked as intervening time. The example seen in (9.87) **mùgéndé mùkágálùkè** 'you go and (after a time in-between) return again' employs the intervening time, as the people are told to go and then come back the next day.

(9.87) **Mù-∅-génd-è**    **mù-ká-gálùk-è** | ú-bú-gáà-ky-à.
     2PL-SBV-go-Fe    2PL-INTV-return-Fe  S.R-14-F2-dawn-Fa

'Go and come back | the next day.' (06 011)

## 9.2.3 Mood

Mood here deals with many manifestations of purpose (including subjunctive purpose, imperatives, frustrated intention, etc.), as well as different sorts of potential/conditionals.

## 9.2.3.1 Purpose / expectation

### 9.2.3.1.1 Imperatives

Here we discuss the singular and plural direct imperatives (as opposed to the indirect subjunctive imperatives listed under 9.2.3.1.2.2).

Direct imperatives (both singular and plural) do not have any prefixes before the macrostem. The understood subject is second-person (singular or plural).

The DIRECT IMPERATIVE, SINGULAR (IMP.SG) consists of the macrostem of the verb (with the optional object)[58] and the final vowel -**a**, as indicated in the following formula:

[macrostem] -F**a**]

This verb form exhibits the Complex LH stem-tone pattern.

The direct imperative is a command which is intended to be carried out immediately and without question, and is often spoken in a rather impolite manner. The direct imperative singular is used in (9.88), where the verb **hùlíkà** simply means 'be quiet!'.

(9.88) Ùyó       mú-gólì         à-ná-mú-bwîr-à: ||  «Ø-Hùlík-à
       that.N+1  1-king's.wife   1-SQ-O1-tell-Fa      be.quiet-Fa

       máàshì!»
       for.goodness.sake

'That king's wife told him: || «Be quiet for goodness sake!»' (24 013)

Some other representative forms are **lólà** 'look (at something)!', **yîjâ** 'come!', **jábùkà** 'cross to the other side!', **sháàgà** 'leave (here)!' Since the direct imperative consists of the macrostem, it can include an object when the verb is transitive, such as the initial cl. 1SG object **m-** 'me' seen in **mbwîrâ** 'tell me'.

The DIRECT IMPERATIVE, PLURAL (IMP.PL) is formed in exactly the same way, except that it has the final vowel -**i**, as indicated in the following formula:

[macrostem] -F**i**]

This verb form has the Complex LH-IP stem-tone pattern.

In (9.89) we observe the direct imperative plural, **lòlí** 'look!'

---

[58] It is more common to use a subjunctive form when an incorporated object is included in a command. In informal speech, however, the direct imperatives are sometimes heard with an incorporated object.

(9.89) À-ná-bwîr-à   á=bà-àbò   ‖   tí=   ‹É=   bà-ánà   ‖   lòl-í
1-SQ-tell-Fa   AU=2-SAME.SET       ‹quote›   O=   2-children   look-Fi

máàwé   |   kw-â=   yì-shùmàs-ír-ì.»
1a+our.mother   how-1=   RFX-sit.sadly-RS-Fi

'And they told their fellows: ‖ ‹quote› «O children ‖ look at our mother | how she is sitting hunched sadly.»' (201 068)

Some other forms include **yîjî** 'come', **jábùkî** 'cross to other side', **shààgî** 'leave here'. An example with the cl. 1 object **mú-** 'him' is seen in **múshúlìkî** 'hit him'.

The EMPHATIC IMPERATIVE, found in both the direct and polite imperative forms, involves the addition of the emphatic **-ag** suffix (8.3.2), meaning 'pay attention!'. Thus in (9.90) the direct imperative form **-lóla** 'look' is modified by the **-ag** suffix.

(9.90) Lól-àg-â!   ‖   Ù-lyá   mú-ndú   w-á=   lù-lyá   lú-sìkú   kàndì |
look-EMP-Fa   1-that.R   1-person   1-A.M=   11-that.R   11-day   again

à-n-yíj-ìr-à.
1-O1.SG-come-APL-Fa

'Look! ‖ That person from that day again | he has come to me.' (Jdg 13:10)

In (9.91) the verb **-lángiiz-** 'look (from a distance)' takes the emphatic imperative plural form, with the emphatic **-ag** suffix and the final vowel **-i**.

(9.91) Lángììz-àg-î!
look-EMP-Fi

'Look (PL)!' (201 118)

The STRONG AND POLITE IMPERATIVES COMBINED can be seen in cases where the command begins with an auxiliary in the direct imperative, such as **gêndâ** 'go', **yîjâ** 'come', **lékâ** 'allow'. This is followed by the command in the polite imperative (simple subjunctive). The first verb in such a pair is always an auxiliary verb,[59] which further defines the command.

In (9.92) the speaker first uses the strong command with the auxiliary **gêndà** 'go', and then the polite (subjunctive) form of the main verb **ùláálíkè** 'invite'.

---

[59] Commands with two separate imperative actions would use the continuative or intervening time for the second command.

*9.2 Detailed inventory of TAM form/meanings*

(9.92) **Ø-Gênd-à    ù-Ø-láálík-è    ‖    ngíìsì  bì-rééré  |  by-ó=**
IMP.S-go-Fa    2SG-SBV-invite-Fe         each    8-simpleton    8-O.R=

**w-à-sìg-à.**
2SG-P1-left-Fa

'Go and invite ‖ every simpleton | which you left behind.' (16 021)

*9.2.3.1.2 Subjunctive*

The SUBJUNCTIVE (SBV) consists of the initial prefixes (subject prefix, optional negative, and a null morpheme in the TAM slot) followed by the macrostem, with a final vowel -**e**, as shown in the following formula:

[S.P [ (NEG) Ø [ (O.P) [ (RFX) [base] -**e**][60]

This verb form, when it has only a standard toneless subject prefix and no further prefixation, exhibits the complex HH stem-tone pattern. However, if there are any prefixes besides the toneless subject marker, even if it is only the addition of a H tone on the subject marker, the verb will instead exhibit the $V_2$ stem-tone pattern.

Although one of the most characteristic features of this form is the use of the final vowel -**e**, it needs to be noted that when a subjunctive form is modified by the addition of any preceding adverbial auxiliaries ending in -**i**, the subjunctive final vowel is lost. This is because the main verb which follows an auxiliary of this type was historically a cl. 5 infinitive, and since an infinitive may not be inflected, it cannot bear the subjunctive FV -**e**. In this case the grammatical tone pattern of the subjunctive is realized on the auxiliary, while the final (lexical) verb exhibits a default infinitive tone.

9.2.3.1.2.1 In purpose/result clauses

In (9.93) we see the subjunctive form (here as a polite command) **ùnáshùbì géndí lìláshà** 'go again and throw it'. In this case, because of the presence of adverbial auxiliaries, the subjunctive FV -**e** is not realized in the surface form of the continuative.

(9.93) **Fùník-á (Sw.)   dúbà    ‖    ù-ná-shùbí       géndí |   làsh-á       í=rw-ījì.**
cover-Fa          quickly      2SG-CON-AGAIN   GOING    throw-Fa   23=11-river

'Cover (it) quickly ‖ and go again and throw (it) | in the river.' (56 020)

---

[60] There are subjunctive forms with other prefixes as well, but these are no longer simple subjunctive. They are given other labels, e.g. with the additive morpheme **ná**-, the form is called continuative, with the **ká**- distal prefix, it is called intervening time, with the -**aaye** auxiliary it is called remote future, etc. The formula for each is presented under its own heading.

The basic underlying meaning[61] of the subjunctive verb is to denote an action or state which is *not yet realized*. There is the connotation of a purpose or desired result. This can take various forms:

- As noted above, the subjunctive can express a polite imperative.
- Often a subjunctive verb follows a phrase such as **gírà** 'in order that' or 'so that', and expresses a purpose or desired result (11.1.1.6).
- Used following a desiderative verb such as 'want', 'hope', or a causative/permissive verb such as 'permit', 'prevent', or 'agree', and followed by complementizer, it can express a *wish* or *desire*, or *plan*, e.g. **àlózììzí kwó** 'he wants that...' (11.1.4.1, g).

9.2.3.1.2.2 Polite imperatives

The POLITE IMPERATIVE is most often expressed by the simple subjunctive form (SBV), and reflects more "social grace" than the direct imperative. In (9.94) the subjunctive form **mùlólérè** 'you (PL) look' is used as a polite imperative.

(9.94) Yîshè       à-ná-bà-bwír-à: ||   «Mù-Ø-lól-ér-é           ú=mú-gánì |
      1a+his.father  1-SQ-O2-tell-Fa     2PL-SBV-look-APL-Fe      AU=3-example

      kú=  yì-zì        n-gónì.»
      17=  these.P-10   10-sticks

'Their father told them: || «Look at the example | concerning these sticks.»' (02 015)

In (9.95) the EMPHATIC POLITE IMPERATIVE verb **ùbáágágè** 'you slaughter' includes the emphatic suffix -**ag**, which here emphasizes a crucial point in the narrative. The trapper has made a deal to give the leopard the liver of everything caught in the trap. The leopard intends to hold him to the agreement, even when it is the trapper's wife who has been caught in the trap!

(9.95) Ù-Ø-báág-ág-è              dúbà  ||  gírá     ú-Ø-m-bèèrèz-é
      2SG-SBV-slaughter-EMP-Fe    quickly    so.that  2SG-SBV-O1-give-Fe

      ú=bú-dìkù.
      AU=14-liver

'Slaughter (her) quickly || so that you give me the liver.' (35 021)

---

[61] The meanings of subjunctive verbs are discussed at length in other sections of this book.

Sometimes a polite command may be expressed by the INTERVENING TIME, marked by **ká-**, indicating that the action will take place only after an intervening time, as seen in (9.96).

(9.96) **Nyínà**        à-ná-mú-bwîr-à: ‖ «Ù̀-ká-té          **gēndì**
1a+her.mother   1-SQ-O1-tell-Fa     2SG-INTV-PRIOR   GOING

**tàndúúl-á** yíb-à-ló    |  í=w-à=       n-dálò.»
check.out-Fa husband-A.M-2SG    23=place-A.M=   9-field

'Her mother told her: ‖ «You (after time) first go check out your husband | at the field.»' (611 031)

### 9.2.3.1.2.3 Mixed imperatives

The mixed imperatives combine more than one verb to express a single command, and include the following forms: very strong imperative, strong and polite imperative combined, polite imperative with mixed subjects, and a polite imperative with mixed time.

The VERY STRONG IMPERATIVE is an idiomatic form using a negative subjunctive form of -**kòlw**- 'dare'.[62] Following that is the complementizer **kwó**, followed by the main verb in the recent past (P1). This form emphasizes the command as strongly as possible. In (9.97) **Ùtákòlwé!** means 'Don't you dare!'.

(9.97) **À-ná-kòmééréz-à**   **mú-ká-à-gé**   w-à-gè    tì= ‖
1-SQ-insist.to-Fa    1-wife-A.M-1    1-A.M-1   ‹quote›

«Ù̀-Ø-mú-bùlìrìz-ê         hàlíndé    à-Ø-kú-bwìr-è. ‖
2SG-SBV-O1-question-Fe    until      1-SBV-O2.SG-tell-Fe

Ù̀-tá-Ø-kòlw-é |           kwó=    w-à-bùl-à         ú=kú-mú-búúz-â.»
2SG-NEG-SBV-dare-Fe       CMP=    2SG-P1-lack-Fa    AU=15-O1-ask-Fa

'And he insisted to his sister-in-law: ‖ «Interrogate him until he tells you. ‖ Don't you dare | to miss asking him.»' (506 023)

Another type of VERY STRONG IMPERATIVE is formed by the idiomatic subjunctive phrase **hàtágírè**[63] 'let there be no', followed by a relative clause such as 'thing which you take', or 'person who breaks this'. An example is found in (9.98), which says 'may there be no (one) who will break it (egg)'.

---

[62] This is an idiomatically used passive form of the verb -**kòl**- 'work'. Thus it would seem to have originally implied being *caused* to do something, so that the idiom would literally mean 'don't let anything make you do this'.

[63] This is an idiomatic use of the verb -**gír**- 'do'. The literal meaning would be 'may there not do', but the freer gloss is 'let there not be'.

(9.98) **Yi-ri    i-gi |    ha-ta-Ø-gir-e    ú-ga-gwan-w-a**
this.P-5   5-egg    16-NEG-SBV-do-Fe    S.R-F2-encounter-PS-Fa

**a-li-ber-a.**
1-O5-break-Fa

'This egg | don't let there be anyone who is encountered having broken it.' (208 006)

To ask someone else to join with oneself in carrying out some action, the POLITE IMPERATIVE WITH MIXED SUBJECTS is used. In such a case there are two polite imperatives together. The first verb is always **-gír-** 'do', with a second-person subject marker (singular or plural) while the second verb has a first-person plural subject marker. In (9.99) the subjunctive verb **ùgírè** 'you do', with 2SG subject prefix **u-**, is immediately followed by **tùgézè** 'let's try', with the 1PL subject prefix **tu-**. In such cases, the speaker is telling the other person to get involved, so they can both do something together.

(9.99) **Ù-Ø-gír-é    tù-Ø-géz-é    lú-sìkù lú-gùmà || gírá**
2SG-SBV-do-Fe    1PL-SBV-try-Fe    11-day   11-one    so.that

**tù-Ø-lól-é |    ú-gáá-sìg-à    ú=w-àbò.**
1PL-SBV-see-Fe    S.R+1-F2-be.left-Fa    AU=1-SAME.SET

'Do let's try one day || in order that we see | who will leave his fellow behind.' (21 009)

In (9.100) we see an example of the same construction, but this time the subject marker is the 2PL **mu-**. Here **mùgírè** 'you do' is followed by **tùtááhè** 'let's go home' with the 1PL subject marker **tu-**.

(9.100) **Bà-lyá    bá-hùmbwà || tì=    |    «Mù-Ø-gír-é**
2-those.R    2-old.lady    ‹quote›    2PL-SBV-do-Fe

**tù-Ø-tááh-è ||    bì-rì    bí-gógó |    by-ó=    w-à-léét-à.»**
1PL-SBV-go.home-Fe    8-is    8-banana.husks    8-O.R=    2SG-P1-bring-Fa

'Those old ladies (assisting in childbirth) || ‹quote›: | «Do let's go home || it's banana husks | that you have brought.»' (201 039)

#### 9.2.3.1.3 Unrealized expectation

'Unrealized expectation' deals with situations which are (or were) expected to take place, but which have not happened yet.

### 9.2.3.1.3.1 Present unrealized expectation

The "present unrealized expectation" (NEG.YET) is a two-word form which expresses a present state in which the action denoted by the verb is expected to take place, but has not yet taken place. The focus is not on the future orientation of the action, but on the *present state* of unrealized action.

The present unrealized expectation form consists of the auxiliary -**zi**[64] to which the initial prefixes (never including the persistive) are attached. After the word break, the macrostem follows, with final vowel -**a**, as shown in the following formula:

[S.P [ (NEG) [ (ADD.V) -**zi**] [(O.P) [ (RFX) [base] -**a**]

This form is exemplified in (9.101) where the man arrives home, and *expecting* a rabbit dinner, asks his wife if she has 'not yet slaughtered' the rabbit he sent home to be prepared for him.

(9.101) Ùyó        mú-shósì ‖ à-ná-shùbí   dēt-à: ‖ «Sí=    n-à-túm-á       |
     that.N+1   1-man          1-SQ-AGAIN     say-Fa    OBV=   1SG-P1-send-Fa

W-à=lú-kwàvù    há-nò!   ‖ Ká=   mù-tà-zì      mú-bààg-â?»
1-A.M-11-rabbit    16-here.P.C   Q    2PL-NEG-YET    O1-slaughter-Fa

'That man ‖ again said: ‖ «But I sent | Rabbit here! ‖ Haven't you slaughtered him yet?»' (626 034-5)

### 9.2.3.1.3.2 Remote past unrealized expectation

The "remote past, expectation, state" (P3.NEG.ST) is a three-word form. The first auxiliary is comprised of the initial prefixes affixed to the P3 auxiliary **áàlì**. Following is the invariable word **záàzì**. The final word is the macrostem of the lexical verb, with the final vowel -**a**, as indicated in the following formula:

[S.P [ (NEG) [**áàlì**] [**záàzì**] [ (O.P) [ (RFX) [base] -**a**]

The first word -**áàlì** exhibits a HL tone contour on the **áà**- and low tone on the copula -**lì**. The second word, **záàzì** also exhibits a HL contour on its penultimate syllable, while the tone of the final syllable is H or L, whatever is the opposite of the initial tone of the following word. The pattern of the final word of the verb form is the Complex LH stem-tone pattern.

---

[64] We interpret this as having a following word break because of its tonal properties. Its tone is the opposite of that of the initial tone of the following word. This is a common tonal phenomenon across word breaks. There are no clear-cut cases in which such interaction takes place at the boundary between a macrostem and a preceding prefix. It is also significant that this form is similar to the adverbial auxiliary -**zíndi** 'NEVER.YET' which differs semantically in that the -**zi** form does not necessarily mean that the action has 'NEVER' yet taken place, just that there is a present state of unrealized expectation.

The meaning of this form is that at a time in the remote past, an action had *not yet* occurred. This, of course, implies that at a later time, the action did actually take place or at least that at the time there was expectation that it would take place.

In (9.102) the statement is made concerning a certain tomb, that 'there was not another person who had yet been buried in there'.

(9.102) **Ndáà=y-è**   **gû-ndì**   **mú-ndù** |   **ú-w-áàlì**   **záàzí**   **zììk-w-á**
NEG.FOC-1   1-other   1-man   S.R-1-P3   YET   bury-PS-Fa

=**mwò**.
=18

'And there was not another person | who had been buried in there.'
(Luk 23:53)

#### 9.2.3.1.4 Intentional

The intentional verb phrase is marked by **gáá-** on the matrix verb (**gáá-** is also used in the unmarked future tense).

##### 9.2.3.1.4.1 Progressive intentional

The progressive intentional is discussed in the progressive section 9.1.2.5 above, since it is both 'progressive' and 'intentional'.

##### 9.2.3.1.4.2 Intentional previous state

The intentional previous state (PREV.INTL) is also a two-word form and again, only a limited number of initial prefixes can occur. No TAM marking is found on the first word. The first word includes only the subject prefix, with an optional NEG marker, followed by the copula **-shùba**. The following word is also an inflected form. The subject prefix of this second word must match that of the first word. The S.P is followed directly by the intentional **gáá-**, then the macrostem, with the final vowel **-a**, according the following formula:

[S.P [(NEG) [-**shùbà**] [S.P [**gáá-** [ (O.P) [ (RFX) [base] -**a**]

This verb form exhibits the complex HL stem-tone pattern on the first word, and the V₂ stem-tone pattern on the second.

The meaning of this form is that an event was intended or expected to have occurred in the recent past, but it did not happen. In (9.103) the accusation **ùshùbà úgálàálà í=wà=ndálò** 'you should/would have slept at the field' implies that the person had recently planned to sleep there, but did not. This form could also be translated as "was/were going to…."

(9.103) **Ná=       w-ô=      yò         mú-kàzà tí=    ‖   «Lééròò   ù-shùbà**
       CNJ=      1-A.M=    that.N+1   2-woman  ‹quote›     this.time  2SG-be.PREV

**ú-gá-làl̀-à   |   í=w-à=        n-dálò.»**
2SG-INTL-sleep    23=place-A.M=  9-field

'And that woman ‹quote›: ‖ «This time you would have slept | at the field (but you did not).»' (111 047)

### 9.2.3.1.5 Frustrated intention

The frustrated recent past (P1.FRUS) is marked by a high tone on **tá-**, which occurs in the TAM slot. In this form, the initial prefixes, including the subject prefix, an optional negative, and the high-toned **tá** in the TAM slot, are followed by the macrostem with the final vowel **-a** or by the macrostem in the resultative form, as indicated in the following formulas:

[S.P [ (NEG) [**tá** [ (O.P) [ (RFX) [base] **-a**]
[S.P [ (NEG) [**tá** [ (O.P) [ (RFX) [base] **-ir-i**]

This verb form exhibits the Complex LH stem-tone pattern. The other tonal characteristic of this form is that the prefix which immediately precedes the TAM marker **tá-** always exhibits H tone, just as is true for the P2 prefix and the F2 prefix, but is *not* the case for *every* H tone TAM marker.

The P1.FRUS form indicates that though the action described by the verb was completed, the expected result of that action has been frustrated. This would be the case, for instance if someone milked a cow and then the milk spilled, so that even though he just milked the cow, there is no milk available.

In (9.104) the recent past, frustrated form is seen in the verb **útángwàsírì** 'you had caught me (frustrated)'. The meaning is that the person had just been caught; however, the expected result does not obtain, as explained in the next verb **wànándíkúùlà** 'and you let me go'.

(9.104) **Kùtí   ú-tá-n-gwàs-ír-ì ‖              w-àná-n-díkúùl-à?**
        how     2SG-FRUS-O1.SG-seize-RS-Fi    2SG-SQ-O1.SG-let.loose-Fa

'How (is it) you had caught me ‖ and you let me go?' (627 047)

Besides its use with the resultative form of the matrix verb as shown in (9.104) above, this **tá-** 'P1.FRUS' prefix can also combine with a recent past form modified by the adverbial auxiliary **málì** 'ALREADY', as shown below in (9.105). Again, this form means that the action of the verb happened, but the expected result was frustrated.

In (9.105) the relative form **úbútámálì** 'which had already (frustrated)' modifies the verb **tòndéérá ú=kúbólà** 'begun to rot'. The idea is that parts of the flesh of a certain child who had been confined in a pit had begun to rot, but that process was cut short by the cleaning of the wounds, so that the child recovered, and the expected result (being rotten) was no longer the case.

(9.105) Bù-lyá    bú-ny-ámà |    ú-bú-tá-málí      tòndéér-á
14-that.R    14-9-meat     S.R-14-FRUS-ALREADY    begin-Fa

ú=kú-ból-à ‖    bà-ná-bù-lyó-s-à.
AU=15-rot-Fa    2-SQ-O14-leave-CS-Fa

'That (pejorative) meat | which had already started to rot ‖ they got rid of it.' (409 072)

### 9.2.3.2 Potential/Conditional

In Kifuliiru the potential/conditional notions are closely related, and share similar formal structures. Thus they are combined in this section. The range of forms is quite varied, with default as well as contrary-to-fact forms, and reflecting time in the past as well as the present.

#### 9.2.3.2.1 Potential

There is a single verb form which is used for both the potential (POT) and conditional[65] (CND) moods. The difference between the two is that the potential occurs with no preceding conjunction, while the conditional is necessarily preceded by the conjunction **ìrí** 'if'.

The potential form of the verb is comprised of the initial prefixes (including the conditional TAM **àngà**-), followed by the macrostem with the final vowel -**a**, as indicated in the following formula:

    S.P [ (NEG) [**àngà**- [ (ADD.V) [ (PERS) [ (O.P) [ (RFX) [base] -**a**]

This verb form exhibits the Complex HL stem-tone pattern.

The potential morpheme **àngà**- means 'might/would/could' and implies potentiality, or even likelihood. In (9.106) **àngàbà** 'he might be' precedes the phrase **yé=wàyàbíírà** 'he's the one who took'.

(9.106) Ù-Ø-té      mù-búúz-á    bw-îjà ‖    à-ngà-b-à     y-é=
2SG-SBV-PRIOR    O1-ask-Fa    14-good     1-POT-be-Fa    1-FOC=

w-à-yàbíír-á    yìzó      fwárángà.
1-P1-take-Fa    those.N+10   10+monies

'First ask him well ‖ he might be the one who took that money.' (33 015)

---

[65] The conditionals are described under adverbial clauses, in 11.1.1.

## 9.2 Detailed inventory of TAM form/meanings

In (9.107) the potential verb **kwàngàbà**, means 'it might be'.

(9.107)  Ø-Lèk-á         à-Ø-lír-è    ‖ kw-àngà-b-à    y-é=    nyínà.
         IMP.S-allow-Fa  1-SBV-cry-Fe   15-POT-be-Fa    1-FOC=  1a+her.mother

'Let her cry ‖ maybe she's the one who is her mother.' (106 140)

In (9.108) we see the potential form **yàngàkúyìtà** 'he might kill you'.

(9.108)  Ù-tá-Ø-gwàt-é         ú=bw-ìrá           |  n-é=     n-dyâlyà ‖
         2SG-NEG-SBV-seize-Fe  AU=14-friendship      CNJ-AU=  9-deceiver

         mú=kúbá ‖ y-àngà-kú-yìt-á |     ù-tà-ná-mény-à.
         because   9-POT-O2.SG-kill-Fa   2SG-NEG-ADD.V-know-Fa

'Don't make a friendship | with a deceiver ‖ because ‖ he might kill you | without your knowing it.' (13 014)

### 9.2.3.2.2 Authentic conditional

#### 9.2.3.2.2.1 Conditional with *àngà-* prefix

The conditionals share the form with the Potential (immediately above) with the added conjunction **ìrí** 'if/when'. In (9.109) we see the conditional form **ìrí nàngàbà ngwétí ngákàlùùkà** 'if/when I would be warming myself by the fire'. Further examples of the conditional forms are found in 11.1.1.

(9.109)  **ìrí**    **n-àngà-b-à**   n-gwétí    n-gá-kàlùùk-à                   |
         if/when   1SG-POT-be-Fa    1SG-PROG   1SG-INTL-warm.self.at.fire-Fa

         n-dà-kìzì       lóóz-á     ú-gá-n-dès-â.
         1SG-NEG-REP     want-Fa    S.R+1-F2-O1.SG-speak+CS-Fa

'When I would be warming myself at the fire | I don't want a person who will speak to me.' (20 023)

#### 9.2.3.2.2.2 Conditional with *mango* temporal adverb

The timeless verb form is basically used in statements which are interpreted as always being true. This form could also be called habitual, in that it indicates something which is habitually applicable. It is thus often used in proverbs. It may also follow the temporal adverb **mángò** 'when', which introduces a dependent temporal clause which is non-past. When combined with **mángò**, the timeless has a conditional meaning which can be translated as 'when/if' or 'whenever' and could be called hypothetical. Observe, for example, the timeless verb 'see it' in the following: **Mángò mùgìbònà, mùgìyìtè** 'When(ever) you see it, kill it.'

### 9.2.3.2.2.3 Conditional with H tone prefix

There are certain Kifuliiru verb forms in which a non-segmental[66] H tone prefix is realized on the subject prefix. Each of the forms has its own basic meaning, to which the factor of hypothetical conditionality is added when the H tone prefix is used. The three non-past forms are all illustrated briefly here using the verb **génd-** 'go'. The basic form of the first, **túgéézìrì** 'if/when we have gone', is the simple resultative (present state resulting from past action), the second, **túgêndà** 'if/when we go', is timeless (unmarked for time and used for something which is always true) and the basic form of the third, **tútàzí gêndà** 'if/when we have not yet gone', i.e. 'before we have gone' or 'without having first gone', is the conditional version of the negative unrealized expectation form which means 'not yet'.[67] Further examples can be found in 11.1.1.3.

The tonal characteristic of the verb stem in these forms is the $V_2$ pattern, the same pattern found in all subjunctive forms and several other irrealis forms. (In their basic forms, i.e. when used *without* the H tone prefix, these forms all exhibit the Complex HL stem-tone pattern instead.) Thus the conditionality overlay consists of a H tone realized on the subject prefix, plus the $V_2$ stem-tone pattern realized on the verb stem.

The timeless form with the H tone prefix is often used to present two alternatives. In such a case it could be translated as 'whether... or...'. Each alternative may be expressed using the timeless verb with H tone conditional prefix. In such a case the second verb often expresses the negation of the first, and the two are juxtaposed. In such a case, the translation is "Whether x or not x...".

In other cases, as seen in (9.110), the alternatives may be expressed using a single timeless verb with conditional H tone subject prefix, followed by the two possibilities separated by **kàndì ìrí** 'or'. It means "whether it is A or B". In (9.110) we see an example in which the choice is between the **byà=mwí=gúlù** 'the things of heaven' and **byá=hànò mú=kíhūgò** 'the things of here on earth'.

---

[66]To say that the prefix is non-segmental means here that it consists only of a H tone. The conditional H tone in these forms is realized on the subject prefix.

[67]This conditional form with the H tone prefix (e.g. **tútàzìgéndà** 'if/when we have not yet gone') contrasts with the negative form of the P1 tense, which has no H tone prefix (e.g. **tùtàzìgéndà** 'we have not yet gone').

(9.110)   …**bí-∅-b-à**         by-à=     mw-í   gúlù  ‖ kàndì ìrí by-á=     hà-nò    |
          8-TL-be-Fa           8-A.M=    18-5   heaven   or           8-A.M=    16-here.P.C

          mú=     kí-hūgò.
          18=     7-earth

'…be it the things of heaven ‖ or the things here | on the earth.' (Eph 1:10)

Another example of the same timeless form with a H tone conditional prefix is seen in (9.111) where the animal hiding in his hole day after day despairs of his life. In this case, there is no alternative expressed and the translation is simply 'if/when'. Note here that the need to realize the H tone prefix on the subject prefix occasions the phonological addition of **í**- preceding the usual (non-syllabic) 1SG subject prefix **N**- (realized here as **m**-).

(9.111) **Ím-∅-bùlúk-ír-à**              í=     m-bùgà |   w-á=n-dàrè
        1SG-WHEN-go.out-APL-Fa    23=    9-outside   1-A.M=9-lion

       à-n-dy-à |        n-vw-ír-ì.
       1-O1.SG-eat-Fa   1SG-die-RS-Fi

'If/when I go out outside | the lion eats me | I'm dead.' (401 090)

#### 9.2.3.2.3 Conditional, contrary to fact

The notion of "contrary-to-fact" is richly exploited in Kifuliiru. There are four forms: the unmarked form with the L tone TAM prefix **àngà**- and the resultative, the past form with the H tone TAM prefix **ángá**- and the resultative, the form with the **kì**- TAM prefix, and the P1 tense preceded by the conjunction **nga** 'if/when'.

##### 9.2.3.2.3.1 Conditional, contrary to fact with L tone *àngà*- prefix

The first potential contrary-to-fact (POT.C.F) (unmarked tense) is comprised of the initial prefixes, including the prefix -**àngà**-, followed by the resultative macrostem, with the final -**ir-i**, as indicated in the following formula:

    [S.P [ (NEG) [**àngà**- [ (ADD.V) [ (PERS) [ (O.P) [ (RFX) [base] -**ir-i**]

This form exhibts the Complex HL stem-tone pattern.

This unmarked form of the POTENTIAL, CONTRARY-TO-FACT (with resultative verb stem) indicates something that is theoretically possible, but is contrary-to-fact.

In (9.112) the use of the **àngà**- prefix on the verb **mwàngànáshóbwìrì** 'and would you be able' implies that it would be highly unexpected that someone would wait long enough until (small children) grew (old enough to marry).

(9.112) Ká=   mw-àngà-ná-shóbw-ìr-ì         ú-kú-línd-írír-à  |   hàlíndé
       Q     2Pl-CON.C.F-ADD-able-RS-Fi    AU=INF-wait-INTS-Fa   until

bà-kùl-è?
2-grow.up-Fe

'Would you (PL) be able to wait | until they grew?' (implied answer: 'No')'

In (9.113) the verb with the contrary-to-fact expectation, **Úwàngàlííri** 'anyone who would eat' communicates the implication that, while someone is theoretically able to eat the potatoes, it is highly unlikely that will happen.

(9.113) **Ú-w-àngà-lí-ír-í**       yì-bí       bí-júmbù ||   ngá=
       S.R-1-POT.C.F-eat-RS-Fi    this.P-8    8-potatoes    like=

bà-mú-shúlìk-à.
2+P1-O1-hit-Fa

'(Anyone) who would eat these potatoes (but no one would eat them) || (like) they would hit him.'

9.2.3.2.3.2 Conditional, contrary to fact with H tone *ángá*- prefix

The past form of the contrary-to-fact is the same as the unmarked one, except that the **ángá**- prefix has a high tone, as follows:

[S.P [ (NEG) [**ángá**- [ (ADD.V) [ (PERS) [ (O.P) [ (RFX) [base] -**ir-i**]
This form exhibits the Complex LL stem-tone pattern.

In (9.114) we see the potential, contrary-to-fact past **byángámúbèrììrì** 'it would have been for him (but was not)' functioning as the independent verb in the sentence. The conjunction **nga** 'like/if' must be cliticized to the potential contrary-to-fact past verb in the second clause, underscoring the contrary-to-fact nature of the statement: 'It would have been well for him if he had not been born (but he was).'

(9.114) **By-ángá-mú-bèr-ì-ìr-ì**       |   bw-îjâ ||    ng-á=
       8-POT.C.F-O1-remain-APL-RS-Fi       14-well      if.C.F-1=

**tá-ngá-bùs-ír-w-ì.**
NEG-CND.C.F-give.birth-RS-PS-Fi

'It would have been for him | well || if he would not have been born (but he was born).' (Mat 26:24)

### 9.2.3.2.3.3 Conditional, contrary to fact with *kì*- prefix

Another type of conditional contrary-to-fact is characterized by the initial prefixes, including the subject prefix, an optional NEG marker, and the TAM prefix **kì-**.[68] There is a H tone on the syllable that precedes the **kì-** prefix. This is the subject marker (if the form is not negative) or the negative marker if there is one,[69] e.g. **túkìgúlìsìbwê** 'if we had been sold (but we were not)'. These prefixes are followed by the default form of the macrostem, with the final vowel **-e**, as indicated in the following formula. The stem-tone pattern is V$_2$.

[S.P [ (NEG) [**kì-** [ (O.P) [ (RFX) [base] **-e**]

In (9.115) the verb in the first clause is the conditional contrary-to-fact persistive subjunctive form **àtákìbè** 'if he were not'. In the second clause, the conjunction **ngá=** 'like/as/if' occurs prior to the recent past verb **wàtùnígà** 'you choked us', giving the meaning 'you would have choked us (but you didn't)'.

(9.115) **Á-tá-∅-kì-b-è**  y-êhê ‖  **ngá=**  **nyìì-tù**
1+CND.C.F.-NEG-PERS-be-Fe  1-CTR.P  then.C.F=  ADD.P-1PL

**tw-éshì** |  **w-à-tù-níg-à.**
1PL-all  2SG-P1-O1.PL-choke-Fa

'If it had not been (for) HIM ‖ then all of US ALSO | you would choke us.'
(23 046)

### 9.2.3.2.3.4 Conditional, contrary to fact with *nga* conjunction

As seen in (9.113)–(9.115) the main clause in a conditional contrary-to-fact statement often consists of the conjunction **nga** preceding a verb in the recent past, and describes what would have happened if the action mentioned in the dependent clause had taken place. The conjunction **nga** is cliticized to the recent past (P1) verb **bàmúshúlìkà** giving the form **ngá=bàmúshúlìkà** 'they would hit him (but they haven't).

In (9.116) we find the conjunction **nga** occurring prior to the past tense (P2) in the form **ngá=bákámúlyâ** 'they would have eaten her (but they did not)'.

---

[68] It is not clear whether this **kì-** is the same as the persistive **kì-** or different. The two have never been observed to co-occur, so they may well be the same morpheme. The placement of the additive **ná-** would also be diagnostic of whether this **kì-** is the persistive (which occurs following additive **ná-**) or a separate TAM marker **kì-** (which would precede the additive **ná-**). However, this conditional C.F form has not been observed with the additive **ná-**. The forms we have observed which have both the additive **ná-** and persistive **kì-** along with the subjunctive final vowel always seem to have the meaning of the continuative plus persistive, and are not conditional contrary-to-fact plus additive.

[69] It is characteristic of structurally subjunctive forms that if they have a negative marker, it is this negative morpheme which bears the H tone that generally characterizes the subjunctive.

In this case, there is no contrary-to-fact form in the preceding clause, it is merely implied. The sentence begins with a fronted object, followed by the focus marker **nie** and the P2 form **ngámúkízâ** 'I am the one who saved her' (implied: if I hadn't....).

(9.116) Ù-yú   mú-kàzì | ni-é=   n-gá-mú-kíz-â ||   <u>ngá=</u>
      1-this.P  1-woman  1SG-FOC=  1SG-P2-O1-save-Fa  if.C.F=

<u>bá-ká-mú-ly-â</u>.
2-P2-O1-eat-Fa

'This woman | I am the one who saved her || like (or) they would have eaten her.' (632 074)

### 9.2.4 TAM in auxiliaries

As is common across the Bantu area, Kifuliiru has a large number of auxiliaries. Some are followed by infinitive forms, whether the currently productive infinitive beginning with the cl. 15 **ú=kú-**, or a remnant of the archaic form which began with the cl. 5 **i-**.[70] The initial **i-** of the latter form has been reinterpreted over time as a suffix on the preceding auxiliary, as will be described below.[71]

Other auxiliaries consist of an inflected verb which precedes another inflected verb form, which together express a unified idea.

#### 9.2.4.1 TAM in infinitive phrases

An infinitive phrase consists of a certain class of auxiliary verb followed by a productive cl. 15 infinitive. The inflectional prefixes of such a phrase are all found on the auxiliary. Infinitives themselves consist of the clitic **ú=**, followed by the cl. 15 prefix **kú-**, plus a macrostem.

As is usual in any language, the verbs which occur before infinitives form a relatively closed set. In over 1,000 pages of Kifuliiru text, there are only 47 different verbs which precede infinitives. Looking at table 9.4, we see that all these auxiliaries which precede infinitives[72] deal with either time (sections

---

[70] These auxiliaries are the only synchronic evidence that cl. 5 infinitives had a place in the history of Kifuliiru. However, the related Bantu J language Kihunde still uses the cl. 5 **i-** as its infinitive prefix.

[71] Thus historically, the auxiliary **géndi** 'GOING' in the phrase **ànágêndì múbwírà** 'and he went and told him' would be derived from something like **ànágéndà íbwírà**. Because of the effects of the coalescence between the final vowel of the auxiliary and the initial vowel of the infinitive, the cl. 5 infinitive prefix **í-** was reinterpreted as the suffix of the auxiliary, and the lexical verb **-gend-** was left with no infinitive marking, except for the Simple stem-tone pattern which is characteristic of the infinitive in Kifuliiru.

[72] The auxiliaries preceding infinitives are similar to the adverbial auxiliaries, in that they

## 9.2 Detailed inventory of TAM form/meanings

a–b) or mood (sections c–n). In each case, the categories are cross-referenced in the first column to categories found in Bybee, et al. (1994), or Palmer (1986). This demonstrates that auxiliary verbs preceding infinitives are not a mishmash of unrelated notions; rather, in every case they fall into commonly accepted temporal and modal categories. The Frequency column notes the number of occurrences of each auxiliary in our texts.

At the same time, as noted above in 9.1.4.2, the auxiliaries preceding infinitive phrases are only semi-grammaticized—some have quite specific meanings, and they can also occur as the main verb of the clause before only a NP, with no infinitive involved.

Table 9.4. Verbs that occur before infinitives

| Bybee/Palmer | Category | Verb | Freq. | Gloss |
|---|---|---|---|---|
| Aspects | | | | |
| a. (Bybee:318) State commences | begin | -tòndeer-/ -tòndeez- | 237 | 'begin' |
| | | -bùtirw- | 1 | 'be born' |
| b. (Bybee:318) State ends | finish | -yús- | 113 | 'end' |
| | | -mál- | 1 | 'end' |
| | leave | -lék- | 27 | 'leave' |
| | | -jánd- | 5 | 'abandon' |
| | | -twikir- | 3 | 'stop' |
| | | -héz- | 1 | 'complete' |
| | | -yìkaany- | 1 | 'cease' |
| c. (Bybee:317) Iterative | add to | -kàviiriz- | 32 | 'add' |
| | | -kàniirir- | 1 | 'add' |
| | | -kávy- | 1 | 'add' |
| | | -génderer- | 58 | 'continue' |
| | | -yùshuul- | 1 | 'add' |
| Moods | | | | |
| d. (Bybee:319) Ability | be able | -lóng- | 155 | 'get' |
| | | -shóbol- | 152 | 'be able' |
| | | -hásh- | 8 | 'be able' |
| | | -zìgir- | 2 | 'be able' |

modify the main verb by adding time and mood notions.

| Bybee/Palmer | Category | Verb | Freq. | Gloss |
|---|---|---|---|---|
| e. (Bybee:321) Obligation | behoove | -kwaniini | 87 | 'behoove' |
| | | -kwiriiri | 52 | 'behoove' |
| f. (Bybee:320) Desire | want | -looz- | 85 | 'want' |
| | | -siim- | 30 | 'like' |
| | | -yìfwij- | 9 | 'desire' |
| | | -yìkùmbul- | 7 | 'miss' |
| | | -tool- | 6 | 'choose' |
| | | -kùnd- | 5 | 'love' |
| | | -sár- | 4 | 'want' |
| | | -fiitirw- | 3 | 'be energetic' |
| | | -lól- | 1 | 'look (for)' |
| | | -shàmbaalir- | 6 | 'rejoice in' |
| g. (Palmer:115) Commissive | refuse/ accept | -láhir- | 27 | 'refuse' |
| | | -yèmeer- | 21 | 'agree' |
| | | -búz- | 3 | 'prevent' |
| | | -shìgini- | 1 | 'prevent' |
| | | -yìyeka | 2 | 'avoid' |
| h. (Bybee:320) Permission | be allowed | -hànguulw- | 25 | 'allow' |
| i. (Palmer:118–119) Fear | be afraid | -yòboh- | 13 | 'be afraid' |
| j. (Bybee:318) State changes | change/ stay same | -hínduk- | 2 | 'change' |
| | | -komeer- | 1 | 'get used to' |
| k. (Bybee:320) Attempt | fight for | -lwir- | 1 | 'fight for' |
| | | -hàmbirir- | 1 | 'contend for' |
| l. (Bybee:320) Root possibility | lack | -bùl- | 2 | 'lack' |
| m. (Palmer:83) Knowledge and belief | know/ forget | -yìji | 18 | 'know' |
| | | -kéngeer- | 4 | 'remember' |
| | | -yíbagir- | 3 | 'forget' |
| | | -mény- | 2 | 'know' |

Examples of several infinitive phrases follow. Note that the object of the infinitive verb may be expressed either by a full nominal referent, or it may

*9.2 Detailed inventory of TAM form/meanings*

be in the form of an object prefix in the infinitive. In (9.117) the auxiliary **ànátòndéérà** 'and she began', demonstrates category (a), "state commences" in table 9.4. The infinitive (the main lexical verb of the phrase) **ú**=k**úmúdùkà** 'to insult him', includes the object of the phrase, the cl. 1 prefix **mú** 'him'.

(9.117) Ùyó mú-kàzì | à-ná-tòndéér-à | ú=kú-mú-dùk-à.
that.N+1 1-woman 1-SQ-begin-Fa AU=15-O1-insult-Fa

'That woman | began | to insult him.' (113 025)

In (9.118) the auxiliary **ágálôngà** 'he will get', exemplifies category (d), "ability".

(9.118) mú=kúbá ná-yè | á-gá-lông-à ú=kú-ly-á í=n-yámà | kú=
because ADD.P-1 1-F2-get-Fa AU=15-eat-Fa AU=9-meat 17=

yùlwò lú-sìkù.
that.N+11 11-day

'because HE ALSO | will get to eat meat | on that day' (26 012)

In (9.119) the auxiliary -**kwàníínì** 'should', exemplifies category (e), "obligation".

(9.119) **Sí**= ni-é= **kwàn-íín-ì** | ú=kú-kìzì kú-yùbák-ír-à |
OBV 1SG-FOC should-RS-Fi AU=15-REP O2.SG-build-APL-Fa

í=n-yûmbà.
AU=9-house

'It's obvious that I am the one who should | be building you | a house.' (617 019)

In (9.120) the auxiliary **ànáláhìrè** 'and she refused', demonstrates category (g), "commissive".

(9.120) **À-ná-láhìr-è** | ú=kú-ly-á | ú=bú-ndù.
1-CON-refuse-Fe AU=15-eat-Fa AU=14-stiff.porridge

'And she refused | to eat | stiff porridge.' (518 013)

It should be noted that these auxiliaries, besides occurring before infinitives in verb phrases, can also occur by themselves as the main verb in a verb phrase, e.g. preceding a non-infinitive NP.[73]

---

[73] The -**ba**- 'be' copular auxiliary, as well as the adverbial auxiliaries which precede an inflected verb can also all be used as main verbs.

Above in (9.118) we observed the verb **ágálôngà** 'he will get' followed by the infinitive **ú=kúlyâ** 'to eat' in the verb phrase **ágálôngà ú=kúlyâ** 'he will get to eat'. In (9.121) the same verb **-lónga** 'receive' does not occur before an infinitive, but rather before the non-infinitive noun **ú=mútīmà** 'heart'.

(9.121) **Mú-k-á**     **ìyó**     **n-góónà** ‖    **à-ná-fw-à** ‖     **mú=kúbâ** |
1-wife-A.M    that.N+9    9-crocodile    1-SQ-die-Fa      because

**bà-tá-ká-kì-lóng-á** ‖    **ú=mú-tīmà** ‖    **gw-á=**    **yìhyó**
2-NEG-P2-PERS-get-Fa    AU=3-heart      3-A.M=    that.N+19

**hí-kólò.**
19-little.monkey

'The wife of that crocodile ‖ died ‖ because | they did not still get ‖ the heart ‖ of that little monkey.' (12 033)

### 9.2.4.2 TAM *in auxiliaries dealing with relative time*

"Relative time auxiliaries" can also be termed "phasal auxiliaries," because they refer to different phases of the event described by the verb. Table 9.5 includes five auxiliaries ending in **-a** which precede an inflected verb (rows a–e). There are also eleven auxiliaries ending in **-i** (related to the archaic cl. 5 infinitive) which precede an uninflected verb stem (rows f–q). The Frequency column notes the number of occurrences of each auxiliary in our texts.

Table 9.5. Auxiliaries dealing with relative time

|    | Auxiliary | Gloss | Freq. |
|----|-----------|-------|-------|
| Ending in -**a** (before inflected verbs) | | | |
| a. | -**laala** | 'ONE DAY AGO' | 1 |
| b. | -**shiiba** | 'THE WHOLE DAY' | 10 |
| c. | -**tuula** | 'HABITUALLY' | 44 |
| d. | -**yàma** | 'IMMEDIATELY' | 52 |
| e. | -**yàma/ yàmiri** | 'ENDURING' | 6 |
| Ending in -**i** (before uninflected verbs) | | | |
| f. | -**búli** | 'SUBSEQUENTLY' | 21 |
| g. | -**kízi** | 'REPEATEDLY (OR HABITUALLY)' | 575 |
| h. | -**máli** | 'ALREADY' | 19 |
| i. | -**shúbi** | 'AGAIN' | 144 |
| j. | -**shúbì** | 'PREVIOUSLY' | 36 |

## 9.2 Detailed inventory of TAM form/meanings

|    | Auxiliary | Gloss | Freq. |
|----|-----------|-------|-------|
| k. | -tàngí | 'FIRSTLY' | 2 |
| l. | -té | 'PRIOR' | 36 |
| m. | -yàmi | 'IMMEDIATELY' | 207 |
| n. | -záàzi/-zí[a] | 'YET (ONLY WITH NEGATIVE)' | 15 |
| o. | -zíndi | 'LASTLY' | 2 |
| p. | -zìndí | 'EVER (ONLY WITH NEGATIVE)' | 14 |
| q. | -zíndukiri | 'EARLY IN MORNING' | 19 |

[a] Both forms have the same meaning: 'yet' (preceded by negative); **-zí** occurs with the recent past tense (P1), while **-záàzi** occurs with the remote past tense (P3). We have seen one instance where **-zi** was used to mean "yet", without the preceding negative, but this is not common.

### 9.2.4.2.1 Relative time auxiliaries which precede inflected verbs

(a) The auxiliary **-laala** 'ONE.DAY.AGO' derives from the verb **kúláálà** 'to spend the night', but has been grammaticized to mean 'one day ago'. In (9.122) **wàláálà** 'you, a day ago' sets the temporal stage for the verb **wàyìtà** 'you killed', so that together the two forms represent the combined idea: 'one day ago you killed'.

(9.122) **Ká= nàà-n-í ù-lóz-ìız-ì ú=kú-n-yīt-à || ngà=**
Q= ADD.P-1SG 2SG-want-RS-Fi AU=15-O1.SG-kill-Fa like=

**kw-ókùlyà w-à-láál-à w-à-yìt-à | ù-lyá**
E-thus.R 2SG-P1-ONE.DAY.AGO-Fa 2SG-P1-kill-Fa 1-that.R

**Mú-mísìrì?**
1-Egyptian

'And ME also do you want to kill me || in the same way you killed yesterday | that Egyptian?' (Exo 2:14)

(b) The auxiliary **-shiiba** 'ALL.DAY' refers to *the entire day*, from sunrise to sunset. In (9.123) the rooster tells the king that his fellow animals have spent the whole day just lying down, being lazy.

(9.123) **Nàlúhàzê   à-ná-shùvy-á   mw-àmì ‖ kw-á=   bà-àbò |**
Rooster   1-SQ-answer-Fa   1-king   CMP-AU=   2-SAME.SET

**bà-shííb-à |   bà-yì-gwèj-ér-fìr-ì.**
2+P1-ALL.DAY-Fa   2-RFX-lie.down-APL-RS-Fi

'Rooster answered the king ‖ that his fellows | spent the whole day | just lying down.' (28 019)

(c) The auxiliary -**tuula** 'HABITUAL' (HAB), deriving from the verb meaning to 'live somewhere', means that something happens *habitually*, or is a usual state. In (9.124) **yáàlí kìzí túúlà** 'he was often habitually' sets the stage for the verb **ágálèngà=mwô** 'he is intentionally passing in there'.

(9.124) **À-tà-ná-kì-lèng-à |   mú=   n-jírá ‖ y-áàlí   kìzí   túúlà |**
1-NEG-SQ-PERS-pass-Fa   18=   9-path   9+O.R-P3   REP   HAB

**á-gá-lèng-à   =mwô.**
1- INTL-pass-Fa   =18

'And he did not still pass | on the road ‖ which he habitually | passed on.' (07 041)

(d) The auxiliary -**yàma** 'IMMED', when followed by a dynamic verb with the intentional **gáá**- prefix, denotes an action which takes place *immediately*, with no temporal space between the preceding action and the one which follows. In (9.125) the verb **ànáyàmà** 'and he immediately' indicates that the man went home with the woman, without any delay.

(9.125) **À-ná-yàm-à   á-gá-mú-tààh-àn-à   ‖ à-ná-gêndíì**
1-SQ-IMMED-Fa   1- INTL-O1-go.home-COM-Fa   1-SQ-GOING

**=b-â   mú-ká-à-gè.**
=become-Fa   1-wife-A.M-1

'And he immediately went home with her ‖ and she went and became his wife.' (06 024)

(e) The auxiliary -**yàma** 'ENDURING', when followed by a copula, a stative verb, or a nominal complement, indicates *always/enduring*. This is the same form seen in (d) immediately above, the only difference being the type of complement that follows. In (9.126) the verb **gúgáyàmà** 'it will remain' provides the context for the copula **gùlì** 'it is', indicating that the number of bricks will *always* remain the very same.

## 9.2 Detailed inventory of TAM form/meanings

(9.126) N-ó=      mú-hárúúró   gw-á=       má-tòfààlì ‖  gú-gá-yàm-à |
        CNJ-AU=   3-count      3-A.M+AU=   6-bricks       3-F2-ENDURING-Fa

        gù-lì |   gwó-gù-lyà.
        3-is      E-3-that.R

'And the count of bricks ‖ it will always be | it is | that very same (number).'

The auxiliary -**yàmiri** 'ALWAYS' is the resultative form of -**yàma**, and has the same meaning, but with a focus on an enduring state. In (9.127) the verb **ààli yàmírì** 'he was remaining' provides the time frame for the verb **àlì** 'he is', meaning that the Lord was *always* remaining with Joseph.

(9.127) Mú=kúbá   Nàhánò ‖   á-àlí   yàmírì |   à-lì   kúgúmá |   nà=
        because    Lord       1-P3    ENDURING   1-is   together   CNJ=

        Yúsèfù.
        Joseph

'Because the Lord ‖ was always | he is with | Joseph.' (Gen 39:23)

*9.2.4.2.2 Relative time auxiliaries which precede an uninflected stem*

(f) The auxiliary -**búli** 'SBSQ' represents an event which is *subsequent* to another one. In (9.128) **ngábùlì tòndéérá ú=kúlírà** 'I then will begin to cry' is subsequent to the previous event, 'I will first cook porridge and eat'.

(9.128) N-àmú=   téé     dùg-á               n-Ø-dy-è ‖
        1SG-F1=   PRIOR   cook.porridge-Fa    1SG-SBV-eat-Fe

        n-gá-búlí         tòndéér-á |   ú=kú-lír-à.
        1SG-INTV-SBSQ    begin-Fa      AU=15-cry-Fa

'I am about to first cook porridge (in order that) I eat ‖ I then will begin | to cry.' (54 009)

(g) The auxiliary -**kìzi** 'REP' shows that something is happening *repeatedly*. The meaning can sometimes shift slightly to the related meaning of *habitually*. In (9.129) the verb **bànákìzí múyìvúgà** states that the people praised him repeatedly.

(9.129) **Yàbó**　　　**bá-ndù** ‖ **bà-ná-kìzí**　**mú-yìvúg-à** ‖ **kw-â**=　**lì**
　　　　 those.N+2　　2-people　　2-SQ-REP　　O1-praise-Fa　　CMP-1=　is

　　　**mú-ndú  mw-îjâ.**
　　　1-person　1-good

'Those people ‖ repeatedly praised him ‖ that he is a good man.' (40 005)

This auxiliary can also be used to emphasize *permanence*, as in example (9.130) where **ngáákìzí yāmà** means 'I will permanently remain'.

(9.130) **N-gáá-kìzí**　　**yāmà** ‖　**n-dì**=　　**kúgùmà  nà**=　　**w-êhè.**
　　　　1SG-F2-REP　　REMAIN　　1SG-am=　together　　CNJ=　　2SG-PRO

'I will habitually always be ‖ I am together with you.' (Jos 1:5)

(h) The auxiliary **-máli** 'ALREADY' refers to something *already* done. (Thus it has the same meaning as the adverb **kéèrà** 'already'.) In (9.131) the verb is in the remote past. Thus the meaning of **áàlí máli bííkà** is that at a time in the past, 'he had already placed' a certain law.

(9.131) **mú=kúbá** ‖　**lw-ó**=　　**lú-bààjá  mw-àmí  w-à-bò** |　**á-àlí**
　　　　because　　　11-FOC=　　11-law　　1-king　　1-A.M-2　　1-P3

　　　**máli**　　　**bíík-à.**
　　　ALREADY　　place-Fa

'because ‖ that was the law that their king | had already established.' (16 004)

(i) The auxiliary **-shùbi** 'AGAIN' when followed by a dynamic (i.e. non-stative) verb stem, denotes something done *again*. In (9.132) the writer uses the phrase **ànáshúbí mwágúlà** 'she again threw down' to refer to the fact that the girl threw down some more money, just as she had done before.

(9.132) **Ùyó**　　　**mú-nyére** ‖　**à-ná-shùbì**　**mwágúl-á**　|　**í=fwárángà.**
　　　　that.N+1　　1-girl　　　　1-SQ-AGAIN　　threw.down-Fa　　AU=10+money

'That girl ‖ again threw down | the money.' (06 022)

(j) When **shùbi** is followed instead by a resultative verb form[74] (which denotes a state) it means *previously* 'PREV' and refers to a former state. In (9.133)

---

[74] The resultative stem is not truly uninflected, but this **shùbi** 'PREVIOUSLY' auxiliary is included here with forms that precede an uninflected stem because they do not precede a verb stem which has its own initial prefixes. In general, the **-i** final auxiliaries are followed by a form with no prefixation and no suffixation except for the default FV **-a**. In the case of **shùbi** 'PREVIOUSLY', the stem-

## 9.2 Detailed inventory of TAM form/meanings

both meanings of **shùbi** occur. In the phrase **ànáshúbí gálúkírà** 'he again returned', -**shubi** means 'AGAIN', while the phrase **àshùbì yìmáázìrì** 'he had formerly been standing', -**shubi** means 'previously'.

(9.133) Iburahimu  **à-ná-shùbì**   gálúk-ír-á       hà-lyá    |   **à-shùbí**
       Abraham    1-SQ-AGAIN      return-APL-Fa    16-there.R    1-PREV

       **yìmááz-ìr-ì**   í=mbere     ly-á=   Nahano.
       stand-RS-Fi     23=before    5-A.M=  Lord

'And Abraham returned again to that place | (where) he had previously stood before the Lord.' (Gen 19:27)

(k) The auxiliary **tàngi** 'FIRSTLY' refers to something done *before others*. In (9.134) the phrase **úgátàngì híkà** 'who would first arrive' refers to whoever would be the first to arrive, before any others did.

(9.134) **Ngíìsì**   **ú-gá-tàngì**        hík-á       há-nò       ‖  í=n-dèhà  |
        whoever    S.R+1-F2-FIRSTLY     arrive-Fa   16-here.P.C     AU=9-gourd

        ì-ná-b-é           ì-yìj-w-ír-í       mw-á=    mī-īījì...
        9-CON-become-Fe   9-fill-PS-RS-Fi    18-AU=   6-water

'Whoever would arrive here first ‖ and her gourd | be full of water...' (43 017)

(l) The auxiliary -**té** 'PRIOR'[75] refers to something done *before other things* (but not necessarily first of all). In (9.135) the speaker uses the phrase **kànáté gèndá kágátàndùùlà** 'and it first went checking out' to indicate that this was the activity the dog did before it did something else.

(9.135) **Kà-ná-té**     gènd-á ‖      ká-gá-tàndùùl-á      |  í=ny-ámîshwà.
        12-SQ-PRIOR    GOING-Fa     12-INTL-check.out-Fa     AU=10-wild.animals

'And it first went ‖ checking out | the wild animals.' (45 003)

The auxiliary -**té** is also often used as an indication of politeness or deference when giving a command. In (9.136), instead of saying 'Give me your harp', the speaker says 'First give me your harp', a respectful way to make the request.

---

tone pattern of the resultative stem which follows it is the Complex HL of the basic resultative form, rather than the Simple stem-tone pattern of the prefixless infinitives which follow most of the -**i** final auxiliaries.

[75]This auxiliary, though it has a H tone, triggers downstep in a following H tone. This means that it underlyingly has a L tone associated with it, or floating to its right. It seems to function as a clitic, and its vowel lengthens when fewer than three morae follow it.

(9.136) **À-ná-bwîr-á kèrè:** ‖ **«Té   Ø-m-bèèrèz-é   nàà-nì** |
     1-SQ-tell-Fa   1a+frog  PRIOR   SBV-O1.SG-give-Fe  ADD.P-1SG

  **yùlwó   lú-làngà   lw-à-wè.»**
  that.N+11  11-harp   11-A.M-2SG

'And he told the frog: ‖ «First give ME ALSO | that harp of yours.»'
(629 021)

(m) The auxiliary -**yàmi** 'IMMED' (always followed by a dynamic verb) refers to something done *immediately*. In (9.137) the writer uses the phrase **ànáyàmí vyūkà** 'and he immediately got up' to indicate that the man got up quickly, without waiting.

(9.137) **À-ná-bòn-à   mú-ká-à-gè** ‖ **kéèrà   à-híndùk-à**
     1-SQ-see-Fa  1-wife-A.M-1  ALREADY  1+P1-change.into-Fa

  **ny-ámíìshwà** ‖ **à-ná-yàmì   vyúk-á** | **dúbá-dúbà.**
  9-wild.animal   1-SQ-IMMED  got.up-Fa  quickly-RDP

'And he saw that his wife ‖ had already turned into a wild animal ‖ and he immediately got up | quickly.' (30 013)

(n) The auxiliary -**záàzí** 'YET' (with P3 forms) or -**zi** (with present forms) is nearly always preceded by the negative and indicates that something has *not yet* happened. In (9.138) the verb **àtàzì lémùùlà** means 'he has not come back from the market'.[76] These two forms differ from the other adverbial auxiliaries listed in this section, in that the verb stem which follows them is not an infinitive form. This fact can be discerned from the tone pattern of the main verb. An infinitive takes the Simple stem-tone pattern, but the stem which follows -**záàzí** or -**zi** (YET) always has the $V_2$ stem-tone pattern characteristic of irrealis forms having subject prefixes.

(9.138) **Kút-àgí   ú-w-à-lém-à**   |   **à-tà-zì   lém-ùùl-à?**
     how-EMP  S.R-1-P1-go.to.market-Fa  1-NEG-YET  go.to.market-RV.T-Fa

'How (is it that) the one who went to the market | he has not yet come back?' (101 046)

In (9.139) the -**zí** form is used in **lùtàzí** 'has not', to show that the day has not arrived yet.

---

[76] By contrast, the simple negative form of the P1 verb tense would yield **àtàlémùùlà** 'he did not come back from market'. This 'NOT.YET' form describes a state, and is semantically the negative of the resultative form **àlémwìrì** 'he has come back from the market'.

## 9.2 Detailed inventory of TAM form/meanings

(9.139) **Yùlwó**    **lú-sìkù** ‖ **kú**=   **ky-ànyà**   **lù-tà-zí**    **hík-â** ‖ **ùyó**
that.N+11    11-day    17=   7-time    11-NEG-YET    arrive-Fa   that.N+1

**mú-nyérè** | **à-ná-gênd-à**    **í**=   **mú-hàndà**.
1-girl    1-SQ-go-Fa    s23=   3-toilet

'That day ‖ when it had not yet arrived ‖ that girl | went to the toilet.'
(620 022)

(o) The auxiliary **-zíndi** 'LASTLY' with a high tone, refers to something done *after everything else*. Thus in (9.140) the writer uses the relative phrase **ábákázíndì yíjà** to refer to the 'ones who came last'.

(9.140) **Yàbó**    **bá-tàbánà** ‖ **á-bá-ká-zíndì**    **yíj-à** ‖ **ná-bò**
those.N+2    2-young.men    S.R-2-P2-LASTLY    come-Fa   ADD.P-2

**bà-ná-síìm-à** | **yàbó**    **bá-hyàkàzì**.
2-SQ-like-Fa    those.N+2    2-new.wives

'Those young men ‖ who lastly came ‖ THEY ALSO liked | those new wives.'
(01 014)

(p) The auxiliary **-zìndi** 'EVER'[77] with a low tone and in a negative form, refers to something that's *not ever* been done. In (9.141) **ndàzìndì yángà** 'I have never married' means that the person has always been single.

(9.141) **Ná-yè** | **à-ná-bà-bwír-à:** ‖ «**Nângà**    **máàshì**    |
ADD.P-1    1-SQ-O2-tell-Fa    no    for.goodness.sake

**n-dà-zìndì**    **yáng-à**.»
1SG-NEG-EVER    marry-Fa

'And HE ALSO | told them: ‖ «No for goodness sake | I haven't ever married.»' (624 013)

In (9.142) we find the construction **àtàkìzìndí zīmbà** 'he has never again stolen'.

---

[77] This auxiliary and the **zi** of (not) YET probably have a common origin.

(9.142) Ùyó    mú-tàbánà |   à-ná-twík-ír-à           ||   à-tà-kì-zìndí
       that.N+1  1-young.man  1-SQ-discontinued-APL-Fa      1-NEG-PERS-EVER

zìmb-á |  hàlíndé  zèènê.
steal-Fa  until    today

'That young | man desisted || and has not again ever stolen | right up to the present time.' (33 024)

(q) The auxiliary -zíndukiri 'EARLY.MORNING', from the verb -zínduk- 'go early in the morning', sets the time as *very early in the morning*. In (9.143) the speaker uses the polite imperative phrase **mùzíndúkírì yíjà** 'you early-in-the-morning come' when he tells people to go home and come back in the morning.

(9.143) Mù-Ø-tááh-ág-è        ||   mù-Ø-zíndúkírì             yíj-à |
        2PL-SBV-go.home-EMP-Fe      2PL-SBV-EARLY.MORNING      come

shéshèèzí |  mw-éshì.
morning      2PL-all

'Go home || come early in the morning | tomorrow | all of you.' (23 021)

### 9.2.4.3 TAM *in auxiliaries dealing with relative location*

Kifuliiru includes quite a few auxiliaries dealing with relative location, presented in table 9.6. Once again these auxiliaries include both forms which precede an inflected verb, and those which precede an uninflected stem. There are four semantic pairs in these locational auxiliaries, -**génda** / -**géndi** 'going', -**yíja** / -**yíji** 'coming', -**lènga** / -**lèngi** 'passing', and -**sìgala** / -**sìgali** 'remaining behind', in which one member occurs before an inflected verb, while the other occurs before an uninflected stem. Only two, the auxiliary -**taaha** 'go home' and -**híkiri** 'arriving (applicative)' have no corresponding form which occurs with the other set of following forms.

## 9.2 Detailed inventory of TAM form/meanings

Table 9.6. Auxiliaries dealing with relative location

|   | Auxiliary | Gloss | Freq. |
|---|---|---|---|
| Ending in -**a** (before inflected verbs) | | | |
| a. | -**génda** | 'GOING (away from deictic center)' | 358 |
| b. | -**lènga** | 'PASSING' | 69 |
| c. | -**sìgala** | 'REMAINING BEHIND' | 43 |
| d. | -**taaha** | 'GOING HOME' | 73 |
| e. | -**yíja** | 'COMING (towards deictic center)' | 199 |
| Ending in -**i** (before uninflected verbs) | | | |
| f. | -**géndi** | 'GOING (away from deictic center)' | 406 |
| g. | -**híkiri** | 'ARRIVING AT' | 12 |
| h. | -**lèngi** | 'PASSING' | 2 |
| i. | -**sìgali** | 'REMAINING BEHIND' | 11 |
| j. | -**yíji** | 'COMING (towards deictic center)' | 201 |

Preceding the discussion of each auxiliary below, a few observations (a-d) should be made.

(a) Whenever the performance of the next event involves movement over a distance, whether toward or away from the deictic center, a directional auxiliary is obligatory. As a result of this rule, the locative auxiliaries are very common throughout narrative text.

In (9.144) the man wakes up and goes to check out his trap. Because the trap is at a separate location from where he wakes up, the use of the auxiliary **géndi** 'GOING' is obligatory.

(9.144) **Ìrí     há-ká-b-á     lú-sìkù  lú-gùmà  ‖  à-ná-gêndì     yúj-à**.
         when  16-P2-be-Fa  11-day   11-one        1-SQ-GOING  check. trap-Fa

'When it was one day ‖ he went to check the trap.' (507 006)

(b) The locative auxiliaries may be used *even after a locative verb* in the immediately preceding clause. In (9.145) the clause containing the auxiliary -**géndi** 'GOING' directly follows a clause where the main verb is -**génd-** 'go'. This may appear redundant in English, but in Kifuliiru it is perfectly natural.

(9.145) N-àmú= **génd-à** ‖ gírà **n-géndì** mú-bòn-a |
      1-F1=    go-Fa    so.that  1SG-GOING  O1-see-Fa

      ín-dà-zíì-fw-à.
      1SG-NEG-YET-die-Fa

'I'm about to go ‖ in order that I may go and see him | when I haven't died yet.' (Gen 45:28)

Likewise the adverbial auxiliary -**yíji** 'COMING' can immediately follow the verb -**yíj**- 'come'. In (9.146) we see an example where the adverbial auxiliary -**yíji** occurs *even within the same clause* as the same verb phrase as the main verb -**yíj**- 'come'. Although it is somewhat rare to have the same root occur both in the auxiliary and its main verb, this example underscores the fact that the locational auxiliary is obligatory when movement is occurring, and that the auxiliary and the main verb have different functions.

(9.146) **Hà-ná-yîjì** yíj-à | mú-tàbánà mú-gùmà.
      16-SQ-COMING  come-Fa  1-young.man  1-one

'And there coming came | one young man.' (101 009)

(c) For at least the two pairs **yiji** / **yija** 'COMING' and **gendi** / **genda** 'GOING', the locational auxiliaries which end in -**a** (i.e. those which precede an inflected verb with intentional **gáá**- or P1 prefix, or with resultative stem) are used when the action of the auxiliary is happening concurrently with the action of the following verb. By contrast, those auxiliaries which end in -**i** (and precede an uninflected stem) indicate that the action of the auxiliary takes the subject to the location where the action of the following verb is taking place. In (9.147) the verb **ànágéndàgà** 'he went' and the verb **ágálóòzà** 'he is looking' occur at the same time. The duration and location of the two events is totally overlapping. The man was 'going, looking'.

(9.147) À-ná-**génd**-àg-à á-gá-lóòz-á | á=bá-kàzì |
      1-SQ-GOING-EMP-Fa  1-INTL-seek-Fa  AU=1-women

      à-tà-ná-bà-bòn-à.
      1-NEG-SQ-O1-see-Fa

'And he went looking for | women | but he did not see them.' (112 007)

In (9.148) **ànáshòkólà í=njírà** 'and he set out on the path' is followed by the subjunctive **àgéndì lóòzà** 'that he going (might) look for'. Here the auxiliary -**géndì** indicates that the man had to go to another spot in order to look for his

## 9.2 Detailed inventory of TAM form/meanings

brother. Thus the two parts of the event represented by **àgéndì lóózà**, 'going' and 'looking', are not overlapping, but successive.

(9.148) **Ìrí**   **há-ká-tám-à**   ‖   **à-ná-shòkól-à**   **í=n-jírà**   ‖   **à-Ø-géndì**
when   16-P2-be.at.last-Fa   1-SQ-set.out-Fa   AU=9-path   1-SBV-GOING

**lóóz-á** |   **ú=mú-lùmúnà.**
seek-Fa   AU=1-younger.brother

'Finally ‖ he set out on the path ‖ to go and look for | (his) younger brother.' (506 012)

(d) As can be seen in the 'Frequency' column of table 9.6 above, **génda / géndi** 'going' occurs about twice as frequently as **yíja / yíji** 'coming'. The rules concerning when to use **géndi** 'GOING' versus **yíji** 'COMING' are presented in 9.2.4.3.3.

### 9.2.4.3.1 Locative adverbial auxiliaries which precede an inflected verb

This section discusses each of the auxiliaries found in table 9.6, as labeled in the table.

(a) The auxiliary **-génda** refers to 'GOING'. In (9.149) the auxiliary **àlì mú=géndà** 'he is GOING' is followed by the intentional **gáá-** (here *not* with future meaning) **ágánjúlìkà** 'he is hitting me'. Together the two parts reflect one unified idea, that is he is going and at the same time he is hitting me.

(9.149) **À-lì**   **mú=**   **génd-á** |   **á-gá-n-júlìk-à.**
1-is   PROG=   GOING-Fa   1-INTL-O1.SG-hit-Fa

'He is going | hitting me.' (14 016)

Besides its use preceding the intentional, the auxiliary **-génda** may also be used with a following resultative verb. In (9.150) the phrase **ànágêndà àkàbètwírì** 'and he went carrying it (on head or shoulder)' indicates that "going" and "carrying" were happening at the same time.

(9.150) **Ùyó**   **mú-ndù** ‖   **à-ná-bòh-à**   **yàkó**   **ká-bwâ** ‖
that.N+1   1-person   1-SQ-wrap-Fa   that.N+12   12-dog

**à-ná-gênd-à**   **à-kà-bètw-ír-í** |   **mú=**   **yìbyó**   **bí-jángálà.**
1-SQ-GOING-Fa   1-O12-carry-RS-Fi   18=   that.N+8   8-banana.leaves

'That person ‖ wrapped that dog ‖ and went carrying it | in those banana leaves.' (14 030)

(b) The auxiliary -**lènga** 'PASSING' refers to *passing* by somewhere. In (9.151) the auxiliary verb **zànálèngà** 'and they passed' combines with the progressive intentional **zìgwétì zígátîmbà** 'they are beating' to reflect the fact that the movement is happening at the same time and location as the event named by the second verb, i.e. horses are passing, while their hoofs are beating out a thumping noise at the same time.

(9.151) **Lyê-ry-ó**   |   **í=fárásì**   ||   **z-àná-lèng-à**   |   **zì-gwétì**
E-5-right.then   AU=10+horses   10-SQ-PASSING-Fa   10-PROG

**zí-gá-tîmb-à** |   **í=bí-sìndò**.
10-INTL-beat-Fa   AU=8-sound

'Right then | the horses || passed | making | a pounding sound.' (Jdg 5:22)

(c) The auxiliary -**sìgala** 'REMAINING' refers to *remaining behind* at some location after someone else has left. In (9.152) the auxiliary verb **ànásìgálà** 'and he remained' combines with the progressive intentional **àgwétì ágályègùùzá á=másù** 'he is passing his eyes carefully back and forth' to reflect one idea, i.e. he is remaining behind, while carefully looking around.

(9.152) **À-ná-sìgál-à**   ||   **à-gwétì** | **á-gá-lyègùùz-á**   |   **á=má-sù**.
1-SQ-REMAINING-Fa   1-PROG   1-INTL-look.around+CS-Fa   AU=6-eyes

'And he remained || he is | looking all around | (with his) eyes.' (22 035)

(d) The auxiliary -**taaha** means 'GO.HOME'. In (9.153) the auxiliary verb **ànáshùbì tááhà** 'and he again went home' combines with the progressive intentional **àgwétí ágálírà** 'he is crying' to reflect one idea, i.e. 'he is going home, crying'.

(9.153) **À-ná-shùbì**   **tááhà**   ||   **à-gwétí**   **á-gáá-lír-à**.
1-SQ-AGAIN   GO.HOME   1-PROG   1-INTL-cry-Fa

'And he again went home || crying.' (07 020)

(e) The auxiliary -**yíja** refers to 'COMING'. In (9.154) the writer uses the auxiliary verb **nàyíjà** 'I have come' with the recent past tense (P1) **nàzìmbà** 'I have stolen' to reflect one idea, i.e. 'I have come, (in the state of) having stolen.'

*9.2 Detailed inventory of TAM form/meanings* 281

(9.154) **Ni-êhê** ‖ **n-à-yíj-à** ‖ **n-à-zìmb-á** ‖ **í=fwárángá** ‖
  1SG-CTR.P  1SG-P1-COMING-Fa  1SG-P1-steal-Fa  AU=9+money

  **z-à=** **mú-ká-à-niè.**
  10-A.M=  1-wife-A.M-1SG

  'ME ‖ I came having stolen ‖ the money ‖ of my wife.' (40 010)

*9.2.4.3.2 Locative auxiliaries which precede an uninflected stem*

(f) The auxiliary **géndi** 'GOING' indicates that the *deictic center* is changing. The subject of the verb is *going towards the new deictic center*. In (9.155) the writer uses the auxiliary **géndi** 'going' to modify the main verb **teekera** 'pack'. The place where the woman is going to pack is another significant location, where the focus of the story now is.

(9.155) **Ùyó** **mú-kàzì** ‖ **à-ná-yàmì** **géndí** **téékér-à** | **í=bí-ndú**
  that.N+1  1-woman  1-SQ-IMMED  GOING  pack-Fa  AU=8-things

  **by-à-gè.**
  8-A.M-1

  'That woman ‖ immediately went and packed | her things.' (40 022)

As can be seen in (9.155), when the auxiliary **-géndi** 'GOING' is combined with temporal auxiliaries, such as **yàmi** 'IMMED' in this case, it is the **-géndi** auxiliary that occurs last in the string. The locational auxiliary **yíji** 'COMING' similarly occurs in the final auxiliary position, closest to the main verb, whenever more than one adverbial auxiliary is used with the same verb.

(g) The auxiliary **-híkiri** refers to 'ARRIVING'. In (9.156) the writer uses the auxiliary **ànáhíkìrì** 'and she arriving' to show that the person first arrived, and then began to **lúkà** 'weave'.

(9.156) **À-ná-híkìrì** **lúk-á** | **ú=mù-gózì** ‖ **à-ná-gù-gér-à**
  1-SQ-ARRIVING  weave-Fa  AU=3-rope  1-SQ-O3-measure-Fa

  **Kályôshò** | **mw-í=** **gósì.**
  Kalyosho  18-5=  neck

  'And she arrived and wove | a rope ‖ and she measured it on Kalyosho | at the neck.' (18 017)

(h) The auxiliary **-lèngí** refers to 'PASSING' by some place. In (9.157) we find the auxiliary **yó=lì mú=lèngì** 'which you are passing' modifying the main verb **sìgírà** 'leaving for'. The person *first* passes by and *then* leaves the livers there.

(9.157) | By-à-bòn-ék-à ‖ | kw-ô= | gw-ét-í | ú=gû-ndì | mú-kàzì |
| 8-P1-see-NEU-Fa | CMP-2SG= | have-RS-Fi | AU=1-other | 1-woman

y-ô= | lì | mú= | lèngì | sìg-ír-á | á=má-dìkù.
1-O.R+2SG= | are | PROG= | PASSING | leave-APL-Fa | AU=6-liver

'It appears ‖ that you have another woman | whom you are passing by and leaving for (her) | the livers.' (632 031)

(i) The auxiliary **-sìgali** refers to 'REMAINING' behind when someone else leaves. In (9.158) the writer uses the auxiliary **ànásìgálì** 'and he remaining' to modify the main verb **lóngà** 'receive'. The **-sigali** auxiliary is used because the sentences which precede this one refer to the fact that the younger brother went off to a different place and became very prosperous. In (9.158) we read that the older one "remained" in the original location of the action, and *after* remaining, he 'received many distresses'. (Note that the finite verb **ákásìgálà** 'he remained' immediately precedes its equivalent auxiliary **ànásìgálì** 'and he remaining'.)

(9.158) Ú=mú-kùlù ‖ í= mûndà á-ká-sìgál-à ‖ à-ná-sìgálì
AU=1-great.one 23= place 1-P2-remain-Fa 1-SQ-REMAINING

lóng-á | á=má-líbú mì-ngì.
receive-Fa AU=6-distresses 6-many

'The older one ‖ where he remained ‖ he remained receiving | many distresses.' (506 011)

(j) The auxiliary **yíji** 'COMING' has one primary use and two extended usages. The primary meaning of the auxiliary **-yíji** refers to *coming towards the established deictic center*, that is, to a place that has already been activated in the hearer's mental representation as significant in the story. In (9.159) the lion is mentioned as being sick. With the lion already established as significant in the hearer's mental representation, the leopard and the eagle are said to *come* to check it out.

## 9.2 Detailed inventory of TAM form/meanings

(9.159) Ìyó    n-dàrè |    y-àná-lwâl-à   ||   ì-ná-hí-ìt-ì       á=bì-ìrá
that.N+9   9-lion    9-SQ-get.sick-Fa   9-ADD.V-has-RS-Fi   AU=2-friends

bá-á-yó bà-bìrì |   í=n-gwî     nà=    nyûndà || <u>bà-ná-yîjí</u>
2-A.M-9  2-two      AU=9-leopard  CNJ=  1a+eagle   2-SQ-COMING

<u>gì-tàndúúl-à</u> | bà-ná-bòn-á   kwó=kéèrá |
O9-check.out-Fa  2-SQ-see-Fa    CMP=ALREADY

y-à-jámb-à.
9-P1-get.skinny-Fa

'That lion | and it got sick || and it has its two friends | leopard and eagle || and they came and checked it out | and they saw that it had already | got skinny.' (11 017-018)

In (9.160) when a person begins to sing, some girls go out and ask who is singing. Then they *come* (not *go*) closer to look at the person singing, who has already been established as the point of interest in the hearer's mental representation. **Yíji** is then repeated in the following point of departure **Ìrí bákáyíjì lóléérà** 'When they came and looked'.

(9.160) Mú-gùmà  à-ná-tòndéér-à: ||  «Pólìngì póó.»|| Bà-lyá    bá-nyéré |
1-one        1-SQ-begin-Fa      Polingi poo       2-those.R  2-girls

bà-ná-hùlúk-à.|| «Bà-nyândì yàbó    | á-bà-lì    mú=   yìmb-á |
2-SQ-go.out-Fa  2-who    those.N+2  S.R-2-are  PROG= sing-Fa

«Pólìngì póò?»|| Bà-lì   b-à=    háyì?»|| <u>Bà-ná-yîj-à</u> |
Polingi poo      2-are  2-A.M=  where?    2-SQ-come

<u>ba-ná-yîjì</u>   <u>lól-éér-à.</u> ||  Írí   <u>bá-ká-yíjì</u>   <u>lól-éér-à</u> ||
2-SQ-COMING   look-APL-Fa   When  2-P2-COMING  look-APL-Fa

bà-lyá    bá-shósì |   bà-ná-géndèrèz-ágy-à |   «Pólìngì póó.»
2-those.R  2-men       2-SQ-continue-EMP+CS-Fa  Polingi poo

'One of them began: || «Polingi poo.» || Those girls | went outside. || «Who are those | who are singing | Polingi poo? || Where are they from?» || And they came | and they came and looked. || When they came and looked || those men | continued | «Polingi poo.»' (206 040-044)

The auxiliary -**yíji** is also commonly used in the extended sense of *something happening after a period of time*, or *some unfolding event*. In (9.161) the use of -**yíji** does not mean that the woman moved over a distance to give birth; rather it means that she *came* to the end of the pregnancy and then gave birth.

(9.161) Ùyó       mú-ká-à-gè ‖   írí    á-ká-yiji     bùt-á       ‖
       that.N+1   1-wife-A.M-1   when   1-P2-COMING   give.birth-Fa

       ky-àná-b-á       ky-ànyá |   ky-ó=      mw-énà.
       7-SQ-become-Fa   7-time      7-A.M+AU=  3-hunger

'That wife of his ‖ when she came to give birth ‖ it was the time | of famine.' (111 004)

As seen in (9.162) the auxiliary **-yíji** is used in its extended sense before the auxiliary **-kéngeera** 'UNINTENDED' to indicate that something happened after a period of time had passed.

(9.162) Ìrí     bá-ká-yándík-á    nà=    kó-òhè ‖   bà-ná-síìm-à   bwénèènè ‖
        when    2-P2-write-Fa     CNJ=   12-PRO     2-SQ-like-Fa   very.much

        bà-ná-yîjì      kéngéér-á        ‖   kéèrà     kà-mál-à.
        2-SQ-COMING     UNINTENDED-Fa        ALREADY   12+P1-finish.off-Fa

'When they had written with it (a pen) ‖ they were very pleased ‖ and they came to realize ‖ it was finished off.' (629 036)

In (9.163) Kalyosho is lying down, and so obviously is not moving from one place to another. Here **-yíji** 'COMING' is used in its 'unfolding event' sense to *mark a significant new event* that leads to the climax of the story.

(9.163) **Kályôshò** ‖   à-gwèj-íír-ì       ‖   à-ná-yîjì      yùvw-â |   bà-kòlà
        Kalyosho        1-lay.down-RS-Fi       1-SQ-COMING    hear-Fa    2-be.NEWLY

        mú=     mú-shwék-à.
        PROG=   O1-tie.up-Fa

'Kalyosho ‖ was lying down ‖ and he came to feel | they are now tying him up.' (302 050)

In (9.164) the **yíji** 'coming' is again used in this same sense, here modifying the verb **lóla** 'look', which comes just before the new and significant event of seeing the lion following.

## 9.2 Detailed inventory of TAM form/meanings

(9.164) Ìrí     á-ká-gír-á           ngw-à=        Ø-sháág-è  |  à-tíbít-è  ||
       when    1-P2-attempt-Fa      FRUS.INT-1=   SBV-leave-Fe   1-run-Fe

       mbw-à=         Ø-yíjì          lól-á  |  í=    ny-úmà |  yéè  ||
       as.soon.as-1=  SBV-COMING      look-Fa   23=   9-behind   Oh.my!

       à-bòn-à        w-á=n-dàrè |    à-lí   í=    ny-úmá   ly-à-gè !
       1+P1-see-Fa    1-A.M=9-lion    1-is   23=   9-behind  5-A.M-1

'When he attempted to leave | and run || when he came to look | back | oh my || he saw Lion | is behind him!' (401 074)

### 9.2.4.3.3 Factors determining use of -géndi versus -yíji

In Kifuliiru, one chooses whether to use **géndi** 'GOING' or **yíji** 'COMING' relative to whether the action is seen as moving toward the current deictic center (Fillmore 1997) or away from it. The choice of -**géndi** versus -**yíji** depends in every case on the context, and the significant mental representation that has (or has not) already been established in the mind of the hearer. This helps us to understand why one is used instead of the other in cases that seem to be otherwise identical. Take for example the following two sentences, which are virtually identical in grammatical form, and which are just a few lines apart in the same story.

**Ìrí ákáyíjì yújà, ànágwânà àgwásá á=kásà.** 'When he *came* to check out the trap, he encountered (that) he has caught a gazelle.'

**Ìrí ákáshùbí géndì yújà, ànágwânà àgwásá í=ngúlúbè.** 'When he again *went* to check out the trap, he encountered (that) he had caught a pig.'

In the context, the factor which triggers either **géndi** 'GOING' or **yíji** 'COMING', is shown here. In (9.165) the trapper is pictured as having set the trap and going home. Then he comes **yíji** to check out the trap, which is already in the mental representation, to see what he has caught.

(9.165) Ùyó        mú-tēzì |       à-ná-yèméér-à  ||  à-ná-sìg-à
        that.N+1   1-trapper       1-SQ-agree-Fa       1-SQ-LEAVING-Fa

        à-tèg-à            || à-ná-táàh-à.      ||  Ìrí     á-ká-yíjì
        1+P1-set.trap-Fa      1-SQ-go.home-Fa       When    1-P2-COMING

        yúj-à          ||  à-ná-gwân-à      |  à-gwá-s-á    |  á=ká-sà.
        check.trap-Fa      1-SQ-encounter-Fa   1-seize-CS-Fa   AU=12-gazelle

'That trapper | agreed || and he left having set the trap || and he went home. || When he came to check out the trap || he encountered | he has caught | a gazelle.' (35 008-009)

In the text shown in (9.166), the trapper sets the trap again and goes home with meat. Then he goes again to check out the trap. In this instance the focus is no longer on the trap which has been set. The trapper is again going back to the same spot, and the suspense concerning the trap is no longer high. This time he simply goes **géndi** to check it out another time.

(9.166) À-ná-shùbí tēg-à | à-ná-tááh-án-á | yìzó ny-ámà. ||
      1-SQ-AGAIN trap-Fa 1-SQ-go.home-COM-Fa those.N+10 10-meats

      Ìrí á-ká-shùbí <u>géndì</u> yúj-à || à-ná-gwân-à |
      When 1-P2-AGAIN GOING check.trap-Fa 1-SQ-encounter-Fa

      à-gwá-s-á | í=n-gúlúbè.
      1-seize-CS-Fa AU=9-pig

'And he again set the trap | and he went home | with those meats. || When he again went to check out the trap || he encountered | he had caught | a pig.' (35 011-12)

Another pair of examples involves **ànágêndí tēgà** 'he went and trapped' versus **ànáyîjí tēgà** 'he came and trapped'. In (9.167) the trapper *goes* to trap in the forest. He has not been there before in the story, and so is moving away from the established deictic center to another location.

(9.167) **Mú-tēzì mú-gùmà** || á-àlí gw-èt-í á=ká-bwá kà-à-gè ||
      1-trapper 1-one 1-P3 has-RS-Fi AU=12-dog 12-A.M-1

      à-ná-<u>gêndì</u> tèg-á | í=ny-ámíìshwá | í= rú-bàkò.
      1-SQ-GOING trap-Fa AU=10-wild.animals 23= 11-forest

'One trapper || had his dog || and he went and trapped | wild animals | at the forest.' (49 002)

In (9.168), from a different narrative, some girls, seen as central in the narrative, report that a certain young man often *comes* to trap at the place where the girls are in the habit of collecting firewood. Thus the trapper is seen as nearing the deictic center.

## 9.2 Detailed inventory of TAM form/meanings

(9.168) **Bà-lyá    bá-nyérè | írí    bá-ká-hík-á |    í=    kā-āyà ||**
2-those.R  2-girls           when   2-P2-arrive-Fa   23=    12-village

**bà-ná-dèt-à: ||  «Í=   w-à=    kú-shéényà  ||   tù-lí**
1-SQ-say-Fa      23=   place-of=  15-get.firewood   1PL-are

**mú=    gwán-á           mú-tàbánà      mú-gùmà  ||   à-lí      mú=**
PROG=  encounter-Fa    1-young.man    1-one           1-is     PROG=

**kìzí    yíjí       tèg-á |    ú=bú-nyúnì.»**
REP    COMING    trap-Fa   AU=15-birds

'Those girls | when they arrived | at the village || they said: || «At the place of getting firewood || we are encountering one young man || he is repeatedly coming to trap | birds.»' (210 075)

The mention of certain locations, especially **kāāyà** 'home' triggers the directional auxiliary **yíji** 'COMING' (rather than -**géndi** 'GOING') in virtually every instance. This is perhaps because the mentioned place, e.g. **kāāyà** is a "home base" that is already in the mental representation of the hearer. One does not "go away" to home. Thus in (9.169) the young man '*coming* collapses at home'.

(9.169) **Ù-lyá    mú-tàbánà |  à-ná-shúbì    gálúk-ír-á       í=    kā-āyà. ||**
1-that.R  1-young.man   1-SQ-AGAIN    return-APL-Fa   23=   12-home

**Ìrí     á-ká-yíjí        yì-tímb-à        há=    kā-āyà ||**
When   1-P2-COMING    RFX-collapse-Fa   16=    12-home

**à-húmààn-á    |   mú-ká-à-gé |   à-kòlà          mú=    ny-ûmbà.**
1+P1-encounter-Fa   1-wife-A.M-1   1-be.NEWLY    18=    9-house

'That young man | again returned to the village. || When he came and collapsed at home || he encountered | his wife | is now in the house.' (101 047)

### 9.2.4.4 TAM *in auxiliaries dealing with relative time plus location*

There are two auxiliaries that relate both to time and to location. Their meanings are polar opposites, as seen in table 9.7.

Table 9.7. Auxiliaries dealing with relative time plus location

| Form | Gloss | Freq. |
|---|---|---|
| **-gwanwa** | 'ENCOUNTERED' | 7 |
| **-sìga** | 'LEAVING' | 20 |

(a) The auxiliary -**gwanwa** 'ENCOUNTERED' refers to some established situation being *encountered*, or come upon at a certain time and place. In (9.170) the auxiliary **àgwánwà** 'she was encountered' modifies the main verb **àhúmbà** 'she dug'. In other words, when the woman is encountered, she has already dug a hole.

(9.170) Ùyó        mú-kàzì ‖ kìzìgà    à-gwánw-à |           à-húmb-à
       that.N+1   1-woman   surprise  1+P1-ENCOUNTERED-Fa  1-dig-Fa

í=kí-shímò.
AU=7-hole

'That woman ‖ surprise she was encountered | having dug a hole.' (409 022)

(b) The auxiliary -**sìga** 'LEAVING' refers to *leaving behind* some person or situation that one has previously been with, and thus is the opposite of -**gwanwa**. Again, both a time and place are involved. In (9.171) the auxiliary **bànásìgà** 'they left behind' modifies the main verb **bàdètà** 'they spoke'. The idea is that before they went, they said something and so left with an understanding established regarding some issue.

(9.171) **Bà-ná-gênd-à** ‖ **hálìkò** ‖ **ba-ná-sig-a**    **bà-dèt-à**
       2-SQ-go-Fa        but        2-SQ-LEAVING-Fa   2+P1-speak-Fa

**kwókùnô:**...
‹quote.MARKED›

'And they went ‖ but ‖ they left having said thus:...' (24 008)

### 9.2.4.5 TAM *in auxiliaries dealing with mood*

The modal auxiliaries in Kifuliiru (table 9.8) include one auxiliary which precedes an inflected verb, i.e. -**kéngeera** 'unintended state' and six which precede an uninflected stem. There are no auxiliary roots in this category that can be used both preceding an inflected verb and preceding an uninflected stem.

## 9.2 Detailed inventory of TAM form/meanings

Table 9.8. Auxiliaries dealing with mood

|   | Form | Gloss | Freq. |
|---|---|---|---|
| Ending in -**a** (before inflected verbs) | | | |
| a. | -kéngeera- | 'UNINTENDED STATE' | 1 |
| Ending in -**i** (before uninflected verbs) | | | |
| b. | -hámbiri | 'ALMOST.TROUBLE' | 0 |
| c. | -líndi | 'AFTER.EFFORT' | 0 |
| d. | -lóózi | 'AS.IF.WANTED' | 0 |
| e. | -lúnguli | 'PREMATURELY' | 2 |
| f. | -ményi/-yìji | 'KNOWING' | 18 |
| g. | -támi | 'AFTER.ALL.THAT' | 3 |

(a) The auxiliary -**kéngeera** 'UNINTENDED' refers to *unintentionally causing a state which is unpleasant and usually unexpected*. In (9.172) the expression **bànáyîjì kéngéérà** 'and they coming caused unintended state' modifies the remainder of the predicate **kèèrà kàmálà** 'it (the ink in a certain pen) was already finished off'. The effect is to communicate that they did not intend or want to finish off the ink in the pen; rather it caught them by surprise, and was a problem.

(9.172) Ìrí bá-ká-yándík-á nà= kó-òhè ‖ bà-ná-síîm-à bwénèènè ‖
   when 2-P2-write-Fa CNJ= 12-PRO 2-SQ-like-Fa very.much

  <u>bà-ná-yîjì</u> <u>kéngéér-á</u> kèèrà | kà-mál-à.
  2-SQ-COMING UNINTENDED-Fa ALREADY 12+P1-finish.off-Fa

'When they had written with it ‖ they were very pleased ‖ and they unintendedly encountered it is already | finished off.' (629 036)

In (9.173) the auxiliary **lyàngàkéngèèra** 'it might cause the unintended state' modifies the main verb **lyàbàhòlézà** 'it causes them to faint'. No one would want or intend that the people faint on the way, but if they were sent away hungry, that's what might end up happening.

(9.173) Hà-lí n-é= ky-ànyà ‖ í-shálí <u>ly-àngà-kéngèèr-à</u> |
   16-is and-AU= 7-time 5-hunger 5-POT-UNINTENDED-Fa

  ly-à-bà-hòl-éz-à mú= n-jírà.
  5-P1-O2-faint-CS-Fa 18= 9-path

'There is also a time ‖ hunger would cause (the unintended state) | of making them faint in the path.' (Mrk 8:3)

(b) The auxiliary -**hámbiri** 'ALMOST.TROUBLE' means that someone has *almost had trouble*. In (9.174) the inflected auxiliary **ànáhámbìrì** 'and he almost' modifies the unprefixed main verb **hóla** 'faint'. A main verb event preceded by -**hámbiri** is always something that would be troublesome and contrary to prior expectation and desire.

(9.174) **Í-zūūbà** ‖ **ly-àná-yák-ìr-à**        **Yónà**   **mw-î-**  **twè** ‖
    5-sun          5-SQ-shine-APL-Fa      Jonah     18-5      head

**à-ná-hámbìrì**                **hól-à.**
1-SQ-ALMOST.TROUBLE         faint-Fa

'The sun ‖ shone on Jonah on the head ‖ and he almost fainted.' (Jon 4:8)

(c) The auxiliary -**líndi** 'AFTER.EFFORT' modifies a verb which marks an event that occurs *after much time/effort*. In (9.175) the writer uses the inflected auxiliary **ànálîndì** 'and he after much effort' to modify the main verb **hísà** 'caused to arrive'. The situation here is that the eagle made a great effort to bring the girl along behind him and finally, at long last, caused her to arrive at the king's place.

(9.175) **Ùyó**     **nyûndà** ‖ **mú=**  **kú-kìzì**  **gír-á**  **kwôkwò** ‖
    that.N+1   1a+eagle    18=      15-REP       do-Fa     thus.N

**à-ná-lîndì**              **hí-s-á**        **ùyó**       **mú-nyéré** |  **í=**
1-SQ-AFTER.EFFORT      arrive-CS-Fa    that.N+1    1-girl                23=

**bw-àmì.**
14-kingdom

'That eagle ‖ in repeatedly doing that ‖ he after much effort caused that girl to arrive | at the king's place.' (616 032)

(d) The auxiliary -**lóózi** 'AS.IF.WANTED' means *as if one wanted to*. It usually means that something *almost* happened, but was prevented. In (9.176) the inflected auxiliary **gànálóòzì** 'and as if they wanted to', to modifies the main verb **zíkà** 'sink'. Although the boats did not sink, they appeared as if they wanted to (were about to) sink.

## 9.2 Detailed inventory of TAM form/meanings

(9.176) Bà-ná-yìjúz-à  ‖  yàgó       má-átò g-ômbì  î=fwì      ‖
       2-SQ-be.full+CS-Fa  those.N+6  6-boat  6-both  AU=10+fish

       hàlíndè |  gà-ná-lóòzì             zík-à.
       until      6-SQ-AS.IF.WANTED       sink-Fa

'They filled | both those boats (with) fish ‖ until | (it seemed) they wanted to sink.' (Luk 5:7)

(e) The auxiliary -**lúnguli** 'PREMATURELY' indicates that the action of the main verb is being done *prematurely*. In (9.177) the inflected auxiliary **àtàngàlúngùlì** 'I would not prematurely' modifies the main verb **liika** 'let go'. The owner of the girl considered it too soon to let go of her.

(9.177) Mw-èné       ú=mw-ānà  ‖  à-ná-láhìr-è  ‖   kw-â-
       1-one.having  AU=1-child   1-CON-refuse-Fe   CMP-1

       tà-ngà-lúngùlì              líík-à   |  ú=mú-nyérè.
       NEG-POT-PREMATURELY         let.go-Fa   AU=1-girl

'The owner of the child ‖ refused ‖ saying that he will not prematurely let go | of the girl.' (513 017)

(f) The auxiliary -**ményi** means 'KNOWING'. In (9.178) the auxiliary verb **tùtàngàményí** 'we would not know' modifies the main verb **dètà** 'speak'. The speaker says that people would just not know how to describe what needed to be said.

(9.178) Hálìkò gw-ôhê ‖ gù-lí mú=       tù-húún-ír-à    í=    mw-à-gè ‖
       but    3-CTR.P   3-is  PROG=    O1-pray-APL-Fa   23=   CON-A.M-1

       mú=           kú-góngéér-à ‖ kú=   n-jírà ‖  y-ó=
       IN.STATE=     15-groan-Fa    17=   9-path    9-O.R=

       tù-tà-ngà-ményí             dèt-à.
       1PL-NEG-POT-KNOWING         speak-Fa

'But HE ‖ is praying for us to him ‖ in groaning ‖ in a way ‖ we would not know how to say.' (Rom 8:26)

The form -**yìji**[78] is the suppletive resultative of -**mény**- and also means 'knowing'. In (9.179) the writer uses the auxiliary verb **ndàyìjì** 'I don't know' to modify the main verb **yōgà** 'swim'.

---

[78]Besides preceding an archaic cl. 5 infinitive (as shown in this example) the auxiliary **yìji** 'KNOWING' can often precede a productive cl. 15 infinitive. Note also that it differs tonally from

(9.179) Y-àná-hì-bwír-à: ‖ «É=  mw-ìrá  w-à-nì ‖   sì=
       9-SQ-O19-tell-Fa     O=   1-friend 1-A.M-1SG    OBV=

   n-dà-yìjí              yōg-à.»
   1SG-NEG-KNOWING        swim-Fa

'And it told him: ‖ «O my friend ‖ it's obvious I don't know (how) to swim!»' (12 018)

(g) The auxiliary -**támi** 'AFTER.ALL.THAT' implies that there is some previous event (or events) which leads up to and influences the action denoted by the main verb. In (9.180) the auxiliary complex **àtálì mú=támì** 'doesn't after all that' modifies the main verb **múkáyìrà** 'be fierce to her'. The husband, who might otherwise have been harsh to his wife, is not harsh to her, in light of something that had happened earlier.

(9.180) **Kírí  nà=   yîbà       ‖ à-tá-l-ì      mú=    támì**
        even  CNJ=  her.husband    1-NEG-is-Fi   PROG=  AFTER.ALL.THAT

   **mú-káy-ìr-à.**
   O1-be.fierce-APL-Fa

'Even and her husband ‖ he is not after all that being harsh with her.' (106 111)

## 9.2.5 TAM with -*ba*- auxiliary in compound verb phrases

The -**ba**- auxiliary can function as the first verb in a compound verb phrase. In such a case, the inflection of the -**ba**- auxiliary sets the TAM of the following matrix verb (see also 9.1.5.1 above).

No matter what the TAM marking on the -**ba**- auxiliary, the matrix verb following it always has a "stative" (as opposed to "dynamic") meaning.

Table 9.9 presents the ten TAM frames communicated by the auxiliary -**ba**- 'become'. In some cases this TAM frame involves primarily "time" as in (a) (P2 past) and (b) (F2 future). In other cases it involves primarily "aspect", as in (d) (progressive). In still other cases it involves "mood", as in (c) (conditional), (g) (subjunctive), (h–i) (conditional, contrary-to-fact), and (j) timeless conditional.

For comparative purposes, each example in table 9.9 is presented with the first-person plural subject prefix. In addition, the lexical verb which follows at the end of the verb phrase in each example is the resultative form **tùshálìsìrì** 'we are in the state of being hungry'. That simple resultative is only one of at

---

the auxiliary meaning "COMING".

## 9.2 Detailed inventory of TAM form/meanings

least 18 possible forms (all expressing state, not a dynamic action) which can follow the -**ba**- auxiliary. For an overview of those forms, see table 9.10.

Immediately following table 9.9 an example of each of the forms of the auxiliary **ba**- 'be' is presented.

Table 9.9. TAM of auxiliary

|   |   | AUX -**ba**- | Lexical verb | Literal gloss |
|---|---|---|---|---|
| a. | P2 past | túkábá | tùshálìsìrì | 'We were in a state of hunger.' |
| b. | F2 future | túgáàbà | tùshálìsìrì | 'We will be hungry.' |
| c. | CND/POT | twàngábà | tùshálìsìrì | 'We would be hungry.' |
| d. | Progressive | tùlì mú=bà | tùshálìsìrì | 'We are habitually hungry.' |
| e. | Sequential | twànábà | tùshálìsìrì | 'We came into state of hunger.' |
| f. | Continuative | tùnábè | tùshálìsìrì | 'We became (predictably) hungry.' |
| g. | Subjunctive | tùbé | tùshálìsìrì | 'Let's be in the state of hunger.' |
| h. | C.F CND PERS | túkìbè | tùshálìsìrì | 'If we had been hungry (C.F)' |
| i. | C.F CND mood | twàngàbíírì | tùshálìsìrì | 'If we were hungry (C.F)' |
| j. | Timeless CND | túbà[a] | tùshálìsìrì | 'be we in the state of hunger' |

[a]In this last form, there is a H-tone morpheme realized on the subject on the timeless form of -**ba**. This gives a conditional/subjunctive meaning, used in a dependent clause which is the first alternative in an either/or clause and can be translated "whether we be...".

In (9.181) the -**ba**- auxiliary **ákábá** 'she was' begins the verb phrase, and sets the time as before yesterday past (P2). This is followed by the copula **akola** 'she is now (not before)'. The overall literal meaning is 'when she was (she is) now (not before)'.

(9.181) Ìrí     á-ká-b-á      à-kòlà          mú=   lú-bàkò ‖  í-bûndà |
        when   1-P2-be-Fa   1-be.NEWLY   18=    11-forest    5-pregnancy

ly-àná-mú-kòm-ér-à    =mwò.
5-SQ-O1-pain-APL-Fa   =18

'When she was | now in the forest ‖ the pregnancy | was paining her there.' (210 019)

In (9.182) the -**ba**- auxiliary **túgáàbà** 'we will be' begins the verb phrase, and sets the time as future (F2). The main verb **tùlí mû**=**nywà** 'we are drinking' marks the progressive aspect. The overall meaning is 'we will be drinking'.

(9.182) Ù-génd-ág-è || gírá    ù-ká-tù-gwàn-è                       hà-líírà ||
        2S-go-EMP-Fe  so.that  2S-INTV-O1PL-encounter-Fe            16-

   tú-gáà-b-à      tù-lì     mû=    nyw-à     á=mī-ījì.
   1PL-F2-be-Fa    1PL-are   PRO=   drink-Fa  AU=6-water

'Go EMP || so that you would find us us there || we will be we are drinking water.' (405 006)

In (9.183) the -**ba**- auxiliary **nàngàbà** 'I would be' begins the verb phrase, and sets the mood as conditional. This is followed by the matrix verb -**lya** 'eat' in the progressive, intentional **ngwétí ngáàlyà** 'I am (intentionally) eating'. The overall literal meaning is 'if I would be (I am intentionally) eating'.

(9.183) **Níè-hè** ||   írí   **n-àngà-b-à**   n-gwétí   n-gáà-ly-à ||   n-dà-kízì
        1SG-CTR.P       if    1-CND-be-Fa      1-PROG    1-INT-eat-Fa    1-NEG-REP

   lóóz-á |  ú-gá-n-dè-s-à.
   want-Fa   S.R+1-F2-O.1S-speak-CS-Fa

'ME || if I would be eating | I don't repeatedly want | one who would converse with me.' (20 016)

In (9.184) the -**ba**- auxiliary **tùlí mû**= **bá** 'we are' begins the verb phrase, and sets the aspect as progressive, which when used with -**ba**- has a 'habitual' meaning. It is followed by the resultative **tùkòlí gwèjììrì** 'we are now (not before) sleeping'. The overall meaning is 'we are (habitually) now (not before) sleeping', i.e. when it becomes night, we always go to sleep, though we hadn't been sleeping earlier.

(9.184) **Tù-lí**   **mû**=   **b-á**   tù-kòlí         gwèj-ììr-ì       bú-shìgì.
        1P-are     PROG=     be-Fa    1P-be.NEWLY     sleeping-RS-Fi   14-night

'We are habitually now sleeping in the night...' (42 012)

In (9.185) the -**ba**- auxiliary **ànábà** 'and he was' begins the verb phrase, and sets the aspect as sequential (SQ). That is followed by the completed recent past **kéérà àgwátwà** 'he is already seized'. The overall meaning is 'and he was (he is) already seized', in this case, seized by thirst.

## 9.2 Detailed inventory of TAM form/meanings

(9.185) <u>À-ná-b-á</u>   kéèrà   à-gwát-w-à   n-é=   n-yótà ‖ kéèrà
1-SQ-be-Fa   already   1+P1-seize-PS-Fa   CNJ-AU=   9-thirst   already

à-ná-shálìk-à.
1-SQ-be.hungry-Fa

'He was already very thirsty ‖ and he was already hungry.' (27 012)

In (9.186) the **-ba-** auxiliary **ànábè** 'and she was' sets the aspect as a predictable continuation. It is immediately followed by the remote past (P3) **áálí rììrí** 'she was'. The overall literal meaning is 'and she was (predictably) (she) was'.

(9.186) **Ùyó**   mú-nyérè ‖ <u>à-ná-b-é</u>   á-àlí   rì-ìr-í   mú-nyéré
that.N+1   1-girl   1-CON-be-Fe   1-P3   is-RS-Fi   1-girl

mw-àmì.
1-king

'And that girl ‖ was the daughter of the king.'

In (9.187) the **-ba-** auxiliary **abe** 'he was' begins the verb phrase in a dependent time clause, and sets the time as 'immediacy, heightened expectation'. This is immediately followed by the progressive **àlì mú=híndá-híndà** 'he is searching, seraching'. The overall literal meaning is 'when he is now (with expectancy for hearer) repeatedly searching'.

(9.187) Lú-sìkù   lú-gùmà   Sényàmà   mbw-à=   <u>Ø-b-è</u>   à-lì
11-day   11-one   Senyama   as.soon.as-1=   SBV-be-Fe   16-is

mú=   hínd-á   híndá   mú=   lú-bàkò...
PROG=   search-Fa   RDP   18   11-forest

'One day, when Senyama (began to) search, search in the forest...' (524 029)

In (9.188) the **-ba-** auxiliary **àtákìbè** 'if he was not already (CF)' begins the verb phrase, which sets the mood as conditional, contrary to fact. It is followed by the recent past, completed **kéèrà àhúúnà** 'he has already asked'. The overall literal meaning is 'if he would not still be (but he is), having already asked'.

(9.188) Ù-yú        mú-ndù  ||  à-tá-kì-b-è              ||   kéèrà       à-húún-á
       this.P-1    1-person   1+if-NEG-PER.ST-be-Fe         already     1+P1-ask-Fa

       kw-ó=       lú-bàajà   lw-à-gè ||  lù-Ø -géndì     tw-íbw-á |    í=
       CMP-AU=     11-case    11-A.M-1    11-SBV-GOING    cut-PS-Fa     23=

       mw-á=       Kàísáàrì...
       CON-A.M=    Caesar

'This man || if he were not || he has already asked that his case || go be cut | with Caesar...' (Act 26:32)

In (9.189) the **-ba-** auxiliary **àngàbíírì** 'if he was' begins the verb phrase, and sets the mood as contrary-to-fact conditional (CF). This is followed by the copula **ali** 'he is'. The overall literal meaning is 'if he were (but is not), (he) is'.

(9.189) É=    Nàhá-mw-ì-tù ||    ngá=     Nàhánò |   à-ngà-bí-ír-í           à-lì
        O=    lord.CON-A.M-1P    if.C.F=  the.lord   1-CND.C.F-be-RS-Fi     1-is

        kúgúmá       ná=       ny-ìì-tù    ||   kí-tùmà      kí-kì |
        together     CNJ=      ADD.P.1-P.R      7-reason     7-what

        tw-àngà-kì-géndìr-ììr-í          |    n-ó=       kú-líbúúk-à?
        1P-CND.C.F-PER.ST-continue-RS-Fi      CNJ-AU=    15-persecuted-Fa

'O our lord || if the Lord | is (C.F) | he is together with us || for what reason | are we still continuing | to be persecuted?' (Jdg 6:13)

In (9.190) the **-ba-** auxiliary **kàbà** 'it would be' begins the verb phrase, and sets the time aspect. This is immediately followed by the copula **kàkòlà** 'it is now (but not before)'. The overall literal meaning is 'when it gets to be (it is) now'.

(9.190) hángó    kà-Ø-b-à      kà-kòlà        ká-lèngé-    rèngé ||   ù-lyá
        when     12-TL-be-Fa   12-be.NEWLY    12-noon      RDP        1-that.R

        kèré à-ná-lyók-è         mwó=   mú-nyéré   mw-îjá   ngà=    n-dóndè
        1a+frog 1-CON-leave-Fe   18+    1-girl     1-nice   like+   10-stars

'When it was now noon || out of that frog came a girl as beautiful as the stars'

In some cases, the auxiliary is marked by the same tense as the matrix clause. In (9.191) the **-ba-** auxiliary **bákábà** 'they were (P2)' is followed by the same P2 past, but with the addition of **kéèrà**, completed, in the form **kéèrà**

*9.2 Detailed inventory of TAM form/meanings*  297

**bákábyálà** 'they have already planted'. The overall literal meaning is 'When they were they had already planted.'

(9.191) ìrí    bá-<u>ká</u>-b-á    kéèrà |   bá-<u>ká</u>-byál-à ||   hà-ná-lèng-á |
       when   2-P2-be-Fa          ALREADY   2-P2-plant-Fa          16-SQ-pass-Fa

í=sìkú         |  nììní.
AU=10+days        few

'When they had already | planted || there passed | a days | a few.' (407 05)

Table 9.10 shows the 18 different TAM forms (seen in the 'Lexical verb' column) that can follow the -**ba**- auxiliary. For purposes of comparison, the forms are all given in the first-person plural with the toneless verb -**taah**- 'go home'. Note that when verbs follow the TAM frame-setter -**ba**-, they all take a "stative" (as opposed to "dynamic") meaning. Some of the glosses in table 9.10 are quite literal.

Table 9.10. Stative verb frames[a] that may follow the auxiliary -**ba**-

|    | AUX -**ba**-[b] | Lexical verb[c] | Gloss |
|----|-----------------|-----------------|-------|
| a. | ìrí twàngàbà    | twàtááhà        | 'If we would be we went home' |
| b. | twànábà         | kéèrà twàtááhà  | 'We had already gone home' |
| c. | twànábà         | tùtááhírì       | 'We were having gone home' |
| d. | ìrí twàngàbà    | tùshùbà mú=táahà | 'If we would be prev. going home' |
| e. | ìrí twàngàbà    | túkátááhà       | 'If we would have gone (P2)' |
| f. | ìrí túkábá      | kéèrà túkátááhà | 'When we had already gone home' |
| g. | ìrí túkábá      | tùtàzì táahà    | 'When we had not yet gone home' |
| h. | twànábà         | twáàlí tààhírì  | 'We had gone home (and still there)' |
| i. | ìrí túkábá      | tùlì[d]         | 'When we were we are...' |
| j. | twànábà         | tùkòlà          | 'We were we are now (not before)...' |
| k. | twànábà         | tùkìrì          | 'We were still...' |
| l. | ìrí túkábá      | tùlì mú=táahà   | 'When we were going home' |
| m. | ìrí túkábá      | tùkòlà mú=táahà | 'When we were now going home' |
| n. | twànábá         | tùkìrì mú=táahà | 'We were still going home' |
| o. | twànábá         | tùgwétì túgátààhà | 'We were intentionally going home' |
| p. | ìrí túkábá      | tùkòlà túgátààhà | 'When we were now going home' |
| q. | ìrí túkábá      | tùkòlá bú=táahà | 'When we were now about to go home' |
| r. | ìrí túkábá      | túgátààhà       | 'When we were going to leave' |

ᵃA verb of any TAM form, if it has a preceding focus copula, or is preceded by the conjunction **nga** 'as if' may also follow the sequential form of the -ba- auxiliary, **-ànába**.

ᵇWhenever possible, we use the sequential form of the auxiliary (**twànába**) in this column. The use of a non-sequential form of the auxiliary here means that the sequential did not co-occur in our texts with the verb form found in the following column. Besides whatever form is found in this AUX column, there may also be other forms of the auxiliary which can co-occur with the verb form that follows. We include only one example of the auxiliary for each of the forms found in the following column.

ᶜNote that any of these verb forms may also include various adverbial auxiliaries of the type that do not require a conjugated verb following, e.g. **-kòli** 'NEWLY', **-kìzi** 'REPEATEDLY' (the **i**-final set of adverbial auxiliaries).

ᵈThis row and the following two rows show the copulas **-li**, **-kola**, and **-kiri**, functioning as copulas, which would precede a NP, rather than used as auxiliaries.

### 9.2.6 Focus

#### 9.2.6.1 Positive focus copulas

When used in a verb phrase, the focus copula (FOC) itself is not marked for TAM. The following verb is what takes the TAM marking. The focus copula itself means 'this is the one (as opposed to others)'.

In (9.192) the cl. 3 focus copula **gwó** 'it is what' adds focus to the recent past (P1) verb **gwánjāāvyà** 'it has made me skinny'. The **gwó** itself is timeless, but is interpreted as being in the same time frame as the following verb.

(9.192) Ú=mw-énà ‖   gw-ó=         gw-á-n-jààv-y-á            kwókùnò.
       AU=3-hunger   3-FOC=        3-P1-O1.SG-get.skinny-CS-Fa   like.this.P.C

'The hunger ‖ is what has caused me to get skinny like this.' (11 019)

In (9.193) the focus copula **byó** occurs prior to the past (P2) in the form **byó bíkátūmà** 'they are what caused' and thus, though itself timeless, may be interpreted in the P2 time frame: 'they are/were the ones that caused'.

(9.193) **Yìbyó** ‖ **by-ó**= **bí-ká-tūm-á** ‖ **n-gá-gír-ír-a** | **ùyó**
that.N+8   8-FOC=   8-P2-cause-Fa   1SG-P2-do-APL-Fa   that.N+1

mw-àná |   kwôkwò.»
1-child    thus.N

'Those (things) ‖ are what caused ‖ that I would do to | that child | thus.' (205 089)

### 9.2.6.2 Negative focus copulas

The negative focus copula (NEG.FOC) means 'there is none' (as opposed to possible existence) and agrees in noun class to some particular referent. Thus it is timeless and completely unmarked for tense. In each case where it is used, semantically there has been a question concerning the referent. The answer, often unexpected, is that the participant does not exist.

In (9.194) the form is **ndáá-yè**, which means 'there is no one from cl. 1 or 1a (person)'.

(9.194) **Ndáá-yè**   **nábwìgírà.**
NEG.FOC-1   1a+do.it.yourself

'There is no do-it-yourself (person who can be completely self sufficient).' (52 021)

In (9.195) the cl. 10 **ndáá-zò** means that 'there is none, from group of cl. 10 (houses)'.

(9.195) **Há-nò**   **n-dì**=   **mw-í**=   **shámbà** ‖ **ndáá-zò**   **ny-ûmbà** ‖
16-here.P.C   1SG-is=   18-5=   desert   NEG.FOC-10   10-houses

í-zì-rí   hò-òfi.
S.R-10-is   16-near

'Here I am in the desert ‖ there are no houses ‖ which are close.' (29 006)

## 10

# Clauses and Information Structure

This chapter begins by describing the syntax of independent clauses.[1] This includes non-verbal clauses, the verbal clause nucleus, and obliques. It also briefly discusses polar questions.

In the second main section, we explore what is referred to in the literature as "information structure," following the model developed by Andrews (1985) and Lambrecht (1994). In particular we give attention to the three types of sentence articulation, i.e. topic-comment, identificational, and presentational. Other relevant notions treated include Levinsohn's (2005) point of departure (PoD) (10.2.4) and dominant focal element (DFE) (10.2.3.1).

Finally, we look at the many ways in which the default word order of the clause is altered by the discourse context, based on the constraints of information structure.

## 10.1 Syntactic structure of independent clauses

### 10.1.1 Non-verbal clauses

The non-verbal clauses in Kifuliiru can be grouped into at least five types. The first four involve variations of identificational structures, either in asking about the identity of a participant, or confirming the identity. In the first type, the general NP is replaced by a question word (what, who, etc.), followed by a demonstrative, which may optionally be modified by a relative clause.

---

[1] In this chapter, self-standing clause constituents (e.g. subjects or objects) are marked by capital letters, e.g. S or O, while bound constituents (i.e. pronoun affixes) are marked by small letters, e.g. s or o.

The second type consists of the cl. 15 question word, **kútì / kútàgì** 'how' followed by a relative clause, but no demonstrative. The third type is the same as the first type, except that the NP is preceded by a question marker, forming a polar question. The fourth type consists of a noun phrase followed by a demonstrative, which may or may not be modified by a relative clause. The fifth type is different, and involves the introduction of a quote. In this type of non-verbal clause, there is no speech verb preceding a quote. Instead, the non-verbal quote marker **ti** 'quote', which is often used following a speech verb, is used alone preceding the quote. In all of the examples below, not only is there no verb; in the context it would be unnatural/ungrammatical to include one.

(a) The structure of QUESTION WORD FOLLOWED BY A DEMONSTRATIVE employs one of the question words e.g. **bi-ki** (8-what). Such constructions are often used in identificational structures where the addressee is being asked to identify the referent of the question word. The request for identification of the referent for (10.1) **Bíkì yíbì?** 'What (is) this?' is answered in the next clause by **shèènyò** 'axe'.

(10.1)

| | | Q word | Dem | | | |
|---|---|---|---|---|---|---|
| À-ná-búùz-à | tì: ‖ | «Bí-kì | yí-bì?» ‖ | Á-bá-ndù | tì: | ‖ |
| 1-SQ-ask-Fa | ‹quote› | 8-what | this.P-8 | AU=2-people | ‹quote› | |

«Shéényò!»
9+axe

'And he asked ‹quote›: ‖ «What (is) this?» ‖ People ‹quote›: ‖ «An axe!»'
(522 037-038)

In (10.2) the question word **bíkì** 'what' is again followed by the demonstrative **yíbì** 'this', but this time a (dependent) relative clause **ùhàgàsírì** '(which) you have hanging on your shoulder' is added.

(10.2)

| | | Q word | Dem |
|---|---|---|---|
| Bà-ná-shùbì | mú-búúz-â: ‖ | «Bí-kì | yí-bí ⎸ |
| 2-SQ-AGAIN | O1-ask-Fa | 8-what | this.P-8 |

Relative clause
ù-hàgàs-ír-ì?»
2SG-carry.over.shoulder-RS-Fi

'And they again asked him: ‖ «What (is) this ⎸ (which) you have over (your) shoulder?»' (603 048)

## 10.1 Syntactic structure of independent clauses

In (10.3) **bíkì** 'what' is the complement of the cl. 8 associative marker (A.M) **byà**. It is followed by the demonstrative NP **yìbí bíjángálà** 'these banana leaves', meaning 'what are these banana leaves for?'. The (dependent) relative clause **byô=gwétì úgákùùmàniâ** 'which you are gathering' is part of the NP and modifies **yìbí bíjángálà**.

(10.3)

| | | | Q word | NP | |
|---|---|---|---|---|---|
| «É | mú-sósì \| | by-à= | bí-kì | yì-bí | bí-jángálà \| |
| O | 1-man | 8-A.M= | 8-what | this.P-8 | 8-banana.leaves |

| | Relative clause | |
|---|---|---|
| by-ó= | gwétí \| | ú-gá-kùùmàn-i-â?» |
| 8-O.R+2SG= | PROG | 2SG-INTL-gather-CS-Fa |

'«O man | for what (are) these leaves | which you are | gathering?»' (14 027)

(b) The second kind of non-verbal clause is also identificational, but of a slightly different type. It contains the cl. 15 **kútì** (or **kútàgì**) QUESTION WORD FOLLOWED BY A RELATIVE CLAUSE. In (10.4) the interrogative **kút-àgì** 'how-EMP' is followed by the relative clause **kwó=túgábàyòngòlòkà** 'that we will be extracting ourselves from them'.

(10.4)

| Q word | | Relative clause |
|---|---|---|
| **Kút-àgì** | kw-ó= | tú-gá-bà-yòngòlòk-à? |
| how-EMP | 15-O.R= | 1PL-F2-O2-extract.selves-Fa |

'How will we extract ourselves from them?' (01 016)

In (10.5) the question word **kútì** 'how' is followed by the relative clause **kwó=yîshò àkúbwîrà** 'that your father told you'.

(10.5)

| Q word | | Relative clause | |
|---|---|---|---|
| **Kútí** | kw-ó= | yîshò | à-kú-bwîr-à? |
| how | 15-O.R= | 1a+your.father | 1+P1-O2.SG-tell-Fa |

'What did your father tell you?' (626 018)

(c) In some cases, a non-verbal clause involves a POLAR QUESTION WITH OMITTED VERB. In (10.6) the question word **ka** precedes the NP and demonstrative, putting the whole non-verbal proposition "that (is) my friend" into question.

(10.6)

| Q | NP | | Dem |
|---|---|---|---|
| **Ká=** | **mw-ìrá** | **w-à-ní** | **ùyó** |
| Q= | 1-friend | 1-A.M-1SG | that.N+1 |
| | | Relative clause | |

**léèrò     ú-w-á-n-dùk-á |            kwôkwô?**
this.time   S.R-1-P1-O1.SG-bad.mouth-Fa   thus.N

'(Is) that my friend | that one | who this time has bad-mouthed me | like this?' (39 016)

(d) The fourth non-verbal clause type is a kind of identificational structure that involves a NOUN PHRASE FOLLOWED BY A DEMONSTRATIVE. In these clauses the demonstratives occur after the other components of the NP, instead of being found in the default position at the beginning of the NP.

In (10.7) the phrase **Ízímáánó lyá=bágéní** 'the guest food of the guests' is followed by the proximal contrastive demonstrative **lìnò** 'this.P.C'.

(10.7)

| NP | | | Dem |
|---|---|---|---|
| **Í-zímáánó** | **ly-á=** | **bá-génì** | **lì-nò.** |
| 5-guest.food | 5-A.M+AU= | 2-guests | 5-this.P.C |

'This (is) the guest food of the guests.' (09 007)

In (8.10) the NP **múgândá wàgè** 'the angel of him' is followed by the nearby demonstrative **ùyó** 'that one'.

(10.8)

| NP | | | Dem |
|---|---|---|---|
| **Ngééká |** | **mú-gândá** | **w-à-gè** | **ùyó.** |
| maybe | 1-angel | 1-A.M-1 | that.N+1 |

'Maybe | that (is) the angel of him.' (Act 12:15)

In (10.9) the cl. 9 **í=ndùsì** 'being full' is followed by the proximal contrastive demonstrative **ínò** 'this one' and then a (dependent) relative clause.

## 10.1 Syntactic structure of independent clauses

(10.9)

| NP | Dem |
|---|---|
| **Í=n-dùsì** | **í-nò** ‖ |
| AU=9-being.full | 9-this.P.C |

| Relative clause | | |
|---|---|---|
| **í-y-à-túm-à** | **n-gì-bwát-íír-í** | **há-nò.** |
| S.R-9-P1-cause-Fa | 1SG-PERS-sit-RS-Fi | 16-here.P.C |

'This (being) full (of food) ‖ is what has caused me to still be sitting here.' (55 006)

In (10.10) the non-verbal clause consists of cl. 3 **múzìmù** 'evil spirit' followed by the nearby demonstrative **yùgwó** 'that.N'. Besides functioning as the non-verbal predicate, **yùgwó** functions as the relativizer for the relative phrase **yùgwó àléétà** 'that.N (thing which) he has brought'.

(10.10)

| NP | Dem | Relative clause |
|---|---|---|
| **Mú-zìmù** | **yùgwó** \| | **à-léét-à.** |
| 3-demon | that.N+3 | 1+P1-bring-Fa |

'It's a demon that one \| (which) he's brought.' (112 036)

(e) Another different sort of non-verbal clause involves the QUOTE MARKER **ti**, with no preceding speech verb. In (10.11) the dependent clause **ìrí bákáhíkágá í=kájábò** 'when they arrived across' is followed by the verbless clause containing the quote marker: **ú=múhyá tí=** 'the new wife ‹quote›', in other words, 'the new wife (said)'.

(10.11)

| **Ìrí** | **bá-ká-hík-ág-á** | **í=** | **ká-jábò** ‖ | **ú=mú-hy-á** \| | **tì=** |
|---|---|---|---|---|---|
| when | 2-P2-arrive-EMP-Fa | 23= | 12-across | AU=1-new.wife | ‹quote› |

**«Éhéè!»**
Oh.my!

'When they arrived across ‖ the new wife \| ‹quote›: «Oh my!»' (112 016)

### 10.1.2 Verbal clause nucleus

The default order within the Kifuliiru verbal clause nucleus is (S) V (C) (O$^1$) (O$^2$), where the complement (C) and the objects (O) cannot co-occur. In ditransitive cases with two objects, we follow the common Bantu practice of marking them as O¹ (first object) and O² (second object),[2] rather than terming one direct object and the other indirect object. Obliques typically occur after the (S) V (C) (O¹) (O²) sequence, but may be preposed in some circumstances, as a result of information structure constraints. In addition, some obliques commonly occur before the nucleus as points of departure (PoD) (10.2.4). Word order is quite strict: except for a few adverbs, nothing else occurs within the (S) V (C) (O¹) (O²) nucleus.

Kifuliiru is a pro-drop language. That is to say that the subject or object noun phrase can be dropped, leaving only the pronoun subject or object prefix on the verb, or, in the case of a second object, a post-clitic following the verb. The subject pronoun prefix on the verb is obligatory, whether or not there is also a self-standing subject NP. The object pronoun prefix can only occur where there is no NP object, or where the object has been left-dislocated to a position preceding the verb.

In the examples below, upper case letters are used for the SVO labeling of free (self-standing) subjects and objects. Lower case letters are used to label the bound prefixes and enclitics.

### 10.1.2.1 Intransitive clauses (S V)

The clause nucleus of intransitive clauses includes only the subject and the verb, with no complement or object of any type. Thus in (10.12) the verb form **byànáyònékà** 'and it poured out' does not have a complement.

| (10.12) | S | | | | s V |
|---|---|---|---|---|---|
| Í=by-ókúlyá | by-á= | àlì | hí-ít-ì ‖ | | by-àná-yònék-à. |
| AU=8-food | 8-O.R+1= | P3 | has-RS-Fi | | 8-SQ-spilled.out-Fa |

'The food which he had ‖ it spilled out.' (34 015)

In (10.13) the verb **ànásháágà** 'and he left' is followed by locative oblique **yàhô** 'there'.

| (10.13) | S | | | s V | Oblique |
|---|---|---|---|---|---|
| Ùyó | nyâmbwè | w-é= | ká-bándà ‖ | à-ná-shââg-à | yà-hô. |
| that.N+1 | 9+jackal | 1-A.M-23= | 12-valley | 1-SQ-leave-Fa | there.N-16 |

'That jackal of the valley ‖ it left there.' (32 041)

In (10.14) the verb is **ànágwà** 'and he fell' and the locative oblique is **kwí=tùmù** 'on his spear'.

---

[2]We use the terms first object and second object to refer only to left-to-right order within the clause, and not to any inherent properties of the referents or to their syntactic function.

10.1 Syntactic structure of independent clauses    307

(10.14)

| S | | s V | | Oblique | |
|---|---|---|---|---|---|
| Ùyó | mú-shósì ‖ | à-ná-gw-à | kw-í= | tùmù. | |
| that.N+1 | 1-man | 1-SQ-fall-Fa | 17-5= | spear | |

'That man ‖ fell on the spear.' (626 039)

In (10.15) the verb **bànágwâtwà** 'and they were grabbed' is passive and is followed by the oblique phrase **nó=lúùgì** 'with jealousy'.

(10.15)

| S | | s V | Oblique | |
|---|---|---|---|---|
| Á=bà-àbò ‖ | | bà-ná-gwât-w-à | n-ó= | lú-ùgì. |
| AU=2-SAME.SET | | 2-SQ-grab-PS-Fa | CNJ+AU= | 11-jealousy |

'His fellows ‖ they were jealous.' (624 005)

In (10.16) the verb **ànáhíkà** 'he arrived' is followed only by an oblique, the locative phrase **mú=kāāyà kágùmà** 'in one city'.

(10.16)

| PoD | | s V | Oblique | | |
|---|---|---|---|---|---|
| Lú-sìkù | lú-gùmà ‖ | à-ná-hík-à | mú= | kā-āyà | ká-gùmà. |
| 11-day | 11-one | 1-SQ-arrive-Fa | 18= | 12-village | 12-one |

'One day ‖ he arrived in one village.' (30 003)

### 10.1.2.2 Clauses with non-object complement (S V C)

In clauses with a non-object complement, predicate complements may follow the identificational copulas **-li** 'is' or **ba** 'become'. In (10.17) we observe that the cl. 2 subject prefix **ba-** on the copula verb **bàlí** 'they are' agrees with the following complement, **bányérè** 'girls'.

(10.17)

| | | | s V | C |
|---|---|---|---|---|
| Á=bà-ndì: ‖ | «Nângà | máàshì | bà-lí | bá-nyérè.» |
| AU=2-other | no | for.goodness.sake | 2-are | 2-girls |

'Others (said): ‖ «No for goodness sake | they are girls.»' (206 027)

In (10.18) the subject **nyókò** 'your mother' is followed by the copula verb **àlí** 'she is' and the complement noun **mwìtánì** 'a killer'.

(10.18)

| S | s V | C |
|---|---|---|
| É= Léézà ‖ nyókó | à-lí | mw-ìtánì. |
| O= Leeza    1a+your.mother | 1-is | 1-killer |

'O Leeza ‖ your mother is a killer.' (628 026)

In (10.19) the subject **yàkó ká-bwâ** 'that.N dog' is followed by the copula phrase **à-ná-b-ágág-à ngá=yé** 'it became like it is the one who is' and the complement **mú-ká-à-gè** 'his wife'.

(10.19)

| S | s V | |
|---|---|---|
| Yàkó    ká-bwâ ‖ | à-ná-b-ágág-à | ngá=   yé= |
| that.N+12    12-dog | 1-SQ-become-EMP-Fa | like    FOC |

| C |
|---|
| mú-ká-à-gè. |
| 1-wife-A.M-1 |

'That dog ‖ became (emphatic) | like he is the one who is his wife.' (106 007)

### 10.1.2.3 Transitive clauses (S V O)

Transitive clauses include a subject, verb, and object. As already mentioned, any given object can be represented by only one element in any one clause. Therefore if an object NP is present, pronominal representation by an object prefix within the verb or by a post-verbal clitic is not allowed. The exception to this occurs when the object is left-dislocated, in which case the pronoun trace still occurs on the verb.

In (10.20), where the verb **bànáyábìirà** 'and they took' takes the object **í=shèènyò íkùmì** 'ten axes'.

(10.20)

| S | s V |
|---|---|
| Yàbó    bà-ànà    bà-à-gè ‖ | bà-ná-yábììr-á | 
| those.N+2    2-children    2-A.M-1 | 2-SQ-took-Fa |

| O | |
|---|---|
| í=shèènyò | í-í-kùmì. |
| AU=10+axes | AU=5-ten |

'Those children of his ‖ took | ten axes.' (32 010)

10.1 Syntactic structure of independent clauses

In (10.21) the verb **ànágêndì lámùsà** 'and he went and greeted' takes the object **návyàlà** 'his mother-in-law'.

(10.21) Mw-ámì ‖ ìrí    á-ká-yús-á       ú=kú-ly-â ‖
        1-king   when  1-P2-finish-Fa  AU=15-eat-Fa

| s V | | O |
|---|---|---|
| **à-ná-gêndì** | **lámùs-à** ‖ | **návyàlà.** |
| 1-SQ-GOING | greet-Fa | 1a+his.mother.in.law |

'The king ‖ when he had finished eating ‖ he went and greeted | his mother-in-law.' (606 042)

In (10.22) the verb **ànábîìkà** 'and she placed' takes the object **í=fwáráŋgá zààgè bíhúmbí bírìndà** 'her money 7,000'.

(10.22)

| s V | O | | | |
|---|---|---|---|---|
| **À-ná-bîìk-á** | **í=fwáráŋgá** | **zà-à-gè** ‖ | **bí-húmbí** | **bí-rìndà** ‖ |
| 1-SQ-place-Fa | AU=10+money | 10-A.M-1 | 8-thousand | 8-seven |

| Oblique | |
|---|---|
| **mú=** | **lú-dáhà.** |
| 18= | 11-bag |

'She placed her money ‖ 7,000 ‖ in the bag.' (33 004)

### 10.1.2.4 Ditransitive clauses (S V O O)

Ditransitive clauses contain a subject, verb, and two objects. The two objects may be allowed by the underlying lexical properties of some verbs, e.g. **-heerez-** 'give'. The ditransitivity may also be the result of the affixation of a valence-increasing extension such as the applicative, causative, or impositive to an already transitive verb. The "extra" objects are found in various semantic roles, such as instrumental, benefactive, malefactive, etc.

#### 10.1.2.4.1 Ditransitive radical with no derivational extensions

Certain verbs are inherently ditransitive.[3] Such verbs may have two objects expressed, either as full noun phrases following the verb, or as incorporated pronominal elements.[4] Such a verb is seen in (10.23), where the verb

---

[3] Though a verb like **-heerez-** does include recognizable extensions, they have been lexicalized as a part of the verb stem. The unextended form of this verb, **-ha-**, is also ditransitive.

[4] We discuss the inclusion of the pronominal object prefixes within the verb here, rather than

ùbàhèèrèzé=kyò 'you give to them it' includes two pronominal objects. The first object prefix bà- is prefixed before the verb root, while the second object kyo is shunted as a clitic to the end of the verb.

(10.23)

| | | s o¹ V | o² |
|---|---|---|---|
| É | dáàtà | ‖ ù-Ø-bà-hèèrèz-é | =kyò. |
| O | 1a+my.father | 2SG-SBV-O2-give-Fe | =7 |

'O my father ‖ give it to them.' (47 008)

In (10.24) the verb -heerez- 'give' has mú- 'he' as its first object and í=kíhândè kyó=bwàmì bwàgè 'a half of his kingdom' as the second. In this case, only the first object is incorporated.

(10.24)

| s o¹ V | o² | | | |
|---|---|---|---|---|
| À-ná-mú-héérez-á ‖ | í=kí-hândè ‖ | ky-ó= | bw-àmì | bw-à-gè. |
| 1-SQ-O1-give-Fa | AU=7-half | 7-A.M+AU= | 14-kingdom | 14-A.M-1 |

'And he gave him | a half | of his kingdom.' (23 048)

The shortened form of 'give', i.e. -ha- 'give', is also ditransitive.[5] The short form of this verb is only used[6] when both objects are incorporated. In (10.25) the o¹ benefactive object kú- 'you' is found as an object prefix preceding the verb and the other object, o², is expressed as a pronominal object clitic following the verb.

(10.25)

| s o¹ V | o² |
|---|---|
| N-dá-gá-kú-h-à | =yê. |
| 1SG-NEG-F2-O2.SG-give-Fa | =O1 |

'I will not give him to you.' (210 123)

Example (10.26) includes two ditransitive verbs. The verb -huun- 'ask' includes the cl. 1 object prefix mú- in the verb kyànámúhúùnà 'and it asked him'. The verb's second object, ízímáánò 'guest food', follows the verb. In the same sentence, the verb -zìmaan- 'serve guest food' has a cl. 7 o¹ prefix kì- 'it', while O² ímbènè 'goat' follows the verb.

---

in the chapter on verbs, because the ability of a nominal to be referenced by a prefix within the verb often seems to be considered by Bantuists a reliable indicator of that nominal's status as an "object."

[5] The much more common form of the verb 'give' includes both frozen applicative and causative extensions, -heez- ~ -heerez-.

[6] We have noted rare occurences which include only one incorporated object, but these are of questionable grammaticality.

## 10.1 Syntactic structure of independent clauses

(10.26)

| s o¹ V | O² | s o¹ V | O² |
|---|---|---|---|
| **Ky-àná-mú-húùn-à** | **í-zímáánò**  ‖ | **à-ná-kì-zímáàn-à** ‖ | **í=m-bènè.** |
| 7-SQ-O1-ask-Fa | 5-guest.food | 1-SQ-O7-serve-Fa | AU=9-goat |

'It (wild animal) asked him for guest food ‖ and he served it | a goat.'
(52 011)

The verb -**ly**- 'eat' is found in unextended form (i.e. with no extensions) as a ditransitive verb in five instances in our texts. In each case, the first object, o¹, is malefactive, that is, being adversely affected by someone else's unauthorized eating, while O² is the thing which is being eaten. The malefactive object, being animate, is the one incorporated into the verb of the relative clause. In (10.27) the verb -**ly**- 'eat' takes the first-person plural object prefix **tú-**, as well as the second object **ámágùshà** 'grubs'.

(10.27) Q word

| | o¹ V | O² |
|---|---|---|
| **Bí-kí**  ‖ | **í-bì-rì**   **mú=**   **tù-ly-à** | **á=má-gùshà** \| |
| 8-what | S.R-8-is PROG= O1.PL-eat-Fa | AU=6-grubs |

| | Oblique | |
|---|---|---|
| **mú=** | **yì-kí**   **kí-byâ.** | |
| 18= | this.P-7 7-small.pot | |

'«What ‖ is eating our grubs (lit., eating us the grubs) | from this pot?»'
(41 009)

Another seemingly ditransitive verb is -**gér**- 'measure'. In (10.28) the cl. 3 prefix, **gù-** 'it' refers back to **úmùgózì** 'rope', mentioned in the previous clause. The O² is the malefactive object, **Kályôshò**, the name of the boy around whose neck she hopes to tie the rope.

(10.28)

| | | | s o¹ V |
|---|---|---|---|
| **À-ná-híkìrì** | **lúk-á** | **ú=mù-gózì** ‖ | **à-ná-gù-gér-à** |
| 1-SQ-ARRIVING | weave-Fa | AU=3-rope | 1-SQ-O3-measure-Fa |

| O² | Oblique | |
|---|---|---|
| **Kályôshò** \| | **mw-í=** | **gósì.** |
| Kalyosho | 18-5= | neck |

'And she arrived and wove a rope ‖ and she measured it (for) Kalyosho | on the neck.' (18 017)

### 10.1.2.4.2 Ditransitive with applicative extension

The applicative -**er** / -**ir** is a valence-increasing derivational extension. When added to a transitive verb, it enables the verb to take two objects.

In (10.29) the ditransitive clause, in which both objects are indicated by nouns, follows the applicativized polite imperative verb **ùlékérè** 'you leave APL'. The $O^1$ **ùyú músósì** 'this man' fills a benefactive role. It is followed by the $O^2$ **í=ngáàvú yàgè** 'his cow'.

| (10.29) | s V | | $O^1$ | | $O^2$ | |
|---|---|---|---|---|---|---|
| | Ù-Ø-lék-ér-é | ‖ | ù-yú | mú-sósí | í=n-gáàvú | y-à-gè. |
| | 2SG-SBV-leave-APL-Fe | | this.P-1 | 1-man | AU=9-cow | 9-A.M-1 |

'(You) leave for ‖ this man | his cow.' (17 017)

In (10.30) the transitive verb -**deek**- 'cook something' is used with the applicative extension -**er**, again allowing the benefactive object to be mentioned. $O^1$ is the prefixed object **gì**- (**í=ngòkò** 'chicken') mentioned earlier in the sentence, while the $O^2$ following the verb is the benefactive, **ú=múkwî** 'the son-in-law'. Here the patient rather than the benefactive is incorporated, because the patient (a chicken) is the topic (old information) of the sentence, and so is not found in the focal position at the end of the clause.

| (10.30) | | | s o¹ V | |
|---|---|---|---|---|
| | Y-àná-háà-bw-à | návyàlà | ‖ | à-Ø-gì-dèèk-èr-è |
| | 9-SQ-give-PS-Fa | 1a+mother.in.law | | 1-SBV-O9-cook-APL-Fe |

| $O^2$ |
|---|
| ú=mú-kwî. |
| AU=1-son.in.law |

'And it was given (to) the mother-in-law ‖ (that) she cook it for the son-in-law.' (513 021)

In (10.31) the verb **mùkómérè** 'you clap for', with the applicative extension -**er**, takes two objects, **mwàmì** 'king' and **á=mágàshà** 'hand (clap)'.

## 10.1 Syntactic structure of independent clauses

(10.31)

| S | | V | O¹ |
|---|---|---|---|
| Á=bá-shósí | mw-éshì ‖ | mù-Ø-kóm-ér-é | mw-àmí \| |
| AU=2-men | 2PL-all | 2PL-SBV-clap-APL-Fe | 1-king |

| O² |
|---|
| á=má-gàshà. |
| AU=6-hand.clap |

'All you men ‖ clap for the king | hands (clap hands for the king.)' (410 008)

In (10.32) the verb **-shwek-** 'tie' takes the applicative extension **-er**. In the clause **nàmúshwékérà ú=mùgózì** 'I tied on him a rope', the malefactive O¹ is represented by the object prefix **mú-** 'him', while the instrumental O² is **úmùgózì** 'rope'.[7]

(10.32)

| | s o¹ V | O² |
|---|---|---|
| Ú-gá-gwàn-à \| | n-à-mú-shwék-ér-à | ú=mù-gózì \| |
| 2SG-F2-encounter-Fa | 1SG-P1-O1-tie-APL-Fa | AU=3-rope |

| Oblique | |
|---|---|
| mw-í= | gósì. |
| 18-5= | neck |

'And you will find | I have tied a rope | on his neck.' (18 015)

In (10.33) the applicative extension is applied to the verb **-ly-** 'eat', making it **-li-ir-** 'eat with'. **Ú=búndù** 'porridge' (the staple starch food of the Bafuliiru) is never eaten by itself. It must be accompanied by a relish of some sort. The applicative extension is used to allow the verb **-liir-** 'eat APL' to take this extra object of accompaniment. In the following example, both objects are expressed as full nouns following the verb.

(10.33)

| s V | O¹ | O² |
|---|---|---|
| À-tá-kìzì lí-ír-à | ú=bú-ndú \| | á=má-gùshà. |
| 1-NEG-REP eat-APL-Fa | AU=14-porridge | AU=6-grubs |

'She doesn't habitually eat porridge | (with) grubs.' (41 004)

---

[7] Either the instrumental object, here the rope, or the malefactive object can be incorporated. See examples (10.42) and (10.43) for two uses of a similar verb, though without the applicative, which show that either the malefactive or the instrumental object may be incorporated, depending on what is topicalized in the sentence.

Generally, only one incorporated object may be represented as a verbal prefix in any one verb. However, two prefixed objects are allowed when one of the two is either first-person singular (1SG), or reflexive (RFX). Such a case, with a first-person singular (1SG) object, is found following the cl. 12 object marker, **kà-** in (10.34) in the phrase **àkòlì kámbìtíírì**[8] 'he has it (value) to me'. In such a case, the first-person singular object is always closer to the verb stem.

(10.34)    O¹                |    s o¹ o² V

| Kìrì | ná= | nàà-nî ‖ | à-kòlì | ká-m-bìt-í-ír-ì. |
|---|---|---|---|---|
| even | CNJ= | ADD.P-1SG | 1-be.NEWLY | O12-O1.SG-have-APL-RS-Fi |

'Even and ME ‖ he is now having it (value) to me.' (Phm 1:11)

### 10.1.2.4.3 Ditransitive with causative extension

The addition of the causative extension to a verb always increases the semantic valence of the verb.[9] In (10.35) the agent/malefactive object **m-** 'me' is expressed in o¹ position, while O² represents the patient, or receiver of the action, **úbútùùzì** 'goods'.

(10.35)         s o¹ V            |         O²

| Zí-gá-yîjì | m-mánúl-íís-â | ‖ ú=bú-tùùzì | bw-à-nî. |
|---|---|---|---|
| 10-F2-COMING | O1.SG-bring.down-CS-Fa | AU=14-goods | 14-A.M-1SG |

'They come making me get down | my goods.' (520 052)

In (10.36) 'the woman filled the basket (O¹) (with) food' (O²) gives another example of a causative verb with two objects. The verb **-yìjul-** 'be full' is a transitive verb whose subject is some sort of "container", and whose object is the substance that is filling that container. When the causative extension is added to this verb, it becomes **-yìjuz-** 'fill', a ditransitive verb whose subject is now the agent who puts some substance into some container, and whose two objects are the container and the substance with which it is filled. In the following example with the causative verb, both of these objects are expressed as full NPs.

---

[8] The **h** on the verb **-hiti-ir-i** 'have for (RS)', changes to **b** when following **m**. As seen in the gloss, this is the applicative form of one of the irregular resultative forms of the verb 'to have'.

[9] A causative verb generally has a causer as well as an agent, but often the agent is not specified with causative verbs. Look at the example **ànáhìngíísà índálò** 'and he had his field farmed', where the subject of the verb is the "causer" as well as the one benefiting from the action, the expressed object, **índálò** 'field' is the patient, and the agent (presumably some paid employee) is left totally unexpressed except by implication.

## 10.1 Syntactic structure of independent clauses

(10.36)

| s V | O¹ | O² |
|---|---|---|
| **À-ná-yìjù-z-é** \| | **í=kí-sâmbà** \|\| | **í=byókúlyà.** |
| 1-CON-fill-CS-Fe | AU=7-large.basket | AU=food |

'And she filled | the large basket | (with) food.' (101 030)

In (10.37) the object **ìyó ndáló yá=yìbyó bígûndù** 'that.N field of those banana plants' has been left-dislocated, and then is referred to again in the verb by means of the object prefix **gì-** 'field'. The causative verb here is **bànágìzùngúlúsà** 'and they surrounded it' and the second object is the instrumental **í=mítēgò** 'traps'.

(10.37)

| O¹ | | | | s o¹ V |
|---|---|---|---|---|
| **Ìyó** | **n-dáló** \| **y-á** | **yìbyó** | **bí-gûndù** \|\| | **bà-ná-gì-zùngúlú-s-â** \|\| |
| that.N+9 | 9-field 9-A.M | that.N+8 | 8-banana | 2-SQ-O9-surround-CS-Fa |

| O² |
|---|
| **í=mí-tēgò.** |
| AU=4-traps |

'That field | of those bananas || they surrounded it || (with) traps.' (25 017)

In (10.38), both the cl. 1 object **mú-** and the reflexive **yì-** are prefixed to the verb base -**lyos**- 'separate from'.[10] The reflexive is always closer to the verb stem than the other object.

(10.38)

| | s o¹ o² V | |
|---|---|---|
| **À-tà-ná-kì-shóbòl-à** | \|\| **ú=kú-mú-yì-lyó-s-á** | **=kw-ò.** |
| 1-NEG-SQ-PERS-be.able-Fa | AU=15-O1-RFX-leave-CS-Fa | =17 |

'And he was not still able || to separate himself from him (a second person).' (53 013)

### 10.1.2.4.4 Ditransitive with impositive extension

The lexicalized (i.e. frozen) impositive[11] extension -**ik** / -**ek** can also trigger two objects. Many impositive ditransitive verbs express aggression with an

---

[10] In this case, the presence of an "extra" object is the result of the promotion of the object of an oblique (locative phrase) to the object of a verb already made transitive by the inclusion of the causative extension. The pronominalized locative marker from the oblique phrase appears as an enclitic on the verb. Such (re)arrangement of clause constituents is done to satisfy information structure constraints regarding the dominant focal element (DFE) (see 10.2.3.1).

[11] This term, employed by Schadeberg (2003:74), denotes an extension which has the central meaning of putting something into some position. This extension is an integral semantic component of the

instrument, such as hitting, beating, scratching, etc. Other ditransitive verbs with this ending include -**shwek**- 'tie up (someone with something)', -**yínik**- 'name (someone some name)', -**hògek**- 'put (garment, etc. on someone)'.

In (10.39) someone is about to tie a headcloth over a woman's eyes against her will. The verb -**shwek**- 'tie up' takes a malefactive object prefix, **kú**- 'you' and an instrumental object, **íkítámbálà** 'headcloth'.

(10.39)

| s o¹ V | O² |
|---|---|
| Tú-gá-<u>kú</u>-shwèk-á \| | í=kí-támbálà. |
| 1PL-F2-O2.SG-tie-Fa | AU=7-headcloth |

'We will tie you | (with) a headcloth.' (201 026)

In (10.40) the O¹ is left-dislocated and is referred to again as a cl. 3 object prefix **gù**- 'it' within the verb **ànágùyínìkà** 'and she named it'. The O² **í-zīīnà (lyà) Kíjōkà-bàgòòzì** 'name (of) Kijoka bagoozi' is a compound object. The verb -**yínik**- contains the impositive extension -**ik**.

(10.40)

| O¹ | | s o¹ V | O² | |
|---|---|---|---|---|
| Yùgwó | mújōkà \|\| | à-ná-gù-yínìk-à | í-zīīnà \|\| | Kíjōkà-bàgòòzì. |
| that.N+3 | 3-snake | 1-SQ-O3-give.name-Fa | 5-name | kijoka-bagoozi |

'That snake || she gave it the name || Kijoka-bagoozi.' (633 006)

The verb -**shúlik**- 'hit' also ends with the frozen impositive extension -**ik**. In (10.41) this verb is followed first by O¹, the receiver of the action, **yìkyó kíshégèshè** 'that.N hedgehog' which, in turn, is followed by O², the instrumental object **í=ngóní ígánà** 'a hundred (strokes of a) stick'.

(10.41)

| | | | s V |
|---|---|---|---|
| Ú=lú-kwàvù \| | lw-àná-bà-bwír-à \|\| | kwó= | bà-Ø-shúlìk-è |
| AU=11-rabbit | 11-SQ-O2-tell-Fa | CMP= | 2-SBV-hit-Fe |

| O¹ | | O² | |
|---|---|---|---|
| yìkyó | kí-shégèshè \|\| | í=n-góní | í-gánà. |
| that.N+7 | 7-hedgehog | AU=10-stick | 5-hundred |

'And the rabbit | told them || to hit that hedgehog | a hundred [strokes of] the stick.' (09 021)

---

Kifuliiru verbs in which it is found; it is not an "add on" extension in the same sense as the causative or applicative. If the impositive is removed from the verb, the remainder is not a complete verb base. Thus we refer to it as a "frozen" or "lexicalized" extension, and it is not glossed separately from the verb root.

## 10.1 Syntactic structure of independent clauses

In (10.42) the incorporated $O^1$ is the receiver of the action. As the boy, referred to in the verb by the cl. 1 object prefix **mú**- 'him' pretends to sleep, his grandmother plots against him. The $O^2$ is the instrument, **ú=mùgózì** 'rope'. The verb -**hògek**- ends with the impositive extension -**ek**.

(10.42)

| S | | s o¹ V | | |
|---|---|---|---|---|
| Á-ká-yùvw-á | náákùlù | ‖ à-kòlà | mú | mú-hòg-ék-á |
| 1-P2-feel-Fa | his.grandmother | 1-NEWLY | PROG | O1-put.on-NEU-Fa |

| $O^2$ | Oblique | |
|---|---|---|
| ú=mù-gózì | mw-í= | gósì. |
| AU=3-rope | 18-5= | neck |

'He felt his grandmother ‖ putting a rope on him | around his neck.' (18 023)

In (10.43) we see the very same verb which was used in (10.42) with the object prefix **mú**- 'him' representing the malefactive object. In (10.43), the instrumental object, **mùgózì** 'rope' is the $O^1$ object, represented in the verb by the cl. 3 object prefix **gù**-. The $O^2$ **náákùlù** 'his grandmother' is now the malefactive object, represented by the NP following the verb.[12]

(10.43) À-ná-hòg-ól-à       yùgwó   mù-gózì   mw-í=   gósí   ly-à-gè ‖
1-SQ-put.around-RV.T-Fa   that.N+3   3-rope   18-5=   neck   5-A.M-1

| s o¹ V | $O^2$ |
|---|---|
| à-ná-gù-hòg-ék-à | ‖ náákùlù. |
| 1-SQ-O3-put.on-IMPS-Fa | his.grandmother |

'And he took that rope off from his neck ‖ and put it on | his grandmother.' (18 025)

### 10.1.3 Obliques

The obliques (i.e. non-nuclear arguments dealing with time, location, instrument, accompaniment, manner, and comparison) are sometimes presented before the clause nucleus (e.g. with temporal points of departure), and in

---

[12] Information structure constraints determine which object is incorporated and which is represented by a NP. The new, focused, information must come in the final position of the clause, while the old, less focal information is downplayed, in this case by pronominalization and incorporation. In (10.43) this focal information is that the one who now has a rope on her neck is the scheming grandma!

other cases they are presented after it. In Kifuliiru the obliques are never found within the clause core, with the exception of a handful of special adverbs.

### 10.1.3.1 Time obliques

Time can be expressed by oblique phrases occurring either at the left or the right of the verbal clause nucleus. If found to the left of the nucleus, these time phrases are functioning as a point of departure (10.2.4).

Some time phrases occur only AT THE BEGINNING OF A CLAUSE, as a point of departure. This is seen in (10.44) where **lyêryô** 'right then is' positioned at the beginning of the clause. Other time phrases normally occurring at the beginning of the clause include **háàhô** 'right then'.

(10.44)

| PoD | S | | | V |
|---|---|---|---|---|
| <u>Lyê-ry-ô</u> \| | ìyó | m-bóngó | ná-yò \|\| | y-àná-náàk-à |
| E-5-right.then | that.N+9 | 9-gazelle | ADD.P-9 | 9-SQ-sass-Fa |

'Right then | that gazelle and IT ALSO || sassed:...' (21 003)

Phrases involving **lúsìkù** 'day' are also interpreted as being points of departure (PoD). Thus in (10.45) the phrase **ngíìsì lúsìkù** 'each day' is a PoD at the beginning of the clause, preceding the subject.

(10.45)

| PoD | | S | | V | | |
|---|---|---|---|---|---|---|
| <u>Ngíìsì</u> | lú-sìkù \|\| | yàbó | bá-nyérè \|\| | bá-àlì | kìzì | génd-á \| |
| each | 11-day | those.N+2 | 2-girls | 2-P3 | REP | go-Fa |

| | Oblique | |
|---|---|---|
| í=w-à= | kú-shéény-à. | |
| 23=place-A.M= | 15-get.firewood-Fa | |

'Each day || those girls || were habitually going to | the place of firewood.' (617 035)

Most other time phrases can occur EITHER AT THE BEGINNING OR AT THE END OF THE CLAUSE. In (10.46) the adverb **búshìgì** 'at night' occurs preposed before the SV clause nucleus, to remove it from the focus position at the end of the sentence. (For information on focus see 10.2.3.1.)

## 10.1 Syntactic structure of independent clauses

(10.46)

| PoD | | S | V |
|---|---|---|---|
| **Lyê-ry-ô** | **bú-shìgì** ‖ | **w-à=kí-hómà** | **à-ná-yîj-à.** |
| E-5-right.then | 14-night | 1-A.M=7-viper | 1-SQ-come-Fa |

'Right then in the night ‖ viper | came.' (632 080)

In (10.47) the same adverb **búshìgì** 'at night' follows the clause nucleus, where it is in the clause-final position and thus in focus.

(10.47)

| S | V | O | Oblique |
|---|---|---|---|
| **Y-êhè** ‖ | **à-ná-gêndì  gánúúz-á** | **yîshè** | **bú-shìgì**... |
| 1-CTR.P | 1-SQ-GOING  converse-Fa | 1a+his.father | 14-night |

'HE ‖ went and conversed with his father at night...' (23 028)

Some more common temporal adverbs that can be positioned either before or after the clause nucleus include: **bígíngò** 'yesterday', **búnò** 'now', **búshìgì** 'night', **bwóbùnò** 'right now', **kàbìgìngwê** 'afternoon', **kálèngé-rēngè** 'noon', **kárê** 'long time ago', **kéèrà** 'long time ago', **kú=lúkùlâ** 'early in the morning', **kú=mbàzì** 'at call of the roosters', **kúshēēzì** 'tomorrow', **músásà** 'early morning'.

### 10.1.3.2 Location obliques

Oblique phrases can also express location. Location phrases are most frequently found to the right of the clause nucleus. For example in (10.48) **mú=yàkó kāāyà** 'into that.N village' tells where Bikoba went.

(10.48)

| S | V | Oblique | | |
|---|---|---|---|---|
| **Ùyó  Bíkòbà** ‖ | **à-ná-gênd-à** | **mú=** | **yàkó** | **kā-āyà.** |
| that.N+1  Bikoba | 1-SQ-go-Fa | 18= | that.N+12 | 12-village |

'That Bikoba ‖ went into that village.' (07 008)

In some cases oblique phrases are represented by locative pronouns, in which case they directly follow the verb. In (10.49) the cl. 16 clitic pronoun **=ho** in the phrase **ànáhíkà=hô** 'and he arrived there' refers to a location that has already been mentioned.

(10.49)

| S | V | Oblique |  |  |
|---|---|---|---|---|
| Kéré ‖ | à-ná-hík-à | =hô ‖ | à-ná-gwân-à | kéèrà |
| 1a+Frog | 1-SQ-arrive-Fa | =16 | 1-SQ-encounter-Fa | ALREADY |

**y-à-gàngábál-à.**
9-P1-be.tired.out-Fa

'The frog | arrived there ‖ and he encountered it has already got very tired.' (21 027)

Locative obliques can also be pronominally expressed by other locative class agreements (cl. 17, cl. 18, and cl. 23). In (10.50) the cl. 23 **í** agreement is the initial element in the phrase **yé=byó=kúlyá** 'there, food'.[13] It refers back to the previous phrase **í=mwá=yìhyó híkólò** 'at the home of that.N monkey'.

(10.50)

| S | | V | Oblique | |
|---|---|---|---|---|
| Ìyó | n-góónà ‖ | y-àná-kìzì génd-á | ngíìsì | lú-sìkú |
| that.N+9 | 9-crocodile | 9-SQ-REP go-Fa | each | 11-day |

| Oblique | | | |
|---|---|---|---|
| í= | mw-á= | yìhyó | hí-kólò ‖ |
| 23= | place-A.M= | that.N+19 | 19-little.monkey |

| Conj | s V | Oblique | O |
|---|---|---|---|
| gírà | ì-Ø-géndì yábíír-á | y-é= | by-ókúlyà. |
| so.that | 9-SBV-GOING take-Fa | 23-AU= | 8-food |

'That crocodile ‖ habitually went every day to the home of that monkey ‖ in order to go and get | food there.' (12 013)

In (10.51) the cl. 18 **mwo** at the end of the phrase **yànásíngòòkèrá=mwò** 'and it burned up in there' refers back to the previous phrase **mú=yùgwó múlírò** 'in that.N fire'.

---

[13] The previous reference marker here is -**o**, just as in the previous example, but coalescence between the **o** and the augment of the following word results in the change from **o** to **e**. Without coalescence, the sequence would be **ìgéndí yàbíírá yò=í=byókúlyà** (lit.) 'that it go receive there food'.

10.1 Syntactic structure of independent clauses

(10.51)

| s V | Oblique | s V |
|---|---|---|
| **Y-àná-tíbùk-ír-à** | **mú=** **yùgwó** **mú-lírò** ‖ | **y-àná-síngòòk-èr-á** |
| 9-SQ-fall-APL-Fa | 18= that.N+3 3-fire | 9-SQ-burn-APL-Fa |

| Oblique |
|---|
| **=mwò**. |
| =18 |

'And it fell into that fire ‖ and it burned up in there.' (20 025)

The cl. 16 locative pronoun **ho** is often used as an "empty" referent to communicate general existence, having nothing to do with previous locational reference. In (10.52) the verb **bàtàkírí=hò** 'they are no longer there' is used to show that the old men no longer exist.

(10.52)

| S | s V | Oblique |
|---|---|---|
| **Á=bá-shààjá á-bá-àlì gì-y-íj-ì** ‖ | **bà-tà-kírí** | **=hò** ‖ |
| AU=2-old.men S.R-2-P3 O9-know-RS-Fi | 2-NEG-is.PERS | =16 |

| Adv | s V |
|---|---|
| **kéèrà** ǀ | **bá-ká-yìt-w-â.** |
| ALREADY | 2-P2-kill-PS-Fa |

'The old men who knew it ‖ no longer exist ‖ already ǀ they were killed.' (23 025)

### 10.1.3.3 Instrument obliques

Instrument is sometimes expressed by an oblique phrase beginning with the conjunctive **na=**. This is seen in (10.53), where **ná=mábòkò gààgè** 'with his hands' is the instrument phrase.

(10.53)

| S | s V |
|---|---|
| **Ùyó** **mú-ndu** ‖ | **à-ná-gì-dàh-à** |
| that.N+1 1-person | 1-SQ-O9-gather.honey-Fa |

| Oblique | | |
|---|---|---|
| **n-á=** | **má-bòkò** | **gà-à-gè.** |
| CNJ-AU= | 6-hands | 6-A.M-1 |

'That man ‖ gathered the honey with his hands.' (Jdg 14:9)

### 10.1.3.4 Accompaniment obliques

Accompaniment, like instrument, can be expressed by the conjunctive **na** plus complement. In (10.54) the person is going home with his hoe on his shoulder.

(10.54)

| s V | | Adverb |
|---|---|---|
| À-ná-táàh-à \| à-kòlà | | mu-lindi-mulindi ‖ |
| 1-SQ-go.home-Fa 1-be.NEWLY | | 3-quick-RDP |

| Oblique¹ | | Oblique² | |
|---|---|---|---|
| **n-e=** **fuka y-a-ge** \| | | **há=** | **lú-tùgò.** |
| CNJ-AU= 9+hoe 9-A.M-1 | | 16= | 11-upper.back |

'And he went home | he is now in a hurry ‖ with his hoe | on (his) back.' (28 016)

### 10.1.3.5 Manner obliques

There are various adverbs which express manner: e.g. **dúbà** 'quickly', **múlîndì** 'fast', **bwîjâ** 'well', etc. Their default position is following the verb.

Manner can also be expressed by a phrase beginning with the conjunctive **na**. In (10.55) the wedding guests spent all day **ní=shálì** 'with hunger'.

(10.55)

| S | | s V | Oblique | |
|---|---|---|---|---|
| **Yàbó** | **bá-génì** ‖ | **bà-ná-shíìb-à** | **n-í=** | **shálì.** |
| those.N+2 | 2-guests | 2-SQ-spend.day-Fa | CNJ-AU+5= | hunger |

'Those wedding guests ‖ spent the day hungry.' (34 020)

### 10.1.3.6 Comparison obliques

A comparison phrase can be formed with **ngá** 'like'. In (10.56) the phrase **ngá= mw-ānà** 'like a child' compares the friend to a person behaving like a child.

(10.56)

|  |  |  |  | s V |
|---|---|---|---|---|
| **É=** **máàshì** | **mw-ìrá** | **w-à-nì** | ‖ **sí=** | **w-à-b-á** |
| O= for.goodness.sake | 1-friend | 1-A.M-1SG | OBV= | 2SG-P1-become-Fa |

Oblique

**ngá=** **mw-ānà!**
like= 1-child

'Oh for goodness sake my friend ‖ it's obvious you've become like a child.' (12 025)

### 10.1.4 Polar questions

In Kifuliiru there are many ways of asking questions. Some employ interrogative pronouns and therefore are discussed under interrogative pronouns (see 3.4). However, polar questions do not use an interrogative pronoun, and apply instead to an entire clause. They are therefore discussed here under clauses.

In (10.57) a question marker **ká** precedes the verb phrase **bìkwíríìrì ú=kúyītà** 'it is fitting to kill…'.

(10.57)

|  | P Ques | s V |  |
|---|---|---|---|
| **É=** **mw-āmì** ‖ | **ká=** | **bì-kwír-îr-ì** | **ú=kú-yìt-á** ǀ |
| O= 1-king | Q= | 8-is.right-RS-Fi | AU=15-kill-Fa |

O

**ú-ká-kú-būt-à?**
S.R+1-P2-O2.SG-give.birth-Fa

'O King ‖ is it right to kill ǀ the one who gave birth to you?' (23 044)

In (10.58) the question marker **ka** is placed just before the verb phrase=**tàlì mú=yùvwá í=shònì** 'is she not feeling shame', while the NP naming the clause subject **Ùyú múkàzì** 'this.P woman' is preposed before the question marker.

(10.58)

|  |  | P Ques | V |  | C |
|---|---|---|---|---|---|
| **Ù-yú** | **mú-kàzì** ǀ | **k-à=** | **tà-lì** **mú=** | **yùvw-á** ǀ | **í=shònì?** |
| 1-this.P | 1-woman | Q-1= | NEG-is PROG= | feel-Fa | AU=9+shame |

'This woman ǀ is she not feeling shame?' (18 011)

## 10.2 Information structure

This section examines information structure, vis-à-vis various "sentence articulations." These include topic-comment articulation (10.2.3), presentational articulation (10.2.5), and identificational articulation (10.2.6), all as used by Andrews (1985) and Lambrecht (1994). Each of these articulations can be preceded by points of departure (PoD) (10.2.4) as used by Levinsohn (2005). Another relevant notion is the dominant focal element (DFE) (10.2.3.1) developed by Levinsohn (2005). Pauses can serve to isolate the above information structure constituents for the hearer. Pauses can also slow down the sentence for rhetorical purposes.

The issues of information structure tend to affect one another, making it difficult to discuss one topic without including the others. While keeping repetition to a minimum, we divide this discussion into three sections: First is a summary of information structure definitions (with examples), as well as an overview of the function of pauses. Following that, information structure is presented in more detail.

In writing Kifuliiru, the message (information) must be structured with great care if the text is to communicate clearly and naturally. The importance of this issue cannot be overemphasized, as it affects clause and sentence construction at every turn.

### 10.2.1 Summary of information structure terminology

There are three distinct SENTENCE ARTICULATIONS.[14] A sentence articulation is "the way that the information in a sentence is presented" Levinsohn (2005:NARR02). The three articulations are topic-comment (often with dominant focal element), presentational, and identificational. A point of departure can precede each one of them.

A referent is interpreted as the TOPIC of a proposition if in a given situation the proposition is construed as being *about* this referent, i.e. as expressing information which is relevant to, and which increases the addressee's knowledge of this referent (Andrews 1985:77, Lambrecht 1994:131). A topic usually consists of *established* information that the hearer has already heard something about.

The COMMENT is the information given about the topic (Andrews 1985:77). In (10.59) the topic (the established referent) **ùyó mùtàbánà** 'that.N young man' is at the beginning of the clause, while **ànáhíndùkà ngúlúbè** 'he changed into a pig' is the comment at the end, increasing the addressee's knowledge about

---

[14]Though this chapter is about clauses, we include here sentence articulations because a minimal sentence consists of a single clause. Many sentences, of course, comprise more than a single clause, but in even many of these, the additional element is less than a complete clause, e.g. a point of departure may consist of a simple noun or NP.

## 10.2 Information structure

the referent. Note that in (10.59) all information within the comment is of equal importance, with none of it being isolated from the rest by a pause. That is, the verb **ànáhíndùkà** 'and he turned into' is presented as equally important as the object **ngúlúbè** 'pig'.

(10.59)

| PoD/topic | | Comment |
|---|---|---|
| Ùyó | mú-tàbánà ‖ | à-ná-hínduk-à n-gúlúbè. |
| that.N+1 | 1-young.man | 1-SQ-change-Fa 9-pig |

'That young man ‖ changed into a pig.' (01 025)

The DOMINANT FOCAL ELEMENT (DFE) is defined as *the portion of the comment that is more important* than the rest. The notion was called DFE by Heimerdinger (1999:167). Levinsohn (2005:NARR04) further developed the idea. In Kifuliiru the DFE is typically isolated in two ways: (a) by being positioned right at the very end of the clause and (b) by being preceded by a short pause. This means that if there is an important new element in the clause, it will typically be introduced at the very end of a topic-comment clause.

In (10.60) the topic/point of departure of the sentence is the already-mentioned NP **Ùyó múshósì** 'that.N man', followed by a long pause. The new information in the comment is **ànágêndà, í=mwàbòvyàlà** 'he went to the in-laws' place'. In this case there is a short pause before **í= mwàbòvyàlà** 'at the place of the in-laws', to isolate it as the DFE, and thus to mark it as especially important.

(10.60)

| PoD/topic | | Comment, with post-pause DFE | |
|---|---|---|---|
| Ùyó | mú-shósì ‖ | à-ná-gênd-á \| í= | mw-à-bò-vyàlà. |
| that.N+1 | 1-man | 1-SQ-go-Fa | 23= place-A.M-2-in.law |

'That man ‖ went \| to the place of the in-laws.' (111 007)

The POINT OF DEPARTURE (PoD) designates an element that is placed at the beginning of a clause or sentence, and that has a dual function:

1. It establishes a starting point for the communication.
2. It cohesively anchors the subsequent clause(s) to something which is already in the context (i.e. to something accessible in the hearer's mental representation) (Levinsohn 2005:NARR03).

When there is more than one PoD in a single sentence, the first one often indicates "the primary basis for relating the sentence to its context" (Levinsohn 2000:11). Two types of PoD are especially common in Kifuliiru: the temporal PoD and the referential PoD.

In (10.61) the first comment shown, **Bànáshòkólà í=njírà** 'and they set off on the path', sets the scene for the next sentence. Thus the temporal dependent clause **Ìrí bákáhíká há=lwījì** 'when they arrived at the river' looks back to the fact that they had already set out, and is also a starting pointing for the new sentence.

(10.61)

| Comment[1] | | PoD | | | |
|---|---|---|---|---|---|
| Bà-ná-shòkól-à | í=n-jírà. ‖ | Ìrí | bá-ká-hík-á | há= | lw-ījì ‖ |
| 2-SQ-set.out-Fa | AU=9-path | when | 2-P2-arrive-Fa | 16= | 11-river |

| Topic | | Comment[2] | | |
|---|---|---|---|---|
| ùyó | mú-nyérè | à-ná-bwîr-à | uyó | mú-tàbánà:... |
| that.N+1 | 1-girl | 1-SQ-tell-Fa | that.N+1 | 1-young.man:... |

'They set out on the path. ‖ When they arrived at the river ‖ that girl told that young man:...' (612 012 )

In (10.62) the already mentioned participants **yàbó bákìnì** 'those dancers' are the referential point of departure, as well as the topic.

(10.62)

| PoD/topic | |
|---|---|
| Yàbó | bá-kìnì ‖ |
| those.N+2 | 2-dancers |

| Comment | | |
|---|---|---|
| bà-ná-háá-bw-à | í=by-ámbálwá \| | í-bì-shúsh-ììn-ì... |
| 2-SQ-give-PS-Fa | AU=8-clothing | S.R-8-resemble-RCP+RS-Fi |

'Those dancers ‖ were given clothes \| that resembled each other...' (36 047 )

IDENTIFICATIONAL articulation involves "a proposition that, except for one element, is assumed to be known." There is then focus on the element that was lacking in the presupposed proposition (Andrews 1985:79).

In (10.63) it is presupposed that something will come out of the pregnancy of the woman. The NP in focus is **bìnó bígógò** 'these husks of banana stems'. The question is asked: 'Are these husks of banana stems what have come out of this my pregnant belly?' (This form of this sentence is a bit abbreviated, as the **ka** question marker is not explicitly stated.)

## 10.2 Information structure

(10.63)

| Focus | | |
|---|---|---|
| **Bì-nó** | **bí-gógó ‖** | |
| 8-this.P.C | 8-banana.stem | |

| | Presupposition | | | | |
|---|---|---|---|---|---|
| **by-ó=** | **by-à-sháág-à** | \| | **mú=** | **lì-nó** | **bûndà?** |
| 8-FOC | 8-P1-come.out-Fa | | 18= | 5-this.P.C | 5+pregnancy |

'(Are) these husks of banana stems ‖ that have come out | of this pregnant belly?' (201 034 )

A sentence has PRESENTATIONAL articulation if it introduces a new entity into a text without linking its introduction "to an already established topic or to some presupposed proposition" (Andrews 1985:80, see also Lambrecht 1994:144).

In Kifuliiru, presentational articulation is commonly realized by the use of a locative subject prefix on the verb, often without a specific preceding locative phrase referent. In (10.64) this is exemplified by the cl. 16 **há** prefix on the verb **háàlì**. The verb then precedes the new entity introduced at the end of the clause. The new entity presented is **múnyéré múgùmà** 'one girl', which occurs in the focus position at the end of the sentence.

(10.64)

| Non-established | | New entity | |
|---|---|---|---|
| **Há-àlì** **rì-ìr-í** | | **mú-nyéré** | **mú-gùmà.** |
| 16-P3 is-RS-Fi | | 1-girl | 1-one |

'There was one girl.' (103 003 )

PREPOSING is "the MOVEMENT of a CONSTITUENT to a POSITION earlier in the SENTENCE" (Crystal 2003:368).

In (10.65) **nyínà** 'his mother' is preposed from its default position just before the verb **ànágêndà** 'she went' and is repositioned as the primary PoD for the sentence.

(10.65)

| PoD¹/topic | PoD² |
|---|---|
| **Nyínà** ‖ | bw-àná-ky-à \| |
| 1a+the.mother | 14-SQ-day.break-Fa |

| Comment |
|---|
| à-ná-gênd-à \|   í=   mûndà   ù-lyá   Kízìmù-ngárà. |
| 1-SQ-go-Fa   23=   place.of   1-that.R   kizimu-ngara |

'The mother ‖ and it dawned | and she went | to the place of that Kizimungara.' (303 033)

POSTPOSING is the movement of a constituent to a position later in the sentence.

In (10.66) the default order of the clause is **bàngá bàlí mú=yó mwānà** 'how many are within that.N child?' Since **ùyó mwānà** 'that.N child' is already established information (observe the previous reference marker **o** in **ùyó**), and since **bàngâ** 'how many' is the new information which needs to be positioned at the end of the sentence, the two constituents are switched, leaving the established information, **ùyó mwānà** 'that.N child', as the PoD/topic and **àlí mwó=bàngâ** 'she has in her how many' as the comment.

(10.66)

| PoD/topic | | Comment | |
|---|---|---|---|
| **Ùyó** | mw-ānà ‖ | à-lì mwó= | bà-ngâ? |
| that.N+1 | 1-child | 1-is 18 | 2-how.many |

'That child ‖ has how many in her?' (303 040)

PROMOTION TO OBJECT involves "a construction in which an oblique element is promoted to the role of an object, with the verb inflected[15] to show that it has this status...This term was coined with reference to Bantu languages" (Matthews 1997).

In Kifuliiru, the object of an oblique phrase may be promoted to the role of object, and thus marked by a prefix in the verb. The locative marker which was the head of the oblique phrase is pronominalized by the addition of the previous reference marker (-**e** / -**o**), and cliticized to the end of the verb, or to the following word if there is one.

The default sentence order of (10.67) would be **nyândì úgábwàtàlà kú=kítûmbì?** 'Who (is the one who) will sit on the chair?' However, the chair

---

[15] Rather than "inflected" it would be more accurate to say that the verb is sometimes "marked" to show that the oblique has been promoted to object. This marking may be a derivational extension in the verb base (VB), or it may be (instead or in addition) an object marker prefix preceding the VB.

## 10.2 Information structure

in the case of (10.67) is not focal, and therefore should not be positioned at the end of the sentence. Thus it is "promoted to object," and so indicated by the prefix **kì-** within the verb, leaving the locative clitic **ku** to be pronominalized and attached to the end of the verb as **kwo**. This construction maintains the relative verb form as the point in focus at the end of the sentence.

(10.67)

| Topic | Comment |
|---|---|
| **Nyândì** | **ú**-gá-**kì**-bwàtàl-à=**kwô**? |
| who | S.R+1-F2-O7-sit-Fa=17 |

'Who will sit on it?' (47 008)

### 10.2.2 Pauses

Pauses are a pervasive feature of Kifuliiru. In independent clauses, they occur in virtually every clause, usually more than once, and with a predictable relation to information structure. Since pause plays such a crucial role in this language, all clause and sentence examples in this book have been carefully marked to show the pauses.[16]

#### 10.2.2.1 Places where pauses are typically found

(a) Except in very rare cases, the clause topic is always followed by a pause. This is typically the longest pause in the clause, and separates established information on the left from new information on the right. This pause occurs in both deliberate speech and in fast speech.[17]

In (10.68) there is a long pause between the topic NP **ùlyá mútàbánà** 'that.R young man' and the comment which follows in the remainder of the sentence.

(10.68)

| Topic | | Comment | | |
|---|---|---|---|---|
| **Ù-lyá** | **mú-tàbánà** ‖ | à-ná-yàm-à \| | á-gá-shààg-à | yà-hô. |
| 1-that.R | 1-young.man | 1-SQ-IMMED-Fa | 1-F2-leave-Fa | there.N-16 |

'That young man ‖ immediately | left there.' (112 049)

---

[16] In slower, deliberate speech (which is followed in most of the examples of this book), long pauses are defined as being of at least one-half second (but often longer). They are marked with double vertical lines ( ‖ ). Short pauses of less than about one-half second are marked with a single vertical line ( | ). Of course general speech speed affects the length of the pauses, which can be longer in deliberate speech than they are in fast speech. In addition, some pauses that occur in deliberate speech do not occur in quick speech. Nevertheless, pauses in general do obtain at all speech speeds, triggered by information structure constraints.

[17] In *very* fast speech, it is difficult to perceive any but the very longest pauses. When an attempt is made to make the rate of speech more moderate, however, the placement of pauses is quite predictable.

(b) Within a comment, a short pause is often employed to help isolate a dominant focal element (10.2.3.1.).

In (10.69) the DFE consists of the locative phrase **í=rànda** 'outside the village'. It is marked as DFE in two ways: by being positioned at the end of the clause, and by being preceded by a short pause.

(10.69)

| Topic | | Comment | |
|---|---|---|---|
| Ùyó | mú-tàbánà ‖ | à-ná-génd-àg-à \| | í= rànda. |
| that.N+1 | 1-young.man | 1-SQ-go-EMP-Fa | 23= outside.of.village |

'That young man | he went | outside of the village.' (112 006)

(c) Besides being used to isolate the DFE (see above paragraph), one or more pauses can also be employed to slow down the information flow of the comment. Since these pauses cannot all mark one "dominant" element, we assume that in such cases pauses are used for rhetorical effect, to lead the listener to slow down and absorb what is happening. Such slowing occurs especially (but not exclusively) at key turning points in a narrative, whether at the beginning of the story when the story theme is first introduced, or near the climax of the story.

The example in (10.70) is taken from a climactic point in a narrative. The comment here contains two pauses, one before **kwí=gosi** 'at the neck' and one before **lyé=yó ngáàvù** 'of that.N cow'.

(10.70) PoD/topic

Í=n-dàrè |
AU=9-lion

| Comment | | | |
|---|---|---|---|
| y-àná-símb-ìr-à \| | kw-í= gósí \| | ly-ê= yó | n-gáàvù. |
| 9-SQ-jump-APL-Fa | 17-5= neck | 5-A.M= that.N+9 | 9-cow |

'The lion | jumped | on the neck | of that cow.' (11 039)

In (10.71) the auxiliary -**ba** 'become' is followed by a pause, before the verb form **áàlí rììrí** 'he was' that follows. This is followed by another pause, before **kíshììrìrì** 'big-mouth'. This clause is key to the theme of the story, as it introduces the thematic character (and the theme itself).

## 10.2 Information structure

(10.71)

| Topic | | Comment | |
|---|---|---|---|
| Mú-gùmà \| | à-ná-b-à \| | á-àlí rì-ìr-í \|\| | kí-shììrìrì. |
| 1-one | 1-SQ-become-Fa | 1-P3 is-RS-F | 7-big-mouth |

'And one | had become | he was || big-mouth.' (503 005)

In the post-climactic section found in (10.72) the comment has two short pauses. One pause comes before **ágáshààgà yàhô** 'he is (intentionally) leaving there' and the other is before **ná=yàbó bándù** 'with those people'.

(10.72)

| PoD/topic | | Comment | | |
|---|---|---|---|---|
| Ù-lyá mú-tàbánà \|\| | à-ná-yàm-à \| | á-gá-shààg-à | yà-hô \| |
| 1-that.R 1-young.man | 1-SQ-IMMED-Fa | 1-F2-leave-Fa | there.N-16 |

| Comment (con't) | |
|---|---|
| ná= yàbò | bá-ndù. |
| CNJ= those.N+2 | 2-people |

'That young man || immediately | intentionally left there | with those people.' (112 049)

In the pre-climactic section in (10.73), the verb phrase **ànátòndéérà ú=kúlírírà** 'and she began to cry for' is broken up by a pause after **ànátòndéérà**. A second pause occurs before **ú=mwàná wàgè** 'her child'.

(10.73)

| Topic | | Comment | |
|---|---|---|---|
| W-à-n-gáàvù \|\| | à-ná-tòndéér-á \| | ú=kú-lír-ír-á \| |
| 1-A.M-9-cow | 1-SQ-began-Fa | AU=15-cry-APL-Fa |

| Comment (con't) | |
|---|---|
| ú=mw-àná | w-à-gè. |
| AU=1-child | 1-A.M-1 |

'The cow || began | to cry for | her child.' (105 036)

In (10.74) the verb phrase **ànáyîjà àgwétí ágábòdòkà** 'and he came (intentionally) hopping' is split by two pauses. Once again, this is in the pre-climactic section.

(10.74)

| Topic | | |
|---|---|---|
| Ùyó | W-á=kèrè | ná-yè \| |
| that.N+1 | 1-A.M-1a+frog | ADD.P-1 |

| Comment | | |
|---|---|---|
| à-ná-yîj-à | \| à-gwétí \| | á-gá-bòdòk-à. |
| 1-SQ-COMING-Fa | 1-PROG | 1-INTL-small.hop-Fa |

'That frog and HE ALSO | came | (intentionally) | hopping.' (104 011)

In (10.75) the comment is split up three times, once by a pause after **yànásìgálà** 'and it remained', once after **ìgwétì** 'PROG' and once before **á=másù** 'eyes'. This clause occurs in the denouement of the story, where the lion realizes the outcome of his actions, as all of the animals that once served him have run off into the bush and are now nowhere to be seen.

(10.75)

| Comment | | | |
|---|---|---|---|
| Y-àná-sìgál-á | \| ì-gwétì \| | í-gá-lyégùùz-â | \| á=má-sù. |
| 9-SQ-REMAINING-Fa | 9-PROG | 9-INTL-focusing.intently-Fa | AU=6-eyes |

'And it remained | intentionally | intently focusing | its eyes.' (16 024)

### 10.2.2.2 *Places where pauses are typically lacking*

(a) Pauses are not normally found within points of departure (PoD), since PoDs involve old information. This is true even when they consist of a fairly long dependent clause, such as **ìrí ákálángíízá yìkyó kítì mú=ndálò** 'when he looked at that.N tree in the field'. There is a pause *following* the PoD, however, to mark it off from the rest of the sentence.

In (10.76) the object of the dependent clause **yìkyó kítì** 'that.N tree' is not preceded by a pause, nor is the oblique **mú=ndálò** 'in the field' preceded by a pause. If these had occurred in an independent clause, however, there would almost certainly have been at least one pause in those positions.

## 10.2 Information structure

(10.76)

| PoD/topic | | | | | |
|---|---|---|---|---|---|
| **Ìrí** | **á-ká-lángííz-á** | **yìkyó** | **kí-tì** | **mú=** | **n-dálò \|** |
| when | 1-P2-look.at-Fa | that.N+7 | 7-tree | 18= | 9-field |

| Comment | |
|---|---|
| **à-ná-hàmágál-à** | **kwókùnô:...** |
| 1-SQ-call-Fa | ‹quote.MARKED› |

'When he looked at that tree in the field | he called thus:...' (626 008)

In (10.77) each of the two sentences has a dependent clause, both ending with **îtwè** 'head': **mángò ngúshúlìkà îtwè** 'when I hit you (with my) head' and **ìrí ákáshúlíká îtwè** 'when he hit (with his) head'. In neither case is the object **îtwè** 'head' isolated by a preceding pause, since it occurs in a clause which is a PoD.

(10.77)

| PoD | | | Comment | |
|---|---|---|---|---|
| **Mángó** | **n-gú-shúlìk-à** | **î-twè** ‖ | **ú-gá-yàmî** | **fw-à!** |
| when | 1SG-O2.SG-hit-Fa | 5-head | 2SG-F2-IMMED | die-Fa |

'When I hit you with my head ‖ you will immediately die!' (626 012)

| PoD | | | Topic | Comment |
|---|---|---|---|---|
| **Ìrí** | **á-ká-shúlík-á** | **î-twè** ‖ | **ná-lyò \|** | **ly-àná-gwât-à.** |
| when | 1-P2-hit-Fa | 5-head | ADD.P-5 | 5-SQ-seize-Fa |

'When he hit him with the head ‖ and IT ALSO | stuck.' (626 013)

In (10.78) the DFE **kú=kítì** 'on the tree' is preceded by a pause in the first independent clause **(híkóló) hyànáshònérà, kú=kítì** 'and it (monkey) climbed on the tree'. However, within the PoD which follows, this same phrase is not preceded by a pause.

(10.78)    Comment
**Hy-àná-shòn-ér-a | kú= kí-tì.** ||
19-SQ-climb-APL-Fa  17=  7-tree

              PoD
**ìrí    hí-ká-shòn-ér-á    kú=    kí-tì** ||
when  19-P2-climb-APL-Fa   17=   7-tree

                Topic
**tw-é=   nô= yó    dáàtá    w-à-nî** |
1PL-FOC= CNJ= that.N+1 1a+father 1-A.M-1SG

        Comment
**tw-àná-tóòl-à  |  á=má-búyè.**
1PL-SQ-pick.up-Fa  AU=6-rocks

'And it (monkey) climbed | the tree. || When it had climbed on the tree || I and that paternal uncle of mine | picked up | stones.' (635 005-6)

(b) Pauses are not found in instances where the entire comment is in focus. In (10.79) the comment is **ànáyìlàshà mú=kíshūkà** 'he threw himself into the bush'. Here there is no short pause to set off a DFE, since the entire comment (including the 'throwing self') is considered to be of equal importance.

(10.79)   PoD/topic    |         Comment
**Mú-gùmá w-à-bò** | | **à-ná-yì-làsh-à    mú=   kí-shūkà.**
1-one    1-A.M-2    1-SQ-RFX-throw-Fa  18=   7-bush

'One of them || threw himself into the bush.' (01 023)

Likewise in (10.80) both words of the comment **ànáhíndùkà mbóngò** 'and he turned into a gazelle' are equally important. Thus there is no pause to set off the last element of the sentence, **mbóngò** 'gazelle'.

(10.80)   PoD/topic     |      Comment
**Ùyó    mú-tàbánà** || **à-ná-híndùk-à    m-bóngò.**
that.N+1 1-young.man   1-SQ-change.into-Fa 9-gazelle

'That young man || changed into a gazelle.' (01 030)

(c) In extremely rare instances, pauses are absent following the topic when the topic names a minor character who is not the center of attention. In

(10.81) the topic **ú=túbwâ** 'the dogs' represents backgrounded characters who are not actively involved in the theme of the story, and thus is not followed by the default pause. Because the story has been referring to a hunt, **ú=túbwâ** 'dogs' are assumed to be part of the scene. The 'trail/scent' of the monkey, by contrast, is isolated by a pause on either side.

(10.81) PoD/topic

<u>**Ú=tú-bwá**</u>
AU=13-dogs

| Comment | | | |
|---|---|---|---|
| **tù-ná-hèmb-é** ‖ | **í=kí-lálí** \| | **ky-á=** | **hì-ryá hí-kólò.** |
| 13-CON-smell-Fe | AU=7-trail | 7-A.M= | 19-that.R 19-monkey |

'The dogs smelled ‖ the trail | of that monkey.' (635 004)

In (10.82) there is no pause within the clause **í=shúúlí bàgìlàshá íráágò** 'that bull they shot a dart at it', even though **í=shúúlì** 'bull' is a preposed object. That is because the entire clause is backgrounded, relative to the following clause **ú=múkó gwànáyîjà: «Zwírìrìrì»** 'and the blood came: «Gush»', as attention is less on the bull than on the results of shooting an arrow at it.

(10.82) 

| PoD/topic | Comment | |
|---|---|---|
| <u>**Í-shúúlí**</u> | **bà-gì-làsh-á** | **í-ráágò** ‖ |
| 9-bull | 2-O9-throw-Fa | 5-dart |

| PoD/topic | Comment | |
|---|---|---|
| **ú=mú-kó** ‖ | **gw-àná-yîj-à:** ‖ | **«Zwírìrìrì».** |
| AU=3-blood | 3-SQ-come-Fa | gush |

'The bull they shot a dart at it ‖ blood | came: ‖ «Gush».'

### 10.2.3 Topic-comment articulation

In topic-comment articulation, the (more) established information is presented in the topic at the beginning of the sentence, and is set off by a pause that is typically the longest in the clause. The new (or less established) information is presented in the comment at the end of the clause.

In (10.83) the established information, the clause object **yìkyó kítì** 'that.N tree', has been preposed to the front of the clause, where it is now the clause topic, and is therefore followed by a long(er) pause. The new information in the clause comment is **ànákìbùgà kwó=búlémbò** 'he smeared it with gluey sap'. Note that the clause subject is represented by the cl. 1 pronoun prefix a- 'he' on the verb.

(10.83)

| PoD/topic | Comment |
|---|---|
| Yìkyó kí-tì ‖ | à-ná-kì-bùg-à kw-ó= bú-lémbò. |
| that.N+7 7-tree | 1-SQ-O7-smear-Fa 17-AU= 14-sap |

'That tree ‖ he smeared it with gluey sap.' (626 006)

### 10.2.3.1 Comment with optional dominant focal element

In many cases there is also a dominant focal element (DFE), defined as the special part of the comment that is more important than the rest. In Kifuliiru the DFE is isolated in two ways: by being right at the end of the clause and by being preceded by a pause. Often constituents such as object and oblique, whose default position is following the verb, are repositioned leftward from their default positions, so that the DFE can be isolated as the only remaining element at the very end of the clause.

The example in (10.84) demonstrates topic-comment articulation: The clause topic **wà=lúkwàvù** 'rabbit' is at the beginning of the clause and followed by a pause. The comment follows, with the DFE **á=kábémbà** 'peanuts' at the very end of the comment, isolated by a preceding pause.

(10.84)

| PoD[18]/topic | Comment, with post-pause DFE |
|---|---|
| W-à-lú-kwàvù \| | à-ná-yîjí zìmb-á \| á=ká-bémbà. |
| 1-A.M=11-rabbit | 1-SQ-COMING steal-Fa AU=12-peanuts |

'Rabbit | came and stole | the peanuts.' (626 007)

In (10.85) we find the command **ùtákìzì zìmbá á=bánámúfwìrì** 'don't steal from widows'. This command consists of only a comment, including a DFE at the end. In Kifuliiru this sentence says that you should not steal from widows, but it strongly implies that you can steal from anybody else! This implication is due to the positioning of the noun **á=bánámúfwìrì** 'widows', which is here isolated in the DFE position (with preceding pause), and therefore put into focal contrast relative to other possible participants.

(10.85)

| Comment, with post-pause DFE |
|---|
| Ù-tá-kìzì zìmb-á \| á=bá-námúfwìrì. |
| 2SG-NEG-REP steal-Fa AU=2-widows |

'Don't steal from | widows.'

---

[18]In this section, the topic is often also the PoD. That is discussed more fully in (10.2.4).

#### 10.2.3.1.1 Syntactic functions of the dominant focal element

Syntactically, lexical items with many different functions can be placed in the DFE position. These include the clause object, a locative phrase, the main lexical verb separated from the auxiliary, etc.

In (10.86) the DFE **í=kígōhè** 'eyelid', is the clause object. Besides being positioned at the end of the clause, it is also isolated by a preceding short pause.

(10.86)

| PoD/topic | Comment, with post-pause DFE |
|---|---|
| **Ny-ûndâ \|** | **à-ná-gìrím-á \| í=kí-gōhè.** |
| 9-eagle | 1-SQ-wink-Fa AU=7-eyelid |

'The eagle | winked | its eyelid.' (11 038)

In (10.87) the DFE at the end of the clause consists of the locative phrase **mú=yìzó nyámà** 'among those meats', which is isolated by a short pause.

(10.87)

| Topic | Comment, with post-pause DFE |
|---|---|
| **Yùgwó \| mú-zīmù ‖** | **gw-àná-sìgál-ág-á \| mú= yìzó ny-ámà.** |
| that.N+3 3-demon | 3-SQ-remain-EMP-Fa 18= those.N+10 10-meats |

'That demon ‖ remained | among those meats.' (112 050)

It is fairly common for a short pause to follow the verbal auxiliary which precedes an infinitive, thus breaking up the verb phrase and making the main lexical verb (i.e. the infinitive) into a DFE. In (10.88) the auxiliary verb **ànátòndèèrè** 'and he then began' is followed by a short pause, marking the main verb **ú=kúlírà** 'to cry' as a DFE.

(10.88)

| Topic | Comment, with post-pause DFE |
|---|---|
| **Kàshéndwà ‖** | **à-ná-tòndèèr-é \| ú=kú-lír-à.** |
| Kashendwa | 1-CON-begin-Fe AU=15-cry-Fa |

'Kashendwa ‖ then began | to cry.' (43 024)

In (10.89) the verb phrase **yànágéndèrèrà úkúyòbóhà bwènèènè** 'and it continued to fear very much' is split by a pause between the auxiliary **yànágéndèrèrà** 'and it continued' and the lexical verb **ú=kúyòbóhà** 'to fear'.

(10.89)

| PoD | Topic |
|---|---|
| ...hálìkò \|\| | í=n-gáàvù \|\| |
| but | AU=9-cow |

| Comment, with post-pause DFE |
|---|
| y-àná-géndèrèr-à \|   ú=kú-yòbóh-á   bwènèènè. |
| 9-SQ-continued-Fa   AU=15-fear-Fa   very.much |

'...but ‖ the cow ‖ continued | to be very afraid.' (11 011)

## 10.2.4 Point of departure

As noted earlier, the term "point of departure" (PoD) is defined by Levinsohn (2005:NARR03:2) as "an element that is placed at the beginning of a clause or sentence, with a dual function. (a) It establishes a starting point for the communication and (b) it cohesively anchors the subsequent clause(s) to something which is already in the context (i.e. to something accessible in the hearer's mental representation)." (See also Dooley and Levinsohn 2001:68.) The different kinds of PoD below are taken from Levinsohn (2005). A sentence can have more than one point of departure; rarely there can be as many as three.

In Kifuliiru the first point of departure in a clause is typically set off by a long pause which follows it. If there is a second PoD, that is usually set off with a pause as well, although the pause after the second PoD is often shorter. Within a PoD itself there is typically no pause.

### 10.2.4.1 Situational points of departure

One of the situational points of departure is the TEMPORAL POINT OF DEPARTURE, which can be a phrase or a dependent temporal clause. In (10.90) the TEMPORAL NOUN PHRASE **lúsìkù lúgùmà** 'one day' provides a temporal point of departure. Note that this PoD is followed by a long pause, a typical feature of the PoD.

(10.90)

| PoD (temporal) | Topic |
|---|---|
| **Lú-sìkù lú-gùmà** \|\| | î=n-gwí |
| 11-day 11-one | AU=9-leopard |

| Comment |
|---|
| y-àná-gênd-à \|  í-gá-hììv-à   \|  mú=  lú-bākò. |
| 9-SQ-GOING-Fa  9-INTL-hunt-Fa  18=  11-forest |

'One day ‖ the leopard went | hunting | in the forest.' (39 023)

In (10.91) the DEPENDENT TEMPORAL CLAUSE **íkyànyà ákábá kéèrà àhìnjúkà** 'The time when he had already passed ahead' provides the temporal point of departure, and is followed by a long pause. Within the PoD clause itself there is no pause.

(10.91)

| PoD (temporal) | | | | |
|---|---|---|---|---|
| **Í=ky-ànyà** | **á-ká-b-á** | **kéèrà** | **à-hìnjúk-à** | ‖ |
| AU=7-time | 1-P2-be-Fa | ALREADY | 1+P1-pass.ahead-Fa | |

| Topic | | Comment | |
|---|---|---|---|
| **bà-lyá** | **bá-nyéré \|** | **bà-ná-sìgálí** | **búúz-án-i-à:…** |
| 2-those.R | 2-girls | 2-SQ-REMAINING | ask-RCP-CS-Fa |

'At the time he had already passed out of sight ahead ‖ those girls | remaining asked each other:…' (506 046)

In (10.92) the dependent clause **Ìrí híkáshònérá kú=kítì** 'When it had climbed the tree' provides the temporal PoD. Again, there is no pause within the PoD itself.

(10.92)

| PoD (temporal) | | | | |
|---|---|---|---|---|
| **Ìrí** | **hí-ká-shòn-ér-á** | **kú=** | **kí-tì** | ‖ |
| when | 19-P2-climb-APL-Fa | 17= | 7-tree | |

| | Topic | | | |
|---|---|---|---|---|
| **tw-é=** | **nô=** | **yó** | **dáàtá** | **w-à-nî** ‖ |
| 1PL-FOC | CNJ= | that.N+1 | 1a+father | 1-A.M-1SG |

| | Comment | |
|---|---|---|
| **tw-àná-tóòl-á \|** | **á-má-búyè.** | |
| 1PL-SQ-pick.up-Fa | AU=6-rocks | |

'When it (monkey) climbed on the tree ‖ I and that paternal uncle of mine ‖ picked up | rocks.' (635 006)

In (10.93) there are two points of departure, each isolated by a long following pause. The second pause is followed by the topic **ùyó múzûngù** 'that.N white person'.

(10.93)

| PoD¹ | PoD² | |
|---|---|---|
| Ngíìsì lú-sìkù ‖ | í=ky-ànyà ky-à= | ká-lèngé-rèngé ‖ |
| Every 11-day | AU=7-time 7-A.M+AU | 12-noon-RDP |

| Topic | Comment |
|---|---|
| ùyó mú-zûngù (Sw.) | á-àlí kìzì yínàmùk-à. |
| that.N+1 white.man | 1-P3 REP straighten.up-Fa |

'Every day ‖ at the time of noon ‖ that white man ‖ habitually straightened up.' (616 006)

SPATIAL POINTS OF DEPARTURE, although quite rarely used in Kifuliiru, do exist. In (10.94) the phrase **í=wà=kúshéényà** 'at the place of getting firewood' provides the spatial point of departure. In this case the oblique phrase has been preposed from its normal place at the end of the clause, in order to give focal prominence to **mútàbánà múgùmà** 'a certain young man', who is being introduced as a participant in the narrative.

(10.94)

| PoD (Preposed oblique) | | |
|---|---|---|
| Í= | w-à= | kú-shéénya ‖ |
| 23= | place.of-A.M= | 15-get.firewood |

| Comment¹ | | |
|---|---|---|
| tù-lì | mú= gwán-á | ǀ mú-tàbánà |
| 1PL-are | PROG= encounter-Fa | 1-young.man |

| Comment² | | | | | |
|---|---|---|---|---|---|
| mú-gùmà ‖ | à-lì | mú= | kìzí | yíjí | tèg-á | ú=bú-nyúnì. |
| 1-one | 1-is | PROG' | REP | COMING | trap-Fa | AU=14-birds |

'At the place of hunting ‖ we are encountering ǀ one young man ‖ he is habitually coming to trap birds.' (210 075)

There are also CONDITIONAL POINTS OF DEPARTURE, in which the PoD is an adverbial clause of condition. In (10.95) the initial referential PoD (see 10.2.4.2) **nyókókùlù** is followed by a long pause, and then **ìrí àngàlúkà ú=mùgózì** 'your grandmother ‖ if she would weave a rope' provides the conditional point of departure for the command that follows.

10.2 Information structure

(10.95)

| | PoD | | | Topic |
|---|---|---|---|---|
| **Nyókókùlù** | ‖ **ìrí à-ngà-lúk-à** | **ú=mù-gózì** ‖ | | **náà-wé** |
| 1a+your.grandmother | if 1-CND-weave-Fa | AU=3-rope | | ADD.P-2SG |

| | Comment | |
|---|---|---|
| **ù-ná-lúk-é** | **ú=gù-ndì.** | |
| 2SG-CON-weave-Fe | AU=3-other | |

'Your grandmother ‖ if she would weave a rope ‖ and YOU ALSO | you weave another.' (18 018)

Finally, there are REASON POINTS OF DEPARTURE, realized by an adverbial clause of reason. In (10.96) the phrase **bwó=wàdètà kwó=tàkìhììtí í=kyōbà** 'since you say that you no longer have fear' provides the adverbial clause of reason to establish a point of departure for what follows. Note (once again) that this reason clause has no internal pauses.

(10.96)

| | PoD | | |
|---|---|---|---|
| **Bwó=** **w-à-dèt-à** | **kw-ó=** | **tà-kì-hì-ìt-í** | **í=ky-ōbà** ‖ |
| since= 2SG-P1-say-Fa | CMP-2SG= | NEG-PERS-have-RS-Fi | AU=7-fear |

| | Comment | | |
|---|---|---|---|
| **ù-Ø-géndì** | **tù-yìt-ír-á** | **ìyó** | **n-dárè.** |
| 2SG-SBV-GOING | O1.PL-kill-APL-Fa | that.N+9 | 9-lion |

'Since you say that you no longer have fear ‖ go and kill that lion for us.' (609 020)

### 10.2.4.2 Referential points of departure

In Kifuliiru there is widespread use of referential points of departure, in the form of nominal constituents. In (10.97) the subject **gùnó mújōkà ngábūtà** 'this snake (which) I gave birth to', functions as both the PoD and the topic of the sentence. This PoD/topic is set off by a long pause.

(10.97)

| PoD/topic | | |
|---|---|---|
| **Gù-nó** | **mú-jōkà** | **n-gá-būt-à**  ‖ |
| 3-this.P.C | 3-snake | 1SG-P2-give.birth-Fa |

| Comment | |
|---|---|
| **gw-à-málì** | **n-góór-à.** |
| 3-P1-ALREADY | O1.SG-distress-Fa |

'This snake (which) I gave birth to ‖ it has already put me in distress.' (633 014)

In (10.98) the NP **Ùyó múndù** 'that.N person' functions as both the clause topic and the referential PoD, and is followed by a long pause.

(10.98)

| PoD/topic | | Comment | | | |
|---|---|---|---|---|---|
| **Ùyó** | **mú-ndu** ‖ | **à-ná-yàmí** | **yàbíír-á** ǀ | **yìhyó** | **hí-shììshì.** |
| that.N+1 | 1-person | 1-SQ-IMMED | take-Fa | that.N+19 | 19-wagtail |

'That person ‖ he immediately took ǀ that little pied-wagtail bird.' (614 051)

Often the referential PoD NP has been preposed to the front of the sentence. In (10.99) the preposed object NP **yìbyó byóshì** 'all of them' (note the previous reference morpheme **o** in **yìbyó**) provides the point of departure, marked by a long pause which follows.

(10.99)

| PoD/topic | |
|---|---|
| **Yìbyó** | **by-óshì** ‖ |
| those.N+8 | 8-all |

| Comment | | | |
|---|---|---|---|
| **ù-Ø-génd-è** | **w-à-bì-hàmb-à** ǀ | **mú=** | **kí-tútúlúgù.** |
| 2SG-SBV-GOING-Fa | 2SG-P1-O8-put.in-Fa | 18= | 7-big.container |

'All those (things) ‖ you go and put them ǀ in a big container.' (208 056)

In (10.100) the phrase **bìnó byó=kúlyà** 'this food', together with the embedded relative clause **byó=wàtùléétérà** 'which you brought us' provides the topic/point of departure.

## 10.2 Information structure

(10.100) Noun of direct address

**«É yâgà** ‖
O comrade

| | Topic/PoD | | |
|---|---|---|---|
| **bì-nó** | **by-ókúlya** | **by-ó=** | **w-à-tù-léét-ér-à** ‖ |
| 8-this.P.C | 8-food | 8-O.R | 1-P1-O1.PL-bring-APL-Fa |

| Comment | |
|---|---|
| **léèrò** \| | **by-à-mét-èèrèr-á** **bwènèènè!»** |
| this.time | 8-P1-be.tasty-INTS-Fa very.much |

'O comrade ‖ this food which you've brought us ‖ this time around \| it's really tasty!' (12 010)

In (10.101) **ná yàbó bàndì báhììvì** 'and those other hunters' serves as a referential PoD involving renewal of referents referred to previously within the narrative (note the previous reference morpheme **o** in **yàbó**).

(10.101)

| | PoD | | | Topic |
|---|---|---|---|---|
| **Ná=** | **yàbó** | **bà-ndì** | **bá-hììvì** ‖ | **mú-gùmà**\| |
| CNJ= | those.N+2 | 2-other | 2-hunters | 1-one |

| Comment | |
|---|---|
| **á-àlí yì-yìk-ììr-í** \| | **ú=mù-mbátì.** |
| 1-P3 RFX-be.with.food-RS-Fi | AU=3-cassava |

'Those other hunters ‖ one (of them) \| had brought himself \| cassava.' (03 004)

### 10.2.5 Presentational articulation

In presentational articulation, a sentence "introduces a new entity without linking its introduction to an already established topic or to some presupposed proposition" Lambrecht (1994:144).

In (10.102) the surface subject is marked on the verb by the cl. 16 prefix **ha-**, which stands here for existence (and not for any specific location). The new entity which is being introduced without being linked to an established topic is **mwàmí múgùmà nà=múkáàgè** 'one king and his wife'.

(10.102)

| Loc. prefix on verb | | New entity | | | |
|---|---|---|---|---|---|
| **Há**-àlì | rì-ìr-í | mw-àmí | mú-gùmà | nà= | mú-ká-à-gè. |
| 16-P2.PS | is-PS-Fi | 1-king | 1-one | CNJ= | 1-wife-A.M-1 |

'There was one king and his wife.' (110 003 )

There are other similar constructions, which technically speaking, do not meet Lambrecht's definition of presentational (since they *do* link to an already established topic). These involve a surface subject consisting of a locative phrase, with the phrase head marked by the cl. 16 **há**, 17 **kú**, 18 **mú**, or 23 **í** clitic. That same prefix is then repeated as the subject prefix of the verb. Examples are the cl. 17 **kú**=bútàmbì bwê=yò njírà kwáàlí bwàtíírì í=mbúmì 'on the side of that.N road there was sitting a blind one' or the cl. 18 **mú**=yìkyó kíshùká mwáàli rììrí í=ndàrè 'in that.N bush there was a lion', etc.

These constructions are used to introduce major participants in focus position at the end of the clause. Such constructions, referred to as locative inversion, are very common in Bantu languages and are also discussed in 12.5.1.1.

## 10.2.6 Identificational articulation

Identificational articulation includes "a presupposed proposition that, except for one element, is assumed to be known." The focus then, is on "the element that was lacking in the presupposed proposition" (Levinsohn 2006; see also Lambrecht 1994:122). The element in focus is what is being "identified." For example, in the sentence "It was an axe that he gave me", the focused element is identified as "axe". The presupposition is that "he gave me something".

Identificational articulation in Kifuliiru can employ the focus copula, the negative focus copula, or one of the non-verbal clauses already mentioned in (10.1.1). The focused element may be the clause subject, object, or an oblique. In a non-verbal clause, the focused element may consist of an NP which is followed only by a demonstrative.

### 10.2.6.1 Subject as focus element

The FOCUS COPULA (FOC)[19] can be used to put focus on the subject of a sentence. In (10.103) the fact that "something was done" is the given information. The element which is unknown is: "By whom?" This question is answered by placing **yàbá bágénì** 'these guests' at the front of a sentence with

---

[19]Though this is called the focus copula, it actually follows the focus element found in sentence-initial position, rather than being a part of the focused element itself. The focused portion is followed by a pause, which separates it from the focus copula and the rest of the sentence. Thus the initial element is the only part which is labeled as focus, while the focus copula forms part of the "presupposition".

identificational articulation. Here the referent of the focused element is also the subject of the main verb in the presupposition.

(10.103)

| Focus | | Presupposition | | |
|---|---|---|---|---|
| Yà-bá | bá-génì ‖ | b-ó= | bà-gír-á | yì-bì. |
| these.P-2 | 2-guests | 2-FOC= | 2-do-Fa | this.P-8 |

'These guests ‖ they are the ones who did these things.' (09 013)

In (10.104) the presupposition is that "someone has been taking money". The question is identifying who did it. This is answered by putting **yêhê** 'HE (in contrast to others)' at the front of the sentence in "focus" position, followed (after a pause) by the focus copula **yé**.

(10.104)

| Focus | | Presupposition | | |
|---|---|---|---|---|
| Y-êhê ‖ | y-é= | w-à-yàbíír-á | yìzò | fwáráng̃á zà-à-nì. |
| 1-CTR.P | 1-FOC= | 1-P1-took-Fa | those.N+10 | 10+monies 10-A.M-1 |

'HE ‖ is the one who took those monies of mine.' (33 017)

In (10.105) the presupposition is that "my child was killed". The focused element, the interrogative **nyândì** 'who', seeks to identify who did it.

(10.105)

| Focus | Presupposition | |
|---|---|---|
| «Nyândì ‖ | ú-ká-n-yìt-ír-á | ú=mw-ānà?» |
| who | S.R+1-P2-O1.SG-kill-APL-Fa | AU=1-child |

'Who (is it) | who killed (relative to me) | the child?' (105 042)

The NEGATIVE FOCUS COPULA (NEG.FOC) can also be used in identificational articulation. The presupposition in (10.106) is that the hunters will eat the meat they kill. (This is usually the case in the Kifuliiru culture.) The focus here is on the fact that among the three hunters, there was not one "who tasted even a bone of that gazelle".

(10.106) Focus

**Ndáá-yè**
NEG.FOC-1

|  | Presupposition |  |  |  |
|---|---|---|---|---|
| **ú-ká-lámb-à** ‖ | **kírí kw-í=** | **vùhà** \| | **ly-ê=** **yò** | **m-bóngò.** |
| S.R+1-P2-lick-Fa | even 17-5= | bone | 5-A.M= that.N+9 | 9-gazelle |

'There is no one who licked ‖ even a bone | of that gazelle.' (03 022)

### 10.2.6.2 Object as focused element

The clause object can also be the focus element in a sentence with identificational articulation. In (10.107) it is given information that the lion will eat someone. The focus here is on identifying who he will eat. The eagle says 'that he be the one that the lion eats'. This includes the cl. 1 focus copula **yé**.

(10.107)

|  |  |  | Focus |
|---|---|---|---|
| **N-yûndà** | **ná-yè** \| | **à-ná-dèt-à** ‖ | **kw-á= Ø-b-é** |
| 9-eagle | ADD.P-1 | 1-SQ-speak-Fa | CMP-1= SBV-be-Fe |

|  | Presupposition |  |
|---|---|---|
| **y-é=** | **n-dàrè** | **í-Ø-ry-à.** |
| 1-O.R+FOC= | 9-lion | 9-TL-eat-Fa |

'The eagle and HE ALSO | said ‖ that he be the one that the lion eats.'
(11 036)

In (10.108) the rat tells the trapper and his wife that they should reward him for his help to them. That he should have a reward then becomes given information for the presupposition of the sentence in (10.108), where **ndáá-yò** 'there is no cl. 9' is in focus to "negatively identify" that the payment that is expected does not exist.

(10.108)

| Focus | Presupposition |  |  |
|---|---|---|---|
| **Ndáá-yó** | **m-bèmbó** | **y-ó=** | **bà-gw-ét-ì.** |
| NEG.FOC-9 | 9-reward | 9-O.R= | 2-have-RS-Fi |

'There is no reward which they have.' (111 035)

### 10.2.6.3 Oblique locative phrase as focus element

Oblique locative phrases can also be marked as the focused element in a sentence with identificational articulation. In (10.109) it is assumed that "I am putting trust" somewhere. The oblique phrase **mwí=gámbó lyàgè** 'in his word' shows where the trust is being put.

(10.109)

| Focus | | |
|---|---|---|
| <u>Mw-í=</u> | <u>gámbó</u> | <u>ly-à-gè</u> ‖ |
| 18-5= | word | 5-A.M-1 |

| | Presupposition | | | |
|---|---|---|---|---|
| mw-ó= | n-dì | mú= | bíík-á \| | ú=mú-lángáálírò. |
| 18-FOC= | 1SG-am | PROG= | place-Fa | AU=3-expectation |

'In the word of him ‖ is where I am placing | expectation.' (Psa 130:5)

### 10.2.6.4 Noun phrase followed by demonstrative

The clauses in this section, when viewed relative to syntactic structure, all involve non-verbal predicates (10.1.1). Relative to information structure, they all have identificational articulation.

In (10.110) the focus is the cl. 1 NP **mwàná wànî** 'my child', which is followed by the presupposition **ùyô** 'that.N'. In other words, a person is presupposed by the demonstrative **ùyô** 'that.N'. The question is: Who is that person? The answer is identified by the focus NP **mwàná wànî** 'my child'.

(10.110)

| | | Focus | | Presupposition |
|---|---|---|---|---|
| É= | Kízìmù-ngárà ‖ | <u>mw-àná</u> | <u>w-à-ní</u> | ùyó. |
| O= | Kizimu-ngara | 1-child | 1-A.M-1SG | that.N+1 |

'O Kizimu-ngara ‖ my child (is) that one.' (617 049)

In (10.111) there are two cases of identificational articulation, this time each in the form of a question: **kútì yùkwô** 'what that.N one' and **lwìmbó lúkì yùlwô** 'what song that.N one'. In the first case the focus is the cl. 15 NP **kútì** 'what' (which includes an understood verbal notion). The presupposition is the demonstrative **yúkwò** 'that'. The focus **kútì** seeks to *identify* what is represented by the demonstrative **yúkwò**. In the same way in the second case the focus **lwìmbó lúkì** 'which song' seeks to identify what is represented by the presupposition **yúlwò** 'that.N'.

(10.111) 

| | Focus | Presupposition | Focus | | Presupposition |
|---|---|---|---|---|---|
| Éhéè! \|\| | Kútì | yùkwô? \|\| | Lw-ìmbó | lú-kì | yùlwô? |
| O my! | what | that.N+15 | 11-song | 11-what | that.N+11 |

'O my! || What is that (thing that is happening)? || What sort of song is that (one)?' (203 023)

## 10.3 Alternations of basic constituent order

The default syntactic word order of the Kifuliiru clause is S V O. There are several ways to alter that basic order, so that in any given context the information structure requirements can be met. Such constituent-order alternations permit the speaker to place old information at the beginning of a topic-comment construction, while new information comes afterwards. At the same time, it allows old information in a presupposition to follow the focused element. It also ensures that the dominant focal element (DFE) is isolated at the very end of a sentence, etc. This section examines various strategies for moving sentence constituents in order to satisfy such information structure requirements.

### 10.3.1 Preposing a clause constituent

To prepose a clause constituent is to move it from its default order within the sentence, and place it in a position earlier in the sentence. Various elements of the sentence may be preposed, as presented below.

#### 10.3.1.1 Preposing the dependent clause subject

In (10.112) the default position of **yîbà** 'her husband' is within the point of departure **í=kyànyà yîbà àlì mú=bàlámúkà** 'the time her husband is returning from a trip'. However **yîbà** has been preposed to the beginning of that PoD. **Yîbà** is also the understood topic of the main clause.

10.3 Alternations of basic constituent order

(10.112)

|  | | PoD |
|---|---|---|
| | Topic | |
| | <u>Yîbà</u> ‖ | í=ky-ànyà  à-lì  mú=  bàlám-úk-à ‖ |
| | her.husband | AU=7-time  1-is  PROG= travel-RV.I-Fa |

|  | Comment |
|---|---|
| à-lì mú= yíj-á    à-bà-gúl-ìr-à    \|  á=má-kânjù \|  b-ómbì. |
| 1-is PROG= COMING-Fa  1+P1-O2-buy-APL-Fa  AU=6-dress  2-both |

'Her husband ‖ the time (when) he is returning from a trip ‖ he is coming having bought | dresses | for both of them.' (628 007)

In (10.113) the proper noun "Piyo" is preposed from its default subject position within the PoD **ìrí Píyò ákáhísá á=mììjí mú=nyûmbà** 'when Piyo brought the water into the house', and is placed at the beginning of the sentence, as topic of the PoD. In the main clause, the topic this time is not **Piyo**, but **nyina** 'her mother'.

(10.113)

|  | PoD | | | | |
|---|---|---|---|---|---|
| <u>Píyò</u> ‖ | ìrí | á-ká-hí-s-á | á=mì-ìjí | mú= | ny-ûmbà ‖ |
| Piyo | when | 1-P2-arrive-CS-Fa | AU=6-water | 18= | 9-house |

| Topic |
|---|
| **nyínà** |
| 1a+the.mother |

| Comment |
|---|
| à-ná-mú-bwîr-à \|  kw-â= géndí gà-fùkúmúl-ír-à \|  mú= ká-bìndì. |
| 1-SQ-O1-tell-Fa  CMP-1= GOING O6-pour-APL-Fa  18=  12-pot |

'Piyo ‖ when she brought the water into the house ‖ the mother told her | to go pour it | into the pot.' (628 016)

### 10.3.1.2 Preposing the clause object

The clause object (normally a post-verbal constituent) can be preposed to the front of the clause, leaving room for the new information in the sentence to be isolated in focal position at the end. When preposed,[20] the clause object is

---

[20] Such preposing followed by later pronominal reference within the sentence to that preposed element is sometimes called left-dislocation (Crystal 2003:262).

obligatorily referenced in the verbal object position within the verb, as seen in (10.114)–(10.116).

In (10.114) one of the objects, **ùyó nyûndà** 'that.N eagle' is preposed to the front of the sentence. Note that this represents (old) given information, with previous reference marker **o** on **ùyó**. Preposing the object makes way for the new information "they gave him half of the country" to be isolated as comment at the end of the sentence.

(10.114)

| PoD/topic | | Comment | | |
|---|---|---|---|---|
| Ùyó | n-yûndà ‖ | bà-ná-<u>mú</u>-hééréz-à | í=kí-hùgò | lú-hândè. |
| that.N+1 | 9-eagle | 2-SQ-O.1-give-Fa | AU=7-country | 11-half |

'That eagle ‖ they gave him half the country.' (616 045)

In (10.115) preposing allows the old information **kìryá kíjùmbà** 'that.R box' to be moved out of the comment portion of the sentence. However it still follows the PoD/topic **ùlyá múnyérè** 'that.R girl', who is also the one referenced by the subject marker of the verb. In this way, **ùlyá múnyérè** 'that.R girl' remains the topic at the beginning of the sentence. Preposing the object keeps the reference clear while properly putting focus on the new information: 'she laid it on the bed'.

(10.115)

| PoD/topic | | Preposed object | |
|---|---|---|---|
| Ù-lyá | mú-nyérè ‖ | kì-ryá | kí-jùmbà \| |
| 1-that.R | 1-girl | 7-that.R | 7-box |

| Comment | | |
|---|---|---|
| à-ná-<u>kì</u>-gwèjé-z-à | kú= | n-gíngò. |
| 1-SQ-O7-lay.down-CS-Fa | 17= | 9-bed |

'That girl ‖ that box \| she laid it on the bed.' (618 006)

In (10.116) the already-mentioned clause object **yìzó nyámà** 'those meats' is preposed from its normal position after the verb to a position before the verb, and after the clause subject. This allows **kwó=bìrì bísíítàrà** 'that they are gristle' to be isolated as the DFE at the end of the sentence.

## 10.3 Alternations of basic constituent order

(10.116)

| PoD¹/topic | | PoD²/preposed object | |
|---|---|---|---|
| **Ùyó** | **mú-kāzì** ‖ | **yìzó** | **ny-ámà** ‖ |
| that.N+1 | 1-woman | those.N+10 | 10-meats |

| Comment, with post-pause DFE | | |
|---|---|---|
| **á-àlí** | **kòlà** | **mú=** |
| 1-P3 | be.NEWLY | PROG= |

| Comment (con't) | | | |
|---|---|---|---|
| **zì-náák-à** | ǀ **kwó=** | **bì-rì** | **bí-síítàrà.** |
| O10-disparage-Fa | CMP= | 8-are | 8-gristle |

'That woman ‖ those meats ‖ she began to disparage them ǀ that they are gristle.' (632 032)

### 10.3.1.3 Preposing a locative oblique phrase

The oblique phrase can be preposed to a position before the SVO nucleus, leaving room for another clause constituent to be in focus at the end of the sentence.

In (10.117) the given information, the locative oblique **mú=kìlīīrà kíshímò** 'in that.D hole' has been moved from clause-final position, and preposed to the front of the clause, where it serves as a PoD. Its trace is the cl. 18 marker **mwo**. The preposing of the oblique phrase takes the clause focus off the old information **mú=kìlīīrà kíshímò** and correctly places it on the comment **àgwètì ágáálírà=mwò** 'she is crying in there'.

(10.117)

| PoD | | |
|---|---|---|
| **Mú=** | **kì-līīrà** | **kí-shímò** ‖ |
| 18= | 7-that.D | 7-hole |

| Comment | | | | |
|---|---|---|---|---|
| **n-à-yúvw-à** | **ú=mú-ndù** | **à-gwètí** | **á-gáá-lír-à** | **=mwò.** |
| 1SG-P1-hear-Fa | AU=1-person | 1-PROG | 1-INTL-cry-Fa | =18 |

'In that hole ‖ I heard a person crying in there.' (107 015)

In (10.118) the given information, the locative oblique **mú=yìkyó kíhūgò** 'in that.N country' has been preposed to the front of the clause, and its trace is again the cl. 18 marker **=mwo** at the end of the clause. This allows **gwànáshùbì**

**téérá=mwò** 'it again attacked in it' to be in focus position at the end of the clause.

(10.118)

| PoD | Topic |
|---|---|
| **Mú= yìkyó kí-hūgò** ‖ | **ú=mw-éná** \| |
| 16= that.N+7 7-country | AU=3-hunger |

| Comment |
|---|
| **gw-àná-shùbì téér-á =mwò.** |
| 3-SQ-AGAIN attack-Fa =18 |

'In that country ‖ hunger \| again attacked in there.' (Gen 26:1)

In (10.119) the given information, the locative oblique **kú=njírá yá=yùgwó múlírò** 'by means of that.N fire', is preposed to the front of the sentence. The preposing of the oblique allows **í=nyámá mbámù** 'large meat' to be in the DFE position, preceded by a short pause.

(10.119)

| PoD | Topic | |
|---|---|---|
| **Kú= n-jírá yá= yùgwó mú-lírò** ‖ | **yàkó** | **ká-fùlò** ‖ |
| 17= 9-way 9-A.M= that.N+3 3-fire | that.N+12 | 12-turtle |

| Comment, with post-pause DFE |
|---|
| **ká-ká-lóng-á \| í=n-yámá m-bámù.** |
| 12-P2-receive-Fa AU=9-meat 9-large |

'And by means of that fire ‖ that turtle ‖ received \| large meat.' (05 009)

Often a preposed oblique follows a PoD/topic, rather than being placed at the very beginning of the sentence. In (10.120) the locative phrase **í=kāāyà** 'at the village' is preposed from its clause-final position, allowing **ànáfwá nó=mwénà** 'she was dying of hunger' to be in focus at the end of the clause. The subject **múkáàgè** 'his wife' is still in clause-initial position as the topic/PoD.

(10.120)

| PoD/topic | Preposed oblique | Comment |
|---|---|---|
| **Mù-ká-à-gè** | **í= kā-āyà** ‖ | **à-ná-fw-á n-ó= mw-énà.** |
| 1-wife-A.M-1 | 23= 12-village | 1-SQ-die-Fa CNJ-AU= 3-famine |

'His wife at the village ‖ was dying of hunger.' (111 015)

In (10.121) the locative oblique **í=rwījì** 'at the river' was preposed from clause-final position to a position as a second PoD, to allow **ànábúlùlà** 'he

## 10.3 Alternations of basic constituent order

pulled' to take the focus position at the end of the clause. **Wà=ngóónà** 'crocodile' is still the main sentence topic.

(10.121)

| PoD/topic | Preposed locative | Comment |
|---|---|---|
| W-à=n-góóná <br> 1-A.M=9-crocodile | í= rw-ījì ‖ <br> 23= 11-river | à-ná-búlùl-à. <br> 1-SQ-pull-Fa |

'Crocodile | at the river ‖ pulled.' (402 031)

In (10.122) the oblique **í=nyúmá lyàgè** 'behind him' is preposed before the verb, so that **lyànásìgálí bèrékà** 'it remained and got broken' could be in focus at the end of the clause.

(10.122)

| PoD¹ | PoD² | Topic |
|---|---|---|
| Léèrò ‖ <br> this.time | ìrí á-ká-bàlám-à ‖ <br> when 1-P2-travel-Fa | lì-ryá î-gì ‖ <br> 5-that.R 5-egg |

| Preposed locative | Comment |
|---|---|
| í= ny-úmá ly-à-gè ‖ <br> 23= 9-behind 5-A.M-1 | ly-àná-sìgálí bèr-ék-à. <br> 5-SQ-REMAINING break-NEU-Fa |

'This time | when he traveled ‖ that egg ‖ behind him ‖ it remained and got broken.' (208 012)

### 10.3.1.4 Preposing the locative phrase complement

The complement of a locative phrase can be preposed to a position preceding the subject, where it serves as a point of departure. In (10.123) the underlying form **ànábyâlà ú=múpûngà mwî=yó ndálò** 'and he planted rice in that.N field' is altered, with the established information, **ìyó ndálò** 'that.N field' preposed to the front of the sentence. The effect is that the new information **múpûngà** 'rice' comes into focus in the comment at the end of the sentence.

(10.123)

| PoD | Comment |
|---|---|
| Ìyó n-dalo ‖ <br> that.N+9 9-field | à-ná-gi-byal-a mwo= mu-punga. <br> 1-SQ-O9-plant-Fa 18= 3-rice |

'That field ‖ he planted in it rice.' (610 008)

### 10.3.1.5 Preposing the associative phrase complement

In (10.124) the established-information NP **ùyó mwānà** 'that.N child' is preposed from its semantic default position as the complement of the associative phrase **kánwá kô=yó mwānà** 'mouth of that.N child'. The default order is **yùlwó lwìmbó lùtàtwíká mú=kánwá kô=yó mwānà** 'that.N song was not cut off in the mouth of that.N child'.

(10.124)

| PoD | | Topic | |
|---|---|---|---|
| **Ùyó** | **mw-ānà** ‖ | **yùlwó** | **lw-ìmbó** \| |
| that.N+1 | 1-child | that.N+11 | 11-song |

| Comment | |
|---|---|
| **lú-tà-Ø-tw-ìk-à** | **mú=** **ká-nwâ.** |
| 11-NEG-TL-cut-NEU-Fa | 18= 12-mouth |

'That child ‖ that song \| did not stop in (his) mouth.' (610 022)

In (10.125) the default order of the NP would be **úmwégó gwóshì gô=yò mútàbánà** 'the whole body of that.N young man'. However, the associative phrase complement, **ùyó mútàbánà** 'that.N young man', being established information, is preposed and presented as the PoD. The new information is then given later in the sentence **ú=mwégó gwóshì gwáàlí dùndùùsírì kwó=lúhérè** 'all the body it was covered with scabies'.

(10.125)

| PoD | | Topic | |
|---|---|---|---|
| **Ùyó** | **mú-tàbánà** ‖ | **ú=mw-égò** | **gw-óshì** ‖ |
| that.N+1 | 1-young.man | AU=3-body | 3-all |

| Comment | | | |
|---|---|---|---|
| **gw-áàlí** | **dùndùùs-ír-ì** \| | **kw-ó=** | **lú-hérè.** |
| 3-P3 | be.sore.covered-RS-Fi | 17-AU | 11-scabies |

'That young man ‖ all of (his) body ‖ it was covered \| with scabies.' (101 010)

In (10.126) the default order is **í=nyûngù yé=mwá=Píyò** 'the pot of Piyo'. The complement of the associative phrase, **Píyò**, has been preposed to topic position and the pronominal trace is seen in the final morpheme of **yé=mwàgè** 'belonging to her'.

## 10.3 Alternations of basic constituent order

(10.126)

| PoD (preposed) | Topic | | |
|---|---|---|---|
| **Píyò** ‖ | í=ny-ûngù | y-é= | mw-à-gè ‖ |
| Piyo | AU=9-pot | 9-A.M+23= | belonging-A.M-1 |

| Comment |
|---|
| **y-àná-yìjúl-à.** |
| 9-SQ-be.full-Fa |

'Piyo ‖ the pot of hers ‖ became full.' (628 015)

### 10.3.1.6 Preposing an intrinsic element of a possessive noun

The word **máàwè** means 'my/our mother', but possession is not expressed by a separate word, or even by a specific morpheme within the word. Still, in (10.127) the semantic notion of possessor found in **máàwè** is preposed, using the contrastive pronoun **niêhè** 'I' to convey the intrinsic first-person possessive sense of **máàwè** 'my mother'. **Niêhè** forms the point of departure for the sentence. The meaning is 'As for ME (in contrast to someone else), my mother died without being buried'. The implication is 'So why should your mother be buried, (as you have just requested)?'

(10.127)

| PoD (preposed) | | Topic | Comment[1] | Comment[2] |
|---|---|---|---|---|
| Sí= | **ni-ê-hè** ‖ | máàwè | á-ká-fw-á ǀ | à-tà-ná-zíìk-w-à. |
| OBV= | 1SG-CTR.P | 1a+my.mother | 1-P2-die-Fa | 1-NEG-SQ-bury-PS-Fa |

'It's obvious that ME ‖ my mother has died ǀ and she was not buried.' (16 009)

### 10.3.1.7 Preposing certain adverbs

There is a limited set of adverbs that can occur in marked positions at points where there is heightened tension in the narrative.

The default position of the auxiliary **kéèrà** 'already' is immediately before the verb. This is its position in more than 95 percent of the cases (221 times in the database). It can also be preposed to a marked position, before both subject and verb. In every marked case, there is heightened tension, as when a lion is hiding behind a door, or a leopard is having plans for a certain place, etc.

In (10.128) we see **kéèrà** 'already' occurring in its default position just before the verb. The child of the lion is already dead, so the tension is lowered.

(10.128)

| PoD/topic | | Adverb | Comment |
|---|---|---|---|
| mw-àná w-á= | n-dàrè \|\| | **kéèrà** | à-fw-à. |
| 1-child 1-A.M= | 9-lion | ALREADY | 1+P1-die-Fa |

'The child of lion ‖ has already died.' (105 011)

In (10.129) **kéèrà** 'already' is preposed to a marked position before the clause topic **íngwî** 'leopard'.

(10.131)

| Preposed | Topic | Comment |
|---|---|---|
| ...**kéèrà** | í=n-gwí \|\| | y-à-hà-híg-ìr-à. |
| ALREADY | AU=9-leopard | 9-P1-O16-purpose-APL-Fa |

'...already the leopard | has schemes for it (this place).' (10 009)

The inherently emphatic adverb **ngànà** 'really'[21] is usually preposed to a marked position, as seen in the dependent clause shown in (10.130). Here the **ngànà** 'really' is placed between the verbal auxiliary **bákábá** 'they were' and the main verb **bágákìjábùkà** 'they will still cross'. It is one of very few words which can occur in this position.

(10.130)

| PoD | | Preposed adverb |
|---|---|---|
| Ìrí | bá-ká-b-á | **ngànà** \| |
| when | 2-P2-be-Fa | really |

| PoD (con't) | |
|---|---|
| bá-gá-kì-jábùk-à | ú=lw-ījì... |
| 2-F2-PERS-cross.over-Fa | AU=11-river |

'When they were really | still about to cross the river...' (631 015)

In (10.131) the adverb **ngànà** 'really' is preposed in marked position between the clause subject **Ú=lwījì** 'river' and the verb **lwànáyàmí yìjúlà** 'and it was immediately full'. Once again, this is one of very few words that can occur between the clause subject and the verb.

(10.131)

| Topic | Preposed adverb | Comment | |
|---|---|---|---|
| **Ú=lw-ìjí** | **ngànà** \|\| | lù-ná-yàmí | yìjúl-à \| |
| AU=11-river | really | 11-CON-IMMED | be.full-Fa |

'The river was really ‖ immediately full.' (103 101)

---

[21] **Ngànà** is a colloquial emphatic particle ("adverb" for lack of a better term) which has little, if any, meaning besides emphasis. It could also be translated 'only/just'.

## 10.3 Alternations of basic constituent order

The adverb **kàndî** 'again' is also often found preposed to a marked position. In (10.132) **kàndî** is preposed within the comment to a position before the infinitive **ú=kúyīmbà** 'to sing'.

(10.132)

| Comment | Preposed adverb | Comment |
|---|---|---|
| **À-ná-tòndéér-à** | **kàndí** | **ú=kú-yīmb-à.** |
| 1-SQ-begin-Fa | again | AU=15-sing-Fa |

'He began again | to sing.' (208 032)

In (10.133) the adverb **kwókùnô** 'thus' is preposed from its default clause-final position to a position just before the verb. This allows **ngwètí íbûndà** 'I have a pregnancy' to be in focal position at the end of the clause.

(10.133)

| PoD¹/topic | PoD² | Comment | |
|---|---|---|---|
| «**Ni-ê-hé** | **kwókùnô** | **n-gw-èt-í** | **í-bûndà.**» |
| 1SG-A.M-CTR.P | like.this.P.C | 1SG-have-RS-Fi | 5-pregnancy |

'ME thus | I have a pregnancy.' (201 010)

In (10.134) **kúshēēzì** 'tomorrow' is preposed from clause final position to a place before the verb. This allows the verb **ngámúgwàtà nààhô** 'I will just seize him' to be in focus position at the end of the clause.

(10.134)

| PoD¹/topic | | PoD² | Comment | |
|---|---|---|---|---|
| **Ù-nó** | **mú-ndù** ‖ | **kúshēēzì** | **n-gá-mú-gwàt-á** | **nààhô.** |
| 1-this.P.C | 1-person | tomorrow | 1SG-F2-O1-seize-Fa | just |

'This person ‖ tomorrow | I will just seize him.' (627 012)

### 10.3.2 Postposing a clause constituent

Postposing a constituent to a position later in the sentence than its default order can be used to give that constituent focal prominence.

#### 10.3.2.1 Subject postposing

The subject of a clause may be postposed by the use of a relative clause. In (10.135) the NP **lúgó lúhámú úlùkòlí yìjwìrí mwè=ngáàvù** 'a large enclosure within which is full of cows' includes a modifying relative clause (underlined). This NP is derived from the default clause **í=ngáàvu zìyìjwìrí mú=lúgò lúhámù** 'cows fill (in) the large enclosure', in which the locative oblique is to the right of the clause nucleus. The alternation of constituent order found in

(10.135) effectively treats the **lúgó lúhámù** 'large enclosure' as established information which precedes comment², while postposing the new (and most in-focus) information, the underlying subject, **ngáàvù** 'cows' to the end of the sentence, where it is the DFE, marked by a preceding pause.

(10.135)

| Comment¹ | | | |
|---|---|---|---|
| À-ná-b-á | n-ó= | lú-gó | lú-hámú \| |
| 1-SQ-become-Fa | CNJ-AU= | 11-enclosure | 11-large |

| Embedded comment² | | | |
|---|---|---|---|
| ú-lù-kòlí | yìjw-ìr-í \| | mw-è= | n-gáàvù. |
| S.R-11-be.NEWLY | fill-RS-Fi | 18-AU= | 10-cows |

'And he had a large enclosure | which was now filled | with cows.' (42 009)

In (10.136) the subject of the temporal PoD clause, **bóóshì** 'all (of them)' is postposed after the auxiliary **bákáyúsâ** 'they had finished', and preceding the following infinitive within the PoD, putting focus on the fact that all of them finished. The default order would be **ìrí bóóshì bákáyúsâ** 'when all had finished'.

(10.136)

| | PoD | | |
|---|---|---|---|
| | | Postposed subject | |
| Ìrí | bá-ká-yús-á | bó-óshì \| | ú=kú-lágáán-à kw-ô-kw-ô \| |
| when | 2-P2-finish-Fa | 2-all | AU=15-agree-Fa Thus |

| Topic | |
|---|---|
| ùyó | kèré \|\| |
| that.N+1 | 1a+frog |

| Comment | | | | | |
|---|---|---|---|---|---|
| à-ná-shùbír-á \| | h-ó= | bá-ká-lágáán-á \| | nê= | yò | m-bóngò. |
| 1-SQ-go.back-Fa | 16-O.R= | 2-P2-agree-Fa | CNJ= | that.N+9 | 9-gazelle. |

'When they finished all of them | to agree thus | that frog || and he went back | to where he had agreed | with that gazelle.' (21 016)

### 10.3.2.2 Focus (of identificational) postposed

In identificational articulation, focus normally occurs first, followed by the presupposition. This default order, discussed in (10.2.6.1) above, is exemplified again here in (10.137) for easy comparison with the postposed order shown in (10.138).

(10.137)

| Focus | | Presupposition | | |
|---|---|---|---|---|
| <u>Yà-bá</u> | bá-génì ‖ | b-ó= | bà-gír-á | yì-bì. |
| these-2 | 2-guests | 2-FOC= | 2-do-Fa | this.P-8 |

'These guests ‖ they are the ones who did these things.' (09 013)

As seen in (10.138) the "focused" constituent, in this case **únò** 'this', can be postposed to the end of the clause, to add to the focus that it already has. This occurs especially with demonstrative pronouns. Thus in (10.138) the mother asks her daughter **yé=mwàná, úkábūtà, únò?** 'Is he the child, you gave birth to, this one?' In this clause **únò** 'this one' has been postposed to the end of the clause, where it is in maximum focus.

(10.138)

| | Presupposition | | | Focus |
|---|---|---|---|---|
| Y-é= | mw-àná ‖ | ú-ká-būt-à | ‖ | <u>ú-nò?</u> |
| 1-FOC= | 1-child | 2SG-P2-give.birth-Fa | | 1-this.P.C |

'Is he the child ‖ (which) you gave birth to ‖ this one?' (303 027)

In (10.139) the focused element **únò** 'this one' of a identificational construction is postposed to the end of the sentence, again for maximum focus.

(10.139)

| Topic | | Comment | |
|---|---|---|---|
| Í-nò | ‖ | ì-tá-lí | ny-ámíìshwà ‖ |
| 9-this.P.C | | 9-NEG-is | 9-wild.animal |

| | Presupposition | Focus |
|---|---|---|
| y-é= | mú-ká-à-niè | <u>ú-nò.</u> |
| 1-FOC= | 1-wife-A.M-1SG | 1-this.P.C |

'This ‖ is not a wild animal ‖ this one is the one who is my wife.' (401 031)

### 10.3.3 Promoting to clause object

In "promoting to object", a trace of the complement of an oblique locative phrase is prefixed in the object slot of the verb. What was formerly the locative marker in the oblique phrase is then pronominalized by the addition of the previous reference morpheme, and appears as a clitic on the end of the verb, or instead on the following word, if there is one. This rearrangement of clause constituents effectively takes the focus off the locative phrase, allowing another constituent to be isolated at the end of the clause in DFE position. Promoting to object is a very common alternation in Kifuliiru.

In (10.140) the form **ànákìzí lùfìná=kwò** 'and he continuously on it tramples' is derived from the default form **ànákìzí fìná kú=lwôhê** 'and he continuously tramples on IT', where the oblique is at the end of the clause. In effect this oblique is promoted into the verb as an object prefix, so that the verb -**fìn**- 'trample' can be in focus at the end of the sentence.

(10.140)

| | | Topic | | |
|---|---|---|---|---|
| Kírí | n-ó= | lú-hú | lw-à-nì | ‖ |
| even | CNJ-AU= | 11-skin | 11-A.M-1SG | |

| | | Comment[1] | | |
|---|---|---|---|---|
| à-lì | mú= | lù-yàj-à | hááshì | ‖ |
| 1-is | PROG= | O11-spread-Fa | on.ground | |

| | Comment[2], Raising to object | | |
|---|---|---|---|
| à-ná-kìzí | lù-fìn-á | =kw-ò. | |
| 1-SQ-REP | O11-trample-Fa | =17 | |

'Even and my skin ‖ he is spreading it on the ground ‖ and he is repeatedly trampling on it.' (14 020)

In (10.141) the form **ànágìshwékérà kwó=mùgózì** 'and he tied to it a rope' is derived from the default **ànáshwékérà ú=mùgózì kú=yôhê** 'and he tied a rope to IT'. Since the object **yôhê** 'IT' is not in focus, instead of appearing as a full contrast pronoun, the reference to it is prefixed to the verb as an object (**gì-**), allowing **mùgózì** 'rope' to be in focus position at the end of the clause.

(10.141)

| Comment[1], raising to object | | |
|---|---|---|
| À-ná-gi-shwék-ér-à | kw-ó= | mù-gózì ‖ |
| 1-SQ-O9-tie-APL-Fa | 17-AU= | 3-rope |

| Comment[2] | |
|---|---|
| à-ná-yîj-à \| | á-gá-gì-búlùl-à. |
| 1-SQ-COMING-Fa | 1-INTL-O9-drag-Fa |

'And he tied it to a rope ‖ and came \| dragging it.' (07 033)

In (10.142) the clause **múgáábàbà=mwô** 'you will among them be' is derived from the default **múgáàbà mú=bóòhê** 'you will be among THEM'. In order to remove **bóòhê** 'THEM' from the place of focus at the end of the sentence, it was prefixed as an object on the verb.

(10.142)

| PoD/topic | Comment, raising to object |  |
|---|---|---|
| **Ná= nìì-nyù** ‖ | **mú-gáá-ba̱-b-à** | **=mwô.** |
| CNJ= ADD.P-2 | 2PL-F2-O2-become-Fa | =18 |

'And YOU ALSO ‖ you will be among them.' (2Th 1:10)

### 10.3.4 Marked placement of pronominal elements

This section deals with the personal pronouns (exemplified here in their cl. 2 forms): **bóónyènè** 'themselves', **bôngwâ** 'themselves', **bóòhê** 'THEY in contrast to others', **bóókì** 'THEY in contrast to expected others', **nábò** 'and THEY ALSO', as well as the set selectors **á=bàndì** 'others' and **á=bààbò** 'their fellows'. It also includes the quantifiers **bìngì** 'many', **bóóshì** 'all', **bómbì** 'both', **bágùmà** 'some', **bàbìrì** 'two', etc., which are used pronominally, and whose default position is at the end of the noun phrase. These pronouns and pronominal elements may also be placed outside of the NP, in a "marked" position, for prominence.

#### 10.3.4.1 *Topical prominence*

Topical prominence can be defined as the prominence of some specific item within the topic of the sentence. In topical prominence in Kifuliiru, this prominence is indicated by the placement of a pronoun or quantifier at the end of the clause topic, just before the verb. In the case of a quantifier, whose default spot is at the end of the NP, this placement at the end of the topic involves displacement from its default position. In the case of the other pronouns, their very presence in the clause always indicates some sort of prominence. Placement in focused position at the end of the topic thus adds to their inherent prominence.

In (10.143) the inherent meaning of the pronoun **yêhê** 'HE (in contrast to others)' is accentuated by its position in the sentence. This pronoun comes at the end of the sentence topic, which is the place of prominence within the topic.

(10.143)

| PoD | Topic | | Comment |
|---|---|---|---|
| | | Topical prominence | |
| **Hálìkò** ‖ | **ú-nò** | **y-êhê** ‖ | **à-ná-m-bwír-ág-à:...** |
| but | 1-this.P.C | 1-CTR.P | 1-SQ-O1.SG-tell-EMP-Fa |

'But | this one HE | he told me:...' (201 076)

In (10.144) the pronoun **náyè** 'and he also' comes at the end of the sentence topic, which begins with **ùyó músósì** 'that.N man'.

(10.144)

|  | | Topic | |
|---|---|---|---|
|  | | | Topical prominence |
| Ùyó | mú-sósí | | ná-yè ‖ |
| that.N+1 | 1-man | | ADD.P-1 |

| Comment | | |
|---|---|---|
| à-ná-dèt-à: ‖ | «Tù-lóóz-é | á=bá-tûngwà.» |
| 1-SQ-say-Fa | 1PL-look.for-Fe | AU=2-judges |

'That man and HE ALSO ‖ said: ‖ «Let's look for | judges.»' (14 004)

In (10.145) the pronoun **bóòhè** 'they, in contrast to others' follows after the coordinate NP **Káshìndì ná=Búkùrù** 'Kashindi and Bukuru', in the position of topical prominence.

(10.145)

| Topic | | | |
|---|---|---|---|
|  | | | Topical prominence |
| Káshìndì \| | nà= | Búkùrù ‖ | bó-òhê |
| Kashindi | CNJ= | Bukuru | 2-CTR.P |

| Comment | | |
|---|---|---|
| bà-ná-sìgál-à | í= | kā-āyà. |
| 2-SQ-remain-Fa | 23= | 12-village |

'Kashindi | and Bukuru ‖ THEY remained at the village.'

In (10.146) the quantifier **byóshì** 'all' is postposed to the prominent position at the end of the sentence topic, which includes the relative clause **byó=bá-àlì hīītì** 'which they had'. This is opposed to its unmarked position, which would be just after **í=byó kúlyâ** 'food', but before the relative clause. With the quantifier in this marked position, special prominence is given to the fact that all of the food (not just part of it) spilled on the ground.

## 10.3 Alternations of basic constituent order

(10.146)

| Topic | | | | | Topical prominence |
|---|---|---|---|---|---|
| Í=by-ókúlyá \| | by-ó= | bá-àlì | hì-ìt-í | | by-óshì ‖ |
| AU=8-food | 8-O.R= | 2-P3 | have-RS-Fi | | 8-all |

| Comment |
|---|
| by-àná-yòn-ék-à. |
| 8-SQ-spill-NEU-Fa |

'The food | which they had all ‖ it spilled.' (34 016)

### 10.3.4.2 Focal prominence

To give focal prominence, pronouns and quantifiers are postposed to the end of the entire clause, in focus position.

In (10.147) some domestic animals are talking to a rat which is caught in a trap. The pronoun **wényènè** 'yourself' occurs in a position of focus at the end of the clause. This helps to focus attention on the fact that the rat itself (in contrast to others) is expected to unspring the trap. The default order would be **wényènè ùhúsé ú=mútēgò** 'you yourself release the trap'.

(10.147)

| Comment | | Focal prominence |
|---|---|---|
| «Ù-Ø-hú-s-é | ú=mú-tègó \| | w-ényènè.» |
| 2SG-SBV-release-CS-Fe | AU=3-trap | 2SG-self |

'You release the trap | yourself.' (48 010)

In (10.148) the quantifier **bóóshì** 'all' is postposed to the end of the clause, to the point of focal prominence. The default order would be **yàbó báhīīvì bóóshì bànáyìgéndèrà** 'those hunters all just went away'.

(10.148)

| Topic | | Comment | Focal prominence |
|---|---|---|---|
| Yàbó | bá-hīīvì ‖ | bà-ná-yì-génd-èr-à | bó-óshì. |
| THOSE.N+2 | 2-hunters | 2-SQ-RFX-go-APL-Fa | 2-all |

'Those hunters ‖ they intentionally went away all of them.' (04 015)

# 11

# Dependent Clauses and Interclausal Relations

This chapter covers adverbial clauses, analytic causatives, concomitant clauses, complement clauses, relative clauses, and relations between independent clauses. In the final section of the chapter we summarize the environments where pause is found within these constructions.

## 11.1 Dependent adverbial clauses

Adverbial clauses are dependent clauses which express adverbial concepts. Those that tend to occur at the beginning of a sentence, preceding the independent clause, include conditionals, temporal, concessive, logical. Those that tend to occur at the end of the sentence, following the independent clause, include purpose/result, focus, attempt, and manner. There is also one type that regularly occurs either before or after the independent clause (reason).

The majority of these dependent adverbial clauses are introduced by conjunctions. Table 11.1 lists the various categories of adverbial clauses and the conjunctions which may introduce each type, along with the gloss of each conjunction. However, some adverbial clauses, rather than being introduced by conjunctions are instead marked by a high tone on the subject prefix of the verb (and no preceding conjunction), or consist only of an infinitive. These are summarized in table 11.2; the examples are given with the verb -**gend**- 'go'.[1]

---

[1] Other, non-dependent contrary-to-fact constructions may be characterized by an auxiliary, such as the form **tùshùbà túgágêndà** 'we would have gone'.

Table 11.1. Conjunctions which may introduce dependent adverbial clauses

| Category | Conjunction | Gloss |
|---|---|---|
| Default conditionals | **írí** | 'if' |
| Contrary-to-fact conditionals | **ngá** | 'if (contrary-to-fact)' |
| Temporal | **írí** | 'when' |
| | **íkyànyà** | 'at the time when (past)' |
| | **mángò** | 'when (timeless)' |
| | **mbú** | 'as soon as (suspenseful)' |
| | **írí** | 'that's when' |
| | **kwó** | 'when, at the time when' |
| Concessive | **kúndù** | 'even though' |
| Logical | **kú=yùkwò** | 'therefore' |
| | **kwôkwô** | 'thus' |
| | **kú=yàhò** | 'therefore' |
| Purpose/result | **hàlíndè** | 'until/result' |
| | **mbú** | 'with intention' |
| | **gírà** | 'so that' |
| Focus | **lyó** | 'that's when' |
| | **lyókì** | 'that's when (contrary to mistaken idea)' |
| Purpose/result, with focus | **hàlíndè lyó** | 'result (w/focus)' |
| | **mbú=lyó** | 'purpose (w/focus)' |
| | **gírá lyó** | 'so that (w/focus)' |
| Attempt | **-gírà with mbú / ngú / kwô** | 'attempted to' |
| Manner | **(ngíìsì) kwô** | '(just) how' |
| Reason | **mú=kúbâ** | 'because' |
| | **bwó** | 'since' |
| | **bwéngè** | 'since' |
| | **mbú=bwò** | 'for alleged reason' |
| | **mbú=bwèngè** | 'since (w/intention)' |

Table 11.2. Dependent adverbial clauses which
do not involve conjunctions

| Category | Dependent verb | Gloss |
|---|---|---|
| Temporal | **ú=kúgéndà** | 'when going' |
| | **túgéézìrì** | 'if/when we have gone' |
| | **tútàzígêndà** | 'before we have gone, when we have not yet gone' |
| Contrary-to-fact conditional | **túkìgêndè** | 'if we had gone (contrary-to-fact)' |

### 11.1.1 Conditional clauses

There are two ways to form conditional clauses: (a) The most common way is to employ the conjunction **ìrí**, before a verb with the conditional prefix **àngà**-. This forms the PROTASIS ("if" clause) of a default[2] conditional. Thus it focuses more on the uncertainty ('if...') of the event named by the verb of the dependent clause than on the relative time of that event. (b) Semantic "conditionals" can be indicated by a certain type of relative clause.

(a) For the most common conditional, the protasis is formed with the preceding conjunction **ìrí** 'if' and the conditional verb prefix **àngà**- 'would'. The independent verb in the APODOSIS ("then" clause, also called independent clause) may be in the continuative (CON), the intervening time (INTV), or the unmarked future (F2).

In (11.1) the protasis of the default conditional **ìrí à-ngà-lùkà** 'if she would braid' is followed by a command expressed by the continuative verb (CON) in the main clause **nàwé ùnálùké ú=gûndì** 'and you also, you braid another'.

(11.1) **É=mwān-è** ‖ **nyókókùlù** **ìrí** **à-ngà-lùk-à**
O=child-pay.attention 1a+your.grandmother if 1-CND-weave-Fa

**ú=mù-gózì** ‖ **nà-wé** **ù-ná-lùk-é** **ú=gû-ndì**.
AU=3-rope ADD.P-2SG 2SG-CON-weave-Fe AU=3-other

'O child (pay attention) ‖ your grandmother if she braids a rope ‖ and YOU ALSO you braid another.' (18 018)

In (11.2) we see the default conditional **ìrí nàngàsíndwà** 'if I lose the case'. The result which will follow if that condition is met is then found in the main clause, where the verb form is the intervening time (INTV) 'after an intervening time' marked by the prefix **ká**- preceded by a low tone subject

---

[2]"Default" is to say that this construction is not contrary-to-fact, and also that it is not primarily temporally oriented.

marker and with the subjunctive final vowel: **ùkánjèègè** 'you will eat me for supper'.

(11.2) **Ìrí**   n-<u>àngà</u>-sínd-w-à   ‖   ù-<u>ká</u>-n-jèèg-è.
     if   1SG-CND-defeat-PS-Fa   2SG- INTV-O1.SG-have.for.supper-Fe

'If I lose the case ‖ you eat me for supper.' (14 005)

It is also quite common to find a verb in the unmarked future (F2) tense in the main clause which follows the default conditional. In (11.3) the default conditional is followed by the F2 form **ngáákùlyà** 'I will eat you'.

(11.3) **Ìrí**   ù-tà-<u>ngà</u>-n-yígùl-ìr-à   ‖   n-gáá-kú-ly-à.
     if   2SG-NEG-CND-O1-open-APL-Fa   1SG-F2-O2.SG-eat-Fa

'If you don't open the door for me ‖ I will eat you!' (105 041)

(b) A RELATIVE CLAUSE, optionally with **ngíìsì** 'whichever/whoever' and obligatorily having a future or conditional verb, can also have a semantically conditional meaning. In (11.4) the relative clause **ngíìsì úgágùgírà** 'whoever will do it' serves as the focus of this sentence in identificational articulation, and semantically, sets forth a condition.

(11.4) **Ngíìsì** |   **ú-gá-gù-gír-à**   ‖   y-é=   ní-gá-hèèrèz-à | ù-yú
     whichever   S.R+1-F2-O3-do-Fa   FOC-1=   1SG-F2-give-Fa   1-this.P

**mú-lùzìnyèrè.**
1-king's.daughter

'Whoever | will do it ‖ he's the one to whom I will give | this king's daughter.' (25 008)

### 11.1.2 Contrary-to-fact conditional/result clauses

A contrary-to-fact[3] conditional is used in the protasis of a contrary-to-fact "if/then" statement. A contrary-to-fact result is found in the apodosis of such a statement.

The contrary-to-fact conditionals/results can be formed in two basic ways, listed here, and exemplified in this section: (a) with the conjunction **nga** 'like' preceding the verb (in certain tenses), or (b) with the conditional, contrary-to-fact persistive subjunctive.

(a) Looking first at the contrary-to-fact forms which employ the contrary-to-fact conjunction **nga** 'like, as if', we see that the CONDITIONAL, CONTRARY-TO-FACT

---

[3] "Contrary-to-fact" could also be called "counter-factual".

is formed in the same way as the default conditional, except that the conjunction **iri**, used with the default conditional, is replaced in the contrary-to-fact conditionals by the conjunction **nga** 'like, as' in the protasis. The conjunction **nga** is used with several different forms of the verb, both in condition clauses and in result clauses. These contrary-to-fact conditional and result forms are listed below:

Conditional, contrary-to-fact, non-past (CND.C.F). This employs the conjunction **nga** followed by a verb with the TAM prefix **àngà-** and the resultative (RS) form of the verb base, (with low tone on both syllables of the prefix, and Complex HL stem tone pattern on the verb stem): **ngá=tw-àngà-gééz-ìr-ì** 'if we were going (but we're not)'.

Conditional, contrary-to-fact, past (CND.C.F.PST). This employs the conjunction **nga** followed by a verb with the TAM prefix **ángá-** and the resultative (RS) form of the verb base, (with high tone on both syllables of the TAM prefix and a Complex LL stem tone pattern):[4] **ngá=tw-ángá-gééz-ìr-ì** 'if we had been going (but we weren't)'.

Result, contrary-to-fact, recent past (P1) **ngá=tw-à-génd-à** 'then we would go (but we won't)'.

Result, contrary-to-fact, unmarked past (P2) **ngá=tú-ká-génd-à** 'then we would have gone (but we didn't)'.

These forms are most often used in clauses which have the meaning "if X were true (but it's not) then Y would be true (but it's not either)". Since such constructions do not tend to occur in traditional narratives, all of the examples below are from biblical text.

In (11.5) the "conditional, contrary-to-fact, past" protasis **ngá=by-ángá-zíz-ìr-ì** 'if it had been (but was not) possible' is used to express that they would have taken out their eyes and given them to the writer, (but of course that was not possible).

(11.5) **Mw-áàlì   rì-ìr-í     mú-gá-jóbòl-à  |  kírí    n-á=      má-sú    gì-ì-nyù ||**
       2PL-P3     is-RS-Fi   2PL-F2-take.out-Fa  even   CNJ-AU=  6-eyes   6-A.M-2PL

   **mù-ná-gá-m-bèèrèz-é |      ngá=    by-ángá-zíz-ìr-ì.**
   2PL-CON-O6-O1.SG-give-Fe    if.C.F=  8-CND.C.F-be.possible-RS-Fi

   'You were (ready to) take out | even your eyes || and give them to me | if it had been possible (it wasn't).' (Gal 4:15)

---

[4]Note that in the surface form of verbs whose stems have H lexical tone (such as -**génd**- 'go'), the Complex LL stem-tone pattern is identical to the Complex HL pattern. In verbs with L lexical tone, or in verbs whose stems have no underlying tone, the differences between the two patterns are evident, and are not neutralized as they are in H-tone verb stems.

In (11.6) the phrase **ngá=w-àngà-mény-ìr-ì** 'if you knew (but you don't)' exemplifies the conditional, contrary-to-fact (non-past) form. Here it has the sense of "if only", because there is no following apodosis ("then" clause).

(11.6) <u>Ngá=</u>   w-àngà-mény-ìr-ì   búnò |
      if.C.F=   2-CND.C.F-know-RS-Fi   now

í-by-àngà-kú-lét-í-ìr-í       ú=mú-tùùlà! ||
S.R-8-CND.C.F-O2.SG-bring-APL-RS-Fi   AU=3-peace

Hálìkò bú-nò | á=má-sú   gà-à-wè |   gà-bì-bìsh-ír-w-ì.
but         14-now AU=6-eyes  6-A.M-2SG  6-O8-hide-RS-PS-Fi

'If (only) you knew (but you don't) now | what would bring you peace! ||
But now | your eyes | (those things) are hidden from them.' (Luk 19:42)

In (11.7), the form is used in wishing something were possible, as the people say "if (only) it were possible, that we could keep getting meat to eat".

(11.7) <u>Ngá=</u>   by-àngà-shóbòs-ìr-ì ||   tù-Ø-kízì   lòng-á   í=ny-ámá
      if.C.F=   8-CND.C.F-be.able-RS-Fi   1PL-SBV-REP  receive-Fa  AU=9-meat

y-ó=     kú-ly-à.
9-A.M+AU=  15-eat-Fa

'If (only) it were possible (but it is not) || we would repeatedly get meat to eat.' (Num 11:4)

(b) The "conditional contrary-to-fact persistive subjunctive" (CND.C.F.PERS) is formed with high tone on the prefix which precedes the aspect marker **kì-** and with the subjunctive final vowel **-e**. This is a past tense contrary-to-fact conditional, meaning 'if something had been true (but was not)' (or in the negative, 'if something had not been true, but was'). In every case, the protasis clause which contains this form is followed by a contrary-to-fact result clause.

Though it can be used with any verb, the CND.C.F.PERS is often used with the copula **-ba-** 'become', as in (11.8), where the point is made that 'if it had not been for him, then all of us, you would have choked us (but he was there, so you didn't)'. Note the **ngá** at the beginning of the 'then' clause, followed, after the preposed object, by the P1 form of the verb **w-à-tù-níg-à** 'you (would have) choked us'.

## 11.1 Dependent adverbial clauses

(11.8) <u>À-tá-kì-b-è</u>　　　y-êhê ‖ ngá= 　　nyìì-tù　　tw-éshí |
1-NEG-CND.C.F.PERS-be-Fe　1-CTR.P 　then.C.F=　ADD.P-1PL　1PL-all

w-à-tù-níg-à.
2SG-P1-O1.PL-choke-Fa

'If it had not been (for) HIM ‖ then all of US | you would have choked us.'
(23 046)

In (11.9) we see another example of the CND.C.F.PERS form, again with the negative, where it marks the verb **-keerez-** 'be late'.

(11.9) <u>Tù-tá-kì-kèèrèz-è</u>　　‖　ngá=　　kééràa　　tw-à-gáluk-à
1-NEG-CND.C.F.PERS-be.late-Fe　　then.C.F=　ALREADY　1PL-P1-return-Fa

=yô | ú=bù-gìrà　kà-bìrì.
=23　AU=14-times　12-two

'If we had not been late ‖ then we could have (gone and) returned (from) there | twice.' (Gen 43:10)

(c) A "relative clause in contrary-to fact form" can also have a somewhat conditional meaning. In (11.10) **úwàngàlíírì** (with the low tone (non-past) **àngà-** prefix and the following resultative form of the verb base, which together signify contrary-to-fact) means 'the one who would eat (but has not)'. In other words, this relative verb semantically presents the hypothetical but still possible condition "if anyone were to eat". In the "then" clause following this hypothetical "condition", the next verb is a P1 form preceded by the contrary-to-fact conjunction **nga: ngá=bàmúshúlìkà** 'then they would hit him (they haven't)'.

(11.10) <u>Ú-w-àngà-lí-ír-í</u>　　yì-bí　　bí-júmbù ‖　ngá=
S.R-1-POT.C.F-eat-RS-Fi　this.P-8　8-potatoes　then.CF.=

bà-mú-shúlìk-à.
2+P1-O1-hit-Fa

'The one who would eat these potatoes ‖ they would hit him (but they haven't).'

### 11.1.3 Temporal clauses

There are several ways to form dependent temporal clauses in Kifuliiru: These clauses generally occur as the initial clause of a sentence and can be introduced by a temporal conjunction, such as **írí** 'when' (followed by unmarked past), **í=kyànyà** 'time' (followed by many possible tenses), **mángò** 'when' (followed by timeless or recent past) or **mbú** 'as soon as' (followed by subjunctive). The conjunction **írí**, used in a clause which follows the main verb, can also mean 'that's when'. In addition, rather than being marked by a conjunction, other dependent temporal clauses can be marked by a high tone on the subject prefix of the verb. Finally, there are two relatively rare forms for temporal clauses, one using the infinitive, and the other employing **kwo** 'when'. In this section we list nine different variations of temporal clauses.

(a) The conjunction **írí**, can introduce a sentence-initial temporal clause. The verb of this dependent clause is nearly always in the P2 tense. The clause introduced by this conjunction often restates some aspect of the previous main clause. Such a construction is used to maintain continuity in a narrative by introducing a new episode/paragraph while at the same time linking back to the event of the previous sentence. This is similar to what is sometimes called "tail-head linkage" (Thompson and Longacre 1985:209–213). In many cases, the main verb of the clause which follows the dependent temporal clause is marked by the sequential tense (SQ), with the prefix **àná-**.

In (11.11) the clause **írí bákáhíká mwí=shámbà** 'when they arrived in the wilderness' is followed by a clause with the sequential tense (SQ) **bànátòndéézá ú=kúhīīvà** 'they began to hunt'.

(11.11) <u>**írí     bá-ká-hík-à**</u>     **mw-í=   shámbá**  ||  **bà-ná-tòndééz-á** |
      when  2-P2-arrive-Fa     18-5=    wilderness       2-SQ-begin-Fa

    **ú=kú-hīīv-à.**
    AU=15-hunt-Fa

'When they arrived in the wilderness || they began | to hunt.' (03 005)

Used in this way, as a link between episodes, the subject of the dependent temporal clause does not necessarily have to be the same as the subject in the second clause, and often it is not. Instead a new subject can be introduced in the second clause. For example, in (11.12) the temporal clause occurs within a point of departure (10.2.4) with a subject which differs from that of the main clause. The subject of the first clause is **ùyó mwānà** 'that.N child', while the subject of the second clause is **yîshè** 'his father'.

## 11.1 Dependent adverbial clauses

(11.12) Ùyó   mw-ānà || írí   á-ká-yús-á   ú=kú-vùn-á   yìzó
that.N+1  1-child   when  1-P2-finish-Fa  AU=15-break-Fa  those.N+10

n-gónì || yîshè   || à-ná-bà-bwír-à:...
10-sticks  1a+his.father  1-SQ-O2-tell-Fa

'That child || when he finished breaking those sticks || his father || told them:' (02 018)

(b) The conjunction **í=kyànyà** '(at the) time (when)' refers to a specific time, and often introduces a dependent clause which, in default order, precedes the main clause. The dependent time clause introduced by **í=kyànyà** may contain a verb with any of a number of different TAM markings, in the past, present, and future. Either stative or dynamic verb forms may occur in the dependent clause. Some examples are given here below.

The conjunction **í=kyànyà** 'time' sometimes (but not nearly as often) functions in a way similar to the conjunction **ìrí**, in that it can mark a temporal discontinuity in a narrative and therefore also indicate a paragraph break. This happens in (11.13) where the conjunction **í=kyànyà** 'time' is part of a clause with the unmarked past (P2) tense marker **ká-** in the clause **í=kyànyà ákábá kéèrà àlùbìshà** 'when he had already hidden it'.

(11.13) **Í=ky-ànyà**   á-ká-b-á   kééerà   à-lù-bìsh-à   ||
AU=7-time  1-P2-become-Fa  ALREADY  1+P1-O11-hide-Fa

à-ná-dóòt-à   í=n-dúùlù || kwó= kééra  yîbà   |
1-SQ-scream-Fa  AU=9-scream  CMP=  ALREADY  her.husband

à-fw-à.
1+P1-die-Fa

'When she had already hidden it || she screamed || that already her husband | has died.' (54 012)

In (11.14) the conjunction **í=kyànyà** 'time' is part of a dependent clause in the recent past tense (P1), in the clause **íkyànyà wàzìhàndúlà** 'when you separate them'.

(11.14) Hálìkò   í=ky-ànyà         w-à-zì-hàndúl-à     ‖   mú-lùmúná
       but      AU=7-time         2SG-P1-O10-separate-Fa  1-little.brother

       w-ì-nyù   ‖   y-é=     w-à-zì-vùn-à |   zóó-shì.
       2SG-A.M-2PL   1-FOC=   1-P1-break-Fa    10-all

'But when you separated them ‖ your little brother ‖ is the one who broke them | all.' (02 017)

In (11.15) the conjunction **í=kyànyà** 'time' is part of a clause in the present progressive.

(11.15) **Í=ky-ànyà** |   à-lì    mú=     fùlúk-à           ‖   à-lì   mú=
       AU=7-time       1-is    PROG=   return.fr.work-Fa      1-is   PROG=

       mù-gír-ír-á   |   í=by-ókúlyâ.
       O2P-do-APL-Fa    AU=8-food

'The time | he is coming home from work ‖ he is making for you | food.' (602 021)

In (11.16) the conjunction **í=kyànyà** is part of a clause in the future tense, **íkyànyà múgáàbà mùkòlà mû=lyâ** 'when you have begun to eat (lit., when you will be you are now eating)'.

(11.16) **Í=ky-ànyà**    mú-gáá-b-à           mù-kòlà        mû=     ly-â   ‖
       AU=7-time       2PL-F2-become-Fa     2PL-be.NEWLY   PROG=   eat-Fa

       ù-ná-mú-bwìr-è:...
       2SG-CON-O1-tell-Fe

'The time you (PL) will be you are now eating ‖ tell him:' (606 038)

The form **í=kyànyà** 'time' can also be followed by an associative phrase with an infinitive complement, as in (11.17) where **í=kyànyà** is modified by the phrase **kyó=kúgéndí yègéréza á=bágénì** 'of going to welcome guests'.

(11.17) **Í=ky-ànyà** |   ky-ó=        kú-géndí    yègéré-z-á       á=bá-génì   ‖
       AU=7-time       7-A.M+AU=    15-GOING    welcome-CS-Fa    AU=2-guests

       à-ná-yì-téér-à      há=   m-bérè.
       1-SQ-RFX-went-Fa    16=   9-before

'The time | of going to welcome the guests ‖ he went on ahead.' (34 007)

Finally, the clause headed by **í=kyànyà** can occur after the main clause, although this is somewhat rare, and perhaps represents an afterthought. In (11.18) the clause **í=kyànyà múgábàyègèrèzâ** 'the time you will welcome them' is sentence final.

(11.18) Kú=   yà-hò      ‖   ni-êhê      n-ié=     mú-gáá-kìzì   lól-ér-á
       17=   there.N-16       1SG-CTR.P   1-O.R=    2PL-F2-REP    look-APL-Fa

=kwó ‖ <u>í=ky-ànyà</u> |   <u>mú-gá-bà-yègèrè-z-â</u>.
=17      AU=7-time         2PL-F2-O2-welcome-CS-Fa

'Therefore ‖ ME I am the one whom you will be continuously looking at ‖ at the time | when you will welcome them.' (34 005)

(c) The conjunction **mángò** 'when' may refer to an unknown, hypothetical time in the future, involving a possibility that has not yet been realized. The verb of a dependent clause introduced by **mángò** is always marked either with timeless (TL) or recent past (P1) tense.

Some speakers, when using the formal speech register, use only a verb in the timeless tense in a temporal clause introduced by **mángò**. In (11.19) **mángò** is used with a following timeless verb in the dependent clause **mángò tùhíká ímwìtù-vyàlà** 'when we arrive at our in-laws' place' to establish the time frame of the independent clause which follows.

(11.19) <u>Mángò</u>   tù-Ø-hík-á      |   í-mw-ì-tù-vyàlà           ‖
        when         1PL-TL-arrive-Fa   23-home-A.M-1PL-in.law

ú-gáà-b-à          nyândì?
2SG-F2-become- Fa  who

'When we arrive | at the place of our in-laws ‖ who will you be?' (09 003)

In (11.20) **mángò** is followed by a verb in the timeless tense: **mùgìbònà** 'you see it'.

(11.20) <u>Mángò</u>   mù-Ø-gì-bòn-à ‖   mù-ná-gì-yìt-è.
        when         2PL-TL-O9-see-Fa   2PL-CON-O9-kill-Fe

'When you see it ‖ kill it.' (09 031)

In (11.21) **mángò** 'if/when' is followed by a negative form of the timeless tense, **ùtàgíndéétérà** 'you don't bring it to me'.

(11.21) Nà=    mángò    ù-Ø-tà-gí-n-déét-ér-à    ‖    n-gá-kú-yìt-à.
       CNJ=   when     2SG-TL-NEG-O9-bring-APL-Fa    1SG-F2-O2.SG-kill-Fa

'And when you don't bring it to me ‖ I will kill you.' (24 017)

In the informal speech register, besides the timeless tense, clauses introduced by **mángò** may also have verbs in the recent past (P1) tense. In (11.22) **mángò** precedes the P1 past **nàhíkà** 'I arrive'.[5]

(11.22) **Mángò**    n-à-hík-à         yà-hô      ‖   n-gá-kú-shúlìk-à.
        when         1SG-P1-arrive-Fa  there.N-16     1SG-F2-O2.SG-hit-Fa

'When I arrive there ‖ I will hit you.' (407 016)

An alternative pronunciation of **mángò** used by some speakers[6] is exemplified in (11.23) where **hángò** 'when' is used, here in a clause with its verb in the timeless tense: **mùtàgìyùbákà** 'you do not build it'.

(11.23) **Hángò**    mù-tà-Ø-gì-yùbák-à       ngá=   kw-ó=    y-áàlí   rì-ír-ì ‖
        when         2PL-NEG-TL-O9-build-Fa   like=  15-O.R=  9-P3     is-RS-Fi

       mú-gá-yì-bòn-èr-à           =kwô.
       2PL-F2-RFX-see-APL-Fa       =17

'When you do not build it just as it was ‖ you will see for yourselves what happens!' (23 020)

(d) The conjunction **mbú** 'as soon as' introduces a dependent clause in which the verb is always in the subjunctive form. The clause expresses immediacy and and triggers a heightened expectation that something important is about to happen. In (11.24) the clause **mbwà=bónè (mbú=àbónè)** 'when he saw' indicates that something important is about to happen soon in the discourse.

---

[5] The corresponding timeless form would be **mbíkà** 'I arrive'.
[6] We have not investigated the parameters regarding the use of this alternative pronunciation. It is much less frequently heard than **mángò**.

## 11.1 Dependent adverbial clauses

(11.24)　Lw-ânwá　mbw-à=　　Ø-bón-é |　kwê=　yò　　n-dáló |
　　　　　11-beard　as.soon.as-1=　SBV-see-Fe　CMP=　that.N+9　9-field

　　　　　bà-gì-táás-à　　lú-hândè ||　à-ná-tòndééz-á |　ú=kú-kīzì　géndí |
　　　　　2+P1-O9-ruin-Fa　11-half　　1-SQ-begin-Fa　　AU=15-REP　GOING

　　　　　gì-lál-íír-à.
　　　　　O9-sleep-APL-Fa

'As soon as Beard saw | that that field | they have ruined half (of it) || he began | to repeatedly go | guard it.' (50 016)

In (11.25) **mbú** precedes the subjunctive form **bàgùbònè** 'they see it'. The idea is that as soon as the girls saw the snake, right then they were startled.

(11.25)　Bá-nyérè　nákìrìrì |　　　mbú=　　　bà-Ø-gù-bòn-è ||　bà-ná-yàmí
　　　　　2-daughters　favorite.wife　as.soon.as=　2-SBV-O3-see-Fa　2-SQ-IMMED

　　　　　yì-káng-à　 ||　mbú=　«Ø-Lòl-á　　gù-lyá |　mú-jōkà!»
　　　　　RFX-startle-Fa　quote　IMP.S-look-Fa　3-that.R　3-snake

'The daughters of the favorite wife | as soon as they saw it || they immediately startled themselves || ‹quote›: «Look at that | snake!»' (512 037)

In (11.26) **mbú** precedes the subjunctive verb **bùhíkè** 'it reached'. The event described here is a turning point in the narrative of which it is a part.

(11.26)　Ú=bú-shìgì　mbú=　　　bù-Ø-hík-é　　　há=　kà-tì　　||　yìkyó
　　　　　AU=14-night　as.soon.as=　14-SBV-arrive-Fe　16=　12-middle　　that.N+7

　　　　　kí-shégèshè |　ky-àná-shálìk-à.
　　　　　7-porcupine　　7-SQ-be.hungry-Fa

'As soon as the night reached the middle || that porcupine | got hungry.' (09 009)

(e) The infinitive (with optional **mú** 'cl.18, in' preceding), can be used as the "main verb" of a temporal clause. This is quite an informal usage, and its grammaticality in formal speech is questionable. The effect of using the infinitive is similar to that of using **mbú** followed by the subjunctive, i.e. there is a sense that some major event is impending.

In (11.27) an infinitive with preceding locative **mú** 'in' is used to express a dependent temporal clause: **mú=kúhìhámbà** 'in putting it in'. Also, in this case, the cl. 19 object **hì-** 'it' seen in the infinitive **kúhìhámbà** refers to the same referent which is the subject in the following main clause **hìnámúbwìrè** 'and it told him'. The effect is to take the focus off the man, who was the subject of the previous sentence, and place it on the little bird which the cl. 19 markers refer to.

(11.27) Ù-lyá   mú-shósì   à-ná-hì-vùn-è.   ‖   Mú=   kú-hì-hámb-á
       1-that.R  1-man      1-CON-O19-break-Fe   18=    15-O19-put.into-Fa

       mú=   lú-dáhà |   hì-ná-mú-bwìr-é:...
       18    11-bag      19-CON-O1-tell-Fe

'That man broke it. ‖ In putting it in the bag | it told him:...' (403 010-011)

In (11.28) only the infinitive **ú=kúgéndì híkà** 'to go and arrive' is followed by the fact that the man finds his wife caught in a trap. The implied, but unexpressed "subject" of **ú=kúgéndì híkà** 'to go arrive' is assumed to be the same as that of the preceding clause.

(11.28) À-ná-yàmì    génd-á   =yò.  ‖   Ú=kú-géndì    hík-á    | í=
        1-SQ-IMMED   go-Fa    =23       AU=15-GOING   arrive-Fa  23=

        w-á=          mí-tēgò ‖   à-gwán-á         |   kéèrà     mú-ká-à-gé |
        place-A.M=    4-traps     1+P1-encounter-Fa    ALREADY   1-wife-A.M-1

        à-gwát-w-à.
        1+P1-seize-PS-Fa

'And he immediately went there. ‖ When (he) went and arrived | at the traps ‖ he encountered | already his wife | has been seized.' (401 027)

(f) A high tone realized on the subject marker of a verb form whose subject marker otherwise has a low tone indicates a dependent clause meaning 'if/when'. Thus **átàlì** 'if/when he is not' contrasts with **àtàlì** 'he is not'. Other examples of such forms are **tútàlì** 'if we are not', **túgèndà** 'if/when we go' (both conditional timeless), **tútàzìgéndà** 'if/when we have not yet gone, or before we have gone' (conditional NOT.YET), and **túgéézìrì** 'if/when we have gone' (conditional resultative).

When the high tone subject prefix occurs with the negative form of the copula -**li**, the meaning, 'if..is/are not', is also translatable as 'except that... be', 'except for...' or 'unless...is/are'. In (11.29) the meaning is that there is no other witness, 'if (he is) not God or except for God'.

## 11.1 Dependent adverbial clauses

(11.29) **Ndáá-kó**    kà-ndì    ká-màsí | á-kà-lì    =hô ‖ <u>á-tà-lì</u>
NEG.FOC-12    12-other   12-witness   S.R-12-is   =16   1+IF-NEG-is

**Rúrémà.**
God

'There is no other witness | which exists ‖ if not (i.e. except for) God.'
(Gen 31:50)

In (11.30) the high-tone subject prefix occurs with the timeless verb **hálèngà** 'when there pass'. This form contrasts with the unmarked recent past (P1) form **hàlèngà**, the latter of which means 'there passed'.

(11.30) <u>**Há-Ø-lèng-à**</u>    ngá=   sìkù    zì-bìrì ‖ kàndì írí zì-shàtù ‖
16-WHEN-pass-Fa   like=   10+days   10-two    or     10-three

**ù-ná-gêndí**     **tàndúúl-á**    **í=kí-tálì.**
2SG-CON-GOING   check.out-Fa   AU=7-banana.pit

'When there have passed about two days ‖ or three ‖ you go and check out the banana pit.' (411 018)

This high tone subject prefix can also be used with the negative form of the timeless tense, meaning 'when X has not (yet) occurred', or put other ways, 'before X occurs', or 'without X having occurred'. In (11.31) the high tone on **bá-** (the subject marker of **bátàzì híkà**) changes the meaning to 'when they had not yet arrived'. (Compare this to the form with the unmarked low tone subject prefix: **bàtàzì híkà** 'they have not yet arrived'.)

(11.31) <u>**Bá-Ø-tà-zì**</u>     **hík-á**    =yò ‖ ù-lyá   dáàtá   | à-ná-b-é
2-WHEN-NEG-YET   arrive-Fa   =23   1-that.R   1a+father   1-CON-be-Fe

**kéèrà** | **á-àlì málì**    **gwánwá** | **à-hík-à.**
ALREADY   1-P3   ALREADY   encountered   1-arrive-Fa

'When they had not yet arrived there ‖ that father | had already | been encountered | arrived.' (506 049)

(g) The conjunction **ìrí** 'while' or 'same time', when occurring *after* the main clause, refers to the *same time* as that main clause. When the dependent clause introduced by **ìrí** occurs after the main clause, the verb of the dependent clause is always marked with the additive morpheme. In addition, the subject of the dependent clause must be the same as that of the preceding main clause.[7]

---

[7] This is not a grammaticized construction, since the verbs in both the dependent clause and the independent clause are chosen from an open class.

In (11.32) the subject of the clause **ànátòndéézà ú=kúlèngà mwó=músísì** 'and he began to tremble' is the same as that of the following clause **ìrí ánálírà** 'while he also cried'. The form **ìrí** indicates that the two events happened at the very same time and with the same subject.

(11.32) **Mw-āmì | à-ná-vyûk-à ǁ à-ná-tòndééz-à ú=kú-lèng-á mw-ó=**
1-king  1-SQ-get.up-Fa  1-SQ-begin-Fa  AU=15-pass-Fa  18-AU=

**mú-sísí | ìrí à-ná-lír-à.**
3-shaking  while  1-ADD.V-cry-Fa

'The king | got up ǁ and began to shake | while crying.' (24 009)

In (11.33) the phrase **ìrí ànáyìbùlágà hááshì** 'while she threw herself down' shows that the action of throwing herself down is happening at the same time as the crying.

(11.33) **À-ná-tòndééz-à ú=kú-lír-à ǁ ìrí à-ná-yì-bùl-ág-à**
1-SQ-begin-Fa  AU=15-cry-Fa  while  1-ADD.V-RFX-throw.down-EMP-Fa

**hááshì.**
down.on.ground

'And she began to cry ǁ while throwing herself down on ground.' (40 017)

In (11.34) the action of the first verb **ànágìyìtà** 'and he killed it' happens at the same time as the action of the following one: **ànálèngà** 'and he passed'. Again, both verbs have the same subject.

(11.34) **Ùyó mú-tēzì ǁ à-ná-gì-yìt-à dúbà | ìrí**
that.N+1  1-trapper  1-SQ-O9-kill-Fa  quickly  while

**à-ná-lèng-à mw-ó= mú-sísì.**
1-ADD.V-pass-Fa  18-AU=  3-shaking

'That trapper ǁ killed it quickly | while shaking.' (35 032)

(h) When **kwó** is used as a conjunction, it means 'at the time when'. The use of this form as a conjunction is quite rare (**kwó** 'that/how' is normally used as a complementizer). In (11.35) **kwó** is used as a conjunction and means 'at the time when', referring here to the time when the lion has not yet come.

## 11.1 Dependent adverbial clauses

(11.35) **Tù-Ø-yám-é     tw-à-bùng-à** ‖ **kwó=   W-á=n-dàrè** |
1PL-SBV-IMMED-Fe   1PL-P1-move-Fa   when=   1-A.M=9-lion

**à-tà-zì    yíj-à.**
1-NEG-YET   come-Fa

'Let's immediately move ‖ at the time when Lion | has not yet come.'
(605 018)

(i) Multiple dependent temporal clauses can occur before a single main clause. In (11.36) the first temporal clause is **zìryá sìkì zìríndà írí zíkáhíkà** 'those seven days, when they came'. The second time clause, which follows it, is **írí bákágéndì yígúlà** 'when they went and opened'. After those two dependent clauses, the main clause follows, **bákágwáná í=kísììkà kyóshì** 'they encountered the whole inner room…'.

(11.36)

| 1st temporal clause | | | | |
|---|---|---|---|---|
| **Zì-ryá** | **sìkù** | **zì-ríndà** ‖ | **írí** | **zí-ká-hík-à** ‖ |
| 10-those.R | 10+days | 10-seven | when | 10-P2-arrive-Fa |

| 2nd temporal clause | | |
|---|---|---|
| **írí** | **bá-ká-géndì** | **yígúl-à** ‖ |
| when | 2-P2-GOING | open-Fa |

| Main clause | | |
|---|---|---|
| **bá-ká-gwán-á** ‖ | **í=kí-sììkà** | **ky-óshì**… |
| 2-P2-encounter-Fa | AU=7-inner.room | 7-all |

'Those seven days ‖ when they arrived ‖ when they went and opened ‖ they encountered ‖ the whole inner room…' (106 143)

In (11.37) there are two dependent temporal clauses preceding the main verb, both introduced by **ìrí** 'when'. They are **ìrí ákáhééká yìryó í=bûndà** 'when she got pregnant' and **ìrí ákáyíjí būtà** 'when she gave birth'. The main verb follows **ànábùtà ú=mújōkà** 'she gave birth to a snake'.

(11.37)

| | 1st temporal clause | | | |
|---|---|---|---|---|
| **Iri** | a-ka-heek-a | yiryo | í-bûndà | ‖ |
| When | 1-P2-carry-Fa | that.N+5 | 5-pregnancy | |

| | 2nd temporal clause | | | Main clause | |
|---|---|---|---|---|---|
| **ìrí** | á-ká-yíjí | būt-à ‖ | | à-ná-bùt-à | \| mú-jōkà. |
| when | 1-P2-COMING | give.birth-Fa | | 1-SQ-give.birth-Fa | 3-snake |

'When she got pregnant ‖ when she came to give birth ‖ she gave birth to | a snake.' (633 005)

Rarely, the introductory temporal clauses can be of different types, and up to three may occur successively preceding a single main clause. In (11.38) the first temporal clause employs the infinitive: **mú=kúgálúkà** 'in returning'. The second one includes an implied **ikyanya** 'time': **(íkyànyà) kìkòlá ngá=kyànyà kyà=kálèngé-rēngè** '(time) it is now about the time of noon', as is the third: **(íkyànyà) kéèrà ízùùbá lyàtùshúlìkà** '(the time) the sun has already beat on us'. Following these introductory temporal clauses, the verb of the main clause is in the sequential tense: **twànálèngà** 'and we passed'.

(11.38)    1st temporal clause

| **Mú=** | kú-gálúk-à ‖ |
|---|---|
| IN.STATE= | 15-return-Fa |

2nd temporal clause

| kì-kòlá \| | ngá= | ky-ànyà \| | ky-à= | ká-lèngé-rēngè ‖ |
|---|---|---|---|---|
| 7-be.NEWLY | like= | 7-time | 7-A.M | 12-noon-RDP |

3rd temporal clause

| kéèrà | í-zùùbá \| | ly-à-tù-shúlìk-à ‖ |
|---|---|---|
| ALREADY | 5-sun | 5-P1-O1.PL-hit-Fa |

Main clause

| tw-àná-lèng-à \| | há-ndú | há-gùmà. |
|---|---|---|
| 1PL-SQ-pass-Fa | 16-place | 16-one |

'In returning ‖ it is now | about the time | of noon ‖ already the sun | has beat on us ‖ and we passed | one place...' (635 003)

### 11.1.4 Concessive clauses

Dependent concessive clauses may be formed in two different ways. (a) The conjunction **kúndù** 'even though', may introduce the clause, or (b) the clause may be formed by a verb having the additive prefix **ná**- (with no introductory conjunction).

(a) The conjunction **kúndù** 'even though' introduces a dependent concessive clause. In (11.39) **kúndú ízùùbá lìkáyìrì** means 'even though the sun is fierce'.

(11.39) <u>Kúndú</u>    í-zùùbá   lì-káy-ìr-ì  ‖ n-gá-yìhàngààn-á   nààhó |
Even.though  5-sun   5-is.fierce-RS-Fi  1SG-F2-persevere-Fa  only

      hàlíndè    n-Ø-gú-hí-s-è.
      until       1SG-SBV-O2.SG-arrive-CS-Fe

'Even though the sun is fierce ‖ I will just persevere | until I cause you to arrive.' (27 029)

The verb of a dependent clause introduced by the conjunction **kúndù** may be marked for any of several TAM categories, including the resultative, as seen above in (11.39), as well as the conditional, the unmarked past tense (P2) and the timeless copula. The clause may also be elided, as in (11.40), where it is followed only by the cl. 15 demonstrative pronoun **kwôkwô** 'thus' with no other verb. In (11.40) **kúndú kwôkwô** means 'even so', or 'even though (it is) like that (referring to an event that was previously mentioned)'.

(11.40) <u>Kúndú</u>    kwôkwô ‖ ùyó    shòòkùlú   w-à-gè |
Even.though  thus.N    that.N+1  1a+old.man  1-A.M-1

      á-tá-ká-lúh-à.
      1-NEG-P2-be.tired-Fa

'Even so ‖ that grandfather of his | did not get tired.' (619 022)

(b) In Kifuliiru the concessive clause can be formed by a verb having the additive prefix **ná**-. In (11.41) the meaning is 'How is it that they don't see evil and (even though) they have eyes?' The concessive meaning is here communicated by the additive **ná**- prefix in the verb **bànáhíìtì**.

(11.41) **Kùtí  bà-tà-lì  mú=  bòn-á  á=má-bî ‖ bà-ná-hí-ìt-ì**
How    2-NEG-are  PROG=  see-Fa  AU=6-evil  2-ADD.V-have-RS-Fi

**n-á=  má-sû?**
CNJ-AU=  6-eyes?

'How (is it that) they are not seeing bad things ‖ and they have eyes?'
(523 039)

In (11.42) the concessive notion 'even when' is communicated by the additive **ná** in **bànákìrì** 'and they still are'. The idea is 'others are buried and (even though) they are alive'.

(11.42) **...n-á=  bà-ndì ‖ bà-ná-kìzì  bà-zíík-à ‖ bà-ná-kìrì |**
CNJ-AU=  2-others  2-SQ-REP  O2-bury-Fa  2-ADD.V-PERS

**bá-gùmààna.**
2-alive.

'...and others ‖ they habitually buried them ‖ and they are still | alive.'
(23 008)

In (11.43) the children ask their father 'where will we pass in coming down and (even though) you have taken away the vine'. This idea 'even though' is communicated by the additive **ná-** in the verb **wànátòlà** 'you have cut'.

(11.43) **É=  dáàtà  |  háy-àgì  tú-gá-lèng-à |  mú=**
O=  1a+our.father  where-EMP  1PL-F2-pass-Fa  IN.STATE=

**kú-shòn-óók-à ‖ kéèrà  w-à-ná-tòl-à      ‖  yù-gú**
15-climb-RV.I-Fa  ALREADY  2SG-P1-ADD.V-cut.off-Fa  this.P-3

**mú-lándírà?**
3-vine

'O Father | where now will we pass | in climbing down ‖ since (even though) already you have cut ‖ this vine?' (32 014)

### 11.1.5 Logical clauses

There are three conjunctions which can introduce a logical dependent clause. Two of these conjunctions involve cl. 15 demonstrative forms: **kú=yùkwò** 'therefore' and **kwôkwô** 'thus'. (Cl. 15 is the class used to indicate infinitives. Thus there is a logical connection being made to some event.) The third conjunction, used much more rarely, and probably with Kiswahili influence, is **kú=yàhò** 'therefore'.

(a) The conjunction **kú=yùkwò** literally means 'in connection with that (event that was already mentioned)'. A shorter, and better, translation would be 'therefore'. As a point of departure (10.2.4), it provides a logical link between an event or events in a previous context and the clause which follows.

In (11.44) the speaker says that he was the one that caused the animal to fall into the trap. This is followed by the logical conclusion: **kú=yùkwò úmbèèrèzàgyé byó=túkálágáánà** 'therefore give me what we agreed on'.

(11.44) **Ni-é=**    w-à-túm-á | í-gáà-gw-à mú= yù-gú mú-tēgò |
       1SG-FOC=  S.R-P1-cause-Fa  9-F2-fall-Fa  18=  this.P-3  3-trap

      <u>kú=yùkwò</u> ‖  ú-Ø-m-bèèrèz-àgy-é | by-ó= tú-ká- lágáán-à.
      therefore    2SG-SBV-O1.SG-give-EMP-Fe  8-O.R=  1PL-P2-agree-Fa

'I'm the one that caused | it to fall into this trap | therefore ‖ give me | what we agreed on.' (632 023)

(b) The conjunction **kwôkwô** 'thus' links, in a logical way, what has already happened to what follows. It is not quite as strong a connection as **kú=yùkwò** 'therefore'. In (11.45) 'the woman agrees, thus she takes that.N young child' is a logical conclusion.

(11.45) **Ùyó**    mú-kàzì | à-ná-yèméér-à. ‖ <u>Kwôkwô</u> ‖  à-ná-yâng-à |
       that.N+1  1-woman  1-SQ-agree-Fa    thus.N       1-SQ-took-Fa

      ù-lyá  mw-àná  mw-ánùkè ‖ à-ná-mú-héèk-à.
      1-that.R  1-child   1-young     1-SQ-O1-carry.on-back-Fa

'That woman | agreed. ‖ Thus ‖ she took | that young child ‖ and carried it on her back.' (307 016-017)

### 11.1.6 Purpose/result clauses

Kifuliiru has three conjunctions that refer to purpose/result, plus one implicit conjunction: One is **gírà** 'in order' (expressing purpose). In addition, **mbú** means 'with the intention' and **hàlíndè** means 'until' (expressing both time and result). In each case the purpose/result clause is followed by the subjunctive.

(a) The conjunction **gírà** expresses purpose, and can be translated 'in order to' or 'so that'.

(11.46) **N-à-yíj-á**     **gírá** | **ú-Ø-n-dágùl-è.**
       1SG-P1-come-Fa    so.that    2SG-SBV-O1-divine-Fe

'I've come *so that* | you divine (for) me.' (10 014)

(11.47) **À-ná-tèg-à**    **á=má-bōkò** || **gírá** | **à-Ø-yábíìr-é** | **á=mī-ījì.**
       1-SQ-trap-Fa    AU=6-hands    so.that    1-SBV-take-Fe    AU=6-water

'And he cupped his hands || *in order* | to get | water.' (07 027)

In (11.48) the conjunction **gírà** 'so that' is followed by the verb **bàlólè** 'they see'.

(11.48) **Bà-ná-lágààn-á**    **ú=lú-sìkù**    **lw-ó=**    **kú-tíbìt-à** ||    **gírá**
       2-SQ-agree-Fa    AU=11-day    11-A.M+AU=    15-run-Fa    so.that

       **bà-Ø-lól-é**    **nyândì** | **ú-gáá-sìg-à**    **ú=w-àbò.**
       2-SBV-see-Fe    who    S.R+1-F2-leave-Fa    AU=1-SAME.SET

'They agreed on the day of running || so that they see who | will leave his fellow behind.' (21 010)

(b) A null (or implicit) conjunction with a subjunctive verb form can also express purpose/result. In (11.49) the subjunctive verb **ábè** '(in order that) he (may) be' again involves purpose/result, but this time the conjunction is implicit.

(11.49) **Ø-Gêndí**    **Ø-bwír-é**    **mw-àmì** || **à-Ø-b-é**    **y-é=**
       IMP.S-GOING    SBV-tell-Fe    1-king    1-SBV-be-Fe    1-FOC=

       **gá-yîjì**    **mú-yáng-à.**
       F2-COMING    O1-marry-Fa

'Go and tell the king || so that he (may) be the one who will come and marry her.' (106 020)

(c) The conjunction **mbú**, when in a clause following the main clause,[8] implies a frustrated intention (FRUS.INT), i.e. although someone is (or might be) intending something, the person will be frustrated.

---

[8] This is in contrast to its use in temporal clauses which *precede* the main clause, where it is translated 'as soon as'.

(11.50)  Ù-Ø-lól-è     ‖ ù-tá-Ø-yì-lyò-s-é        kú=    bà-ndì ‖
         2SG-SBV-look-Fe  2SG-NEG-SBV-RFX-leave-CS-Fe  17=   2-other

   **mb-ù**=    Ø-kúlíkír-é |   y-à-wè-yàwè      n-jírà.
   FRUS.INT-2SG=  SBV-follow-Fe   9-A.M-2SG-RDP   9-path

'Look ‖ don't remove yourself from others ‖ *with the intention* of following | your own unique path *(because you will be frustrated)*.' (11 042)

(11.51)  N-dà-ná-kí-hí-ìt-í          hà-ndì       h-ó=     n-gáá-hùm-à ‖
         1SG-NEG-ADD.V-PERS-have-RS-Fi  16-other   16-O.R=  1-F2-touch-Fa

   **mbú**=    nì-Ø-mù-gúl-ìr-é       |   í=by-ámbàlwà.
   FRUS.INT   1SG-SBV-O2.PL-buy-APL-Fe     AU=8-clothing

'I no longer have another place where I could touch (to find money) ‖ *with the intention* that I buy you | clothes.' (33 012)

(d) The conjunction **hàlíndè** means 'until', combining the *temporal element* with the notion of *result*.

(11.52)  À-ná-mú-bíng-ìríz-à ‖   **hàlíndè** |   à-ná-mú-gwât-à.
         1-SQ-O1-chase-INTS-Fa    until       1-SQ-O1-grab-Fa

'He chased her ‖ *until (and with the result that)*| he caught her.' (06 023)

(11.53)  À-ná-lwâl-à       í=kí-hándò ‖   **hàlíndè**    ky-àná-mú-yìt-à.
         1-SQ-get.sick-Fa   AU=7-sore      until          7-SQ-O1-kill-Fa

'And he got sick with a sore ‖ *until (and with the result that)* it (the sore) killed him.' (48 014)

In (11.54) the conjunction **hàlíndè** 'until (with the eventual result that…)' is followed by the subjunctive **nìmúyìtè** '(that) I kill him'. In this case the person speaking wants to kill someone, and uses **hàlíndè** to express time and result.

(11.54)  **Kútì n-gáá-gír-à** ‖   **hàlíndè**    nì-Ø-mú-yìt-è?
         what  1SG-F2-do-Fa       until           1SG-SBV-O1-kill-Fe

'What will I do ‖ *until (and with the result that)* I kill him?' (619 043)

### 11.1.7 Focus clauses

Dependent focus clauses in Kifuliiru are a type of non-initial clause which puts focus on the preceding clause in an identificational sentence articulation

(10.2.6). There are three different introductory conjunctions which are used in focus clauses, all of which can be generally translated 'that's when'.

(a) The conjunction **lyó** 'that's when', puts contrastive focus on the preceding clause, when used in identificational articulation. In identificational articulation, it is presupposed that the event of the second clause (the presupposition) will obtain. Normally, the initial, focus element of such a construction is a noun phrase. However, when the cl. 5 focus copula, **lyó** 'that's when' is used in a identificational construction, the focused element is a clause. This initial clause of the sentence identifies the prerequisite for the second clause to happen. In (11.55) the main verb **ngábàlàmà** 'I will travel' identifies what must happen in order for the second clause to obtain: **lyó=ngírá kwó=ngámùpángírà** 'that's when I (will) do what I planned for you'. Note that the verb which follows **lyó** is not a subjunctive form, but the timeless. Sometimes the verb which follows **lyó** is instead a future (F2) form.

(11.55)

| Focus | Presupposition | | |
|---|---|---|---|
| **N-gá-bàlàm-à** ‖ | **ly-ó=** n-gír-á ‖ | kwó= | n-gá-mù-páng-ír-à (Sw.). |
| 1SG-F2-travel-Fa | 5-FOC= 1-do-Fa | what= | 1-P2-O2.PL-plan-APL-Fa |

'I will travel ‖ that's when I do ‖ what I planned for you (PL).' (201 006)

In (11.56) it is presupposed that people want to be many in their tribe. The main verb **mùkízí būtá** 'be continuously giving birth' identifies the prerequisite that must happen for the second clause **lyó=mùlùgà** means 'that's when you will be many' to obtain.

(11.56)

| Focus | Presupposition | | |
|---|---|---|---|
| **mù-Ø-kízí** | būt-à | ‖ **ly-ó=** | mù-lùg-à. |
| 2PL-SBV-REP | give.birth-Fa | 5-FOC= | 2PL-be.many-Fa |

'(You pl.) repeatedly give birth ‖ that's when you will be many.' (Gen 1:28)

(b) The conjunction **lyókì** means 'that's when (as opposed to another time or situation you mistakenly had in mind)'. This conjunction, which includes a cl. 5 prefix, is a lexicalized use of the cl. 5 member of the set of alternative pronouns, such as **yeki** 'HE (as opposed to the one mistakenly assumed)', **booki** 'THEY (as opposed to the one mistakenly assumed)', etc. (3.3.2.2).

In (11.57) the presupposition is that circumcision has value. The prerequisite for this to be true, according to the writer, is **ìrí wàngàkìzí sìmbáhá yìzó màajà** 'if you would obey those laws'; that's when circumcision will have value (as opposed to an alternative mistaken notion).

(11.57)

| | | Focus | | | |
|---|---|---|---|---|---|
| **Ìrí** | w-àngà-kìzí | sìmbáh-á | yìzó | | màajà ‖ |
| IF | 2SG-CND-REP | obey-Fa | those.N+10 | | 10+laws |
| | | Presupposition | | | |
| **ly-ókì** ‖ | ú=kú-téngúúl-w-á | | kw-à-wè | kú-gáà-b-à | |
| 5.ALT | AU=15-circumcise-PS-Fa | | 15-A.M-2SG | 15-F2-be-Fa | |

Presupposition (con't)

| **n-á=** | ká-márò. |
|---|---|
| CNJ-AU= | 12-value |

'If you would continually obey those laws ‖ that's when ‖ your circumcision | will have | value.' (Rom 2:25)

(c) The conjunction **ìrí**, can also be used to introduce the dependent clause in identificational articulation. In this context **ìrí** means 'that's when it's true', in the sense of the general truth of a statement (as opposed to **lyó** which means 'that's when, relative to a particular time').

In (11.58) the first clause **ìrí wàngàyúvwá ú=lúhàzì lwàní lwàbìkà** 'if/when you would hear my rooster crowing' is a dependent conditional clause, and the conditional conjunction **ìrí** means 'if/when'. In the following clause, **ìrí ndàrè àhíkà** 'that's when the lion has come', **ìrí** has a different meaning, communicating the result: 'that's when'. Relative to identificational articulation, it is assumed that the lion will come, the question is when. The answer is given in the focus clause: "when you hear my rooster crow".

(11.58)

| | | Focus | | |
|---|---|---|---|---|
| **Ìrí** | w-àngà-yúvw-á | ú=lú-hàzì | lw-à-ní | lw-à-bìk-à ‖ |
| if | 2SG-CND-hear-Fa | AU=11-rooster | 11-A.M-1SG | 11-P1-crow-Fa |
| | Presupposition | | | |
| **ìrí** | n-dàrè | à-hík-à. | | |
| FOC | 9-lion | 1+P1-arrive-Fa | | |

'When you would hear my rooster | crowing ‖ then the lion | has come.' (105 020)

(d) The focus clause can also consist of a relative clause. In (11.59) **ngíìsì yé=yíshè ágáyèmèèrà** 'whomever the father agrees to' is followed by **ìrí yé=gámúyângà** 'that's when he's the one who will marry her'. Relative to identificational articulation, it is assumed that the daughter will be married by someone. The first clause puts focus on who that person is, the one that the father will agree to.

(11.59)

| | | | Focus | | | |
|---|---|---|---|---|---|---|
| Mú= | kà-tì | kà-à-bò ‖ | ngíìsì | y-é= | yîshè | \| |
| 18= | 12-middle | 12-A.M-2 | whoever | 1-O.R= | 1a+her.father | |

| Focus (con't) | | Presupposition | | |
|---|---|---|---|---|
| á-gá-yèmèèr-à ‖ | ìrí | y-é= | gá-mú-yâng-à. | |
| 1-F2-agree-Fa | that's.when | 1-FOC= | F2-O1-marry-Fa | |

'Among them ‖ whomever her father | will agree to ‖ that's when he's the one who will marry her.' (06 007)

### 11.1.8 Purpose/result clauses, together with focus

The focus conjunction **lyó** is often preceded by another conjunction, producing a form that includes both purpose/result and focus. Composite conjunctions of this type include the forms **gírá lyó** 'so that (purpose), with focus', **hàlíndé lyó** 'until (and with the result that), with focus', and **mbú=lyó** 'with intention, with focus'. The second conjunction **lyo** 'that's when' functions according to identificational articulation (10.2.6). These forms are translated rather literally here to give a better feel for the meaning. Though the purpose clauses introduced by **gírà, mbu, and hàlíndè** are all followed by the subjunctive form of the verb, when they are combined with **lyó**, the subjunctive form is no longer used. Instead, the verb of the following clause is always timeless, as is the case when the conjunction **lyo** is used alone.

(a) The composite conjunction **gírá lyó** (lit. 'so that that's when') combines the notions of purpose and focus. In (11.60) the main focus clause **tùgéndè áháyìhèríírì** 'let's go to a private place' identifies what must happen in order for the second clause to obtain **mùlóngá ú=kúlùhúúkà** 'you get to rest'. It also expresses purpose.

## 11.1 Dependent adverbial clauses

(11.60)

|  | Focus | |
|---|---|---|
| Tù-Ø-génd-é \| | á-hà-yìhèr-íír-ì | ‖ |
| 1PL-SBV-go-Fe | S.R-16-private-RS-Fi | |

|  | Presupposition | | |
|---|---|---|---|
| **gírá** | **ly-ó**= | mù-Ø-lóng-á \| | ú=kú-lùh-úúk-á \| hínììnî. |
| so.that | 5-FOC= | 2PL-TL-get-Fa | AU=15-be.tired-RV.T-Fa  a little |

'Let's go | to where it's private ‖ so that that's when you get | to rest | a bit.' (Mrk 6:31)

In (11.61) the main focus clause **Kú=yùkwò nàmùyìngíngà múlyè** 'Therefore I beg you to eat' identifies what is necessary for the dependent clause **mùlóngà ú=búlyó bwó=kúkīrà** 'you get the means to be saved' to obtain. This sentence again involves both purpose and focus, expressed by **gírà lyó**.

(11.61)

|  | Focus | | |
|---|---|---|---|
| Kú= | yùkwò ‖ | n-à-mù-yìngíng-à \| | mú-Ø-ly-è  ‖ |
| 17= | that.N+15 | 1SG-P1-O1-beg-Fa | 2PL-SBV-eat-Fe |

|  | Presupposition | | |
|---|---|---|---|
| **gírá** | **ly-ó**= | mù-Ø-lóng-á | ú=bú-lyó \| bw-ó= |
| so.that | 5-FOC= | 2PL-TL-receive-Fa | AU=14-means  14-A.M+AU= |

| Presupposition (con't) |
|---|
| **kú-kīr-à.** |
| 15-be.saved-Fa |

'Therefore ‖ I beg you | eat ‖ so that/that's when you get the means | of being saved.' (Act 27:34)

(b) The composite conjunction **hàlíndè lyó** combines the meanings of 'until (and with the result that)' and 'that's when (with focus)'. In (11.62) the main focus clause **ágánákìmùyèrèkà kìrí né=bìhímìrì yíbì** 'he will also still show you even what surpasses these (things)' identifies the prerequisite for the dependent clause to happen, i.e. **mùsóómérwà bwénèènè** 'you are very amazed'.

(11.62)

| Focus | | | |
|---|---|---|---|
| À-gá-ná-kì-mù-yèrèk-à | ‖ kìrí | n-é= | bì-hím-ìr-ì |
| 1-F2-ADD.V-PERS-O1-show-Fa | even | CNJ-AU= | 8-surpass-RS-Fi |

| Focus (con't) | | Presupposition | | |
|---|---|---|---|---|
| yí-bì ‖ | halinde \| | ly-ó= | mù-Ø-sóómér-w-á | bwénèènè. |
| these.P-8 | until | 5-FOC= | 2PL-TL-amazed-PS-Fa | very.much |

'And he will still show you ‖ even what surpasses these ‖ until/with the result | that's when you are very amazed.' (Jhn 5:20)

In (11.63) it is assumed that the person wants to praise God before the people. The focus clause **é=nàhánò, únyígùlè á=kánwâ** 'O Lord, open my mouth' identifies the prerequisite to make that happen. The second clause has both a result component and a focus component.

(11.63)

| | | Focus | | |
|---|---|---|---|---|
| É= | Nàhánò ‖ | ú-Ø-n-yígùl-è | á=ká-nwâ | ‖ |
| O= | Lord | 2SG-SBV-O1.SG-open-Fe | AU=12-mouth | |

| | | Presupposition | | | |
|---|---|---|---|---|---|
| hàlíndè | ly-ó= | n-Ø-gìzì | kú-yìvúg-á | \| í= | m-béré |
| until | 5-FOC= | 1SG-TL-REP | O2.SG-praise-Fa | 23= | 9-before |

| Presupposition (con't) | |
|---|---|
| ly-á= | bá-ndù. |
| 5-A.M+AU= | 2-people |

'O Lord ‖ open for me the mouth ‖ until/with the result that I repeatedly praise you | in front of the people.' (Psa 50:15)

(c) The composite conjunction **mbú=lyó** combines the meanings of 'with the (frustrated) intention' and 'that's when, with focus'. In (11.64) there was a rock from which milk was flowing. It is assumed that the person intended to have much milk, and thus the main focus clause **ànáfûndà hó=múshólò** 'and he forced in there an iron digging stick' identifies the prerequisite for that to happen, i.e. digging around. That's when **gàhùlúká mwó=mìngì** '(the milk would) come out from in there much'.

## 11.1 Dependent adverbial clauses

(11.64)

| | Focus | |
|---|---|---|
| À-ná-fûnd-à \| | h-ó= | mú-shólò ‖ |
| 1-SQ-force.in-Fa | 16-AU= | 3-iron.stick |

| | Presupposition | | | |
|---|---|---|---|---|
| mbú= | ly-ó= | gà-Ø-hùlúk-á \| | mwó= | mì-ngì |
| FRUS.INT= | 5-FOC= | 6-TL-come.out-Fa | 18= | 6-much |

'And he forced in | there the iron stick (for digging) ‖ with the presumption/that's when (milk would) come out | from in there much.' (22 026)

In (11.65) the main (embedded) focus clause **kwó=nyìkérè kú=lúhú lwànî** 'that I cut some of my skin' identifies what might have to happen for the intention to obtain **mbú=lyó=ngútábúlà** meaning '(with (frustrated) intention/that's when) I assist you'.

(11.65)

| | Focus | | |
|---|---|---|---|
| Bì-tà-ngà-shóbòk-à ‖ | kwo= | n-yì-kér-è \| | kú= |
| 8-NEG-POT-be.able-Fa | CMP= | 1SG-RFX-slice.off-Fe | 17= |

| Focus (con't) | | Presupposition | | |
|---|---|---|---|---|
| lú-hú | \| lw-à-nî | ‖ mbú= | ly-ó= | n-Ø-gú-tábúl-à. |
| 11-skin | 11-A.M-1SG | FRUS.INT= | 5-FOC= | 1SG-TL-O2.SG-assist-Fa |

'It would not be possible ‖ that I slice off from myself | part of my skin ‖ with the intention/that's when I assist you.' (31 015)

### 11.1.9 Manner clauses

There are two ways of introducing a manner clause:

(a) The relativizer **kwó** 'how' often includes an implicit **ngíìsì** 'each/every', (which combines to produce **ngíìsì kwó** 'just how') to communicate manner. In (11.66) the relativizer **kwó** 'how' is found in the relative clause **kwó=bágááyìtà nyínà** 'how they will kill the mother'.

(11.66) **Bà-ná-yàm-à    bà-hùlúk-à         mú=  ká-bìndì || bà-ná-yàmí**
2-SQ-IMMED-Fa   2+P1-come.out-Fa   18=   12-jar      2-SQ-IMMED

**púúmúk-à || gírá    bà-Ø-géndì    lól-á |  kw-ó=    bá-gáá-yìt-à**
dash.off-Fa   so.that 2-SBV-GOING   see-Fa  15-O.R=   2-F2-kill-Fa

**nyínà.**
1a+their.mother

'They immediately came out of the jar || and they immediately dashed off || so that they could go and see | how they will kill their mother.' (201 086)

(b) The conjunction **nga** 'like/as(if)' can also introduce a manner clause. In (11.67) the conjunction **nga** 'like/as' is found in the relative clause **ngá=kàgwétí íshúúshírà** 'like it had a fever'.

(11.67) **Ka-lya    ka-bwa    ka-na-yij-a  ||  na-ko      ka-na-beer-a**
12-that.R  12-dog   12-SQ-come-Fa   ADD.P-12   12-SQ-remain-Fa

**yà-hô   |  ngá    kà-gw-ét-í       í-shúúshírà.**
there.N-16  like  12-have-RS-Fi    5-fever

'That dog came || and IT stayed there | like it had a fever.' (106 167)

**11.1.10 Reason clauses**

There are four conjunctions/composite conjunctions which can introduce a dependent reason clause: **mú=kúbà** 'because', **bwó** 'since', **í=bwèngè / kú=bwèngè** 'since', **mbú=bwó / mbú=bwèngè** 'for the alleged reason that'. The verb in the reason clause may be marked for any one of a variety of tenses/aspects.

(a) The conjunction **mú=kúbà** means 'because' (lit., 'in the to be').

(11.68) **Yùgwó    mw-énà || gw-àná-yìt-à  bá-ndú  bì-ngì ||  mú=kúba |**
that.N+3  3-hunger    3-SQ-kill-Fa  2-people 2-many      because

**gú-ká-hèb-à   sìkú     ny-ìngì |  mú=  yìkyó     kí-hūgò.**
3-P2-finish-Fa 10+days  10-many   18=  that.N+7  7-country

'That hunger || killed many people || because | it finished many days | in that country.' (20 003)

In (11.69) the independent clause **nàkúbwîrà kwókù** 'I've told you this' is followed by the dependent clause **mú=kúbá ngúyìjì kwô=tàbàlà mwâzì** 'because I know you that you don't spread news'.

## 11.1 Dependent adverbial clauses

(11.69) N-à-kú-bwîr-à         kwókù ||  mú=kúbá     n-gú-y-ìj-ì                     ||
       1SG-P1-O2.SG-tell-Fa   thus.P    because     1SG-O2.SG-know-RS-Fi

kw-ô=      tà-Ø-bàl-à              mw-âzì.
CMP-2SG=   NEG-SBV-spread-Fa       3-news

'I've told you this || because I know you || that you don't spread news.'
(40 011)

(b) The conjunction **bwo** is a bit weaker than **mú=kúbà** 'because' and could be translated 'since' or 'in that'.

(11.70) Ni-é=       hì-ìt-ì           á=ká-máró |   ú=kú-mù-hím-à              ||
       1SG-FOC=    having-RS-Fi      AU=12-value    AU=15-O2.PL-surpass-Fa

**bwó**=     ni-é=        rì mú=    láng-á |    á=kā-āyà.
since=       1SG-FOC=     is PROG=  guard-Fa    AU=12-village

'I'm the one with more value | than you (PL) || since I'm the one who is guarding | the village.' (37 007)

In (11.71) the dependent clause **bwó=wàdètà kwô=tàkìhíítí í=kyōbà** 'since you say that you no longer have fear' precedes the independent clause **ùgéndí tùyìtírá ìyó ndàrè** 'go kill for us that.N lion'.

(11.71) **Bwó**=   w-à-dèt-à    |    kw-ô=       tà-kì-hí-ít-í
       since=     2SG-P1-say-Fa      CMP-2SG=   NEG-PERS-have-RS-Fi

í=ky-ōbà ||    ù-Ø-géndí          tù-yìt-ír-á ||        ìyó        n-dàrè.
AU=7-fear      2SG-SBV-GOING     O1.PL-kill-APL-Fa      that.N+9   9-lion

'Since you say | that you no longer have fear || go and kill for us || that lion.' (609 020)

(c) The conjunction **bwèngè** 'since' is used in the same way as **bwó** just above. The form **bwèngè** can be preceded by the cl. 17 locative clitic **kú**, the cl. 23 locative clitic **í**, or by nothing at all, and in each case means 'since' or 'in that'. In (11.72) it is preceded by the cl. 23 **í**.

(11.72) Í=     bw-èngè    mù-lì      bá-ná-kíkwì      ‖   mù-tà-kwán-íìn-í |
       23=    14-since    2PL-are    2-CNJ-uncleanness    2PL-NEG-should-RS-Fi

   mù-Ø-kízì          láál-à    kú=     by-ájò     ‖   sí=     mù-Ø-kízí          láál-á |
   2PL-SBV-REP        lay-Fa    17=     8-bedding      OBV=    2PL-SBV-REP        lay-Fa

   hááshì.
   down.on.ground

'Since you (PL) are dirty ‖ you should not | lie on bedding ‖ but you should habitually lie | on the ground.' (515 033)

(d) The composite conjunction **mbú=bwó** 'for the alleged reason that' (or 'merely because'). The use of this conjunction implies that a stated or supposed reason is not adequate grounds for a certain reaction.

In (11.73) the independent clause **nyíná wà=Píyò ànágwâtwà nó=lúùgì hí=gúlú lyà=Lééza** 'the mother of Piyo was seized with jealousy over Leeza' is followed by the dependent clause beginning with **mbú=bwó**. By this the narrator of the story is indicating that he finds the stated reason to be inadequate justification for the mother's jealousy over her step-daughter.

(11.73) Nyíná         w-à=     Píyò   ‖   à-ná-gwât-w-à        nó=     lú-ùgì
        1a+her.mother 1-A.M    Piyo       1-SQ-seize-PS-Fa     CNJ=    11-jealousy

   hí=gúlú lyà=   Léézà  ‖   mbú=              bwó=          yîbà        | í=ky-ànyà
   16+5=over 5-A.M Leeza     for.alleged.reason              her.husband     AU=7-time

   à-lì    mú=    bàlám-úk-à   ‖   à-lì    mú=      yíj-á         à-bà-gúl-ìr-à  |
   1-is    PROG=  travel-RV.I-Fa   1-is    PROG=    COMING-Fa     1+P1-O2-buy-APL-Fa

   á=má-kânjù |      bó-mbì.
   AU=6-robes        2-both

'The mother of Piyo ‖ was seized with jealousy over Leeza ‖ for the alleged reason that her husband | when he is coming home from a trip ‖ is coming having bought | dresses | for both of them (i.e. for Leeza as well as for Piyo).' (628 007)

In (11.74) **mbú=bwô=lì mú=gírá í=míkòlèzì míìjâ** means 'for (the alleged) reason that you are doing good deeds'. The implication is that they aren't stoning the person for the alleged reason that he is doing good works, but for another reason. The implication is that the reason is not adequate, and that there is another one.

(11.74) **Tù-tá-gá-kú-làsh-à** =gô ‖ **mbú**= **bw-ô**= **lì**
1PL-NEG-F2-O2.SG-throw-Fa =6 for.alleged.reason+2SG= are

**mú**= **gír-á** **í=mí-kòlèzì** **mí-ìjâ.**
PROG= do-Fa AU=4-works 6-good

'We will not throw them (rocks) at you ‖ for the alleged reason that you are doing good deeds.' (Jhn 10:33)

In (11.75) the independent clause **mùtákìzì shàmbáálà** 'don't be rejoicing' is followed by the dependent clause **mbú=bwó=yìbyó bísīgò bìgwétí bígámùsìmbàhà** which means 'for (the alleged) reason these demons are obeying you'. The implication is that this reason is not adequate, and that they should rejoice for another reason.

(11.75) **Mù-tá-kìzì** **shàmbáál-à** ‖ **mbú**= **bwó**= **yìbyó** **bí-sīgò** ‖
2PL-NEG-REP rejoice-Fa for.alleged.reason those.N+8 8-demons

**bì-gwétí** **bí-gá-mù-sìmbàh-à.**
8-PROG 8-INTL-O2.PL-obey-Fa

'Don't always rejoice ‖ merely because those demons ‖ are obeying you.' (Luk 10:20)

## 11.2 Analytic causatives

The analytic[9] causative, using the verb -**tùm**-[10] means 'cause (something to happen)'. This verb can also be used with the meaning 'send (something to someone, or someone to some place)'.[11] The tense marking on the verb -**tùm**- is quite free and can include the unmarked past (P2) tense, the unmarked future (F2) tense, the sequential (SQ) tense. The verb -**tùm**- used as an analytic causative can also be used in the resultative (RS) tense.

The most common tense in the verb following the analytic causative is the unmarked future (F2), where the idea of "intentional" comes into play. In (11.76) the unmarked past (P2) tense form on the **gúkátūmà** 'it caused', is followed by an unmarked future (F2)[12] on the following verb **ágáàlyà** 'he will eat'.

---

[9] The analytic causative consists of "a matrix verb (expressing the notion of CAUSE whose sentential complement refers to the caused event) (Payne 1997:181).

[10] The default meaning of the verb -**tùm**- can be 'send' *or* 'send for'.

[11] Its meaning as a causative is reflected in the derived noun **kítùmà** 'cause', used exclusively in the question: **Kítùmà (kíkì)**? 'Why?'.

[12] Though the second verb in the analytic causative in Kifuliiru takes what is structurally a future form, it is not used in a time-related way in this form. Analytic causatives in other languages may use a verb of some other non-future form, such as a subjunctive, in an analytic causative.

(11.76) **Ú=mú-géndó-géndò** || **gú-ká-tùm-á**   **ú=mù-ndú** |   **á-gáà-ly-à** |
AU=3-going-RDP        3-P2-cause-Fa        AU=1-person     1-F2-eat-Fa

**jòngò.**
9+commotion

'Going here and there || is what caused the person | to eat | commotion.'
(30 016)

In (11.77) the analytic causative **bákátūmà** 'they caused' is unmarked past (P2) and is followed by another P2 verb **túkáhábúkírà** 'we got lost'.

(11.77) **Tú-ká-húmáánán-á**   **n-á=**    **bá-húlúlà** ||   **b-ó=**    **bá-ká-tùm-á** |
1PL-P2-encounter-Fa       CNJ-AU=   2-bandits         2-FOC=    2-P2-cause-Fa

**tú-ká-hábúk-ír-à** |    **mú=**   **kì-nó**       **kí-shúkà.**
1PL-P2-get.lost-APL-Fa    18=      7-this.P.C     7-bush

'We encountered bandits || they are the ones who caused | us to get lost | in this bush.' (01 042)

## 11.3 Reduced clauses indicating concomitant "state"

A clause indicating a CONCOMITANT STATE can be expressed by a locative **mú** 'within' with infinitive complement. We interpret this construction as a grammatically reduced clause, in which the understood time constraints as well as subject are identical to those of the verb in the modified main clause. The dependent **mú**-plus-infinitive phrase can either precede or follow the independent clause.

In (11.78) the dependent verb phrase **mú=kúgéndí lwísâ** 'in going to fight', is placed before the independent verb phrase **gúkásīgà gwàbwírà** 'left having told' and indicates the state which obtains in that second phrase.

(11.78) **Yùgwó**    **mú-jōkà** ||    **mú=**       **kú-géndí**    **lw-ís-á**
that.N+3    3-snake          IN.STATE=    15-GOING       fight-CS-Fa

**mú-rámú**         **w-à-gè** ||   **gú-ká-sīg-à**      **gw-à-bwír-á**
1-brother-in.law   1-A.M-1         3-P2-LEAVING-Fa     3-P1-tell-Fa

**mú-ká-à-gè:...**
1-wife-A.M-1

'That snake || in going to fight its brother-in-law || it left telling its wife:...'
(608 038)

In (11.79) the dependent verb phrase **mú=kúshònérá kú=yìkyó kítì** 'in climbing on that.N tree' indicates the state which is the setting for the main verb **bàléngè** '(that) they pass'.

(11.79) **À-ná-bwîr-à     yàbó         bà-àná       bà-à-gè ‖ kwó=   mú=**
        1-SQ-tell-Fa    those.N+2   2-children   2-A.M-1    CMP=   IN.STATE=

**ku̱-shòn-ér-á     kú=    yìkyó      kí-tì ‖ bà-Ø-léng-é |   kú=**
15-climb-APL-Fa   17=   that.N+7   7-tree   2-SBV-pass-Fe   17=

**yùgwó       mú-lándírà.**
that.N+3    3-vine

'And he told those children of his ‖ that in climbing on that tree ‖ they should pass | on that vine.' (32 011)

In (11.80) **mú=kúgálúkà** 'in returning' occurs before the main verb **àlì mú=yíjà** 'he is coming' and indicates the setting for the event expressed by the main verb.

(11.80) **Ná=   mú=          ku̱-gálúk-à |    à-lì    mú=     yíj-á**
        CNJ   IN.STATE   15-return-Fa     1-is   PROG   COMING-Fa

**á-gá-n-júlìk-à.**
1-F2-O1.SG-hit-Fa

'And in returning | he is coming hitting me.' (14 017)

In (11.81) the phrase **mú=kúshònóókà** 'in climbing' comes after the main verb **túgálèngà** 'we will pass' and indicates the state in which the main verb obtained.

(11.81) **É   dáàtà              ‖ háy-àgì          tú-gá-lèng-à |    mú=**
         O   1a+my.father       where-EMP        1PL-F2-pass-Fa     IN.STATE=

**ku̱-shòn-óók-à?**
15-climb-RV.I-Fa

'O my father ‖ where will we pass | in climbing down?' (32 014)

## 11.4 Complement clauses

Complementation[13] is defined as when "a notional sentence or predication is an argument of a predicate" Noonan (1985:42). Thus in sentence (11.82) the

---

[13] Under complementation, we do not include infinitives which follow a verb, as the verb-plus-

verb **bànálágààn à** 'and they agreed together' takes the complement clause **kwó=bàgéndí hīīvà** 'that they go hunt'. The complementizer in this case is the cl. 15 clitic **kwó** 'that'.

(11.82) Yàbó       bá-sósì ‖  bà-ná-lágààn-à ‖  kwó=      bà-géndí    hīīv-à.
        those.N+2  2-men       2-SQ-agree-Fa    that=     2-GOING     hunt-Fa

'Those men ‖ agreed ‖ that they go hunt.' (03 002)

The complementizers are limited to basically two forms, **kwó** 'that' and **mbú** 'that'.[14] Of the two, **kwó** is much more common as a complementizer. **Mbú**, when used as a complementizer, also can be translated as 'that', but often has the secondary connotation of '(often frustrated) intention'. Complement clauses in Kifuliiru are presented here, roughly following the complementation classes laid out by Noonan (1985:110–133). Although some verbs might seem to fit into more than one class, the idea of classes is still helpful in considering complement clauses.

### 11.4.1 Classes of complement clauses

(a) INDIRECT SPEECH VERBS commonly precede the complementizer **kwó** 'that'. In (11.83) the main verb **ànáyìdòdómbà** 'and she grumbled' is followed by the complement clause **kwó=yîbà àmúsúmìrá í=bísììtàrà** 'that her husband bought for her gristle'.

(11.83) À-ná-yìdòdómb-à ‖  kwó=   yîbà           | à-mú-súm-ìr-á |
       1-SQ-grumble-Fa       CMP=   her.husband   1+P1-O1-buy-APL-Fa

       í=bí-sììtàrà.
       AU=8-gristle

'And she grumbled ‖ (saying) that her husband | bought her | gristle.' (26 010)

There are many other "utterance" verbs and verb phrases in the data (which may precede **kwó** or **mbú**) in marking speech, including the following: -**biik- ndáhírò** 'make oath', -**buuz-** 'ask', -**bwir-** 'tell', -**dèt-** 'say', -**doot- í=ndúùlù** 'cry out', -**dùk-** 'insult', -**gánuul-** 'tell', -**hàmagal-** 'call', -**huun-** 'ask for', -**kànukir-** 'scold', -**kyul-** 'decree', -**lágaan-** 'agree', -**lágaani-** 'promise', -**láhir-** 'deny', -**laalik-** 'invite', -**lèg-** 'accuse', -**lír-** 'cry', -**naak-** 'speak disrespectfully', -**seezer-** 'say good-bye', -**shékeerez-** 'laugh at',

---

infinitive phrases all communicate aspect or mood, and are described in chapter 9, "Verb Words and Phrases". The group of verbs which precede infinitives includes the phasals 'begin', 'end', 'cease', etc. Nor do we consider here the quote introducers **tí=** «quote» or **kwókùnó** '(like) that'.

[14] Another pronunciation of **mbú** 'that' is **ngú** 'that'.

## 11.4 Complement clauses

-**shiikiz**- 'swear', -**shùvy**- 'answer', -**tákir**- 'beg', -**tèndeer**- 'beg', **ú=mwâzì kúhíkírà** 'news arriving', -**yèmeer(ezani)**- 'agree (together)', -**yèrek**- 'show', -**yìbuuz**- 'ask self', -**yìdès**- 'say to self', -**yìdòdomb**- 'mutter, grumble', -**yìdùndulik**- 'boast', -**yìháy**- 'praise self', -**yīmb**- 'sing', -**yìnging**- 'plead', -**yìmómoot**- 'grumble', -**yìgányir**- 'moan about problems'.

(b) PROPOSITIONAL ATTITUDE VERBS include 'think, agree (with something), guess', etc. In (11.84) the main verb **gùtànákìtònà** 'and it did not any more think' is followed by **kwê=yò** (**kwó** + **ì**-**yó**) 'that that.N quail...' and thus identifies what was not thought about.

(11.84) Gù-tà-ná-kì-tòn-à  |  kw-ê=   yò         n-gwârè |  y-ó=
       3-NEG-SQ-PERS-think-Fa   CMP=  that.N+9  9-quail     9-FOC=

y-à-túm-á |  gù-tà-Ø-kì-síngòòk-à  |  ná=  yùgwó     mú-lírò.
9-P1-cause-Fa  3-NEG-SBV-PERS-burn.up-Fa  CNJ=  that.N+3  3-fire.

'And it did not any more think | that that quail | is what caused | it did not get burned up | by that fire.' (13 013)

Verbs and verb phrases in this class include -**ba**- **kálángíkízô** 'be a sign', -**sálir**- 'think (consider)', -**sáliz**- 'think (consider)', -**tòn**- 'think (have opinion)', -**yèmeer**- 'agree', -**yèmeeza**- 'cause to agree', -**yìkeek**- 'guess, assume'.

(c) PRETENSE VERBS include those with meanings like 'hide something, trick, deceive, go ahead (in pretense)', etc. In (11.85) the main verb **wámbìshà** 'you hid from me' is followed by the complement **kwó=ngáávù àtàlèngà hánò** 'that the cow did not pass here'.

(11.85) W-á-m-bìsh-à       ||  kwó=  W-à-n-gáávù |  à-tà-lèng-à
       2SG-P1-O1.SG-hide-Fa    CMP=  1-A.M-9-cow    1-NEG+P1-pass-Fa

há-nò.
16-here.P.C

'You hid from me || that Cow | did not pass here.' (605 028)

Verbs in this class include -**beesh**- 'lie', -**bìsh**- 'hide', -**hènd**- 'trick', -**hènduul**- 'deceptively put off', -**yìhúnd**- 'pretend', -**yìgír**- 'pretend', **yìhùmeer**- 'pretend'.

(d) COMMENTATIVE VERBS include ideas like 'count as/consider, be certain, be appropriate', etc. In (11.86) the main verb **àshùbà mú=múhárúúrà** 'who were counting him' is followed by the complement **kwâ=lì múshííjá wàbò** 'that he is their brother'.

(11.86) N-á=      bá-nyéré  b-á=     kà-nó      kā-āyà |   á-bà-shùbà
       CNJ-AU=   2-girls   2-A.M=   12-this.P.C  12-village  S.R-2-be.PREV

   mú=      mú-hárúúr-á |   kw-â=     lì  mú-shííjá      w-à-bò ||
   PROG=    O1-count-Fa     CMP-1=    is  1-brother.of.girl  1-A.M-2

   bà-Ø-tángír-é |   ú=kú-mú-bòn-à |   ngá=   yîshè.
   2-SBV-begin-Fe   AU=15-O1-see-Fa    as=    1a+their.father

'And the girls of this village | who were formerly counting | that he is their brother || let them begin | to see him | as their father.' (410 016)

Other such verbs and verb phrases in this class include -**ba- né=mbùzì-mbùzì** 'be uncertain', -**bwinikiiri** 'be clear', -**huuz-** 'praise', -**kwaniini / kwiriiri** 'be appropriate', -**yìvúg-** 'praise', **yó=háàhê** 'it is more'.

(e) KNOWLEDGE VERBS include ideas like 'know, remember, show, guess', etc. In (11.87) main verb **ànákéngèèrà** 'and she remembered' is followed by the complement clause **kwâ=hììtí mwìrá wàgè wà Nábààlyà** 'that she has her friend Nabaalya'.

(11.87) À-ná-kéngèèr-à ||  kw-â=    hì-ìt-í       mw-ìrá    w-à-gè ||  w-à=
       1-SQ-remember-Fa   CMP-1=   has-RS-Fi    1-friend   1-A.M-1    1-A.M=

   Nábààlyà.
   Nabaalya

'And she remembered || that she has her friend || Nabaalya.' (19 004)

Other verbs or verb phrases in this class include -**kébukw-** 'become aware', -**kéngeer-** 'remember', -**ba- ná=kásīīsà** 'be certain', -**lúmbuuk-** 'be known extensively', -**mény-** 'know', -**ményees-** 'make known', -**ményeekan-** 'be known', -**yùvikaan-** 'be heard', -**rùnguruk-** 'be aware', -**sóm-** 'read', -**tàng- ú=búmàsì** 'give witness', -**tòn-** 'think', -**yándisirwi** 'be written', -**yèrek-** 'show', -**yìkeek-** 'guess', -**yìji** 'know(ire RS)', -**yìgiriza-** 'teach'.

(f) FEAR VERBS include the ideas of 'worry, concern', etc. In (11.88) the main verb **bákáyòbóhà** 'they were afraid' is followed by the complement **kwó=bàngàkòlí tùmítá mwāmì** 'that they would now spear the king'.

11.4 Complement clauses          403

(11.88)  ...mú=kúbá   bá-ká-yòbóh-à ‖  kwó=   bà-ngà-kòlí      tùmít-á
         because      2-P2-fear-Fa      CMP=   2-POT-NEWLY      spear-Fa

         mw-āmì.
         1-king

'...because they were afraid ‖ that they might now spear the king.' (51 017)

Other "fear" verbs include -**gérani**- 'be worried', -**taani**- 'be concerned'.

(g) DESIDERATIVE VERBS include the notions of 'hope, wait for, want, like', etc. In (11.89) the main verb **twàngàsíímírì** 'we would like' is followed by the complement **kwó**=**tùmútwàlè** 'that we take him away'.

(11.89) Tw-àngà-síím-ír-í    kwó=    tù-Ø-mú-twàl-è.
        1PL-POT-like-RS-Fi   CMP=    1PL-SBV-O1-take-Fe

'We would like that we take him away.' (106 048)

Other verbs and verb phrases in this category include -**bòn**- **búlìgò** 'be upset', -**ba**- **nó**=**múlángáálírò** 'have hope', -**huun**- 'ask for', -**lángaliiri** 'wait', -**líndir**- 'wait', -**looz**- 'want', -**lóziizi** 'want', -**siim**- 'like', -**tàluulw**- 'be set aside for', -**tool**- 'choose', -**vyuk**- **í**=**mbâmbà** 'raise an argument'.

(h) CAUSATIVE/PERMISSIVE VERBS include notions like 'permit, prevent, cause, agree, send for', etc. In (11.90) the main verb **nàlúngìkà** 'I sent' is followed by the complement **kwó**=**mùmúyìtè** 'that you kill him'.

(11.90) Mw-é=    bá-ndù ‖  n-à-lúngìk-à |   kwó=    mù-Ø-mú-yìt-è ‖
        2PL-FOC=  2-people  1SG-P1-send-Fa   CMP=    2PL-SBV-O1-kill-Fe

        mw-àná-shùbì      mú-sìg-à.
        2PL-SQ-AGAIN      O1-leave-Fa

'You people ‖ I sent | that you kill him ‖ and you left him again.' (210 108)

Other verbs and verb phrases of this type include -**biik**- 'place in position', -**biik**- **í**=**ndáhírò** 'place oath', -**bùz**- 'prevent', -**gáshaaniz**- 'pray', -**gúliisibw**- 'be sold', -**hámbir**- 'argue', -**hàmbaaz**- 'force', -**hámbanw**- 'contend', -**hángirir**- 'prevent', -**hànguul**- 'allow', -**hàngwirwi** 'be allowed', -**hánuul**- 'advise', -**kómeerez**- 'insist', -**láhirir**- 'refuse', -**lék**- 'allow', -**shímy**- 'cause', -**shúngikw**- 'be planned', -**tègaanurw**- 'be prepared', -**tíz**- 'court', -**tool**- 'choose', -**tùmir**- 'send for', -**yèmeer**- 'agree'.

(i) ACHIEVEMENT VERBS include notions like 'make a law, do, plan, give up, decide, dare', etc. In (11.91) the main verb **ànáshúngìkà** 'and he planned' is followed by the complement **kwá=báshààjà bóóshì bàyítwè** 'that all the old men be killed'.

(11.91) **À-ná-shúngìk-à** || **kw-á=** bá-shààjà bó-óshí | bà-Ø-yít-w-è.
1-SQ-purpose-Fa  CMP-AU=  2-old.men  2-all  2-SBV-kill-PS-Fe

'And he purposed || that all the old men | be killed.' (51 007)

Other such verbs include -**biik**- **ú=lúbààjà** 'make a law', -**biik**- **ú=lúhángò** 'decide', **bùlì bwîjâ** 'it is good', -**gír**- 'do', -**hèbuur**- 'give up', -**híg**- 'resolve', -**kéngeer**- 'remember', -**kòl**- 'do', -**kòlwe** 'dare', -**lúngik**- 'send', -**shóbok**- 'be possible', -**shúngik**- 'purpose, plan', -**twir**- **ú=lúbààjà** 'make judgment (lit., cut case)', -**zìg**- 'be able'.

(j) IMMEDIATE PERCEPTION VERBS include 'see, hear, feel', etc. In (11.92) the main verb **ànábònà** 'and he saw' takes the complement **kwó=kéèrà kàshálìkà** 'that it was already hungry'.

(11.92) **À-ná-bòn-à** || **kwó=** kéèrà || kà-shálìk-à.
1-SQ-see-Fa  CMP=  ALREADY  12-be.hungry-Fa

'And he saw || that it was already || hungry.' (45 023)

Similar verbs include -**bòn**- 'see', -**bònek**- 'appear', -**lól**- 'look', -**lóleer**- 'look at', -**yìyùvw**- 'feel self', -**yùvw**- 'hear'.

(k) Although less frequent, the COMPLEMENTIZER **mbú** can also function to introduce a dependent complement, with the connotation of 'with the (frustrated) intention that'. Usually the verb which follows **mbú** indicates an action not yet completed, or which has been frustrated in some way. As in example (11.93), the verb in a complement clause introduced by **mbú** is always in the subjunctive.

(11.93) **Lyêryô** | **ùyó** **mú-nyérè** || **à-tà-ná-kì-línd-ír-à**
right.then  that.N+1  1-girl  1-NEG-SQ-PERS-wait-APL-Fa

**mbú=** nyíná | à-Ø-gálúk-è || à-ná-yàmí
FRUS.INT=  1a+her.mother  1-SBV-return-Fe  1-SQ-IMMED

gálúk-ír-á | í= mw-á= yîbà.
return-APL-Fa  23=  place-A.M=  husband

'Right then | that girl || did not still wait (with intention) that her mother | return || and she immediately returned | to the place of her husband.' (620 028)

## 11.4.2 Idiom of attempt

The idiom which means "to attempt" uses a form of the verb -**gir**- 'do', followed by one of the complementizers **kwó**, **mbú**, or **ngú**, and a subordinate complement clause with a subjunctive verb. In (11.94) the construction **byànágírà mbú=bìdétè** means 'they attempted to speak (lit., they made that they speak)'.

(11.94) Yìbyó      bí-nyámíìshwà ná-byò ‖ <u>by-àná-gír-à</u>   <u>mbú</u>=
       those.N+8  8-wild.animals  ADD.P-8   8-SQ-attempt-Fa  FRUS.INT=

   **bì-Ø-dét-è.**
   8-SBV-speak-Fe

   'Those wild animals and THEY ALSO ‖ attempted to speak.' (28 022)

In (11.95) the complement **ànágírá kwâ=shúbí bètúlà yùgwó múlóngè** means 'and she attempted that she again carry (on her head) that.N bamboo stick'.

(11.95) **À-ná-yìmúk-à** ‖ <u>à-ná-gír-á</u>    <u>kw-â</u>=  Ø-shúbí     bètúl-á |
       1-SQ-get.up-Fa    1-SQ-attempt-Fa  CMP-1=  SBV-AGAIN  carry-Fa

   **yùgwó    mú-lóngè.**
   that.N+3  3-bamboo

   'And she got up ‖ and attempted to again carry (on her head) | that bamboo stick.' (27 017)

A somewhat rarer variation of **mbú** is **ngú**, seen in (11.96), where **ànágírà ngwà=gálùkè** means 'and he attempted to go back'.[15]

(11.96) **À-ná-bòn-à   mù-lí   ú=mú-jòkà** ‖ <u>à-ná-gír-á</u>    ‖ <u>ngw-à</u>=
       1-SQ-see-Fa   18-is   AU=3-snake     1-SQ-attempt-Fa    FRUS.INT-1=

   **Ø-gálùk-è.**
   SBV-return-Fe

   'And he saw a snake is in there ‖ he attempted ‖ to go back.' (108 016)

---

[15] The first clause of this same example exhibits an instance of a null complementizer following the verb -**bòn**- 'see'. Such instances with a null complementizer are attested, but only in a very informal register (see speech registers in 12.1).

### 11.4.3 Idiom of number

A clause introduced by the complementizer **kwó** is an idiomatic way to put focus on number. In (11.97) the subject **yàbó báshósì** 'those men' is followed by the complement clause **kwó=bàlí bàshàtù** 'being three (lit., that they are three)'. This construction puts focus on the fact that they are three, as opposed to the alternative unmarked noun phrase **yàbó báshósí bàshàtù** 'those three men'.

(11.97) Yàbó    bá-shósí  <u>kwó=</u>  <u>bà-lí</u>  <u>bà-shàtù</u> ||
those.N+2  2-men  that=  2-are  2-three

bà-ná-gì-bètúl-ír-à  mw-í=  dàkò  ly-é=  kí-tì ||  h-ó=
2-SQ-O9-carry-APL-Fa  18-5=  under  5-A.M+AU=  7-tree  16-O.R=

bá-àlí  bwàt-íír-ì.
2-P3  sit-RS-Fi

'Those men being three || they carried it (to) under the tree || where they were sitting.' (03 016)

In (11.98) the number clause modifies the incorporated object of the verb. Here **bànázìkúúmánià** 'and they gathered them' is followed by **kwó=zìrì múnààna** 'being eight (lit., that they were eight)'.

(11.98) Bà-ná-zì-kúúmán-i-á  <u>kwó=</u>  <u>zì-rì</u>  <u>múnààna</u> |  bà-ná-zì-hééréz-à
2-SQ-O10-gather-CS-Fa  that=  10-are  eight  2-SQ-O10-give-Fa

yîshè.
1a+their.father

'And they gathered them (sticks) together being eight | and they gave them to their father.' (02 011)

### 11.4.4 Idiom of comparison with *kè=tàlì yò=háàhè* 'isn't it all the more'

Finally, the complementizer **kwó** 'that' is used to introduce the clause which follows the idiomatic clause **kè=tàlì yó=háàhè (kwó...)** 'isn't it all the more so (that...)'. This idiom expresses a comparative link between two entire sentences. In (11.99) the preceding context is that God clothes the lilies of the field. The phrase which follows **kè=tàlì yó=háàhè** 'isn't it all the more so' presents the case that he will also clothe people.

## 11.5 Relative clauses

(11.99) **Àahô!** ‖ K-è= tà-lì y-ó= háàhè ‖ kwó= nì-ìnyù |
OK.then Q-9= NEG-is 9-FOC= more CMP= ADD.P-2PL

á-gáá-kìzì mù-yámbík-à?
1-F2-REP O2.PL-clothe-Fa

'OK then! ‖ Isn't it all the more ‖ that YOU ALSO | he will habitually clothe you?' (Luk 12:28)

In (11.100) the fact that God has already chosen people makes it all the more sure that he will give them their justice. This again is signaled by the phrase **kè=tàlì yó=háàhè**.

(11.100) **Àahô!** ‖ N-á= bá-ndú b-ó= Rúrémà kéèrà
OK.then CNJ-AU= 2-people 2-O.R= God ALREADY

á-ká-tóól-à ‖ k-è= tà-lì y-ó= háàhè | kw-á=
1-P2-choose-Fa Q-9= NEG-is 9-FOC= more CMP-1=

gá-bà-hèèrèz-â | ú=kú-lí kw-à-bò?
F2-O2-give-Fa AU=15-truth 15-A.M-2

'OK then! ‖ And people whom God has already chosen ‖ isn't it all the more | that he will give them | their justice?' (Luk 18:7)

## 11.5 Relative clauses

A relative clause is a dependent clause embedded within a NP, which always modifies the head of that phrase. The definitions for the following terms are well established and we quote Levinsohn (2005:NARR10):

Head noun:[16] the entity being modified by the relative clause.

Relative clause: the clause that modifies the head noun.

Relativizer: a particle or word in the relative clause that is substituted for the head noun.

Relative clauses are used only in certain discourse contexts in Kifuliiru, and basically function in background material to mark items of thematic salience. Information that is thematically salient is defined by Levinsohn (2005:NARR10) as being "significant for what follows in the narrative".

In addition, relative clauses in Kifuliiru are typically *restrictive*, identifying or defining the head noun they modify. (Some languages also use non-restrictive relatives, a term used for relative clauses which merely describe, rather than identify the head noun.)

---

[16] The head noun stands for any part of the NP, including, for instance, only a demonstrative, or even an understood null form.

In Kifuliiru, constituents in the following syntactic roles have been found to be modified by a relative clause: subject, object, time, location.

There are two different types of relative clauses in Kifuliiru. These differ in structure, and are called subject relative clauses and object relative clauses. In a subject relative clause, the subject of the relative clause is the same referent which is named by the head noun. In an object relative clause, it is the object of the relative clause which is the same referent as that named by the head noun. Both subject relative clauses and object relative clauses function as a modifier in a noun phrase.

Note below in the discussion of both subject relative clauses and object relative clauses, the item labeled "head noun" may not actually be a structural noun, but rather may be another structural element such as a determiner, a pronoun, or an adjective which is serving as the only element in a noun phrase, and thus is representing the understood noun.

### 11.5.1 Subject relative clauses

A subject relative clause (S.R) is a relative clause in which the subject of the relative clause is referenced to the NP being modified. For example, in the phrase 'the boys who hit the dog', the relative clause 'who hit the dog' modifies the noun 'boys'. To be a subject relative clause does *not* mean that the head noun necessarily functions as the subject of the main or matrix clause.[17] The head noun may be functioning as the subject, object, or other constituent of the main clause.

The relativizer for a subject relative clause is an initial high-tone vowel on the verb.[18] (This vowel is generally identical to the vowel of the following subject prefix.)[19] The subject relativizers are as follows: cl. 1 ú-, cl. 2 á-, cl. 3 ú-, cl. 4 í-, cl. 5 í-, cl. 6 á-, cl. 7 í-, cl. 8 í-, cl. 9 í-, cl. 10 í-, cl. 11 ú-, cl. 12 á-, cl. 13 ú-, cl. 14 ú-, cl. 15 ú-, cl. 16 á-, cl. 18 ú-, cl. 19 í-. The subject relativizer is in addition to, and precedes, the subject prefix and whatever other prefixes, if any, that are required by the TAM of the verb.[20]

In (11.101) the NP being modified by the relative clause is the subject of the matrix clause **yàbó bátàbánà** 'those young men'. It is modified by the subject relative clause **ábákázíndì yíjà** 'who came last', in which the cl. 2 subject, indicated by the initial prefixes **á-bá-** refers to **yàbó bátàbánà**.

---

[17] A matrix clause is a clause within which another clause is embedded.

[18] The subject relativizer has the same shape (including high tone) as the augment.

[19] The exception to this is in relatives of cl. 1, which do not have the normal cl. 1 subject prefix **a-**. In these cases the relativizer/subject prefix is simply **ú(ú)-**. In cl. 4 and cl. 9 the subject prefix is identical to the relativizer, so the two are elided into a single vowel, **í-**.

[20] Again, the exception to this is with the third-person singular (cl. 1), for which the normal cl. 1 subject prefix **a-** is replaced by **ú-**.

## 11.5 Relative clauses

(11.101)

| Head NP | | Subject relative clause | |
|---|---|---|---|
| Yàbó | bá-tàbánà | á-bá-ká-zíndì | yíj-à |
| those.N+2 | 2-young.men | S.R-2-P2-LASTLY | come-Fa |

| ná-bò | bà-ná-síìm-à | yàbó | bá-hyákàzì. |
|---|---|---|---|
| ADD.P-2 | 2-SQ-like-Fa | those.N+2 | 2-new.wives. |

'Those young men who came last | and THEY ALSO liked | those new wives.'
(01 014)

In (11.102) the subject relative clause **ábákátùmwá ná=mwāmì** 'those who were sent by the king' modifies **yàbó** 'those', which is the object of the dependent temporal clause **ìrí ákábòná yàbó** 'when he saw them'.

(11.102)

| | | | | Head NP | |
|---|---|---|---|---|---|
| Ùyó | mú-sósì ‖ | ìrí | á-ká-bòn-á | yàbó | |
| that.N+1 | 1-man | when | 1-P2-see-Fa | those.N+2 | |

| Subject relative clause | | |
|---|---|---|
| á-bá-ká-tùm-w-á | ná= | mw-āmì ... |
| S.R-2-P2-send-PS-Fa | CNJ= | 1-king |

'That man ‖ when he saw those | who were sent by the king...' (47 005)

In (11.103) the subject relative clause **úgwáàlì sòkànììnwí nó=lúbàkò** 'which was surrounded by forest' modifies the complement of the locative phrase **ku=múgàzì múgùmà** 'on one mountain'.

(11.103)

| | | | LM | Head NP | |
|---|---|---|---|---|---|
| Bó-óshì ‖ | bá-àlí | tùùz-ìr-í | kú= | mú-gàzì | mu-guma ‖ |
| 2-all | 2-P3 | live-RS-Fi | 17= | 3-mountain | 3-one |

| Subject relative clause | | | |
|---|---|---|---|
| ú-gw-ááli | sòkàn-ììn-w-í | n-ó= | lú-bàkò. |
| S.R-3-P3 | surround-RS-PS-Fi | CNJ-AU= | 11-forest |

'All of them ‖ lived on one mountain ‖ that was surrounded | by forest.'
(02 003)

In (11.104) the cl. 18 subject relative marker and subject agreement **ú-mù-** is used to reference an understood rather than explicitly stated NP, the cl. 18 'place inside'. Thus the head noun is not explicit in this case, but its understood referent is still the same one which is the subject of the relative clause. Such an understood referent is common with subject relative clauses which have a locative class subject (usually cl. 16 or 18).

(11.104) Ùyó | Àbùsàlúmù ‖ à-ná-yîj-à | à-ná-yìngír-á |
that.N+1    Absalom       1-SQ-come-Fa    1-SQ-enter-Fa

Subject relative clause
<u>ú-mù-lí   mw-àmì</u>.
S.R-18-is  1-king

'That | Absalom ‖ came | and he went in | where the king was.' (2Sa 14:33)

Stative verbal adjectives can also be used as relative clauses.[21] In (11.105) the subject relative **íbíyándìkè** '(things) written' modifies **byoshi** 'all', which is the object of the matrix clause.

(11.105)                                   Head NP
Yí-bì   ‖ by-ó=   bì-shwés-ìr-ì   by-óshì |
this.P-8  8-FOC=  8-tie-RS-Fi     8-all

Subject relative clause
<u>í-bí-yándìk-é   mú=   Màajà   z-à=    Músà</u>.
S.R-8-written-Fe  18=   laws    10-A.M= Moses

'This ‖ is what ties up everything | (that is) written in the laws of Moses.' (Mat 7:12)

## 11.5.2 Object or complement relative clauses

In an object relative clause (O.R) it is the object of the relative clause that is referenced to the head noun which is modified. Take again the example of the boys and the dog. In the phrase 'the dog which the boys hit', the noun "dog" is the head noun, modified by the relative clause. And 'dog' is also the object of the verb found in the relative clause.

The relativizer in an object relative clause is formed by the normal GNP morpheme, followed by the previous reference marker -e (for cl. 1) or -o (for the other classes). This produces cl. 1 **yé**, cl. 2 **bó**, cl. 3 **gwó**, cl. 4 **yó**, cl. 5 **lyó**, cl. 6 **gó**, cl. 7 **kyó**, cl. 8 **byó**, cl. 9 **yó**, cl. 10 **zó**, cl. 11 **lwó**, cl. 12 **kó**, cl. 13 **twó**, cl. 14 **bwó**, cl. 15 **kwó**, cl. 16 **hó**, cl. 18 **mwó**, cl. 19 **hyó**. This relativizer is joined to

---

[21] Whether **íbíyándìkê** consists of an augment on a noun phrase which is structurally in apposition to **byoshi**, and is headed by the stative verbal adjective, or whether it should instead be seen as a deverbal adjective which undergoes relativization is a matter of interpretation.

## 11.5 Relative clauses

the following verb as a proclitic. Structurally, this relativizer is identical to the focus copula which means 'he/she/it, etc. is the one'.

The object relativizer may be omitted when the head noun being modified is a demonstrative pronoun **yùkwó** 'that.N' or **yìbyó** 'those (things)' when it is the one of the time words **kyànyà** 'time' or **kíhê** 'time', or when it is the locative words **í=mûndà** 'there' or **yàhó** 'there'. These are all common, generic words, for which the relativizer seems to be understood. The relativizer is also omitted by some of the younger generation, who are influenced by the national language French.

In (11.106) the head noun **ú=lúsìkù** 'day' is simultaneously the clause subject of the dependent clause **ìrí ú=lúsìkù ìrí lúkáhíkà** 'when the day arrived' and the object of the object relative **lwó=bákálágáánà** 'which they agreed'; **lwó** is the relativizer.

(11.106) Head noun | Object relative clause

| Ú=lú-sìkù | lw-ó= bá-ká-lágáán-à ‖ | ìrí | lú-ká-hík-à ‖ |
|---|---|---|---|
| AU=11-day | 11-O.R= 2-P2-agree-Fa | when | 11-P2-arrive-Fa |

| m-bóngó | y-àná-yîj-à. |
|---|---|
| 9-gazelle | 9-SQ-come-Fa |

'The day which they agreed (upon) ‖ when it arrived ‖ that gazelle | came.' (21 017)

In (11.107) the specifier **ngíìsì** 'whatever' modifies the understood object **bíndù** 'things', which is not explicitly stated. That phrase **ngíìsì bíndù** is simultaneously the object of the main verb **mùlólé**, and the object of the relative clause **byó=múndú ágáshàlà** 'what the person will vomit up'.

(11.107)                            Head NP

| Mù-Ø-tù-shà-z-é | ‖ gírá | mù-Ø-lól-é | ngíìsì |
|---|---|---|---|
| 2PL-SBV-O1.PL-vomit-CS-Fe | so.that | 2PL-SBV-look.at-Fe | whatever |

Object relative clause

| by-ó= | mú-ndú | á-gáá-shàl-à. |
|---|---|---|
| 8-O.R+AU= | 1-person | 1-F2-vomit-Fa |

'Make us vomit ‖ so that you (may) look at | just what (things) the person | will vomit up.' (09 016)

In (11.108) the head noun **íkíhùgó** 'country' is the subject of the main verb **kíkátéérwá** 'it was attacked'. At the same time it is the complement of a locative clause headed by the cl. 18 **mú**. The relative clause can be translated as 'the country which frog and rat lived in'. The locative marker of the semantically underlying locative phrase has been moved to the end of the verb as a pronominal element (underlined here): **íkíhùgó kyó=kèré né=mbébà báàli tùùzìrí=mwò** 'the country which frog and rat lived in'. This clause derives from the more basic clause **kèré né=mbébà báàlì tùùzírì mú=kíhūgò** 'frog and rat lived in a country'. The constituents have been rearranged to fit the point which the speaker wants to make: that the country was attacked by hunger. Expressing as a relative clause the fact that frog and rat lived there also marks that fact as being important to the theme of the story (11.5.6).

(11.108)   Head noun
    Í=kí-hùgó   |
    AU=7-country

   Object relative clause
   **ky-ó=** | **kèré** | **n-é=** | **m-bébá** | **bá-àlì** | **tùùz-ìr-í** | **=mwò** ||
   7-O.R= | 1a+frog | CNJ-AU= | 9-rat | 2-P3 | live-RS-Fi | =18

   **kí-ká-téér-w-á** | **n-ó=** | **mw-énà**.
   7-P2-attack-PS-Fa | CNJ-AU= | 3-hunger

'The country | which frog and rat | lived in || was attacked | by hunger.'
(20 002)

Likewise in (11.109) the head noun **íbíjángálà** 'banana leaves' is the object of the main verb **útwé** 'you cut', as well as the complement of the understood locative phrase **kú=bíjángálà** 'on the leaves'. The relative clause **byó=ngákúbààgìrà=kwô** 'that I will slaughter you on' derives from the understood clause **ngákúbààgìrà kú=(bíjángálà)** 'I will slaughter you on (banana leaves)'.

(11.109)                              Head noun
   **Ø-Gênd-á**  |  **ú-Ø-tw-é**  |  **í=bí-jángálà**   ||
   IMP.2SG-go-Fa   2SG-SBV-cut-Fa   AU=8-banana.leaves

         Object relative clause
   **by-ó=**  **n-gá-kú-bààg-ìr-à**           **=kwô**.
   8-O.R=    1SG-F2-O2.SG-slaughter-APL-Fa    =17

'Go | and cut | the banana leaves || which I will slaughter you on.' (14 024)

### 11.5.3 Null relativizers

As already mentioned, the relativizer may optionally be omitted in object relative phrases—often by younger speakers with French influence or by people speaking in an informal speech register. The absence of a relativizer is also found, even in formal speech register, with constructions involving **yùkwó** 'that.N', **yìbyó** 'those', **kú=kyànyà** 'at the time', **í=mûndà** 'there', and **yàhó** 'there'. The following seven examples illustrate environments in which the relativizer is usually omitted.

(a) When the head noun (modified by the relative clause) is the cl. 15 demonstrative pronoun **yùkwó** 'that', then the relativizer **kwó** is dropped, perhaps because it would take the same form as the last syllable of the pronoun itself (i.e. it would be **yùkwó kwó**). In (11.110) **yùkwó** 'that.N' refers to things the father had told them. The underlying clause is **yîshè ákábàbwírá yùkwó** 'his father had told him that.N'.

(11.110)

| | | | | Head noun |
|---|---|---|---|---|
| Yàbó | bà-ánà | bà-à-gè ‖ | bà-ná-yèméér-à | yùkwó |
| those.N+2 | 2-children | 2-A.M-1 | 2-SQ-agree-Fa | that.N+15 |

        Object relative clause
        ―――――――――――――――――――
    **yîshè**    ‖  **á-ká-bà-bwír-à**.
    1a+their.father  1-P2-O2-tell-Fa

'Those children of his ‖ agreed to that (which) their father ‖ told them.' (110 009)

(b) In (11.111) the nearby demonstrative pronoun **yìbyó** 'those' refers to the understood **byókúlyâ** 'food' which the monkey is eating. Again, the relativizer has been omitted, perhaps because it would take the same form as the last syllable of the pronoun itself (i.e. **yìbyó byó**).

(11.111)

| | | | | Head NP |
|---|---|---|---|---|
| Ú-m-bèèrèz-é | nàà-nì | ‖ | kú= | yìbyó |
| 2SG-O1.SG-give-Fe | ADD.P-1SG | | 17= | that.N+8 |

        Object relative clause
        ―――――――――――――――――――
    **ù-gwétí**    **ú-gáà-ly-à**.
    2SG-PROG  2SG-INTL-eat-Fa

'Give ME ALSO ‖ some of that (which) you are eating.' (12 006)

(c) In (11.112) **yàhó** 'where' (without a following relativizer) is followed by the relative clause **íkásìgá í=zààbò** 'it had left its fellows'. The basic underlying construction is **íkásìgá í=zààbò yàhô** 'it left its fellows there'. Here the relativizer has been omitted, perhaps because it would take the same form as the last syllable of the pronoun itself (i.e. **yà-hó hó**).

(11.112) Ìrí    í-ká-b-á         kéèrà      y-à-yìgút-à ‖ y-àná-gálùk-à ‖
        when   9-P2-become-Fa   ALREADY    9-P1-full-Fa    9-SQ-return-Fa

| | Head NP | Object relative clause | |
|---|---|---|---|
| y-àná-húb-à | yà-hó | í-ká-sìg-á | í=zà-àbò. |
| 9-SQ-miss-Fa | there.N-16 | 9-P2-leave-Fa | AU=10-SAME.SET |

'When it (cow) had already gotten full ‖ it returned ‖ and it missed that place | (where) it had left | its fellows.' (11 004)

(d) In (11.113) there is no relativizer after **kyànyà** 'time'. This phrase alone introduces the following dependent clause **ndí=mú=kúhàmágálírà í=byó=kúlyâ** 'I am calling you to food'.

(11.113) Sí=    nàà-nì       n-dí=    mú=      mény-á | kwó=   w-é=
         OBV=   ADD.P-1SG    1-am=    PROG=    know-Fa  CMP=   2SG-FOC=

rì     mú=      n-dùk-à ‖         kú=
is     PROG=    O1.SG-insult-Fa   17=

| Head noun | Object relative clause | | |
|---|---|---|---|
| ky-ànyà | n-dì mú= | kú-hàmágál-ír-á | í=by-ókúlyâ. |
| 7-time | 1-am PROG= | O2.SG-call-APL-Fa | AU=8-food |

'It's obvious that ME ALSO I know | that you're the one who is insulting me ‖ at the time | I am calling you | to food.' (39 026)

(e) In the same way in (11.114) there is no relativizer after **kíhè** 'time'. That word alone introduces the time relative clause **yêhé kéèrà àhúnìràgà** '(when) he was already sleeping EMP'.

## 11.5 Relative clauses

(11.114)

|  |  |  |  |  | Head noun |
|---|---|---|---|---|---|
| **Bù-lyá** | **bú-nyúní** | **bw-óshì** \| | **bw-àná-yîj-à** \|\| | **kú=** | **kí-hé** |
| 14-that.R | 14-birds | 14-all | 14-SQ-come-Fa | 17= | 7-time |

Object relative clause

| **y-êhé** \| | **kéèrà** \| | **à-húnìr-àg-à.** |
|---|---|---|
| 1-CTR.P | ALREADY | 1+P1-sleep-EMP-Fa |

'All those birds | came || at a time that HE | was already | sleeping.' (204 022)

(f) The word **í=mûndà** 'there' can also introduce a locative relative clause, with no following relativizer. In (11.115) **í=mûndà** 'there' is followed directly by the object relative clause **àbùngírà** 'there (where) he moved to'.

(11.115) **À-ná-gêndí túúl-á bw-îjá ná= mú-ká-à-gè** \|\|
1-SQ-GOING live-Fa 14-good CNJ= 1-wife-A.M-1

| Head noun | Object relative clause |
|---|---|
| **í=** **mûndà** | **à-bùng-ír-à.** |
| 23= place | 1-move-APL-Fa |

'And he went and lived well with his wife || at the place (where) he moved to.' (44 011)

(g) The object relativizer is sometimes dropped even in constructions where it would normally be found. The object relativizer **yé** would normally occur in **ùyú mwāmì yé twàbííkà yáhà** 'this king whom we have placed here'. However, in (11.116), the **yé** relativizer does not occur in that position. Possibly this is due to the following focus clause, which also begins with **yé**.

(11.116)

| Head noun | | Object relative Clause | |
|---|---|---|---|
| **Ù-yú** | **mw-āmì** | **tw-à-bíík-à** | **yá-hà** \|\| |
| 1-this.P | 1-king | 1PL-P1-place-Fa | here.P-16 |

| **y-é=** | **w-à-yìngír-à** \| | **á=há-ndú** | **hà-à-gè.** |
|---|---|---|---|
| 1-FOC= | 1-P1-enter-Fa | AU=16-place | 16-A.M-1 |

'This king (which) we have placed here || he is the one that enters | his place.' (410 013)

### 11.5.4 Headless relative clauses

There are quite a few instances of headless relative clauses, where the head noun is implicit, but not actually stated. For example whenever a relative clause modifies a cl. 16 locative head noun, that head noun (**á=hándù** 'place') is usually left unexpressed. (This may be because **áhándù** is the only noun found in cl. 16.) In (11.117) the cl. 16 locative relativizer **hó** '(there) where' is seen introducing the relative clause **túgálôngà íbyó kúlyâ** 'we will get food'.

(11.117) Ø-Yîj-â       n-Ø-gú-twàl-é         |
         IMP.S-come-Fa 1SG-SBV-O2.SG-take-Fe

|  | Object relative clause |  |
|---|---|---|
| h-ó= | tú-gá-lông-à | í=by-ókúlyâ. |
| 16-O.R= | 1PL-F2-receive-Fa | AU=8-food |

'Come (that) I take you | there (where) we will get food.' (20 009)

In (11.118) the head noun **á=hándù** 'place' is again implicit. (Here the vowel of the relativizer **hó** elides before the cl. 1 subject prefix **à-**, to form **ha**.)

(11.118) À-ná-híkìrì    lól-à      ||
         1-SQ-ARRIVING  look.at-Fa

|  | | Object relative Clause | | |
|---|---|---|---|---|
| h-â= | kìzì | bíík-ír-á | í=fwárángà || | à-tà-ná-zì-bón-à. |
| 16-O.R+1= | REP | place-APL-Fa | AU=10+money | 1-NEG-SQ-O10-see-Fa |

'And she arrived and looked || where she habitually put | her money || and she did not see them (money).' (40 016)

### 11.5.5 *Kútì* 'how' grammaticized in a relative construction

The question word **kútì** 'how?' when combined (in an informal speech register) with the cl. 15 object relative marker **kwó** 'that', no longer has its basic interrogative function. In (11.119) **kútì kwó** instead functions to introduce a relative clause. This relative clause, in standard speech register, would be introduced with **ngíìsì kwo** 'just what' and not **kútì kwo**.

(11.119) **Hálìkò | n-gá-gêndì    lágúz-â         ‖ gírá    ú=mú-lágúzì    ‖**
         but       1SG-F2-GOING get.fortune.told-Fa  so.that AU=1-fortune.teller

**á-Ø-m-bwìr-é     |   kútí    kw-ó=    n-gáá-gír-à**.
1-SBV-O1.SG-tell-Fe    that    15-O.R=  1SG-F2-do-Fa

'But | I will go and get fortune told ‖ so that the fortune teller ‖ will tell me | that which I will do.' (10 007)

### 11.5.6 Relative clause function: denoting thematic salience

Relative clauses are not used indiscriminately in Kifuliiru stories. Rather, their typical function is to mark thematic salience (highlighting material central to the theme of the story).

In all of narrative 13 there are only two relative clauses. The first occurs in the second line of the story, where the object relative **byé=gáàlyà (byo=ígáàlyà)** 'that which it (quail) would eat' highlights the theme of the story, which is "How the Snake Eventually *Ate* the Quail". In this example, the head noun, **byókúlyâ** 'food' is implicit.

(11.120) **Y-áàlí  kìzì   génd-á      í-gá-lóòz-â    ‖ by-é=     gáà-ly-à**.
         9-P3   REP    GOING-Fa    9-F2-search-Fa   8-O.R+9=   F2-eat-Fa

'It (quail) was repeatedly going looking for ‖ what it will eat.' (13 002)

The second relative clause of narrative 13, found in line 10, is nearly identical, still referring to the theme of *eating*, but this time the snake is the subject, as the quail tells the snake "to get down, to look for what it would eat". Here again the theme is highlighted by the object relative clause **byó=gúgáàlyà** 'what it would eat'.

(11.121) **ìyó       n-gwârè ‖ y-àná-gù-bwír-à | kwó=   gù-Ø-túúlík-è   ‖**
         that.N+9   9-quail   9-SQ-O3-tell-Fa   CMP=   3-SBV-get.down-Fe

**gírà     gù-Ø-génd-é        gú-gá-lóòz-á |  by-ó=    gú-gáà-ly-à**.
so.that  3-SBV-GOING-Fe     3-INTL-look-Fa   AU=8-O.R=  3-F2-eat-Fa

'That quail ‖ told it (snake) | that it get down ‖ so that it could go and look for | what it would eat.' (13 010)

Narrative 105 revolves around the lion's desire to catch whoever killed its child. This theme is reflected by the subject relative clause **úkányìtírà ú=mwānà** 'who killed to me the child'.

(11.122) É= W-á-n-gáàvù ‖ nyándì ú-ká-n-yìt-ír-á       ú=mw-ānà?
       O=  1-A.M-9-cow      who   1+S.R-P2-O1.SG-kill-APL-Fa  AU=1-child

'O cow ‖ who (is) the one who killed my child?' (105 042)

The theme of narrative 112 is that a certain young man wants to marry a girl who looks like his mother. This theme is reflected in the two subject relative constructions in line 3, **úkálóózá ú=kúyángá úmúkàzì** 'who wanted to marry a woman' and **úshúshììnì nà=nyínà** 'who resembles his mother'.

(11.123) Há-àlírì-ìr-í | ú=mú-tàbánà mú-gùmà ‖ ú-ká-lóóz-á |
       16-P3 is-RS-Fi   AU=1-boy     1-one      1+S.R-P2-want-Fa

       ú=kú-yáng-á    ú=mú-kàzì | ú-shúsh-ììn-í            | nà=
       AU=15-marry-Fa AU=1-woman  1+S.R-resemble-RCP+RS-Fi   CNJ=

       **nyínà.**
       1a+his.mother

'There was | a young man ‖ who wanted | to marry a woman | who resembled | his mother.' (112 003)

The same theme is again reflected in line 4, in the object relative **yâ=síímà** (**yé=àsíímà**) 'whom he liked'.

(11.124) À-ná-dèt-à ‖ kwó= y-êhê | ndáá-yè mú-nyérè | y-â=
       1-SQ-say-Fa   CMP=  1-CTR.P  NEG.FOC-1 1-girl     1+O.R-1+P1=

       **síím-à.**
       like-Fa

'And he said ‖ that HE | there's no girl | that he likes.' (112 004)

In narrative 503 the theme of the story revolves around the wisdom of not talking about everything that you have seen. This theme is reflected by the relative clause in the title: **Byóshí íbìbónwà bìtàdètwâ** 'all that is seen is not spoken'.

(11.125) By-óshí | í-bì-Ø-bón-w-à ‖ bì-tà-Ø-dèt-w-á.
       8-all     S.R-8-TL-see-PS-Fa  8-NEG-TL-say-PS-Fa

'All | that is seen ‖ is not spoken.' (503)

The theme is again reflected in the subject relative **íhyáàlì kìzí bònékà** 'which appeared', found in the fifth line, again underscoring that the man was repeating everything that he saw.

(11.126) **Ndááhyò** ‖ **í-hy-áàlì   kìzí   bòn-ék-à** ‖ **í=   mûndà**
NEG.FOC-19   S.R-19-P3   REP   see-NEU-Fa   23=   place

**bà-shííb-à**   ‖ **á-tà-yìjí**   **hì-bwír-á   mw-āmì**.
2-spend.day-Fa   1+IF-NEG-COMING   O19-tell-Fa   1-king

'There's no ‖ small thing that appeared ‖ at the place where they spend the day ‖ without his coming telling it to the king.' (503 005)

## 11.6 Relations between independent clauses

There are several relationships which may obtain between two independent clauses in a sentence, or between two sentences.

COORDINATION is signaled by the use of a verb having either the sequential or the continuative TAM, both of which include the prefix **ná-**. CONTRAST between two independent clauses can be signaled by the conjunction **hálìkò** 'but'. In verbs of certain tenses, contrast can also be expressed by the inclusion of the additive prefix **ná-** in the verb of the second clause. Clauses expressing different ALTERNATIVES are conjoined by the conjunction **kàndí írí** 'or'.

### 11.6.1 Coordination between clauses

Coordination between clauses of equal status is basically indicated by the use of a verb with the sequential (SQ) TAM marker **ná-**. In addition, the continuative (CON) **ná-** (with final vowel **-e**) can be used in *predictable* environments or with subjunctive verbs. Several coordinated clauses may follow each other within the same sentence when the clauses are part of a "same-event complex".

Example (11.127) provides an example of several coordinated clauses. The verb **ànálángīīzà** 'and he looked at' (marked by the sequential **àná-**)[22] is followed by other verbs marked by the sequential (SQ) in the same event complex: **ànágìbònà** 'he saw it', **ànágìlángīīzà** 'and he looked at it', **ànáyàmà àtíbìtà** 'and he immediately ran'. There is no need to repeat the noun referent **shòòkùlú wàgè** 'his grandfather', or even to use a free pronoun. Instead, the subject prefix **a-** 'he' is sufficient to reference the same subject.

---

[22] With a cl. 1 subject marker, **a-**, the subject marker elides with the initial **a** of the sequential marking, i.e. **a-ana** > **aana**, which is shortened to **ana-** when three or more morae follow.

(11.127) Ìrí     shòòkùlú           w-à-gè ‖   á-ká-hík-à     mw-í=
        when   1a+grandfather    1-A.M-1    1-P2-arrive-Fa  18-5=

dékérè              ‖ à-**ná**-lángììz-á   í-ryá       ny-ámíìshwà ‖
elephant.ear.leaves   1-SQ-look.at-Fa    9-that.R    9-wild.animal

à-**ná**-gì-bòn-à ‖   à-**ná**-gì-lángīīz-à |   à-**ná**-yàm-à    à-tíbìt-à.
1-SQ-O9-see-Fa      1-SQ-O9-look.at-Fa      1-SQ-IMMED-Fa   1+P1-run-Fa

'When his grandfather ‖ arrived in the elephant-ear leaves ‖ he looked at that wild animal ‖ and he saw it ‖ and he looked at it | and he immediately ran.' (302 011-012)

The sequential aspect can also be used to coordinate clauses within an event complex in which the verbs have different subjects. In (11.128) the initial verb **bànázìkúúmánià** 'and they gathered them' has a cl. 2 subject ("children", mentioned in the preceding context) marked by the prefix **ba-**. This is followed in the next independent clause by another verb with the same subject, **bànázìhéérézà** 'and they gave them'. The following two verbs both have a different subject, who has just been mentioned within the discourse as the object of the second verb. The change of subject is indicated by the cl. 1 subject prefix **a-** on the verb **ànázìshwékérà kúgùmà** 'and he tied them together' and **ànákìzì bàhéérézá=zò múgùmà-múgùmà** 'and he gave them (sticks) to them (children), one (child) at a time'. An intervening verb, in the dependent complement clause, **kwâ=zìvùnè** 'that he break them', has yet another cl. 1 subject: the child referred to by **múgùmà-múgùmà**. The verb of the fifth independent clause in the event complex has yet another subject, the sticks, indicated by the cl. 10 subject prefix **z-** on the verb **zànábàyàbírà** 'and they (sticks) defeated them'. Such concatenation of clauses marked by the sequential is extremely common throughout Kifuliiru texts, since the sequential is used to indicate verbs which are on the event line (noting events) of a narrative discourse.

## 11.6 Relations between independent clauses

(11.128) **Bà-<u>ná</u>-zì-kúúmán-i-á | kwó= zì-rì múnààna ||**
2-SQ-O10-gather-CS-Fa    in.that= 10-are eight

**bà-<u>ná</u>-zì-héérèz-à yíshè | à-<u>ná</u>-zì-shwék-ér-à kúgùmà ||**
2-SQ-O10-give-Fa  1a+their.father          1-SQ-O10-tie-APL-Fa
together

**à-<u>ná</u>-kìzì  bà-héérèz-á  =zò   mú-gùmà-múgùmà |**
1-SQ-REP  O2-give-Fa   =10   1-one-RDP

**kw-â=   Ø-zì-vùn-è   || z-<u>àná</u>-bà-yàbír-à.**
CMP-1=  SBV-O10-break-Fe   10-SQ-O2-defeat-Fa

'And they gathered them (sticks) | being eight || and they gave them to their father | and he tied them together || and repeatedly gave them (sticks) to them one (child) at a time | so that he break them || and they (sticks) defeated them.' (02 011)

### 11.6.2 Contrast between clauses

(a) The conjunction **hálìkò** 'but' introduces an idea which is in contrast (or contrary to expectation) to what is presented in the immediately preceding context. In (11.129) the sentence begins with **Bànávyûlà íngwí, bànágìyìmúlà** 'the hunters roused up a leopard and chased it'. That is immediately followed by **hálìkò yànábàsìgà** 'but it left them behind'.

(11.129) **Bà-ná-vyûl-à        í=n-gwí    || bà-ná-gì-yìmúl-à |**
2-SQ-cause.to.get.up-Fa  AU=9-leopard  2-SQ-O9-chase.off-Fa

**hálìkò |  y-àná-bà-sìg-à.**
but      9-SQ-O2-leave-Fa

'They made a leopard get up || and they chased it | but | it left them behind.' (04 003)

In (11.130) a boy throws something at a bird, hoping to kill it. The conjunction **hálìkò** 'but' introduces something that is contrary to the boy's expectation, i.e. **kànáyìpúrúmúkírà** 'it just dashed off'.

(11.130) À-ná-làsh-à     yàkó      ká-nyúnì ‖ hálìkò |
       1-SQ-throw.at-Fa  that.N+12  12-bird    but

kà-ná-yì-púrúmúk-ír-à.
12-SQ-RFX-dash.off-APL-Fa

'And he shot at that bird ‖ but | it just dashed off.' (07 014)

(b) Contrast can also be expressed by the use of a continuative verb. In (11.131) contrast between the two clauses is expressed by the use of continuative **ná-** in the negative verb of the second clause: **ùtà<u>ná</u>lèèt<u>é</u>** 'and you do not bring'. The wife has expected that her husband will bring her the liver of the animals he traps, and the use of the negative-plus-continuative construction in the following clause signals a displeasing contrast to that expectation.

(11.131) Lééròò     lú-sìkù    lú-gùmà   mú-ká-à-gè tì=   ‖ «Kút-àgì
        this.time  11-day     11-one    1-wife-A.M-1 ‹quote›=  how-EMP

w-êhé |     ù-lì      mú=     kìzì    gwá-s-á |    í=ny-ámîishwà ‖
2SG-CTR.P   2SG-are   PROG=   REP     grab-CS-Fa   AU=9-wild.animal

ù-tà-<u>ná</u>-lèèt-<u>é</u>      | ú=bú-dìkù?
2SG-NEG-ADD.V-bring-Fe    AU=14-liver

'This time one day his wife ‹quote›: ‖ «Why do YOU | repeatedly seize | wild animals ‖ and (but) you do not bring | the liver?»' (401 019)

**11.6.3 Clause level alternatives: ìrí...kàndí írí 'if...or'**

An alternative to the option presented in a clause introduced by **ìrí** 'if' may be presented by a following clause introduced by the conjunction **kàndí írí / kàndí** 'or'. (This same conjunction is used at the phrase level to present alternatives, e.g. this or that). In (11.132) **kàndí írí** indicates the alternative between **ìrí àlì múgúmááná** 'if he is well' and the following phrase **àkòlà múlwāzì** 'he is now sick'.

(11.132) Bá-àlí kìzì   mú-hènándúl-á ‖  gìrá     bà-Ø-lól-é  |  ìrí  à-lì
        2-P3   REP    O1-examine-Fa    so.that  2-SBV-look-Fe  if   1-is

mú-gùmààná ‖    <u>kàndí</u> ‖  <u>írí</u>    à-kòlà |         mú-lwāzì.
1-well          or          if     1-be.NEWLY       1-sick

'They repeatedly examined him ‖ so that they see | if he is well ‖ or ‖ if he is now | sick.' (38 007)

## 11.7 Pauses at the sentence level

Pauses are important in marking off various constituents of information structure (as described in chapter 10), as well as constituents of sentence structure (described here below). Since pause is such an important part of Kifuliiru discourse, the phenomenon will be presented in some detail here, although not exhaustively. A pause within a sentence is typically found in certain grammatical environments, listed here and exemplified below:

- after nouns of direct address
- after a point of departure (PoD), whether this involves a conjunction, an adverb, locative phrase, or a dependent clause with tail-head linkage. If there is more than one PoD in a clause, there is typically a pause after each one. This is described at some length in 10.2.4 and will not be further exemplified below.
- after mid-sentence conjunctions
- before a relative clause
- before a complement clause
- before a quote (direct or indirect)
- between clauses marked by a string of sequential verbs

(a) After noun of direct address

A noun of direct address is typically followed by a long pause. In (11.133) the noun of direct address **é=mwìrá wànì** 'O my friend' is followed by a long pause.

(11.133) Noun of direct address

<u>É= mw-ìrá w-à-nì ‖</u>
O= 1-friend 1-A.M-1SG

**ú-Ø-n-gìz-é** | **ná= yù-gú mú-lírò!**
2SG-SBV-O1.SG-save-Fe CNJ= this.P-3 3-fire

'O my friend ‖ save me | from this fire!' (13 003)

Similarly, in (11.134) the noun of direct address, **é=mwānà** 'O my child', is followed by a long pause.

(11.134) Noun of direct address

    É=   mw-ānà ‖
    O=   1-child

| ù-tà-yúvw-á | ngíìsí | by-ó= | yîshó | à-kú-bwîr-à. |
|---|---|---|---|---|
| 2SG-NEG-hear-Fa | whatever | 8-O.R= | 1a+your.father | 1-O2.SG-tell-Fa |

'O child ‖ you have not heard | exactly | what your father | has told you.'
(626 020)

(b) After a mid-sentence conjunction

There is typically a pause after a mid-sentence conjunction followed by another clause. In (11.135) the conjunction **mú=kúbá** 'because' is preceded and followed by a long pause.

(11.135) 
| Ù-tá-Ø-gwàt-é | ú=bw-ìrá | n-é= | n-dyâlyà ‖ |
|---|---|---|---|
| 2SG-NEG-SBV-seize-Fe | AU=14-friendship | CNJ-AU= | 9-deceiver |

Conjunction

| mú=kúbà ‖ | y-àngà-kú-yìt-à... |
|---|---|
| because | 9-POT-2SG-kill-Fa |

'Don't become friends | with a deceiver ‖ because ‖ he could kill you...'
(13 014)

Similary, in (11.136) the conjunction **hálìkò** 'but' is preceded and followed by a long pause.

(11.136) 
                                Conjunction

| N-àngà-kú-kìz-ííz-ì | ‖ hálìkò ‖ |
|---|---|
| 1SG-POT.C.F-2SG-save-RS+APL-Fi | but |

| ndáá-kwò | n-gá-kú-tèlùl-à. |
|---|---|
| NEG.FOC-15 | 1SG-F2-O2.SG-lift.up-Fa |

'I would save you ‖ but ‖ there's no way | I can lift you up.' (13 004)

(c) Before a relative clause

Pauses are typically found before relative clauses. When a relative clause is found within a point of departure, however, there is typically not a pause preceding it. In (11.137) the relative clause **úwàléngà** 'who has passed' is preceded by a pause.

## 11.7 Pauses at the sentence level

(11.137)  W-à-n-gáàvù | à-ná-dèt-à: ‖ «W-á-n-dàrè  ùyó |
        1-A.M-9-cow   1-SQ-say-Fa   1-A.M-9-lion   that.N+1

       Relative clause
       ―――――――――
       ú-w-à-léng-à.»
       S.R-1-P1-pass-Fa

'Cow | said: ‖ «That (was) Lion | who passed.»' (105 028)

In (11.138) the relative clause **úkáyángà ú=múkàzí wàgè** 'who had married his wife' is preceded by a pause.

(11.138)  Há-àlí   rì-ìr-ì   mú-shósí   mú-gùmà |
        16-P3   is-RS-Fi   1-man   1-one

                Relative clause
             ―――――――――――――――
       ú-ká-yáng-á   |   ú=mú-kàzí   w-à-gè.
       S.R-P2-marry-Fa   AU=1-woman   1-A.M-1

'There was a certain man | who married | his woman.' (412 001)

In (11.139) the relative clause **ábáàlí bwàtììrì yàhô** 'who were sitting there' is preceded by a pause.

(11.139)  N-àná-zì-gáb-ìr-à      ‖   bá-lùmúnà       bà-à-nî |
        1SG-SQ-O10-divide-APL-Fa   2-young.brother   2-A.M-1SG

                Relative clause
            ―――――――――――
       á-bá-àlí   bwàt-ììr-í   yà-hô.
       S.R-2-P3   sit-RS-Fi   there.N-16

'And I divided them among ‖ my younger brothers | who were sitting there.' (635 024)

(d) Before a complement clause

Complement clauses are typically preceded by a pause. In (11.140) the complement clause **kwó=nàrágìrà** 'that I am grazing animals' is preceded by a long pause.

(11.140) Ù-Ø-lék-ág-è         ‖   n-gá-téb-à              nyókò              ‖
        2SG-SBV-allow-EMP-Fe      1SG-F2-deceive-Fe       1a+your.mother

| Complement clause |
| --- |
| kwó= n-à-rágìr-à. |
| CMP= 1SG-P1-graze.animals-Fa |

'Let (EMP) ‖ me deceive your mother ‖ that I am grazing animals.' (412 026)

In (11.141) the complement clause **kwó=lùlì lwà=múbóndò** 'that is yellowish' is preceded by a pause.

(11.141)

| | | Complement clause | | |
| --- | --- | --- | --- | --- |
| Bà-ná-lù-bòn-à \| | kwó= | lù-lì | lw-à= | mú-bóndò. |
| 2-SQ-O11-see-Fa | CMP= | 11-is | 11-A.M= | 3-yellowish |

'And they saw it (rooster) | that it is yellowish.' (634 016)

(e) Before a quote (direct or indirect)

Both direct and indirect quotes are typically preceded by a pause.
In (11.142) the direct quote **Nângà! Ndàngàlyà ùyú, mwìrá wànì** 'No! I would not eat this one, my friend' is preceded by a long pause.

(11.142) **Ì=n-dàrè | y-àná-dèt-à: ‖**
         AU=9-lion   9-SQ-said-Fa

| | Quoted material | | | |
| --- | --- | --- | --- | --- |
| «Nângà! ‖ | N-dà-ngà-ly-à | ù-yú \| | mw-ìrá | w-à-nì.» |
| No | 1SG-NEG-POT-eat-Fa | this.P-1 | 1-friend | 1-A.M-1SG |

'The lion | said: ‖ «No! ‖ I would not eat this one | my friend.»' (11 022-023)

In (11.143) the indirect quote **kwó=Wàlúkwàvù àlì múgéní wà=yîshè** 'that Rabbit is a guest of his father' is preceded by a long pause.

## 11.7 Pauses at the sentence level

(11.143)

| Ìrí | bá-ká-hík-à | há= | kā-āyà ‖ | à-ná-bwîr-à | nyínà ‖ |
|---|---|---|---|---|---|
| when | 2-P2-arrive-Fa | 16= | 12-village | 1-SQ-tell-Fa | 1a+his.mother |

Quoted material
--------

| kwó= | W-à-lú-kwàvù \| | à-lì | mú-géní | w-à= | yîshè. |
|---|---|---|---|---|---|
| CMP= | 1-A.M-11-rabbit | 1-is | 1-guest | 1-A.M= | 1a+his.father |

'When they arrived at the village ‖ he told his mother ‖ that Rabbit | is a guest of his father.' (626 025)

(f) Between coordinate clauses

Typically when independent coordinate clauses follow each other in a sequence, each is separated from the next by a long pause. In (11.144) there are coordinate clauses, as seen in **yùgwó mújōkà gwànáyìzòngézà=mwò** 'that.N snake wrapped itself there', **yànágùbálàlànà** 'and it (quail) flew off with it', **yànátwá í=kájábó kó=lwījì** 'and it landed on the other side of the river'. Each of these is separated from the following one by a long pause.

(11.144)

Clause[1]
--------

| Yùgwó | mú-jōkà \| | gw-àná-yì-zòngéz-à | =mwò ‖ |
|---|---|---|---|
| that.N+3 | 3-snake | 3-SQ-RFX-wrap-Fa | =18 |

Clause[2]
--------

| y-àná-gù-bálàl-àn-à ‖ |
|---|
| 9-SQ-O3-fly-COM-Fa |

Clause[3]
--------

| y-àná-tw-à | í= | ká-jábó \| | k-ó= | lw-ījì ‖ |
|---|---|---|---|---|
| 9-SQ-land-Fa | 23= | 12-across | 12-A.M+AU= | 12-river |

'That snake (cl. 3) | it wrapped itself there ‖ and it (quail) flew off with it ‖ and it landed on the other side | of the river.' (13 006-008)

# 12

# Narrative Forms

This chapter deals with linguistic notions that relate to narrative texts. The patterns described here apply to folktales as well as to non-fictional narratives.

The chapter opens with a summary of speech registers, since these different registers are relevant to the material presented in later sections of the chapter. Following that, we turn to the major components of the narrative. These include the introduction, the story body (with discussion of episodes, as well as sequential tenses), the story peak, and the conclusion. Next is a discussion of highlighting devices of various types. These include demonstratives in their function as thematic salience markers, the use of the verbal suffix -**ag** for emphatic prominence, various slowing-down devices, and the use of stylized songs. This is followed by a short look at reported speech. The chapter ends with a discussion of participant reference and tracking.

## 12.1 Speech register summary

Narratives can be told along a continuum of different speech registers, from formal written register, to the quite informal spoken register. There is a less-defined middle ground, here called the somewhat informal register, in which the degree of formality is less than formal but greater than quite informal. The basis for claiming that these three different speech registers even exist comes from two facts.

First, the same story can be told in different registers. For example, the story of a farmer who was outfoxed by a rabbit is told in both the formal written register (#626) and in the quite informal spoken one (#406).

Secondly, the same individual can use different registers. Sengoronge Katyera normally writes stories in the formal written register, but when he speaks, he uses a quite informal register.

The different registers are distinguished here by at least four objective criteria (summarized in table 12.1):

- The formal and informal registers each use a distinct system for marking thematic salience with demonstratives. The formal register uses only the nearby demonstrative to indicate thematic salience marking (TSM), without distinguishing between levels of salience. The two informal registers, by contrast, distinguish between default thematic salience marked by the nearby demonstrative, and major thematic salience marked by the remote demonstrative (12.3.1).
- The formal and informal registers also use different systems for conveying reported speech. The formal register introduces every speech act with a full speech verb (such as 'said', 'told him', 'answered', etc.), but the informal registers use a speech verb only in the first speech of a closed conversation, while the rest of the speeches in that group are marked with quote markers but no full speech verb.
- The formal register does not often use the continuative verb form for "predictable" sequential events, while this is commonly done (often 10–20 times per story) in the informal registers.
- In the formal register the emphatic verbal extension -**ag** is used rarely (maybe once or twice per story) and then only in direct speech reporting a command. In the quite informal register the emphatic is used much more often (often 10–20 times) and foreshadows material which is thematically prominent. The somewhat informal register tends more toward the formal in this regard, using the emphatic quite sparingly. Thus the emphatic is common only in the quite informal register.

Table 12.1. Speech register summary

|  | Formal written | Somewhat informal | Quite informal spoken |
|---|---|---|---|
| Thematic salience marking | Default | Default/major ||
| Speech verbs | Only speech verbs | Speech verbs and other quote forms ||
| Continuative | Very rare | Common ||
| Emphatic marker -**ag** | Very rare || Common |

## 12.2 Narrative text units

### 12.2.1 Story introduction

The story introduction typically includes some or all of the following three elements: (a) the introduction of the main participants by the use of the remote past stative tense (P3) or the unmarked past tense (P2), (b) the use of the quantifier -**gùmà** 'one/some' to mark the major character(s), and (c) the use of a relative clause, or other similar construction, to help identify the story theme.[1]

#### 12.2.1.1 Stories beginning with the P3 past tense

The main participant of the story is typically introduced by means of the remote past tense (P3 ) in the context of a sentence with presentational articulation ('there was a...') or locative inversion ('in that village, there were...') (12.5.1.1).

In (12.1) the first sentence of the story introduces the main participant by means of presentational articulation (i.e. 'there was...') with the verb in the P3 tense. The initial verb begins with cl. 16 subject prefix **ha-** at the beginning of **háálí rììrí** 'there was'. Also in typical narrative style, the main participant being introduced, **múshósì** 'man', is modified by the adjective -**gùmà** 'a certain'. Finally, the main participant is also modified by a relative clause, **úwáàlí tùùzìrwí né=mítègó yàgè** 'who lived by his traps'. The relative clause serves to highlight the theme of the story, which concerns those traps.

---

[1] By "theme" here we mean the pervading idea (Oxford English Dictionary), i.e. what the author is primarily talking about.

(12.1) **Há-àlí rì-ìr-í**   **mú-shósí mú-gùmá mú-tēzì** ∥ **ú-w-áàlí tùùz-ìr-w-í** |
    16-P3   is-RS-Fi   1-man   1-one   1-trapper   S.R-1-P3   live-PS-Fi

**n-é=**   **mí-tègó y-à-gè.**
CNJ-AU=   4-traps   4-A.M-1

'There was one man a trapper ∥ who lived | by his traps.' (35 001)

The same basic pattern is seen in (12.2), with the use of a presentational verb with cl. 16 subject prefix. Again the main participant is marked by **múgùmà** 'one'. In this case there is not a relative clause; rather more information is given about 'the young man' in a following clause which gives his name.

(12.2) **Há-àlí rì-ìr-í**   **ú=mú-tàbánà**   **mú-gùmà** ∥ **í=i-zīīnà**   **ly-à-gè** ∥
    16-P3   is-RS-Fi   AU=1-young.man   1-one   AU=5-name   5-A.M-1

**y-é=**   **Bíkòbà.**
1-FOC=   Bikoba

'There was one young man ∥ his name ∥ he is Bikoba.' (07 002)

In (12.3) locative inversion is used to introduce the major participants. This involves the cl. 18 **mu** as the head of the surface locative phrase at the beginning of the clause, together with the corresponding **mw-** subject prefix on the verb. Note also the use of **kágùmà** 'a certain' to describe **kāāyà** 'village', and the relative clause at the end of the sentence to add thematic information concerning the major participants (the three girls). This construction is similar to the presentational ones in (12.1) and (12.2) above, with the addition of the locative phrase at the beginning of the clause, and a different locative class marker (cl. 18 **mú** instead of cl. 16 **há**).

(12.3) **Mú=**   **kà-àyá**   **ká-gùmà** ∥ **mw-âli**   **rì-ìr-í**   **á=bá-nyéré**
    18=   12-village   12-certain   18-PS.ST   is-RS-Fi   AU=2-girls

**bà-shàtù** |   **á-bâ-lí**   **kùnd-íín-ì**   **bwènèènè.**
2-three   S.R-2-P3   love-RCP+RS-Fi   very.much

'In a certain village ∥ there were three girls | who loved each other very much.' (01 002 )

Example (12.4) illustrates participant introduction with no locative subject marker on the verb. However the P3 past is still used in the verb phrase **áàlí gwètí** 'she had'. In addition, once again the quantifier **-gùmà** 'one' serves to introduce the main participant **múvīīrè** 'mother of young children', while the quantifier **bàbìrì** 'two' introduces **bààná bààgè** 'her children'. The nouns in apposition, **ú=múnyéré nó=mútàbánà** 'girl and boy', provide added introductory information about the children.

(12.4) **Mú-vììré mú-gùmà á-àlí gw-èt-í bà-ànà bà-à-gé bà-bìrì ||**
  1-mother 1-one    1-P3  has-RS-Fi 2-children 2-A.M-1 2-two

  **ú=mú-nyéré |  n-ó=    mú-tàbánà.**
  AU=1-girl    CNJ-AU=  1-young.man

'One young mother had her two children || a girl | and a boy.' (33 002)

### 12.2.1.2 Stories beginning with the P2 past tense

In perhaps a less classic style, narrative introductions may also begin with the unmarked past (P2) tense, marked by **ká-** in the verb TAM slot. In (12.5), for example, the author was presenting information about himself and his paternal uncle. In the middle of his speech he embedded a narrative text. Since he had already been talking about himself and his uncle, there was no need to introduce either of them again. Thus, following a temporal setting, **lúsìkù lúgùmà** 'one day', he jumped right into the story, using the P2 tense in the first verb **túkágéndí hīīvà** 'we went hunting'. Note that just as seen in the examples in (12.2.1.1), the adjective -**gùmà** is used in the introduction, here modifying **lúsìkù** 'day' in the temporal setting.

(12.5) **Lú-sìkù lú-gùmà || ni-êhé | ni-é=    ná=   dáàtà**
  11-day 11-one      1-CTR.P 1SG-FOC+O.R= CNJ= 1a+my.paternal.uncle

  **w-à-ní    w-à=   Rúshūbì || tú-ká-géndì  hììv-á | í=m-bóngò.**
  1-A.M-1SG  1-A.M= Rushubi   1PL-P2-GOING  hunt-Fa AU=9-gazelle

'One day || ME | I together with (lit., it is I and) my paternal uncle Rushubi || we went to hunt for | gazelle.' (635 001)

In (12.6) the P2 **ká-** tense again introduces the story, together with **mú-gùmà** 'one' modifying the main character and the relative clause **útàshúshíìnì nà=nyínà** 'who does not resemble his mother', which highlights the theme of the story.

(12.6) **Mú-tàbánà mú-gùmà ‖ á-ká-dēt-à | kwó= y-êhè |**
     1-young.man 1-one      1-P2-say-Fa   CMP=   1-CTR.P

    **à-tá-gá-yâng-à    ú=mú-kàzí | ú-tà-shúsh-îìn-í |**
    1-NEG-F2-marry-Fa   AU=1-woman   S.R+1-NEG-resemble-RCP+RS-Fi

    **nà= nyínà.**
    CNJ= 1a+his.mother

  'One man ‖ said | that HE | will not marry a woman | who does not resemble | his mother.' (36 002)

In (12.7) the P2 past **ká-** tense is again used to introduce the story. Though not used to modify the main participant, the introductory adjective **lúgùmà** 'certain' occurs twice here, modifying both the temporal setting **lúsìkù** 'day' and the locational setting, **lúbàkò** 'forest'.

(12.7) **Lú-sìkù lú-gùmà ‖ ú=lú-kwàvù | lú-ká-b-á     | lù-gwétì |**
    11-day 11-one    AU=11-rabbit   11-P2-become-Fa   11-PROG

    **lú-gá-génd-à   gèndà | mú= lú-bàkò lú-gùmà.**
    11-INTL-go-Fa   RDP   18=   11-forest   11-one

  'One day ‖ the rabbit | was | intentionally | going going | in a certain forest.' (46 002)

In (12.8) the P2 **ká-** tense again introduces a story, together with the quantifiers **múgùmà** 'one' and **bàshàtù** 'three' modifying the main participants.

(12.8) **Ú=mw-àmì mú-gùmà ‖ á-ká-tùm-á   á=bá-shósí bà-shàtù | gìrá**
    AU=1-king   1-one      1-P2-send-Fa   AU=2-men   2-three   so.that

    **bà-Ø-génd-é    bá-gá-tàndùùl-à | í=m-bìbí    | z-é=**
    2-SBV-GOING-Fe   2-INTL-check.out-Fa   AU=10-borders   10-A.M+AU=

    **kí-hūgò   ky-à-gè.**
    7-country   7-A.M-1

  'A certain king ‖ sent three men | to go check out | the borders | of his country.' (47 002)

### 12.2.2 Story body

The story body is here defined as the material that comes between the story introduction and the story conclusion. The story body is usually divided into episodes, which feature "discontinuities" relative to time, place, participants, and actions. The sequential verbs are used within episodes to move the event line forward.

#### 12.2.2.1 Episode boundaries

Givón notes that episode boundaries are characterized by discontinuities of time, place, participants, and actions (Givón 1984:245; see also Grimes 1975). In the Kifuliiru corpus, discontinuities of time are more predominant, but there are also a few discontinuities of participants. Discontinuities for actions and location are extremely rare, and are thus not discussed here.

##### 12.2.2.1.1 Discontinuity of time

Very often new episodes begin with a discontinuity of time from the preceding episode. The discontinuity is indicated either by a dependent time clause or by a temporal phrase. Typically, when a dependent clause of time is used (generally the conjunction **ìrí** 'when' plus a verb with the unmarked past (P2) marked by the prefix **ká**-) the discontinuity between episodes is more significant than when only a temporal phrase is used. This is consistent with the principle of "iconicity", which says that a bigger grammatical structure represents something bigger.

(a) The conjunction **ìrí** 'when', together with a verb in the P2 past tense (with **ká**- TAM marker) usually indicates a new episode, marked as a paragraph break. In the text samples studied, well over half of new episodes are marked in this way.[2]

The dependent clause which is introduced by **ìrí** links back to information from the previous episode, while at the same time beginning a new episode. Such linkage is called "tail-head linkage" (Thompson and Longacre 1985:209–213). Tail-head linkage is defined by Dooley and Levinsohn (2001:16) as "the repetition in a subordinate clause, at the beginning (the 'head') of a new sentence, of at least the main verb of the previous sentence (the 'tail')." In Kifuliiru, however, the main verb of the previous sentence is not usually repeated in the "link", so technically this is not tail-head linkage by the above definition. All the same, some aspect of that previous clause is usually echoed, along with the presentation of some new piece of information, thus defining an episode boundary. This can be seen below in examples (12.9), (12.10), and (12.11).

Narrative 112 (12.9) begins with the introduction **Háàlí rììrí ú=mútàbánà múgùmà úkálóózá ú=kúyángá ú=múkàzì** 'There was a young man who wanted to marry a woman'. After that comes a subordinate time clause with

---

[2] In one set of six folk tales, approximately 24 new episodes were marked by the conjunction **ìrí** 'when', followed by the P2 tense, marked by -**ká**-. By contrast, 17 were marked in other ways. In almost every case where the conjunction **ìrí** was employed, it marked a discontinuity.

the conjunction **iri** 'when' and the P2 tense marked by the prefix **ka-**, signaling the beginning of the first episode. That clause, **ìrí bákámúyèréká á=bányéré bóóshì** 'when they showed him all the girls', refers back to what has already been explained in the context. (It follows that when he was seeking a girl to marry, that they would be showing him girls.) Thus this second sentence (marked by **iri** 'when' and **ka-** 'P2') begins the first episode (also seen as the first set of events).

(12.9) Há-àlí rì-ìr-í    ú=mú-tàbánà    mú-gùmà |   ú-ká-lóóz-á
     16-P3 is-RS-Fi   AU=1-young.man   1-one    S.R+1-P2-want-Fa

ú=kú-yáng-á |   ú=mú-kàzì. ||   Ùyó    mú-tàbánà || <u>ìrí</u>
AU=15-marry-Fa   AU=1-woman.   that.N+1   1-young.man   when

<u>bá-ká-mú-yèrék-á</u> |   á=bá-nyéré bó-óshì...
2-P2-O1-show-Fa    AU=2-girls   2-all

'There was one young man | who wanted to marry | a woman. || That young man || when they showed him | all the girls...' (112 103-104)

In (12.10) **ìrí bákáhíká mú=njírà** 'when they arrived in the path' indicates a change to the time as well as highlighting a new location. It is, in a way, redundant to say that they "arrived in the path", when the previous sentence just stated that they had set out in it. The reason the information is repeated is to indicate a discontinuity of time, and thus to mark a new episode. Again, note that although the verb **-gwat-** 'grab' is not repeated word-for-word in the following dependent clause, the idea of arriving in the path still presents the same idea.

(12.10) Bà-ná-gwàt-àg-é    í=n-jírà. ||  <u>ìrí</u>   <u>bá-ká-hík-à</u>   mú=   n-jírà ||
     2-CON-grab-EMP-Fe   AU=9-path   when  2-P2-arrive-Fa   18=   9-path

bà-ná-hík-à   kú=   lw-ījì.
2-SQ-arrive-Fa  17=   11-river

'And they set out (grabbed path). || When they arrived in the path || they arrived at the river.' (112 012-013)

There is a similar occurrence in the next paragraph of that same narrative. This is seen in (12.11), where it is stated that they crossed the river (clearly implying that they reached the other side). The following dependent temporal clause **ìrí bákáhíkàgà í=kájábò** 'when they reached EMP the other side' repeats that thought. Such redundancy is not necessary from the point of view of presenting new information, but it is necessary to introduce new episodes.

## 12.2 Narrative text units

(12.11) **Bà-ná-jábùk-à** | **ú=lw-ījì**. ‖ **Ìrí    bá-ká-hík-àg-à    í=  ká-jábò** |
     2-SQ-cross-Fa   AU=11-river  When  2-P2-arrive-EMP-Fa  23= 12-across

     **ú=mú-hyà**  |  **tì=**  ‖  «**Éhèè!**»
     AU=1-new.wife  ‹quote›=  Oh.my

'And they crossed | the river. ‖ When they had reached the other side | the new wife | ‹quote›: ‖ «Oh my!»' (112 015)

In other cases, a time clause may introduce a new temporal setting which is not directly linked back to the previous sentence. In (12.12) the clause **ìrí hákábá lúsìkù lúgùmà** 'when it was one day' marks the beginning of a new episode. This is followed by another dependent time clause which also mentions a new location: **ngwà=jábúkágé úlwījì** 'when he was intending to cross the river'. This doubling of dependent time clauses is the speaker's way of introducing a major new episode in the story; there is temporal as well as locational discontinuity. In this case, it is at the point of the story when the young man finally comes across the kind of girl he has been looking for to marry. The importance of this sentence is also marked by the frequent pauses.

(12.12) **Ìrí    há-ká-b-à    lú-sìkù lú-gùmà** ‖ **ngw-à=**
     when  16-P2-become-Fa  11-day  11-one    as.soon.as-1=

     **Ø-jábúk-ág-é      ú=lw-ījì**  ‖  **à-húmààn-à**  ‖
     SBV-cross.over-EMP-Fe  AU=11-river  1+P1-encounter-Fa

     **ú=mú-nyéré** |  **à-bwát-îîr-ì** |  **mw-í=  dākò ly-é=    kí-tì.**
     AU=1-girl     1-sit-RS-Fi    18-5=  under 5-A.M+AU=  7-tree

'When it became one day ‖ when he crossed the river ‖ he encountered ‖ a girl | sitting | under a tree.' (112 008)

In (12.13) a new time is indirectly linked to the previous episode, marked by the phrase **ísìkù ìrí zíkálùgà** 'the days, when they were many...'. In other words, there has been a major lapse of time (many days) between the episode introduced here and the previous episode.

(12.13) **Í-sìkù** | **ìrí** **zí-ká-lūg-à** ‖ mw-àná w-à= n-gáàvù ‖
10-days when 10-P2-are.many-Fa 1-child 1-A.M= 9-cow

à-ná-fw-á | n-í= shálì.
1-SQ-die-Fa CNJ-AU+5= hunger

'The days | when they were many ‖ the child of Cow ‖ died | of hunger.' (105 035)

(b) On rare occasions, the cl. 18 marker **mú**, together with the infinitive, is used as a dependent time clause, while also setting the state of the following verb (see 11.3). The reduced clause in (12.14) **mú=kútááhà** 'in going home' is used to present a temporal discontinuity which introduces a new episode. (The previous episode was talking about how the porcupine was beaten.)

(12.14) **Mú=** **kú-tááh-à** ‖ yìkyó kí-shégèshè |
18= 15-return.home-Fa that.N+7 7-porcupine

ky-àná-kúúdúk-à.
7-SQ-stalk.off.angrily-Fa

'In returning home ‖ that porcupine | stalked off angrily.' (09 023)

### 12.2.2.1.2 Discontinuity of participants

Occasionally an episode begins with a discontinuity in the cast of participants. Within the body of one story, the presentational clause in (12.15) introduces new participants: **hànáyîjà ábátàbáná bàshàtù** 'there came three young men'. This represents a discontinuity from the participants previously involved in the narrative.

(12.15) **Hà-ná-yîj-à** | **á=bá-tàbáná** **bà-shàtù** ‖ bá-àlí kìzì génd-á |
16-SQ-come-Fa AU=2-young.men 3-three 2-P3 REP GOING-Fa

bá-gá-lóòz-à | á=bá-kàzì | b-ó= bá-gá-yâng-à.
2-INTL-search.for-Fa AU=2-women 2-O.R= 2-F2-marry-Fa

'There came | three young men ‖ they were repeatedly going | looking | for women | to marry.' (01 004)

### 12.2.2.2 P3 past tense used for background material

The remote past (P3) is used to present background information within the body of the narrative. In (12.16) the P3 past tense (with its characteristic tense marker **ááli**) is used in two verbs which give background information.

## 12.2 Narrative text units

(12.16) **Kú**= yìkyó ky-ànyá mw-àmì | **á-àlí** màlí zìmb-w-á |
17= that.N+7 7-time 1-king 1-P3 ALREADY steal-PS-Fa

í=n-gáàvù. || Á=bá-lémbérézí bà-à-gè || **bá-àlí** kòlà
AU=9-cow AU=2-assistants 2-A.M-1 2-P3 be.NEWLY

mú= génd-á | bá-gá-gì-lóóz-à.
PROG= GOING-Fa 2-INTL-O9-seek-Fa

'At that time the king | had already been robbed of | his cow. || His assistants || were now going | looking for it.' (22 006)

In (12.17) the P3 is used in a dependent time clause which provides background information about a certain fearful man. The use of the auxiliary **kizi** 'repeatedly' in **bwáàlí kìzí yīrà**[3] 'it was (repeatedly) getting dark' makes the verb apply to multiple occurrences of the action of getting dark, and thus describes a habitual state in the past.

(12.17) Ùyó mú-shósì || **ìrí** **bw-áàlí** kìzí yīr-à ||
that.N+1 1-man when s14-P3 REP get.dark-Fa

à-tá-gá-kì-bòn-èk-à | há= m-bùgà.
1-NEG-F2-PERS-see-NEU-Fa 16= 9-outside

'That man || whenever it was getting dark || he will no longer be seen | outside.' (609 004)

### 12.2.2.3 Sequential tenses to move the episode forward

There are two tenses which indicate sequential action. The SEQUENTIAL tense is marked in the TAM slot by verb prefix **àná-**, with a final vowel **-a**. It is used to move the event line forward within an episode. The CONTINUATIVE[4] tense, is marked by **ná-** in a verb with the final vowel **-e**. It is also used to move the event line forward, but only in contexts that are *predictable*. In this sense the continuative could be said to mark an "extension" of a previous thought, conversation, action. The subject prefix pronouns of successive verbs are often different, even in the same "event complex".

---

[3] The cl. 14 subject prefix of the verb refers to the understood subject **búshìgì** 'evening'.
[4] Besides this discourse usage of the continuative, it can also be used in a sequence of imperatives, or in a sequence of subjunctive verbs.

### 12.2.2.3.1 Sequential chaining within episode

The sequential[5] tense[6] moves the event line forward. In the selection given in (12.18) all of the verbs are marked by the sequential tense, with no other tense occurring in between: **ànáyūmià** 'and she hardened', **àtànábàbìshúúkà** 'and she did not reveal (to) them', **bànáyìgéndèrà** 'and they went', **yànábìshúúkà** 'and it unhid itself', and **yànáyìbúgùmùlà** 'and shook itself off'. As can be seen from the subject markers, the subjects of the verbs are different: cl. 1 **a-**, the cl. 2 **ba-**, and cl. 9 **i-** (which changes to **y-** when followed by a vowel).

(12.18) Ùyó    mú-kàzì |   <u>à-ná</u>-yùm-i-á |      ú=mú-tīmà |
        that.N+1  1-woman    1-SQ-dry-CS-Fa        AU=3-heart

<u>à-tà-ná</u>-bà-bìsh-úúk-à. ||   Yàbó         bá-hīīvì |   <u>bà-ná</u>-yì-génd-èr-à
1-NEG-SQ-O2-hide-RV.I-Fa       those.N+2    2-hunters    2-SQ-RFX-go-APL-Fa

bó-óshì. ||   Há=   ny-úmá    ly-à-bò |   ìyó         n-gwí    ||
2-all         16=   9-after   5-A.M-2    that.N+9    9-leopard

<u>y-àná</u>-bìsh-úúk-à ||   <u>y-àná</u>-yì-búgùmùl-à |   ú=lú-vù.
9-SQ-hide-RV.I-Fa        9-SQ-RFX-shake.off-Fa      AU=11-dust

'That woman | hardened (her) heart | and did not reveal (to) them. || Those hunters | all of them left. || After them | that leopard || came out of hiding || and he shook off from himself | dust.' (04 015)

In (12.19) progress of the event line is again marked by sequential verbs and again the various verbs recount actions of different participants, marked by the cl. 9 **i-** and the cl. 3 **gu-** (which surface as **y-** and **gw-**, respectively): **yànáyèméérà** 'it agreed', **yànágóòlà** 'it stretched out', **gwànáyìzòngézà** 'it wrapped self around', **yànágùbálàlànà** 'it flew with it', **yànátwà** 'it landed', and **yànábwîrà** 'it told'.

---

[5] The initial **à-** of **àná-** is elided when it follows a subject marker ending in **a-** and is followed within the word by three or more morae (including **ná-**).

[6] Thus it could also be called the "narrative tense" or the "consecutive tense".

## 12.2 Narrative text units

(12.19) **Ìyó    n-gwârè** ‖ **ìrí    í-ká-yùvw-á    kwôkwó** ‖ **y-àná-yèméér-à** ‖
that.N+9  9-quail    when  1-P2-hear-Fa    thus.N        9-SQ-agree-Fa

**y-àná-góòl-à    í-í-gósì.** ‖ **Yùgwó    mú-jōkà** ‖ **gw-àná-yì-zòngéz-à**
9-SQ-stretch-Fa  AU=5-neck    that.N+3   3-snake        3-SQ-RFX-wrap-Fa

**=mwò** ‖ **y-àná-gù-bálàl-àn-à** ‖      **y-àná-tw-á** |   **í=**
=18        9-SQ-O3-fly-COM-Fa             9-SQ-land-Fa      23=

**ká-jábó** | **k-ó=**    **lw-ījì** ‖ **y-àná-bwîr-à    yùgwó    mú-jōkà:...**
12-across    12-AU=       11-river    9-SQ-tell-Fa    that.N+3   3-snake

'That quail ‖ when it heard thus ‖ it agreed ‖ and it stretched out (its) neck. ‖ That snake ‖ wrapped itself around there ‖ and it (quail) flew with it ‖ and it landed | across | the river ‖ and it told that snake:...' (13 006-008)

### 12.2.2.2.3.2 Continuative marking predictable sequences

The continuative TAM marker (CON) is very similar to the sequential (SQ), in that it includes the TAM prefix **ná-**, and can describe sequential events. It is different in that it does not include the recent past marker **a-** in the TAM slot. Also, it has the final vowel **-e** instead of **-a**. The continuative TAM is used in the more informal registers to mark items that are somehow *predictable* from the context. In some of the very informal texts, almost half of the event line verbs are in the continuative.

In (12.20) the boy tells his mother to take the rooster and serve it to the rabbit. Once she is told, it is considered predictable that the mother does just that. This predictable information is coded by four continuatives in a row, not all of the same subject class: the cl. 1 **ànágwàtè** 'and she grabbed', **ànálùbààgè** 'and she butchered it', **ànálùzímààné** 'and she served it as guest food' and the cl. 2 **bànámúbììkè** 'and they placed him'.

(12.20) Ìrí    bá-ká-hík-à    há=    kā-āyà ‖ ù-lyá    mw-ānà |  à-bwír-à
       When   2-P2-arrive-Fa  16=   12-village  1-that.R  1-child   1+P1-tell-Fa

   nyínà              |   kwó=    bà-Ø-gwát-é |   lù-lyá      lú-hāzì |
   1a+his.mother          CMP=   2-SBV-seize-Fe   11-that.R   12-rooster

   bà-Ø-lù-zímààn-é                 w-à-lú-kwāvù |   kwó=    yîshè          |
   2-SBV-O11-give.guest.food-Fe    1-A.M-11-rabit    CMP=    1a+his.father

   á-gá-fùlùk-à.            ‖    Nyínà          ‖
   1-F2-return.from.work-Fa     1a+his.mother

   à-ná-gwàt-è |    lù-lyá      lú-hāzì ‖    à-ná-lù-bààg-è          ‖
   1-CON-grab-Fe    11-that-R   11-rooster   1-CON-O11-slaughter-Fe

   à-ná-lù-zímààn-é               |  w-à-lú-kwāvù. ‖   W-à-lú-kwāvù ‖
   1-CON-O11-give.guest.food-Fe     1-A.M-11-rabbit    1-A.M-11-rabbit

   bà-ná-mú-bììk-é |    mú=    n-dáárò.
   2-CON-O1-place-Fe    18=    9-guest.room

'When they arrived at the village ‖ that child | told his mother | that they seize | that rooster | and give it as guest food to Rabbit | that his father | will come home after work. ‖ The mother ‖ grabbed | that rooster ‖ and butchered it ‖ and gave it as guest food | to Rabbit. ‖ Rabbit ‖ and they placed him | in the guest room.' (406 010-012)

In the first section of (12.21) the mother tells the daughter to 'go hide; don't go revealing yourself, but go hide'. The following sentence codes this predictable information (where she does exactly what her mother had just told her) by the continuatives: **ànágéndè** 'and she went', **ànágêndì híkà**[7] 'and she going arrived', and **ànábèèrè** 'and she remained'.

---

[7] Note that the continuative final vowel -**e** does not appear on multiword forms (like **ànágêndì híkà**) in which an **i**-final auxiliary precedes an uninflected verb stem.

## 12.2 Narrative text units

(12.21) **Ná**= **w-à**= **nyínà:**  ‖  **«Ù-Ø-génd-é**  
CNJ= 1-A.M= 1a+her.mother  2SG-SBV-GOING-Fe

**ú-gá-bìsh-àm-à.** ‖  **Ù-tá-Ø-gênd-è**  **ù-gwétí**  
2SG-INTL-hide-POS-Fa  2SG-NEG-SBV-GOING-Fe  2SG-PROG

**ú-gá-bìsh-ùùk-à** ‖ **sì**= **ù-Ø-génd-é** | **ù-gwétí**  
2SG-INTL-hide-RV.I-Fa  OBV= 2SG-SBV-GOING-Fe  2SG-PROG

**ú-gá-bìsh-àm-à.** ‖ **Ù-lyá** **mú-nyéré**| **à-ná-gênd-è**|  
2SG-INTL-hide-POS-Fa  1-that.R 1-girl  1-CON-GOING-Fe

**à-gwétí á-gá-bìsh-àm-à** ‖ **à-ná-gêndì** **hík-à** | **kú**=  
1-PROG 1-INTL-hide-POS-Fa 1-CON-GOING arrive-Fa  17=

**lw-âlà** | **à-ná-bèèr-è** | **í**= **rú-gúlú** | **ly-á**= **yùlwó** **lw-âlà.**  
11-cave  1-CON-remain-Fe  23= 11-above  5-A.M= that.N+11  11-cave

'And the mother (said): ‖ «Go and hide. ‖ Don't go revealing yourself ‖ but go | and hide.» ‖ That girl | went | hiding herself ‖ and she went and arrived | at the cave | and she remained | above | that cave.' (111 035-036)

From the above examples it might appear that the continuative is used only after a command (which indeed would make the following action predictable). However, a command is not what triggers the continuative, as seen in the (12.22). Here the young man has been looking for a special girl to marry, one who resembles his mother. When he finally finds one (as recounted in the first sentence of (12.22), the following sentence gives information that is somewhat predictable given the theme of the story: the young man proposes to her, she accepts, and they head down the road together.

(12.22) Ìrí      á-ká-mú-bòn-á tì=         «Nângà ‖ y-ô-yú | y-é=
When   1-P2-O1-see-Fa   ‹quote›=   no        E-this.P-1   1-FOC=

shúsh-ììn-í              nà=        máàwè          ‖ n-ó=      mú-tûmbà |
resemble-RCP+RS-Fi   CNJ=      1a+my.mother    CNJ-AU=   3-size

ngá=   gw-à=    máàwè.»    ‖ Ù-lyá      mú-tàbánà |
like=   3-A.M=   1a+my.mother   1-that.R   1-young.man

à-ná-mú-bwìr-e: ‖ «É=   mú-nyérè ‖ n-à-kú-síìm-à      ‖
1-CON-O1-tell-Fe      O=   1-girl         1SG-P1-O2.SG-like-Fa

n-àmú=     kú-yáng-à.»   ‖ Ná-yé ‖ tì=        ‖ «Èè ‖
1SG-P1=   O2.SG-marry-Fa    ADD.P-1   ‹quote›=    yes

ú-Ø-n-yâng-è.»            ‖ Bà-ná-gwàt-àg-é |   í=n-jírà.
2SG-SBV-O1.SG-marry-Fe    2-CON-grab-EMP-Fe   AU=9-path

'When he saw her ‹quote›: «No way! ‖ This very one | is the one that resembles my mother ‖ and the size | is like that of my mother.» ‖ That young man | told her: ‖ «O girl ‖ I like you ‖ I'm about to marry you. ‖ And SHE ‖ ‹quote›: ‖ «Yes ‖ marry me.» ‖ And they set out | on the path.'
(112 009-012)

In (12.23) it can again be seen that there is no preceding command. The young man has been seeking a way to get rid of the demon (the girl), who has been sitting on his back. When she finally flies to the meat, he gets his chance and dashes off. The predictability of the event is marked by the continuative form in the auxiliary verb of the phrase **bànáyàmàgè bágápùùmùkà** 'and they immediately dashed off'.

## 12.2 Narrative text units

(12.23) **Yùgwó mú-zīmù** ‖ gw-àná-yàmí bálál-á ngànà nà= kú=
that.N+3 3-demon 3-SQ-IMMED flew-Fa just CNJ= 17=

zì-ryá n-yámà! ‖ Ù-lyá mú-tàbánà ‖ à-ná-yám-à |
10-those.R 10-meats! 1-that.R 1-young.man 1-SQ-IMMED-Fa

á-gá-sháàg-à yà-hô ‖ ná= yàbó bá-ndù |
1-INTL-leave-Fa there.N-16 CNJ= those.N+2 2-people

**bà-ná**-yàm-àg-è | bá-gá-pùùmùk-à. ‖ Bà-ná-jábùk-à |
2-CON-IMMED-EMP-Fe 2-INTL-dash.off-Fa 2-SQ-cross.over-Fa

lù-lyá lw-ījì.
11-that.R 11-river

'That demon ‖ immediately just flew to those meats! ‖ That young man ‖ immediately | left there ‖ and those people | and they immediately | dashed off. ‖ And they crossed | that river.' (112 048-049)

### 12.2.3 Peak

The peak of a narrative may be defined as "any episode-like unit set apart by special surface-structure features and corresponding to the climax or denouement in the notional structure" (Longacre 1996:37). The peak, then, represents the climax of the story. In Kifuliiru, the peak episode is often marked by an increase in the concentration of *thematic salience markers* (TSMs) (12.3.1, 12.3.2) and by the use of *slowing down* devices (12.3.4). In the quite informal register, the peak is also often marked by the heavy use of the *emphatic extension* -**ag** (12.3.3). Finally, it is marked by a *higher concentration of pauses*, which also serve to slow down the flow of information. These features are all described elsewhere and thus not described again here.

### 12.2.4 Story conclusion

The conclusion of a typical narrative is characterized in one of two ways, either by a moral or else by a formulaic ending.

#### 12.2.4.1 *Story moral*

The moral of the story refers to "the moral significance or practical lesson... to be drawn from a story" (Gove 1971:550). In quite a few instances, Kifuliiru stories end with a moral which drives home the practical lesson of the story. The moral may, or may not, be expressed by a proverb.

In (12.24) we see the moral which ends story 13. In this story, the snake ate the quail, even though the quail had just saved it from the fire. The moral is that we should not do as the quail did and make friends with a deceiver. Note that this moral is not in the form of a proverb.

(12.24) Ù-tá-Ø-gwàt-é        ú=bw-ìrá     | n-é=       n-dyâlyà ||
       2SG-NEG-SBV-seize-Fe  AU=14-friendship  CNJ-AU=  9-deceiver

   mú=kúbá ||   y-àngà-kú-yìt-á |   ù-tà-ná-mény-à.
   because      9-POT-O2.SG-kill-Fa  2SG-NEG-SQ-know-Fa

'Don't make a friendship | with a deceiver || because || he could kill you | without you knowing it.' (13 014)

In (12.25) the story concludes as the king says proverbially, 'If it (cl. 6, referring to water, etc.) has spilled out, it is not still picked up'. In this case nothing has been literally spilled out, rather, someone has been choked to death mistakenly. Nevertheless the deed is irreversible and this proverbial saying is what ends the story.

(12.25) Ìrí  gà-Ø-yòn-ék-à        || gà-tà-Ø-kì-shàmàt-w-â.
       If   6-TL-pour.out-NEU-Fa    6-NEG-TL-PERS-pick.up-PS-Fa

'If it is spilled || it is not still picked up.' (503 030)

### 12.2.4.2 Formulaic ending

There are two formulaic endings that are often used with Kifuliiru folktales. Each of these endings includes two parts which combine to communicate a sense of finality. Both use verbs in the timeless tense, which is also used in proverbs.

In (12.26) we see one of the formulaic expressions found at the end of many stories.

(12.26) H-ó=    lú-fùmò ||  h-ó=    lù-Ø-hék-èr-à  ||  nà=   h-ó=
       16-FOC=  11-story    16-FOC=  11-TL-end-APL-Fa   CNJ=  16-FOC=

   lù-Ø-hùmb-ír-à.
   11-TL-rain.end-APL-Fa

'That's where the story || that's where it comes to an end || and that's where it finishes.'

An alternate formulaic end to a folktale is shown in (12.28) and is also very commonly used.

(12.27) Ú=lú-fùmò | h-ó= lù-Ø-hùmb-ír-à yà-hò || sí=
       AU=11-story 16-FOC= 11-TL-rain.end-APL-Fa there.N-16 OBV=

   lù-tà-Ø-hùmb-á | ngá= n-vùlà.
   11-NEG-TL-rain.end-Fa like= 9-rain

   'The story | that's where it ends there || but it does not end | like rain.'

## 12.3 Highlighting

"Sentences are typically highlighted when they relate to a climax, or when a significant development or a change of directions occurs" (Levinsohn 2005:NARR05). In this section we discuss various highlighting devices: (a) demonstratives as thematic salience markers, (b) thematic salience expressed by the cl. 16 locative marker **ha** 'place', (c) emphatic prominence expressed by the -**ag** suffix on the verb, (d) slowing-down devices, and (e) cryptic songs.

### 12.3.1 Demonstratives as thematic salience markers

In narrative texts[8] the nearby and remote demonstratives function as thematic salience markers[9] (TSMs). This means that they mark material that is deemed important (salient) to the story theme, according to the author/speaker's intended purpose. Thus points that one speaker may consider thematically salient might not be marked as salient by another speaker. However, where the participants *are* marked as salient is always significant.

The most commonly marked elements are key thematic participants. In addition, TSMs can also mark objects/locations/abstractions which are important to the story theme, especially at the end of episodes, where they function to summarize.

The type of demonstrative used as a TSM varies depending on the story register:

- In formal, written speech, only the nearby demonstratives are used as TSMs. Where salience is marked, no distinctions are made in degrees of salience.

---

[8] In other contexts, these demonstratives have meanings based on position relative to speaker and hearer, as discussed in 3.5.2.

[9] Thematic salience markers (TSM) might also be referred to as development markers (DM), because they "constrain the reader to *move on to the next point*...they indicate that the material so marked represents a new development in the story or argument, as far as the author's purpose is concerned" (Dooley and Levinsohn 2001:93). The Kifuliiru TSMs do exactly that, basically occurring whenever a new thematic development occurs. In addition, however, Kifuliiru TSMs (more rarely) mark thematic summarization through objects/locations/abstractions, etc., especially at episode boundaries. This could be viewed as summarization of the theme at key points. Thus we used the term TSM instead of DM. All of these points will be illustrated in the examples that follow below.

- In all informal registers, two types of thematic salience are distinguished; the nearby demonstratives mark default thematic salience, while the remote demonstratives indicate major thematic salience.

The following points are made by way of general introduction:

- In no story does the major TSM occur before a default TSM has appeared in the story. Rather, the default TSM always occurs first in the story, after which the major TSM may be used. As a corollary, major TSMs tend to be concentrated toward the end of the story.
- At higher points of tension in the story TSMs tend to occur more frequently, and are often found "stacked" as many as three or four per sentence, instead of the normal one or two.
- While TSMs routinely occur in clauses which are on the event line,[10] it is not the event line itself which triggers these demonstratives. Many of the "events" that occur in a story are not new thematic developments and are therefore not marked with TSMs. TSMs are used to mark only new thematic developments in the story.
- As would be expected, the use of the TSMs is to some degree subjective, since the speaker/writer is highlighting what is important to the theme of the story as he/she interprets it. Although there is a common, predictable pattern as to when TSMs could likely occur, the extent to which they are employed remains, in the final analysis, up to the intuition of the speaker/writer.

In section (12.3.1.1) we present four different narratives in which we have marked the TSMs. The first narrative is in formal written register, so only nearby demonstratives (marked as ***that.N*** in a bold italic font) function as TSMs. In the three texts of informal register, both the nearby (marked as ***that.N*** in bold italic) and the remote demonstratives (marked as **that.R** in bold) are used as TSMs.

### 12.3.1.1 *Written register, formal; nearby (default) only*

The story in (12.28) is written in the formal speech register, and thus contains only nearby demonstratives to mark thematic salience. This story is representative of 55 stories of the formal register (01–55) where only the nearby demonstratives are used.

---

[10]The event line consists of the clauses which express the events that form the narrative, as opposed to clauses which express descriptive or background material, material within reported speech, or narrator evaluations.

(12.28) Kifuliiru story 11. Theme: "The danger of losing fear"
  Episode 1 (Introduction)

| 1a. | Background material, no TSMs | There were cows of one man, grazing.<br>When they arrived in the wilderness, one of them wandered off on its own unique path to feed.<br>When it had become already satisfied, it returned, but it missed the place it had left its fellows and it took a different path and got lost. Its fellows went home.<br>Its owner, he went looking for it and he gave up on it. |
|---|---|---|
| 1b. | Cow encounters Lion | ***that.N cow*** went and came out into the forest of the lion.<br>The lion saw it and welcomed it. |
| 1c. | Cow is afraid of Lion | ***that.N cow*** was afraid and said: «O for pity's sake, my comrade, aren't you going to eat me?»<br>The lion refused. |
| 1d. | Cow draws near to Lion | ***that.N cow*** neared ***that.N lion*** and they greeted each other,<br>but the cow continued to be very afraid. |
| 1e. | Cow tries to escape danger | ***that.N cow*** said that it is about to return.<br>The lion told it like this: «Allow that we live together, because me also, I'm living alone. I have already refused to you that I will not eat you, you who are my friend and you are also now my neighbor.» |
| 1f. | Cow is persuaded to live with Lion. | ***that.N cow*** agreed that they live together, because it no longer knew the path which would return it (to where it came from). |
| 1g. | Fear (non-participant) ends episode | ***that.N fear*** which it had had, ended. |

## Episode 2

| 2a. | Lion gets sick, friends arrive | When some days had passed, ***that.N lion*** got sick. It had its two friends, leopard and eagle. They came and checked it out and they saw that it was already very skinny, and they asked it: «What caused you to become so skinny like this?» |
|---|---|---|
| 2b. | Lion explains why he is sick | ***that.N lion*** answered: «Hunger is what made me skinny like this. Just a sickness would not cause me to get this skinny.» |
| 2c. | Friends propose that Lion eat Cow  Proposal rejected | ***that.N leopard*** and ***that.N eagle*** whispered to ***that.N lion*** and told it: «Would you not eat this cow?» The lion said: «No! I would not eat this friend of mine. Let me die rather than eat him!» The eagle was very sad that their friend the lion was about to die of hunger. |
| 2d. | Eagle makes second proposal to Lion  Proposal accepted | ***that.N eagle*** again said to ***that.N lion***: «This cow, if it would say itself that you eat it, in the place of (instead of) dying of this hunger, would you not eat it?» The lion said: «You my friends from long ago, if you said that I eat it, I would eat it.» |
| 2e. | Friends leave, expecting proposal to be realized | ***that.N eagle*** and ***that.N leopard*** went home; with an expectation that they also will get supper there. |

## Episode 3 (Climactic)

| 3a. | Friends come back to see if Lion ate Cow | When a few days had passed, they came and looked if ***that.N lion*** had already eaten ***that.N cow***. |
|---|---|---|
| 3b. | Friends find that Lion still with hunger | This time they encountered ***that.N lion*** was now about to die of ***that.N hunger***. The leopard asked the lion: «O you, why did you not do that which we told you?» |
| 3c. | Leopard makes a proposal  focus on: Leopard | ***that.N leopard*** said: «Ok then, May I be the one you will eat, in the place of dying of hunger!» The lion refused, saying it will not eat ***that.N leopard***. |

## 12.3 Highlighting

| 3d. | focus on: Eagle | The eagle and he also said that he be the one that the lion eat, but the lion again refused, saying it will not eat **that.N eagle**. |
|---|---|---|
| 3e. | Cow falls for the trick | **that.N cow**, when it heard its comrades say that it eat them, and it did not eat them, it also said: «May I be the one that you eat.» |
| 3f. | Pre-climax: Lion pauses | **that.N lion** was quiet and eagle winked its eyelid. |
| 3g. | Climactic event experiencer: Cow | The lion jumped on the neck of **that.N cow** and knocked it down and it immediately died. |
| 3h. | Dénouement with Lion, Leopard, Eagle, and Cow | **that.N lion** and **that.N leopard** and **that.N eagle** surrounded the corpse of **that.N cow**. And they began to tear it apart. |

The theme of this story centers around *the danger of losing fear*.

Where TSMs are absent

TSMs do not occur in any of the clauses of (12.28.1a). Although the material is on the event line, the events still consist of only background material. This includes how the cow wandered off on its own and got lost, taking a different path, with the owner not being able to find it. This paragraph does not deal with the theme (i.e. cow's fear of the lion, or with the effects of the loss of that fear).

Secondly, there are no TSMs in events that do not move the theme line forward. Thus in (12.28.1b) the lion welcomes the cow, which is no cause for fear. In (12.28.1c) the cow asks if it will be eaten, and again the lion refuses. In this case, the cow is marked by a TSM, because the question gives voice to his fear, but the lion, who answers kindly, is not marked at that point. In (12.28.1e) the (unmarked) lion again speaks in a friendly way, saying that he will not eat the cow.

Likewise, in the following episode, in (12.28.2c) when the leopard and lion suggest that the lion eat the cow, the lion's refusal is not marked, as it involves old information (the lion has already said that he will not eat the cow).

### Where TSMs are present

In this formal written text, only default salience markers are used, distinguishing only one level of thematic salience.

TSMs are used in (12.28.1b) when the cow first meets the lion (the source of fear), again in (12.28.1c) when the cow asks if he will be eaten (reflecting fear), in (12.28.1d) where the cow is still afraid, and in (12.28.1e) when he is thinking about returning (because of fear). In (12.28.1f) when the cow agrees to live with the lion, he is marked again, as the cow loses his fear. As the episode ends, the abstraction "fear" is marked, as it now ended, contributing to the cow's eventual demise.

In the second episode, the lion is marked in (12.28.2a) when he gets sick, because that sets up the danger for the cow. Thematic marking also is seen in (12.28.2b) when Lion answers that hunger is what made him skinny (again foreshadowing the eating of the cow). There is stacked marking (three times) in (12.28.2c) when the suggestion is made that lion actually eat the cow. There is also marking in (12.28.2d) when the eagle asks the lion if he would eat the cow if the cow asks him to, and in (12.28.2e) where eagle and leopard now have an expectation of eating the cow before too long.

In the third and final episode, the lion is marked in (12.28.3a) and (12.28.3b) as dying of hunger (heightening the danger for the cow). The leopard and eagle are marked in (12.28.3c) and (12.28.3d) when the lion refuses to eat them (because this sequence is setting up the lion eating the cow). The cow is then marked in (12.28.3e) when he falls for the trick and asks to be eaten. In (12.28.3f) and (12.28.3g) the lion, and then the cow, are both marked as lion pauses dramatically, and cow is finally attacked. Then at the end, there is a high concentration of TSMs in (12.28.3h), as the lion, leopard, and eagle, each marked by a TSM, surround the corpse of the cow, also marked by a TSM.

#### 12.3.1.2 *Spoken, somewhat informal; both nearby (default) and remote (major)*

The narrative in (12.29) is in the somewhat informal (spoken) speech register.

(12.29) Kifuliiru story 105. Theme: "The wronged one gets revenge"

Episode 1 (Introduction)

| 1a. | Lion and Cow are friends<br><br>They are living together | There was Lion and Cow.<br>*that.N Lion* and *Cow* became friends and they went to cut and gather trees for building.<br>*There.N* where they were gathering trees, they encountered a very nice plain and they built there.<br>And they went and looked for what (animals) they could come and tend in *that.N house*. |
|---|---|---|
| 1b. | Background, no TSMs | After a few days, Lion got pregnant and gave birth to a child and she went looking for food for him.<br>In a few days, Cow also got pregnant and she also gave birth to a child and she also kept going looking for food for him. |
| 1c. | Their children are friends | *Those.N children* both remained playing. |
| 1d. | Child of cow kills child of lion<br>Past events are not marked | In *that.N playing* the child of the cow killed the child of the lion.<br>Cow, when she returned, encountered the child of lion has already died.<br>Cow asked: «What killed this child of the lion?»<br>The child of the cow answered her: «We were playing and I killed it.» |
| 1e. | Cow tries to escape danger | *that.N cow*, when it saw *that.N child* had already died, it told itself that it should leave there.<br>And it took its child and immediately ran. |

Episode 2

| 2a. | Old man introduced | When it arrived in the path, it encountered there one old man and it told him (the man) to hide it. |
|---|---|---|
| 2b. | Old man asks what the problem is | *that.N old man* asked it: «Why am I going to hide you?»<br>And it told him: My child was playing with the child of the lion and it killed him. |
| 2c. | Old man hides them | *that.N old man* took Cow and her child and went and hid her in his *house*. |
| 2d. | Old man gives sign of danger | *that.N old man* told Cow: «If you would hear my rooster crowing, that's when lion has arrived.» |

## Episode 3

| 3a. | Past events not marked | The lion, when she came from looking for food, she encountered her child has already died.<br>When Lion encountered her child already has died, she began to cry.<br>When she looked for the place of Cow and her child, she did not see them.<br>And she said that Cow is the one who killed her child. |
|---|---|---|
| 3b. | Lion asks old man where cow is (Real tension begins) | Right then she immediately went and looked for Cow.<br>When she arrived in the path, she came upon **that.R old man**.<br>Lion asked **that.R old man**: «O grandfather, is there no cow which passed here? |
| 3c. | Rooster crows (sign of lion's coming) | **That.R rooster** immediately crowed.<br><br>When **that.N rooster** crowed, then Cow said: «That's Lion who has passed.» |

## Episode 4

| 4a. | Lion follows dead-end path, causing her to return | When Lion followed **that.N path**, he arrived at where it ended. |
|---|---|---|
| 4b. | Lion asks old man again about the cow | Lion again returned to where **that.R old man** was and told him: «O grandfather, is there no cow which passed here?» |
| 4c. | Old man tries to save the cow | **that.N old man** told Lion, «Allow that I go and drink some water, after that we can come and converse.» |
| 4d. | Old man reveals danger to cow | **That.R old man** went in the house and told Cow: «Lion is waiting for you here outside.»<br>Cow always remained right there in the house with her child. |

Episode 5 (Climactic)

| 5a. | Lion accuses old man of lying about cow | The days, when they were many, the child of the cow died of hunger.<br>Cow began to cry for her child.<br>Lion heard that she is crying for her child.<br>Lion said to **that.N old man**: «It's obvious you denied that Cow is here. It's obvious that very one is now crying.» |
|---|---|---|
| 5b. | Old man denies | **that.N old man** said: «No she is not Cow, she is Goat.»<br>Lion told him: «Open the door so I can if it is not Cow.» |
| 5c. | Old man forced to open door | Lion told **that.R old man**: «If you do not open for me, I will eat you.» |
| 5d. | Old man opens the door | **That.R old man** opened. Lion saw Cow and it asked her: «O Cow, who killed my child?»<br>Cow said: «I don't know!»<br>Lion asked her: «What did you run from?» |
| 5e. | Climax (automatic, not marked) | Right then Lion began to fight Cow and she killed her. |
| 5f. | Conclusion | That's where the story ends, but it doesn't stop like rain. |

The theme centers on "The wronged one gets revenge." In this story both default and marked thematic salience markers are employed, to distinguish different levels of thematic salience.

Where TSMs are absent

There are no TSMs in (12.29.1b), where the animals get pregnant and go looking for food, since this background material has nothing to do with revenge. Likewise in (12.29.1d), there are no TSMs to mark the conversation of how the lion's child was killed, since that deals with past information.

The entire paragraph in (12.29.3a), where the lion comes back and finds his child dead, does not have a TSM, as it also deals with past events. Likewise in (12.29.5a) there is no marking where the cow begins to cry for its dead child, as it is not related to getting revenge.

Finally the end of the story is not marked, including the climax where the lion questions the cow and then eats her. This seems to reflect the fact that once the old man opens the door the die has been cast, and the killing of the cow is taken for granted. (This is opposite from the previous story, where the conclusion of the story is marked by stacked demonstratives. This variation in usage patterns shows that the use of TSMs involves the speaker's interpretation and discretion.)

Where TSMs are present

In (12.29.1a) the lion and cow are friends, doing things together. The house, where they lived together, highlights their friendship, and is marked. There are markings in (12.29.1c) and (12.29.1d) as the child of the lion is killed, and in (12.29.1e), when the cow decides to leave.

In episode 2 only the old man is marked in (12.29.2b), (12.29.2c), and (12.29.2d) as he works to hide the cow.

In episode (12.29.3b) and (12.29.3c) the old man and the rooster are each marked twice, as the lion comes looking for the cow, and the rooster crows at the end of the episode to mark the danger.

In episode 4 the old man is marked three times, in (12.29.4b), (12.29.4c), and (12.29.4d), as he again attempts to hide the cow from the probing lion.

In episode 5, the old man is again marked four times in (12.29.5a), (12.29.5b), (12.29.5c), and (12.29.5d), as he is forced to give away the cow's hiding place.

To summarize, from episode 2 through 5, the old man is extensively marked (ten times!) and the rooster (whose crowing is the symbol of danger) is marked twice. The old man is obviously important to the end of the story, as he is the one who will either keep the cow hidden, or give her up to the lion's revenge. By contrast, neither the lion or the cow is marked at all after the first episode.

Nearby/remote distinction

The chart in (12.30) shows only the lines with TSM marking. Default TSM (marked by the nearby demonstrative) is shown in the left-hand column, while major TSM (marked by remote demonstrative) is shown in the right-hand column. The items marked by a TSM are shown below in bold.

(12.30) Default and major thematic salience in narrative 105

| | Default TSM (nearby demonstrative) | Major TSM (remote demonstrative) |
|---|---|---|
| 1a. | **Lion** and **cow** became friends at **house** | |
| 1c. | **Children** were playing | |
| 1d. | **In playing** child of cow kills child of lion | |
| 1e. | **Cow** sees **child** dead and runs away | |

## 12.3 Highlighting

|  | Default TSM (nearby demonstrative) | Major TSM (remote demonstrative) |
|---|---|---|
| 2b. | **Old man** asks why hide | |
| 2c. | **Old man** hides cow and child | |
| 2d. | **Old man** warns cow to say put | |
| 3b. | | **Old man** encountered by lion<br>Lion asks **old man** about cow |
| 3c. | | **Rooster** crows - danger |
| 3c. | When **rooster** crows, cow sees danger | |
| 4a. | Lion leaves **that path** temporarily | |
| 4b. | | Lion returns to **old man** |
| 4c. | **Old man** tries to stall | |
| 4d. | | **Old man** tells Cow Lion is waiting outside! |
| 5a. | Lion challenges **old man** | |
| 5b. | **Old man** denies having Cow | |
| 5c. | | Lion tells **old man** «Open up!» |
| 5d. | | **Old man** opens door |

If one reads just the marked TSM column in the right-hand column, the points of major salience in the story are quickly seen. The default TSMs on the left also mark salient material, but not to the same degree as those in the major TSM column on the right.

In this story (as in all other informal texts) default salience is marked first before major salience. Thus the first thematically salient events up through (12.30.2d) are all marked with the default TSM (the nearby demonstrative). The old man is first marked with the major TSM (the remote demonstrative) in (12.30.3b), as that is the point where the real action begins (where the lion encounters the old man in looking for the cow).

Throughout the rest of the story default is used twice when the old man tries to get the lion off the cow's track (12.30.4c, 5b). The major TSM occurs when the lion returns (12.30.4b) and when the old man tells the cow that the lion is there (12.30.4.d) and when the lion tells the old man to open up or be eaten and he opens up (12.30.5c, d).

To summarize, the major TSMs (remote demonstratives) are used to mark especially salient points of thematic development. The default TSM (nearby demonstrative), still marks points of thematic development, but only those seen by the author as of lesser importance.

### 12.3.1.3 Written, somewhat informal; both nearby (default) and remote (major)

The narrative story in (12.31) is again in the somewhat informal speech register.

(12.31) Kifuliiru story 503. Theme: "All that is seen is not spoken"

Episode 1 (Introduction)

| 1a. | King just introduced | In the past there was a king. ***that.N king*** had his three favorite friends. |
|---|---|---|
| 1b. | Friends just introduced | ***that.N king*** told ***those.N good friends*** of his to go hunt for him a wild animal. |
| 1c. | Friends go hunting First mention of big-mouth not highlighted | ***those.R good friends*** went hunting for him. One was a big-mouth. There wasn't any small thing that was seen where they spent the day, that he did not come and tell to the king. |
| 1d. | Habit of talking too much mentioned | His comrades tried hard to scold him harshly relative to ***that.N habit***, but he defeated them. Two more times they again told him that it is not everything that a man sees in the forest that he speaks in the village. |
| 1e. | Man does not heed warning | ***that.N father*** did not hear (listen). |

Episode 2

| 2a. | Setting for theme which follows | This time, one day, he went his own way. He encountered a head without a body and he hit it with his stick and asked it: «Why did you die?» It answered him: «Because of saying everything». He went home with the happiness of having got news to go tell the king. |
|---|---|---|
| 2b. | Man blurts out news | When he arrived, before he swallowed saliva, he immediately blurted out ***that.R news*** of his. |
| 2c. | News is questioned | The king immediately called his assistants and told them that ***that.N good friend*** of his had already told a lie. This time they should go together and he going show them ***that.N head*** which speaks, though it doesn't have a body. And he gave them permission that if he is lying, they should leave him right there (kill him). |

12.3 Highlighting

| 2d. | Three set out to examine news | **those.R attendants** set out on the path with **that.R father**. |
|---|---|---|

Episode 3 (Climactic)

| 3a. | The head still there | When they arrived there, they encountered **that.R head** still there.<br>And they told him (the man) that he do just as he did so the head speaks. |
|---|---|---|
| 3b. | Man strikes the head with the stick | And he took **that.R stick** of his and he struck **that.R head**.<br>And he asked it: «Why did you die?» |
| 3c. | Head does not answer | **that.R head** did not answer. |
| 3d. | Attendants kill big-mouth | **those.R attendants** immediately grabbed him and they choked him. |
| 3e. | Head finally speaks, saying, «I told you so!» | When they had already left him lying there, **that.R head** said: «What did I tell you? Did I not tell you that I died because of speaking many things! Have you as well not died!» |
| 3f. | Attendants are horrified | **those.R attendants** were astonished.<br>And they went home with sadness that already they have done the unmentionable and the things (big-mouth had said) had been true. |
| 3g. | Consequences of speaking | And they arrived and told the king just how they went and that they had killed **that.R father** and afterwards the head spoke. |
| 3h. | Conclusion: no TSMs | The king said: «If it (water) has spilled out, it is no longer gathered up!» |

The theme of this story revolves around "the problem of spreading news indiscriminately".

<u>Where TSMs are absent</u>

The entire setting in (12.31.2a) is unmarked by TSMs, as there is nothing about exposing news or talking too much, and thus it does not move forward the theme of speaking indiscriminately. The order to kill the big-mouth if it is seen that he is lying is presented without nominal reference to any participants (they are only pronominally referenced), so is also unmarked. In addition the king's conclusion (in the form of a proverb) is not marked.

### Where TSMs are present

In episode 1, the king tells his friends to go hunting. "Those friends" are marked twice in this episode, probably just to establish their reference. In (12.31.1c) the big-mouth is introduced as one of the three friends. Their trying to rid him of his habit in (12.31.1d) and his not listening in (12.31.1e) are also marked.

In episode 2, big-mouth blurts out to the king the news about the talking head he saw (12.31.2b). The king then accuses him of telling a lie (12.31.2c). The order is then given that if it is seen that he is really lying, he should be killed on the spot, setting things up for the climax (12.31.2d).

In episode 3 we reach the climax of the story. This time there is marking on the head (12.31.3a), asking why it died (12.31.3b), the lack of an answer (12.31.3c), and the killing of big-mouth (12.31.3d). In (12.31.3e) the TSM-marked head speaks about inappropriate speaking, which astonishes the TSM-marked attendants (12.31.3f). In (12.31.3g) those attendants told the king the fate of the TSM-marked big-mouth: he had been killed even though he hadn't been lying.

This story shows a definite tendency to concentrate the default TSMs at the beginning of the story, while the major forms are concentrated at the end (with only two occurring in the first half of the story). The second of those two, the telling of the news in (12.31.2b), is obviously very thematic. The last default TSM of the narrative occurs in (12.31.2c), where the king challenges the fact that "that head" is talking, and everything which is marked as thematic after that, from (12.31.2d) onwards, is marked by the remote demonstrative as an item of major thematic importance.

## 12.3 Highlighting

Nearby/remote distinction

(12.32) Major and default thematic salience in narrative 503, by line

| | Default TSM (nearby) | Major TSM (remote) |
|---|---|---|
| 1a. | The **king** had three good friends | |
| 1b. | That **king** told those **good friends** to hunt | |
| 1c. | | Those **good friends** went hunting |
| 1d. | Fellows tried to stop the bad **habit** of their friend | |
| 1e. | That **father** did not listen | |
| 2b. | | Big-mouth tells that **news** |
| 2c. | King says that **big-mouth** has told him a lie | |
| 2c. | They should go show him that **head** which speaks | |
| 2d. | | Those **attendants** took path with that **father** |
| 3a. | | They encountered that **head** |
| 3b. | | They took that **stick** and hit **head** |
| 3c. | | That **head** did not answer |
| 3d. | | Those **attendants** grabbed and choked him |
| 3e. | | That **head** said |
| 3f. | | Those **attendants** were astonished |
| 3g. | | They told king how they killed that **father** |

As can be seen above, (12.32) lays out the occurrences of the default and major TSMs, clearly revealing the tendency in this narrative to concentrate the default TSMs at the beginning of the story, while the major TSMs are concentrated at the end, with only two occurring in the first half of the story.

### 12.3.1.4 Spoken, quite informal; both nearby (default) and remote (major)

The narrative in (12.33) is in the quite informal register.

(12.33) Kifuliiru story 112. Theme: "The results of being too picky"

Episode 1 (Introduction)

| 1a. | Introduction: no TSM | There was one young man who wanted to marry a woman. |
|---|---|---|
| 1b. | Young man too picky | *that.N young man*, when they showed him all the girls in that village of theirs, and he said that HE, there is no girl that he likes, he said that he must marry a woman who resembles his mother, and of the size which is like that of his mother. |
| 1c. | Young man looks for a girl | *that.N young man* he went outside of the village. And he went looking for women and he did not find them. |

Episode 2

| 2a. | Intro of girl: no TSM | When it was one day, when he was about to cross the river, he encountered a girl sitting under a tree. When he saw her, quote=«Oh no, this very one is the one who resembles my mother, with a size like that of my mother!» |
|---|---|---|
| 2b. | Young man proposes | *that.R young man* told her: «O girl, I like you, I'm about to marry you.» And she quote=«OK, marry me!» And they took the path. |

Episode 3

| 3a. | Girl agrees, needs to be carried | When they were in the path, they reached a river, *that.R girl* quote=«No, I will not cross this river, but you carry me on your back». |
|---|---|---|
| 3b. | Young man agrees | *that.R young man* quote=«Oh, surely! Will you be too hard for me to take across the river?» |

## 12.3 Highlighting

| | | |
|---|---|---|
| 3c. | Young man puts her on his back | **that.N young man** placed her on his back. In the river «splash-splash», the river «swish swish swish» and they crossed the river.<br>When they reached the other side, the new wife quote=«On my! Will the new wife get down here? You take me into the house. I the new bride, would I go with my feet again, we who are the ones now about to go to the village?» |
| 3d. | Young man sees that girl has trouble<br>No more new thematic developments in this section | **that.R young man** quote=«No! We will go.» And he arrived at their place (when) it's now dusk and he went into the house.<br>And he told his mother quote=«O my mother, I've brought the new bride. You give me some food».<br>His mother quote=«Will you not eat in here?» and he quote=«Oh no! You bring (it) to me in here.»<br>To tell (i.e. when he told) the young wife get down from the back,<br>«It's obvious I will not get down!»<br>«Get down from the back!»<br>«It's obvious I will not get down!» And he spent the night with her on his back, and he spent the day with her on his back. A week «puu», month «puu»! O comrades! Oh my! The person will die! |

Episode 4

| | | |
|---|---|---|
| 4a. | Other men hear news | **that.N news** they brought to other men. |
| 4b. | Men realize the "girl" is a demon | **those.N men** when they heard it and they said quote=«Oh my! A demon, **that.N one** he has brought! That's right! A demon, Oh!»<br>Others quote=«How are you going to get rid of it?»<br>As soon as they try something, no results! |
| 4c. | Setting up resolution involving bull meat | Other men told them quote=«You get a big bull, a bull which you castrated and now has much fat. Let him take her (the demon) right there where he took her from. You (PL) going slaughter for her **that.N bull** and you place all of **that.N meat** and, intestinal fat, and intestinal fat on the fire.» |

Episode 5 (Climactic)

| 5a. | Young man with bull brought to the same tree | Ok then! They led to the river **that.R young man** and **that.R bull**; and they took it under **that.R tree** and they stabbed in the knife; the fatty inner meat they piled up on the firewood; **that.R bull** it began to cook; the smell of roasting meat kept being smelled. |
|---|---|---|
| 5b. | Story slows down as the young man talks | **that.R young man** continuously told her: «Roast it well, you've burnt it! Roast it well, you've burnt it!» |
| 5c. | Demon tempted to jump off back | In saying thus: «Roast it well, you've burnt it,» **that.R demon** that's when she pulled her fingernails/claws out (from his back). |
| 5d. | Demon flies off to the meat | **that.N demon** when she sensed really that the roasting smell it was very sweet in her nose, she immediately just flew to **that.R meat**! |
| 5e. | Young man escapes | **that.R young man** he immediately left there with **those.N people** and they immediately dashed off and they crossed **that.R river** and they went home. |
| 5f. | Demon stays with meat | Thus **that.N demon** remained with **that.N meat**. |
| 5g. | Conclusion | That's where the story ends and where it ends off. |

The theme of the story is "The results of being too picky" (in looking for a wife).

Where TSMs are absent

As usual, there are no TSMs in the introduction of the young man (12.33.1a) or of the girl (12.33.2a). There are also two places in the middle of the story where there are no TSMs. The first is in (12.33.3c) as the new bride refuses to get off the young man's back and go into the house. This is not new information, as she has already refused to get down earlier.

Then in (12.33.3d) there is a relatively long section where the wife is adamantly refusing to get down off his back (again, already alluded to), and which notes that a week went by, and then a month, with her constantly on his back.

## 12.3 Highlighting

Where TSMs are present

In episode 1 the young man is marked, as he refuses all the village girls (12.33.1b), and even when he went outside the village but did not find a wife (12.33.1c). This shows that he is too picky.

In (12.33.2b) he is marked when he asks the young girl to marry him, setting up the problem.

In (12.33.3a) the girl is marked when she refuses to cross the river. The young man is marked in (12.33.3b) when he agrees to let her get on his back, and when he actually puts her on his back (12.33.3c). He is marked again at the beginning of (12.33.3d) as he agrees to let the girl stay on his back after they had crossed the river.

In (12.33.4a) the thematic material begins with the marked "that news" being taken to other men. This is the beginning of the solution. Those men who heard the news are marked (12.33.4b) as they decide that that girl (also marked in (12.33.4b) is an evil spirit. The vital elements of their solution, a bull and its meat, are also both marked (12.33.4c).

In (12.33.5a) the young man, the bull (marked twice), and the fateful tree are all marked with TSMs as the story leads to the climax. The young man is marked (12.33.5b) as the aroma of roasting meat grows stronger and he reports the details of the roasting process. The demon is marked (12.33.5c) as she begins to loosen her grip on him. In (12.33.5d) both the demon and the meat are marked as she flies off the young man's back and descends on the meat. There is a concentration of TSMs again in (12.33.5e) as the young man and the people with him all dash across "that river". The demon and the meat are marked again, with default marking, in the closing sentence (12.33.5f) of the narrative.

Nearby/remote distinction

In (12.34) the left-hand column lists the default TSMs, while the right-hand column lists the major TSMs. Once again, if one just reads down the right-hand column, the thematic essence of the story is quickly seen. The default TSMs on the left also mark important material, but not to the same degree as those in the major TSM column on the right.

(12.34) Major and default thematic salience in narrative 112, by line

| | Default TSM (nearby) | Major TSM (remote) |
|---|---|---|
| 1b. | **Young man** looks for special woman | |
| 1c. | **Young man** looks, does not find her | |
| 2b. | | **Young man** proposes to girl |
| 3a. | | **Girl** wants to be carried |
| 3b. | | **Young man** agrees |
| 3c. | **Young man** puts her on his back | |
| 3d. | | **Young man** agrees to keep carrying her |
| 4a. | **News** brought to men | |
| 4b. | **Men** say that **that one** is a demon | |
| 4c. | Getting a **bull** and roasting its **meat** | |
| 5a. | | **Young man** and **bull** taken under **tree**, **bull** cooks |
| 5b. | | **Young man** tells them to not burn it |
| 5c. | | **Demon** loosens fingernails |
| 5d. | **Demon** can no longer resist the aroma | Flies to that **meat** |
| 5e. | | **Young man** leaves there |
| 5f. | With those **people** **Demon** remains behind with the **meat** | They all cross the **river** |

As in all other stories, the first TSMs in the story are default ones, as the theme begins to be developed. The first major TSM is used to mark the young man as he proposes marriage, while the second and third major TSMs mark the fact that the girl wants him to carry her, and that he agrees to do so.

The news that is brought to the men, and their solution, is marked by default TSMs, while the actual implementation of the plan is indicated by major TSMs. The demon smelling the aroma of the meat is marked by a default TSM, while her actually flying to the meat is has a major TSM, as does the young man who escapes from her. The other people with the young man are marked by default TSMs, but their crossing the river is marked in a major way. The spirit remaining behind with the meat is anti-climactic, but still important and thus marked with the default TSM.

### 12.3.2 Thematic salience expressed by the cl. 16 locative marker *ha* 'place'

In addition to its function as a locative marker, in narrative texts the cl. 16 locative phrase headed by **há** marks a location or setting in the story where a *significant new development* of the story theme is *about to* take place. That development often, but not always, involves the emergence of an important participant. By marking such a location by the LM **há**, the speaker is in effect shining a spotlight on that place in the story, encouraging the hearer to pay special attention.[11]

While **há** is used only in the context of a significant thematic development in the story, it is important to note that such a thematic development does not mandate the occurrence of **há**. The use of **há** is dependent on whether or not the speaker chooses to highlight the location of the next significant development.

Evidence for this text-oriented analysis of the cl. 16 **há** marker is seen by observing the occurrence of the LM **há** vis-à-vis the alternative cl. 23 LM **í**, which occurs within the same general environment, but which lacks the semantic component of thematic development. Such evidence is abundant, as the LMs **há** and **í** occur profusely throughout the texts studied.

In (12.35) the cl. 16 marker **há** occurs before the position noun **nyúmà** 'behind' in the locative phrase **há=nyúmá lyé=nyûmbà** 'at the place (TSM) behind the house'. That place behind the house is marked by **há**, because it is the location where a significant thematic development in the story is about to occur, i.e. where the young king is suddenly, and unpredictably, seized by a python.

---

[11] It is interesting to note that this discourse meaning of the class 16 LM head **há** is very similar to the meaning of the Thematic Salience Marking (TSM) implied by demonstrative pronouns (3.5.2), i.e. both mark a new thematic development. The main difference is that the LM head **há** refers to the *location* where a new thematic development takes place, whereas the demonstrative TSM commonly alludes to an *already mentioned discourse participant* that is involved in the new thematic development.

(12.35) Ùyó     mw-àmì   mú-sòrè   ‖ à-ná-sóók-ér-à   **há=**
   that.N+1  1-king   1-young.man   1-SQ-turned-APL-Fa   16.TSM=

   **ny-úmá   ly-é=**   **ny-ûmbà** ‖   í-shàtò   y-àná-mú-gwât-à ‖
   9-behind   5-A.M+AU=   9-house   9-python   9-SQ-O1-grab-Fa

   y-àná-mú-yì-zìng-ír-à   =kwò ‖   y-àná-mú-tîmb-à   hááshì.
   9-SQ-O1-RFX-wrap-APL-Fa   =17   9-SQ-O1-throw.down-Fa   on.ground

'That young king ‖ turned the corner behind the house ‖ and a python grabbed him ‖ and wrapped itself around him ‖ and threw him down.'
(51 013)

By contrast, in (12.36) the cl. 23 LM **í** occurs with the position noun **nyúmà** 'behind', but it does not mark a place where thematic action will take place. The wife was simply following behind, and when her husband encountered the first trap, he saw it had not sprung. This does not represent a new thematic development.

(12.36) Ùyó   mú-kàzì   ná-yè |   à-ná-gênd-à **í=**   **ny-úmá**   **ly-à-gè**
   that.N+1  1-woman   ADD.P-1   1-SQ-go-Fa   23=   9-behind   5-A.M-1

   lú-tó-lútô.   ‖ Yîbà |   ìrì   á-ká-hík-á   kú=
   11-unobtrusively-RDP   her.husband   when   1-P2-arrive-Fa   17=

   mú-tègò |   gw-à=   m-bérè | à-ná-gwân-à   |   gù-tà-húk-à.
   3-trap   3-A.M=   9-before   1-SQ-encounter-Fa   3-NEG+P1-sprung-Fa

'That woman and SHE also | went behind him unobtrusively. ‖ Her husband | when he arrived at the trap | the first | he found | it had not sprung.'
(632 034-635)

## 12.3.3 Emphatic prominence (-*ag*)

According to Callow emphatic prominence is used where "the speaker feels strongly about a particular item, or feels that an event is unexpected" (Callow 1974:52). Both of these meanings of emphatic prominence may be expressed in Kifuliiru by the inclusion of a prefinal -**ag**[12] suffix in the verb.

In QUOTED speech of both formal and informal texts this suffix is used in commands to mean '*pay attention* to what I am saying'. This device usually occurs in quoted speech no more than once or twice per story.

In texts of quite informal register, this extension can also be used in NON-QUOTED material to mean '*pay attention*, because something important is about

---

[12]The structural considerations and placement of the emphatic -**ag** suffix are discussed under verbal extensions (Volume 1, 6.1.3).

to happen'. This use of the emphatic suffix typically occurs before the thematically salient event actually occurs, and can appear 10–20 times in a story.

#### 12.3.3.1 Emphatic marker in speech quotes

When found within direct speech quotes, -**ag** means 'pay attention', adding emphasis to a command. Used with this meaning it rarely occurs more than once or twice per story. In story 13 it is employed once at the beginning of the climax section, where the quail tells the snake: **Tùlùùk-ág-à** 'get down!'

(12.37) Y-àná-bwîr-à   yùgwó   mú-jōkà: ‖ «Ø-Tùlùùk-<u>ág</u>-à.»
      9-SQ-tell-Fa   that.N+3   3-snake    IMP.S-get.down-EMP-Fa

'And it told that snake: ‖ «Get down.»' (13 008)

In (12.38) the harvesters command: **Ùtùhèèrèzàgyé=zò** 'you give them to us!' Here again, the emphatic -**ag**[13] extension gives emphasis to a command.

(12.38) Yàbó      bá-géshì  ‖  bà-ná-mú-bwìr-è   tî=   ‖
      those.N+2   2-harvesters   2-CON-O1-tell-Fe   ‹quote›=

      «Ù-Ø-tù-hèèrèz-<u>àg</u>-y-é      =zò.»
      2SG-SBV-O1.PL-give-EMP-CS-Fe   =10

'Those harvesters ‖ told him ‹quote›: ‖ «Give them to us!»' (204 017)

#### 12.3.3.2 Emphatic marker in non-quoted material

When used with verbs other than commands in reported speech, -**ag** still means 'pay attention', but in a different sense, meaning pay attention *just before a thematically salient event*. The effect is "Pay attention, what is about to happen is particularly important."[14] The emphatic -**ag** is used with this function only in narratives of the informal register. The frequency with which -**ag** is used in this way is proportional to the degree of informality of the style: the more informal the story, the more the emphatic is used.

Story 406 is in the quite informal register. In example (12.39) -**ag** occurs on **ànáhíkàgè** 'and he arrived EMP' and **ànádètàgè** 'and he said EMP'. These verbs occur just before a thematic development and serve as a signal that what follows is important. What follows in (12.39) is that the man discovers that the rabbit which he had sent ahead with his child to be cooked as his supper was

---

[13] In this example morphological constraints cause -**ag** to be followed by -**y**, a repeated form of the causative morpheme, reflecting the lexicalized causative found in -**heerez**- 'give'.

[14] In this way, the suffix -**ag** has a function similar to that of the Greek particles **idou** / **ide** (Van Otterloo 1988).

not cooked for him. Note that the thematic event itself is not marked by the -**ag**, but only the material preceding it.

(12.39) À-ná-hík-**àg**-è     há=   kā-āyà   ||   bà-ná-mú-hèèrèz-é |
      1-CON-arrive-EMP-Fe    16=   12-village    2-CON-O1-give-Fe

      á=mī-ījì   ||   à-ná-yì-kàràb-é    í=bí-dáká |   kú=   má-gúlú
      AU=6-water    1-CON-RFX-wash-Fe    AU=8-mud    17=   6-legs

      nà=   kú=   má-bòkò   ||   à-ná-dèt-**àg**-è      tî=:   ||
      CNJ=   17=   6-hands    1-CON-speak-EMP-Fe    ‹quote›=

      «Ø-m-béérèz-í    í=by-ókúlyà.»   ||   Bà-ná-mú-hèèrèz-é
      IMP.P-O1.SG-give-Fi    AU=8-food      2-CON-O1-give-Fe

      í=byókúlyà.   ||   Mbw-à=    Ø-yíjí     bōn-à |   ú=bú-ndú     |
      AU=food       as.soon.as-1=   SBV-COMING   see-Fa   AU=14-porridge

      ná=   mí-rûndá    |   tî=:   ||   «Ê |   ká=   n-à-tùm-à
      CNJ=   4-bitter.vegetable    ‹quote›=    O     Q=    1SG-P1-send-Fa

      mí-rûndá?   ||   Sí=    n-à-sìg-á     |   í-shógó    y-à-ní     |
      4-bitter.vegetable    OBV=   1SG-P1-leave-Fa    AU=9+meat   9-A.M-1SG

      há-nò.   ||   Háyí   |   y-à-génd-à?»
      16-here.P.C    where    9-P1-go-Fa

'And he arrived in the village || and they gave him | water || and he washed the mud | from his feet and from his hands || and he said ‹quote›: || «Give me food.» || And they gave him food. || As soon as he came and saw | the porridge | and the bitter vegetable | he ‹quote›: || «O | did I send for bitter vegetable? || Isn't it obvious that I left | my main dish food | here. || Where | did it go?»' (406 016-017)

Story 112 is also in the quite informal register, containing 17 occurrences of the suffix -**ag**. In (12.40) there are three instances of it, in **ànáhíkàgè** 'and he arrived', **ànáyìfúndàgè** 'and he went inside uninvited', and **ànábwìràgè** 'and he told'. The actions of these verbs are not in themselves prominent, but they set up the listener to pay attention to what follows, that is, he has brought a wife and there is a problem with her, so that the young man will not eat in the place where others normally eat.

(12.40)  À-ná-hík-**àg**-è     há=   mw-à-bò ‖  hì-kòlà
         1-CON-arrive-EMP-Fe  16=   place-A.M-2   19-be.NEWLY

hí-hwéhwérwê. ‖  À-ná-yì-fúnd-**àg**-è    mú=   ny-ûmbà ‖
19-dusk          1-CON-RFX-go.in-EMP-Fe   18=   9-house

à-ná-bwìr-**àg**-è    nyíná           | tî=       ‖ «É=   máàwè           ‖
1-CON-tell-EMP-Fe     1a+his.mother   ‹quote›=   O=     1a+my.mother

n-à-léét-á        | ú=mú-hyà.         ‖ Mú-Ø-m-bèèrèz-é  |
1SG-P1-bring-Fa   AU=1-new.bride      2PL-SBV-O1.SG-give-Fe

í=by-ókúlyâ.» ‖ Nyínà            tî=       | «K-ò=   tá-gá-lì-ìr-à
AU=8-food       1a+his.mother   ‹quote›=   Q-2SG=   NEG-F2-eat-APL-Fa

mú-nò?» ‖ Nà=   w-á=    ná-yè     tî=        ‖ «Nângà |
18-here.P.C CNJ= 1-A.M= ADD.P-1  ‹quote›=      no

ú-Ø-n-dèèt-èr-è             |  mú-nò.»
2SG-SBV-O1.SG-bring-APL-Fe     18-here.P.C

'And he arrived at their place ‖ it is now dusk. ‖ And he went straight into the house ‖ and he told his mother | ‹quote›: ‖ «O mother ‖ I have brought | a new bride. ‖ Give me | some food. ‖ The mother ‹quote› | «Will you not eat in here?» ‖ And HE ‹quote›: ‖ «No | bring (it) to me | in here.»'
(112 021-026)

In (12.41) the emphatic -**ag** extension is found suffixed to the verbal auxiliary -**ba** 'to become' (here in the reduplicated form -**agag**, because this is a single syllable verb root). The fact that they finished the food is not important, but what follows is very important; the father begins to dance with the daughter and to brag about how clever he was in tricking his wife. This leads to his demise.

(12.41)  Ìrí   bá-ká-b-**ágág**-á       kéèrà     bà-yús-á |  ú=kú-ly-á
         when 2-P2-become-EMP-Fa       ALREADY   2-finish-Fa  AU=15-eat-Fa

í=by-ókúlyà ‖ yîbà          | à-géndì      yábíír-á |  ù-lyá
AU=8-food     her.husband    1+P1-GOING   take-Fa     1-that.R

mw-ānà ‖   à-Ø-kín-é           ‖  àkínè.
1-child    1-SBV-dance-Fe        RDP

'When they had already finished | eating the food ‖ her husband | went and took | that child ‖ that he dance ‖ that he dance.' (111 052)

Because the emphatic extension **-ag** appears on verbs which lead up to the climactic point in the narrative, it is commonly found on verbs of motion, such as -**kùlikir**- 'follow', -**génd**- 'go', -**jábuk**- 'cross over', -**hík**- 'arrive', -**fù-luk**- 'return from work', -**gwata ínjírà** 'set out on path'. In each case when such a verb is marked, something important is about to happen in the story.

In (12.42) the emphatic **-ag** extension occurs only once, found in **ákákùlíkírágà** 'he had followed'. Again, there is nothing at all thematic about this verb, except that its emphatic suffix indicates that the climactic episode is about to begin.

(12.42) W-á-n-dàre ‖ ìrí   á-ká-kúlíkír-ág-á   ìyó        n-jírà ‖
      1-A.M-9-lion   when 1-P2-follow-EMP-Fa   that.N+9   9-path

      à-ná-gêndì    hík-á   | h-ê=     hék-ì-ìr-ì.
      1-SQ-GOING   arrive-Fa   16-O.R+9=   end-APL-RS-Fi

'Lion ‖ when he followed that path ‖ he went and arrived | where it ends.'
(105 030)

### 12.3.4 Slowing-down devices

A common highlighting device is to slow down the rate of information presented in the story, especially just before the climax, or at the climax itself. This is often accomplished by repetition of information and presentation of greater detail, in order to increase suspense. It can also include an increased number of pauses. These slowing-down devices occur in all speech registers.

In the formal written register in story 13, in the section just prior to the climax, the quail tells the snake: **tùlùùkágà** 'get down EMP'. When the snake says that it is very hungry, the quail's request is *repeated*, with greater detail, this time as indirect speech: **kwó=gùtúlúùkè...** 'that it get down...'.

## 12.3 Highlighting

(12.43) **Y-àná-bwîr-à    yùgwó    mú-jōkà:** ‖ «**Ø-tùlùùk-ág-à.**» ‖
9-SQ-tell-Fa    that.N+3    3-snake    IMP.S-get.down-EMP-Fa

**Yùgwó    mú-jōkà** ‖ **gw-àná-dèt-à** | kwó= kéèrà
that.N+3    3-snake    3-SQ-speak-Fa    CMP= ALREADY

**gw-à-shálìk-à** |    bwénèènè. ‖    **ìyó**    **n-gwârè** ‖
3-P1-be.hungry-Fa    very.much    that.N+9    9-quail

**y-àná-gù-bwír-á** | kwó=    **gù-Ø-túlúùk-è** |    gírá |
9-SQ-O3-tell-Fa    CMP=    3-SBV-get.down-Fe    so.that

**gù-Ø-génd-è**    **gú-gá-lóòz-à** |    í=by-ó=    **gú-gáà-ly-à.**
3-SBV-GOING-Fe    3-INTL-search-Fa    AU=8-O.R    3-F2-eat-Fa

'And it told that snake: ‖ «Get down.» ‖ That snake ‖ said | that already it was hungry | very much. ‖ That quail ‖ told it | that it get down | so that | it go and search for | what it will eat.' (13 008-011)

Likewise in the informal register in story 11, the climax comes when the cow finally says: "May I be the one you eat!" At that point the story is slowed down with the details that **ìyó ndàrè yànáhùlíkà** 'that.N lion was quiet' and **nyûndà ànágìrímà í=kígòhè** 'the eagle winked his eyelid'. This immediately precedes the point where the lion jumps on the cow to kill it.

(12.44) **Y-àná-dèt-à:** ‖ «**M-Ø-b-é**    ni-ó=    **gáa-ly-à.**» ‖
9-SQ-say-Fa    1SG-SBV-become-Fe    1SG-FOC+O.R+2SG=    F2-eat-Fa

**Ìyó    n-dàrè** ‖ **y-àná-hùlík-à.** ‖    **Ny-ûndâ** |    **à-ná-gìrím-à**
that.N+9    9-lion    9-SQ-be.quiet-Fa    9-eagle    1-SQ-wink-Fa

**í=kí-gòhè.** ‖    **Í=n-dàrè** ‖ **y-àná-sìmb-ír-à**    kw-í=    gósì |    ly-ê=
AU=7-eyelid    AU=9-lion    9-SQ-jump-APL-Fa    17-5=    neck    5-A.M=

yò    n-gáàvù ‖ **y-àná-gì-tímb-à**    hááshì    |
that.N+9    9-cow    9-SQ-O9-throw.down-Fa    down.on.ground

**y-àná-yàm-à    í-gáà-fw-à.**
9-SQ-IMMED-Fa    9-F2-die-Fa

'And it said: ‖ «May I be the one that you eat.» ‖ That lion ‖ was quiet. ‖ The eagle | blinked the eyelid. ‖ The lion ‖ jumped on the neck | of that cow ‖ and threw it down | and it immediately died.' (11 037-39)

In story 105, again of the informal register, just before the climax, Lion asks the old man if there isn't a cow who has passed by. The old man, instead of answering, says that he first wants to get a drink of water, before continuing to discuss the matter. This addition of detail effectively slows the story down at the point of suspense.

(12.45) W-á-n-dàrè ‖ à-ná-shùbì gálúk-ír-à | á-hà-lì ù-lyá
1-A.M-9-lion    1-SQ-AGAIN    return-APL-Fa    S.R-16-is    1-that.R

mú-sháàjà ‖ à-ná-mú-bwîr-à: ‖ «É= shòòkùlù ‖ ndáá-yò
1-old.man    1-SQ-O1-tell-Fa    O=    1a+old.man    NEG.FOC-9

n-gáàvù | í-y-à-lèng-á    há-nò?» ‖ Ùyó    mú-sháàj-à ‖
9-cow    S.R-9-P1-pass-Fa    16-here.P.C    that.N+1    1-old.person-Fa

à-ná-bwîr-à    w-á-n-dàrè: ‖ «Ù-Ø-lék-è | n-Ø-dé
1-SQ-tell-Fa    1-A.M-9-lion    2SG-SBV-allow-Fe    1SG-SBV-PRIOR

gêndíì    nyw-á |    á=mā-āji ‖ tù-ká-bùlì    yíjì |
GOING    drink-Fa    AU=6-water    1PL-INTV-SBSQ    COMING

gánúúl-à.»
converse-Fa

'Lion ‖ again returned | where the old man was ‖ and he told him: ‖ «O old man ‖ (is there) no cow | that passed here?» ‖ That old man ‖ told Lion: ‖ «Allow | I first go and drink | water ‖ then we will subsequently come | and converse.»' (105 031-032)

One more example from the informal register, story 112, shows how the action is slowed down at the climax by the addition of details: The knife is brought out, the intestinal fat is placed on the firewood, the bull begins to burn, the roasting smell is sensed. Then the young man says twice: **Ùyókyé bwîjá, wàgàsìríízà! Ùyókyé bwîjá, wàgàsìríízà!** 'Roast it well, you've burnt it! Roast it well, you've burnt it!' That same phrase is repeated in the next sentence: **Mú=kúdètá Ùyókyé bwîjá, wàgàsìríízà!** 'In saying roast it well, you've burnt it!' Yet another detail is that the demon then removes her fingernails from his back. All of this detail serves to slow down the story just before the climax.

(12.46) **Ààhô!** || **Bà-ná-shòlér-á** | **ù-lyá**    **mú-tàbánà** |  **n-ê=**    **ryà**
OK.then   2-SQ-led.off-Fa   1-that.R    1-young.man    CNJ-9=   that.R

**shúúlì.** ||  **Bà-ná-gì-hí-s-àgy-á**    |    **mw-í=**    **dàkó**    **ly-á=**    **kì-ryá**
bull         2-SQ-O9-arrive-CS-EMP-Fa       18-5=       under        5-A.M=    7-that.R

**kí-tì** ||   **bà-ná-gì-lùnd-ág-á** |   **í-kéétà.** ||   **Ú=lú-shá**   |
7-tree       2-SQ-O9-stab-EMP-Fa       5-knife          AU=11-intestine.fat

**bà-ná-lù-gùngìk-è** |    **kú=**       **shāālì.** ||    **Ì-ryá**    **shúúlí** |
2-CON-O11-pile.up-Fe       17=        firewood           9-that.R    bull

**ì-ná-tòndèèr-àg-é** |    **ú-kú-híír-ág-à**    ||    **ú=mú-shììrìrì**
9-CON-begin-EMP-Fe       AU=15-burn-EMP-Fa          AU=3-barbecue.smell

**gw-àná-kìzí**    **lāk-à.**  ||   **Ù-lyá**     **mú-tàbánà** ||    **à-ná-kìz-àg-í**
3-SQ-REP         occur-Fa        1-that.R      1-young.man        1-SQ-REP-EMP-Fi

**gù-bwír-à:** ||   **«Ù-Ø-yóky-é**    **bw-îjá** |   **w-à-gà-sìrííz-à!** ||
O3-tell-Fa           2SG-SBV-roast-Fe    14-well      2SG-P1-O6-burn-Fa

**Ù-Ø-yóky-é**      **bw-îjá** |   **w-à-gà-sìrííz-à!»** ||    **Mú=**
2SG-SBV-roast-Fe    14-well      2SG-P1-O6-burn-Fa             18=

**kú-dèt-á**    **kwôkwò:**    **«Ù-Ø-yóky-é**    **bw-îjà** |
15-speak-Fa    thus.N        2SG-SBV-roast-Fe    14-well

**w-à-gà-sìrííz-à** ||    **gù-lyá**    **mú-zìmù**    **ná-gwò** ||
2-P1-O6-burn-Fa         3-that.R    3-demon        ADD.P-3

**irí**            **gù-ná-kùùl-àg-è** ||    **í=ny-úùnù**    **zá-á-gwò.**
that's.when    3-CON-pull.out-EMP-Fe    AU=10-fingernails    10-A.M-3

'OK then! || And they led away | that young man | and that bull. || And they caused it to arrive | under that tree || and they stabbed in | the knife. || The intestinal fat | they piled it up | on the firewood. || That bull | and it began | to burn || and roasting smell repeatedly came. || That young || man told it: || «Roast it well | you've burnt it! || Roast it well | you've burnt it!» || In saying like this: «Roast it well | you've burnt it» || that demon and IT ALSO | that's when it pulled out || its fingernails.' (112 044-045)

## 12.3.5 Songs which provide key information

In Kifuliiru folk tales, one common highlighting strategy is to introduce a song, usually consisting of just a few clauses. The song is usually repeated verbatim once or twice (for rhetorical effect), or sometimes even more. In normal story-telling situations, the songs are set apart from the rest of the story by actually being sung by the speaker, while the rest of the story is spoken. Occasionally all or part of the song is also set apart by being in Kiswahili. In most other cases the songs are in Kifuliiru, but in a different style from the rest of the narrative: a poetic form which includes repetition and a relaxation of normal grammatical rules. The songs are often introduced by the "marked" quote marker **kwókùnô** 'like this.P.C' to highlight the following speech.

These short songs function to give an insider's view of the story, usually dealing with the main thematic problem in the story. They often reveal information key to the resolution of the thematic conflict. In this section we discuss five examples, chosen from many others in the data.

In the selection seen in (12.47), Piiyo has lost favor with her stepmother, who has thrown her into a deep pit. She has remained there without anyone knowing where she is. The following songs sung by her and her younger half-sister Leeza, who misses her, are repeated three times in the story, in lines 047, 053, and 066–067. The song of Leeza includes the Kiswahili words **baba amekuja** 'father has come'. The rest of Leeza's song and the reply from Piiyo are in Kifuliiru. The noun of direct address in the first sentence of Leeza's song, **Piiyo**, is seen at the beginning and the end of the line **O Piiyo, baba amekuja, Piiyo** 'O Piiyo, father has come, Piiyo'. In the second quote, from Piiyo, the noun of direct address **Leeza** is used five times. Such use of the nouns of direct address would occur only once in normal speech, and certainly not five times.

This song sung by the mourning Leeza receives an unexpected reply from deep in the hidden pit, and communicates to Leeza that her mother is a witch who has thrown Piiyo into a deep hole. Leeza's knowing about Piiyo's predicament leads directly to the resolution, whereby Piiyo is saved from the hole.

## 12.3 Highlighting

(12.47) **À-ná-tòndéér-à kàndí ú=kú-yīmb-à:** ‖ «**Ó** **Pííyò** ‖ **bábà** (Sw.) |
1-SQ-begin-Fa again AU=15-sing-Fa O Piiyo father

**à-mè-kúj-à** (Sw.) | **Pííyò**.» ‖ Lyéryò Pííyò | ìrí
1-RS-come-Fa Piiyo Right.then Piiyo when

**á-ká-yùvw-á î-zù** | ly-à= mú-lùmúná w-à-gè ‖
1-P2-hear-Fa 5-voice 5-A.M= 1-younger.sister 1-A.M-1

**à-ná-tòndéér-à** | ú=kú-mú-shùvy-â: ‖ «**Léézà** **Léézà** ‖
1-SQ-begin-Fa AU=15-O1-answer-Fa Leeza Leeza

**nyókò** | **à-lí** **mú-lózì** | **é**= **Léézà** | **á-m-búmb-ìr-à**
1a+your.mother 1-is 1-witch O= Leeza 1-O1.SG-dig-APL-Fa

**í=kí-shímò** | **Léézà** | **mú**= **má-tàmbì** | **ná**= **mú**=
AU=7-hole Leeza 18= 6-width CNJ= 18=

**bú-làà-búlà** | **é**= **Léézà**.»
14-length-RDP O= Leeza

'And she began again to sing: ‖ «O Piiyo ‖ father | has come | Piiyo. ‖ Right then Piiyo | when she heard the voice | of her younger sister ‖ she began | to answer: ‖ «Leeza Leeza ‖ your mother | is a witch | O Leeza | she dug for me a hole | Leeza | in length | and width | O Leeza.' (409 047, 053, and 066, 067)

In the narrative from which (12.48) is taken, a song occurs twice, in line 44 and soon after in lines 46–47. In this case, a woman receives a girl, by magic, from inside a peanut. The woman is warned to be careful and not let the girl get rained on. When the girl does get rained on, the mother starts to sing: «**É=Nábómbwé, Nábómbwê**.» (**Nábómbwê** means 'the one who is softened'). The girl's answer is introduced by **kwókùnô** 'quote.MARKED', indicating a very prominent speech. The words **fyo, fyo, fyo, fyo, fyo, fyo-fyoo** are strong interjections of provocation.

This is a very crucial part of the story, as the wonderful girl who has been doing so much work in the house and in the field is about to be lost, just because she got wet. That fact is highlighted by the song.

(12.48) À-ná-tòndéér-á   ú=kú-yīmb-à: ||   «É= **Nábómbwé** |  **Nábómbwê**.» ||
1-SQ-begin-Fa      AU=15-sing-Fa         O=  Nabombwe        Nabombwe.

**Nábómbwé**    **ná-yé**   **à-ná-yìtáb-à**     kwókùnô:       ||
Nabombwe        ADD.P-1     1-SQ-respond-Fa      ‹quote.MARKED›

«<u>Fyò</u> | <u>fyó</u> | <u>fyò</u> <u>fyó</u>   <u>fyò</u> | <u>fyó</u> | <u>fyó</u> | <u>fyó</u> | <u>fyóò</u>.»
provocation                 provocation

'And she began to sing: and SHE answered like this: || (provocation).'
(613 044; 046-047)

In (12.49) the song is again introduced with the marked complementizer **kwokuno** 'thus'. In this song the "problem" of the story is presented: twins were born in the forest, and the boy, who sings to his sister the song in (12.49) was abandoned there, while the mother brought the girl home instead.

(12.49) **À-ná-yìmb-à**   kwókùnô:       || «<u>Ni-êhê</u> |   <u>n-dà-lí</u>      <u>mú-já</u>
1-SQ-sing-Fa       ‹quote.MARKED›     1SG-CTR.P      1SG-NEG-am     1-slave

<u>w-à-wè</u>. ||   <u>Nyókò</u>            | <u>á-ká-sìg-à</u>    <u>á-n-jând-à</u>       |
1-A.M-2SG        1a+your.mother      1-P2-left-Fa       1-O1.SG-abandon-Fa

<u>mú</u>=    <u>lú-bàkò</u> ||   <u>à-ná-kú-léèt-à</u>   |   <u>w-é</u>=      <u>mw-ānà</u>
18=     11-forest       1-SQ-O2.SG-bring-Fa       2SG-FOC=    1-child

<u>mú-nyérè</u>.»
1-girl

'And he sung like this: || «ME | I am not your slave. || Your mother | abandoned me | in the forest || and she brought you | you the one who is a girl child.»' (617 033)

In (12.50) the quote is again introduced by **ànátòndèèré ú=kúyīmbà** 'and she began to sing', together with the marked complementizer **kwókùnô** '‹quote.MARKED›'. The girl, Nanjira, had a special potato which she called her child and treated like a doll, but her brother peeled it and cut it up. The girl will not be consoled. The mother's song tells the girl twice, with the very same words, to take another potato. In song of reply the girl uses the very same words twice in refusing. This represents the key problem of the story.

## 12.3 Highlighting

(12.50) **Nyínà** ‖ à-ná-tòndèèr-é   ú=kú-yìmb-á   kwókùnô:   ‖ «**É=**
1+her.mother  1-CON-begin-Fe   AU=15-sing-Fa  ‹quote.MARKED›   O=

<u>**máàwè**</u>   ‖ **Nánjírà** ‖   Ø-yábììr-á   |   í=kí-júmbú   <u>ky-à-wè</u>. ‖
1a+my.mother   Nanjira     IMP.S-take-Fa   AU=7-potato   7-A.M-2SG

<u>É=</u> **máàwè**   |  **Nánjírà** ‖   Ø-yábììr-á   í=kí-júmbú
O=  1a+my.mother    Nanjira      IMP.S-take-Fa   AU=7-potato

<u>ky-à-wè</u>.» ‖ Ùyó   mú-nyéré   ná-yè  | à-ná-mú-shūvy-à: ‖
7-A.M-2SG   that.N+1   1-girl   ADD.P-1   1-SQ-O1-answer-Fa

«<u>N-dà-ngà-b-à</u>   **Nánjírà** ‖   <u>ú-ká-n-gér-á</u>   |
1SG-NEG-POT-become-Fa   Nanjira   2SG-P2-O1.SG-cut.up-Fa

<u>í=kí-júmbù</u>. ‖ <u>N-dà-ngà-b-à</u>   **Nánjírà** ‖
AU=7-potato    1SG-NEG-POT-become-Fa   Nanjira

<u>ú-ká-n-gér-á</u>   |   <u>í=kí-júmbù</u>.»
2SG-P2-O1.SG-cut.up-Fa   AU=7-potato

'The mother ‖ began | to sing like this: ‖ «O my mother ‖ Nanjira ‖ take | your potato. ‖ O my mother ‖ Nanjira ‖ take your potato.» ‖ That girl and SHE ALSO | answered: ‖ «I would not be Nanjira ‖ you cut up | my potato. ‖ I would not be Nanjira ‖ you cut up | my potato.»' (618 019)

In (12.51) the song is again introduced by **ànátòndèèré ú=kúyīmbà** 'and she began to sing', this time together with the quote marker **ngu**. This song is sung by a girl who is the only girl in the village whose mother will not allow her to use a cooking pot to cook some mushrooms she has brought back from the field. When the mother refuses, the girl begins to sing. In the song, the girl asks the mother again, twice, with the very same words, for a pot. The mother's refusal to give her daughter a pot represents the key problem of the story.

(12.51) À-ná-tòndèèr-è  ú=kú-yìmb-à  ngù:  ‖ «É=  máàwè
1-CON-begin-Fe  AU=15-sing-Fa  ‹quote›  O=  1a+my.mother

**máàwè**  |  **Ø-m-b-è**  **ny-ûngù  nàà-nî.**»  ‖  Ngù:
1a+my.mother  SBV-O1.SG-give-Fe  9-bowl  ADD.P-1SG  ‹quote›

«É=  **máàwè**  **máàwè**  |  **Ø-m-b-è**
O=  1a+my.mother  1a+my.mother  SBV-O1.SG-give-Fe

**ny-ûngù  nàà-nî.**»
9-bowl  ADD.P-1SG

'And she began to sing (quote): ‖ «O my mother my mother | give and ME ALSO a pot. ‖ (quote) O my mother my mother | give ME ALSO a pot.»'

There are many other stories which include a short song (often repeated) that gives an insider's point of view into the problem of the story. To include such a song is not obligatory, but it is a frequently used highlighting device.

### 12.4 Reporting of conversation

Kifuliiru has a variety of ways to report speech, both direct and indirect, and preceded by various speech introducers. These are described below.

### 12.4.1 Reported speech in quite formal written register

The quite formal register involves several characteristics of speech reporting. First, direct quotes, rather than indirect, are the default in this register. Indirect quotes are employed only for presenting reported speech acts which the author wishes to background (Levinsohn 2005 sec. 7.1.1).

Secondly, in the formal register, each instance of reported speech, whether direct or indirect, is introduced by a complete speech verb such as: **-dèt-** 'say', **-bwir-** 'tell', **-buuz-** 'ask', **-gánuul-** / **-gánuuz-** 'converse', **-kòmeerez-** 'insist', **-láhir-** 'disagree', **-lóngool-** 'dispute', **-naak-** 'speak disrespectfully', **-shùvy-** 'answer', **-tèndeer-** 'beg', **-yèmeer-** 'agree', **-yìdòdomb-** 'mutter', etc.

Finally, the marker **kwókùnô** '‹quote.MARKED›' may be used following the speech verb when introducing a quote which is especially significant to the story.

An example of the speech forms found in formal register is seen in (12.52).[15] The English transcription is given in the chart below, in which each new row begins with a different speech. In (12.50), direct speech is bolded and indirect speech is bold italicized. (The D/I column signals direct or indirect speech.)

---

[15]This story is representative of 56 formal, written texts, which all display the same basic system of reported speech.

## 12.4 Reporting of conversation

As can be seen in the "speech verb" column, each speech is introduced by a separate speech verb.

(12.52) Reported speech in quite formal written register

|   | D/I | Speech orienters ||| Story |
|---|---|---|---|---|---|
|   |   | Subject | Speech verb | Quote marker |   |
| a. | D | NP | 'said' | --- | The quail always going looked for what it could eat. It encountered a snake now slithering along, because the bush that it was in, it was now burning. That snake said to that quail: «**O my friend, save me from this fire.**» |
| b. | D | NP | 'answered' | --- | The quail answered: «**I would save you, but there's no way to lift you up.**» |
| c. | D | NP | 'told' | --- | That snake told that quail: «**I will wrap myself around your neck, and you will fly with me until (we reach) the other side of the river.**»<br><br>That quail, when it heard that, agreed and stretched out its neck. That snake wrapped himself around it, and it (quail) flew off with it, and it landed on the other side of the river. |
| d. | D | --- | 'told' | --- | And it told that snake: «**Get down.**» |
| e. | I | NP | 'said' | **kwó** | That snake said <u>that</u> *it was already very hungry.* |
| f. | I | NP | 'told' | **kwó** | That quail told it <u>that</u> *it get down, in order to go look for what it would eat.* |

|   | D/I | Speech orienters | | | Story |
|---|---|---|---|---|---|
|   |   | Subject | Speech verb | Quote marker |   |
| g. | D | --- | 'told' | **kwó-kùnô** | And it told that quail ‹quote.MARKED›: «**I no longer have the strength to go looking for other food. You are the one I'm about to eat.**» That snake swallowed that quail.<br><br>And it no longer thought that that quail is what caused it to not be burned by that fire. |

### 12.4.2 Direct versus indirect speech

In the formal register, direct speech is used for reported speech which is considered prominent in the story line. Indirect speech is used for backgrounded material, which is given less prominence.

The beginning of the climactic episode calls for direct speech to be used in the first sentence: and it told that snake: «Get down!». The prominence of the next two sentences is lowered by indirect speech. First, the snake gives a vague response about being hungry, and not yet directly refusing to get down. The quail then repeats the request, which as a repetition is not prominent, and so is reported as indirect speech.

This indirect speech is in contrast to (and sets up) the snake's stunning response which immediately follows in the climax of the story. This example of indirect speech can be seen as a kind of "foil", defined by the *Oxford English Dictionary* as "anything that serves to set off another thing distinctly or to advantage by contrast". Here the less prominent indirect speech serves to make the following direct speech, by contrast, all the more prominent.

As seen in the chart, direct speech most often does not involve a quote marker following the speech verb. The exception to this is the special-prominence quote marker **kwókùnô** '‹quote.MARKED›', used only for the thematically prominent speech at the climactic turning point in (12.52g). **Kwókùnô** is never used to introduce indirect speech. Rather, indirect speech is most often introduced by the complementizer **kwo**. In formal register, the quote marker **ti** is never employed.

### 12.4.3 Reported speech in informal registers

The text in (12.53) exemplifies the treatment of reported speech in a quite informal register. In this story each row contains a new speech, and the heavy lines separate new groups of speakers. Looking at the text, the following generalizations can be made here (and expanded below after the chart).

- Indirect speech is used only for backgrounded material. Indirect speech is bold and italicized in the righ-hand column, while direct speech is bold.
- The speaker, i.e. the subject of the speech verb, if any, may be indicated by a noun phrase, especially at the beginning of a tight-knit conversation. In the middle of such a conversation, the speaker, i.e. the subject of the speech verb, if any, is often marked by **ná=wà=náyè** 'and he also' (or an equivalent in another person/number, e.g. **ná=wà=nábò** 'and them also'), or a non-pronominal version of the preceding, e.g. **ná=wà=nyínà** 'and his mother also', **nà=wá=mwāmì** 'and the king also'.
- The speech verb typically is found only at the beginning of a tight-knit speech. In (12.53), such verbs are found in rows a, b, d, j, m, q, s, t, u.
- The quote marker, if used, is most commonly **tî** ‹quote›. Other quote markers are **mbû** ‹quote›, **ngû** ‹quote›, or **kwôkwô** '‹thus.N›'. Just as in the formal register, **kwókùnô** '‹quote. MARKED›' highlights prominent speech.
- In some cases there is no speech orienter of any kind, but only the speech itself is reported, as the speakers take turns talking back and forth; see (12.53n–p).

(12.53) Speech forms in formal register

| Speakers | Speech orienters | | | Story |
|---|---|---|---|---|
| | Subject | Speech verb | Quote marker | |
| | NP | said | **kwó** | a. There was one young man who wanted to marry a woman. That young man, when they showed him all the girls in that village of theirs, said that HE, **there is no girl that he likes**, |
| | --- | said | **kwó** | b. He said that **he must marry a woman who resembles his mother, and of the size which is like that of his mother.** That young man went outside of the village. And he went looking for women, but did not find any. |
| man to himself | --- | --- | **tí** | c. Then one day, when he was about to cross the river, he encountered a girl sitting under a tree. When he saw her, ⟨quote⟩ «**No way, she's the one who resembles my mother, and a size like that of my mother!**» |

## 12.4 Reporting of conversation

| Speakers | Speech orienters | | | Story |
|---|---|---|---|---|
| | Subject | Speech verb | Quote marker | |
| man and girl | NP | told | --- | d. That young man told her: «**O girl, I like you, I'm about to marry you.**» |
| | **Naye** | --- | tí | e. And she ⟨quote⟩ «**OK, marry me!**» And they took the path. |
| | NP | --- | tí | f. When they were in the path, they reached a river. That girl ⟨quote⟩ «**No, ME, I will not cross this river, but you carry me on your back.**» |
| | NP | --- | tí | g. That young man ⟨quote⟩ «**Oh surely. Will you be too much for me to take across the river?**» That young man placed her on his back. In the river «kagata-kagata», the river «vwo vwo vwo», and they crossed the river. |
| | Noun | --- | tí | h. When they reached the other side, the new wife ⟨quote⟩ «**Oh my! Will the new wife get down here? You take me to the house. Me the new wife, would I go with my feet again, we who are the ones now about to go to the village?**» |
| | NP | --- | tí | i. That young man ⟨quote⟩ «**No, we will go.**» |

| Speakers | Speech orienters ||| Story |
|---|---|---|---|---|
| | Subject | Speech verb | Quote marker | |
| man and mother | --- | told | **tí** | j. And he arrived at their place at dusk, and he went into the house. And he told his mother ‹quote› «**O my mother, I've brought the new bride. You give me some food**». |
| | Noun | --- | **tí** | k. His mother ‹quote› «**Will you not eat in here?**» |
| | **Ná=wà= náyè** | --- | **tí** | l. And he ‹quote› «**Oh no! You bring (it) to me in here.**» |
| man and wife | Ø | to tell | --- | m. To tell the young wife: «**Get down from the back!**» |
| | --- | --- | --- | n. «**It's obvious I will not get down!**» |
| | --- | --- | --- | o. «**Get down from the back.**» |
| | --- | --- | --- | p. «**It's obvious I will not get down!**» And he spent the night with her on his back, and he spent the day with her on his back. A week «puu», month «puu»! O comrades! Oh my! The person will die! |
| man and other men | NP | said | **tí** | q. They took that news to other men. Those men, when they heard it, they said ‹quote› «**Oh my! What he has brought is a demon! That's right! A demon. Yes!**» |
| | N | --- | **tí** | r. Others ‹quote› «**How are you going to get rid of it?**» As soon as they try something, no results! |

12.4 Reporting of conversation

| Speakers | Speech orienters | | | Story |
|---|---|---|---|---|
| | Subject | Speech verb | Quote marker | |
| other men | NP | told | tí | s. Other men told them ‹quote› «**You get a big bull, a bull which you castrated, one that now has much fat. Let him take it (demon) right there where he got her. You go and slaughter that bull for her, and you place all of that meat, and the fatty intestine, and the fatty intestine, on the fire.**» Ok then! They led that young man and that bull to the river, and they took it under that tree, and they stabbed the knife into it. The fatty intestine they piled up on the fire; that bull began to cook; roasting odor kept being smelled. |
| man and wife | NP | told | --- | t. That young man told her: «**Roast it well, don't burn it! Roast it well, don't burn it!**» |
| | --- | to say | kwôk-wô | u. In saying like this: «**Roast it well, don't burn it**,» that's when that demon pulled out her fingernails. That demon, when she sensed that the roasting smell was was really very sweet in her nose, she immediately flew right to that meat! That young man immediately left there with those people, and they immediately dashed off and they crossed that river and they went home. So that demon remained among that meat. That's where the story finishes and that's where it ends. |

### 12.4.3.1 Direct versus indirect speech

The use of indirect speech is quite rare in informal register. In the story in (12.53), indirect speech occurs only twice. Both occurrences are in the setting in rows a and b, where the man is not talking to anyone in particular. As was true in the more formal register, indirect speech is used mainly for less prominent or backgrounded information.

Direct speech with a speech verb is used to introduce the great majority of speeches in informal register. In the story above, it is found in (12.53d, j, m, q, s, t, u).

### 12.4.3.2 Reduced speech orienters in tight knit conversations

The typical pattern is to employ a speech verb at the beginning of each new tight-knit (also called "closed") conversation.[16] Subsequent repartee in the conversation is not introduced by the use of a speech verb. Instead, it is either preceded by some type of quote marker, or in rare cases it may completely lack any speech orienter.

The Kifuliiru text at the beginning of a conversation (lines 12.53d, e) is presented here in (12.54). The new conversation is opened with the speech verb **ànámúbwìrè** 'he told her'. The reply, by contrast, is not preceded by a speech verb, but is minimally introduced by **Náyè tî** 'And she ‹quote›'.

(12.54) **Ù-lyá    mú-tàbánà |    à-ná-mú-bwìr-é:   ||    É=    mú-nyérè ||**
1-that.R   1-young.man   1-CON-O1-tell-Fe      O=    1-girl

**n-à-kú-síìm-à   ||   n-àmú=   kú-yáng-à.   ||   Ná-yè**
1SG-P1-O2.SG-like-Fa   1SG-F1=   O2.SG-marry-Fa   ADD.P-1

**tí=   | «Èè ||   ú-Ø-n-yâng-è.»**
‹quote›=   Yes   2SG-SBV-O1.SG-marry-Fe

'That young man | told her: || «O girl || I like you || I'm about to marry you.» || And SHE also ‹quote›: |«Yes || marry me.»' (112 010-011)

Once a closed conversation has been introduced using a speech verb, further responses in that same conversation are introduced only by a minimal quote marker like **ti** ‹quote›, **mbu** ‹quote›, or **ngu** ‹quote›, and/or by an idiomatic form like **ná=wà=náyè** 'and he also (said)'.

---

[16] A tight-knit conversation is where "each successive speaker takes up the same topic as that of the previous speech and develops the conversation from the point at which the last speaker left off" Levinsohn (2005:NARR07).

## 12.4 Reporting of conversation

In (12.55)–(12.58), we see a conversation between a young man and his mother. The opening of this conversation (spoken by the young man) in (12.55), is marked by a speech verb plus quote marker: **ànábwírágè tí** 'and he told EMP ‹quote›'. The young man tells his mother: 'I have brought home a new wife; give me some food'.

In (12.56), now within a closed conversation, the mother's response is introduced by the reduced form **nyínà tí** 'the mother ‹quote›'. No speech verb is used for the reply, but only the quote marker **tí**.

In (12.57), still within the same closed conversation, the young man's response is introduced by **ná=wà=náyè tí** 'and he also ‹quote›', again with no speech verb involved.

(12.55) a. <u>À-ná-bwìr-àg-è</u>   nyínà    | <u>tì</u>=       É=       máàwè    |
         1-CON-tell-EMP-Fe       1a+his.mother  ‹quote›=  O=   1a+my.mother

   n-à-léét-à            ú=mú-hyà     ||  mú-Ø-m-bèèrèz-é
   1SG-P1-bring-Fa       AU=1-new.wife     2PL-SBV-O1.SG-give-Fe

   í=by-ókúlyâ. ||
   AU=8-food

b. <u>Nyínà</u>        || <u>tí</u>=    «K-ò=    tá-gá-lì-ìr-à          mú-nò?» ||
   1a+his.mother        ‹quote›=     Q-2SG=   NEG-F2-eat-APL-Fa      18-here.P.C

c. <u>Ná</u>=        w-à=       ná-yè     <u>tí</u>=    || «Nângà ||
   CNJ=            1-A.M=     ADD.P-1   ‹quote›=       No

   ú-Ø-n-dèèt-èr-è                 mú-nò.»
   2SG-SBV-O1.SG-bring-APL-Fe       18-here.P.C

'And he told his mother | ‹quote›: «O mother | I have brought a new bride || give me food. || The mother || ‹quote›: «Won't you eat it in here?» || And HE also ‹quote›: || «No || bring it to me in here.»' (112 022-026)

The two texts presented in (12.52) and (12.53) did not happen to include **mbu** '‹quote›' (or the alternative pronunciation **ngu**) as quote markers. Basically **mbu**[17] and **ngu** function in just the same way as **ti**, but are used much less frequently. In (12.56) **mbu** '‹quote›' introduces the direct quote **bóóshì bàlí í=wà=ndálò** 'all are at the (place of) the field'.

---

[17] **Mbu** (and not **ti** as in Kifuliiru) is the main quote marker in Chitembo, a related zone J language.

(12.56) **Mú-shììjá   w-à-wè      ná-yè |   à-génd-à   háyì? ||   Mbù=**
       1-brother    1-A.M-2SG   ADD.P-1   1-go-Fa    where      ‹quote›=

   **«Bó-óshì ||   bà-lí    í=w-à=            n-dálò.»**
   2-all         2-are    23=place-A.M=     9-field

'«Your brother and HE also | where has he gone?» || ‹quote›: «All || are at the field.»' (106 041-42)

More rarely, some speakers use the alternative pronunciation, **ngu**, rather than **mbu** for this quote marker, as seen in (12.57), where **ngu** introduces the direct quote **Ká=wàngàbònà ágàlì hánò?** 'Would you see what is here?'

(12.57) **Tí=       «É=    bà-lyá       ||  bì-kì      í-bì-rì     ì-yó         mûndà? ||**
        ‹quote›=   O=     2-comrades      8-what     S.R-8-is    there.N-23   place

   **Lú-bí     lú-kì?» ||   Ngù=    «Ká=   w-àngà-bòn-à |   á-gà-lí**
   11-noise  11-which     quote    Q=     2SG-POT-see-Fa    S.R-6-is

   **há-nò?»**
   16-here.P.C

'‹Quote›: «O comrades || what is over there? || What noise?» || ‹quote›: «Would you see | what is here?»' (401 040-41)

### 12.4.3.3 Absence of speech orienter

In some cases of reported direct speech, speech orienters are absent altogether. No speech verb like 'tell' or 'say' is used, nor is there a reduced speech orienter such as **ti** '‹quote›'. The repartee consists only of the direct speech of the participants as they take turns speaking. This is seen in (12.53 n–p), where the young man and his new bride are talking back and forth.

This closed conversation is presented again below in (12.58). It begins with the infinitive form of a speech verb: **kúbwírágá** 'to tell' (meaning 'when he told') in the phrase **kúbwírágá ú=múhyá shònòòkágà kú=múgóngò** 'to tell the new wife: «Get down from the back!»'. The reply of the wife in (12.58a) is not introduced by any speech orienter. Only her words themselves are reported: **Sì=ndágáshònòòkà** 'It's obvious I will not get down'.

The same exchange is repeated in (12.58c) and (12.58d), again with no speech orienter of any kind. This sort of reporting of direct speech communicates a very rapid argument back and forth, where it is clear who is talking to whom without belaboring the point by using speech orienters.

(12.58) a. **Kú-bwír-ág-á   ú=mú-hyà:** ‖ **«Ø-shòn-òòk-ág-à** |
  15-tell-EMP-Fa   AU=1-new.wife    IMP.S-climb-RV.I-EMP-Fa

  **kú=   mú-góngò.»** ‖
  17=    3-back

b. **«Sì=   n-dá-gá-shòn-òòk-à.»** ‖
  OBV=   1SG-NEG-F2-climb-RV.I-Fa

c. **«Ø-Shòn-óók-à        kú=   mú-góngò.»** ‖
  IMP.S-climb-RV.I-EMP-Fa  17=   3-back

d. **«Sì=   n-dá-gá-shòn-òòk-à.»**
  OBV=   1SG-NEG-F2-climb-RV.I-Fa

'To tell the young wife: ‖ «Get down | from the back!» ‖ «It's obvious I won't get down.» ‖ «Get down from the back!» ‖ «It's obvious that I won't get down.»' (112 027-028)

## 12.5 Participant reference

### 12.5.1 Introduction of participants

In narrative texts the nouns used to introduce major participants are always found at the end of a clause. This positions them as the dominant focal element (DFE) in the sentence (10.2.3.1). The introduction of a major participant often involves a clause with presentational articulation (or locative inversion). Minor characters and props, on the other hand, require no special placement at the end of the clause, and can be introduced anywhere in the sentence.

#### 12.5.1.1 Introduction of major participants

One basic way to introduce major characters is with presentational articulation. Presentational articulation includes a verb with a cl. 16 locative subject marker **ha**-, but with no expressed location involved. (This corresponds to the English 'There was...') The verb in the introductory clause is generally in the remote (P3) or unmarked (P2) past tense. The introduction of a major participant also usually includes the use of the adjective -**gùmà** 'a certain'. In addition, there is often a relative clause which further describes the major participant.

In (12.59) presentational articulation is used when the main character of the narrative is introduced. The cl. 16 **ha**- is used as subject marker in the verb **háálí rīīrì** 'there was'. The participant being introduced in DFE postion of the clause is the phrase **mútàbánà múgùmà** 'a young man'. This DFE is isolated by a short preceding pause, together with a long pause afterwards, preceding the next clause. This example also includes the typical introductory adjective **múgùmà** 'one, certain' and a relative clause which relates the major participant to the theme of the story.

(12.59) **Há-àlì**   rì-ìr-í |   **ú=mú-tàbánà**   mú-gùmà ||   **ú-ká-lóóz-á**
   16-P3   is-RS-Fi   AU=1-young.man   1-one   S.R+1-P2-want-Fa

   **ú=kú-yáng-á** |   **ú=mú-kàzì.**
   AU=15-marry-Fa   AU=1-woman

'There was | a certain young man || who wanted to marry | a woman.'
(612 003)

In cases of locative inversion, the class marker on a surface subject locative phrase matches the class of the subject prefix on the verb. The "underlying" subject (the major participant) is then presented at the end of the clause. In (12.60) the cl. 18 (surface subject) locative phrase **mú=kíshùkà** 'in the bush' triggers the subject marking of the verb, **mwáàlì rīīrì** 'there was' (**mw-** before vowels). This then introduces the main character **í=kínyúní kíhámú bwènèènè** 'a very large bird'.

(12.60) **Mú=**   **kí-shùkà** ||   **mw-áàlì**   rì-ìr-í |   **í=kí-nyúní**   **kí-hámú** |
   18=   7-bush   18-P3   is-RS-Fi   AU=7-bird   7-large

   **bwènèènè.**
   very.much

'In the bush || there was | a large bird | very.' (610 006)

Major participants can also be introduced without presentational articulation or locative inversion, and therefore without positioning the major participant at the end of the clause. This is a less "classic" (or less standard) style. In (12.61) we see the first sentence of a story, where the major character is introduced as the subject of the sentence: **mútēzì múgùmà** 'a certain trapper'. With no presentational articulation (or locative inversion) in this clause, the fact that this is a main participant is marked by **múgùmà** 'one/certain' and by the background P3 tense.

## 12.5 Participant reference

(12.61) **Mú-tēzì    mú-gùmà** ‖ **á-àlí    gw-èt-í    á=ká-bwá    kà-à-gè.**
       1-trapper 1-one    1-P3   have-RS-Fi  AU=12-dog  12-A.M-1

'One trapper ‖ had his dog.' (49 002)

Major participants introduced in the middle of the story are usually introduced in a sentence which begins with a point of departure (PoD) (10.2.4). This serves to move them into the focal position at the end of a clause. The constructions which introduce such "local VIPs" often involve verbs like -**gwan**- 'encounter', -**hís**- 'cause to arrive', -**hùlukir**- 'appear', -**húmaan**- 'meet up with, encounter', -**lyok**- 'come out of'.

In (12.62) a main participant is introduced following the clauses **ìrí hákábá lúsìkù lúgùmà, ngwà=jábúkágé úlwījì** 'when it became one day, when he was intending to cross the river'. These two PoDs provides material at the beginning of the sentence which allows the new information **ú=múnyérè** 'a girl' to occur as a DFE at the end.

(12.62) **Ìrí    há-ká-b-á    lú-sìkù  lú-gùmà** ‖ **ngw-à=**
       when  16-P2-become-Fa  11-day  11-one    when-1=

      **Ø-jábúk-ág-è** | **ú=lw-ījì** ‖ **à-húmààn-à** | **ú=mú-nyérè** ‖
      SBV-cross.over-EMP-Fe  AU=11-river  1-encounter-Fa  AU=1-girl

      **à-bwát-íìr-ì    mw-í= dàkó** | **ly-é=**   **kí-tì.**
      1-sit-RS-Fi   18-5=  under   7-A.M+AU=  7-tree

'When it was one day ‖ when he was going to cross | the river ‖ he encountered | a girl ‖ sitting under | a tree.' (112 008)

In (12.63) the phrase **kú=màànà nyîjá zô=yó mùkáàgè** 'by the good luck of that.N wife of his' provides material at the beginning of the sentence which allows the **í=mbébá yànáhùlúkírá=hô** 'a rat appeared there' to be more in focus toward the end, after a long pause.

(12.63) **Kú=    màànà    ny-îjá    z-ô=    yó    mù-ká-à-gè** ‖
       17=   9+luck   9-good  10-A.M=  that.N+1  1-wife-A.M-1

      **í=m-bébá** | **y-àná-hùlúk-ír-á    =hô.**
      AU=9-rat   9-SQ-appear-APL-Fa  =16

'By the good luck of that wife of his ‖ a rat | appeared there.' (35 023)

### 12.5.1.2 Introduction of minor participants and props

Minor characters can be presented anywhere in the clause, but usually not in the DFE slot at the end of the clause, as they are usually of passing importance.

In (12.64) **á=bàndì bándù** 'other people' is in the subject slot at the beginning of the sentence. These people do not have a major role, but are just bystanders who go to tell the mother something. In this case the existence of 'other people' is assumed, and they can be topical, without ever being formally introduced. Thus the author introduces them in the initial position of the sentence and not at the end of the clause in the DFE slot.

(12.64) <u>Á=bà-ndì</u>   bá-ndù ‖   bà-ná-gêndì   bwír-á |   ù-lyá
AU=2-other   2-people   2-SQ-GOING   tell-Fa   1-that.R

nyíná   |   w-à=   mú-hyà:...
1a+her.mother   1-A.M=   1-new.wife

'Other people ‖ went and told | that mother | of the newlywed...' (111 020)

In (12.65) the locative phrase **í=mwàbò-vyàlà** 'at the in-laws' place' includes the first mention of the in-laws, who are implied, because the couple is married. They are introduced at the beginning of the sentence, because the in-laws themselves are not central to the theme of the story.

(12.65) S-í=   <u>mw-à-bò-vyàlà</u> ‖   y-àná-b-à   |   y-ò=   y-áàlì
OBV+23=   place-A.M-2-in-law   23-SQ-become-Fa   23-FOC=   23-P3

yèz-ír-í   |   í=by-ókúlyà.
crop.yield-RS-Fi   AU=8-food

'But at the in-laws' ‖ it was (the place) | where was growing | food.' (111 005)

However, in (12.66) a prop that is important (the vine) is introduced by locative inversion. Even though it is not an animate being, still the children of the fox need to climb on it, in order to reach a beehive where their father sends them to collect honey. (This vine is important to the theme of the story, because when their father then cuts it down, the children have no way to climb down, and fall from the tree to their deaths on the ground.) In this case the locative subject marker is the cl. 17 **ku-**, where the subject is <u>kú=yìkyó kítì</u> 'on that.N tree' followed by a verb with a cl. 17 prefix **kw-**, in <u>kwáàlí</u> **shònírí** 'there climbed'.

(12.66) <u>Kú</u>=    <u>yìkyó</u>      <u>kí-tì</u> ||    <u>kw-áàlí</u>    <u>shòn-ír-í</u> ||    ú=mú-lándírà.
       17=     that.N+7     7-tree       17-P3         climb-RS-Fi           AU=3-vine

'On that tree || there climbed || a vine.' (32 007)

## 12.5.2 Tracking of major participants

Some of the material in this section is discussed elsewhere and thus is cross-referenced.

(a) Prefix pronouns

As already mentioned, in sentences referring to the same event complex, pronominal prefixes are often used in back-to-back clauses with sequential tenses, even when different speakers are being referred to. This is a typical Bantu feature that occurs throughout the event line.

(b) Free pronouns

There are many kinds of free personal pronouns in Kifuliiru (see 3.3.2), and each of them has a specialized meaning relating to the notions of contrast, alternation, inclusion, exclusion, addition, etc. In addition, the demonstrative pronouns communicate notions of speaker/hearer orientation and distance in terms of here, near, far, remote, contrast, thematic salience, etc.

Except in rare cases where they occur clause-finally, pronouns always carry a special meaning like the ones listed in the previous paragraph. Free pronouns are never used merely to keep track of referents. If they are used in such a way, this probably reflects influence from French.

(c) Consistency of names for characters

Characters are usually are referred to throughout a story by one consistent noun or noun phrase rather than being called by different names simply to introduce variety into the narrative, as is often done in English. For example in story 105, the lion is referred as **wándàrè** 'Lion' or **ùyó / ùlyá wándàrè** 'that.N/R lion' 11 times. By contrast, she is not referred to as "that tricky one" or "that persistent animal" or any other descriptive name. Cow is referred to as **wàngáàvù** 'cow' 11 times, but never as "the frightened one" or "the unfortunate bovine", etc. In the case of the old man, he is referred to as **músháàjà** 'old man' or **ùyó / ùlyá músháàjà** 'that.N/R old man' seven times and as **ùyó múshósì** 'that.N man' twice, so there is a slight variation. However, he is never referred to as "the courageous one", "the soft-hearted old fellow", etc. Thus the names of the characters tend to remain quite consistent throughout the story.

# 13

# Proverbs and Riddles

## 13.1 Proverbs

There are many Kifuliiru proverbs,[1] literally thousands of them. Speaking a known proverb effectively heightens the truth value of what is being said, and is akin to quoting holy writings. Thus they are commonly employed to lend veracity to a statement. In addition, proverbs often make a point in a way that can only be processed by cultural "insiders."

### 13.1.1 Proverb formal considerations

#### 13.1.1.1 Usually quite pithy

Kifuliiru proverbs tend to be quite pithy. In the corpus studied, the proverbs averaged only 3.95 words each, assuming one does not count the one-syllable clitics (e.g. nominal augment, locative markers, associative markers, etc.) as separate words. If the clitics are counted as separate words, the proverbs still average only 4.83 words per proverb. Sixty-six percent of the proverbs are two to four words long: thirteen percent are two words long, twenty-seven percent are three words long, and twenty-six percent are four words long. These figures reflect the fact that Kifuliiru proverbs "minimize" grammatical complexities wherever possible.

The two-word proverb in (13.1) explains that there is no one who does things all by himself. Other people always need to be involved and depended on.

---

[1] A corpus of 1,105 proverbs was the basis for the analysis presented in this chapter.

(13.1) **Ndáá-yè nábwìgírà.**
      NEG.FOC-1   1+do.it.yourself

'There's no one doing things by himself.'

The three-word proverb in (13.2) states that the gazelle suckles its child. This is to say that though the gazelle is perceived as an animal that is always running and jumping around, even it must stop to suckle its offspring. Therefore people, too, should take breaks from their work.

(13.2) **Á=ká-sà ‖ kà-Ø-yó-z-á mw-ānà.**
      AU=12-gazelle   12-TL-suckle-CS-Fa   1-child

'The gazelle ‖ suckles the child.'

The four-word proverb in (13.3) says that if one does not kill a friendship, he/she does not get hold of another. Sometimes it is necessary to retreat from a certain relationship, if it is in conflict with another relationship that you want to establish.

(13.3) **Ú-tá-Ø-yìt-á bw-ìrà ‖ à-tà-Ø-gwát-á bù-ndì.**
      S.R+1-NEG-TL-kill-Fa   14-friendship   1-NEG-TL-get.hold-Fa   14-other

'The one who does not kill a friendship ‖ does not get hold of another.'

### 13.1.1.2 Nouns

#### 13.1.1.2.1 Augments on initial nouns, sometimes on non-initial

In all proverbs which begin with a noun, that initial noun includes the augment. However, the augment is found with only about half of the nouns occurring at the end of a proverb.

The augment is always attached to the initial word in a noun phrase. Thus when it appears on an adjective, it indicates that the adjective is being used substantively (as the head of the NP). In (13.4) the augment appears on the stative verbal adjective **ú=mútòlé** 'the one who is cut off', creating something akin to a relative clause.[2] This is seen in (13.4) in **ú=mútòlé îtwè** 'the one whose head is cut off'.

(13.4) **Ú-mú-tòl-é î-twè ‖ à-tà-Ø-génd-à.**
      AU-1-cut-e   5-head   1-NEG-TL-go-Fa

'The one who has his head cut off ‖ does not go.'

---

[2] Relative clauses are also very common in proverbs.

## 13.1 Proverbs

At the end of a proverb, the use of the augment is optional. This is demonstrated by (13.5) and (13.6), which are very similar to each other, except that in the first, the augment appears on the object noun, while in the second, it does not.

In (13.5), the object **í=njūkì** 'honey' includes the augment **í**.

(13.5) **Á=bá-twá    ìrí    bà-∅-lùg-à    ‖    bà-tà-∅-dààh-á    | í=n-jūkì.**
AU=2-pygmy   if    2-TL-be.many-Fa    2-NEG-TL-raid.hive-Fa   AU=10-beehive

'The pygmies if they are many ‖ they don't raid | beehives.'

In (13.6) the object **njùkì** 'beehive' does not have the augment.

(13.6) **Á=bá-twá    ìrí    bà-lí b-ìngì ‖    bà-tà-∅-dààh-á    n-jùkì.**
AU=2-pygmy   if    2-are 2-many   2-NEG-TL-raid.hive-Fa   10-beehive

'The pygmies if they are many ‖ they don't raid beehives.'

### 13.1.1.2.2 Preference for use of singular subject

Proverbs having a singular subject are more common than those which have a plural subject, by a ratio of almost ten to one. Sometimes the noun which names the subject is used, while other times the singular subject is shown only by the subject concord on the verb. In (13.7) a verb (in a relative clause) with a third-person singular subject is used: **úgwētì** 'the one who has (things)'.

(13.7) **Ú-gw-ēt-ì    ‖    à-tà-∅-hánùùl-w-à.**
S.R+1-have-RS-Fi    1-NEG-TL-advise-PS-Fa

'The one who has something ‖ is not advised (does not take advice easily).'

### 13.1.1.3 Verb forms

#### 13.1.1.3.1 Many negative forms

It is significant that approximately 65 percent of the 1,105 proverbs have negative verb forms, marked by the negative **ta-** prefix. In (13.8) the negative potential verb **ìtàngàhúbà** 'it would not miss' is typical.

(13.8) **Í=ngwî** || **ì-tà-ngà-húb-á** **ú=lw-íví** | **lw-ê=** **kìzí**
AU=9+leopard 9-NEG-POT-miss-Fa AU=11-door 11-A.M+9= REP

**yìgúl-à.**
open-Fa

'The leopard || would not miss the door | which he habitually opens.'

The negative focal copula **ndaa** 'there is no' occurs 22 times in the corpus of proverbs, as another way of negating the proposition. In (13.9) the cl. 1 negative focal copula **ndáá-yè** means 'there is no one'.

(13.9) **Ndáá-yè** **ú-báág-ír-á** || **á-há-zírá** | **í-sáázì.**
NEG.FOC-1 S.R+1-slaughter-APL-Fa S.R-16-without 10-flies

'There's no one who slaughters || at a place without | flies.'

### 13.1.1.3.2 Many focal copulas

The focal copula (e.g. **hó** 'that's where', **yé** 'that's who') is used 140 times (12.3 percent of the time). In (13.10) the second **hó** 'that's where' is a focal copula.

(13.10) **H-ó=** **lwìjí** **lù-hóóh-ír-ì** || **h-ó=** **lù-Ø-jábùk-w-â.**
16-AU= 11-river 11-be.calm-RS-Fi 16-FOC= 11-TL-cross.over-PS-Fa

'Where the river is calm || that's where it is crossed.'

### 13.1.1.3.3 Timeless verb form most common

The timeless tense with null tense marker (used in a habitual sense), is the most commonly occurring tense in proverbs, occurring in well over half the proverbs. Also occurring, but much less frequently, are the unmarked future (F2) **gaa-** and recent past (P1) **a-**, and the unmarked past (P2) **ka-**. The background P3 tense marked by **áàli** never occurs in the corpus of proverbs. In (13.11) the timeless tense is seen on the verb **kíhùlúkà** 'it comes out'.

(13.11) **Í=kí-nwâ** || **kì-Ø-hùlúk-á** **n-é=** **m-bàlì.**
AU=7-mouth 7-TL-come.out-Fa CNJ-AU= 9-outsider

'A word || can also come from the person who is not in our conversation.'

### 13.1.1.4 Clauses

Relative clauses are more common in proverbs than in other genres, occurring in about 15 percent of the proverbs. In (13.12) the subject relative is seen in

**úhúúnà** 'the one who asks'. Relative clauses in Kifuliiru are always restrictive (i.e. identificational) rather than descriptive or modifying.

(13.12) **Ú-Ø-húún-á**     **lûngwé**     | **á=mī-ījì**     || **à-Ø-mú-h-à**     **=gô.**
S.R+1-TL-ask-Fa     1a+certain.lake     AU=6-water     1-TL-O1-give-Fa     =O6

'The one who asks the lake | for water || he gives it to him.'

### 13.1.1.1.4.1 Conjunctions

Eighty-nine percent of the proverbs include only one independent clause, while 11 percent have two independent clauses. When clauses are joined by conjunctions, we find that the conjunctions are chosen from a very limited set: basically **ìrí** 'if' or 'that's when', **si** 'but', and **mbu** 'with (frustrated) intention'.

The most common conjunction used is **ìrí**, used in 8.6 percent of the proverbs. This conjunction has two different meanings. Used in the initial clause, it means 'if/when'. It is used in this way 27 times in the proverb corpus. In (13.13) **ìrí bàlí bìngì** means 'if they are many'. It should be noted that in non-proverbs the verbal complement would have included the conditional auxiliary **bàngàbà** 'they would be', as in **ìrí bàngàbà bàlí bìngì** 'if they would be they are many'. However, in the proverb, a shortened version is used, without **bàngàbà**.

(13.13) **Á=bá-ndù** || **ìrí**    **bà-lí**    **bì-ngì** || **bà-tà-Ø-shúlìk-à**    **m-bébà.**
AU=2-people    if    2-are    2-many    2-NEG-TL-hit-Fa    9-rat

'People || if they are many || they don't (i.e. can't) hit the rat.'

The second meaning of **ìrí** is 'that's when'. It has this meaning when used to introduce the second clause. It is used in 68 proverbs at the beginning of the second clause to mean 'that's when'. As in (13.14), the sentence would make perfectly good sense without the use of **ìrí**. Thus the use of this conjunction is quite marked, emphasizing the factuality of the second half of the sentence. In this case, the emphasis is on the fact that the person who killed the king would not be the one to go around announcing his death (as he would not want people to think he was the first to know the news).

(13.14) Ú-w-à-dèt-à   kwó=   mw-àmì   à-fw-à   ‖   ìrí   à-tà-lì
        S.R-1-P1-say-Fa   CMP=   1-king   1+P1-die-Fa   that's.when   1-NEG-is

      y-é=   w-à-mú-yìt-à.
      1-FOC=   1-P1-O1-kill-Fa

'The one who says that the king has died ‖ that's when he's not the one who killed him.'

The other conjunction common in proverbs, **si** 'but', is used 52 times (in about 5 percent of the proverbs.)

(13.15) Í=n-gónì   ì-Ø-vùn-à   í-vùhà ‖   sì=   ì-tà-Ø-vùn-à   n-géshò.
        AU=9-stick   9-TL-break-Fa   5-bone   BUT=   9-NEG-TL-break-Fa   9-habit

'The stick breaks bones ‖ but it does not break habits.'

Other conjunctions are used less often: **Mbu** is used 18 times (1.6 percent), the analytic causative -**tùma** 'that's why/that's what caused' is used 9 times (.8 percent), and **í=kyànyà** 'the time (when)' and **gírà** 'so that' are used once each. In the corpus there is no use of **kwôkwô** 'thus', **hàlíndè** 'until', **mángò** 'when', **kúndù** 'though', or **kú=yùkwò** 'therefore'.

### 13.1.2 Proverb meaning considerations

#### 13.1.2.1 *Straightforward meanings, versus "insider" ones*

Some proverbs are relatively straightforward in their meaning and can be understood without having "insider" information about the culture. In (13.16) the meaning is quite obvious: 'Work, let's eat, is not slavery', meaning 'we should work so we can eat, there's no shame or injustice in that'.

(13.16) «Ø-Kòl-á   tú-Ø-ly-è»   ‖   bù-tà-lì   bù-jâ.
        IMP.S-work-Fa   1PL-SBV-eat-Fe   14-NEG-is   14-slavery

'Work let's eat ‖ is not slavery.'

Many other proverbs, however, are not as transparent and need "inside" information before they can be properly understood. In (13.17) it says that the fly which dies on the sore is not a misfortune. The meaning is that the fly was doing its duty in eating where it was supposed to eat. If it got killed in the process, it was not because of any impropriety on its part.

## 13.1 Proverbs

(13.17) **Ú=rú-sáází | ú=kú-fw-ír-à kú= kí-hándò || bù-tà-lí**
　　　　AU=11-fly　　AU=15-die-APL-Fa　17=　7-sore　　14-NEG-is

**bú-hányà.**
14-misfortune

'The fly | to die on the sore || is not a misfortune.'

To understand the proverb in (13.18) one also needs a bit of inside information. In "two bowls are not scraped clean with the finger", it means that if you are scraping one bowl clean with the finger, you cannot simultaneously scrape the other one as well. This proverb shows that one should not overextend him/herself and try to do too much at a time.

(13.18) **Í=m-bàngàlà zì-bìrì || zì-tà-Ø-kòmb-w-â.**
　　　　AU=10-bowl　　10-two　　10-NEG-TL-scrape.clean-PS-Fa

'Two bowls || are not scraped cleaned with the finger.'

### 13.1.2.2 Common participants

Of the proverbs studied, most have singular, human (cl.1) subjects. This is exemplified in (13.19) where the cl. 1 subject relative **ú-** refers to 'the one who'.

(13.19) <u>**Ú**</u>**-tà-dès-ír-ì　　||　　à-tà-Ø-zìng-w-â.**
　　　　S.R+1-NEG-say-RS-Fi　　1-NEG-TL-tell.untruth-PS-Fa

'The one who does not speak || is not lied about.'

In proverbs where the subject is not expressed by a relative clause (meaning "humans in general") there are many other nouns used as subject. In (13.20) is a list of the other most common nouns found as subjects in the corpus, besides unspecified human referents. Included are all the subject nouns that are found five times or more, listed with the number of occurrences.

(13.20)

| Word | Gloss | No. | Word | Gloss | No. |
|---|---|---|---|---|---|
| úmwānà | 'child' | 51 | múgéézì | 'traveler' | 8 |
| lwījì | 'river' | 22 | mbènè | 'goat' | 8 |
| kábwâ | 'dog' | 18 | múngérè | 'shepherd' | 8 |
| ábákàzì | 'woman' | 17 | ndándà | 'payment' | 8 |
| mwîjâ | 'good person' | 17 | nyâmbwè | 'fox' | 8 |
| ínjírà | 'path' | 15 | ámìínò | 'teeth' | 7 |
| múkùlù | 'important one' | 15 | íngwî | 'leopard' | 7 |
| músósì | 'man' | 15 | ívùhà | 'bone' | 7 |
| kánwâ | 'mouth' | 14 | múkô | 'blood' | 7 |
| ngónì | 'walking stick' | 14 | nvúlà | 'rain' | 7 |
| íkítì | 'tree' | 13 | ákàáyà | 'village' | 6 |
| mwīrà | 'friend' | 13 | búshìgì | 'night time' | 6 |
| ngāāvù | 'cow' | 13 | nálúgânda | 'craftsman' | 6 |
| bwéngè | 'intelligence' | 12 | úmújōkà | 'snake' | 6 |
| -vyàlà | 'in-laws' | 12 | ámáví | 'feces' | 5 |
| yîshè | 'father' | 12 | íkíbūzì | 'sheep' | 5 |
| ámásû | 'eyes' | 11 | mágálà | 'body' | 5 |
| nyínà | 'mother' | 11 | mbébà | 'rat' | 5 |
| mwāmì | 'kind' | 10 | mútīmà | 'heart' | 5 |
| áhālì | 'the place where' | 9 | úbwîjâ | 'goodness' | 5 |
| íngòkò | 'chicken' | 9 | mútēgò | 'trap' | 5 |
| nyûmbà | 'house' | 9 | | | |

## 13.2 Riddles

There is a strong tradition in Kifuliiru of telling riddles, especially around the fireplace after supper, at the time of **máyìzâ** 'time of telling stories, or riddles'. Riddles (**Sákúúzô**) are typically told mainly by the grandmother, or the mother. Some examples of riddles are presented in the explanation below.

The riddles all share certain grammatical characteristics, which are enumerated in 13.2.1.

## 13.2.1 Riddle formal considerations

### 13.2.1.1 Formulaic introduction

Every riddle begins with a formulaic introduction: The riddle asker says: **sáákwè**, someone answers: **rúúzè** and then the first person gives the riddle. Saying **sáákwè** immediately lets one's listener know that there is a riddle coming. Replying **rúúzè** means that the listener wants to hear the riddle and try to guess the answer. The literal meaning of these verbal words is obscure.

(13.21) **Sáákwè! ǁ Rúúzè! ǁ** N-dì= mû= ly-â
        1SG-is= PROG= eat-Fa

    n-dá-gá-ná-hám-à. ǁ      Ú=mú-shítò.
    1SG-NEG-F2-ADD.V-get.big-Fa    AU=3-roasting.stick

'Riddle! ǁ Ask! ǁ I am eating but I will not get fatter. ǁ Roasting stick.'

There is no effort to couch riddles in a "pithy" abbreviated version of the grammar, as is done in proverbs. In fact the grammar of the riddles does not significantly differ from the grammar found in normal narrative text. Thus in (13.22) the longer progressive form of the verb is used in **ndì mú=shwékà** 'I am tying'. (A proverb, by contrast, would likely employ the shorter timeless form **njwékà** 'I tie', which still has the same 'habitual' meaning.)

(13.22) **Sáákwè! ǁ Rúúzè! ǁ** N-gw-ét-í    í=m-bèné   y-à-ní    n-dì
        1SG-have-RS-Fi    AU=9-goat   9-A.M-1SG   1SG-am

    mú=   shwék-à ǁ   ú-lì    mú=    lēng-à ǀ   à-ná-lèngì
    PROG=   tie-Fa    S.R+1-is   PROG=   pass-Fa   1-SQ-PASSING

    té-z-â. ǁ      Kí-mê.
    be.loose-CS-Fa    7-dew

'Riddle! ǁ Ask! ǁ I have my goat (that) I am tying ǁ the one who is passing ǀ lets (it) loose. ǁ Dew.'

### 13.2.1.2 First person, the most common reference

The riddles are most often cast in the first-person form (over 75 percent of the time), and less often are found in the third-person or have a non-personal subject (just under 25 percent). In (13.23) the use of the first-person singular subject is seen in **ngwétì** 'I have'.

(13.23) **Sáákwè!** || **Rúúzè!** || N-gw-ét-í    í=ny-ûmbá   y-à-nî ||
                                   1SG-have-RS-Fi  AU=9-house  9-A.M-1SG

n-zírá      mú-lyángò. ||  Î-i-gì.
9-without   3-door         AU-5-egg

'Riddle! || Ask! || I have my house || without a door. || Egg.'

In (13.24) the verb **nàtùmítà** 'I spear' is in the first-person singular form.

(13.24) **Sáákwè!** || **Rúúzè!** || N-à-tùmít-á |   bú-gálàmà. || Í=shódù.
                                    1SG-P1-spear-Fa  14-on.back   AU=9+grass

'Riddle! || Ask! || I spear | lying down on my back. || Sharp grass.'

In (13.25) the riddle is expressed in the first-person plural, as seen in the 1PL copula **tùlì** 'we are'.

(13.25) **Sáákwè!** || **Rúúzè!** || Tù-lì    kí-húmbì |  tù-lì    mú=    hánd-à
                                    1PL-are  7-thousand   1PL-are  PROG=  rent-Fa

mú=    hí-ny-ûmbà |  hí-nìnììnî. || Ng-é=      kì-bìríítì.
PROG=  19-9-house    19-small       like-AU=   7-match

'Riddle! || Ask! || We are a thousand | and we stay in a house | very small. || Like matches.'

In (13.26) a cl. 10 subject is used in the riddle, even though the answer is marked by cl. 6. Probably cl. 10 is used as a general plural class, so it will not give away the answer. The cl. 10 subject is seen in the verbs **zàyùmà** 'they dry out' and **zìtágánátwánwà** 'and they will not be lit'.

(13.26) **Sáákwè!** || **Rúúzè!** || Z-à-yùm-à |  zì-tá-gá-ná-twàn-w-â.  ||
                                    10-P1-dry-Fa  10-NEG-F2-ADD.V-light.fire-PS-Fa

Á=má-hèmbè |  g-é=         n-gáávù
AU=6-horns    6-A.M+AU=    9-cow

'Riddle! || Ask! || They dry out | and they will not be lit. || The horns | of a cow.'

### 13.2.1.3 *Higher proportionate use of the additive morpheme*

Compared to normal narrative speech, the riddles contain a larger proportion of verbs which contain the additive morpheme. This is seen in (13.27) where the additive **ná** is found in the verb **yó=ngánálèngà** 'that's where I will and pass'. Other examples which include the additive are found in (13.21), (13.26), and (13.30).

(13.27) **Sáákwè!** ‖ **Rúúzè!** ‖ **Í**=n-jírá    bà-lì mú=    ny-èrék-à ‖
                                  AU=9-path  2-are PROG=  O1.SG-show-Fa

   y-ó=    n-gá-**ná**-lèng-à        =mwô. ‖ **Ú**=**mú-dùgà**.
   9-FOC=  1SG-F2-ADD.V-pass-Fa      =18     AU=3-car

'Riddle! ‖ Ask! ‖ The path that they show me ‖ is the one I will also pass through. ‖ Car.'

### 13.2.1.4 nga often introduces answer

In just under a quarter of the riddles, the answer to the riddle is preceded by **nga** 'like'. This may imply the answer is something that was searched for. For example, when one is looking for something on the ground and then spots it, he will say **ngà**=**byébìnô** 'like these very things (which I was looking for)'.

In (13.28) the answer **lúlìmì** 'tongue' is preceded by **nga** 'like'.

(13.28) **Sáákwè!** ‖ **Rúúzè!** ‖ N-gw-ét-í       í-béngá ly-à-nî ‖ mù-lí
                                  1SG-have-RS-Fi  5-pool  5-A.M-1SG  18-is

   í=mòtó       n-gùmà  nààhô. ‖ Ngà=  **lú-lìmì**.
   AU=9+fish    9-one   only      like=  11-tongue

'Riddle! ‖ Ask! ‖ I have my pool ‖ there is only one fish in there. ‖ Like the tongue.'

### 13.2.1.5 Augment sometimes used in the answer

The augment is sometimes used with the noun which states the answer, but that is not necessary. In example (13.28) above, the augment was not included in the answer. (If the augment had been present, the answer would have been **ngó=lúlìmì** 'like the tongue' rather than **ngà=lúlìmì**.) However in (13.29) the augment is used with the noun which is the answer: **ngó=múshákù** 'like the head of hair'. The presence or absence of the augment does not make a difference semantically in the meaning of the answers in (13.28) and (13.29). Thus one concludes that the use of the augment in that context is optional.

(13.29) **Sáákwè!** ‖ **Rúúzè!** ‖ **Kándá-hárùùr-w-â.** ‖ **Ng-ó=** **mú-shákù.**
　　　　　　　　　　　　thing.not-count-PS-Fa　　like-AU=　3-head.of.hair

'Riddle! ‖ Ask! ‖ A thing not counted. ‖ Like a head of hair.'

### 13.2.2 Riddle meaning considerations

Most of the riddles are designed to make one guess what is being described. Quite often an inanimate object is described in animate terms, as if it had personality. In (13.30) the riddle is 'I am going and will not return'. Although this is described in first-person singular animate terms, the answer is actually an inanimate object, 'the river which flows over a rock'.

(13.30) **Sáákwè!** ‖ **Rúúzè!** ‖ **N-dì=**　　**mú=**　　**génd-à** ‖
　　　　　　　　　　　　1SG-am=　　PROG=　　go-Fa

**n-dá-gá-ná-gálùk-à.**　　‖　　**Ú=lw-ìjí**　|　**n-í=**　　**búyè.**
1SG-NEG-F2-ADD.V-return-Fa　　AU=11-river　CNJ-AU=　5+rock

'Riddle! ‖ Ask! ‖ I am going ‖ and I will not return. ‖ A river | with a rock.'

Likewise in (13.31) the inanimate 'sun and moon' are described by the animate terms 'my father and my mother'.

(13.31) **Sáákwè!** ‖ **Rúúzè!** ‖ **Dáátá**　　|　**à-lì**　**mú-káyù** ‖ **nà=**
　　　　　　　　　　　　1a+my.father　1-is　1-fierce　　　CNJ=

**máàwé**　　　**à-lì**　**mú-tùùdù.** ‖ **Í=zùùbá** | **n-ó=**　　**mw-ēzì.**
1a+my.mother　1-is　1-gentle　　　AU=5+sun　CNJ-AU=　3-moon

'Riddle! ‖ Ask! ‖ My father | is fierce ‖ and my mother is gentle. ‖ The sun | and moon.'

# 14

# Reduplication

Reduplication is a rich and pervasive feature of Kifuliiru. It can occur in nouns, verbs, adverbs, adjectives, locative phrases, numbers, associative pronouns,[1] different-set demonstrative pronouns (see 3.5.1.4), and other demonstrative pronouns (see 3.5).

Reduplication is part of a tendency to grammaticize rather than just lexicalize real-world phenomena that reflect time, space, repetition, etc. In line with this tendency, items that are viewed as being repeated in the real world often are represented by reduplicated structures, whether of verbal actions or states, or the same things in a group, the same type of thing, etc. Other meanings of reduplication include extensiveness, emphasis, and pejorative.

Reduplication in Kifuliiru may be either productive or non-productive:

PRODUCTIVE REDUPLICATION is distinguished by two features. First, the reduplicated form has a non-reduplicated equivalent. Secondly, the meaning of the reduplicated form is predictable, given the meaning of the non-reduplicated equivalent. Reduplication is always productive in adjectives, e.g. **bí-nììnì-bínììnì** (8-small-RDP) and numbers, e.g. **gà-bìrì-gàbìrì** (6-two-RDP). It is sometimes productive in verbs, e.g. **à-ná-génd-à-gèndà** (1-SQ-go-Fa-RDP), nouns, e.g. **mú-tèèkó-mútéékò** (3-groups-RDP), and adverbs, e.g. **mú-lîndì-múlîndì** (3-quickly-RDP).

NON-PRODUCTIVE REDUPLICATION involves forms which generally have no non-reduplicated equivalent; if there is a non-reduplicated equivalent, the meaning of the reduplicated whole cannot be deduced from the meaning of the original word.

---

[1] The associative pronouns are forms such as **hāāgè** '(place) of his', **byāābò** '(things) of theirs', etc., which are pronominal forms of an associative phrase, e.g. **há=mwāmì** 'of the king', **byá=bāāmì** 'of the kings', etc.

Non-productive, lexicalized reduplicated forms include most reduplicated nouns, e.g. **kí-yíngí-yíngì** (7-mentally.impaired.person) 'mentally handicapped person (pejorative)', adverbs, e.g. **bw-îjâ-bwîjâ** (14-slowly-RDP) 'slowly', cf. **bw-îjâ** 'well, nicely' and demonstrative pronouns, e.g. **gú-ndí-gúndì** (3-other-RDP) 'other (pejorative)' ('other questionable one'), cf. **gú-ndì** (3-other) 'other'.

## 14.1 Reduplication structural considerations

### 14.1.1 Parts of speech where reduplication occurs

A summary of all parts of speech that exhibit reduplication, together with a representative sample of each, is presented in table 14.1.

Table 14.1. Parts of speech exhibiting reduplication

| Part of speech | Only stem repeated | Entire word/phrase repeated | |
|---|---|---|---|
| Verbs | **tù-bì-y-ìj-í-yîjì** | **n-àná-gênd-à** | **nànágêndà** |
| | 2-O8-know-RS-Fi-RDP | 1SG-SQ-go-Fa | RDP |
| | 'we've always known' | 'I went and went' | |
| Adverbs | **ká-síngé-síngè** | **mú-lîndí** | **múlîndì** |
| | 12-speed-RDP | 3-quickly | RDP |
| | 'quickly' | 'in a very big hurry' | |
| Nouns | **ká-shánwé-shánwè** | **n-dèèkó** | **ndēēkò** |
| | 12-pinky-RDP | 9-group | RDP |
| | 'pinky finger' | 'one group at a time' | |
| Adjectives | | **má-núnù** | **mànùnû** |
| | | 6-sweet | RDP |
| | | 'all of them sweet' | |
| Locative phrases | | **kú=n-góókólò** | **kú=ngóókólò** |
| | | 17-9-shore | RDP |
| | | '(keeping going) along the shore' | |
| Numbers | | **zì-bìrì** | **zìbìrì** |
| | | 10-two | RDP |
| | | 'two by two (or price of two each)' | |
| Associative pronouns | | **hà-à-gé** | **hàágè** |
| | | 16-A.M-1 | RDP |
| | | 'his own unique place' | |

## 14.1 Reduplication structural considerations

| Part of speech | Only stem repeated | Entire word/phrase repeated | |
|---|---|---|---|
| Different-set demonstrative pronouns | | **kú-ndí** | **kúndì** |
| | | 15-other | RDP |
| | | 'another kind (contrary to norm)' | |
| Demonstrative pronouns | | **gwó-gù-lyá** | **gwógùlyâ** |
| | | E-3-that.R | RDP |
| | | 'that very one' | |

Table 14.1 presents two types of reduplication: first (in the middle column) where only the stem is repeated (excluding prefixes), and second (in the right-hand column) where the entire word or phrase is repeated (including prefixes).

- The pattern in which only the stem is repeated, and the prefixes or clitics occur only once is observed in nouns which have been lexicalized as reduplicated items, in many reduplicated verbs, and in most adverbs.[2] An example of a noun which demonstrates this pattern is the cl. 7 **kíngóró-ngórò** 'coin', in which only the stem **ngórò** is repeated, and not the cl. 7 prefix **kí-**. Since this is a lexicalized form, there is no synchronic form *__kíngóró__. Verbs, on the other hand, always have a non-reduplicated equivalent, e.g. -**símbá-símbá** 'to jump around' is derived from the unreduplicated form -**símb-** 'to jump'.
- The pattern in which the entire word or phrase is repeated, including prefix(es) and stem(s), as well as any phrase-internal clitics, is found in all reduplicated adjectives, locative phrases, numbers, associative pronouns, different-set pronouns, and demonstrative pronouns. It also pertains to some reduplication in verbs, adverbs, and non-lexicalized nouns.

Any locative clitics following a reduplicated verb stem are added following reduplication, and thus not repeated. In (14.1) the verb base -**géndá-géndà** 'going, going' is reduplicated, while the attached locative clitic **mwô** 'in there' is not repeated.

---

[2]In the cases where the reduplicated word has been lexicalized, there may be no more than one long vowel in the entire word, e.g. **kíngóró-ngórò** is phonetically **kíngóróóngórò**. In cases where the reduplication is productive, both sections retain any original vowel length found in the unreduplicated form, e.g. **kúsímbà-símbà** is phonetically **kúsíímbá-síímbà**, and **kúgéndá-géndà** is **kúgééndá-gééndà**.

(14.1) Ø-Lól-àg-í!    || sì=   n-gòlí        bw-ìn-ì     mw-á=   bá-ndú
      IMP.P-look-EMP-Fi   OBV=  1-be.NEWLY    see-RS-Fi   18+AU=  2-people

bá-ná ||   bà-gwétí   bà-gá-génd-à-géndà       =mwò.
2-four     2-PROG     2-INTL-go-Fa-RDP         =18

'Look! || It's obvious I now see four people in there || they are moving around in there.' (Dan 3:25)

Any verbal extensions[3], however, are repeated in reduplication, since they are part of the verb stem. Thus in (14.2) the applicative extension -er is repeated along with the verb root -**shék**- 'laugh'.

(14.2) **Návyàlà**   || à-ná-yàmì    bwír-á   ú=mú-kwî       | kw-â=
      1a+mother-in-law   1-SQ-IMMED   tell-Fa   AU=1-son.in.law   CMP-1=

Ø-mú-bwìr-è ||  bí-kí     by-â=    lì    mú=    shék-ér-á-shékérà.
SBV-O1-tell-Fe   8-what   8-O.R+1=   is   PROG=   laugh-APL-Fa-RDP

'Mother-in-law || immediately told son-in-law | to tell her || what he is laughing about.' (502 032)

## 14.1.2 Two phonological constraints affecting reduplication

Firstly, single syllable CV roots may be not be reduplicated without also repeating the prefix. For example, in the noun **búlàà-bùlà** 'length', the cl. 14 prefix **bú-** must be repeated as well as the stem -**la**. Thus *búlàà-là is not an option. Other examples, are the cl. 14 adverb **búshàà-bùshà** 'worthless' (cf. **búshâ** 'empty, bare, free') and the cl. 12 **káré-kárê** 'early in the morning'.

It should be noted however, that this constraint does not apply to single syllable stems if they contain a glide (CyV) or (CwV). Stems of this shape may be reduplicated without repeating their prefix, e.g. **búlyâ-lyà** 'deceitfulness', **hí-hwâ-hwà** 'thin person', and **búhwé-hwè** 'whispering'.

Secondly, when a prefix is phonologically part of the first syllable of the reduplicated stem, that prefix must be reduplicated along with the stem, regardless of the length of the stem. A first-person singular object prefix N- or a cl. 9/10 noun prefix N- is always a phonological part of the syllable to which it belongs, because these morphemes consist only of a non-syllabic nasal. For this reason, in the verb **ú=kú-m-bìr-á-mbírà** (AU=15-O1. SG-call-Fa-RDP) 'to call *me*, call *me*', the first-person singular prefix **m-** is repeated in the reduplicated verb stem. Compare this with the lack of repetition of the CV- cl. 3 object prefix **gù-** in **à-ná-gù-góny-à-gònyà**

---
[3] Extension is the term commonly used for non-final, semantically definable derivational verbal suffixes in Bantu languages.

(1-SQ-O3-fold-Fa-RDP) 'and she folded, folded *it*'. Two similar examples, the noun **lúmbèhó-mbéhò** 'timid person' in which the root of the stem is N-**hēhò** (9-cold), and the adverb **ká-ngálí-ngálì** (14-backwards-RDP), cf. **lúgálì** (11-flat.on.back) (Adv).

### 14.1.3 Reduplicating only part of the stem

There is extensive partial reduplication in the lexicon, in which a single syllable is repeated within a stem. This is especially common in verbs: e.g. -**gógombek**- 'intrude, forcefully enter', -**gòlolomb**- '(water) flow, trickle'. In many cases, there have been phonological changes, such as loss of prenasalization preceding another prenasalized segment, which altered the segments and obscured the presence of reduplication. An example is the lack of prenasalization in the initial syllable of -**gòngobok**- 'be thin from lack of food'. Lexicalized reduplication of a single syllable is also evident in some nouns, e.g. **í=íháhà** 'a person on last breaths'. In all such cases of submorphemic single syllable reduplication, there is no corresponding unreduplicated form. To discuss all of these sublexical frozen reduplications is beyond our scope here. Only lexical-level reduplication is treated here.

## 14.2 Functions of reduplication

The various meanings of Kifuliiru reduplication can all be subsumed under four major categories: repetition, extensiveness (or lack of it), emphasis, and pejorative. The first three meanings all iconically reflect the "repeated" nature of reduplication. The fourth meaning, pejorative, though not having an inherent relation to reduplication, is nevertheless very common in the language.

### 14.2.1 Repetition

#### 14.2.1.1 Repeated action in dynamic verbs

REPEATED action is often expressed by reduplicated verbs. Virtually any dynamic verb stem can be productively reduplicated. The most basic meaning of Kifuliiru reduplication is iteration (the same semantic concept repeated). But it can also subsume the related meanings of 'continual' or 'habitual'.

In (14.3) ITERATIVE action, i.e. repeated, is seen in the verb -**buuza-buuza** 'ask, ask (repeatedly)' (from -**buuz**- 'ask'). In this case, the king's workers went into the village looking for information, repeating their question each time they encountered children.

(14.3) Á=bá-ndú | á-bá-àlí  kìzí  kòl-á  yà-hó  í=  bw-àmì ||
AU=2-people  S.R-2-P3  REP  work-Fa  there.N-16  23=  14-kingdom

bà-ná-gênd-à  bá-gá-bùùz-à-bùùzá |  á=bà-ànà  mú=  kā-āyà.
2-SQ-GOING-Fa  2-INTL-ask-Fa-RDP  AU=2-children  18=  12-village

'The people | who worked there at the king's place || went asking asking | the children in the village.' (22 015)

In (14.4) the same action is repeated with a CONTINUAL connotation. The verb base -**zùrumb**- 'buzz around', when reduplicated to -**zùrumba-zurumba** 'buzz, buzz' has the predictable meaning of 'buzzing around and around'. In this example a bee is speaking, and tells the young man to watch carefully: whichever lady the bee goes buzzing (continually) around her head, that's the one who is to be his wife.

(14.4) Ù-Ø-lóléékéz-é  ngíìsì  y-é=  n-gá-zùrùmb-à-zùrùmbà
2SG-SBV-look.well-Fe  whoever  1-O.R=  1-F2-buzz.around-Fa-RDP

kw-î=  twê ||  ù-ná-mú-gwàt-ìr-è  kú=  kú-bōkò |  ìrí
17-5=  head  2SG-CON-O1-grab-APL-Fe  17=  15-hand  thats.when

mù-ká-à-wè.
1-wife-A.M-2SG

'Watch carefully whichever one I buzz buzz around at the head || you grab her by the hand | that's the one who is your wife.' (36 050)

In (14.5) there is repeated action with a HABITUAL connotation. The verb base -**huun**- 'request', when reduplicated to -**huuna-huuna** 'ask-ask' has the predictable meaning of 'requesting habitually (or begging)'. The sentence depicts the character Kokobola starting to beg food from his neighbors, something that was repeated on a habitual basis.

(14.5) Ùyó  Kókòbòlâ ||  à-ná-tòndééz-à  ú=kú-génd-á |
that.N+1  Kokobola  1-SQ-began-Fa  AU=15-GOING-Fa

á-gá-hùùn-à-hùùná  í=by-ókúlyá |  mú=  n-yûmbà |  z-á=
1-INTL-ask-Fa-RDP  AU=8-food  18=  10-houses  10-A.M+AU=

bá-túúlání  bà-à-gè.
2-neighbors  2-A.M-1

'That Kokobola || began to go | begging, begging food | from among the houses | of his neighbors.' (40 023)

## 14.2 Functions of reduplication

In (14.6) we present further examples of some of the reduplicated dynamic (action) verbs (here including only verb stems beginning with **b** through **h** as found in fifty-six texts). This subset gives an idea of the widespread nature of reduplication in verbs.

(14.6) 

| Reduplicated verb stems | Gloss |
|---|---|
| -**bàlanduka-balanduka** | 'roll over and over' |
| -**bànga-banga** | 'keep lying about something' |
| -**bùnda-bunda** | 'sneak along hiding, crawl along in underbrush' |
| -**bùka-buka** | 'nurse along' |
| -**buuza-buuza** | 'keep asking' |
| -**bùya-buya** | 'delay, not knowing what to do, where to go' |
| -**bwànda-bwanda** | 'pace around and around' |
| -**daaya-daaya** | 'keep stepping or acting carefully, purposefully' |
| -**dèta-deta** | 'keep talking' |
| -**dòza-doza** | 'keep badgering someone to make them angry' |
| -**dwira-dwira** | 'fast-talk, trying to get out of an unpleasant situation' |
| -**gaaya-gaaya** | 'writhe in pain, not be able to get comfortable because of pain' |
| -**gèhya-gehya** | 'lurk around spying on someone or some place' |
| -**génda-genda** | 'keep going' |
| -**génga-genga** | 'be nosy' |
| -**gónya-gonya** | 'fold repeatedly' |
| -**gúmya-gúmya** | 'persevere in difficulty, keep steeling oneself' |
| -**gùga-guga** | 'keep gathering' |
| -**gùsha-gusha** | 'gather something together' |
| -**gwata-gwata** | 'keep grabbing things' |
| -**haasa-haasa** | 'keep stubbornly trying what is impossible' |
| -**heema-heema** | 'resent something and keep complaining' |
| -**héra-hera** | 'keep touching; attend to, care for' |
| -**hínda-hinda** | 'circle around and around' |

### 14.2.1.2 *Same referent repeated: Nouns, adjectives*

Reduplication in nouns and adjectives is commonly employed for items of the same kind occurring in succession, or in groups.

In (14.7) the reduplicated noun **mwémbé-mwémbè** 'mango, mango' (cf. **mwémbè** 'mango') indicates items of the same kind successively acted upon in the same way. In this case there are multiple mangoes given out, one at a time, one to each worker.

(14.7) À-ná-kìzí hééréz-á   ngíìsì mú-kòzì |   mw-émbé-mwémbè |   gírà
     1-SQ-REP   gave-Fa    each  1-worker   3-mango-RDP   so.that

     bà-Ø-dátúùl-è |   mw-á=   má-tê.
     2-SBV-suck.out-Fe  18-AU=  6-saliva

'And he gave each worker | a mango | in order that they suck out | from it saliva (wet their mouths with it.)' (520 062)

In (14.8) the noun **mábéngà** 'ponds' is reduplicated to **mábéngá-mábéngà** 'ponds of the same type, in the same situation'. The assertion is that in the time of heavy rains, there are repeated occurrences of pools of standing water (here and there).

(14.8) N-é=   ky-ànyà |   ky-á=   má-hònànvùlà || lì-Ø-ná-b-é |
     CNJ-AU=  7-time   7-A.M+AU=  6-dropping.rain  5-SBV-ADD.V-is-Fe

     mw-á=   má-béngá-mábéngà.
     18-AU=  6-ponds-RDP

'And at the time | of the rains || there would be | ponds all over in there.' (Psa 83:6)

In (14.9) the word **kíshùngù-shùngù** 'thicket' seems to underscore the multiplicity of plants that grow together in a thicket.

(14.9) ìyó   m-bóngó | y-áàlí tùùz-ír-í   mú=   ká-bándá ká-gùmá kí-ìjâ |
     that.N+9  9-gazelle  9-P3  live-RS-Fi  18=  12-valley 12-one 12-good

     ká-àlí rì-ìr-í |   n-é=   kí-shùngù-shùngú || ky-é=   bí-tí |
     12-P3  is-RS-Fi  CNJ-AU=  7-thicket-RDP   7-A.M+AU=  8-tree

     by-é=   mì-mbátì.
     8-A.M+AU=  4-cassava

'That gazelle | was living in a certain nice valley | it (valley) had | a thicket || of trees | of cassava.' (10 003)

## 14.2 Functions of reduplication

In (14.10) the reduplicated substantive adjective **hínììnì-hínììnì** 'little bit, little bit' reflects the fact that the cutter was cutting multiple bits of meat, each of which was small.

(14.10) Ùyó    mú-shìshúzí || à-ná-kìzí   shìsh-á | <u>hí-nììnì-hínììnì</u>.
that.N+1  1-cutter.of.bits  1-SQ-REP  cut-Fa  19-small-RDP

'That cutter || repeatedly cut | little by little.' (614-005)

In (14.11) the reduplicated adjective **mákáyù-màkàyù** 'fierce, fierce', modifying troubles, indicates that each of the troubles will be severe.

(14.11) **Ù-Ø-mény-è**    **bw-îjá** || **kwò**=  **mú**=  **sìkù**  **z-é**=  **m-bèrúúkà** ||
2SG-SBV-know-Fe  14-good  CMP=  18=  days  10-AU=  19-very.last

**há-gáà-b-à**    **á=má-líbú** |  <u>**má-káyù-mákáyù**</u>.
16-F2-be-Fa  AU=6-distress  6-severe-RDP

'Know well || that in the last days || there will be troubles | severe.' (2Ti 3:1)

The meaning of multiple like items or like sets of items is also found in reduplicated quantifiers. The reduplication of a quantifier signifies that the repeated groups are of the same type, and each consists of the same number of items.

In (14.12) each of the children jumps, one at a time. This is expressed by the reduplicated **múgùmà-múgùmà** 'one, one' or 'one at a time'.

(14.12) **Bó-óshì** || **bà-ná-kìzí símbúk-á** | <u>**mú-gùmà-múgùmà**</u> || **à-ná-kìzí**
2-all    2-SQ-REP  jump-Fa  1-one-RDP    1-SQ-REP

**bà-sám-á** |  **ìrí**  **à-ná-bà-tèrék-éz-á** |  **hààshì**.
O2-catch-Fa  while  1-SQ-O2-placing-INTS-Fa  on.ground

'All of them || repeatedly jumped | one at a time || and he repeatedly caught them | while putting them | on the ground.' (32 040)

In (14.13) we present a chart of more examples where reduplication signifies items of the same kind in the same circumstances, either in succession, or in a group.

(14.13) Reduplication indicating repetition, similar items

| | Reduplicated form | Gloss |
|---|---|---|
| Groups | **mìhízá-mìhízà** | 'groups coming at different times' |
| | **bííró-bíírò** | 'bunches of the same type' |
| | **ndèèkó-ndēēkò** | 'groups of the same type of thing' |
| | **bígùgù-bígùgù** | 'crowds of the same type' |
| | **mábéngá-mábéngà** | 'ponds of the same type' |
| Quantities | **múgùmà-múgùmà** | 'one at a time' |
| | **zìbìrì-zìbìrì** | 'two at a time' |
| | **mákùmì gàshàtù-gàshàtù** | '30 at a time' |
| | **mákùmì gàlíndàtù-gàlíndàtù** | '60 at a time' |
| | **íígáná-íígánà** | '100 at a time' |
| Qualities | **hínììnì-hínììnì** | 'small, small' |
| | **mákáyú-mákáyù** | 'fierce, fierce' |
| | **bíkùlù-bíkùlù** | 'great, great (things)' |
| Body parts | **bígèrè-gèrè** | 'ankle or wrist joint (repeated movements)' |
| Sights and sounds | **kíkòrò-kòrò** | 'windpipe (repeated breaths)' |
| | **bùhwé-hwè** | 'whisper' |
| | **mútèèrà-tèèrà** | 'small flute' (repeated noise) |
| | **lúnyèzí-nyèzì** | 'something sparkling' (repeated light) |
| Spotted/speckled | **bútòbèké-bútòbèkê** | 'speckled' (animals, house etc.) |
| | **ndòbé-ndòbê** | 'speckled sheep or goat' (repeated spots) |
| | **bùjéré-jérè** | 'speckled sheep or goat' (repeated spots) |

## 14.2.2 Extensiveness (or the lack of it)

Reduplication can indicate extensiveness or, for nouns in the diminutive class, the lack of it.

### 14.2.2.1 Enduring state in a closed set of stative verbs

The reduplication of six stative verbs implies the meaning 'always'. In some cases there is a strong implication that there was never a time when any other state was in effect. These stative verbs include various resultative forms (RS), and are all listed in (14.14).

(14.14) Reduplicated stative verbs

| Unredup form | Gloss | Reduplicated form | Gloss |
|---|---|---|---|
| **-ri-ir-i** | 'be' (RS of **-li** 'be') | **-riiri-riiri** | 'always being' |
| **-kòla** | 'be now, not before' | **-kòla-kola** | 'always being (before present)' |
| **-yàm-ir-i** | 'endure' (RS of **-yàma** 'always be') | **-yàmiri-yamiri** | 'always enduring' |
| **-mény-a** | 'know' | **-ménya-menya** | 'always knowing' |
| **-y-ìj-i** | 'know' (RS of **-mény-** 'know') | **-yìji-yiji** | 'always knowing' |
| **-h-iit-i** | 'have' (RS of **-h-** 'give') | **-hiiti-hiiti** | 'always having' |

In (14.15) the use of the reduplicated copula **-riiri-riiri** implies that the referents' deeds were always bad, and by implication never good.

(14.15) **Í**=**mí-kòlèzí**   **y-à-bò** ‖   **y-áàlí**       <u>**rì-ìr-ì-ríírí**</u>      **mí-bì.**
  AU=4-works      4-A.M-2       4-P3              is-RS-Fi-RDP              4-bad

  'Their deeds ‖ were (always) bad.' (Jhn 3:19)

The verb base **-mény-** 'know' has an irregular resultative form **-yìji**. When reduplicated, both involve an emphatic meaning communicating that something is known for certain. This is exemplified in (14.16), where the speakers are contending that they know well all the things they are saying.

(14.16) **Yí-bì**   ‖ **by-ó**=  **tù-gwétí**    **tú-gáá-dèt-à**    ‖
  these.P-8  8-O.R=  1PL-PROG    1PL-INTL-speak-Fa

  <u>**tù-bì-yìj-í-yījì.**</u>
  1PL-O8-know+RS-Fi-RDP

  'These things ‖ which we are speaking about ‖ we know them well.' (Jhn 3:11)

In (14.17) the reduplicated verb **àbìményà-mènyà** 'he knew them completely' along with the preceding auxiliaries **áàlì málí gwánwá** 'he had already been encountered' (i.e. with foreknowledge) implies that 'he always knew them (and there was never a time when he did not)'.

(14.17) Hà= n-yúmá     Yêsù | à-ná-tāng-w-à       í=mw-ìnyù ‖ ngá= kwó=
16=  9-behind   Jesus  1-SQ-offer-PS-Fa   23=CON-2PL   like= that=

Rúrémá | á-àlí málí    gwánw-á         | <u>à-bì-mény-à-mènyà</u>.
God     1-P3  ALREADY ENCOUNTERED-Fa   1-O8-know-Fa-RDP

'Afterwards Jesus | was delivered to you ‖ just as God | had already been encountered | knowing would happen.' (Act 2:23)

### 14.2.2.2 Reduplication in nouns expressing extended length

Reduplication is often used to indicate extension in objects, including long things, tall things, and deep things. It includes the words for length, width, etc., as in (14.18).

(14.18) Reduplication in nouns expressing extended length

| Reduplicated form | Gloss |
|---|---|
| **búlàà-bùlà** | 'length' |
| **bútàmbì-tàmbì** | 'width, side to side' |
| **kálàmbà-làmbà** | 'long thin thing' |
| **kánywángí-nywángì** | 'very tall thing' |
| **káshùngù-shùngù** | 'very tall thing' |
| **kírímbí-rímbì** | 'a very deep pit' |
| **lírà-lìrà** | 'quite long' |
| **kálándó-lándò** | 'tall, long thing' |
| **kíshàngé-shāngè** | 'a type of tall tree' |
| **múbàngà-bàngà** | 'a type of large fish' |

In (14.19) the phrase **kánywàngì-nywàngì kó=múgāzì** can be literally translated 'very tall thing of a mountain'.[4]

---

[4] Kifuliiru has a whole set of "expressive" nouns which denote qualities of size, character, etc., e.g. **kánywàngì-nwyàngí ké'nyûmbà** 'a very tall thing of a house', **kánywàngì-nywàngí ké'kítì** 'a very tall thing of a tree', etc. This is similar to the way English uses "a giant of a man", "a monster of a fish", "a doozy of a headache", etc. except that in Kifuliiru the expressive nouns are not used without a following associative phrase telling what the noun is describing. Several of these "expressive" nouns involve reduplication.

## 14.2 Functions of reduplication

(14.19) À-ná-mú-twâl-à | kú= ká-nywàngì-nywàngí | k-ó=
1-SQ-O1-take-Fa    17    12-tall.thing-RDP    12-A.M+AU=

mú-gāzì.
3-mountain

'And he took him | up a tall thing | of a mountain.' (Mat 4:8)

#### 14.2.2.3 Reduplication in nouns expressing extended conditions

In (14.20) we see a list of conditions that could be assumed to be extended, such as light,[5] darkness, sounds, and emotions.

(14.20) Reduplication in nouns expressing extended conditions

| Category | Reduplicated form | Gloss |
|---|---|---|
| Light | kírùgú-rūūgù | 'time of hot sun' |
|  | kálèngé-rēngè | 'noon' |
|  | ú=múlègè-règè | 'daylight hours' |
|  | káré-kárê | 'very early in the morning' |
| Darkness | káhúúná-húùnà | 'dusk' |
|  | lúhúúná-húùnà | 'dusk' |
|  | hìmbùzá-mbúzà | 'just before dawn, while still dark' |
| Sound | múvùgù-vùgù | 'sound made by a thing thrown' |
| Emotions | mágèngé-gēngè | 'joy' |
| Other | káhóndó-hóndò | 'deep sleep' |
|  | kítóngò-tóngò | 'place of very rich soil' |
|  | búlèmbè-rèmbè | 'full to the brim' |
|  | kítùkú-tūkù | 'purple' |

#### 14.2.2.4 Reduplication in nouns expressing diminutive

In (14.21) we see some reduplicated nouns which have a diminutive connotation. Perhaps this reflects the tendency for these items to be found repeated in groups of like kind.

---

[5] When a Mufuliiru wants to tell you that the headlights of your car are on during the daylight, he will open and shut his hand repeatedly. This seems to reflect the idea that light is something viewed as repeated or prolonged.

(14.21) Reduplication in nouns expressing diminutive

| Reduplicated form | Gloss |
|---|---|
| í=kíngóró-ngórò | 'coin' |
| híjéré-jérè | 'very small specks' |
| ú=túlèmbé-rêmbê | 'small birds' |
| káshánwé-shánwè | 'pinky finger' |
| mbágá-mbágà | 'small sheep ear' |

### 14.2.2.5 Reduplication in adverbs expressing great many

Some reduplicated adverbs which express the idea of "very many" or "in great numbers" are given in (14.22). These are derived from verbs, as shown, and have no unreduplicated equivalent.

(14.22) Reduplication expressing large amounts

| Reduplicated adverb | Gloss | Cf. verb base | Gloss |
|---|---|---|---|
| **dwàvwé-dwàvwè** | 'very many' | -dwàng- | 'to mix together, |
| **yòndó-yōndò** | 'many, many" | -yòndolok- | 'be great many' |
| **ngàndá-ngàndà** | 'very many' | -kànd- | 'press down' |

In (14.23) **yòndó-yōndò** 'in great numbers' refers to an especially good catch of fish.

(14.23) Î-fwí    z-à-fw-á    yòndó-yōndò.
      10-fish  10-P1-die-Fa  in.great.numbers-RDP

'The fish have died in great numbers.'

### 14.2.2.6 Reduplication in adverbs expressing speed (or lack of it)

The reduplication of many adverbs of motion express speed or the lack of it.

## 14.2 Functions of reduplication

(14.24) Reduplication in adverbs expressing speed (or lack of it)

| Category | Reduplicated adverb | Gloss | Compare | Gloss |
|---|---|---|---|---|
| Quickly | **dúbà-dúbà** | 'quickly' | **dúbà** | 'quickly' |
| | **kángúbí-ngúbì** | 'in a hurry' | **-kúbiriz-** | 'do quickly' |
| | **múlîndì-múlîndì** | 'fast' | **múlîndì** | 'quickly, fast' |
| | **dúgùlì-dúgùlì** | 'a quick pace' | **dúgù-dúgù** | 'sound of liquid pouring out' |
| Slowly | **bwîjâ-bwîjâ** | 'slowly, carefully' | **bwîjâ** | 'well' |
| | **lújóbé-jóbè** | 'slowly in shame' | **-jòjober-** | 'walk in shame' |
| | **lútóó-lútô** | 'follow furtively' | **-yìtónd-** | 'be careful' |
| | **búhòlò-búhòlò** | 'gently-gently' | **búhòlò** | 'weakness' |
| | **kírámú-kírámù** | 'occasionally' | **kírámúkò** | 'once in a while' |

#### 14.2.2.7 *Extension of various kinds:* **kwìngì** 'different varieties'

When **-ìngì** 'many' is used with the cl. 15 **kú-** prefix, as in **íbírúgú byá=kwìngì** 'vessels of many (different kinds)', it has the meaning of 'several different varieties' of the same basic concept or item. In its reduplicated form, **kwìngí-kwìngì**, the multiplicity of varieties is emphasized: **málwàzí gá=kwìngí-kwìngì** 'sicknesses of many, many different kinds'.

### 14.2.3 Reduplication expressing emphasis

The emphatic demonstrative pronouns, in their non-reduplicated form have the emphatic meaning 'those same ones, in contrast to any other possibility'. The reduplication of these pronouns puts even further emphasis on the fact that the referent of the pronoun has exactly the same identity as one which was mentioned before.

In (14.25), by describing the number of bricks using the reduplicated version of the emphatic remote demonstrative pronoun, **gwógùlyá-gwógùlyâ** 'that very same', the speaker is placing special emphasis on the fact that the number had to remain exactly the same as before.

(14.25) **Bwó**= yà-bá bá-ndú | bà-lí bò-òló bwènèènè || ú=mú-hárúúró
since= these.P-2 2-people 2-is 2-lazy very.much AU=3-count

gw-á= má-tàfààlì || gù-Ø-yám-é | gù-lì **gwó-gù-lyá** |
3-A.M+AU= 6-bricks 3-SBV-remain-Fe 3-is E-3-that.R

**gwógùlyà.**
RDP

'Since these people | are very lazy || the count of bricks || must remain | that very same | very same (count).' (Exo 5:8)

In (14.26) the reduplicated emphatic demonstrative **lyêryó-lyêryô** 'right then, at that very same time' is used adverbially to put extra emphasis on the fact that the leopard comes at the precise moment when the gazelle is talking about him.

(14.26) **Lyêryò-lyêryò** | ùyó mú-lágúzí || à-ná-bòn-à í=n-gwí |
right.then-RDP that.N+1 1-fortune.teller 1-SQ-see-Fa AU=9-leopard

y-à-yíj-à || à-ná-gì-bwír-à: || «Ù-yì-bìsh-é dúbà.»
9-P1-come-Fa 1-SQ-O9-tell-Fa 2SG-RFX-hide-Fe quickly

'Right then | that witch || saw a leopard | coming || and he told it (gazelle): || «Hide yourself quickly!»' (10 011)

In (14.27) the use of the reduplicated form **léèrò-léèrò** 'this time, emphasized' shows that things are really serious. In its unreduplicated form **léèrò** means 'this time, as opposed to previous times'.

(14.27) **Léèrò-léèrò** || kút-àgi n-àmú= gír-à? || Ú=mw-éná
this.time-RDP what-EMP 1SG-F1= do-Fa AU=3-hunger

gú-gá-n-yìt-ìr-á | á=bā-ānà.
3-F2-O1.SG-kill-APL-Fa AU=2-children

'This time || what am I about to do? || Hunger will kill (to me) | the children.' (56 007)

In (14.28) the adverb **ngànà** 'really' can be reduplicated as **ngàná-ngànà** 'really, really', to emphasize the speaker's strong opinion on the truth of the preceding predication.

## 14.2 Functions of reduplication

(14.28) À-lí ng-í= zùùbá **ngàná-ngànà**.
1-is like-AU+5= sun really-RDP

'She is like the sun really really.' (106 016)

### 14.2.4 Reduplication (usually) expressing pejorative

Reduplication is sometimes used to express a pejorative connotation.

#### 14.2.4.1 Reduplicated nouns

There are many, many Kifuliiru nouns with reduplication of the stem which have a pejorative connotation. In (14.29) the reduplicated noun **kímbìrí-mbìrì** 'headless body' has pejorative connotations.

(14.29) À-ná-húmààn-án-á | î=twé | lí-zírá | kí-mbìrí-mbìrì ||
1-SQ-encounter-RCP-Fa AU=5-head 5-without 7-headless.body-RDP

à-ná-lì-shúlìk-á | kw-é= n-góní.
1-SQ-O5-hit-Fa 17-AU= 9-stick

'And he came across | a head | without a body || and he hit it | with a stick.' (503 010)

In (14.30) we see a fairly extensive list of reduplicated nouns (and a few substantive adjectives) taken from our texts. Most of these denote character traits or ongoing states with a pejorative connotation.

(14.30) Reduplication expressing ongoing conditions or traits (usually pejorative)

| Reduplicated form | Gloss |
|---|---|
| bítwì-twî | 'deaf person' (cf. kú-twīrì 'ear') |
| búlèngú-lēngù | 'frivolity, passing the time' |
| búlyâ-lyà | 'trickiness, deception' |
| búngísí-ngísì | 'hesitancy' |
| búngólwé-ngólwè | 'weakness' |
| búshà-búshà | 'worthlessness, emptiness' |
| búyíngí-yíngì | 'foolishness' |
| gòbwé-gòbwé | 'danger' |
| hípéré-pérè | 'lazy idler, loitering riff-raff' |
| híhwâ-hwà | 'very thin person' |
| káhímwé-hímwè | 'lack of effort, half-heartedness' |

| Reduplicated form | Gloss |
|---|---|
| káhólé-hôlé | 'soft spot in infant's skull' |
| kanjígí-njígì | 'slowpoke, person who doesn't hurry' |
| kímbálá-mbálà | 'depravity' |
| kímbìrí-mbìrì | 'headless body' |
| kíngányá-ngányà | 'deformed, misshapen person' |
| kíngíshó-ngíshò | 'unknown creature, monster' |
| kíngòlé-ngōlè | 'smell of burned food (overcooked till burnt)' |
| kípàrà-pàrà | 'mischievous person, troublemaker' |
| kíshámbà-shámbà | 'good for nothing, empty' |
| kíyíngí-yíngì | 'mentally impaired person' |
| lúléhè-rèhè | 'craving' |
| lúmbèhó-mbéhò | 'reserved, reticent' |
| lújándì-jándì | 'insignificance, triviality, unimportance' |
| lútyôgò-tyôgò | 'meaningless pledges' |
| mákùbì-kùbì | 'contending for something not your right' |
| málàngù-làngù | 'luke-warm water, or very weak beer' |
| mánjòká-njòkà | 'snake venom; (cf. **mújōkà** 'snake') |
| mbúzí-mbūzì | 'hesitancy, fearing possible bad consequences' |
| múdààlí-dāālì | 'quarrelsome person' |
| múngátá-ngátà | 'one sick for many days' |
| ngùmbí-ngùmbì | 'with nothing at all' |
| njwègé-njwēgè | 'much noise and commotion' |

#### 14.2.4.2 Reduplicated pronouns

The reduplication of the associative pronoun communicates the pejorative nature of a *difference*, most often an undesired non-conformity. (The associative pronoun in its non-reduplicated form expresses an association of one antecedent with another, e.g. **íí=nyúmá lyàgè** 'behind of him', **í=bíndú byàgè** 'the things of him'.) When reduplicated, these pronouns always carry the emphatic meaning of 'own unique things, distinct from others'.

In (14.31) the associative pronoun **háágè** 'at his place' occurs in its reduplicated form **háágé-hāāgè** 'at his own distinct place (as opposed to the places of others)'.

(14.31) **Ngíìsì mú-gùmà** || **à-ná-gêndì**   **yùbák-á** || **hà-à-gé-hāāgè**.
      Each  1-one       1-SQ-GOING  build-Fa  16-A.M-1-RDP

'And each one || went and built || at his own separate place.' (02 023)

In (14.32) the reduplicated associative pronoun **byágé-byāgè** 'his own unique things' has a clearly pejorative implication, implying that someone is off doing his own thing, rather than fulfilling expectations as a normal member of the group.

(14.32) **À-lì  mú=    gír-á  by-á-gè-byàgè** ||  **mù=kúbá  à-tá-lì    mú=**
      1-is   PROG=  do-Fa  8-A.M-1-RDP      because    1-NEG-is  PROG=

      **lóóz-á** |    **kw-â=**    **hánúùlwè**.
      want-Fa    CMP-1=   SBV-advise-PS-Fe

'He does his own things (in his own way) || because he does not want | to be advised.' (53 003)

### 14.2.4.3 Reduplicated demonstratives

The different-set demonstrative pronoun, **-ndi** 'other', when reduplicated, always has the pejorative connotation of 'different, not within the expected norm'.

In (14.33) the reduplicated cl. 9 different-set pronoun **gîndì-gîndì** 'another-another' emphasizes that one cow takes a different path not followed by the others. The result of this foolish behavior is that the cow gets lost, while the rest of the cows are able to return home.

(14.33) **Y-àná-gwât-à  gî-ndì-gîndì  n-jírà** ||  **y-àná-téér-ék-à** ||
      9-SQ-take-Fa    9-other-RDP   9-path     9-SQ-get.lost-NEU-Fa

      **í=zá-àbò**     ||   **z-àná-tááh-à**.
      AU=10-SAME.SET   10-SQ-go.home-Fa

'And it (Cow) took another (different) path || and it got lost || and its fellows || returned home.' (11 005)

In (14.34) **kúndí-kūndì** 'other-other' contrasts with **kwábò-kwábò** 'their own distinct way' earlier in the sentence. Again the yelling is put in a pejorative light.

(14.34) **Bá-gùmà** | bà-ná-kìzí yàmíz-á kw-à-bò-kwábò || n-á= bà-ndí |
  2-ones  2-SQ-REP  yell-Fa  15-A.M-2-RDP  CNJ-AU= 2-others

**kù-ndì-kúndì.**
15-other-RDP

'Some | were repeatedly yelling in their own unique way || and others | in a different (sort of way).' (Act 19:32)

### 14.2.4.4 Reduplicated adjectives

Reduplication of adjectives sometimes carries a pejorative meaning. This often seems to be the case with the reduplicated form of -**ìngì** 'many', which can carry the pejorative connotation of things being too many. In (14.35) the use of the reduplicated quantifier **bìngí-bìngì** '(too) many' refers to 'too many doctors'.

(14.35) **Ùyó** mú-kàzí | á-àlí màlí lìbúúk-á bwènèèné | mù=
  that.N+1 1-woman  1-P3  ALREADY  distressed-Fa  very.much  18=

**kú-bùk-w-â** | ná= bá-fùmú **bì-ngí-bìngì**.
15-treat-PS-Fa CNJ= 2-doctors 2-many-RDP

'That woman | had suffered very much | in being treated | by (too) many doctors.' (Mrk 5:26)

# Appendix: Texts

For each text, the register indicators are presented, which distinguish "formal written," "somewhat informal," and "quite informal spoken," (see table 12.1). These indicators include whether only default, or default *and* marked TSMs are employed (see 12.3), the frequency of use of the **ti** quote marker (12.4.3), the use of the continuative (12.2.2.3), and the use of the emphatic -**ag** (12.3.3), as follows:

    Thematic Salience Marking used:
    Reported speech introduced by **ti**:
    Sequential action expressed by continuative:
    Emphatic -**ag**:

Folktale: Quite formal register
Text 1: "The cow that lost its fear" (no. 11) Writer: Sengoronge Katyera
    Thematic Salience Marking used: Default TSM only
    Reported speech introduced by **ti**: 0
    Sequential action expressed by continuative: 0
    Emphatic -**ag**: 1

**Há-àlí rì-ìr-ì  í=n-gáàvù** || **z-à=  mú-sósí mú-gùmà** ||
16-P3  is-RS-Fi  AU=10-cows  10-AM=  1-man  1-one
There were cows || of a certain man ||

**z-àná-rágìr-à.** ||  **Ìrí  zí-ká-hík-á   mw-í=  shámbà** || **í=n-gùmà** ||
10-SQ-eat.grass-Fa  When  10-P2-arrive-Fa  18-5=  wilderness  AU=9-one
and they were grazing. || When they arrived in the wilderness || one ||

y-àná-hwábúk-à | kw-á-yò-kwáyò || ì-rì   mú=      génd-á |
9-SQ-wander.off-Fa  15-AM-9-RDP     9-be  PROG=    GOING-Fa
wandered off | in its own way || going off |

í-gá-lì-ìs-â. ||      Ìrí    í-ká-bá  kéèrà      y-à-yìgút-à ||  y-àná-gálùk-à ||
9-INTL-eat-CS-Fa   When  9-P2-be  ALREADY   9-P1-be.full-Fa  9-SQ-return-Fa
eating. || When it was already satisfied || it returned ||

y-àná-húb-á   yàhó |       í-ká-sìg-á      í=z-ààbò ||         y-àná-gwât-à |
9-SQ-miss-Fa  there.N+16  9-P2-leave-Fa  AU=10-SAME.SET    9-SQ-take-Fa
and it missed there (where) | it left its fellows || and it took |

gî-ndì-gîndì  n-jírà ||  y-àná-téér-ék-à ||  í=z-ààbò |
9-other-RDP   9-path     9-SQ-lose-NEU-Fa    AU=10-SAME.SET
another different path || and it got lost || its fellows |

z-àná-táàh-à. ||         Mw-èné  =y-ô |   à-ná-gênd-à
10-SQ-return.home-Fa   1-owner   =9-PR   1-SQ-GOING-Fa
returned home. || The owner | went

á-gá-gì-lóóz-à ||         à-ná-gì-hèbúúr-à. ||   Ìyó        n-gáàvù ||  y-àná-gêndí
1-INTL-O9-search-Fa   1-SQ-O9-give.up-Fa     that.N+9   9-cow       9-SQ-GOING
looking for it || and he gave up on it. || That cow || went

hùlúk-ír-à ||       mú=    lú-bàkó |  lw-é=        n-dàrè. ||   Í=n-dàrè |
appear-APL-Fa    18=      11-forest  11-AM+AU=   9-lion       AU=9-lion
and appeared || in the forest | of the lion. || Lion |

y-àná-gì-bòn-à ||    y-àná-gì-yégèr-éz-à. ||      Ìyó        n-gáàvù ||
9-SQ-O9-see-Fa      9-SQ-O9-come.near-CS-Fa    that.N+9   9-cow
saw it || and welcomed it. || That cow

y-àná-yòbóh-à ||   y-àná-dèt-à: ||   «É=   máàshì              yâgà ||     k-ó=
9-SQ-fear-Fa      9-SQ-day-Fa      O=    for.goodness.sake   comrade,   Q-2SG=
|| was afraid || and it said: | «O for pity's sake comrade ||

tá-gáà-n-dy-à?» ||      Í=n-dàrè |   y-àná-làhír-à. ||   Ìyó        n-gáàvù ||
NEG-F2-O1.SG-eat-Fa   AU=9-lion   9-SQ-refuse-Fa     that.N+9   9-cow
aren't you going to eat me?» || The lion | said no. || That cow ||

y-àná-yégèèr-à |     ìyó        n-dàrè ||  bà-ná-lámùs-án-i-à ||    hálìkò ||
9-SQ-come.near-Fa  that.N+9   9-lion     2-SQ-greet-RCP-CS-Fa    but
neared | that lion || and they greeted each other || but ||

í=n-gáàvù || y-àná-géndèrèr-à | ú=kú-yòbóh-á bwènèènè. || Ìyó
AU=9-cow 9-SQ-continued-Fa AU=15-fear-Fa very.much that.N+9
the cow || continued | to be afraid very much. || That

n-gáàvù | y-àná-dèt-à | kwó= y-àmú= gálúk-à. || Í=n-dàrè |
9-cow 9-SQ-speak-Fa CMP= 9-F1= return-Fa AU=9-lion
cow | said | that it is about to return. || Lion |

y-àná-gì-bwír-à kwó-kù-nô: || «Ù-Ø-lék-è |
9-SQ-O9-tell-Fa <quote.MARKED> 2SG-SBV-allow-Fe
told it like this: || «Allow |

tù-Ø-túúl-ánw-è || mú=kúbá nàà-nì | n-dúúz-ír-ì ni-ényènè. ||
1PL-SBV-live-MUT-Fe because ADD.P-1SG 1SG-live-RS-Fi 1SG-self
that we live together || because and me also | I live by myself. ||

Kéèrà n-à-kú-láhìr-ìr-á || kwó= n-dá-gáá-kú-ly-à ||
ALREADY 1SG-P1-O2.SG-refuse-APL-Fa CMP= 1SG-NEG-F2-O2.SG-eat-Fa
Already I have refused || that I will not eat you ||

w-é= mw-ìrá w-à-nì || ù-ná-kòlá | mú-túúlání
2SG-FOC= 1-friend 1-AM-1SG 2SG-ADD.V-are.NEWLY 1-neighbor
you who are my friend || and you now | are neighbor ||

w-à-nì.» || Ìyó n-gáàvù | y-àná-yèméér-á | bà-Ø-túúl-ánw-è ||
1-AM-1SG that.N+9 9-cow 9-SQ-agreed-Fa 2-SBV-live-MUT-Fe
of mine. || That cow | agreed | that they live together ||

mú=kúbá | ì-tà-kì-yì-j-í
because 9-NEG-PERS-know-RS-Fi
because | it no longer knew

í=n-jírá | í-y-àngà-gì-gálúl-à. || Yìkyó ky-òbá ky-áàlì
AU=9-path S.R-9-POT-O9-return-Fa that.N+7 7-fear 7-O.R+1+P3
the path | which would return it home. || That fear which it

gw-ét-ì | ky-àná-mál-à. || Ìrí há-ká-lèng-á | í-sìkù n-débè ||
have-RS-Fi 7-SQ-finish.off-Fa When 16-P2-pass-Fa 10-days 10-some
had | was finished off. || When there passed | some days ||

ìyó n-dàrè | y-àná-lwâl-à || ì-ná-hí-ìt-ì | á=bì-ìrà
that.N+9 9-lion 9-SQ-got.sick-Fa 9-ADD.V-has-RS-Fi AU=2-friends
that lion | got sick || and it has | friends

bá-á-yò | bà-bìrì || í=n-gwí | nà= ny-ûndà. || Bà-ná-yîjì
2-AM-9    2-two      AU=9-leopard  CNJ=  9-eagle      2-SQ-COMING
of it | two || leopard | and eagle. || And they came

gì-tàndúúl-à || bà-ná-bòn-à kwó= kéèrà y-à-jàmb-á |
O9-check.out-Fa  2-SQ-saw-Fa  CMP=  ALREADY  9-P1-become.thin-Fa
and checked it out || and they saw that it was already skinny |

bwènèènè || bà-ná-gì-búúz-à: || «Bí-kí | í-by-à-kú-jàà-vy-á |
very.much    2-SQ-O9-ask-Fa       8-what   S.R-8-P1-O2.SG-be.thin-CS-Fa
very much || and they asked it: || «What | is it that caused you to be skinny |

kwó-kù-nô?» || ìyó       n-dàrè | y-àná-shùvy-à: || «Ú=mw-énà ||
E-15-thus.P.C   that.N+9  9-lion   9-SQ-answer-Fa      AU=3-hunger
like this?» || That lion | answered: || «Hunger ||

gw-ó=   gw-á-n-jàà-vy-á        kwó-kù-nô. || Í=n-dwàlà
3-FOC=  3-P1-O1.SG-be.skinny-CS-Fa  E-15-thus.P.C   AU=9-sickness
is what made me skinny like this. || Sickness

nààhô || ì-tà-ngà-tùm-ír-ì |   n-gá-jàmb-à  kw-ó-kù.» ||
only    9-NEG-POT-cause-RS-Fi  1-F2-be.thin-Fa  E-thus.P-15
only || would not cause | me to get thin like this.» ||

ìyó      n-gwî ||  nô=   yò       ny-ûndà || bà-ná-hwéhwét-éz-à |[1]
that.N+9 9-leopard  CNJ=  that.N+9  9-eagle     2-SQ-whispered-CS-Fa
That leopard || and that eagle || whispered |

ìyó      n-dàrè ||  bà-ná-gì-bwír-à: || «K-ò  tà-ngà-ly-à     ì-yí
that.N+9 9-lion     2-SQ-O9-tell-Fa      Q-2SG NEG-POT-eat-Fa  this.P-9
to that lion || and they told it: || «Would you not eat this

n-gáàvù?» || í=n-dàrè | y-àná-dèt-à: || «Nângà! || N-dà-ngà-ly-à
9-cow        AU=9-lion  9-SQ-said-Fa      No         1SG-NEG-POT-eat-Fa
cow?» || Lion | said: || «No! || I would not eat

ù-yú |   mw-ìrá w-à-nî. ||  N-gáá-lék-à      ní-Ø-fw-è ||     h-ó=
this.P-1 1-friend 1-AM-1SG   1SG-F2-allow-Fa  1SG-SBV-die-Fe   16-O.R=
this | friend of mine. || I would allow myself to die || instead

n-àngà-mú-ly-à» || Ny-ûndâ | à-ná-jéngèèrw-á    bwènèènè || kw-é=
1SG-POT-O1-eat-Fa  9-eagle    1-SQ-be.very.sad-Fa  very.much    CMP-AU=
of eating him.» || The eagle | was sad very much || that

---

[1] May also be pronounced as the variant -hohwetez-.

**n-dàré** | **mw-ìrá** **w-à-bò** | **à-mú=** **fw-à** **n-ò=** **mw-énà.** || **Ùyó**
9-lion 1-friend 1-AM-2 1-F1= die-Fa CNJ-AU= 3-hunger that.N+9
the lion | their friend | is about to die of hunger. || That

**ny-ûndà** || **à-ná-shùbì** **bwír-á** **iyó** **n-dàrè** | **kwó-kù-nô:** ||
9-eagle 1-SQ-AGAIN tell-Fa that.N+9 9-lion <quote.MARKED>
eagle || again told that lion | like this: ||

«**Ì-yí** **n-gáàvù** || **ìrí** **y-àngà-dèt-à** **y-ónyènè** || **kw-ô=**
This.P-9 9-cow if 9-CND-say-Fa 9-self CMP-2SG=
«This cow || if it would say itself || that

**Ø-gì-ry-è** | **h-ó=** **w-àngà-fw-á** | **ná=** **yù-gú** **mw-énà** **k-ò=**
SBV-O9-eat-Fe 16-O.R= 2SG-POT-eat-Fa CNJ= this.P-3 3-hunger Q-2SG=
you eat it | instead of you dying | of this hunger ||

**tà-ngà-gì-ry-â?**» || **ìyó** **n-dàrè** **y-àná-dèt-à:** || «**Mw-é=** **bì-ìrà**
NEG-POT-O9-eat-Fa that.N+9 9-lion 9-SQ-say-Fa 2PL-FOC= 2-friends
would you not eat it?» || That lion said: || «You the friends

**bà-à-nì** **bà=** **kéérà** || **bwó=** **mw-à-dèt-à** **kwó=** **nì-Ø-gì-ry-è** ||
2-AM-1SG 2+A.M= long.ago since= 2PL-P1-say-Fa CMP= 1-SBV-O9-eat-Fe
of me of long ago || since you say that I eat it ||

**n-àngà-gì-ly-à.**» || **Ùyó** **ny-ûnda** || **nê=** **yó** **n-gwî** ||
1SG-POT-O9-eat-Fa that.N+1 9-eagle CNJ= that.N+9 9-leopard
I would eat it.» || That eagle || and that leopard

**bà-ná-tááhà** || **bà-kòlì** **lángààl-íír-ì** | **kwó=** **ná-bò** |
2-SQ-GO.HOME 2-are.NEWLY expect-RS-Fi CMP= ADD.P-2
|| went home || now expecting | that and they also |

**bá-gá-lóng-èr-à** | **h-ó=** **mú-shéégò.** || **Ìrí** **há-ká-lèng-á**
2-F2-receive-APL-Fa 16-O.R+AU= 3-evening.meal When 16-P2-pass-Fa
they will get | supper there. || When had passed

**í-sìkù** **n-gérwà** || **bà-ná-yîjì** **lól-à** || **ìrí** **ìyó** **n-dàrè** ||
10-days 10-some 2-SQ-COMING look.at-Fa if that.N+9 9-lion
some days || they came to see || if that lion ||

**kéérà** **y-à-ly-á** | **ìyó** **n-gáàvù** || **bà-ná-gwân-à** **léèrò** |
ALREADY 9-P1-eat-Fa that.N+9 9-cow 2-SQ-encounter-Fa this.time
had already eaten | that cow. || And they found this

ìyó        n-dàrè ‖ ì-kòlà        bú=    dèngúúk-á² ∣    ná=    yùgwó
that.N+9    9-lion    9-is.NEWLY    F1=    finished.off-Fa    CNJ=    that.N+3
time ∣ that lion ‖ was about to be finished off ∣ by

mw-énà. ‖    Í=n-gwí        y-àná-búùz-à ∣    í=n-dàrè: ‖    «Éwè ‖    kí-tùmà
3-hunger    AU=9-leopard    9-SQ-ask-Fa    AU=9-lion    Hey    7-reason
that hunger. ‖ The leopard asked ∣ the lion: ‖ «Hey ‖ for what reason

kí-kì ∣    ù-tá-ká-gír-á ‖        kù-lyá ∣    tú-ká-kú-bwír-à?» ‖    ìyó
7-what    2SG-NEG-P2-do-Fa        15-that.R    1PL-P2-O2.SG-tell-Fa    that.N+9
∣ you have not done ‖ that ∣ which we told you?» ‖ That

n-gwí ∣    y-àná-dèt-à: ‖    «Ààhô!    M-Ø-b-é            ni-ó=
9-leopard    9-SQ-say-Fa    OK.then    1SG-SBV-become-Fe    1SG-FOC+O.R+2SG=
leopard ∣ said: ‖ «OK then ‖ may I be the one

gá-ly-àgàg-à ‖³    h-ó=    w-àngà-fw-à ∣    n-ó=    mw-énà.» ‖
F2-eat-EMP-Fa    16-O.R=    2SG-POT-die-Fa    CNJ-AU=    3-hunger
you will eat ‖ instead of you dying ∣ of hunger.» ‖

Í=n-dàrè ‖    y-àná-làhír-á    kw-é=    tá-gáà-ly-à ∣    ìyó    n-gwî. ‖
AU=9-lion    9-SQ-refuse-Fa    CMP-9=    NEG-F2-eat-Fa    that.N+9    9-leopard
The lion ‖ refused that he will not eat ∣ that leopard.

Ny-ûndà ná-yè ∣    à-ná-dèt-à ‖    kw-â=    Ø-b-è    y-é=
9-eagle    ADD.P-1    1-SQ-say-Fa    CMP-1=    SBV-be-Fe    1-FOC+O.R+AU=
‖ The eagle and he also ∣ said ‖ that he be the one

n-dàrè ∣    î-ry-à. ‖    Hálìkò ‖    y-àná-shùbì    làhír-á ‖    kw-é=    tá-gáà-ly-à ∣
9-lion    9-eat-Fa    but    9-SQ-AGAIN    refuse-Fa    CMP-9=    NEG-F2-eat-Fa
lion ∣ eats. ‖ But ‖ it again refused ‖ that it will not eat ∣

ùyó    ny-ûndà. ‖    Ìyó    n-gáàvù ∣    ìrí    í-ká-yùvw-á ∣    kw-á=
that.N+1    9-eagle    that.N+9    9-cow    when    9-P2-hear-Fa    CMP-AU=
that eagle. ‖ That cow ∣ when it heard ∣ that

bà-à-bò        bà-dèt-à ‖    kw-ê=    Ø-bà-ly-è ‖
2-A.M-SAME.SET    2+P1-say-Fa    CMP-9=    SBV-O2-eat-Fe
its fellows said ‖ that it eat them ‖

---

²May also be pronounced as the variant -dènduuk-.

³As confirmation that the emphatic extension is a rarely used optional feature in this formal speech register, the author inadvertently omitted it here when reading his own story.

**ì-tà-ná-bà-ly-à ǁ    ná-yò     y-àná-dèt-à: ǁ   «M-Ø-b-é |**
9-NEG-SQ-O2-eat-Fa    ADD.P-9   9-SQ-say-Fa      1SG-SBV-become-Fe
and it did not eat them ǁ and it also said: ǁ «May I be

**ni-ó=             gáà-ly-à.» ǁ    Ìyó       n-dàrè | y-àná-hùlík-à. ǁ  Ny-ûndâ |**
1SG-FOC+O.R+2SG    F2-eat-Fa       that.N+9   9-lion    9-SQ-be.quiet-Fa   9-eagle
the one | that you eat.» ǁ That lion | was quiet. ǁ Eagle |

**à-ná-gìrím-á |  í=kí-góhè. ǁ   Í=n-dàrè |   y-àná-símb-ìr-à |    kw-í=   gòsì |**
1-SQ-wink-Fa     AU=7-eyelid    AU=9-lion    9-SQ-jump-APL-Fa       17-5=    neck
winked | an eyelid. ǁ The lion | jumped | on the neck |

**ly-ê=    yò         n-gáàvù ǁ     y-àná-gì-tímb-à |          hááshì ǁ**
5-AM=    that.N+9    9-cow         9-SQ-O9-throw.down-Fa     down.on.ground
of that cow ǁ and it knocked it down | on ground ǁ

**y-àná-yàm-à |    í-gáà-fw-à. ǁ    Ìyó        n-dàrè ǁ   nê=     yò         n-gwî ǁ**
9-SQ-IMMED-Fa    9-INTL-die-Fa     that.N+9   9-lion     CNJ=    that.N+9   9-leopard
and it immediately | died. ǁ That lion ǁ and that leopard ǁ

**nô=     yò         ny-ûndâ ǁ    bà-ná-sók-ánán-á |       ú=mú-túmbá |   gw-ê= |**
CNJ=    that.N+1    9-eagle      2-SQ-go.behind-MUT-Fa    AU=3-corpse    3-AM=
and that eagle ǁ circled around | the corpse | of

**yò         n-gáàvù ǁ    bà-ná-tòndééz-á |   ú=kú-gù-tètémb-à. ǁ    Í-í-hánò: ǁ**
that.N+9   9-cow        2-SQ-begin-Fa       AU=15-O3-tear.apart-Fa   AU=5-advice
that cow ǁ and they began | to tear it apart. ǁ Advice: ǁ

**Ù-Ø-lól-è ǁ           ù-tá-Ø-yì-lyò-s-é |         kú=    bà-ndì |**
2SG-SBV-look-Fe       2SG-NEG-SBV-RFX-leave-CS-Fe   17=    2-others
Look! ǁ Don't remove yourself | from others |

**mb-ù=       Ø-kúlíkír-é ǁ    y-à-wè-yàwè |       n-jírà ǁ**
INTL-2SG=   SBV-follow-Fe    9-AM-2SG-RDP        9-path
with the intention of following ǁ your own unique path ǁ

**ù-tá-kéngèèr-è |         w-à-géndì |        yì-fúnd-à |       h-ô= |**
2SG-NEG-UNINTENDED-Fe    2SG-P1-GOING       RFX-go.in-Fa      16-O.R
so that you don't unintentionally | go getting yourself into | a place where

**tá-gá-lyòk-à. ǁ**
NEG-F2-leave-Fa
you will not leave. ǁ

Folktale: Somewhat informal register
Text 2: "Enmity between the lion and the cow" (no. 105) Speaker: Rumwaga
    Thematic Salience Marking used: Both default TSM (15) and remote TSM (7)
    Reported speech introduced by **ti**: 1
    Sequential action expressed by continuative: 0
    Emphatic -**ag**: 2

**Há-àlí**   **rì-ìr-ì**   **w-á-n-dàrè** | **ná=**   **w-à-n-gáàvù.** || **Ùyó**   **w-á-n-dàrè** |
16-P3   is-RS-Fi   1-A.M-9-lion   CNJ=   1-A.M-9-cow   that.N+1   1-A.M-9-lion
There was lion | and cow. || That lion | and

**ná=**   **w-à-n-gáàvù** | **bà-ná-gwât-à**   **ú=bw-ìrà** ||   **bà-ná-gêndì**
CNJ=   1-A.M-9-cow   9-SQ-seize-Fa   AU=14-friendship   2-SQ-GOING
cow | made a friendship || and they went

**húmb-ír-á** | **í=mí-gándà.** ||   **Ìyó**   **mûndà** | **bá-àlì**
dig-APL-Fa   AU=4-trees.for.building   that.N+23   place   2-P3
and cut trees | for building. || There (where) | they were

**húmb-ír-à**   **í=mí-gándà** ||   **bà-ná-húmààn-à** | **hà-lì**   **í=n-dèkèèrà**
dug-APL-Fa   AU=4-trees.for.building   2-SQ-encounter-Fa   16-is   AU=9-plain
cutting trees for building || they encountered | there is a plain

**ny-íìjâ**   **bwènèènè** || **bà-ná-hà-yùbák-à.** || **Bà-ná-gênd-à**
9-good   very.much   2-SQ-O16-build-Fa   2-SQ-GOING-Fa
very good | and they built there. || And they went

**bá-gá-lóòz-â** ||   **by-ó=**   **bá-gá-yîjì**   **tùng-ír-à** |   **mw-î=**
2-INTL-search-Fa   8-O.R=   2-F2-COMING   take.care.of-APL-Fa   18=
looking || for what (animals) they could tend | in

**yò**   **ny-ûmbà.** || **Há=**   **ny-úmá**   **ly-é=**   **sìkù**   **n-gêrwà** ||
that.N+9   9-house   16=   9-after   5-AM+AU=   days   9-few
that house. || After a few days ||

**W-á-n-dàrè** | **à-ná-yìm-à** |   **à-ná-bùt-à**   **ú=mw-ānà** ||
1-AM-9-lion   1-SQ-conceive-Fa   1-SQ-give.birth-Fa   AU=1-child
lion | got pregnant | and gave birth to a child ||

**à-ná-gênd-à** |   **á-gá-mú-lóóg-èz-á** |   **í=by-ókúlyà.** || **Mú=**
1-SQ-GOING-Fa   1-INTL-O1-search-APL+CS-Fa   AU=8-food   18=
and it went | looking | for food for him. || In

**sìkú  nìnììnî |  w-à-n-gáàvù  ná-yè |   à-ná-yìm-à ||      ná-yè |**
days   few        1-A.M-9-cow    ADD.P-1    1-SQ-conceive-Fa    ADD.P-1
a few days | the cow and she | also got pregnant || and she also |

**à-ná-bùt-à            ú=mw-ānà ||  ná-yè |   à-ná-kìzì   génd-á |**
1-SQ-give.birth-Fa    AU=1-child    ADD.P-1   1-SQ-REP    GOING-Fa
gave birth to a child || and she also | repeatedly went |

**á-gá-mú-lóóg-èz-á |          í=by-ókúlyà. ||  Yàbó      bà-ànà**
1-INTL-O1-search-APL+CS-Fa    AU=8-food       Those.N+2  2-children
searching for | food for it. || Those children

**bó-mbì ||  bà-ná-kìzì  sìgál-à |   bà-gwétì  bá-gá-shààt-à. ||  Mú=      yùkwó**
2-both    2-SQ-REP    remain-Fa   2-PROG    2-INTL-play-Fa      18=     that.N+15
both || they habitually remained | playing. || In that

**kú-sháát-à |  mw-ànà  w-à=     n-gáàvù ||  à-ná-yìt-á   mw-àná |  w-á=**
15-play-Fa    1-child   1-A.M=   9-cow      1-SQ-kill-Fa   1-child    1-AM=
playing | the child of the cow || killed the child | of

**n-dàrè. || W-à-n-gáàvù  ìrí     á-ká-fùlúk-à ||       à-ná-húmààn-à |**
9-lion      1-A.M-9-cow    when   1-P2-return.home-Fa    1-SQ-encounter-Fa
the lion. || The cow when it returned home from work || it encountered |

**mw-ànà  w-á=    n-dàrè |  kéèrà      à-fw-à. ||   W-á-n-gáàvù |**
1-child   1-AM=   9-lion     ALREADY    1+P1-die-Fa   1-A.M-9-cow
the child of the lion | is already dead. || The cow |

**à-ná-búùz-à: ||  «Bí-kí   í-by-à-yít-á |    ù-nó       mw-ànà |   w-á=**
1-SQ-ask-Fa        8-what   S.R-8-P1-kill-Fa   1-this.P.C   1-child     1-A.M=
asked: || «What killed | this child | of

**n-dàrè?» ||  Mw-àná  w-á=    n-gáàvù |  à-ná-mú-bwîr-à: ||  «Tù-shùbà**
9-lion         1-child   1-A.M=   9-cow     1-SQ-O1-tell-Fa      1PL-PRIOR
the lion?» || The child of the cow | told it: || «We were

**mú=       sháát-à ||  n-àná-mú-yìt-à.» ||  Ìyó       n-gáàvù |  ìrí**
PROG=     play-Fa      1SG-SQ-O1-kill-Fa    that.N+9   9-cow       when
playing || and I killed it.» || That cow | when

**í-ká-bōn-à ||    kwó=    kéèrà |      ùyó        mw-ānà**
9-P2-see-Fa       CMP=    ALREADY     that.N+1    1-child
it saw || that already | that child

à-fw-à ‖ y-àná-yì-búúz-à ‖ kwê= Ø-sháág-è yà-hô. ‖
1+P1-die-Fa 9-SQ-RFX-ask-Fa CMP+9= SBV-depart-Fe there.N-16
had died ‖ it asked itself ‖ that it leave there. ‖

Y-àná-yábììr-à | ú=mw-àná w-à-gè ‖ y-àná-yàm-à | í-gá-tíbìt-à. ‖
9-SQ-take-Fa AU=1-child 1-A.M-1 9-SQ-IMMED-Fa 9-INTL-run-Fa
And it took | its child ‖ and it immediately | ran. ‖

ìrí í-ká-hík-á mú= n-jírà ‖ y-àná-gwán-án-à ‖ mw-ó=
when 9-P2-arrive-Fa 18= 9-path 9-SQ-encounter-RCP-Fa 18-AU=
When it arrived in the path ‖ it encountered there ‖

mú-shààjà mú-gùmà ‖ y-àná-mú-bwîr-à ‖ kw-â= Ø-mú-bìsh-è. ‖
1-old.man 1-one 9-SQ-O1-tell-Fa CMP-1= SBV-O1-hide-Fe
one old man ‖ and it told him ‖ that he hide it. ‖

Ùyó mú-shààjà | à-ná-gì-búúz-à: ‖ «N-gá-kú-bìsh-ìr-à
that.N+1 1-old.man 1-SQ-O9-ask-Fa 1SG-F2-O2.SG-hide-APL-Fa
That old | man asked it: ‖ «I will hide you for

bí-kì?» ‖ Y-àná-mú-bwîr-à: ‖ «Ú=mw-àná w-à-nî ‖ à-shùbà mú=
8-what 9-SQ-O1-tell-Fa AU=1-child 1-A.M-1SG 1-PRIOR PROG=
what?» ‖ And it told him: ‖ «My child ‖ was

sháát-à ‖ ná= mw-ànà w-á= n-dàrè ‖ à-ná-mú-yìt-à.» ‖ Ùyó
play-Fa CNJ= 1-child 1-A.M= 9-lion 1-SQ-O1-kill-Fa that.N+1
playing |with the child of the lion | and it killed him.» ‖ That

mú-shósì | à-ná-twâl-à W-à-n-gáàvù | n-ó= mw-àná w-à-gè ‖
1-man 1-SQ-carry-Fa 1-A.M-9-cow CNJ-AU= 1-child 1-A.M-1
man | took that cow | and its child ‖

à-ná-gêndì mú-bìsh-à | mú= mw-à-gè ‖ Ùyó mú-shósì |
1-SQ-GOING O1-hide-Fa 18= home-A.M-1 that.N+1 1-man
and he went and hid him | in his place. ‖ That man |

à-ná-bwîr-à w-à-n-gáàvù: ‖ «Ìrí w-àngà-yúvw-á ú=lú-hàzì
1-SQ-tell-Fa 1-A.M-9-cow if 2SG-CND-hear-Fa AU=11-rooster
told that cow: ‖ «If you hear that rooster

lw-àn-í | lw-à-bìk-à ‖ ìrí n-dàrè | à-hík-à.» ‖ N-dàrè |
11-A.M-1SG 11-P1-crow-Fa that's.when 9-lion 1+P1-arrive-Fa 9-lion
of me | is crowing ‖ that's when the lion | has arrived.» ‖ The lion |

**ìrí á-ká-sháág-á** ǁ **í=w-à= kú-lóóz-á** | **í=by-ókúlyâ** ǁ
when 1-P2-depart-Fa 23=place-A.M= 15-search-Fa AU=8-food
when it left ǁ the place where it was looking | for food ǁ

**à-ná-gwán-án-á** ǁ **ú=mw-àná w-à-gè** ǁ **kéérà à-fw-à** ǁ
1-SQ-encounter-COM-Fa AU=1-child 1-A.M-1 ALREADY 1+P1-die-Fa
it encountered ǁ its child ǁ is already dead.

**W-á-n-dàrè** ǁ **ìrí á-ká-húmáán-á** ǁ **ú=mw-àná w-à-gè kéérà**
1-A.M-9-lion when 1-P2-encounter-Fa AU=1-child 1-A.M-1 ALREADY
ǁ The lion ǁ when it encountered ǁ its child already

**à-fw-à** ǁ **à-ná-tòndéér-à** | **ú=kú-lír-à.** ǁ **Ìrí á-ká-lól-ág-á** |
1+P1-die-Fa 1-SQ-begin-Fa AU=15-cry-Fa when 1-P2-look-EMP-Fa
is dead ǁit began | to cry. ǁ When it looked |

**á-hà-lì W-à-n-gáàvù** | **n-ó= mw-àná w-à-gè** ǁ
S.R-16-is 1-A.M-9-cow CNJ-AU= 1-child 1-A.M-1
at where the cow was | and its child ǁ

**à-tà-ná-kì-bà-bòn-à** ǁ **à-ná-dèt-à** ǁ **kwó= W-à-n-gáàvù** ǁ
1-NEG-SQ-PERS-O2-see-Fa 1-SQ-speak-Fa CMP= 1-A.M-9-cow
it no longer saw them ǁ and it said ǁ that the cow

**y-é= w-à-mú-yìt-ír-à** | **ú=mw-àná w-à-gè.** ǁ **Lyêryô** ǁ **à-ná-yàmì**
1-FOC= 1-P1-O1-kill-APL-Fa AU=1-child 1-A.M-1 right.then 1-SQ-IMMED
ǁ is the one who killed | its child. ǁ Right then ǁ it immediately

**génd-á á-gá-lóóz-á** | **W-à-n-gáàvù.** ǁ **Ìrí á-ká-hík-á mú=**
GOING-Fa 1-F2-seek-Fa 1-A.M-9-cow when 1-P2-arrive-Fa 18=
went looking for | the cow. ǁ When he arrived in

**n-jírà** ǁ **à-ná-hùlúk-ír-à** | **kû= lyà mú-shààjà** ǁ **W-á-n-dàrè** |
9-path 1-SQ-appear-APL-Fa 17= that.R+1 1-old.man 1-A.M-9-lion
the path ǁ he appeared to | that old man. ǁ The lion |

**à-ná-búùz-à** | **ù-lyá mú-shààjà:** ǁ «**É= shòòkùlù** ǁ **kà= ndáá-yò**
1-SQ-ask-Fa 1-that.R 1-old.man O= 1a+old.man Q= NEG.FOC-9
asked | that old man: ǁ «O grandfather ǁ is there no

**n-gáàvù** | **í-y-à-lèng-á há-nò?**» ǁ **Lù-lyá lú-hāzì** ǁ
9-cow S.R-9-P1-pass-Fa 16-here.P.C 11-that.R 11-rooster
cow | which passed here?» ǁ That rooster ǁ

lw-àná-yàm-à       lú-gáá-bìk-à ||    Yùlwó      lú-hāzì |   ìrí
11-SQ-IMMED-Fa     11-INTL-crow-Fa    that.N+11  11-rooster  when
it immediately crowed. || That rooster | when

lú-ká-bīk-à ||    ìrí           W-à-n-gáàvù |   à-ná-dèt-à: ||   «W-á-n-dàrè
11-P2-crow-Fa     that's.when   1-A.M-9-cow     1-SQ-say-Fa      1-A.M-9-lion
it crowed || that's when the cow | said: || «Lion

ùyó |       ú-w-à-léng-à.» ||   W-á-n-dàrè ||   ìrí     á-ká-kùlíkír-ág-à
that.N+1    S.R-1-P1-pass-Fa    1-A.M-9-lion    when    1-P2-follow-EMP-Fa
is that one | who passed.» || The lion || when it followed

ìyó        n-jírà ||   à-ná-gêndì       hík-à |      h-ê=     hék-īīr-ì. ||   W-á-n-dàrè ||
that.N+9   9-path      1-SQ-GOING       arrive-Fa    16-9=    end-RS-Fi       1-A.M-9-lion
that path || it went and arrived | at where it ends. || The lion ||

à-ná-shùbì       gálúk-ír-á |     á-hà-lì       ù-lyá        mú-shààjà |
1-SQ-AGAIN       return-APL-Fa    S.R-16-is     1-that.R     1-old.man
again returned | to where that old man was |

à-ná-mú-bwîr-à: ||     «É=     shòòkùlù ||    ndáá-yò       n-gáàvù
1-SQ-O1-tell-Fa        O=      old.man        NEG.FOC-9     9-cow
and said to him: || O grandfather || is there no cow

í-y-à-lèng-á         há-nò?» ||    Ùyó         mú-shààjà |    à-ná-bwîr-à
S.R-9-P1-pass-Fa     16-here.P.C   that.N+1    1-old.man      1-SQ-tell-Fa
which passed here? || That old man | told

W-á-n-dàrè: ||     «Ù-Ø-lék-è ||           n-dé=       géndíì    =nyw-à |
1-A.M-9-lion       2SG-SBV-allow-Fe        1SG-PRIOR=  GOING     drink-Fa
the lion: || «Allow || (that) I first go and drink |

á=mā-ājì ||       tù-ká-bùlì       yíjì |      gànúúl-à.» ||    Ù-lyá       mú-shààjà |
AU=6-water        1PL-F2-SBSQ      COMING      converse-Fa      1-that.R    1-old.man
water || then we come and | converse.» || That old man |

à-ná-gêndì       bwír-á     W-à-n-gáàvù |    mú=      ny-ûmbà: ||   «W-á-n-dàrè |
1-SQ-GOING       tell-Fa    1-A.M-9-cow      18=      9-house       1-A.M-9-lion
went and told that cow | in the house: || «Lion |

à-kú-líndìr-ììr-ì       há-nò |        há=      m-bùgà.» ||    W-à-n-gáàvù |
1-O2.SG-wait-RS-Fi      16-here.P.C    16=      9-outside       1-A.M-9-cow
is waiting for you here | outside.» || The cow

à-ná-yàmì       béér-á      mwô-mw-ô ‖    mú=   ny-ûmbà |   n-ó=
1-SQ-ALWAYS     remain-Fa   E-18-in.there.N  18=   9-house     CNJ-AU=
| always remained right there ‖ in the house | together with

mw-àná   w-à-gè. ‖   Í=sìkù |      ìrí     zí-ká-lūg-à ‖         mw-ànà  w-á=
1-child  1-A.M-1     AU=10+day    when    10-P2-be.many-Fa      1-child  1-A.M=
its child. ‖ The days | when they were many ‖ the child of

n-gáàvù |  à-ná-fw-à |   n-í=           shálì. ‖  W-à-n-gáàvù ‖
9-cow      1-SQ-die-Fa   CNJ-AU+5=      hunger    1-A.M-9-cow
the cow | died | from hunger. ‖ The cow ‖

à-ná-tòndéér-à |  ú-kú-lír-ír-á |       ú=mw-àná   w-à-gè. ‖  W-á-n-dàrè |
1-SQ-began-Fa    AU=15-cry-APL-Fa      AU=1-child  1-A.M-1    1-A.M-9-lion
began | to cry for | its child. ‖ The lion |

à-ná-yūvw-à |   kw-â=       kòlà       mú=     lír-ír-á |     ú=mw-àná ‖
1-SQ-hear-Fa    CMP-1=      is.NEWLY   PROG=   cry-APL-Fa    AU=1-child
heard | that it is now crying | for its child. ‖

W-á-n-dàrè |    à-ná-bwîr-à |  ùyó      mú-shààjà: ‖  «Sí=
1-A.M-9-lion    1-SQ-tell-Fa   that.N+1  1-old.man     OBV=
The lion | told | that old man: ‖ «It's obvious

w-à-láhìr-à |      kwó=      W-à-n-gáàvù |    à-tà-lì     há-nò. ‖     Sì=
2SG-P1-refuse-Fa   CMP=      1-A.M-9-cow      1-NEG-is    16-here.P.C  OBV=
you refused | that the cow | is not here. ‖ It's obvious

yô-yô |     à-gwétí    á-gáá-lír-à. ‖  Ùyó      mú-shààjà |  à-ná-dèt-à: ‖
E-that.N+1  1-PROG     1-INTL-cry-Fa   that.N+1  1-old.man    1-SQ-say-Fa
that very one | is crying.» ‖ That old man | said: ‖

«Nângà ‖    à-tà-lì      W-à-n-gáàvù ‖  à-lì    w-á-m-bènè. ‖   W-á-n-dàrè |
no          1-NEG-is     1-A.M-9-cow    1-is    1-A.M-9-goat    1-A.M-9-lion
«No ‖ it's not a cow ‖ it's a goat.» ‖ The lion |

à-ná-mú-bwîr-à: ‖     «Ù-Ø-yígúl-è        n-Ø-dól-è ‖         ìrí   à-tà-lí |
1-SQ-O1-tell-Fa       2SG-SBV-open-Fe     1SG-SBV-look-Fe     if    1-NEG-is
told him: ‖ «You open up (so) I (may) see ‖ if it is not |

W-à-n-gáàvù. ‖   W-á-n-dàrè ‖    à-ná-bwîr-à |  ù-lyá    mú-shààjà: ‖   «Ìrí
1-A.M-9-cow      1-A.M-9-lion    1-SQ-tell-Fa   1-that.R  1-old.man      if
the cow.» ‖ The lion ‖ told | that old man: ‖ «If

ú-tà-ngà-n-yígùl-ìr-à ‖ n-gáá-kú-ly-à.» ‖ Ù-lyá
2SG-NEG-CND-O1.SG-open-APL-Fa 1-F2-O2.SG-eat-Fa 1-that.R
you do not open up for me ‖ I will eat you.» ‖ That

mú-shààjà | à-ná-yígùl-à. ‖ W-á-n-dàrè | à-ná-bòn-à W-á-n-gáàvù |
1-man 1-SQ-open-Fa 1-A.M-9-lion 1-SQ-see-Fa 1-A.M-9-cow
old man | opened up. ‖ The lion | saw the cow |

à-ná-mú-búùz-à: ‖ «É= W-à-n-gáàvù ‖ nyândí |
1-SQ-O1-ask-Fa O= 1-A.M-9-cow who
and it asked it: ‖ «O cow ‖ who |

ú-ká-n-yìt-ír-á | ú=mw-ānà?» ‖ W-à-n-gáàvù |
S.R+1-P2-O1.SG-kill-APL-Fa AU=1-child 1-A.M-9-cow
killed ‖ my child?» ‖ The cow |

à-ná-dèt-à: ‖ «N-dà-yì-j-ì.» ‖ W-a-n-dare | à-ná-mú-búùz-à: ‖
1-SQ-say-Fa 1SG-NEG-know-RS-Fi 1-A.M-9-lion 1-SQ-O1-ask-Fa
said: ‖ «I don't know.» ‖ The lion | asked it: ‖

«Bí-kì by-ó= ká-tíbít-ír-à?» ‖ Lyêryò W-á-n-dàrè ‖
8-what 8-O.R+2SG= P2-run-APL-Fa right.then 1-A.M-9-lion
«What did you run from?» ‖ Right then the lion ‖

à-ná-tòndéér-á ú=kú-lwí-s-á W-à-n-gáàvù | à-ná-mú-yìt-à. ‖
1-SQ-began-Fa AU=15-fight-CS-Fa 1-A.M-9-cow 1-SQ-O1-kill-Fa
began to fight with the cow | and it killed it. ‖

Ú=lú-fūmò ‖ h-ó= lù-hùmb-ír-à yà-hô ‖ sí=
AU=11-story 16-FOC= 11-rain.end-APL-Fa there.N-16 OBV=
The story ‖ that's where it ends there. ‖ But it's obvious

lù-tà-hùmb-á | ngá= n-vùlà. ‖
11-NEG-rain.end-Fa like= 9-rain
it does not end | like rain. ‖

Folktale: Quite informal register
Text 3: "The young man who was too picky about girls" (no. 112) Speaker: Njiginya

    Thematic Salience Marking used: Both default TSM (12) and remote TSM (13)

    Reported speech introduced by **ti**: 12

    Sequential action expressed by continuative: 12

    Emphatic **-ag**: 21

**Há-àlí  rì-ìr-í |  ú=mú-tàbáná     mú-gùmà | ú-ká-lóóz-á**
16-P3   is-RS-Fi  AU=1-young.man   1-one    S.R+1-P2-seek-Fa
There was | one young man | who wanted

**ú=kú-yáng-á |   ú=mú-kàzì. ||  Ùyó      mú-tàbánà || ìrí**
AU=15-marry-Fa   AU=1-woman     that.N+1  1-young.man   when
to marry | a woman. || That young man || when

**bá-ká-mú-yèrék-á  á=bá-nyéré  bó-óshí ||  mú=    yàkó      kà-àyá**
2-P2-O2-show-Fa    AU=2-girls   2-all        18=    that.N+12  12-villlage
they showed him all the girls || in that village

**k-é       mw-à-bò ||  à-ná-dèt-à ||  kwó=  y-êhê |  ndáá-yè**
12-A.M+23  place-A.M-2  1-SQ-say-Fa   CMP=  1-CTR    NEG.FOC-1
of theirs || he said | that HE | there is no

**mú-nyéré ||  y-â=       síím-à. ||  À-ná-dèt-à |  kwó=  y-êhê | à-kwírí-ìr-ì**
1-girl       1-O.R+1=   like-Fa     1-SQ-say-Fa   CMP=  1-CTR    1-must-RS-Fi
girl || which he likes. || And he said | that HE | must |

**ú=kú-yáng-á |   ú=mú-kàzì |  ú-shúsh-ììn-í |            nà=**
AU=15-marry-Fa   AU=1-woman   S.R+1-resemble-RCP+RS-Fi   CNJ=
marry | a woman | who resembles |

**nyínà ||      nà=  w-é=    kì-ìmó | í-kì-rì |  ngá=  ky-à=**
1a+his.mother  CNJ=  1-A.M=  7-size   S.R-7-is   like=  7-A.M=
his mother || and of a size | which is | like that of

**nyínà. ||       Ùyó      mú-tàbánà | à-ná-génd-àg-á | í=**
his.1a+his.mother  that.N+1  1-young.man   1-SQ-go-EMP-Fa   23=
his mother. || That young man | went.EMP |

ràndà ‖ à-ná-génd-àg-à | á-gá-lóòz-à | á=bá-kàzì |
outside.of.village  1-SQ-GOING-EMP-Fa  1-INTL-seek-Fa  AU=2-women
outside of the village ‖ and he went EMP | looking | for women |

à-tà-ná-bà-bòn-a. ‖  Ìrí  há-ká-b-á  lú-sìkù lú-gùmà ‖
1-NEG-ADD-O2-see-Fa  when  16-P2-become-Fa  11-day  11-one
and he did not see them. ‖ When it was one day ‖

ngw-à=  Ø-jábúk-ág-é |  ú=lw-ījì ‖  à-húmààn-à |
as.soon.as-1=  SBV-cross.over-EMP-Fe  AU=11-river  1-encounter-Fa
just when he crossedEMP | the river ‖ he encountered |

ú=mú-nyérè ‖ à-bwàt-íír-ì mw-í= dàkò | ly-é= kí-tì. ‖ Ìrí
AU=1-girl  1-sit-RS-Fi  18-5=  under  5-AM+AU=  7-tree  when
a girl ‖ sitting underneath | a tree. ‖ When

á-ká-mú-bōn-à ‖ tî= ‖  «Nângà ‖ y-ô-yù | y-é=
1-P2-O1-see-Fa  ‹quote›= no  E-this.P-1  1-FOC=
he saw her ‖ ‹quote›: ‖ «No! ‖ This very one | is the one

shúsh-ììn-í |  nà=  máàwè ‖  n-ó=  mú-tûmbà ‖ ngá=
resemble-RCP+RS-Fi  CNJ=  1a+my.mother  CNJ-AU=  3-size  like=
that resembles | my mother ‖ and of a size | like

gw-à= máàwè!» ‖  Ù-lyá  mú-tàbánà | à-ná-mú-bwìr-è: ‖ «É=
3-A.M=  1a+my.mother  1-that.R  1-young.man  1-CON-O1-tell-Fe  O=
that of my mother!» That young man | told her: ‖ «O

mú-nyérè ‖ n-à-kú-síim-à ‖  n-àmú=  kú-yáng-à.» ‖ Ná-yè |
1-girl  1SG-P1-O2.SG-like-Fa  1SG-F1=  O2-marry-Fa  ADD.P-1
girl ‖ I like you ‖ I'm about to marry you.» ‖ And she also |

tì= |  «Éé | ú-Ø-n-yâng-è.» ‖  Bà-ná-gwàt-àg-è  í=n-jírà. ‖
‹quote›= Yes  2SG-SBV-O1-marry-Fe  2-CON-grab-EMP-Fe  AU=9-path
said: | «Yes | marry me.» ‖ And they took toEMP the path. ‖

Ìrí  bá-ká-hík-à  mú=  n-jírà ‖ bà-ná-hík-à  kú=  lw-ījì. ‖ Ù-lyá
when  2-P2-arrive-Fa  18=  9-path  2-SQ-arrive-Fa  17=  11-river  1-that.R
When they arrived in the path ‖ they arrived at the river. ‖ That

mú-nyérè | tì=  «Nângà ‖ ni-êhê ‖ n-dá-gá-jábùk-à |
1-girl  ‹quote›= No  1SG-CTR  1SG-NEG-F2-cross.over-Fa
girl | said: «No! ‖ ME ‖ I will not cross |

**ú=lw-ījì! ǁ    Sí=    ú-Ø-m-bèèk-é |            í=      mú-góngò.» ǁ    Ù-lyá**
AU=11-river   OBV=  2SG-SBV-O1.SG-carry-Fe    23=    23-back          1-that.R
the river. ǁ It's obvious that you carry me | on(your) back.» ǁ That

**mú-tàbánà ǁ    tì=        «É=mámà! ǁ    K-ó=    gá-n-yàbìr-àg-à |**
1-young.man   ‹quote›=   Oh=surely    Q-2SG=  F2-O1.SG-defeat-EMP-Fa
young man ǁ said: «Sure! ǁ Will it defeat.EMP me

**ú=kú-jáb-úl-á |            ú=lw-ījì?» ǁ   Ù-lyá    mú-tàbánà ǁ**
AU=15-cross-RV.T-Fa         AU=11-river   1-that.R  1-young.man
| to take you across | the river?» ǁ That young man ǁ

**à-ná-mú-bììk-é |         í=      mú-góngò. ǁ   Mú=     lw-ījì ǁ**
1-CON-O1-place-Fe         23=    3-back         18=    11-river
placed her | on his back. ǁ In the river ǁ

**«Kágàtà | kágàtà.» ǁ        Ú=lw-īji |        «Vwò | vwò | vwò.» ǁ**
(ideophone) splash, splash   AU=11-river      (ideophone) swish, swish
kagata | kagata. ǁ The river | vwo | vwo | vwo. ǁ

**Bà-ná-jábùk-à |         ú=lw-ījì. ǁ   Ìrí     bá-ká-hík-ág-á |     í=     ká-jábò ǁ**
2-SQ-cross.over-Fa       AU=11-river   when   2-P2-arrive-EMP-Fa   23=   12-across
And they crossed over | the river. ǁ When they arrived.EMP | on the far side |

**ú=mú-hyá      tì= |     «Éhéè! ǁ    K-ó=    mú-hyà |**
AU=1-new.wife   ‹quote›=   O.my        Q-AU=   1-new.wife
the new wife ‹quote›: | «Oh my! ǁ The new bride |

**á-gá-shòn-òòk-èr-à     há-nò? ǁ    Ú-m-bí-s-é |              mú=**
1-F2-climb-RV.I-APL-Fa  16-here.P.C   2SG-O1.SG-arrive-CS-Fa    18=
will she get down here? ǁ Take me | into

**ny-ûmbà. ǁ   Ni-é=       mú-hyà ǁ      ká=    n-gá-génd-àg-à |     ná=**
9-house      1SG-FOC=    1-new.wife    Q=     1SG-F2-go-EMP-Fa      CNJ=
the house. ǁ Me the new wife ǁ will I goEMP | by

**má-gúlú kàndî ǁ   tw-é=       tù-kòlà          tú-gá-gênd-à | há=**
6-feet    again    1PL-FOC=   1PL-are.NEWLY    2PL-F2-go-Fa    16=
foot again ǁ we the ones who are now going | to

**kā-āyà? ǁ   Ù-lyá     mú-tàbánà | tì=       «Nângà | tú-gá-gênd-à.» ǁ**
12-village   1-that.R  1-young.man  ‹quote›=   no       1PL-F2-go-Fa
the village?» ǁ That young man | ‹quote› ǁ «No | we will go.» ǁ

**À-ná-hík-àg-è |**     **há=**   **mw-à-bò |**   **hì-kòlà**     **hí-hwéhwérwê ||**
1-CON-arrive-EMP-Fe    16=   home-A.M-2   19-is.NEWLY   19-dusk
And he arrived.EMP | at their home | it's now dusk ||

**à-ná-yì-fúnd-àg-è |**     **mú=**   **ny-ûmbà ||**   **à-ná-bwìr-àg-è**
1-CON-RFX-go.in-EMP-Fe    18=   9-house    1-CON-tell-EMP-Fe
and he went straight.EMP | into the house || and he told.EMP

**nyínà ||**    **tì=**    **É=**   **máàwè ||**    **n-à-léét-à**     **ú=mú-hyà ||**
1a+his.mother   ‹quote›=   O=   1a+my.mother   1SG-P2-bring-Fa   AU=1-new.wife
his mother: || ‹quote› «O my mother || I have brought a new bride ||

**mú-Ø-m-bèèrèz-é |**     **í=byókúlyâ. ||**   **Nyínà ||**    **tì=**     **«K-ò=**
2PL-SBV-O1.SG-give-Fe    AU=food    1a+his.mother   ‹quote›=   Q-2SG=
Give me | food.» || The mother || quote: «Will you

**tá-gá-lì-ìr-à**     **mú-nò?» ||**   **Ná=**   **w-à=**   **ná-yè**    **tì= ||**
NEG-F2-eat-APL-Fa    18-here.P.C   CNJ=   1-A.M=   ADD.P-1   ‹quote›=
not eat in here?» || And he ‹quote›: ||

**«Nângà! ||**   **ú-Ø-n-dèèt-èr-è**     **mú-nò.» ||**   **Kú-bwír-ág-á |**
No    2SG-SBV-O1.SG-bring-APL-Fe   18-here.P.C   15-tell-EMP-Fa
«No! || Bring it to me in here.» || To tell.EMP |

**ú=mú-hyà: ||**   **«Ø-Shòn-óók-ág-à**     **kú=**   **mú-góngò!» ||**   **«Sì=**
AU=1-new.wife    IMP.S-climb-RV.I-EMP-Fa   17=   3-back      OBV=
the new wife: || «Get downEMP off the back!» || «It's obvious

**n-dá-gá-shòn-òòk-à!» ||**   **«Ø-Shòn-óók-à**    **kú=**   **mú-góngò!» ||**   **«Sì=**
1SG-NEG-F2-climb-RV.I-Fa   IMP.S-climb-RV.I-Fa   17=   3-back      OBV=
I will not get down!» || «Get down off the back!» || «It's obvious

**n-dá-gá-shòn-òòk-à!» ||**   **À-ná-mú-làal-àn-è**     **kú=**
1SG-NEG-F2-climb-RV.I-Fa   1-CON-O1-spend.night-COM-Fe   17=
I will not get down!» || He spent the night with her on

**mú-góngò ||**   **à-ná-mú-shììb-àn-è**     **kú=**   **mú-góngò. ||**   **Í-yíngá |**
3-back    1-CON-O1-spend.day-COM-Fe   17=   3-back    5-week
his back || and he spent the day with her on his back. || A week |

**«pùù!» ||**   **Mw-ézì |**   **«pùù!» ||**   **É=**   **bà-lyâ |**   **=yê ||**
sound.of.finish   3-month   sound.of.finish   O=   2-comrades   =O.my
puu! || A month | puu! || Hey guys | look out ||

ú=mú-ndú   á-gáà-fw-à! ‖ Yùgwó   mw-âzì ‖ bà-ná-gù-hí-s-à |
AU=1-person   1-F2-die-Fa   that.N+3   3-news   2-SQ-O3-arrive-CS-Fa
the person will die! ‖ That news ‖ they caused it to arrive |

mú=   bà-ndì   bá-shósì. ‖ Yàbó       bá-shósì |  ìrí    bá-ká-gù-yùvw-á ‖
18=   2-other  2-men        those.N+2  2-men     when  2-P2-O3-hear-Fa
to other men. ‖ Those men | when they heard it ‖

bà-ná-dèt-à |   tì=       «Yéhéè! Mú-zìmù yùgwó |   à-léét-à!» ‖
2-SQ-say-Fa     ‹quote›=   O.my    3-demon  that.N+3  1-bring-Fa
they said: | ‹quote› «O my! It's a demon this one | he has brought!» ‖

«Éégò ‖    mú-zīmù?» ‖ «Èè!»   Á=bà-ndì ‖   tì=        «Kút-àgì |
Is.that.so!  3-demon    Yes    AU=2-others   ‹quote›=   how-EMP
«Is that so? ‖ A demon?» ‖ «Yes.» ‖ Others ‖ ‹quote›: «How.EMP |

mú-gá-gù-sààz-â?» ‖ Mbù=         bà-Ø-gír-ág-è          yá-gà ‖
2PL-F2-O3-get.rid-Fa  as.soon.as=  2+P1-SBV-do-EMP-Fe    this.P-6
will you get rid of it?» ‖ When they try.EMP these ‖

shóóbè! ‖   Á=bà-ndì    bá-shósì | bà-ná-bà-bwír-à |  tì= ‖
emptiness   AU=2-other  2-men      2-SQ-O2-tell-Fa    ‹quote›=
«It's no use!» ‖ Other men | told them: | ‹quote› ‖

«Mù-Ø-yábíìr-è |   í=fììzì ‖     shúúlí |  y-ó=    mú-ká-sáyúúl-à ‖
2PL-SBV-take-Fe    AU=9+bull     9+bull    9-OR=   P2-P2-castrate-Fa
«Take | a big bull ‖ a bull | that had you castrated ‖

ì-ná-kòlì         hí-ìt-ì |    á=má-vùtá  mì-ngì. ‖ À-shúbí
9-ADD.V-is.NEWLY  have-RS-Fi   AU=6-fat   6-much     1-AGAIN
and which now has | much fat. ‖ Let him again

gù-twál-à ‖   háá-hà-lyà |   á-ká-gù-sááz-â. ‖    Mù-Ø-gír-è |
O3-carry-Fa   E-16-there.R   1-P2-O3-take.from-Fa  2PL-SBV-do-Fe
take it back ‖ right there(where) | he took it(the demon) from. ‖ Make sure

|mù-Ø-géndí        gù-báág-ír-à |      iyó        shúúlì ‖ mù-ná-bììk-é |
2PL-SBV-GOING     O3-slaughter-APL-Fa  that.N+9   9+bull   2PL-CON-place-Fe
you go and slaughter for it | that bull ‖ and place |

yìzó         ny-ámá     zó-óshì ‖  n-ó=       lú-shá           n-ó=
those.N+10   10-meats   10-all     CNJ-AU=    11-intestine.fat  CNJ-AU=
all those meats ‖ and the intestinal fat and

lú-shá | kú= mú-lírò.» || Àahô! || Bà-ná-shóól-ér-à ù-lyá
11-intestine.fat 17= 3-fire OK.then 2-SQ-lead-APL-Fa 1-that.R
the intestinal fat | on the fire. || OK then! || They led to the river that

mú-tàbánà | n-ê= lyà shúúlì || bà-ná-gì-hí-s-āgy-à || mw-í=
1-young.man CNJ-9= that.R 9+bull 2-SQ-O9-arrive-CS-EMP-Fa 18-5=
young man | and that bull || and they made it arrive EMP ||

dàkò ly-á= kì-ryá kí-tì || bà-ná-gì-lùnd-ág-á | í-kéétà. ||
under 5-A.M= 7-that.R 7-tree 2-SQ-O3-stab-EMP-Fa 5-knife
underneath that tree || and they killed.EMP it | with the knife. ||

Ú=lú-shâ || bà-ná-lù-gùngìk-è | kú= shààlì. || Ì-ryá
AU=11-intestine.fat 2-CON-O11-pile.up-Fe 17= 9+firewood 9-that.R
The intestinal fat || they gathered it up in a heap | on the firewood. || That

shúúlì | ì-ná-tòndèèr-àg-é | ú=kú-híír-ág-à. || Ú=mú-shìrìrì |
9+bull 9-CON-begin-EMP-Fe AU=15-burn-EMP-Fa AU=3-roasting.smell
bull | and it began.EMP | to burn.EMP. || And roasting smell |

gw-àná-kìzí lāk-à. || Ù-lyá mú-tàbánà | à-ná-kìz-àg-í
3-SQ-REP sound-Fa 1-that.R 1-young.man 1-SQ-REP-EMP-Fi
was repeatedly sensed. || That young man | repeatedly.EMP

gù-bwír-à: || «Ù-Ø-yóky-é bw-îjâ | w-à-gà-sìrííz-à! ||
O3-tell-Fa 2SG-SBV-roast-Fe 14-well 2SG-P1-O6-burn-Fa
told it(demon): || «Roast it well | you are burning it! ||

Ù-Ø-yóky-é bw-îjâ | w-à-gà-sìrííz-à!» || Mú= kú-dèt-à
2SG-SBV-roast-Fe 14-well 2SG-P1-O6-burn-Fa 18= 15-speak-Fa
Roast it well | you are burning it!» || In saying

kwô-kw-ò: || «Ù-Ø-yóky-é bw-îjâ | w-à-gà-sìrííz-à!» || gù-lyá
E-15-thus.N 2SG-SBV-roast-Fe 14-well 2-P1-O6-burn-Fa 3-that.R
like this: || «Roast it well | you are burning it!» || that

mú-zìmù ná-gwò || ìrí gù-ná-kùùl-àg-è ||
3-demon ADD.P-3 that's.when 3-CON-pull.out-EMP-Fe
demon and it also || pulled out.EMP ||

í=ny-úùnù zá-á-gwò. || Yùgwó mú-zīmù || ìrí gú-ká-yùvw-á
AU=10-fingernails 10-A.M-3 that.N+3 3-demon when 3-P2-hear-Fa
its fingernails. || That spirit || when it smelled ||

**ngànà** || **ìrí**   **ú=mú-shìrìrì** ||   **gw-à-nún-à**   **bwènèènè** | **mw-í**
really   when AU=3-roasting.smell   3-P1-be.sweet-Fa   very.much   18-5
really the roasting smell || was sweet very much | in

**zūūlù** || **gw-àná-yàmí bálál-á ngànà** | **nà=**   **kú=**   **zì-ryá**   **ny-ámà.** ||
nose   3-SQ-IMMED   fly-Fa   really   CNJ=   17=   10-that.R   10-meat
the nose || it immediately flew really | to those meats. ||

**Ù-lyá**   **mú-tàbánà** || **à-ná-yàm-à** |   **á-gá-shààg-à yà-hô** ||   **ná=**
1-that.R   1-young.man   1-SQ-IMMED-Fa   1-F2-leave-Fa   there.N-16   CNJ=
That young man || he immediately | left there || with

**yàbó**   **bá-ndù** || **bà-ná-yàm-àg-è** |   **bá-gá-pùùmùk-à** ||
those.N+2   2-people   2-CON-IMMED-EMP-Fe   2-INTL-dash.off-Fa
those people || and they immediately.EMP | dashed off ||

**bà-ná-jábùk-à** |   **lù-lyá**   **lw-ījì** |   **bà-ná-táàh-à.** ||
2-SQ-cross.over-Fa   11-that.R   11-river   2-SQ-return.home-Fa
and they crossed | that river | and they went home. ||

**Kwô-kw-ô|**   **yùgwó**   **mú-zīmù** ||   **gw-àná-sìgál-ág-á** |   **mú=**   **yìzó**
E-15-thus.N   that.N+3   3-demon   3-SQ-remain-EMP-Fa   18=   those.N+10
Thus | that demon || remained.EMP | with those

**ny-ámà.** ||   **H-ó=**   **lú-fùmó** ||   **h-ó=**   **lù-hék-èr-à** |   **nà=**
10-meats   18-FOC=   11-story   16-FOC=   11-come.to.end-APL-Fa   CNJ=
meats. || That story || that's where it comes to end | and

**h-ó=**   **lù-hùmb-ír-à.** ||
16-FOC=   11-rain.end-APL-Fa
that also is where it ends (like rain). ||

# References

Alexandre, Pierre. 1966. *Systeme verbal et predicatif du Bulu*. Paris: Librairie C. Klincksieck.

Andrews, Avery. 1985. The major functions of the noun phrase. In Timothy Shopen (ed.), *Language typology and syntactic description*, Vol. 1, 62–154. Cambridge: Cambridge University Press.

Ashton, E. O. 1959. *Swahili grammar (including intonation)*. London: Longmans.

Bastin, Yvonne. 2003. The Lacustrine zone (Zone J). In Derek Nurse and Gerard Philippson (eds.), *The Bantu languages*, 501–528. New York: Routledge.

Busongoye, Kamaro. 2004. Complement clauses in Kifuliiru. M.A. thesis. Nairobi Evangelical Graduate School of Theology.

Bybee, Joan, Revere Perkins, and William Pagliuca. 1994. *The evolution of grammar*. Chicago: The University of Chicago Press.

Callow, Kathleen. 1998. *Man and message*. Lanham: University Press of America.

Carter, Hazel. 1973. *Syntax and tone in Kongo*. London: School of Oriental and African Studies.

Crystal, David. 1997. *The Cambridge encyclopedia of language*. Cambridge: Cambridge University Press.

Crystal, David. 2003. *A dictionary of linguistics and phonetics*. 5th edition. London: Blackwell.

Dahl, Östen. 1985. *Tense and aspect systems*. Oxford: Basil Blackwell.

Delobeau, Jean-Michel. 1984. *Phonologie du kifuliru (langue bantoue du groupe J)*. Mass Market Paperback.

Dik, Simon. 1978. *Functional grammar*. Amsterdam: North Holland.

Doke, Clement M. 1938. *Textbook of Lamba grammar*. Johannesburg: Witwatersrand University Press.

Doke, Clement M. 1943. *Outline grammar of Bantu*. Grahamstown: Rhodes University.

Dooley, Robert A., and Stephen H. Levinsohn. 2001. *Analyzing discourse: A manual of basic concepts*. Dallas: SIL International.

Dugast, Idelette. 1971. *Grammaire du Tunen*. Paris: Éditions Klincksieck.

Fillmore, Charles J. 1997. *Lectures on deixis*. Stanford, Cal.: Center for the Study of Language and Information.

Firbas, Jan. 1964. From comparative word-order studies. *BRNO Studies in English* 4.111–126.

Gauton, Rachélle. 1999. Locative prefix stacking as a earlier viable locativising strategy in Bantu. In Paul F. A. Kotey (ed.), *Trends in African linguistics 3: New dimensions in African linguistics and languages*, 217–232. Trenton, N.J.: Africa World Press.

Givón, Talmy. 1984/1990. *Syntax: A functional-typological introduction*. 2 vols. Amsterdam and Philadelphia: John Benjamins.

Gordon, Raymond G. Jr. 2005. *Ethnologue: Languages of the world*. 15th edition. Dallas: SIL International.

Gove, Philip B. 1971. *Webster's seventh new collegiate dictionary*. Chicago: Rand McNally & Company.

Grimes, Joseph E. 1976. *The thread of discourse*. The Hague: Mouton.

Grimes, Joseph E. 1978. How does a language acquire gender markers? In Joseph Greenberg (ed.), *Universals of human language* 3:47–82. Stanford: Stanford University Press.

Guldemann, Tom. 1999. Head initial meets head final: Nominal suffixes in Eastern and Southern Bantu from a historical perspective. *Studies in African Linguistics* 28:49–91.

Guthrie, Malcolm. 1948. *The classification of the Bantu languages*. London: Oxford University Press for the International African Institute.

Guthrie, Malcolm. 1970. *Collected papers on Bantu linguistics*. Gregg International Publishers. England (from the article originally published as Bantu word division, International African Institute Memorandum XXII, 1948).

Guthrie, Malcolm. 1971. *Comparative Bantu*, vol. 2. Farnborough, Hants, England: Gregg International Publishers.

Hayes, Bruce. 1989. The prosodic hierarchy in meter. In P. Kiparsky and G. Youmans, (eds.) *Phonetics and phonology: Rhythm and meter,* 201-260. Orlando: Academic Press.

Hedinger, Robert. 2001. Bakossi grammar. Unpublished manuscript. SIL Cameroon.

Heimerdinger, Jean-Marie. 1999. Topic, focus and foreground in Ancient Hebrew narratives. *Journal for the Study of the Old Testament:* Supplement Series 295.

Hyman, Larry M. 2003a. Basaá(A43). In Derek Nurse and Gérard Philippson (eds.), *The Bantu languages.* New York: Routledge.

Lambrecht, Knud. 1994. *Information structure and sentence form.* Cambridge: Cambridge University Press.

Levinsohn, Stephen H. 2000. *Discourse features of New Testament Greek: A coursebook on the information structure of New Testament Greek.* 2nd edition. Dallas: SIL International.

Levinsohn, Stephen H. 2004. Non-narrative lecture notes. SIL International.

Levinsohn, Stephen H. 2005. Self-instruction materials on narrative discourse analysis (NARR files). Online at https:// mail.jaars.org/~bt/narr.zip SIL International.

Levinsohn, Stephen H. 2006. The relevance of Greek discourses studies to exegesis. *Journal of Translation,* 2.2. Dallas: SIL International.

Longacre, Robert E. 1996. *The grammar of discourse.* New York: Plenum Press.

Matthews, P. H. 1997. *Oxford concise dictionary of linguistics.* Oxford/NewYork: Oxford University Press.

Meeussen, A. E. 1959. *Essai de grammaire Rundi.* Tervuren.

Meinhof, Carl. 1899. Grundriss einer Lautlehre der Bantusprachen. Leipzig: Brockhaus. 2$^{nd}$ edition 1910. Berlin: D. Reimer.

Meinhof, Carl. 1904. Das Dahlsche Gesetz. *Zeitschrift der Deutschen Morgenländischen Gesellschaft* 57:299–304.

Meinhof, Carl. 1932. *Introduction to the phonology of the Bantu languages.* Translated and revised (from Meinhof 1910) by N. J. Warmlo. Berlin: D. Reimer/E.Vohsen.

Noonan, Michael. 1985. Complementation. In Timothy Shopen (ed.), *Language typology and syntactic description Vol. 2,* 42-140. Cambridge: Cambridge University Press.

Nurse, Derek. 2003. *Aspect and tense in Bantu Languages.* In Derek Nurse and Gérard Philippson (eds.), *The Bantu languages,* 90–102. New York: Routledge.

Palmer, F. R. 1986. *Mood and modality.* Cambridge: Cambridge University Press.

Payne, Thomas. 1997. *Describing morphosyntax.* Cambridge: Cambridge University Press.

Schadeberg, Thilo C. 2003. *Derivation.* In Derek Nurse and Gérard Philippson (eds.), *The Bantu languages,* 71–89. New York: Routledge.

Thompson, Sandra A., and Robert E. Longacre. 1985. Adverbial clauses. In Timothy Shopen (ed.), *Language typology and syntactic description, Vol 1,* 171–234. Cambridge: Cambridge University Press.

Van Otterloo, Roger. 1988. Towards an understanding of "lo" and "behold": Functions of *idou* and *ide* in the Greek New Testament. *Occasional Papers in Translation and Textlinguistics* 2.1:34–64.

Welmers, William. E. 1973. *African language structures.* Berkeley and Los Angeles: University of California Press.

Ziervogel, D. 1959. *A grammar of Northern Transvaal Ndebele.* Pretoria: J. L. van Schaik.

Ziervogel, D. 1971. The Bantu locative. *African Studies* 30.3–4:371–384.

# Person index

Alber, Barbara..................................................................ii
Andrews, Avery ...................................................301, 324, 326
Ashton, E. O. .......................................................................37
Augustin, Maryanne.........................................................xx
Banyimwire wa' Rusati, Mushonio ....................................... xxii, 2
Black, Cheryl......................................................................xx
Bleek, Wilhelm..................................................................20
Brown, Bonnie ............................................................. ii, xx
Bukuru, Nakalali ..................................................................2
Busongoye, Kamaro........................................................xx, 2
Bybee, Joan .................. 9, 100, 203, 214, 215, 217, 228, 237, 243, 244, 265, 266
Cahill, Mike......................................................................xix
Callow, Kathleen ............................................................468
Carter, Hazel....................................................................214
Crystal, David.........................................8, 108, 124, 212, 327, 349
Dahl, Östen .....................................................................217
Doke, Clement M .......................................................195, 214
Dooley, Robert A...............................................230, 338, 435, 447
Dugast, Idelette ..............................................................214
Fillmore, Charles ............................................................285
Fivaz, Derek.................................................................xx, 19
Floor, Sebastian................................................................xx
Follingstad, Carl................................................................xx
Gauton, Rachélle ............................................................198
Gilley, Leoma...................................................................xx
Givón, Talmy...................................................................435
González, Margaret .........................................................xx

Gordon, Raymond G. Jr. ................................................ 1
Gourley, Lois .................................................... ii, xx
Gove, Philip B. ................................................... 445
Grimes, Joseph E. ................................................. 435
Guthrie, Malcolm ........................................... xxiv, xxv, 1
Hampshire, Jon. .................................................. xix
Heimerdinger, Jean-Marie ......................................... 325
Huttar, George ................................................. ii, xx
Hyman, Larry M. ......................................... xxv, xxvii, 91
Jones, Rhonda Hartell ........................................... ii, xx
Jouannet, Francis. .................................................. 2
Kashindi, Asile .................................................... 2
Kashindi, Ye' Mwana Adrien ...................................... xix
Katyera, Sengoronge ...................................... xx, 2, 5, 430, 529
Kinyamagoha, Juma. ............................................ xx, 2
Koehler, Loren ................................................... xx
Kwangiba, Kifuvyo. ................................................ 2
Kyula, Kazera ..................................................... 2
Lambrecht, Knud ................................. 301, 324, 327, 343, 344
Lauber, Ed ...................................................... xix
Levinsohn, Stephen H. ..... v, xx, 14, 99, 230, 300, 301, 323, 324, 325, 338, 344, 407,
    435, 447, 480, 488
Longacre, Robert E. .................................... v, xx, 372, 435, 445
Martens, Lana. .................................................... xx
Matthews, P. H. .................................................. 328
Meeussen, A. E. ............................................... 1, 214
Meinhof, Carl ................................................... 20
Mushonio Banyimwire Warusati .................................... 2
Musobwa, Bahabwa. ............................................... 2
Mwemera, Bugulube ................................................ 2
Ngalonga, Mulubi. ................................................. 2
Noonan, Michael .............................................. 399, 400
Nurse, Derek .............................................. xx, xxiii, 9
Pagliuca, William. ........................................... 9, 100, 214
Palmer, F. R. ................................................ 265, 266
Payne, Doris ..................................................... xx
Payne, Thomas ........................................... 158, 169, 397
Perkins, Revere. ........................................... 9, 100, 214
Philippson, Gérard. ............................................. xxiv
Rasmussen, Kent ................................................. xx
Schadeberg, Thilo C. .......................................... 81, 315

Stegen, Oliver .......................................................... xx
Thompson, Sandra A. ............................................... 372, 435
Thwing, Rhonda ....................................................... xx
Welmers, Wm. E. ...................................................... 20
Wise, Mary Ruth ...................................................... ii, xx
Yunga, Mulogoto ...................................................... 2
Ziervogel, D. ........................................................ 20, 35, 198
Zihindula, Kibambazi ............................................. xx, xxii, 2

# Language index

Basaá . . . . . . . . . . . . . . . . . . . . . . . . . . . . . . . . . . . . . . . . . . . . . . . . . . . . . . . . . . . . . . 91
Cambodian. . . . . . . . . . . . . . . . . . . . . . . . . . . . . . . . . . . . . . . . . . . . . . . . . . . . . . . 214
Chitembo . . . . . . . . . . . . . . . . . . . . . . . . . . . . . . . . . . . . . . . . . . . . . . . . . . . . . 1, 489
French . . . . . . . . . . . . . . . . . . . xviii, xxi, xxvii, xxx, 2, 8, 10, 11, 97, 411, 413, 495
Gusii . . . . . . . . . . . . . . . . . . . . . . . . . . . . . . . . . . . . . . . . . . . . . . . . . . . . . . . . . . . . 1
Havu . . . . . . . . . . . . . . . . . . . . . . . . . . . . . . . . . . . . . . . . . . . . . . . . . . . . . . . . . . . . 1
Hema . . . . . . . . . . . . . . . . . . . . . . . . . . . . . . . . . . . . . . . . . . . . . . . . . . . . . . . . . . . 1
Kihunde . . . . . . . . . . . . . . . . . . . . . . . . . . . . . . . . . . . . . . . . . . . . . . . . . . . . . 1, 264
Kinande . . . . . . . . . . . . . . . . . . . . . . . . . . . . . . . . . . . . . . . . . . . . . . . . . . . . . . 1, 221
Kinyarwanda. . . . . . . . . . . . . . . . . . . . . . . . . . . . . . . . . . . . . . . . . . . . . . . . . . 1, 2, 6
Kinyindu . . . . . . . . . . . . . . . . . . . . . . . . . . . . . . . . . . . . . . . . . . . . . . . . . . . . . . . . . 1
Kirundi. . . . . . . . . . . . . . . . . . . . . . . . . . . . . . . . . . . . . . . . . . . . . . . . . . . . . . . . . . . 1
Kiswahili . . . . . . . . . . . . . . . . . . . xxi, xxvii, xxxvi, 10, 16, 40, 127, 208, 384, 476
Kivira . . . . . . . . . . . . . . . . . . . . . . . . . . . . . . . . . . . . . . . . . . . . . . . . . . . . . . . . . . 1, 2
Luhya . . . . . . . . . . . . . . . . . . . . . . . . . . . . . . . . . . . . . . . . . . . . . . . . . . . . . . . . . . . 1
Mashi . . . . . . . . . . . . . . . . . . . . . . . . . . . . . . . . . . . . . . . . . . . . . . . . . . . . . . . . . . 1, 2
Proto-Bantu. . . . . . . . . . . . . . . . . . . . . . . . . . . . . . . . . . . . . . . 9, 20, 35, 81, 148, 210
Talinga . . . . . . . . . . . . . . . . . . . . . . . . . . . . . . . . . . . . . . . . . . . . . . . . . . . . . . . . . . 1

# Overall index

## A

**abbreviations** xxxiii
abstract (nouns)  4, 19, 23, 34, 97, 151, 174-176, 179
accompaniment  47-48, 158, 161-162, 313
    noun phrases  **161-162**
    obliques  **162**, 313, 317, 322
additive adverbs  105-106
additive noun phrases  159-160
additive pronoun  11, 42, **44-45**, 50-51
additive prefix, verb  15, **206-207**, 214-215, 244, 250, 262, 379, **383-384**, 419, **506**
address, forms of  71, 135-136
**adjectives**  3, 4, 10, 19, 24, **81-89**
    adjective stems  81-83
    comparison strategies  89-90
    concord  84-85
    "expressive" nouns  11, 107, 137, **152-154**
    lexical adjectives  81-82
    stative verbal adjectives  3, 81, **85-88**, 410
adverbial clauses  365-397. *See also* dependent clauses

adverbs  3, 10, **99-106**, 214, 219, 306, 318-319, 322, 355, 509-511, 522-523
    additive adverbs  105-106
    confirmatory adverbs  105
    intensifier and limiter adverbs  104-105
    manner adverbs  102-104, 322
    positional adverbs  102
    preposing  355-357
    reduplication  522-523
    temporal adverbs  99-102, 318-319
agent of passive construction  160
agreement  19-35, 153, 169, 196
    conjoined NPs of different genders  28
    of copula with complement  28-29
    singular/plural class pairings  22
alternations of basic constituent order  348-363. *See also* preposing; postposing
alternatives
    clause level  419, 422
    phrase level  162-163
alternative pronoun(s)  11, 38, 42-45, 47-48, 388
animate/animacy
    gender classes  27, 111

and locatives 169, 173-174, 176, 180
object incorporation 41, 311
in riddles 508
same-set demonstrative 76
apodosis 367-370
aspect (in verbs) 203, 227, 237 579, 582
completive (**kéèrà**) **100-102, 227, 242**
**continuative 244-247**, 293, 367, 419, 422, 439, 441-445
habitual (*See* habitual)
intervening time (distal **ká-**) 247-248
progressive 215, 238-242, 293
progressive, intentional 218-219, 227, **241-242**, 280
progressive, newly 240-241
progressive, persistive 240
progressive, recent past 239-240
progressive, unmarked 239, 241
resultative (perfective) 9, 243-244
sequential 244, 293, 439-441
state changes/continues 238
timeless /habitual **237-238**, 246, 259-261, 293, 500, 505
timeless, conditional 293
associative marker 3, 24, 30, 97, 150, 153, 155, 157, 197
associative phrases 4, 11, 137-138, 142, **150-155**
expressive nouns 11, 107, **152-154**, 521
special focus idiom 154-155
associative pronouns 3, 10, 24, 26-27, 138-142, **157-158**, 509, 511
augment (initial vowel) 3, 8, 19, 21, 24-25, 60, 64 , 78, 88, 137-140, **143-150**, 205
in proverbs 498
in riddles 507
on infinitives 146, 208

where found/precluded **146-150**, 172
auxiliary(ies) 3, 203, 213-227, 238-242, 255, 264-298
adverbial auxiliaries 13, 213-216, **219-224**, 250-251, **268-292**, 298
auxiliary **ba- 292-298**
grammaticization of 213-215
of mood 288-292
of relative location 276-292
of relative time 268-276
of relative time plus location 287-288
progressive (*See* progressive)
semi-grammaticized, with infinitives 216, 264-267
and the subjunctive 250-251
TAM in auxiliaries 12, 217, 264, **268-298**
with inflected main verb 219-220, 269-271, 279-280, 287-288
with uninflected verb stem 221-222, 271-276, 281-285, 290-292

**B**

-**ba** 'to be' as auxiliary **292-298**
background information, in narratives 17, 231-232, 335, 407, 438-439, 480
fewer pauses 335
indirect quotes 17, 480-483, 488
P3 past tense 231-232, 438-439
relative clauses 407
Bantu xvii, xxv, xxvii, xxxi, 9, 11, 21, 195, 198, 214, 264, 328, 344, 495, 512
**zone D 1**
zone J xvii, 1, **489**
base 5, 7-8, 10, 85, **204-205**, 208, 242
benefactive 309-310, 312

Overall index 563

## C

cardinal numbers 93-97
causative 309, 314-315, 403
 analytic causative 15, 397-398, 502
chaining, sequential 435-436, **440-441**
circumflex accent 7
class agreement (gender-number). *See* noun class
classification of Kifuliiru 1
clause nucleus 4, 99, 107, 111, 301, **305-317**
 default order 305-306
clauses 14-15, 251, 301-363, 365-427. *See also* complement clauses; dependent clauses; independent clauses; relative clauses
cleft constructions 212
closed conversation. *See* tight-knit conversation
"coming" vs "going" auxiliary 276-282, **285-287**
comment (vs. topic) 14, 301, **335-338**, 348-355
comparison **89-90**, 163, 166, 183, 317, 322, 406
complement 86, 88-89, 138, 143, 164, 307-308
 ideophone as 112
 of associative 154-155, 167, 353-355
 of conjunctive 162, 168, 321-322
 of locative phrase 353, 359, 411, 412
complement clauses 400-406, 423, 425
complementizer(s) 3, 53, **400-401**, 404-406, 478, 482
completive aspect (**kéèrà**) **100-102**, **227**, **242**
concessive clauses 15, 207, 365-366, **383-384**
conditional 257, 259-263, 367

conditional clauses 246, 257, 259, 261-263, 296, 367-368
 contrary-to-fact 261-263, 293, 368
 past 261-264, 369-371
conjunctions 4, 138, 365-367, 380, 384-397
 compound 15, 366, 390-394, 396
 introducing dependent clauses 365-366
 conjunctive **kandi iri** 'or' 137-138, 162-163, 419, 422
 conjunctive **na** 44, **138**, 158-162, 321
 conjunctive **nga** 'like, as' 163-164, 394
 conjunctives used with noun phrases 158-164
 in proverbs 501-502
constituent order, basic 348
continuative **244-247**, 293, 367, 419, 422, 439
 marking predictable sequences 430, 439, 441-445
contrary-to-fact
 clauses 365-366, 368-371
 verb forms 261-264, 292-293, 295, 368
contrast between clauses 421-422
conventionalizing implicatures 13
conventions used in this work 5-10
 texts and their numbering 5
 transcription conventions 6-10
conversation. *See* reported speech
coordination in noun phrases 158-159
coordination between clauses 419-421
copulas 38, 150, 162, **209-213**, 215, 238
 agreement with complement 28-29
 **ba-** copula 210-211, 217-218, 307 (*See also*, auxiliary, **ba-**)
 be.NEWLY (new state) 209, 220, 215, 231, 233, 238

be.PREV (former state) 209, 220, 238-239
equational -**li** copula 209, 307
focus (contrastive) copula 38, 48, 89, **212-213**, 221, 226, 344-345
    negative 38, 212-213, 226, 299, 345
    positive 212, 221, 298-299, 344
persistive -**kiri** 209, 231, 238

# D

deictic center 13, 277, 281-282, 285-287
demonstratives 4, 62, 57-80, 147
    as thematic salience markers 4, 16, 37, 64-65, **429-431**, 445, **447-467**
    distal 57, 59, 61-63, 65, 70-71, 78
    emphatic 60-63, 72-75, 78-79
    in non-verbal clause 347-348
    locative 63, 78-80
    nearby 56-58, 60-63, 65, 69-70
    proximal 56-63, 65-68
    proximal contrastive 59, 61-65, 68-70, 73
    remote 16, 59, 61-65, 71-72
    same/different set demonstratives 64-65, 75-78, 509
denouement 332, 445, 451
dependent/adverbial clauses 15, 365-419
    complement clauses, classes of 400-404
    concessive 366, 383-384
    conditional 246, 257, 259, 261-263, 296, 367-368
    conjunctions which may introduce 366
    contrary to fact conditional/result 368-371
    focus 387-390
    logical 384-385
    manner 393-394
    protasis 367-370
    purpose/result 251, 385-387, 390
    purpose/result, with focus 390-393
    reason 394-397
    reduced clauses, concomitant state 398-399
    relative clauses 407- 419
    temporal 15, 230, 259, 319, 325-326, 338-339, 366-367, **371-382**
    with **kwo** 399, 400-404, 423, 425, 579
    with **mbu** 404
    without conjunctions 367
dialects, Kifuliiru 2
different set demonstratives 64-65, 75-78, 509
diminutive 4, 19, 35, 519, 522
direct versus indirect speech 8, 17, 426, 480, **482**, 488
discontinuity in narrative 15, 16, 230, 435
    of location 230, 437
    of participants 438
    of time 16, 230, 373, **435-438**
discourse. See information structure
distal **ká-**. See **intervening time**
dominant focal element 14, 15, 301, 315, **324-325**, 330, **336-338**
dynamic verbs 217- 219, 270, 272, 274, 292
    reduplication in 513-516

# E

emphatic demonstratives 57, 59-63
emphatic suffix (verb) / emphatic prominence 9, 15, 16, 205, 249-250, 252, 308, 429-431, 445, 447, **468-472**
episode(s) 16, 17, 230, 372, 434-447

Overall index                                                             565

established (old) information (topic)
    xvii, 245, 288, 324, 327-329, 335-
    336, 343-344, 353-354, 358
exclusive pronouns  2, 38, 42-45, **48-49**
expressive nouns  11, 107, **152-154**, 521

**F**

final vowel  5, 9, 203-204, 208, 210, 221
focus/ focal  xvii, 15, 17, 154-156, 227,
    312, 317-319, 326-327, 329, 334,
    340, **344-348**, 350-361, **363**, 365-
    366, 493
    clauses  387-390
    conjunctions  366
    purpose clause with focus  390-393
    (*See also* dominant focal element)
focus (contrastive) copula (FOC)  38,
    48, 89, 212-213, 221, 226, 344-345
    positive  212, 221, 264, 298-299, 344
    negative  38, 213, 226, 299, 345
free (self-standing) pronouns  42-56,
    495
fronting. *See* preposing
frustrated intention (verbs)  204, 248,
    257-258
frustration (interjections/ideophones)
    8, 124-125, 129
future  233-237
    immediate  233-234
    unmarked  234-236
    remote  236-237
    simple immediate  233

**G**

gender resolution in conjoined nouns
    28
gender-number prefix (GNP)  19-35,
    153, 169, 196
    singular/plural class pairings  22
glide formation  6, 27, 57-58, 60, 512

"going" vs "coming" auxiliary  276-
    282, 285-287
grammaticization of auxiliaries
    213-215
greetings  107, 134-136
    forms of address  136

**H**

habitual
    -**kizi** as  13, 49, 84, 105, 129, 246, 268,
        271-272, 313, 318, 320, 340, 384,
        396, 407, 416, 439, 500, 537
    progressive state as  293-294,
    reduplication indicating  513-515
    timeless as  **237-238**, 259, 500, 505
    -**tuula** as  13, 220, 268, 270
headless relative clause  416
head noun  **407**-416
hierarchy  28, 41, 207
highlighting in narratives  447-**480**
    emphatic prominence (-**ag**)  464
    slowing-down devices  330, 445,
        472-475
    use of songs  17, 471

**I**

identificational articulation  14, 212,
    324, **326**, **344-348**, 358, 368, 388-
    389, 390
ideophones  4, 6, 8, 12, **108-124**
    examples in context  116-124
    general characteristics of  109-111
    meanings by domain  112-116
    used nominally  111-112
initial vowel. *See* augment
interjections  4, 6, 8, 12, 107, **124-134**,
    477
imperatives  247, **249-253**, 439
    direct  249-251
    mixed  12, 253-254
    polite  252-253

implication (interjections) 124, 125, 129
implicatures, conventionalized 13
inanimate/inanimacy
    and locatives 169, 173, 182
    and locative inversion 494
    and same-set demonstrative 76
    in riddles 508
independent clauses 301, 367-370, 419-422
    alternatives between 422
    apodosis 367-370
    coordination of clauses 419-421
    contrast between clauses 421-422
    ditransitive clauses (SVOO) 309-317
    intransitive clauses (SV) 306-307
        with non-object complement 307-308
    non-verbal clauses 301-305
    polar questions 302, 303, 323
    relations between 419-422
    syntactic structure 301- 323
    transitive clauses (SVO) 308-309
    verbal clause nucleus 305-317
indirect speech 400, 472, 480, **482-483**, **488**,
infinitive 13, 35, 169, **208-209**, 216, 224, 264-268, 337, 367, 490
    archaic cl. 5 infinitive 205, 221, 251, 264, 268, 291
    augment on 146
    expressing concomitant state 14, 377-378, 382, 398-399, 438
    infinitives in noun phrases 67, 89, **143**
    as location 174, 179
    prefixless 221, 233, 239
    verbs that precede infinitives 13, 216-217, 264-268, 291
informal registers. *See* speech registers

information structure 301, **324-348**
    alternations of basic constituent order 348-363
    constraints on xvii, 41, 301, 306, 315, 317, 329
    dominant focal element 14, 15, 301, 315, 324-325, 330, **336-338**, 348, 491
    focal prominence of pronouns and quantifiers 14, 340, **361-363**
    locative inversion 15, 170, 344, **431-432**, **491-492**
    new/old information xvii, xx, 14, 15, 312, 317, 324, 325, 328,329, 332, 335, 344, 346, 348-363
    pauses 10, 14, 329-335, 419, 420, 562
    point of departure 101, 111, 185, 283, 301, 318, 324-326, **338-343**, 348, 353, 355, 372, 385, 423, 424, 493
    polar questions 302, 303, 323
    postposing a clause constituent 14, **328**, **357-359**, 362, 363
    preposing a clause constituent 14, 39, 100-101, 306, 318, 323, **327**, 335, 340, 342, **348-357**
    promoting to clause object 14, 315, 328-329, 359-361
    sentence articulations 301, 324
        identificational 14, 212, 324,**326**, **344-348**, 358, 368, 388-389, 390
        presentational 150, 301, 324, 327, **343-344**, 431-432, 438, 491-492
        topic-comment 14, 324-326
    tail-head linkage 230, 372, 423, 435
    terminology, summary of 324-329
    topic-comment articulation 14, 324, 335
        comment with optional DFE 336

topical prominence 361-363
instrument 158, **161**, 309, 313, 315-317, **321-322**
intentional 204, 218-219, 224-225, 227, 241-242, 256-258
intention(al) 204, 218-219, 225, 256-258
    frustrated intention 257-258
    intentional, previous state 256-257
    intentional, progressive 218-219, 227, 241-242
interclausal relations 15, 419-422
interjections 4, 6, 8, 12, 107, 124-134
intervening time (verb aspect) 206, 227, **247-248**, 250-251, 253, 367
intransitive clauses (SV) 306-307
introduction of participants 491-493
iterative 265, 513

## K

Kifuliiru
    classification 1
    dialects 2
    previous works 2
kinship terms 4, 20, 31-32, 135, 165-166
Kiswahili xxi, 10, 16, 40, 208, 384, 476

## L

LH stem-tone pattern. *See* tone patterns
locative inversion 15, 170, 344, 431-432, 491-492
locatives 4, 39, 41, 169-201, 467
    cl. 16 11, 22, 53, 73, 93, 181, 343-344, 410, 416, 431, 432, 447, 467, 491
    cl. 17 181-187, 344
    cl. 18 188-192, 344, 410
    cl. 23 11, 178-181, 344, 467
    co-occurrence restrictions 175, 198-199
    idioms with frozen locative markers 192-195
    structure 169-175
locative phrases 4, 10, 11, 15, 142, 150, 168, **169-201**, 463

## M

macrostem 204, 205, 207
major participant(s). *See also* participant reference
    introduction 15, 17, 344, 432, **491-493**
    tracking 17, 428, **495**
major thematic salience 16, 65, 430, 448, 456-458. *See also* thematic salience
malefactive 309, 311, 313, 314, 316, 317
manner
    adverbs 3, **102-104**
    clauses 365, 366, **393-394**
    expressed by cl. 15 /17 166, 186
    obliques 317, 322
maps xxxvii- xxxviii
minor participants 494-495
modal auxiliaries 288-292
mood (in verbs) xxvi, 12, 13, 203-204, 206, 214, 222, 225, 227, **248-263**, **264-268**, 288-292, 293-298
    conditional 257, 259-263, 367
    conditional, contrary-to-fact 261-263, 293, 368
    imperatives 248-254 (*See also* imperatives)
    intention, frustrated 256-257
    intentional 204, 219, 225, 256-258
    intentional, previous state 256
    intentional, progressive 218-219, 227, 241-242
    potential 257-258
    subjunctive 10, 204, 210, 221, 236, 245, 247-250, **251-254**, 260, 263,

278, 292-293, 368, 370, 372, 376-377, 385-388, 390, 397, 404, 405, 419, 439
  unrealized expectation, present (not.yet) **254-256**, 260, 274-275, 297, 367, 378-379
  unrealized expectation, remote past 255-256
movement 12, 112, 114, 178-181, 277-287
multiple embedding, noun phrase 167-168

# N

names
  personal 4, 20, 30-32, 34, 111, 135
  place 34-35, 174, 178
narrative discourse 429-495
  background information 17, 231, 407, **438-439**, 480
  body of story 434
  chaining, sequential 435-436, 440-441
  conclusion/moral 445-447
  denouement 332, 445, 451
  direct versus indirect speech 8, 17, 426, 480, **482-488** (*See also* reported speech)
  discontinuity in 15, 16, 230, 435
    of location 230, 437
    of participants 438
    of time 16, 230, 373, **435-438**
  emphatic prominence 447, 468-472
  episode boundaries 230, 372, 434-447
  formulaic ending 446-447
  highlighting 447-480
  introduction 431-434
  moral 445-446
  participant reference 17, 491-496
  peak 445
predictability shown by continuative 419, 430, 439, **441-445**
quoted speech (*See* reported speech)
sequential chaining 435-436, 440-441
slowing-down devices 330, 445, **472-475**
songs 17, 447, **475-480**
speech registers (*See* speech registers)
tenses, use of in narratives 431-434, 438-445
texts studied 5-6
text units 431-447
thematic salience in 431, 445, 447-468
nearby demonstrative 4, 56-**58**, 60-63, 65, **69-70**, 78, 304, 305, 413
  emphatic form 60, **78**
negation, negative marking 10, 15, **206**, 207, 208, 211, 213, 214, 222, **225-226**, 229, 231, 236, 247, 253, 260, 263, 269, 274-275, 370-371, 378-379
  as thematic salience marker 4, 16, 37, 64-65, 69, **429-431**, 445, **447-467**
  in proverbs 499-500
negative focus copula 38, **212-213**, 226, **299**, 345-346
new/old information xvii, xx, 14, 15, 312, 317, 324, 325, 328, 329, 332, 335, 344, 346, 348-363
new state 234, 235, 238
not.yet/not.ever 222, 274, 378
non-verbal clauses **301-305**, 344, 347-348
noun(s) 4, 19-35
  expressive nouns 11, 107, **152-154**, 521

position nouns  4, 178, 181, **195-201**, 467-468
   in proverbs  498
noun classes (gender- number)  19-35
   class agreement (gender-number)  24-31
   copula agrees with complement  28-29
   count nouns by gender  22-23
   different GNP's for same referent  28
   gender resolution with conjoined nouns  28
   lexicalized noun prefixes  30
   mismatches between classes  29
   non-count nouns  23
   personification of animate noun  30
   prefixes  19, 24-25
   semantic categories in  31-35
   singular-plural correspondences  21-22
noun phrase(s)  25-28, 137-168
   additive noun phrases  159-160
   associative phrases  4, 11, 137-138, 142, **150-155**
   augments in  143-150
   constituents used substantively  140-142
   default/ marked order of constituents  138-139
   expressive nouns  11, 107, **152-154**, 521
   infinitives in  143
   multiple embedding  167-168
   reciprocal  160
   structure of  137-139
   with noun of apposition  166-167
noun phrases with **mwene**  138, **164-166**
   comparative 'like X'  166
   kinship terms/family  165-166
   ownership or authority  164-165
numbers  4
   cardinal numbers  93-97
   idiom of number  405-406
   ordinal numbers  97-98

## O

o of reference  9, **37-38**, 41-43, 58-63, 91, 93, 142, 157, 212-213, 320, 328, 342-343, 350, 359, 410
object (of verb)  305
   as focused element in identificational articulation  346
   enclitics  38, 41-42, 210, 308, 310, 319, 328-329, 359-361,
   first/ second  204-205, 208-209, 305, 306, 309-317
   prefix on verb  204-205, **207-209**, 249, 266, **309-317**
   preposed/fronted  264, 335-336, 342, **349-351**
   promoting to  14, 315, **328-329**, **359-361**
   with intransitive verb  210
object relative clause  213, **408**, **410-413**
oblique(s)  306, 307, 309, 311, **318-323**
   accompaniment obliques  322
   comparison obliques  322-323
   instrument obliques  321
   location obliques  319-321
   locative oblique as focus  347
   manner obliques  322
   time obliques  318-319
old information  xvii, 245, 288, 324, 327-329, 335, 343-344, 353-354, 358
onomatopoeia  108
ordinal numbers  97-98
ownership  155-156, 164-165

## P

paragraphs 15-16, 230, 372, 435-436, 455
participant reference
    major participants
        introduction 15, 17, 344, 432, **491-493**
        tracking 17, 428, **495**
    minor participants/props 494-495
parts of speech, inventory 3-5
passive 85, 103, 253, 307,
    agent of 158, 160-161
past 227-228, 366. *See also* conditional; progressive; resultative
    completive 100-101, 242-243
    recent (P1) 204, **227-229**, 244, 253, 280-281, 294, 295, 372-373, 375-376, 379, 500
    remote (P3) (past state) 204, 210, 222, 231-**232**, 255, 269, 272, 295, **431-433, 438-439**
    sequential (narrative past) 204, 207, 211, 216, **244**, 293-294, 298, 372, 382, 397, **419-420**, 423, 430, 435, **439-441**
    unmarked (P2) 15, 206, 218, 220, **229-230**, 269, 292, 293, 296, 298, 371-373, 383, 397-398, **433-434**, 435
    unrealized expectation, remote past 255
pause(s) 10, 14, 166, 324-325, **329-335**, 336-342, 344-345, 351-352, 358, 365
    long pause 10, 325, 335, 338-342
    short pause 10, 325, 334, 337, 352
    summary of usage 423-427
    where typically found 329-332
    where typically lacking 332-335
pejorative
    cl.14 as 258
expressive nouns as 152
reduplication indicating 509-510, 513, **525-528**
persisting state 203
    contrary to fact conditional 263, 368, 370-371
    expressed by resultative 9, 243 (*See also* resultative)
    expressed by copula -**kiri** 13, 209, 232, 238, 240
    expressed by prefix **ki-** 13, 207, 222, 209, 222, 255, 263, 368
    progressive 232, 240
place names 34-35, 174, 178
point of departure (PoD) 101, 301, 324, **325-326**, 332, **338-342**, 423
    referential 111, 326, **341-343**, 353, 355
    situational 338-341, 493
        conditional 340
        logical/reason 185, 341, 385
        spatial 340
        temporal 101, 283, 318, 338-339, 348-349, 372
polar questions 302, 303, **323**
position noun(s) 4, 178, 181, **195-201**, 467-468
possession
    associative marker showing 151
    associative pronouns 3, 25-28, 157-158, 526-527
    contrastive possession 155-156
    inherent (in kinship terms) 355
    ownership 155-156, 164-165
    same-set 75-77
postposing a clause constituent 14, **328, 357-359**, 362, 363
    postposing subject 357-358
    postposing focus 358-359
potential/conditional 257, 259-263, 367

pre-prefix. *See* augment
predictable continuation in narrative 16, 203, 227, 245, 293, 295, 419, 430, 439, **441-445**
preposing a clause constituent 14, 39, 100-101, 306, 318, 323, **327**, 335, 340, 342, **348-357**
preposing certain adverbs 355-357
    preposing associative phrase complement 353-355
    preposing intrinsic element of possessive 355
    preposing locative oblique 351-353
    preposing locative phrase complement 353
    preposing object 349-351
    preposing subject 348-349
prepositional. *See* verb suffixes, associative
prepositions. *See* position nouns
presentational articulation 150, 301, 324, 327, **343-344**, 431-432, 438, 491-492
previous language work 2
previous reference morpheme 9, **37-38**, 41-43, 58-63, 91, 93, 142, 157, 212-213, 320, 328, 342-343, 350, 359, 410
previously occurring state 13, 209, 215, 222, 227, **238-239**, 268, 272-273
    intentional 256-257
proclitics 163, 171, 172, 233, 411
pro-drop 306
progressive 215, 238-242, 293
    progressive intentional 218-219, 227, 241-242
    progressive, newly 240-241
    progressive, persistive 240
    progressive, recent past 239-240
    progressive, unmarked 239

promoting to object 14, 315, **328-329**, **359-361**
pronoun(s) 5, 10, 11, **37-56**
    additive 11, 38, 42-45, 47, **50-51**
    alternative 11, 42-43, **47-48**
    associative 3, 157-158, 511
    contrastive 11, 25, 27, 37-38, 42-44, **45-47**, 355
    exclusive 2, 38, 42-45, **48-59**
    interrogative **51-56**, 139, 302, 397
    object pronoun (enclitic) **41-42**, 319, 321, 511-512
    marked placement of 361-363
    personal pronoun(s) 11, 42-51
    prefixes (verb) 38-41
proper names 4, 20, 30-32, 34, 111, 135
protasis 367-370
Proto-Bantu 9, 20, 35, 81, 148, 210
proverbs 17, 146, 259, **497-504**
    form 497-502
    meaning 502-504
    use of augment in 498-499
purpose/result clauses 251-252, 365, **385-387**
    with focus 390-393

## Q

quantifier(s) 14, 37-38, 81, **91-93**, 98, 142, 147-148, 149, 158, 166, 361-363, 431, 432, 434, 517, 528
question marker 5, 302, 303, 322
questions 302-304
    interrogative pronouns 52-57, 139, 302, 397
    polar 302, 303, **323**
quote(s). *See* reported speech
quote marker 4, 8, 107, 109, 111, 116-123, 302, 305, 430, 476, 479, 482-**483**, 488-489, 490, 529

## R

reason clauses  341, 365, 366, **394-397**
reciprocal noun phrases  160
reduplication  4, 8, 10-11, 85, 95, 108, 110, 183, **509-528**
    emphatic demonstratives  37-38, 57, 74-75, 78
    functions of  513-528
    phonologically motivated  471
    structural considerations  509-513
referential point of departure. *See* point of departure
referentiality  145, 147
reference, participant. *See* participant reference
reference, previous. *See* previous reference morpheme
reflexive prefix  40, 41, 48, 204, 207, 208, 221, 314-315
registers, speech. *See* speech registers
relative clause(s)  3, 15, 140, 142, 159, 162, 166, 180, 245, 302-305, 329, 365, 389, 393-394, 404, **407-419**, 498
    contrary-to fact conditional  371
    denoting thematic salience  407, **417-419**
    headless  416
    in proverbs  501
    in strong imperatives  253
    null relativizers  413-415
    object /complement relative  38, 213, 303, 342, 362, 407, **410-412**
        marker (pronoun)  38, 41, 59, 162
    restrictive  15, 407, 501
    subject relative  212, 231, 257, 357, 368, 405, 406, **408-410**
        marker (pronoun)  25, 204
relativizer  408, 410-411, 413-416

reported speech  17, 430, 448, 468-469, **480-491**
    absent/reduced speech orienter  488-491
    closed (tight-knit) conversation  17, 430, **488-489**, 490
    direct/indirect quotes  8, 17, 426, 476, **482-488**
    emphatic extension in  468-469
    formal vs. informal register  426, 480-491
    quote marker  4, 8, 107, 109, 111, 116-123, 302, 305, 430, 476, 479, 480, 482-**483**, 488-489, 490, 529
    use of speech verbs  225, 302, 305, 430-431, 476-478, 480-483, 488-490
resultative  9, 242-243, 256, 259, 261, 272
riddles  497, 505-508

## S

same-event complex  419
same-set demonstratives  64-65, 75-78, 509
sentence articulations  301, 324
    identificational  14, 212, 324, **326, 344-348**, 358, 368, 388-389, 390
    presentational  150, 301, 324, 327, **343-344**, 431-432, 438, 491-492
    topic-comment  14, 324-326
sequential (narrative past)  204, 207, 211, 216, **244**, 293-294, 298, 372, 382, 397, **419-420**, 423, 430, 435, **439-441**
simple stem-tone pattern. *See* tone patterns
singular-plural correspondences, noun class  21-22
slowing-down devices  324, 330, 445, **472-475**

Overall index 573

songs in narratives  17, 447, **475-480**
speech. *See* reported speech
speech rate  7, 329
speech registers  15, 17, 244
    formal written register  15, 17, 375, 425, 534
    quite informal  15, 376, 413, 416, 425, 457, 483
    somewhat informal  15, 425, 448
    speech register summary  429-431
    use of continuative in informal  12, 244, 430, 439, 441-444, 529, 536, 543
    use of emphatic extension  17
    use of speech verb(s)  225, 302, 305, 430-431, 480-483, 488-490
spirantization  243
stative verb(s)  12, 217-220, 270, 519-520
    frames with auxiliary -**ba**-  3, 297-298
stative verbal adjectives  3, 81, **85-88**, 410, 498
stem-tone patterns. *See* tone patterns
subject postposing  328, **357-358**
subject prefixes  24-25, 28-29, **39, 205-206**, 214, 218
subject relative clause  **408-410**
subject relative marker  205, 408
subjunctive  10, 204, 210, 221, 236, 245, 247-250, **251-254**, 260, 263, 278, 292-293, 368, 370, 372, 376-377, 385-388, 390, 397, 404, 405, 419, 439

# T

tail-head linkage  230, 372, 423, 435
TAM (tense/aspect/mood)  7, 12, 203, 206, 227. *See also* tense; aspect; mood
TAM in auxiliaries  12, 217, 264, **268-298**. *See also* auxiliaries
TAM in infinitive phrases  264-268
TAM with -**ba**- auxiliary  13, 292-298
tense  5, 7, 12, **203-206**, 210, **227-237**. *See also* future; past
text linguistics  15-17
thematic salience  447
    demonstratives marking  4, 16, 37, 64-65, 69, **429-431**, 445, **447-467**
    expressed by cl. 16  171, 173, 176, **181**, 447, **467-468**
    major vs default  15, 16, 65, 430-431, 447-467
    marking peak  445
    relative clause as marking  15, 407, **417-419**
tight-knit (closed) conversation  17, 430, 483, **488**-489
timeless  205, **237-238**, 246, 259-261, 292-293, 500, 505
tone marking conventions  7
tone patterns (verbal stem- tone)  85, 203, 206, 208, 221, 239, 251
    complex HH stem-tone pattern  236, 250
    complex HL stem-tone pattern  228, 237, 239, 241, 242, 244, 256, 258, 260, 261, 272, 369
    complex LH stem-tone pattern  248, 255, 257
    complex LH-IP stem-tone pattern  249
    complex LL stem-tone pattern  262, 369
    simple stem-tone pattern  221, 229, 233-234, 239, 264, 272
    $V_2$ stem-tone pattern  231, 234-235, 236, 241, 244, 247, 250, 256, 260, 263, 274

topic-comment articulation  14, 301, 324, **335**
   comment with optional DFE 336-338
topical prominence  361-363
tracking of participants. *See* participant reference
transcription conventions  6-10
transitive (verbs)  308-309
translation, possible mismatches in 10-18

## U

**unintended outcome  13, 124, 220, 284, 288-289, 535**
unrealized expectation  254-256, 260, 274-275, 297, 367, 378-379

## V

$V_2$ stem-tone pattern *See* tone patterns
valence (of verbs)  309, 312, 314
verb(s)
   aspect (*See* aspect)
   auxiliaries (*See* auxiliaries)
   base  5, 7-8, 10, 85, **204-205**, 208, 242
   basic affixation  204-208 (*See also* verb prefixes; verb suffixes)
   copulas (*See* copulas)
   "defective" verbs  214
   macrostem  5, 205, 221
   mood (*See* mood)
   negation  226
   overview of verb form types 204-227
   phrase ( multiword verb)  3, 13, 14, 39, 146, **203**, 212, **214**-218, 227, 242, 256, 267-268, 278, **292-298**, 323, 331, 337, 398-403, 432
   phrases with -**ba**  210-211, 217-218, **292-298**, 307
   preceding infinitives  264-268
   single-word verbs  5, 203-213
   stative vs. dynamic  217-219, 270, 272, 274, 292-293, 297, 373, 513
   stem  5, 8, 40, 48, 85, 203, 205-206, 208
   TAM (*See* tense; aspect; mood)
   TAM in auxiliaries (*See* auxiliaries)
   TAM in infinitive phrases (*See* infinitive)
   tense (*See* tense)
   tone in  7 (*See also* tone patterns)
   toneless  7, 39, 88, **208**, 297
   transitivity
      ditransitive  305, **309-315**
      intransitive  210, **306-308**
      transitive  308-309
   uninflected verb stem  8, 210, 214, 221-222, 268, 271-272, 276-278, 281, 288-289, 438
verb prefixes  204-208. *See also* future; past
   additive prefix  15, **206-207**, 214-215, 244, 250, 262, 379, **383-384**, 419, **506**
   distal **ka-**  206, 227, **247-248**, 250-251, 253, 367
   initial prefixes  205
   negative  10, 15, **206**, 207, 208, 211, 213, 214, 222, **225-226**, 229, 231, 236, 247, 253, 260, 263, 269, 274-275, 370-371, 378-379
   object prefix  5, 24-25, **39-41**, 204, 207-208, 214, 215-218, 223-224, 267, 306, 308-317, 360, 512
   persistive  207, 209, 222, 255, 263, 368
   reflexive  40-41, 48, 204, 207, 208, 221, 314, 315
   subject prefix  24-25, 28-31, **39**, 85, **203-206**, 208, 214-218, 221, 223,

225, 229, 231, 233, 235, 241, 251, 254, 256, 257, 260, 261, 263, 274, 327, 378, 379, 431-432, 439, 492
  subject relative marker  24-25, 205, 408-410, 417-418, 500, 503
verb suffixes/extensions/enclitics
  applicative  86, 180, 210, 309, 312-314, 512
  causative  309, 310, 314-315, 469
  emphatic  9, 16, 205, 250, 252, 308, 429-431, 445, 447, **468-472**
  enclitic pronouns  38, **41-42**, 170, 210, 226
  final vowel  5, 9, 203-204, **208**, 210-211, 221-222, 228, 229, 233-238, 241, 244, 247, 249-251, 255-258, 263-264, 368, 370, 419, 439, 441-442
  impositive  309, 315-317
  resultative final  9, 242-243, 256, 259, 261, 272
vowel coalescence  7, 8, 58, 60, 77, 155, 167, 195, 197

# W
word order, basic  138-139, 305-306

# Z
**zone D**  1
zone J  xvii, 1, **485**

# SIL International Publications

Additional Releases in the **Publications in Linguistics** Series

146. **The Kifuliiru language, Volume 1: Phonology, tone, and morphological derivation**, by Karen Van Otterloo, 2011, 512 pp., ISBN 978-1-55671-261-6
145. **Language death in Mesmes**, by Michael B. Ahland, 2010, 155 pp., ISBN 978-1-55671-227-2
144. **The phonology of two central Chadic languages**, by Tony Smith and Richard Gravina, 2010, 267 pp., ISBN 978-155671-231-9
143. **A grammar of Akoose: A northwest Bantu language**, by Robert Hedinger, 2008, 318 pp., ISBN 978-1-55671-222-7
142. **Word order in Toposa: An aspect of multiple feature-checking**, by Helga Schröder, 2008, 213 pp., ISBN 978-1-55671-181-7
141. **Aspects of the morphology and phonology of Kɔnni**, by Michael C. Cahill, 2007, 537 pp., ISBN 978-1-55671-184-8
140. **The phonology of Mono**, by Kenneth Olson, 2005, 311 pp., ISBN 978-1-55671-160-2
139. **Language and life: Essays in memory of Kenneth L. Pike**, edited by Wise, Headland, and Brend, 2003, 674 pp., ISBN 978-1-55671-140-4
138. **Case and agreement in Abaza**, by Brian O'Herin, 2002, 304 pp., ISBN 978-1-55671-135-0
137. **Pragmatics of persuasive discourse in Spanish television advertising**, by Karol J. Hardin, 2001, 247 pp., ISBN 978-1-55671-150-3
136. **Quiegolani Zapotec syntax: A principles and parameters account**, by Cheryl A. Black, 2000, 365 pp., ISBN 978-1-55671-099-5

SIL International Publications
7500 W. Camp Wisdom Road
Dallas, TX 75236-5629

Voice: 972-708-7404
Fax: 972-708-7363
publications_intl@sil.org
www.ethnologue.com/bookstore.asp

www.ingramcontent.com/pod-product-compliance
Lightning Source LLC
Chambersburg PA
CBHW071216290426
44108CB00013B/1193